Future Advancements for CSR and the Sustainable Development Goals in a Post-COVID-19 World

Andrea Pérez
University of Cantabria, Spain

A volume in the Advances in Human Resources Management and Organizational Development (AHRMOD) Book Series

IGI Global
PUBLISHER of TIMELY KNOWLEDGE

Published in the United States of America by
IGI Global
Business Science Reference (an imprint of IGI Global)
701 E. Chocolate Avenue
Hershey PA, USA 17033
Tel: 717-533-8845
Fax: 717-533-8661
E-mail: cust@igi-global.com
Web site: http://www.igi-global.com

Library of Congress Cataloging-in-Publication Data

Names: Perez, Andrea, 1984- editor.
Title: Future advancements for CSR and the sustainable development goals in a post-COVID-19 world / Andrea Perez, editor.
Description: Hershey, PA : Business Science Reference, [2022] | Includes bibliographical references and index. | Summary: "In light of the new reality imposed by the COVID-19 outbreaks, this book urges the scientific community to study corporate and stakeholder reactions that may lead to changes in CSR, corporate approaches to sustainability and the stakeholders' (consumers, employees, etc) psychology and behavior"-- Provided by publisher.
Identifiers: LCCN 2021026039 (print) | LCCN 2021026040 (ebook) | ISBN 9781799880653 (hardcover) | ISBN 9781799880660 (paperback) | ISBN 9781799880677 (ebook)
Subjects: LCSH: Social responsibility of business. | Sustainable development. | COVID-19 (Disease)--Economic aspects.
Classification: LCC HD60.3 .F87 2022 (print) | LCC HD60.3 (ebook) | DDC 658.4/08--dc23
LC record available at https://lccn.loc.gov/2021026039
LC ebook record available at https://lccn.loc.gov/2021026040

This book is published in the IGI Global book series Advances in Human Resources Management and Organizational Development (AHRMOD) (ISSN: 2327-3372; eISSN: 2327-3380)

British Cataloguing in Publication Data
A Cataloguing in Publication record for this book is available from the British Library.

Advances in Human Resources Management and Organizational Development (AHRMOD) Book Series

Patricia Ordóñez de Pablos
Universidad de Oviedo, Spain

ISSN:2327-3372
EISSN:2327-3380

Mission

A solid foundation is essential to the development and success of any organization and can be accomplished through the effective and careful management of an organization's human capital. Research in human resources management and organizational development is necessary in providing business leaders with the tools and methodologies which will assist in the development and maintenance of their organizational structure.

The **Advances in Human Resources Management and Organizational Development (AHRMOD) Book Series** aims to publish the latest research on all aspects of human resources as well as the latest methodologies, tools, and theories regarding organizational development and sustainability. The **AHRMOD Book Series** intends to provide business professionals, managers, researchers, and students with the necessary resources to effectively develop and implement organizational strategies.

Coverage

- Executive Education
- Upward Feedback
- Talent Identification and Management
- Change Management
- Performance Improvement
- Personnel Policies
- Disputes Resolution
- Employee Benefits
- Training and Development
- Human Resources Development

IGI Global is currently accepting manuscripts for publication within this series. To submit a proposal for a volume in this series, please contact our Acquisition Editors at Acquisitions@igi-global.com or visit: http://www.igi-global.com/publish/.

The Advances in Human Resources Management and Organizational Development (AHRMOD) Book Series (ISSN 2327-3372) is published by IGI Global, 701 E. Chocolate Avenue, Hershey, PA 17033-1240, USA, www.igi-global.com. This series is composed of titles available for purchase individually; each title is edited to be contextually exclusive from any other title within the series. For pricing and ordering information please visit http://www.igi-global.com/book-series/advances-human-resources-management-organizational/73670. Postmaster: Send all address changes to above address.

Titles in this Series

For a list of additional titles in this series, please visit: www.igi-global.com/book-series

Building Competencies for Organizational Success Emerging Research and Opportunities
Donta S. Harper (University of Washington, USA)
Business Science Reference • © 2021 • 217pp • H/C (ISBN: 9781799865162) • US $195.00

Role of Leadership in Facilitating Healing and Renewal in Times of Organizational Trauma and Change
Lynda Byrd-Poller (Thomas Nelson Community College, USA) Jennifer L. Farmer (Renewed Mindset LLC, USA) and Valerie Ford (ISP Global Communications LLC, USA)
Business Science Reference • © 2021 • 291pp • H/C (ISBN: 9781799870166) • US $195.00

Impact of Infodemic on Organizational Performance
Muhammad Waseem Bari (Government College University, Faisalabad, Pakistan) and Emilia Alaverdov (Georgian Technical University, Georgia)
Business Science Reference • © 2021 • 380pp • H/C (ISBN: 9781799871644) • US $195.00

Handbook of Research on Advancements in Organizational Data Collection and Measurements Strategies for Addressing Attitudes, Beliefs, and Behaviors
Mihai C. Bocarnea (Regent University, USA) Bruce E. Winston (Regent University, USA) and Debra Dean (Regent University, USA)
Business Science Reference • © 2021 • 400pp • H/C (ISBN: 9781799876656) • US $295.00

Transgender Discrimination in the Workplace
Qaiser Rafique Yasser (Preston University, Islamabad, Pakistan)
Business Science Reference • © 2021 • 315pp • H/C (ISBN: 9781799873129) • US $195.00

Effective Strategies for Communicating Insights in Business
Ross Jackson (Wittenberg University, USA) and Amanda Reboulet (Jacoulet, USA)
Business Science Reference • © 2021 • 261pp • H/C (ISBN: 9781799839644) • US $195.00

Handbook of Research on Remote Work and Worker Well-Being in the Post-COVID-19 Era
Daniel Wheatley (University of Birmingham, UK) Irene Hardill (Northumbria University, UK) and Sarah Buglass (Nottingham Trent University, UK)
Business Science Reference • © 2021 • 420pp • H/C (ISBN: 9781799867548) • US $265.00

IGI Global
PUBLISHER of TIMELY KNOWLEDGE

701 East Chocolate Avenue, Hershey, PA 17033, USA
Tel: 717-533-8845 x100 • Fax: 717-533-8661
E-Mail: cust@igi-global.com • www.igi-global.com

Table of Contents

Detailed Table of Contents

The 2030 Agenda implies an important commitment that should be achieved by companies, countries, and governments, and the goals set should be worked on with the aim to boost the areas they address. Corporate social responsibility is a tool for organizations to act on behalf not only of the public but also of all stakeholders, as affirmed by the stakeholders' theory. Given the interest the stakeholders have in achieving the Sustainable Development Goals, it is important to observe the attitudes and behaviors that the organizations develop to achieve their intended contribution. This chapter analyzes the companies´ attitudes and behaviors developed to fulfill five SDGs (from 1 to 5). The study is focused on the content analysis of the corporate social responsibility reports of 16 car manufacturing companies. At the end, the authors propose some future lines of research.

This chapter explores how luxury fashion and accessories firms are adapting their CSR strategies to be more sustainable considering that the firms have been impacted by the COVID-19 pandemic. In this context, the authors explore how companies are communicating their efforts and how they engage consumers according to sustainable development. The methodology followed in this study is based on case studies analyzing the activities of luxury fashion and accessories brands operating in different countries, such as LVMH, Kering, Richemont, Chanel, EssilorLuxottica, Chow Tai Fook, PVH, and Swatch Group. The results show that almost all luxury fashion and accessories firms include the SDGs in their CSR/sustainability strategies and communicate how their efforts contribute to achieving the 17 SDGs. Nearly all these companies set long-term objectives including areas, such as 1) environmental protection as a key axis of their strategy, 2) support for the communities where they operate, and 3) promotion of equality and inclusion of their employees.

This chapter investigates whether sustainability practices of one of the leaders of the coffee industry, Starbucks, have changed during the COVID-19 pandemic as compared to the period before the virus outbreak. In particular, the authors ask which dimensions, or sub-dimensions, of sustainability in particular have been cut off first. Secondary data in the form of industry and company reports, websites, as well as research articles has been used. The findings of this study are particularly important for practitioners and researchers interested in changes in the coffee market, corporate sustainability, and consumer behavior, particularly during a systemic crisis, such as the COVID-19 pandemic. The topic is very current, and high-quality interdisciplinary research on a continuously deepening crisis with an unknown expiration date promises value-added potential, much more than "filling a gap" in the literature.

In 2015, the United Nations adopted 17 major Sustainable Development Goals (SDGs) to address current economic, social, and environmental challenges. Governments play a key role in achieving the SDGs through advocacy, awareness, and regulation. In this work, the authors focus on SDG 3, "Guarantee a Healthy Life and Promote Well-Being for All Ages." Specifically, the articulation of citizen participation for health promotion in health schools is reviewed. They have been selected by choosing four schools and a Spanish entity that show how health education can facilitate the development of citizen participation in the field of health. The health schools and their corresponding training programs show the multiplicity of ways that citizens acquire access to the health field, ranging from information to decision-making in the system.

Compliance with the Sustainable Development Goals (SDGs) and the 2030 Agenda represents a large investment that cannot be obtained solely through public resources. Therefore, it is necessary for the private sector to align itself with the SDGs and integrate them into its business model. In an attempt to align private interests with the SDGs, various impact measurement initiatives have emerged in recent years. However, none of them have been universally accepted, in part, because they still have weaknesses. As an alternative, some companies have chosen to become certified. The figures show that the B Corp certification is one of the most important ones internationally, since it has been growing at a rapid pace since its creation. In fact, there are currently almost 4,000 certified companies throughout the world. Despite this fact, there are very few studies which analyze the main effects of this certification yet. Therefore, the objective of this chapter is to validate a questionnaire that collects these effects through a Delphi study, formed by a panel of experts in the B Corp movement.

Entrepreneurship conditions the sustainable development of a society by the economic, social, and environmental impact of new ventures. Specifically, startups, due to their high level of innovation and scalability, have an important role in fostering and accelerating the implementation of sustainable practices. An empirical analysis is carried out through data collected in the framework of the GEM

Preface

The COVID-19 global pandemic has had a profound impact on the global business community. Amidst the ongoing crisis, countries around the world are opening up again to a business world in which both consumer behaviors and company practices have started to change. Numerous companies are using corporate social responsibility to demonstrate their commitment to fighting against COVID-19 and alleviating the negative consequences of the pandemic for their stakeholders; due to this, corporate social responsibility is expected to become a core issue for managers and researchers in the post-pandemic era.

Future Advancements for CSR and the Sustainable Development Goals in a Post-COVID-19 World discusses the challenges and opportunities of corporate social responsibility and studies the reactions to the COVID-19 global pandemic that may lead to changes in corporate social responsibility, corporate approaches to sustainable development goals, and stakeholders' reactions to the post-COVID-19 era. This book addresses the opportunities for businesses to shift towards more genuine and authentic corporate social responsibility that contributes to addressing urgent social and environmental challenges. In doing so, the many academic areas covered in this publication include Corporate Social Responsibility, Corporate Sustainability, Entrepreneurship, Greenwashing, Organizational Development, Politization of Corporations, Social Entrepreneurship, Social Media, Socially Responsible Attitudes and Behaviors, Sustainability Leaders, Sustainable Development Goals (SDGs) and Value-Driven Management.

Covering these topics, the book is ideal for managers, executives, entrepreneurs, business professionals and practitioners, policymakers, academicians, researchers, and students.

The book includes 13 chapters where scholars and practitioners from six different countries provide their views on how businesses and the society can take advantage of the COVID-19 global pandemic situation to commit themselves to the UN Sustainable Development Goals through the application of more meaningful corporate social responsibility and entrepreneurship practices. Contributors are based on Canada, Denmark, Turkey, India, Oman, and diverse Spanish cities. Therefore, the range of nationalities included in the book represents an opportunity to reflect on the multiple perspectives adopted in different continents and regions to comply with the UN Sustainable Development Goals.

Although the book is not divided into sections, the chapters have been organized based on a top-down structure that moves from the theoretical underpinnings of sustainability, corporate social responsibility, and the UN Sustainable Development Goals (Chapters 1-5), to empirical representations of how public and private companies and institutions are dealing with their commitments to sustainability after the Covid-19 pandemic (Chapters 6-10). Finally, the book presents chapters where the authors have mainly focused on the role of entrepreneurship (Chapters 11-12), and social media (Chapter 13) to contribute to sustainability.

In Chapter 1, the authors explore the role that the private sector assumes in promoting sustainable development and fighting economic, social and environmental international challenges by working on the United Nations Sustainable Development Goals. From a theoretical approach, the chapter provides a literature review on business strategies (i.e. corporate social responsibility and social entrepreneurship) that can align business goals with the SDGs. It also presents a discussion on the main benefits of working on the SDGs (i.e., social impact and business value) that serves as a rationale for companies to invest in social and environmental programs. The chapter concludes with an overview of recent literature that has explored the corporate-SDGs intersection, which assists the authors in identifying gaps in current literature and relevant areas of future research on the involvement of the private sector in the Agenda 2030. In summary, the chapter aims to serve as an introduction to the book in which many of the topics discussed over the rest of chapters are introduced and briefly presented to create a common thread for the book.

Chapter 2 explores the evolving field of Corporate Social Responsibility (CSR) research and practices in the Sustainable Development Goals era. The authors introduce a contemporary definition of CSR reflective of the SDGs era. Section-1 provides an exploration of the conceptual and theoretical foundations underpinning the evolution of CSR approaches. Section-2 advocates for the SDGs framework in support of the proliferation of sustainability management across business settings. Section-3 delineates how adopting the SDGs as a framework for corporate sustainability can enhance corporate resilience towards economic shocks. Section-4 discusses strategic perspectives on corporate sustainability management and elaborates on the role of business in satisfying promises of sustainable development. Illuminating the legitimacy of the SDGs as a framework for positioning corporations as global sustainability leaders, this chapter serves as a roadmap outlining how business can advance their CSR strategies to align business goals with societal needs in a post-COVID-19 World.

In Chapter 3, the author proposes to analyze the theory of the political enterprise with focus on the concept of ethical values-driven management in the contemporary debate on the politization of business in service of sustainability in cosmopolitan society. By service of cosmopolitan society of the political enterprise the chapter investigates the idea of the political enterprise as being a responsible political, ethical, and social agent with focus on the 17 UN sustainable development goals (SDGs) that is required to justify its mission and role in society as a political actor that makes a different for its social and political community. The company is embedded in a social and political order with a diversity of political values, and the discussion about the meaning of the concept of values-driven management is therefore fundamental if one is to analyze the concept of the political enterprise in service of sustainable development goals.

Following the stakeholder theory and the resource-based view, Chapter 4 attempts to specify value creation of companies to preserve strategic position while satisfying the demands and interests of their stakeholders. In this sense, corporate social responsibility seems as a viable way of providing help and support to stakeholders during the fight against the pandemic as well as a catalyzer for the integration of sustainable development goals that can bridge the widened gap in the society. Hence, this chapter seeks to present an understanding on socially responsible value creation, dynamic and digital capabilities, and implementation of sustainability driven CSR initiatives to ensure recovery, growth and achieve sustainable development goals.

Chapter 5 focuses on the disclosure of non-financial information by companies in their annual reports as an increasingly important duty of companies due to its interest for stakeholders' decision-making. This chapter aims to map research articles that have addressed the study of non-financial information in the last twenty years and have been published in journal indexed in the Web of Science (JCR) and Scopus (SJR) databases. The analyses carried out are described from a triple perspective: meta-perspective, content-based perspective and methodological perspective. The main results obtained show the growing interest in research on non-financial information in terms of both quantity and quality of the publications.

Starting in Chapter 6, the book moves from the theoretical discussion of sustainability to the empirical exploration of corporate and institutional commitment to CSR and the UN SDGs in diverse industries. For instance, the authors of Chapter 6 argue that, given the interest the stakeholders have in achieving the Sustainable Development Goals, it is important to observe the attitudes and behaviors that the organizations develop to achieve their intended contribution in the sustainability sphere. Based on this idea, the chapter analyzes the companies´ attitudes and behaviors developed to fulfill five SDGs (from 1 to 5). The study is focused on the content analysis of the Corporate Social Responsibility reports of 16 car manufacturing companies.

Chapter 7 explores how luxury fashion and accessories firms are adapting their CSR strategies to be more sustainable by considering how they have been impacted by the COVID-19 pandemic. In this context, the authors explore how companies are communicating their efforts and how they engage consumers according to sustainable development. The methodology followed in the study presented in this chapter is based on case studies analyzing the activities of luxury fashion and accessories brands operating in different countries, such as LVMH, Kering, Richemont, Chanel, EssilorLuxottica, Chow Tai Fook, PVH and Swatch Group. The results show that almost all luxury fashion and accessories firms include the SDGs in their CSR/sustainability strategies, and communicate how their efforts contribute to achieving the 17 SDGs. Nearly all these companies set long-term objectives including areas, such as: i) environmental protection as a key axis of their strategy, ii) support for the communities where they operate, and iii) promotion of equality and inclusion of their employees.

In Chapter 8, the authors investigate whether sustainability practices of one of the leaders of the coffee-industry, Starbucks, have changed during the Covid-19 pandemic as compared to the period before the virus outbreak. In particular, the authors ask which dimensions, or sub-dimensions, of sustainability in particular have been cut off first. Secondary data in the form of industry and company reports, websites as well as research articles are used. The findings of the study are particularly important for practitioners and researchers interested in changes in the coffee market, corporate sustainability, and consumer behavior, particularly during a systemic crisis, such as the Covid-19 pandemic.

In Chapter 9, the authors focus on SDG 3 "Guarantee a healthy life and promote well-being for all ages". Specifically, the articulation of citizen participation for health promotion in Health Schools is reviewed. For their empirical analysis, the authors have chosen four schools and a Spanish entity that show how health education can facilitate the development of citizen participation in the field of health. The Health Schools and their corresponding training programs show the multiplicity of ways that citizens acquire access to the health field, ranging from information to decision-making in the system.

Chapter 10 explores B Corporations as an interesting certification movement that can take for-profit companies to commit to SDGs more deeply. As defended by the authors of the chapter, compliance with the SDGs and the 2030 Agenda represents a large investment that cannot be obtained solely through public resources. Therefore, it is necessary for the private sector to align itself with the SDGs and integrate them into its business model. In an attempt to align private interests with the SDGs, the B Corp certification is one of the most important initiatives internationally, since it has been growing at a rapid pace since its creation. In fact, there are currently almost 4000 certified companies throughout the world. Despite this fact, very few studies analyze the main effects of this certification yet. Therefore, the objective of this chapter is to validate a questionnaire that collects these effects through a Delphi study, formed by a panel of experts in the B Corp movement.

Chapter 11 focuses on entrepreneurship intentions as another interesting way to advance sustainability efforts worldwide. Entrepreneurship condition the sustainable development of a society by the economic, social and environmental impact of new ventures. Specifically, startups, due to its high level of innovation and scalability, have an important role in fostering and accelerating the implementation of sustainable practices. In this chapter, an empirical analysis is carried out through data collected in the framework of the GEM project to define the extent in which startups innovation impact SDGs. The results highlight that the most frequently addressed goals belong to the economic sphere, (e.g., SDG 8 and SDG 9), while environmental and social aspects are scarcely considered. More than half of the SDGs are addressed by less than 10% of the startups. The chapter concludes that a change in policies to promote SDGs is needed to foster the implementation of CSR strategies from early entrepreneurial stages, increase startups awareness and face the lack of attention that some SDGs are receiving from the currently emerging innovation.

In a similar vein, Chapter 12 goes in-depth into the definition and study of social entrepreneurship (SE). The authors argue that, despite the increasing research in the field of SE, unfortunately there is not yet consensus on its conceptualization. The main points of disagreement are related to the business' mission and to the source of income. Based on these two dimensions and a bottom-up approach, this chapter contributes to previous literature by proposing and empirically exploring a categorization of three types of social entrepreneurs: socially responsible entrepreneur (SRE), social enterprise entrepreneur (SEE) and social initiative entrepreneur (SIE), which is applied empirically to explore the social entrepreneurs' personal characteristics (gender, age and education), similarities and differences. Multinomial logistic regressions are applied on an international sample of GEM data that includes 11,280 commercial entrepreneurs and 3,373 social entrepreneurs. The findings of the study will permit researchers and practitioners to understand previous empirical findings on social entrepreneurship more clearly and to advance in the study of this evolving phenomenon.

The book concludes with Chapter 13, in which the authors aim to explore the ways in which targeted consumers engage with CSR activities on social media platforms, specifically when discussing their opinions and experiences regarding the CSR activities of their favorite brands. For this purpose, the variable moral norms was integrated in the theory of reasoned action. The study data about consumers' engagement (CE) in corporate social responsibility communication (CSRC) over social media (SM) platforms – electronic word of mouth, or e-WoM - was collected from 290 actual engaged consumers in online ordering and involved in social media groups. The findings confirmed that the antecedent factors (consumers' attitude, subjective norms and moral norms) have a positive influence on consumers' intention to use e-WoM, while no effect was found on CE in CSRC in SM. Furthermore, e-WoM found to have direct significant impact on CE in CSRC in SM as well as it mediates the relationship between the antecedent factors and CE in CSRC in SM.

Covering this vast range of topics, many of them relatively new in the research field, the content of *Future Advancements for CSR and the Sustainable Development Goals in a Post-COVID-19 World* contributes significantly to previous academic research. The contribution lays on the constitution of the book as one of the first collective works that focus specifically on the consequences of the Covid-19 outbreak for the advancement of sustainability efforts and the consecution of the 17 UN Sustainable Development Goals programmed in the 2030 Agenda. Going through this book, the reader will either find inspiration to engage more deeply with CSR if he/she is a practitioner, or find interesting new lines of research if he/she is an academic. In any other case, the book is a good start to learn the ways in which private and public companies and institutions are dealing with the consequences of the pandemic and its impact on their sustainability efforts.

Chapter 1
Companies and the UN Sustainable Development Goals:
At the Intersection Between Social Impact and Business Value

Elsa Diez-Busto
University of Cantabria, Spain

Paula San-Martín
University of Cantabria, Spain

Andrea Pérez
https://orcid.org/0000-0003-3521-1783
University of Cantabria, Spain

ABSTRACT

This chapter explores the role that the private sector assumes in promoting sustainable development and fighting economic, social, and environmental international challenges by working on the United Nations Sustainable Development Goals. From a theoretical approach, the chapter provides a literature review on business strategies (i.e., corporate social responsibility and social entrepreneurship) that can align business goals with the SDGs. It also presents a discussion on the main benefits of working on the SDGs (i.e., social impact and business value) that serves as a rationale for companies to invest in social and environmental programs. The chapter concludes with an overview of recent literature that has explored the corporate-SDGs intersection, which assists the authors in identifying gaps in current literature and relevant areas of future research on the involvement of the private sector in the Agenda 2030.

DOI: 10.4018/978-1-7998-8065-3.ch001

INTRODUCTION

In the context of the Covid-19 pandemic, economies are facing a deep and growing crisis. Although the trajectory of the crisis is still uncertain, it is evident that the world will change markedly after the pandemic as a consequence of its important implications for public health, the economy, social stability or world politics, among other factors. However, if crisis management is approached correctly, important positive lessons can be learned for the future. Thus, the Covid-19 pandemic may also represent opportunities for better governance, and this is a crucial time to make high-level commitments that build a better world (Sachs et al., 2020).

Working to achieve the Sustainable Development Goals (SDGs) is one of the high-level commitments that can help rebuild and sustain our planet into the future. The SDGs are the global goals, of a shared nature, for sustainable development, and the Covid-19 crisis makes them more relevant than ever. In this sense, the implementation process of the SDGs offers unparalleled opportunities to advance equal opportunities and promote social and economic empowerment, helping countries to promote further the cause of sustainable development in their territories, thus benefiting their populations (Leal Filho et al., 2019). More precisely, the SDGs can help international governments chart medium and long-term responses so that countries can recover more quickly from the health, economic, social and environmental impacts of the pandemic (Sachs et al., 2020).

Nevertheless, national-level progress on the SDGs, and therefore, sustainable development of the planet, cannot be achieved solely with work coming from public administration. As budgets for public development continue to shrink (Scheyvens et al., 2016), the need for financial support and collaborative partnerships becomes increasingly salient. On the contrary, progress in the fulfilment of the SDGs requires the awareness and involvement of agents and institutions from very diverse spheres, such as government organizations, the private sector, civil society and individual citizens (Bebbington & Unerman, 2018). For example, the private sector has many strengths to contribute to meeting the SDGs, including innovation, responsiveness, efficiency, and provision of specific skills and resources (Scheyvens et al., 2016). The importance of the private sector is such that many experts affirm that the SDGs cannot be achieved without the contribution of companies (van Zanten & van Tulder, 2018).

However, we must be aware that the involvement of the private sector in the achievement of the SDGs depends largely on their ability to create business value derived from their investments in social and environmental activities (Busco et al., 2017). In this regard, it is understood that companies will align with the SDGs and integrate them into their business models in a more solid way when they perceive that these goals help them generate new income, increase synergies in their supply chains, recruit and retain talent and/or awaken the interest of investors (Busco et al., 2017). After all, companies committed to sustainable development want to achieve the same goals as any other company: driving revenue growth, creating value and accelerating business expansion. Otherwise, if working on the SDGs does not bring direct benefits to companies in the form of business value, it will be difficult for them to be proactive in integrating these objectives into their business models (Schönherr et al., 2017). This fact will greatly hinder the possibility of achieving true long-term sustainable development at the national level, preventing the achievement of the 2030 Agenda on time.

As will be further discussed in this chapter, some scholars have started to identify a clear business logic behind companies' involvement in the SDGs (van Zanten & van Tulder, 2018), as they can unlock millionaire annual opportunities for value creation in terms of accounting-based measures of financial performance (e.g., ROA, ROE, etc) (Byun & Oh, 2018) or significant increases in the value of companies in financial markets (Pérez et al., 2020). As a consequence, it seems that the world might be facing the emergence of a new purpose-led business era in which the private sector may turn towards more sustainable business practices not only based on normative causes but also on voluntary, conscious and self-motivating goals. In this context, the SDGs can be used as a framework for companies to smoothly synergize business value creation and social impact delivery, which have been traditionally perceived as being mutually exclusive (Dorado, 2006). Some examples of the nice fit between business value and social impact provided by the SDGs framework will be further discussed in this chapter. This is the case of some new forms of business practices, such as social entrepreneurship and the B Corporations movement, which have a social impact at the core of their mission (Stubbs, 2017; Tabares, 2021) while they still work to be financially self-sufficient and even profitable (Carriles-Alberdi et al., 2021).

In any case, the scientific research existing to date barely covers the role of the private sector in achieving international policy objectives in terms of sustainable development, so that very little is still known about how the SDGs contribute to the creation of business value (Adams, 2017) or how various companies and sectors are supporting the implementation of each of the 17 SDGs concretely (ElAlfy et al., 2020a). The academic literature shows that certain studies have discussed the influence of companies on some specific sustainable development challenges, such as poverty and inequality, peace or energy and climate change (Kolk et al., 2018). However, global and integrative studies that analyse the business contribution to the totality of the SDGs have not yet been provided, while the analysis of the specific impacts that social and environmental activities are having on the creation of business value and/or social impact is still scarce (Kolk, 2016). As a result, a detailed analysis is needed on how companies are contributing to sustainable development, which will allow monitoring and making a more comprehensive evaluation of the effectiveness of CSR and sustainable development policies that can contribute to meeting the 2030 Agenda on time (Scheyvens et al., 2016). As explained by Blowfield (2012), the request for more information to understand the potential of companies as development agents expresses a genuine need to know the possibilities, limitations and conditions of the business role in sustainable development so that, in turn, opportunities can be better exploited, risks can be contained and complementary contributions from different types of agents can be optimized. Also, more information can provide deepened understanding as to how best practices can be transferred and scaled across geo-political and industrial contexts. In this sense, important questions persist that require a more critical stance on the business contribution to the fulfilment of the SDGs. For example, can for-profit companies make a significant contribution to achieving the SDGs, or is it more likely that in the future we will continue to see only business "as usual", resulting in higher profits for some, but notable losses of opportunities for many? (Scheyvens et al., 2016). Or, more specifically, how are business performance measures integrated into compliance with the SDGs at the country level? (Bebbington & Unerman, 2018).

Along these lines, the main objective of this chapter is to reflect on both the potential and the current limitations of the private sector to contribute to the fulfilment of the SDGs within the framework of the 2030 Agenda. More specifically, an extensive literature review is carried out by revising the research that, to date, have addressed the interrelation between corporate social responsibility (CSR), sustainability, SDGs, business value and social impact. In doing so, the authors aim at clarifying how social and environmental activities of the private sector contribute to advance in the achievement of the SDGs, while also clarifying whether these activities generate social impact and business value for the organizations that implement them. With this proposal, the authors intend that the chapter serves as an introductory conceptual framework to the book "Future Advancements for CSR and the Sustainable Development Goals in a Post-COVID-19 World", in such a way that the main concepts within the book are clarified in advance for a correct understanding of the rest of the chapters included in this collective work, which will delve into more specific concepts and strategies on the matter under discussion in this research book.

BACKGROUND

UN Sustainable Development Goals (SDGs)

In September 2015, following the decision made at the Rio+ 20 Conference 2012 and after more than three years of intergovernmental work through the Open Working Group, the member states of the United Nations (UN) proposed a new set of Sustainable Development Goals (SDGs) at the 70th UN General Assembly. The SDGs were conceived to succeed the Millennium Development Goals (MDGs), with an expiration date of 2015, as the main benchmark for international development in the period 2015-2030. They were included in the 2030 Agenda for Sustainable Development (United Nations, 2015). Developing the SDGs was widely seen as an ambitious challenge, as these goals covered a much broader range of sustainability issues than their predecessors (Leal Filho et al., 2019). While the MDGs primarily focused on human development outcomes, such as poverty alleviation, the SDGs took a more holistic approach, broadening their range of goals to capture all aspects of the so-called 'triple bottom line' approach, including social development, environmental results and economic achievements of countries (Bebbington & Unerman, 2018). The Synthesis Report of the Secretary-General on the Post-2015 Sustainable Development Agenda, published on December 4, 2014, included six 'essential elements' to achieve the SDGs, in which inclusion, dignity and justice were prominent (Scheyvens et al., 2016). Along this line, the SDGs act mainly in the areas of justice, governance and association among the state members (Leal Filho et al., 2019). Unlike the MDGs, the SDGs were also intended to be universal, that is, applicable to all countries and not just developing countries (van Zanten & van Tulder, 2018). They should also serve as guides for a difficult transition to sustainable development, which the international community has been avoiding since the 1992 Earth Summit (Le Blanc, 2015). The consultative approach adopted to develop the SDGs was also praised (Scheyvens et al., 2016). More precisely, the SDGs were established after a massive consultation with stakeholders (Kharas & Zhang, 2014) that involved governments, companies, civil society organizations and knowledge institutions (van Zanten & van Tulder, 2018). During the development of the proposal, over 4.5 million responses were collected in the MY World Survey of the UN Development Programme (UNDP), a process that was part of the hyper-participatory approach assumed for the preparation of the SDGs.

As an intergovernmental negotiated document, the SDGs represent a delicate political balance (Ahmed et al., 2015), which is presented in the form of 17 goals, including several target indicators each, which add up to a total of 169 specific objectives. Furthermore, the SDGs and their target indicators can be seen as a network, in which there are links among all the goals through numerous targets that refer to multiple SDGs (Le Blanc, 2015). As explained by Boto-Álvarez & García-Fernández (2020), the 2030 Agenda is indivisible and must be implemented as a whole, in an integrated and not fragmented way, since all the SDGs are closely related. Some studies have explored causal relationships among the SDGs (Le Blanc, 2015) determining that, in the same way, that a chain is only as strong as its weakest link, sustainable development can only be achieved to the limits of the weakest SDG (Leal Filho et al., 2019). These 17 SDGs aim to stimulate action, over a period of 15 years, in areas of critical importance for humanity and the planet (United Nations, 2015), including the fight against poverty, epidemics and global warming, to name just a few (Boto-Álvarez & García-Fernández, 2020). As indicated by Kumar et al. (2016), the SDGs can be classified into three main groups: the first group refers to the extension of the MDGs until 2030 (SDGs 1-7); the second group focuses on social inclusion (SDGs 8-10); the third group refers to urban sustainability (SDGs 11-17).

SDG1 emphasizes ending all forms of extreme poverty in the world. More specifically, it focuses on reducing poverty to half the proportion of people of all ages in any country, according to the respective national definitions of poverty. SDG2, which aims to end hunger and achieve food security with better nutrition, relates to the promotion of sustainable agriculture and provides a cushion for achieving the goal of poverty eradication. SDG3, which focuses on ensuring healthy lives and promoting well-being for all, has a direct impact on quality of life by especially ending premature mortality. SDG4 relates to one of the most important areas of sustainable development, inclusive and quality education. Ensuring gender equality in all forms and all areas is the key focus of SDG5. SDG6 and SDG7 together are necessary to ensure environmental justice in a global context, providing universal and safe access to water and renewable energy sources. SDG8 seeks to promote inclusive and sustainable economic growth with productive and decent working conditions for all. This SDG links economic sustainability at the country level with labour dignity at the individual level. SDG9 aims to achieve inclusive and sustainable industrialization, focusing on technology, innovation and sustainable infrastructures. Reducing inequalities among countries is the focus of SDG10. SDG11 focuses on ensuring that cities are inclusive, safe, resilient and sustainable. While climate change and environmental sustainability issues are integrated into most of the SDGs, SDG13 is particularly focused on combating climate change and its impact on the planet. SDG14 aims to ensure the sustainable use of the ocean, seas and marine resources. Another important development aspect is the sustainable use of terrestrial ecosystems and forests, which is captured in SDG15. SDG16 focuses on promoting peaceful and inclusive societies with access to justice. In doing so, it calls for equal access to knowledge and justice services for all. Finally, SDG17 focuses on issues related to the effective implementation of all the other SDGs through the establishment of alliances among numerous institutions in society. Graphic 1 summarises the 17 SDGs and their main objectives.

The Role of Companies in Driving SDGs

The implementation of the SDGs globally requires very ambitious financing programs to achieve the goals in time. The traditional approach to sustainable development financing, mainly based on public investments, is insufficient and requires a radical paradigm shift (Ahmed et al., 2015). Due to the transformative nature of the new development agenda, together with the large scale of the economic requirements that it entails, all possible resources must be mobilized for the world to be successful in meeting the 17 SDGs (Ahmed et al., 2015). For example, in the last United Nations Conference on Trade and Development, experts estimated that the investment required to advancing in the SDGs achievement stays between 5 and 7 trillion dollars per year (Avrampou et al., 2019). Only in developing countries, investment estimates range from 3.3 to 4.5 trillion dollars to work on key areas such as basic infrastructure, food security, mitigation of climate change, health and education. For this purpose, developing countries have an annual financing gap of approximately 2.5 trillion dollars (Salazar & Katigbak, 2016). Therefore, the SDG framework recognizes that achieving these goals will require concerted action among numerous social actors, including governments, public and private sector organizations, civil society, and individual citizens (Bebbington & Unerman, 2008; Avrampou et al., 2019).

Table 1. The 17 Sustainable Development Goals of the 2030 Agenda

Goal	Description
	SDG1. No poverty End poverty in all its forms everywhere
	SDG2. Zero hunger End hunger, achieve food security and improved nutrition and promote sustainable agriculture
	SDG3. Good health and well-being Ensure healthy lives and promote well-being for all at all ages
	SDG4. Quality education Ensure inclusive and equitable quality education and promote lifelong learning opportunities for all
	SDG5. Gender equality Achieve gender equality and empower all women and girls
	SDG6. Clean water and sanitation Ensure availability and sustainable management of water and sanitation for all
	SDG7. Affordable and clean energy Ensure access to affordable, reliable, sustainable and modern energy for all
	SDG8. Decent work and economic growth Promote sustained, inclusive and sustainable economic growth, full and productive employment and decent work for all
	SDG9. Industry, innovation and infrastructure Build resilient infrastructure, promote inclusive and sustainable industrialization and foster innovation
	SDG10. Reduced inequalities Reduce inequality within and among countries
	SDG11. Sustainable cities and communities Make cities and human settlements inclusive, safe, resilient and sustainable
	SDG12. Responsible consumption and production Ensure sustainable consumption and production patterns
	SDG13. Climate action Take urgent action to combat climate change and its impacts
	SDG14. Life below water Conserve and sustainably use the oceans, seas and marine resources for sustainable development
	SDG15. Life on land Protect, restore and promote sustainable use of terrestrial ecosystems, sustainably manage forests, combat desertification, and halt and reverse land degradation and halt biodiversity loss
	SDG16. Peace, justice and strong institutions Promote peaceful and inclusive societies for sustainable development, provide access to justice for all and build effective, accountable and inclusive institutions at all levels
	SDG17. Partnership for the goals Strengthen the means of implementation and revitalize the global partnership for sustainable development

Source: UN Department of Economic and Social Affairs website (https://sdgs.un.org/goals)

A crucial actor in this context is the private sector, which is expected to play its role not only through the financing of SDGs initiatives but also by integrating the 2030 Agenda as a core pillar that drives corporate decision-making to align global value chains with today's most pertinent societal needs. The start of the new millennium has been marked by great enthusiasm for how the private sector can contribute to achieving the SDGs, by increasing available funds and bringing relevant knowledge to address major sustainable development issues (Scheyvens et al., 2016). For instance, when designing the SDGs, business leaders sat alongside politicians and civil society actors, becoming one of the main stakeholders in the Open Working Group in charge of setting up the SDGs (van Zanten & van Tulder, 2018). The close involvement of the private sector in the process of designing the SDGs reflected a conscious change in business mentality, which has led to the private sector being more intertwined in the world of sustainable development policy and planning. Consequently, many progressive companies have developed business models that are imbued with social values and responsibilities, and that seek commercial success hand in hand with more sustainable approaches and positive social and environmental impacts. Corporate Social Responsibility (CSR) and Social Entrepreneurship are the two most successful approaches that have emerged and extensively developed over the last decades to accommodate the private sector's work on sustainable development issues. As it will be further discussed in this section, these two concepts constitute notable strides in corporate sustainability efforts as they reflect a change of mentality in companies from the traditional purely financial perspective (i.e., the maximization of economic benefits) (Friedman, 1962) towards a way of doing business based on the win-win philosophy and the balance between business value and social impact (Pérez, 2011).

Corporate Social Responsibility

Although early CSR conceptualizations developed in the 1950s, it was not until the 1960s that the concept and its academic study were especially developed. In this decade, numerous definitions were proposed under two frameworks: the orthodox paradigm and the stakeholder approach. While the orthodox paradigm defends CSR as a one-dimensional concept in which the only responsibility of a company is to provide goods and services to society and maximize shareholder profit (Friedman, 1962); the stakeholder approach replaces this orientation with a more social and abstract vision of CSR, under which companies must take a leading role in enhancing society, by accepting economic, legal, ethical and philanthropic responsibilities towards all their stakeholders (Carroll, 1979).

Along the stakeholder approach to CSR, Maignan & Ferrell (2004) proposed a classification of CSR definitions based on the orientation that lies behind them. According to these authors, CSR can be understood as:

- **Social obligation:** CSR involves various corporate responsibilities that include financial, legal, ethical and philanthropic obligations; CSR is primarily focused on corporate financial and legal responsibilities.
- **Stakeholder obligation:** Companies should not be responsible for the whole society but only for those groups who directly affect or are affected by businesses. The company's main CSR activities should be focused on satisfying stakeholders' demands.
- **Voluntary ethical behaviour:** CSR is a voluntary, proactive and preventive commitment of the company, regardless of any obligation imposed by society or stakeholders.
- **Set of management processes**: CSR as corporate social responsiveness that includes monitoring changing environmental conditions, addressing the needs of target audiences and developing policies and strategic action plans to improve corporate image.

Based on the numerous definitional approaches, it appears that there is no unanimous definition for CSR (Whitehouse, 2006), although most of the proposals point out the relationship between CSR and business sustainability and ethics, as well as with the company's commitment to the interests of its stakeholders (Panapannan et al., 2003). From a close analysis of previous definitions, it follows that CSR should be understood as a global concept that includes a whole range of philanthropic and normative issues related to the role of companies in society (Maignan & Ferrell, 2001), as well as all moral obligations that maximize the positive impact while minimizing the negative effect of the company in its surroundings (Pérez, 2011).

Since the 1990s, CSR has gained increased attention from practitioners and scholars because CSR investment has been demonstrated to lead to numerous corporate benefits such as the recovery of corporate credibility after product and company crises (Lin et al., 2011), employee attraction and retention (Kim & Park, 2011) or beneficial relationships with consumers and other primary stakeholders (Peloza & Shang, 2011). Most commonly, companies implement various forms of CSR activities, such as charitable donations, the use of green materials, or diversity initiatives, among others (Yoo & Lee, 2018). For instance, only in Spain, in 2017 companies invested over 846 million euros in CSR activities, which represented a 10% increase over CSR investment in 2016 (SERES, 2018), while the growth increase has been maintained over the years. Additionally, the Covid-19 crisis has lead numerous companies around the world to proactively engage in new CSR activities, particularly those that can offer immediate assistance to the fight against the virus (He & Harris, 2020). As an example, He & Harris (2020) referred to the case of UK manufacturing companies, which had "transformed their factories to produce ventilators, personal protective equipment, hand sanitiser, and so on, with some of them donating, instead of selling, these products". They also referred to examples within the telecommunications sector, supermarkets or banking companies.

However, it is also true that, in most countries, the work carried out until now by companies in the CSR realm has been framed in a legislative context characterized by the so-called "soft law", which means that companies usually apply some internal CSR norms that can influence the general legislative situation, but whose lack of obligation relegates them to the scope of voluntariness (Yan, 2019). This lack of legislative obligation has resulted in the actual implementation of many CSR policies that, in numerous cases, rely on merely generic commitments that are not transferred to real business strategies. As an example, a recent report on corporate sustainability highlighted that only 48% of companies in the world currently adopt the SDGs, and only 21% of CEOs feel that their business activities are contributing to the SDGs achievement (Accenture, 2019). As an example, on many occasions, we find companies that lack a strategic orientation in their CSR policies as their leaders often struggle to find paths to achieve CSR-related goals. Such a lack of a strategic focus leads to frustration, sunken time and financial costs and eventual disengagement with deepened sustainability efforts.

These figures highlight the contradiction that seems to have settled internationally for several years now: that of a society that claims to put aside empty words vs. a private sector whose social purposes are not always translated into concrete action measures. Consequently, an extensive line of research related to the use of CSR as a greenwashing strategy by companies has developed and it is now central to any discussion on the involvement of the private sector in the 2030 Agenda (van Zanten & van Tulder, 2018). Greenwashing refers to corporate actions of misleading stakeholders (especially consumers) regarding the social and environmental activities implemented by the company (firm-level greenwashing) or the social and environmental benefits of its products and/or services (product-level greenwashing) (Izzo et al., 2020). Most commonly, it is the case that a greenwashing company engages in two behaviours simultaneously: poor CSR performance and positive communication about such a CSR performance (Delmas & Burbano, 2011). Many detractors of companies' CSR involvement also criticise that, when investing and communicating on CSR, these organizations tend to focus only on salient CSR activities from which they can directly gain profit, whereas they slack off the unobservable activities that are not expected to provide them direct economic benefits (Wu et al., 2020). Therefore, the motives behind CSR investment and corporate sincerity have repeatedly been called into question when a company invests in CSR-related initiatives and green marketing (Parguel et al., 2011).

Among other relevant concerns, the context described in the lines above highlights the need for greater regulatory consistency around CSR (Buijink et al., 2019). In this sense, milestones such as the increasingly common non-financial reporting laws that are beginning to emerge worldwide open a path to be explored (Jackson et al., 2020). The relevance of these standards is due to the progress they represent towards the consolidation of CSR since they contribute to measuring, supervising and managing corporate CSR performance and the impact of companies on society (Buijink et al., 2019). In this sense, non-financial reporting has acquired a fundamental role as a mechanism of accountability with investors, these being increasingly aware of the relationship between financial sustainability and economic, social and environmental sustainability (Gao et al., 2016). For instance, in a survey conducted by PwC (2015), a significant gap was identified between (a) the number of companies committed to the SDGs and (b) the number of these companies that indicated they did not know how they would evaluate their performance concerning the SDGs. This gap highlights the need for new forms of accounting measurement in this regard (Bebbington & Unerman, 2018). Another study on the reporting practices of the SDGs suggested that, although 62% of companies mention the SDGs in their non-financial reports, only 28% of them establish quantitative goals linked to their social, environmental and economic impacts in the form of at least one key performance indicator (KPI) (PwC, 2017). Similarly, in the exploratory study by Izzo et al. (2020), it was observed that, even though the knowledge of the SDGs by the private sector is high and a significant number of large companies have already introduced the SDGs in their non-financial reports and their storytelling practices, the nature and requirements of the SDGs, as well as the definition of KPIs specifically related to these objectives, is still very scarce.

Given all of the above, it seems evident that academic research and corporate practice still have a long way to reflect on the capacity for current CSR policies to satisfy the SDGs. Both spheres still have to determine whether the extent of CSR policies is enough for advancing sustainable development, while also designing new ways to set real changes in the CSR-SDGs intersection.

Social Entrepreneurship

An alternative to advance in the achievement of the SDGs from the perspective of the private sector, which is perhaps less controversial than CSR, is the one proposed by the so-called social entrepreneurship. Although social entrepreneurs have always existed everywhere around the world (Bacq & Janssen, 2011), it was not until the 1980s that social entrepreneurship was introduced in academic literature and the concept became internationally renowned (Brock & Steiner, 2009). In this regard, and even though unified definitions of social entrepreneurship do not exist within academic literature or in the management arena (Dacin et al., 2010), it is generally agreed that social entrepreneurship mainly refers to "the process through which entrepreneurs follow a social mission, which can be expressed in terms of social change, social transformation, social value creation or social impact, and that aims to address social problems and needs or create social rather than personal and shareholder wealth" (Bonfanti et al., 2016, p. 391).

Even though the concepts of social entrepreneurship and CSR have sometimes been used interchangeably, both approaches to the involvement of the private sector in sustainable development are notably different and they should be distinguished (Dorado, 2006). In this regard, CSR refers to the practices, strategies or programs that a commercial enterprise or an entrepreneur (i.e., a company) implements to generate a positive or responsible impact on society, without this being its core mission or main objective. CSR refers to actions to mitigate the impact derived from the commercial activities previously established by the company (Silva, 2015). On the contrary, social entrepreneurship refers to initiatives that use business models to promote social value and sustainable development and that are not dominated by direct financial benefits for the entrepreneurs (Mair & Marti, 2006). Thus, and contrary to early general literature in the entrepreneurship field, which suggested that the primary function of an entrepreneur is starting new profit-seeking business ventures, literature on social entrepreneurship makes it clear that entrepreneurship does not necessarily require a profit motive (Mort et al., 2003). Whereas companies that implement CSR have the objective to maximize profits, social entrepreneurs, on the contrary, supply needs primarily focused on improving social wealth, even if they do not work on a profit-making basis (Mair & Marti, 2006; Estrin et al., 2013). Companies that implement CSR and businesses that opt for social entrepreneurship are therefore distinguished by their primary objective (financial value creation and social value creation, respectively), although they also have much in common, such as the central role of innovation, the necessity to bear the risk and the ability to be proactive (Mort et al., 2003; Estrin et al., 2013).

Since the 1980s, social entrepreneurship has become an increasingly important research topic, getting public policymakers to show special interest in promoting the creation of social businesses (Bacq & Janssen, 2011). This interest stems from the widespread recognition of social entrepreneurs when it comes to tackling serious social and environmental problems (Zahra et al., 2008) and the inability of governments to fully solve these problems on their own (Wry & York, 2017). This way, social entrepreneurship emerges as a possible solution to achieve the SDGs by building alternative economic models in which the social end is considered over the traditional economic objectives of other companies within the private sector (Carriles-Alberdi et al., 2021). These social entrepreneurs, as already argued in the "Think Global Trade Social" report, have a potentially crucial role to play in achieving the global SDGs (Social Enterprise UK, 2015). In this regard, the idea of the SDGs has quickly gained ground because of the growing urgency of sustainable development for the entire world (Sachs, 2012). Achieving these goals will require the efforts of governments, businesses and third sector actors, often working in collaboration (Littlewood & Holt, 2018). To meet these objectives and face the great challenges that society currently encounters, committed businesses are needed, which not only seek to maximize the benefit of their shareholders, or reduce their negative impact but also seek to maximize their positive social, environmental or governance impact. In this sense, social entrepreneurship, with its ability to generate innovative, efficient and sustainable initiatives and its objective of causing systemic change, has emerged as a key model to reduce the financial deficit observed when it comes to the implementation of SDGs (PwC, 2020).

Therefore, public and governmental policies should consider not only the needs of for-profit companies, in general, but also especially foster social entrepreneurs because of their direct impact on the economic, social and environmental development of nations. Providing specific education and tax-incentive programmes and, most importantly, easier access to funding for future social entrepreneurs can meet the objectives of a better, fairer society based on entrepreneurship success. The promotion of social entrepreneurship worldwide can also be beneficial for existing for-profit companies that seek to transform their business models (Halme et al., 2012; Alt & Craig, 2016). The nature and complexity of the problems and challenges experienced by consumers, employees and other relevant stakeholders continuously evolve and grow (Nandan et al., 2014). These challenges call for numerous departments in for-profit companies, such as marketing and selling units (Alt & Craig, 2016), to lead and facilitate social change to keep running their business tasks while having a lasting impact on communities and people. Therefore, developing a special sensitivity towards social entrepreneurship among society can promote an earlier and easier identification of social needs within companies that lead to a natural and strong change in corporate practices and business models through social intrapreneurship (Nandan et al., 2014).

The Positive Impacts of Company Involvement in SDGs

A recurring topic of interest for scholars on CSR and social entrepreneurship literature focuses on understanding the benefits for companies and the society that derive from the implication of the private sector in social and environmental issues. Along this line, the outcomes of company involvement in SDGs are most commonly differentiated between social benefits (i.e., social impact, purpose) and business value and financial performance.

Social Impact

As Baraibar et al. (2020) indicated, the concept of social impact is not easy to define, considering it even the most volatile term in the entire field of social studies. Therefore, and as it is common in most literature related to CSR, social entrepreneurship and SDGs, there is currently no single and universally accepted definition of social impact (Perrini, 2020). Furthermore, this concept is often replaced by terms such as "social value" (Santos, 2012), "social return" (Clark et al., 2004), "social performance" (Mair & Marti, 2006) and "social return on investment" (Hall et al., 2015), which contributes to the current difficulties in properly understanding and limiting the scope of social impact.

For instance, Dietz (1987) defined a social impact as a significant improvement or deterioration in the well-being of people or a significant change in an area of community interest. Hadad & Gauca (2014) defined it as the positive shifts (changes) in the status quo of people (affected by a specific social problem) as a consequence of an action, activity, process, project and even policy undertaken by individuals, companies, NGOs or governments, among other agents. More recently, Rawhouser et al. (2019) defined social impact as the beneficial outcome resulting from prosocial behaviour that is enjoyed by the intended targets of that behaviour and/or by a broader community of individuals, organizations, and/or environments.

Based on these definitions, it is therefore clear that to generate a social impact, the role of numerous and diverse stakeholders is fundamental, including the implication of the private sector. For instance, the role of social businesses, as examples of social entrepreneurship, is critical because the social impact is the main result of the activities they carry out (Perrini, 2020). More precisely, social businesses can demonstrate that their activities and interventions are directly related to some beneficial change for society and, therefore, they derive into desirable social impacts (Daye & Gill, 2017). Social impact is an important piece of the phenomenon of social entrepreneurship (Dacin et al., 2010; Rawhouser et al., 2019) and could even be considered the most relevant dependant variable based on related performance within social entrepreneurship (Rawhouser et al., 2019).

Close to social entrepreneurship, there are also some other initiatives from the private sector that contribute to the generation of social impact. This is the case of the B Corporations (B Corps) movement, a certification that measures a company's entire social and environmental performance through the B Impact Assessment methodology. This assessment evaluates how a company's operations and business model impact its employees, community, environment, and customers from the supply chain and input materials to the charitable giving and employee benefits implemented by the company. More precisely, the B Impact Assessment evaluates five impact areas: Workers, Governance, Community, Environment, and Customers (B Lab, 2020). The B Corp Certification proves the company is meeting the highest standards of verified performance and is committed to considering stakeholder impact for the long term by building it into the company's legal structure. Therefore, B Corps are companies that aim to create positive social impacts for the planet and internalize aspects of their social context through business leadership and sustainability to foster social change (Stubbs, 2017). Along this line, Tabares (2021) showed that B Corps are great contributors to the solution of social problems, such as agriculture-related challenges, corruption, climate change, labour, poverty, and unsustainable habits, so they conduct activities that fulfil the UN mission and the SDGs by reinforcing their social impact in a broad sense. In this context, a recent report by the United Nations Development Program strengthened that the generation of social impact and its measurement should be one of the main objectives of the 2030 Agenda since it is a great opportunity to learn about the contribution of companies to the SDGs (United Nations Development Program and Global Reporting Initiative, 2016).

Business Value and Financial Performance

In addition to creating social impact, companies that get involved in CSR or social entrepreneurship also have to search for some sort of profit-making goal to be economically sustainable in the long run. Therefore, the business value and financial performance derived from corporate social and environmental involvement is another outcome to bear in mind when analyzing the contribution of the private sector to SDGs and the 2030 Agenda (Busco et al., 2017; Schönherr et al., 2017).

Van Zanten & van Tulder (2018) saw a clear business logic behind companies' involvement in the 2030 Agenda: contributing to the SDGs can unlock up to $12 trillion annually in business opportunities and value creation for companies. To corroborate this idea, previous CSR literature has notably focused on exploring the link between CSR investment (or performance) and financial performance (CFP) (Pérez et al., 2020), with most of these studies identifying a positive correlation between both constructs (Byun & Oh, 2018). These studies have been frequently classified along two streams of research depending on how they measure CFP. On the one hand, numerous studies have explored CSR against accounting-based measures of CFP (e.g. ROA, ROE and EPS) (Feng et al., 2008). On the other hand, more recent research assesses CSR effectiveness in terms of its contribution to market value as a more adequate measure of CFP to evaluate the CSR-CFP link (Flammer, 2013).

For instance, numerous scholars have paid special attention to examining the impact of CSR on accounting-based measures of CFP (Pérez et al., 2020). Nonetheless, empirical findings along this line have shown an inconsistent relationship between CSR and CFP (Hendarto & Purwanto, 2012). Most studies suggest that the correlation between CSR and CFP is positive because, although the cost of implementing CSR activities can be high, CSR generates significant management revenues, while also reducing corporate transactional costs (Feng et al., 2018). For instance, CSR leads companies to higher morale of employees, attracts and retains quality employees, and improves consumers' attitude towards the company and its products (El Ghoul et al., 2017). However, there are also studies arguing that CSR detracts from CFP because any discretionary expenditure on social betterment unnecessarily puts the company at an economic disadvantage in a competitive market (McWilliams & Siegel, 1997).

In contrast, when exploring the effects of CSR on market-based measures of CFP (i.e. abnormal returns for companies in stock markets, price per share or share price appreciation), scholars have more consistently reported that CSR is strongly and positively correlated with CFP (Flammer, 2013). More precisely, CSR performance allows companies to attract external resources because shareholders appreciate the opportunities and rewards that a good CSR reputation brings in terms of obtaining quality employees or market products and services to consumers (Flammer, 2013). From this perspective, CSR is a source of competitive advantage. Along this line, previous research has shown that positive and negative CSR perceptions, or even CSR news in the media, affect market reactions differently. For instance, Patten (2008) found that the market reacted significantly to corporate press releases announcing charitable giving. Additionally, Flammer (2013) found that companies receiving awards for their voluntary CSR programs and eco-friendly activities experienced significant and positive stock price changes. On the opposite, discriminatory practices and eco-harmful activities were associated with significant and negative stock returns.

In any case, the study by Salazar & Katigbak (2016) highlighted that, on a global scale, the real participation of the private sector in areas associated with the SDGs still appears to be relatively low due to the fear of CEOs to some important economic dilemmas. For example, the study by Accenture (2019) highlighted some of the most significant economic and business constraints that prevent business action along the SDGs. In this report, 28% of the consulted CEOs cited the "absence of market pull" as a top barrier to implementing sustainable businesses. Additionally, 43% of the world's largest companies cited competing for strategic priorities as another top barrier, while 55% identified the pressure to operate with extreme cost-consciousness against investing in longer-term strategic objectives, and 63% referred to political uncertainty across markets as another key constraint that is reducing or stalling their sustainability efforts. Another recent study from the United Nations Conference on Trade and Development revealed that only a small fraction of the assets invested by banks, pension funds, insurers, foundations and multinational companies were associated with the key areas of the SDGs, and the figures were still smaller in developing countries, particularly in the poorest economies (Salazar & Katigbak, 2016). One of the most meaningful obstacles is the inadequate risk profile in the return of many of the investments in sectors considered sensitive or of a public service nature, such as health, education, basic infrastructure and public services.

Based on these ideas, it is evident that future research has to keep working on reducing the stigma associated with CSR, social entrepreneurship and SDGs investment by demonstrating the benefits that contributing to the 2030 Agenda can report to the private sector in terms of business value and financial performance.

OVERVIEW OF ACADEMIC LITERATURE ON THE CORPORATE-SDGS INTERSECTION

To conclude this introductory chapter on the potential and limitations of the private sector to contribute to the SDGs, the authors aim to provide a brief literature review on the latest and most relevant studies that have explored the corporate-SDGs intersection from an academic perspective. In doing so, the authors want to shed some light on the main lines of research and the gaps of knowledge identified in previous literature that will assist future researchers to advance in this topic while objectively measuring the role of the private sector in contributing to the SDGs. In this regard, the degree to which the private sector has been involved in the development and implementation of the SDGs has barely transcended the scientific field and at present, there is a profound lack of knowledge about the scope of the results, the achievements obtained and the pending tasks of companies in this area. More specifically, today there is very little scientific research on the contribution of the private sector to the achievement of the SDGs, with the exact contribution that can be attributed to different companies and sectors in the fulfilment of the 17 SDGs at the country level being specifically unknown.

At implementing a search of academic articles in Google Scholar, which included terms related to companies, CSR and SDGs in their titles, the search returned as a result mostly papers from 2020, with only a few being published in internationally renowned journals. Table 2 presents a summary of the most relevant papers identified in the search, which are commented next.

Table 2. Overview of recent papers on the Corporate-SDGs intersection

Authors	Goal	Method	Findings
Schönherr et al. (2017)	To explore whether and how the SDGs may serve as a reference framework that can support companies in improving their CSR engagement in a way that contributes to sustainable development	(general) Theoretical literature review	Systematically measuring and managing corporate impacts on sustainable development is a prerequisite for demonstrating a net contribution to the SDGs. Existing corporate measurement and evaluation systems need to be adapted and new management instruments have to be developed
ElAlfy et al. (2020a)	To analyze whether and how companies communicate about the SDGs on social media	Empirical study (content analysis + regression analysis)	The SDGs are communicated by companies in a way that addresses strategic corporate sustainability and social responsibility. Companies mostly communicate those SDGs that are linked to the company's core business, which allows them to increase their legitimacy on the market
ElAlfy et al. (2020b)	To determine to what ends the SDGs have impacted CSR research from 2015 to 2020	(systematic) Theoretical literature review	Research has placed a particular emphasis on certain SDGs. Nevertheless, the voluntary nature and lack of a single ubiquitous reporting standard threatens the capacity for CSR to positively drive the 2030 Agenda
Lu et al. (2021)	To discuss the issues relevant to the CSR evaluation and to develop a model of CSR assessment by taking into account SDGs	(general) Theoretical literature review	Previous CSR assessment models present limitations to evaluate the SDGs addressed by companies. Therefore, a novel model of CSR assessment is proposed
Gallardo-Vázquez et al. (2021)	To identify to what extent companies address the SDGs through their CSR practices	Empirical study (content analysis + latent class analysis)	Not all the SDGs are related to CSR. Companies perform differently in their CSR practices and, consequently, have different contributions to the SDGs. There is little difference in the companies' profile regarding their performance in CSR towards the SDGs

Source: Compiled by the authors

One of the first approaches in academic literature to explicitly connect companies within the private sector and the SDGs was provided by Schönherr et al. (2017). Through a theoretical review of previous research taken from the CSR literature, these scholars aimed at linking CSR and the SDGs to explore how the 2030 Agenda becomes a reference framework that supports transnational companies in improving their CSR engagement in a way that contributes to sustainable development. As part of their argumentation, Schönherr et al. (2017) identified that we still know very little of the actual impacts of CSR engagement on sustainable development, mainly because there are still few measurement tools to assess corporate impacts against the SDGs. Therefore, this study pointed to an important gap in academic literature, related to the necessary development of impact assessment tools as a prerequisite for demonstrating a net corporate contribution to the SDGs. To fill this gap, the scholars proposed a research agenda for this purpose. The study by Lu et al. (2021) also focused on the measurement issue and discussed the CSR evaluation methods proposed in previous literature to find their limitations and justify the development of a new model of CSR assessment that particularly took into account the SDGs. Lu et al. (2021) observed that the main limitations of previous CSR assessment models were: the selective implementation of SDGs, greenwashing, the lack of integration of all stakeholders, the lack of consideration for small and medium-sized enterprises (SMEs) and the difference in CSR practices among countries. Based on their findings, they proposed a CSR assessment model that aimed at solving these major problems. Similarly, Gallardo-Vázquez et al. (2021) developed a proxy measurement scale to assess the commonalities between CSR and the SDGs, which they used afterwards to derive conclusions on the extent to which companies addressed the SDGs in their CSR practices. Based on the application of their own CSR & SDG communality matrix, they concluded that: not all the SDGs were related to CSR practices, companies performed differently in their CSR practices, and consequently have different contributions to the SDGs, and there was little difference in the companies' profile regarding their performance in the CSR practices towards the SDGs.

As a development of the research method implemented by Schönherr et al. (2017), other scholars have focused on providing systematic reviews of academic literature on the link between CSR literature and the SDGs (ElAlfy et al., 2020b). For instance, ElAlfy et al. (2020b) applied a scoping methodology for mapping concepts within the CSR-SDGs research domain to deepen the understandings of how global adoption of the SDGs has influenced academic literature on strategic CSR. More precisely, they aimed at providing a holistic perspective on how and why companies integrate CSR into their core planning, processes and structures while attempting to create both social and business value through their commitment to the SDGs. As previously suggested in this chapter, their findings also showed that peer-reviewed articles on CSR and the SDGs have increased substantially over the years, especially since 2019, while they have focused specifically on corporate contributions to SDGs 1, 4, 6, 8, 12, and 17. Nevertheless, ElAlfy et al. (2020b) also agreed that this sort of scoping review falls short in establishing causality between the evolution of CSR research trends and progress on the SDGs. Therefore, they called for further scientific inquiry, especially based on empirical studies that connect CSR actions with advances in the SDGs.

In another recent study, ElAlfy et al. (2020a) focused on corporate communication of the SDGs as part of the CSR strategy of companies. With the main goal of analyzing whether and how companies communicate about the SDGs on social media, these scholars demonstrated that companies communicate their CSR actions in a way that sets naturally within their corporate strategy. In doing so, they mostly communicate about those SDGs that are closely linked to their company's core business, which is a natural route to increase their competitive advantage at the same time that they improve their legitimacy. Therefore, recent literature on the CSR-SDGs intersection also points to marketing and communication issues as another relevant line of research to take into consideration in future research.

CONCLUSION AND FUTURE RESEARCH DIRECTIONS

Because the corporate-SDGs intersection has been scarcely addressed in previous academic literature, in this chapter the goal of the authors has been to provide a general overview of the key role that the private sector can play in promoting sustainable development by investing and working on the SDGs promoted by the United Nations since 2015. For this purpose, CSR and social entrepreneurship have been revised as the main business strategies available for companies to work on the SDGs. Key advantages for companies and the society when the private sector invests in the SDGs, that is, the creation of social impact and business value and financial performance, have also been discussed. Finally, the authors have presented a brief review of recent studies found in the academic literature that explore the corporate-SDGs intersection. In reviewing these issues, the chapter does not only aim at providing new light along this line of research, but also at presenting some of the key concepts that will be explored more in-depth over the rest of the chapters and, therefore, serving as an introduction to this book.

The presented review has demonstrated that there are already extensive lines of research that support the involvement of companies in economic development, social advancement and environmental protection across nations, either because of their positive impacts on society or due to their evident correlation to the financial returns for companies. In this regard, CSR has been the traditional way in which companies have contributed to sustainable development since the 1950s. However, CSR has frequently faced criticism based on the profit-making motivations that may be hidden behind a company's contribution to CSR activities. Greenwashing accusations have become frequent and lead entrepreneurs to search for new alternatives to contribute to sustainable development, such as social entrepreneurship. Nonetheless, social entrepreneurship is a quite recent concept that still lacks a clear definition and, consequently, its connection to the SDGs is still to be conceptualized more clearly.

Despite these advances in research, it has also become evident that academic literature on the specific role played by the private sector on the development and achievement of the 17 SDGs has been scarce so far and significant research gaps persist that may lead to exploring new lines of study:

- The analysis of the most recent literature along this line of the study suggests that there is still a predominance of theoretical works, whereas empirical evidence on the CSR-SDGs link is still minimal and, therefore, the establishment of causality between CSR and the SDGs is a neglected task. Future research should focus on providing quantitative data on the CSR and/or social entrepreneurship activities implemented within the private sector and how they are correlated to the achievement of SDGs milestones across countries. For this purpose, there are interesting public databases that can be useful for researchers interested in this line of study. The United Nations Global SDG Database (https://unstats.un.org/sdgs/indicators/database/) may be a good starting point as it provides access to data compiled through the UN System in preparation for the Secretary-General's annual report on "Progress towards the Sustainable Development Goals" and it can be easily crossed with private records on CSR investment, activities and results to find correlations and causality patterns.
- Similarly, significant gaps have been observed in the development and application of impact measurement tools to assess companies' contribution to the SDGs. However, without exhaustive measurements on the contribution of the private sector to the achievement of the SDGs, it is difficult to assert with certainty to what extent the paradigm shifts in the business world, directed towards a more sustainable economic activity aligned with the principles of the triple bottom line, is truly

effective and correctly focused. Impact measurement is, therefore, one of the main challenges within the SDGs framework (Schönherr et al., 2017) and researchers still have a long way to go to provide solid measurement tools and systematically implement impact measurement and management. Again, the lack of quantitative information in this regard makes it impossible to draw solid conclusions that can guide the strategies and future actions of governments, companies and civil institutions for the timely achievement of the goals set out in the 2030 Agenda.

- Finally, previous literature points to the relevance of business communications to translate CSR and social entrepreneurship strategies into business value and financial performance, which presents itself as another interesting line for further research. New marketing studies to determine how CSR and social entrepreneurship efforts should be transmitted to stakeholders and society are necessary. By working along this line, research can determine what is the best formula to spread the word about the SDGs framework and keep progressing on the paradigm shift of the private sector towards more sustainable business models.

By addressing these research gaps, scholars can begin to increase the utility of management research to corporate practice and, in turn, increase the absolute positive impact of corporate activities on the SDGs. Towards this end, the content of this book in subsequent chapters will aim to fill some of these gaps in the literature by presenting specific projects, methodologies and research questions along the diverse concepts discussed above.

REFERENCES

Accenture. (2019). *The decade to deliver a call to business action. The United Nations Global Compact - Accenture Strategy CEO study on sustainability 2019* [Report]. Accenture.

Adams, C. (2017). Conceptualising the contemporary corporate value creation processes. *Accounting, Auditing & Accountability Journal, 30*(4), 906–931. doi:10.1108/AAAJ-04-2016-2529

Ahmed, H., Mohieldin, M., Verbeek, J., & Aboulmagd, F. (2015, May). *On the Sustainable Development Goals and the role of Islamic finance* [Working paper]. Policy Research World Bank Group.

Alt, E., & Craig, J. B. (2016). Selling issues with solutions: Igniting social intrapreneurship in for-profit organizations. *Journal of Management Studies, 53*(5), 794–820. doi:10.1111/joms.12200

Avrampou, A., Skouloudis, A., Iliopoulos, G., & Khan, N. (2019). Advancing the Sustainable Development Goals: Evidence from leading European banks. *Sustainable Development, 27*, 743–757. doi:10.1002d.1938

Bacq, S., & Janssen, F. (2011). Structuring the field of social entrepreneurship: A transatlantic comparative approach. In O. J. Borch, A. Fayolle, P. Kyrö, & E. Ljunggren (Eds.), *Entrepreneurship research in Europe: Evolving concepts and processes* (pp. 153–188). Edward Elgar Publishing Limited. doi:10.4337/9780857931757.00017

Baraibar-Diez, E., Luna, M., Odriozola, M. D., & Llorente, I. (2020). Mapping social impact: A bibliometric analysis. *Sustainability, 12*(22), 1–20. doi:10.3390u12229389

Bebbington, J., & Unerman, J. (2018). Achieving the United Nations Sustainable Development Goals: An enabling role for accounting research. *Accounting, Auditing & Accountability Journal, 31*(1), 2–24. doi:10.1108/AAAJ-05-2017-2929

Blowfield, M. (2012). Business and development: Making sense of business as a development agent. *Corporate Governance: The International Journal of Business in Society, 12*(4), 414–426. doi:10.1108/14720701211267775

Bonfanti, A., Battisti, E., & Pasqualino, L. (2016). Social entrepreneurship and corporate architecture: Evidence from Italy. *Management Decision, 54*(2), 390–417. doi:10.1108/MD-08-2014-0532

Boto-Álvarez, A., & García-Fernández, R. (2020). Implementation of the 2030 Agenda Sustainable Development Goals in Spain. *Sustainability, 12*(2546), 1–31. doi:10.3390u12062546

Brock, D. D., & Steiner, S. (2009). *Social entrepreneurship education: Is it achieving the desired aims?* [Working paper]. Policy Research World Bank Group.

Buijink, W. F. J., Sellhorn, T., & Wagenhofer, A. (2019). Special issue: Regulation of corporate disclosure. *Schmalenbach Business Review, 71*(2), 131–136. doi:10.100741464-019-00075-w

Busco, C., Fiori, G., Frigo, M. L., & Riccaboni, A. (2017). Sustainable Development Goals: Integrating sustainability initiatives with long-term value creation. *Strategic Finance*, (September), 28–37.

Byun, S. K., & Oh, J. (2018). Local Corporate Social Responsibility, media coverage, and shareholder. *Journal of Banking & Finance, 87*, 68–86. doi:10.1016/j.jbankfin.2017.09.010

Carriles-Alberdi, M., López-Gutiérrez, C., & Fernández-Laviada, A. (2021). The influence of the ecosystem on the motivation of social entrepreneurs. *Sustainability, 13*(922), 1–17.

Carroll, A. B. (1979). A three-dimensional conceptual model of corporate performance. *Academy of Management Review, 4*(4), 497–505. doi:10.5465/amr.1979.4498296

Clark, C., Rosenzweig, W., Long, D., & Olsen, S. (2004). *Double bottom line project report: Assessing social impact in double bottom line ventures. Methods catalog*ue [Working paper]. UC Berkeley Working Paper Series.

Dacin, P. A., Dacin, M. T., & Matear, M. (2010). Social entrepreneurship: Why we don't need a new theory and how we move forward from here. *The Academy of Management Perspectives, 24*(3), 37–57.

Daye, M., & Gill, K. (2017). Social enterprise evaluation: Implications for tourism development. In P. J. Sheldon & R. Daniele (Eds.), *Social entrepreneurship and tourism. Philosophy and practice* (pp. 173–192). Springer International Publishing. doi:10.1007/978-3-319-46518-0_10

Delmas, M. A., & Burbano, V. C. (2011). The drivers of greenwashing. *California Management Review, 54*(1), 64–87. doi:10.1525/cmr.2011.54.1.64

Dietz, T. (1987). Theory and method in social impact assessment. *Sociological Inquiry, 57*(1), 54–69. doi:10.1111/j.1475-682X.1987.tb01180.x

Dorado, S. (2006). Social entrepreneurial ventures: Different values so different process of creation, no? *Journal of Developmental Entrepreneurship, 11*(04), 319–343. doi:10.1142/S1084946706000453

El Ghoul, S., Guedhami, O., & Kim, Y. (2017). Country-level institutions, firm value, and the role of Corporate Social Responsibility initiatives. *Journal of International Business Studies*, *48*(3), 360–385. doi:10.1057/jibs.2016.4

ElAlfy, A., Darwish, K. M., & Weber, O. (2020a). Corporations and Sustainable Development Goals communication on social media: Corporate social responsibility or just another buzzword? *Sustainable Development*, *28*(5), 1418–1430. doi:10.1002d.2095

ElAlfy, A., Palaschuk, N., El-Bassiouny, D., Wilson, J., & Weber, O. (2020b). Scoping the evolution of Corporate Social Responsibility (CSR) research in the Sustainable Development Goals (SDGs) era. *Sustainability*, *12*(5544), 1–21. doi:10.3390u12145544

Epstein, M. J., & Yuthas, K. (2014). *Measuring and improving social impacts. A guide for nonprofits, companies, and impact investors*. Berrett-Koehler Publishers.

Estrin, S., Mickiewicz, T., & Stephan, U. (2013). Entrepreneurship, social capital, and institutions: Social and commercial entrepreneurship across nations. *Entrepreneurship Theory and Practice*, *37*(3), 479–504. doi:10.1111/etap.12019

Feng, Z., Chen, C. R., & Tseng, Y. J. (2018). Do capital markets value corporate social responsibility? Evidence from seasoned equity offerings. *Journal of Banking & Finance*, *94*, 54–74. doi:10.1016/j.jbankfin.2018.06.015

Flammer, C. (2013). Corporate social responsibility and shareholder reaction: The environmental awareness of investors. *Academy of Management Journal*, *56*(3), 758–781. doi:10.5465/amj.2011.0744

Friedman, M. (1962). *Capitalism and freedom*. University of Chicago Press.

Gallardo-Vázquez, D., Hourneaux, F., da Silva, M. L., & Valdez-Juárez, L. E. (2021). On earth as in heaven: Proxy measurements to assess the Sustainable Development Goals at the company's level through CSR indicators. *Sustainability*, *13*(2), 1–16. doi:10.3390u13020914

Gao, F., Dong, Y., Ni, C., & Fu, R. (2016). Determinants and economic consequences of non-financial disclosure quality. *European Accounting Review*, *25*(2), 287–317. doi:10.1080/09638180.2015.1013049

Hadad, S., & Gauca, O. D. (2014). Social impact measurement in social entrepreneurial organizations. *Management & Marketing*, *9*, 119–136.

Hall, M., Millo, Y., & Barman, E. (2015). Who and what really counts? Stakeholder prioritization and accounting for social value. *Journal of Management Studies*, *52*(7), 907–934. doi:10.1111/joms.12146

Halme, M., Lindeman, S., & Linna, P. (2012). Innovation for inclusive business: Intrapreneurial bricolage in multinational corporations. *Journal of Management Studies*, *49*(4), 743–784. doi:10.1111/j.1467-6486.2012.01045.x

He, H., & Harris, L. (2020). The impact of Covid-19 pandemic on corporate social responsibility and marketing philosophy. *Journal of Business Research*, *116*, 176–182. doi:10.1016/j.jbusres.2020.05.030 PMID:32457556

Hendarto, K. A., & Purwanto, B. M. (2012). Market reactions of mandatory implementation of corporate social responsibility: Indonesia context. *Asia Pacific Management Review*, *17*(4), 379–402.

Izzo, M. F., Ciaburri, M., & Tiscini, R. (2020). The challenge of Sustainable Development Goal reporting: The first evidence from Italian listed companies. *Sustainability*, *12*(3494), 1–18. doi:10.3390u12083494

Kharas, H., & Zhang, C. (2014). New agenda, new narrative: What happens after 2015? *SAIS Review (Paul H. Nitze School of Advanced International Studies)*, *34*(2), 25–35. doi:10.1353ais.2014.0019

Kim, S., & Park, H. (2011). Corporate Social Responsibility as an organizational attractiveness for prospective public relations practitioners. *Journal of Business Ethics*, *103*(4), 639–653. doi:10.100710551-011-0886-x

Kolk, A. (2016). The social responsibility of international business: From ethics and the environment to CSR and sustainable development. *Journal of World Business*, *51*(1), 1–38. doi:10.1016/j.jwb.2015.08.010

Kolk, A., Rivera-Santos, M., & Rufín, C. (2018). Multinationals, international business, and poverty: A cross-disciplinary research overview and conceptual framework. *Journal of International Business Policy*, *1*(1), 92–115. doi:10.105742214-018-0004-1

Kumar, S., Kumar, N., & Vivekadhish, S. (2016). Millennium Development Goals (MDGs) to Sustainable Development Goals (SDGs): Addressing unfinished agenda and strengthening sustainable development and partnership. *Indian Journal of Community Medicine*, *41*(1), 1–4. doi:10.4103/0970-0218.170955 PMID:26917865

Lab, B. (2020). *Certified B corporation*. https://bcorporation.net/

Le Blanc, D. (2015). Towards integration at last? The Sustainable Development Goals as a network of targets. *Sustainable Development*, *23*(3), 176–187. doi:10.1002d.1582

Leal Filho, W., Tripathi, S. K., de Andrade Guerra, J. B. S. O., Giné-Garriga, R., Orlovic Lovren, V., & Willats, J. (2019). Using the sustainable development goals towards a better understanding of sustainability challenges. *International Journal of Sustainable Development and World Ecology*, *26*(2), 179–190. doi:10.1080/13504509.2018.1505674

Lin, C., Chen, S., Chiu, C., & Lee, W. (2011). Understanding purchase intention during product-harm crises: Moderating effects of perceived corporate ability and Corporate Social Responsibility. *Journal of Business Ethics*, *102*(3), 455–471. doi:10.100710551-011-0824-y

Littlewood, D., & Holt, D. (2018). How social enterprises can contribute to the Sustainable Development Goals (SDGs) – A conceptual framework. In Entrepreneurship and the Sustainable Development Goals (pp. 33-46). Emerald Publishing Limited.

Lu, J., Liang, M., Zhang, C., Rong, D., Guan, H., Mazeikaite, K., & Streimikis, J. (2021). Assessment of corporate social responsibility by addressing sustainable development goals. *Corporate Social Responsibility and Environmental Management*, *28*(2), 686–703. doi:10.1002/csr.2081

Maignan, I., & Ferrell, O. C. (2001). Antecedents and benefits of corporate citizenship: An investigation of French businesses. *Journal of Business Ethics*, *23*(3), 283–294. doi:10.1023/A:1006262325211

Maignan, I., & Ferrell, O. C. (2004). Corporate social responsibility and marketing: An integrative framework. *Journal of the Academy of Marketing Science*, *32*(1), 3–19. doi:10.1177/0092070303258971

Mair, J., & Marti, I. (2006). Social entrepreneurship research: A source of explanation, prediction, and delight. *Journal of World Business*, *41*(1), 36–44. doi:10.1016/j.jwb.2005.09.002

McWilliams, A., & Siegel, D. (1997). Event studies in management research: Theoretical and empirical issues. *Academy of Management Journal*, *40*(3), 626–657.

Mort, G. S., Weerawardena, J., & Carnegie, K. (2003). Social entrepreneurship: Towards conceptualisation. *International Journal of Nonprofit and Voluntary Sector Marketing*, *8*(1), 76–88. doi:10.1002/nvsm.202

Nandan, M., London, M., & Bent-Goodley, T. (2014). Social workers as social change agents: Social innovation, social intrapreneurship, and social entrepreneurship. *Faculty Publications*, *3770*, 1–34.

Panapanaan, V. M., Linnanen, L., Karvonen, M., & Phan, V. T. (2003). Roadmapping corporate social responsibility in Finnish companies. *Journal of Business Ethics*, *44*(2-3), 133–148. doi:10.1023/A:1023391530903

Parguel, B., Benoît-Moreau, F., & Larceneux, F. (2011). How sustainability ratings might deter 'greenwashing': A closer look at ethical corporate communication. *Journal of Business Ethics*, *102*(1), 15–28. doi:10.100710551-011-0901-2

Patten, D. M. (2008). Does the market value corporate philanthropy? Evidence from the response to the 2004 tsunami relief effort. *Journal of Business Ethics*, *81*(3), 599–607. doi:10.100710551-007-9534-x

Peloza, J., & Shang, J. (2011). How can corporate social responsibility activities create value for stakeholders? A systematic review. *Journal of the Academy of Marketing Science*, *39*(1), 117–135. doi:10.100711747-010-0213-6

Pérez, A. (2011). *A study of corporate social responsibility image: Its formation process and its integration in banking service users behavior* [Thesis]. University of Cantabria, Santander, Spain.

Pérez, A., López, C., & García de los Salmones, M. M. (2020). Do all CSR news affect market value equally? *Social Responsibility Journal*, *16*(8), 1107–1123. doi:10.1108/SRJ-03-2019-0116

Perrini, F., Costanzo, L. A., & Karatas-Ozkan, M. (2020). Measuring impact and creating change: a comparison of the main methods for social enterprises. *Corporate Governance: The International Journal of Business in Society.*

PwC. (2015). Make it your business: Engaging with the Sustainable Development Goals [Report]. PriceWaterhouseCoopers.

PwC. (2017). *SDG reporting challenge 2017. Exploring business communication on the global goals* [Report]. https://www.pwc.com/gx/en/sustainability/SDG/pwc-sdg-reporting-chal-lenge-2017-final.pdf

PwC. (2020). *Retos del emprendimiento social en España y su contribución para el cumplimiento de los ODS* [Report]. https://www.pwc.es/es/publicaciones/tercer-sector/informe-emprendimiento-social-pwc-y-ashoka.pdf

Rawhouser, H., Cummings, M., & Newbert, S. L. (2019). Social impact measurement: Current approaches and future directions for social entrepreneurship research. *Entrepreneurship Theory and Practice*, *43*(1), 82–115. doi:10.1177/1042258717727718

Sachs, J., Schmidt-Traub, G., Kroll, C., Lafortune, G., Fuller, G., & Woelm, F. (2020). *The Sustainable Development Goals and COVID-19. Sustainable development report 2020* [Report]. Cambridge University Press.

Sachs, J. D. (2012). From millennium development goals to sustainable development goals. *Lancet*, *379*(9832), 2206–2211. doi:10.1016/S0140-6736(12)60685-0 PMID:22682467

Salazar, V. A., & Katigbak, J. J. P. (2016). Financing the Sustainable Development Goals through private sector partnership. *CIRSS Commentaries*, *3*(10), 1–2.

Santos, F. (2012). A positive theory of social entrepreneurship. *Journal of Business Ethics*, *111*(3), 335–351. doi:10.100710551-012-1413-4

Scheyvens, R., Banks, G., & Hughes, E. (2016). The private sector and the SDGs: The need to move beyond 'business as usual'. *Sustainable Development*, *24*(6), 371–382. doi:10.1002d.1623

Schönherr, N., Findler, F., & Martinuzzi, A. (2017). Exploring the interface of CSR and the Sustainable Development Goals. *Transnational Corporations*, *24*(3), 33–47. doi:10.18356/cfb5b8b6-en

SERES. (2018). SERES, valor social 2018. V Informe del impacto social de las empresas [Report]. SERES.

Silva, A. C. (2015). Social entrepreneurship and corporate social responsibility: Differences and points in common. *Journal of Business & Economic Policy*, *2*(2), 85–93.

Social Enterprise UK. (2015). *Think global trade social* [Report]. https://www.britishcouncil.org/sites/default/files/seuk_british_council_think_global_report.pdf

Stubbs, W. (2017). Characterising B Corps as a sustainable business model: An exploratory study of B Corps in Australia. *Journal of Cleaner Production*, *144*, 299–312. doi:10.1016/j.jclepro.2016.12.093

Tabares, S. (2021). Do hybrid organizations contribute to Sustainable Development Goals? Evidence from B Corps in Colombia. *Journal of Cleaner Production*, *280*, 124615. doi:10.1016/j.jclepro.2020.124615

United Nations. (2015). Transforming our world: The 2030 agenda for sustainable development [Report]. Author.

van Zanten, J. A., & van Tulder, R. (2018). Multinational enterprises and the Sustainable Development Goals: An institutional approach to corporate engagement. *Journal of International Business Policy*, *1*(3-4), 208–233. doi:10.105742214-018-0008-x

Whitehouse, L. (2006). Corporate social responsibility: Views from the frontline. *Journal of Business Ethics*, *63*(3), 279–296. doi:10.100710551-005-3243-0

Wry, T., & York, J. G. (2017). An identity-based approach to social enterprise. *Academy of Management Review*, *42*(3), 407–416. doi:10.5465/amr.2013.0506

Wu, Y., Zhang, K., & Xie, J. (2020). Bad greenwashing, good greenwashing: Corporate Social Responsibility and information transparency. *Management Science*, *66*(7), 3095–3112. doi:10.1287/mnsc.2019.3340

Yan, M. (2019). Corporate Social Responsibility versus shareholder value maximization: Through the lens of hard and soft law. *Northwestern Journal of International Law & Business*, *40*(1), 47–85.

Yoo, D., & Lee, J. (2018). The effects of Corporate Social Responsibility (CSR) fit and CSR consistency on company evaluation: The role of CSR support. *Sustainability*, *10*(2956), 1–16. doi:10.3390u10082956

Zahra, S. A., Rawhouser, H. N., Bhawe, N., Neubaum, D. O., & Hayton, J. C. (2008). Globalization of social entrepreneurship opportunities. *Strategic Entrepreneurship Journal*, *2*(2), 117–131. doi:10.1002ej.43

KEY TERMS AND DEFINITIONS

B Corporations (B Corps): A model of companies that meet the highest standards of social and environmental performance, public transparency, and corporate responsibility to balance profit with purpose.

Business Value: Standard measure to evaluate the global value of a company, taking into consideration the total sum of all tangible (e.g., monetary assets, stockholder equity, fixtures, and utility) and intangible (e.g., brand, recognition, goodwill, public benefit, and trademarks) assets.

Corporate Social Responsibility: Global concept, closely related to sustainability and ethics, that gathers all the philanthropic and normative issues related to the role of companies in society, as well as all moral obligations that maximize the positive impact while minimizing the negative effect of the company in its economic, social, and environmental context.

Financial Performance: A quantitative measure of how well a company uses its business assets and generates revenues. It refers to the company's overall financial health over a given period.

Non-Financial Reporting: A process of data collection and formal disclosure on non-financial aspects of corporate performance that helps the company measure, understand and communicate its impact.

Private Sector: The part of the economy that is run by individuals and for-profit companies and is not state-controlled. It has to be clearly distinguished from the public sector (ruled by governments) and the voluntary sector (ruled by charities and other nonprofit organizations).

Social Entrepreneurship: A corporate perspective from which companies implement a business model whose final objective is not the maximization of their economic benefits, but the search for social benefit, providing innovative solutions to social, cultural and environmental problems.

Social Impact: Beneficial outcomes resulting from prosocial behaviour that are enjoyed by the intended targets of that behaviour and/or a broader community of individuals, organizations, and/or environments.

Sustainable Development Goals: A collection of 17 interlinked global goals proposed by the United Nations in 2015 and designed to end poverty, protect the planet, and ensure that all people enjoy peace and prosperity by 2030.

Chapter 2
Positioning Corporations as Sustainability Leaders:
A Roadmap to Align Strategic Corporate Social Responsibility With the SDGs

Nicholas Palaschuk
https://orcid.org/0000-0001-6866-846X
University of Waterloo, Canada

Amr El Alfy
University of Waterloo, Canada

Jeffrey Wilson
University of Waterloo, Canada

ABSTRACT

This chapter explores the evolving field of corporate social responsibility (CSR) research and practices in the Sustainable Development Goals era. The authors introduce a contemporary definition of CSR reflective of the SDGs era. Section 1 provides an exploration of the conceptual and theoretical foundations underpinning the evolution of CSR approaches. Section 2 advocates for the SDGs framework in support of the proliferation of sustainability management across business settings. Section 3 delineates how adopting the SDGs as a framework for corporate sustainability can enhance corporate resilience towards economic shocks. Section 4 discusses strategic perspectives on corporate sustainability management and elaborates on the role of business in satisfying promises of sustainable development. Illuminating the legitimacy of the SDGs as a framework for positioning corporations as global sustainability leaders, this chapter serves as a roadmap outlining how business can advance their CSR strategies to align business goals with societal needs in a post-COVID-19 world.

DOI: 10.4018/978-1-7998-8065-3.ch002

INTRODUCTION

In a time of heightened climate risk and social consciousness, the era of efficiency-based corporate sustainability management is insufficient. Businesses once viewed as leaders, targeting returns along the intersection of the triple bottom line are now being surpassed by a new age of responsible corporations actively transforming markets to address multiple societal values. Fully entrenched in what Klaus Schwab's 2020 Davos Manifesto dubs a purpose-led era for business, research and evidence-based practices have shown that issues of sustainability continue to find increasing resonance in the values of civil society, activities of industrial organizations, and intentions of nation-state regulatory frameworks (Hoffman, 2010). A landscape once dominated by environmental activists and ethically motivated NGOs, market transparency, and rising accountability standards in the wake of the popularization of social media-based mechanisms now favor innovative firms and conscious leaders who embody the promises of sustainable development (Broman & Roberts, 2017). As a result, sustainability has become an integral part of business across various sectors and industries (Galpin et al., 2015).

This chapter explores the evolving realm of Corporate Social Responsibility (CSR) research and practices in the era of the United Nations Sustainable Development Goals (SDGs). Sustainable development has emerged as an integrative framework for theorizing the interface between businesses, society, and nature (Marcus et al., 2010; Vermeulen & Witjes, 2016). While scholars and CSR practitioners have been critical of the nebulousness of the SDG domains (Jamali and Karam, 2016), we argue that the SDGs offer a robust framework to guide CSR given the objectivity and specificity of the goals, targets, and indicators. With the current debates regarding the definition of "materiality", reporting on the SDGs by corporations across various sectors has been shown to enhance reporting quality, along with the organizational-level capabilities to align strategic planning with a diverse array of stakeholder needs. Rather than a strategy in-of-itself, strategic CSR provides a paradigm (by which we perceive and act on issues of sustainability) that, when embedded into corporate language, theory, and practice, provides a systems approach to delivering multiple values, spanning beyond the service of wealth creation, organizational boundaries, and traditional stakeholder groups (Dyllick & Muff, 2016). Both a process and outcome in-of-itself, the authors introduce a contemporary definition of strategic CSR reflective of corporate realities in the SDGs era.

Corporate Social Responsibility is the integration of a holistic perspective across all levels of a firm's strategic planning and decision-making so that the firm is managed knowledgeably in the interests of a broad set of stakeholders, spanning beyond firm boundaries, to achieve maximum shared value over the medium to long-term while providing sufficient short-term returns to warrant continued investment, iteration, and innovation necessary for business, society and nature to thrive (ElAlfy et al., 2020, p. 1).

First noted by Gladwin et al. (1995), then elaborated upon over the last two and a half decades, management theory and organizational sciences are undergoing a paradigm shift from mechanistic to systems thinking. Section 1 provides an in-depth exploration of the conceptual foundations and normative elements that underscore the evolution of corporate social responsibility approaches, highlighting three transformative shifts in thinking.

1. **From Agency to Communion**: The shift towards business as the dominant institution driving social responsibility.
2. **From Exterior to Interior:** The shift in drivers of the corporate sustainability journey and relevant impacts on the rate and efficacy of corporate change.
3. **From Conceptual to Material:** The shift from sustainability's conceptual roots towards a renewed focus on materiality and strategic implementation.

Interconnections, tensions and trade-offs, and the nature of relationships between core tenants and analytic tools are reviewed from a co-evolutionary systems perspective.

Section 2 advocates for the legitimacy and applicability of the United Nations Sustainable Development Goals (SDGs) framework in supporting the proliferation of CSR across business settings. Transformative in their operationalization of systems-thinking, the SDGs are indicative of considerable progress along the business-society-nature interface and illustrate the ability of responsible corporate policy to be an end in-of-itself for facilitating a dynamic equilibrium among (competing) sustainability objectives (Ozanne et al., 2016). The SDGs represent a transformative touchpoint in the domain of CSR and sustainability management as the 17 goals were developed under the governance of a tripartite of governments, the private sector, and civil society members. The section positions how the SDGs play a critical role in the advancement of CSR and corporate sustainability domains on academic research as well as industry perspectives. In this section, the authors outline how the SDGs support companies in defining their aspirational purpose in a way that is relevant and inspiring to stakeholders, allow purpose to become the foundation for its strategy, and ignite long-lasting positive change that may increase shareholder value over the long term.

Moreover, the COVID-19 crisis has caused severe disruption to global supply chains, drops in supply and demand of goods and services, and stark increases in unemployment. The calamity has exposed vulnerabilities in the current paradigm of corporate management thinking and operational structures. Based on recent academic literature and industry reports, section 3 highlights how adopting the SDGs as a framework for corporate sustainability can enhance a companies' resiliency towards economic shocks. As a reflection on the existing global COVID pandemic, the authors argue that while the immediate need is to help mitigate and stabilize the economy and employment in the short-term, in the longer term a business resiliency approach will support a sustainable, robust, and systematic economic recovery that is in-line with the 17 global goals.

Section 4 discusses strategic perspectives and implications for corporate operating models, demonstrating the legitimacy of corporate sustainability management as a foundation for internalizing social responsibility as a core managerial principle; elaborate on the role businesses play in the global sustainability transition and satisfying promises of sustainable development. In doing so, the authors seek to provide tangible and transferable lessons on how businesses can make an effective contribution to addressing the sustainability challenge.

The chapter concludes with a discussion on how businesses can avoid the dangerous trap of incrementalism that impedes timely progress toward sustainable scenarios (Burch et al., 2014). With an eye towards the future, the authors advocate for management researchers and practitioners alike to use the SDGs as a compass, providing a North Star that both directs and catalyzes purpose-led corporate transitions well beyond the 2030 agenda. By outlining the evolution of corporate social responsibility scholarship and practice and underscoring the current state of affairs, this chapter provides readers with a roadmap, detailing 'how' and 'why' strategic CSR: 1) has become a pre-requisite to legitimate business practice; 2) can be advanced through integrative reporting against the SDGs; and 3) is a differentiating factor in building future-oriented and resilient business models. All of which we believe is desperately needed in a post-COVID-19 World.

BACKGROUND

Evolution of Corporate Social Responsibility

Wave 1: Enterprise Integration

As the visual signs of global scarcity spill over into social discourse, the rising sentiment of protectionism/conservationism has driven a paradigm shift in the way we view our organizations. Notably outlined by Andrew Hoffman's 2018 Harvard Business Review article titled "*The Next Phase of Business Sustainability*", the author categorizes this ontological evolution in CSR from a practitioner lens' through three waves. The first, otherwise noted as 'enterprise integration', saw corporate leadership realize that through sustainability management systems, efficiency gains can help organizations save costs, reduce risks, and build a differentiated reputation, both in product and job markets. Treating business, society, and nature as separable units, corporate responses (to pressing social and ecological issues) were reduced to linear causal flows that are both presumed predictable and controllable (Folke et al., 2002). Such logic has helped to not only further insulate traditional (growth-ladened) economic thinking in contemporary business practice but creates moral justifications for the loosening of regulatory 'shackles and proliferation of time-discounting practice(s).

Wave 2: Market Transformation

The second wave precludes the transformation of markets, which sees corporate leadership overcome cognitive biases surrounding (inconsequential implications) limitless substitutability of natural capital, consumption, and economic growth. The departure lies in a broadening stakeholder perspective that now reached beyond the shareholders to include customers, suppliers, government, creditors, and employees. Pursuing what can be likened to John Elkington's (1997) Triple-bottom line[1] (TBL) approach to value creation, value chains include broader stakeholder groups and social values in accompaniment with traditional economic value. This iteration of CSR emerged as a functional response to the 1987 Brundtland Commission of Sustainable Development[2] and environmental movement of the late 90s. Maintaining an embedded view of the firm, albeit still an inward-out view of corporate activities, the mission for corporate governance under this paradigm was to manage and maximize synergies at the intersection between economic growth, social equity, and environmental wellbeing.

Paving the path for the advent of the Sustainable Development Goals, this second wave has helped catalyze scholarly inquiry into how and why organizations are responding to society's most pressing grand challenges. According to Serafeim (2020), more than 250,000 publications focused on environmental, social, and governance (ESG) issues were published in 2018 alone, covering 8000 companies worldwide. If trends in academic research are meant to mirror today's market realities, than this growth can be viewed as a responseto the growing scale and magnitude of challenges today's businesses face. Subject to unprecedented levels of transparency and visibility, popular media and disclosure standards have gained considerable power creating public pressures for businesses and researchers alike (Schaltegger & Burritt, 2018). Whether viewed as coercive or mimetic, These forces dictate that it is the responsibility of management to devise strategy for organizations that helps broaden their value chains and deepen the impacts of operations on addressing societal needs (Bapuji et al., 2018; Porter & Kramer, 2011). This second wave has been experienced as a gradual paradigm shift, whereby the 'DNA' and purpose of the firm, spanning back nearly 50 years now rewards those business models with sustainability at their core (Schaltegger et al., 2012).

Wave 3: True Business Sustainability

The third and final iteration, 'true' business sustainability, sees businesses engage in the deployment of systems logic during strategy formulation, strategic CSR planning, and program development. This wave is multi-dimensional, multi-level, and interconnected through feedback loops (Williams et al., 2017). When fully understood and supported by collaborative processes/structures to problem-solving, organizations (and the people occupying them)begin to engage in transformative learning, create conditions for self- organization, and direct information flows in a manner that supports the emergence of CSR-oriented innovations (Lozano, 2012). For senior managers and leadership, this is the challenge of finding a balance between the urgent and the important. If strategic CSR is to enable companies to reach these aspirational goals, it must be characterized as a shared managerial (organizational) and scientific (sustainability; management) problem. In doing so, corporations are better equipped to devise and deploy strategies that help bridge procedural (know-how), conceptual (know-what), and propositional (know-that) knowledge deemed necessary to deal with the complexity of sustainability challenges (Laasch et al., 2020).

With multiple goals active at any given point in time, strategic CSR decision-making and strategy formulation becomes much more than simply processing information and becoming aware of sustainability. This implicit prioritization of the economic dimensions of TBL-thinking, or enlightened self-interest leads to the inevitable result where CSR is promoted by management and supported by leadership only when profitable (Schaltegger & Burritt, 2018). Thus, the economic dimensions of TBL-thinking continue to be treated as a keystone element of sustainable development discourse, a catalyst for organizational change, and the first-order incentive driving strategic CSR (Eccles et al., 2012).

True business sustainability requires a boundary-spanning perspective (defined as "work to enable exchange between the production and use of knowledge to support evidence-informed decision-making in a specific context") (Benarek et al., 2018, p. 1176), a systemic re-design of corporate strategy, and reconceptualization of entire business models. With a renewed focus on the firm's capability to not only create competitive advantage but sustain it, future-oriented businesses are required to transform their business models continuously in response to a dynamic natural environment and changing societal values. According to Hoffman (2018) and other highly acclaimed business scholars, this at the very least requires a shift to outside-in thinking where senior leadership must start from society and its problems by asking themselves "which opportunities arise by solving todays' most pertinent grand societal challenges". When operationalized, this leads practitioners to a conceptual broadening compared to previous neo-liberal interpretations of CSR as a philanthropic add-on.

For firms to not only identify, but capture value from opportunities that emerge from an economy that is increasingly geared towards stakeholder models of capitalism, than that firms must come to understand how individuals, organizations, and societies can environmentally and socio-economically flourish in the long- term while allowing shareholders to also flourish by ensuring that their respective organizations' CSR programs reduce costs, increase revenues, add value to assets-under-management, or reduce risks and liabilities (Starik and Kanashiro, 2013). For leadership to proactively and knowledgeably manage these trade-offs between different stakeholder needs surrounding sustainable development, strategic CSR dictates corporations must: 1) integrate competing demands in a triple-bottom-line (TBL) (Elkington, 1997; Porter & Kramer, 2006) 2) integrate paradox logic balancing short-term and long-term targets (Baumgartner & Rauter, 2017); and 3) consume income, not capital (Donaldson & Preston, 1995; Gladwin et al., 1995).

CORPORATE SOCIAL RESPONSIBILITY IN THE SDGS ERA

Advancing Strategic CSR using the SDGs

The United Nations Sustainable Development Goals

On September 25th, 2015, constituents of 193-member countries of the United Nations co- produced a framework delineating the 17 Sustainable Development Goals (SDGs), which remains the most widely adopted and comprehensive roadmap supporting collective action on today's most pertinent grand societal challenges. At an organizational level, this framework is being used to shape CSR agendas and corporate reporting practices in a manner that is globally relevant and contextually nuanced (Williams et al., 2019). Differentiated from their predecessors, the Millennium Development Goals, the SDGs mark a seismic shift in government-private sector cooperation. With a renewed focus, these goals explicate that organizations are central to sustainable development as both contributors and drivers of solutions to grand challenges. Embedded within socio-ecological systems, businesses are "integrated and indivisible" (p. 355) in shaping our collective trajectory on the SDGs (Howard-Grenville et al., 2019).

Challenges to Aligning Corporate Reporting Practice with the SDGs

Leading businesses have slowly come to realize that they no longer must choose between climate action and strong bottom lines. On the contrary- ethical and equitable corporate practices have become a strategy for building business legitimacy and purpose in the communities they are embedded in. Highlighted by the global advisory services giant KMPG in their 2020 Survey of Sustainability Reporting, the Lionshare of today's most successful companies are connecting their activities with the SDGs. Catalyzing firm-level service/product delivery by drawing on global insights and best practices, 96% of N100 (i.e. top 100 companies by revenue in each of the 52 countries surveyed by KMPG) and 72% of G250 (i.e. world's largest 250 companies by revenue as defined in the 2019 Fortune 500 rankings) are integrating the SDGs into corporate reporting. Using science-based targets, the SDGs provide leadership with a 'toolkit' for identifying and actioning the methodologies, requirements, processes, benefits, and measurements most material to their context. Addressing a well-known managerial knowledge deficit surrounding issues of sustainability, leadership can come to better understand, communicate, and manage their absolute contributions to today's most pertinent grand societal challenges.

Underscored by Target 12.6 of the SDGs, transparency has quickly become the new paradigm for conducting socially responsible business. While the Global Reporting Initiative (GRI) remains the dominant global standard for sustainability reporting, a notable increase in the relative proportion of companies reporting against the SDGs has occurred since their (2015) inception. As leadership becomes more comfortable and familiar with the SDGs, and pressure from investors and industry peers for more ethical and equitable practices throughout entire value chains mount, this trend should be expected to continue. However, the depth and degree to which the SDGs are being integrated vary significantly. . That being, the majority of companies (86% of N100 and 90% of G250) reporting against the SDGs have been found disclosing only their positive impacts while hyper- emphasizing SDGs 8, 12, and 13 at the expense of biodiversity (e.g. SDG 14, 15) and social equity (e.g. SDG 1-6, 10) (KPMG 2020). Both unbalanced and one-sided, this style of reporting distorts public opinion and gives society a false sense of security by overestimating our positive contributions while underestimating our negative ones.

Sustainability in Corporate Reporting Practice

While the promises of the United Nations Sustainable Development Goals provide material and measurable framework for grounding transformative systems thinking into business strategy, organizations continue to struggle with the normativity (leading to false starts and frustration), complexity (leading to confusion and reductionist conceptualizations), and radical uncertainty (leading to resistance and fatalism) associated with the SDGs (Howard-Grenville et al. 2019). This underscores a lingering need to address what many refer to as the 'greatest challenge' facing management research- the seemingly ever-widening science-practice gap(Banks et al. 2016). In doing so, universities and governments can support corporation's by contributing to an evidence-based research agenda that directly addresses the knowledge deficit among practitioners and by deepening understandings of 'how' and 'why' proven strategies for addressing the SDGs can be successfully transferred, scaled, and sustained across emergent markets/ industry landscapes (Rynes & Bartunek, 2017).

Today, a proliferation of reporting and disclosure standards have empowered companies to measure and manage their CSR-related performance. The Carbon Disclosure Project (CDP) and Global Reporting Initiative (GRI), as examples, have emerged as some of the most widely adopted frameworks for corporate reporting. The Task Force on Climate-related Financial Disclosures (TCFD) or Sustainability Accounting Standards Board (SASB) are renowned for empowering businesses to align financial and non- financial disclosures. The Dow Jones Sustainability Index provides material criteria across industries and parity along the economic, environmental, and social dimensions of sustainable development. Now GRESB, the global ESG benchmark for real assets in the global commercial real estate sector is providing specificity to an industry-level. The modern CEO, at least in theory, has never been better positioned to tackle issues of sustainability and transform business operating for good in a purpose-led era. While the proliferation of sustainability reporting standards might be viewed as progress, quantity does not preclude quality and limits the comparability of the results given the lack of harmonization and standardization of sustainability reporting (Kolk, 2016). The SDGs can help solve the ambiguity in the reporting domain as the 17 goals serve as a global agenda towards corporate sustainability and strategic CSR. The 17 goals, along with defined 169 targets and 232 indicators, can shape a decision-making framework for managers within firms to measure and report on their performance to their stakeholders (Clement & Laurent, 2017).

Legitimacy of the SDGs as a Corporate Reporting Framework

A core limitation to existing sustainability reporting frameworks, which encompasses the whole CSR domain, is a lack of clarity regarding the scope and scale of corporate responsibility operating boundaries. Discussions on what precisely constitutes a "material" report remains contentious among corporate sustainability experts (Gray, 2002) and has been recently given the monkier of "aggregate confusion" by Berg et al. (2020). This ambiguity negatively impacts practitioners who struggle with identifying the "right" disclosure(s) that align business goals with the SDGs. Of the three levels of corporate management (normative, strategic, operational), strategic perspectives on CSR provide important insights into the desired goals, resulting benefits, and requisites for implementation (Baumgartner & Rauter, 2017). These benefits include but are not limited to productivity and efficiency process gain, risk mitigation and cost reduction, and improved reputation and legitimacy (Eccles et al., 2012; Hahn et al., 2010). However, mobilizing sustainability-oriented change at the organizational level necessitates that firms move beyond conceptual visions and goal setting towards evidence-based approaches that group corporate activities in material assessments (Baumgartner & Rauter, 2017; Hahn et al., 2010).

Chandler and Werther (2013) highlight four key underpinnings that distinguish strategic CSR from other approaches to corporate stewardship. First, managers must develop and implement their sustainability agendas via a strategic planning process that cascades corporate-level to functional and operational-level strategies. Second, CSR is regarded as a 'core' competency across all of a firm's operations rather than mere 'function,' (i.e. marketing or public relations). Third, firms incorporate a stakeholder perspective that goes beyond shareholders to include non-traditional groups including customers, employees, and the communities they are embedded in. Fourth, and maybe most importantly, is the bridging short- term and long-term temporal outlooks, which lie at the core of the Brundtland definition of sustainable development (Gibson, 2006). Given the uncertainty of transition processes, strategic CSR requires an adaptive (reporting) framework that enhances the corporation's capacity to broker interactions between technology, policy-power-politics, economics-business-markets, and culture-discourse-public opinion (Geels, 2011).

The SDGs, when compared to other (sustainability) reporting standards, seek to bridge the interactions and interdependencies between different stakeholder groups, technologies, institutions, infrastructures (Williams et al., 2017). With grounded understandings of how entrenched cognitive, institutional, socio-economic processes lock business into trajectories while locking out more sustainable alternatives, the SDGs should be considered as a 'blueprint', helping to reduce barriers that impede timely progress on the adoption of new corporate practices (Loorbach & Wisjman, 2018). Lock-in mechanisms include scale economies, existing infrastructure, sunk investments, competencies (cognitive, normative, regulative), and institutional commitments (shared beliefs, power relations, incumbent interests) (Truffer & Coenen, 2012; van Mossel et al., 2018). Given the tripartite nature of this framework (consisting of government, business, and public stakeholders), SDG targets and indicators provide a level of materiality to industry metrics that constitute a notable leap forward in helping bridge global relevance with firm-level action. When applied to strategic decision-making and resource allocation in a corporate setting, this instills a level of pragmatism by strengthening the capacity of management systems to balance short-term benefits while maintaining interest in the long-term vision of sustainable development (Meadowcroft, 2009). In doing so the SDGs help address three fundamental gaps that continue to impede collective action towards a more sustainable future. That being; the attitude-behavior (also referred to as value-action) gap of organizational behavioural (Kollmus & Agyeman, 2002; Whitmarsh, 2009); the intent-implementation gap in policy (Lorenzoni et al., 2007; Portney, 2013); and competitive-sustainability strategy gap in management systems (Lo & Sheu, 2007; Wright & Nyberg 2017). By supporting deepened understandings as to 'how' and 'why these gaps exist, the higher-order gap between research and practice might be addressed in parallel.

The SDGs address a delimited number of sustainability issues that are relevant to businesses and their operations. In a time where stakeholders, not only demand but reward (most notably through legitimacy building) proactive green positions, the 17 goals incorporate 169 targets along with 232 indicators, that cumulatively, help organizations measure their performance and progress towards these grand challenges in an objective manner (PWC, 2018; Scheyvens et al., 2016). As the COVID-19 crisis has most recently shown us, business resilience is foundational in an organization's ability to both cope with and take action to capture value from many opportunities that emerge from times of crises. Constituting a blueprint for navigating the most pertinent grand societal challenges of today and into the future, integrating the SDGs as a framework that guides strategic CSR initiatives enables corporations to respond with both speed and agility in the face of uncertainty. More specifically, the SDGs allow decision-makers to align firms resources and local values and needs in a manner that more directly addresses material targets associated with each goal, and in turn, helps institutions identify their socio-ecological impacts in a way that can help managers map their CSR agendas from an "inside-out" approach. A core requisite of 'true' business sustainability (Dyllick & Muff, 2016; Hoffman, 2018).

The COVID-19 crisis has challenged all the business-as-usual models in a way that calls not only for adaptive tactics but also for anticipatory strategies that can achieve business resilience (Burnard, Bhamra, & Tsinopoulos, 2018). Strategic CSR can help firms achieve resilient models that can allow them to thrive during economic turbulences. This stems from the long-term planning models of strategic CSR has highlighted by Chandler and Werther (2013). Firms that work on enhancing their economic, social and environmental footprints have higher tendencies to balance their short-term profits while assuring long-term gains from a TBL lens. To elaborate, firms with strong CSR strategies care for their employees and their working conditions which enhances the engagement and ownership thus creating purpose throughout the workforce (Matute-Vallejo, Bravo, & Pina, 2011). During the pandemic, organizations with higher trust in their employees as well as training and leadership programs have significant implications on employee and firm performance (Wolor, Solikhah, Fidhyallah, & Lestari, 2020).

As a policy framework guiding human development towards long-term prosperity, the SDGs represent important steps in the evolution of disclosure standards (Griggs et al., 2013). Transformative in its operationalization of systems-thinking, the SDGs are indicative of considerable progress along the business-society-nature interface to be an end in-of-itself for facilitating a dynamic equilibrium among (competing) sustainability objectives (Ozanne et al., 2016). For example, SDG# 8 calls for decent work and economic growth and has many targets and indicators for equity and employee safety. These universal targets can help aligning growth strategies with societal needs (Sachs, Schmidt-Traub, Kroll, Lafortune, & Fuller, 2018). From an equity standpoint, the SDGs framework represents considerable progress where outcomes for developed vs. developing economies or business vs. society are no longer considered as being mutually exclusive (Sachs, 2012).

USING THE SDGs TO BUILD BUSINESS RESILIENCE

The Value of the SDGs Framework During Times Of Crisis

A core tenant of the Sustainable Development Goals is the interconnectivity of economic, social, and environmental domains of human development which emphasizes aspects of inclusivity, connectivity, equity, prudence, and security (Griggs et al., 2013). Implicit in the definition of sustainable development is progress towards an improved state of well-being (Daly, 1990). CSR strategy contributes to that end if designed to build purpose, catalyze change agency, clarify roles, encourage employee mobilization, and identify mechanisms for meaningful engagement (Lorenzoni et al., 2007). Purpose-led organizations become particularly relevant during times of crisis as it helps stakeholders (e.g., employees, managers, investors, customers) navigate uncertainty, inspires engagement and commitment, and in some cases, even reveals untapped market potential. The challenge facing leadership and senior managers lies in identifying the appropriate design elements and translating those into effective programs and policies.

The SDGs constitute a corporate value agenda that helps build resilience by embedding purpose in strategy. The power of a needs-focused, values-oriented agenda is that it enables organizations to achieve strategic priorities more effectively today while providing a line of sight into how to shift resources as priorities change in future scenarios. If performance is driven by behaviour, and behaviour is driven by context, then using the SDGs to ground CSR strategy can clarify business objectives that align needs and priorities deemed most poignant by civic society. To fully harness purpose requires that employees identify with and feel connected to corporate purpose. Symbolic artifacts (overt and obvious elements of an organization) are important parts of organizational culture, but the purpose is forged by tangible strategy and actionable behaviour change (Schein, 2017). In doing so, future-oriented companies can identify and clarify where value is created in the organization. The key here is to use the 2030 agenda to focus organizational efforts and instill a sense of what matters to every employee.

The COVID-19 pandemic has illuminated a 'readiness' gap in many firms' ability to tailor CSR programs in a manner that aligns with changing employee needs and values in a dynamic work environment. Whether disruption comes in the form of international travel restrictions impacting partnership development or work-from-home orders altering team-level coordination and collaborative processes, the 'health' (defined as an organization's ability to function effectively, to cope with change, and to grow from within to sustain superior performance) of today's organizations are under threat (Di Fabio, 2017). While it may be common wisdom that organizations and work arrangements have profound effects on the meaning people derive from their lives, the human dimensions of sustainability have largely remained in the background of corporate strategy and academic discourse (Pfeffer, 2010). The stark reality remains, only a few organizations fully realize the power of purpose. This requires that businesses become clearer in their communications, agile in their strategy and decision-making, and local in their partnerships. Future-oriented companies will be able to use the SDGs to focus on mobilizing sustainability- oriented corporate values as purpose-building that is part of broader efforts to ensure talent primacy and resilience. In doing so, the current viral pandemic, along with those unforeseen crises of the future might be viewed as an opportunity to innovate and transform, rather than hurdles to overcome.

Common to most crises, is the importance of speed in response to external events and the ability to capitalize on new emerging opportunities. The SDGs can be used as a toolkit by leadership to target specific areas for improvement, identifying and linking key performance indicators across each level of a CSR program. Prioritizing improvements to specific sustainable development goals and targets will empower companies to allocate their workforce aggressively, dynamically, and continuously against their core priorities recognizing that this activity is both an economic engine and long-term competitive strength.

Operationalizing SDGs Logic To Advance Strategic CSR

Bansal and Hoffman's (2012) review of the *Business and Natural Environment* research field is indicative that despite novel insights provided by SDGs-related research, business continues to underestimate the complexity and urgency associated with issues of sustainability. Driven by an inability to understand, much less address the interconnectivity of systems logic in strategic decision-making corporate responses to the SDGs materializes through Goldilocks syndrome. That being, corporations become paralyzed in the face of imminent and mounting risks yet remain unconcerned with planning in the face of future disasters. This poses the question if the path development for elaborating on the role organizations play in sustainable development is so clear, why does industrial activity continue to fall short?

Rather than preparing for any specific grand challenge, the SDGs provide an assortment of pathways by which businesses might build resilience which includes building strong cross-sectoral business relationships and improving supply chains (SDG 17); reducing waste streams, and increasing the circularity of value chains (SDG 12); taking a proactive stance on employee well-being and psychological safety that support productive activities (SDG 8); and create redundancies through integrated policy frameworks to secure resource reserves for climate action (SDG 13). Collectively, when organizations operationalize strategic CSR initiatives that action these themes, they enhance the ability of employees across all levels of an organization to respond with agility and adapt to emerging business landscapes. Replacing the 3-to-5- year planning horizons of traditional strategic planning, the SDGs provide an aspirational 15-year agenda to inform scenario planning. The SDGs enable longer-term scenario-based planning that provides evidence-based interpretations about how and why multiple futures might unfold. In an economy "where the only certainty is uncertainty, the one sure source of lasting competitive advantage is knowledge" (Nonaka, 1994, p.96).

When crafted correctly, a strategic CSR portfolio and evaluative metrics informed by the SDGs provide leadership with meaningful insights into the health and performance of an organization. Maybe more importantly, such an exercise helps leadership identify where within the organization value is created. In addition, the SDGs provide mechanisms of transparency, accountability, and security while cumulatively help to foster purpose across an organization. The goal of any measurement and monitoring system is to ultimately drive action. Those companies who are most future- oriented will take steps to integrate the SDG indicators into their culture by regularly tracking and communicating progress with stakeholders as well as embedding them in performance reviews.

Recent studies have started analyzing the long-term implications of the pandemic on corporate policies and governance (Purwanto et al., 2020; Wulandari, Hertati, Antasari, & Nazarudin, 2021). The results show that governance and sustainability leadership is key to corporate success. According to a (2021) McKinsey article, future-ready companies share 3 commonalities that are intertwined by clear communication. These organizations provide clarity to purpose, value creation and market differentiation, and strong and distinct cultures. This requires that businesses become clearer in their communications, agile in their strategy and decision-making, and local in their partnerships. Future- oriented companies will be able to use the SDGs to focus on mobilizing sustainability-oriented corporate values as purpose-building that is part of broader efforts to ensure talent primacy and resilience.

Emerging From Crisis as Sustainability Leaders'

Sustainable development is a complex myriad of interconnected grand challenges, which cannot be achieved through political means alone. To build prosperous bridges between government and business, policy development must constitute a joint venture- directing best practices to deepen understandings of socio-ecological systems at the firm level and aligning CSR with competitive strategies (Gibbs & O'Neill, 2017). Mirroring a shift in societal concerns from financial survival toward quality-of-life issues, building resilience has transitioned from being a supplemental benefit to a strategic priority for organizations (Di Fabio, 2017). This growing attention is reflected in a proliferation of theories, constructs, and studies seeking to explain why employees flourish or fail, and the effect of purpose on individual behaviours and the organization at large. Research studying fluctuations in employee purpose over time is needed to extend and inform the study of between individual differences as it allows us to identify proximal predictors of resilience as well as to capture the effects of episodic situational influences on resilience and whether interactions can predict productivity. Intraindividual purpose states cannot be assessed through a balanced scorecard approach given that it is dynamic, with its parts being influenced simultaneously by personal and situational factors at different magnitudes. This underscores the need to establish whether all are integral to changes in job demands/resources or whether they have differing salience over time.

During every crisis lies a great opportunity. As organizations move from a mindset of coping to competing, leading companies will seize opportunities and create new pathways to the heightened responsibility that are more flexible, integrated, and ultimately more resilient. The systematic and inclusive nature by which the SDGs have been developed should help mitigate stress during times of uncertainty by linking strategy with purpose. In doing so, organizations can build resilience where employees adapt and grow during a crisis. Through self-concordant strategies that align business goals with societal needs, leadership can help build resilience as a bridge across uncertainty that will not only sustain the organization through crisis and help them manage risk going forward but also lead people to surprisingly positive and purposeful outcomes as they emerge on the other side.

STRATEGIC PERSPECTIVES ON CORPORATE SOCIAL RESPONSIBILITY

Positioning Businesses For A Post-COVID-19 Economy

Over the last two decades, CSR has become a mainstay of business strategy, where stakeholders require organizations to move towards more sustainable business models. Navigating, much less strategizing for future business scenarios is daunting. As this chapter is being written, the modern corporation is experiencing markets more dynamic and uncertain than those compared to the 2008 financial crisis. As the COVID-19 crisis wages on, businesses are struggling with market upheaval, the disrupted of supply chains and the suspension of international trade. The employees who occupy them are facing disrupted work environments, social distancing regulations, job uncertainty and declines across a number of societal wellbeing indicators. These are but just a few of the consequences today's organizations are facing in the wake of the COVID pandemic. With increasing scholarly and practitioner attention being focused on trying to envision the future of industries- delineating what commerce and work look like in the 'next normal' of a post-pandemic world, Amidst such social unrest sits the fact that natural systems and climates continue to change at an unprecedented rate and scale fueled by biodiversity losses and carbon-intensive industrial activities. The greatest transfer of wealth in history is expected to see $30 trillion in wealth to younger generations embodying a more conscious and value-oriented employee, consumer, and stakeholder as the knowledge economy grows. In the wake of such change, businesses are left with one choice- transform or perish.

Given that the pursuit of CSR goes far beyond traditional business practices, business model innovation, at some level, is required (Loorbach & Wijsman, 2018). Positive performance implications are rendered by satisfying innovation criteria (i.e., strong sustainability; systems thinking; radicalism; long-term orientation; mindset change) regarding how more sustainable technologies and structures can be used to improve a firm's products/services (value proposition), customer relationships (value capture), partner networks and infrastructure (value network), and financial aspects of all the above (Bocken et al., 2014). The argument for strategic CSR as an effective driver of building better organizations requires CSR initiatives be managed sustainably to provide five key elements (Harris & Crane, 2002; Salzmann et al., 2005; Schaltegger & Burritt, 2018; Schaltegger et al., 2012; Schrettle et al., 2014).

1. **Commercial Viability:** Minimum levels of cost recovery
2. **Strategic alignment:** Interlinking competitive strategy and moral purpose
3. **Scalability:** Within and across industries/geographies
4. **Collaborative Models:** Leveraging private-public partnership's
5. **Positive outcomes:** Communicated for society and the environment

Designing CSR Strategy To Fit

In light of calls for transformative change, the business case for CSR remains a keystone element within management discourse, expanding to include more holistic conceptions of strategic CSR. A positive relationship has been theoretically grounded by the *Social Impact Theory*, which shows that CSR activities result in greater business reputation and thus, better performance. Additionally, Waddock and Graves's (1997) *Theory of Good Management* sheds light on how companies that choose to focus on social dimensions improve stakeholder relationships have better economic and environmental performance (Martinez-Ferrero et al., 2015). Nevertheless, the degree to which a positive relationship can be expected to exist is largely dependent on stakeholder awareness, which currently, favors markets in developed countries. Business case development remains the only means by which organizations can feasibly link competitive and sustainability strategies (Whelan & Fink, 2016). While this sentiment may not hold entirely true in today's purpose-led and values-oriented market, strategic CSR requires sustainability management systems that at minimum provide sufficient returns to warrant continued investment while satisfying multiple societal values.

It is the ability of a firm to govern sustainability vision among stakeholders that defines the strength to which any (positive) performance link is realized (Aras & Crowther, 2008). A governance challenge at its core, the business case question facing decision-makers is how profit increasing, opposed to cost increasing CSR measures can be identified and integrated into core business activities (Baumgartner & Ebner, 2010). To elaborate, the practices of highly responsible companies are differentiated due to differences in governance structures. Empirical evidence supporting a positive link between corporate governance and financial performance attributes this to improved: agency, stakeholder engagement, access to capital, human capital development, and public profile through appropriate disclosure (Martinez-Ferrero et al., 2015; Robinson et al., 2016).

From a strategic perspective, this requires senior managers and corporate leadership to identify inputs, processes, structures, and metrics to operationalize, evaluate, and adapt CSR strategies (Horisch et al., 2015). It is this ability to identify and action the strategic elements of sustainability management systems that shape the extent to which a firm can align itself with market conditions, societal norms, and the resilience of the natural ecosystem within which it is embedded. This is defined as a sustainability "fit" (Metcalf & Benn, 2012). It is the fit of a firm that serves as a determinant of the diffusion (how widely it is experienced), depth (how deeply it is valued), and degree (the extent to which it is manifested in behaviour and practice) to which corporate social responsibility is realized (Harris & Crane, 2002).

Aligning CSR Strategy With Personal Values

One of the main barriers to CSR as an effective driver of corporate sustainability management is rooted in organizational and personal values (Kiesnere & Baumgartner, 2019). Thus, a key component of this journey involves embedding sustainability in organizational culture (Bertels et al. 2010). However, there is little theoretical understanding of what constitutes a CSR-driven culture, much less how organizations realize and implement cultural change (Linnenluecke & Griffiths, 2010). The concept of organizational culture has become popular within the CSR paradigm as it provides an access point to develop explanations for an organization's sustainability performance (Linnenluecke & Griffiths, 2010). Developing a socially responsible corporate culture could be defined as a decision (or series of decisions) of when to implement a sustainably oriented practice in organizations and or why, where, and how it should be implemented, not to mention who should oversee the process (Schein, 2017). This journey is unique to a given corporate context, the processes by which cultural change is managed, and the target objectives and key results outlined by leadership. It is the degree of alignment and congruence between these elements that is central to building self-concordance (Tian & Robertson, 2019). With origins in behavioral psychology, the roots of self-concordance lie in Self-Determination theory, describing the fulfilment of individual needs that comes from pursuing and, in turn, achieving goals that align with core personal values. Today, the self-concordant model has proven particularly useful in theorizing the relationship between the design of CSR strategies and changes in employee wellbeing and indicators of work performance (Tian & Robertson, 2019).

When self-concordant, employees develop an innate, values-based identification with goals of CSR, meaning that individuals internalize societal responsibility as a part of their self-identity (Tian & Robertson, 2019). For practice, designing cultural interventions that align with personal values, individuals are inclined to have more positive perceptions of a given intervention, enhancing goal attractiveness, and the effort an individual is willing to exert to behave in a manner that aligns with the values and satisfies the goals of their organization (Kurz et al., 2015). The product- a management system that creates a positive feedback loop between purpose and productivity, which over the long-term is a self-reinforcing, more sustainable form of enterprise. Social enterprises, which aim to have a positive impact on their stakeholders, can help achieve long-term profitability through developing a positive corporate image, which should satisfy stockholders' interests (Al Mubarak et al., 2018). CSR also increases employees' loyalty to their firms, which results in reducing turnover rates and increasing employee motivation and engagement (Angeli, 2017). These responsible practices from an organization enhance the performance of a firm, not only from an economic aspect but also the social and environmental performance parameters (Hammer & Pivo, 2017).

Bringing organizational culture to the bottom line is not a new concept (Hofstede et al., 1990; Quinn & Rohrbaugh, 1981). In macro-economic terms, sustained superior financial performance and competitive advantage can be attained from supportive organizational culture (Barney, 1986). However, it is notable that the economic dimensions of culture change have been neglected and under-researched in comparison to its social and environmental counterparts (Gregory et al. 2009). While it is agreed that strong CSR culture(s) must be strategically developed and systematically managed, there is little consensus on matters of acceptable profit margins relative to other investment opportunities; time horizons to cost recovery; impact expectations; and measurement and reporting frameworks (Chang & Kuo, 2008). The incipient nature of the 'business case' for CSR, and the variation in which it is measured has allowed for subjective interpretations on behalf of corporate leaders (Bansal & Hoffman, 2012). Given the complexity and contextual embeddedness of change required, managers suffer from a lack of clarity regarding what constitutes the right business model. Even with nearly 1400 companies, spanning 160 countries operating as signatories to the United Nations Global Compact (Schrettle et al., 2014), the transferability and comparability of empirical evidence surrounding the 'what' and 'how' of CSR literature is bounded.

However, the most significant gap impeding CSR development continues to be the lack of descriptive studies explaining 'how' companies approach BoCS in practice (Eccles et al., 2012; Martinez- Ferrero et al., 2015; Rouseau, 2012; Salzmann et al., 2005). While previously the authors suggest that practitioners suffer from a knowledge deficit concerning CSR decision-making, this appears to also hold true for researchers responsible for the current state-of-the-art. Admittingly still a nascent area of practice, the business case of CSR as a driver of corporate sustainability management lacks the comprehensive empirical evidence necessary to support the proliferation of evidence-based decision-making in practice.

Futureproofing Business By Managing Strategic CSR

Emerging from the COVID-19 crisis, a new social contract is needed between businesses and society. One that prioritizes the sustainable business agenda, recognizes the importance of purpose-led ethical leadership and supports resilience building through management systems designed to change people, culture and behaviour. To support this transition, CSR practitioners must re-imagine strategic CSR. Moving beyond traditional conceptions of "doing good by doing well", businesses must engage with broader range of stakeholders with the aim of integrating social purpose across all levels of an organization. A journey which requires a fundamental change in organizational culture, the goal becomes of instilling strong stewardship principles across all business activities and deploying long-term strategies that deliver on social as well as business outcomes simultaneously. In doing so, organizations might position themselves as market leaders through futureproofing- a strategic planning exercise that maintains a long-term view of CSR, integrates business and social purpose, and in turn builds trust and resilience (Burnard et al., 2018). When treated iteratively, organizations can better identify and communicate their purpose to relevant stakeholders (employees, customers, investors, local communities, suppliers) whereby management systems deliver more consistent responsible business practices that integrate meaning into the lives of people. Over the long-term, this contributes to sustained competitive advantages and constitutes a dynamic organizational capability that enables practitioners to cope with uncertainty, respond with agility, and flourish during times of crisis.

Mediators of this CSR integration, particularly knowledge management and learning, offer powerful research tools for leveraging and directing successful culture change and influence on the effectiveness of sustainable development (Austin & Claassen, 2008). Moving forward, there is a lingering need for a cohesive synthesis of business case drivers and business models to provide a language and performance link that aligns with TBL thinking (Schaltegger et al., 2012). Such an endeavor would support the development of an evidence-based blueprint for corporate sustainability management, that when operationalized, would equip senior management with the type of knowledge necessary to make agile and informed decisions in the face of uncertainty. Or even yet, in times of crises. After all, an organization is only effective to the extent that it can convert new knowledge into products and services valued by stakeholders. With the potential to support improved corporate governance and decision-making, research should continue to investigate the capacity of strategic CSR to align cultural change with market requirements and dynamics in a manner that enhances firm performance (Baumgartner & Rautner, 2017). As the capacity for cultural forecasting develops, the better the potential for diagnosing, directing, and managing an organization's knowledge creation processes. While research indicates that most companies seem to have the potential to realize one or more business cases, this potential is seldom realized in practice due to issues of complexity and materiality (Kahn et al., 2016).

In a 2016 study, Kahn et al. demonstrated that firms with superior ratings on material sustainability issues outperformed firms with poor ratings on the same issues. More importantly, no significant differences in performance outcomes were found between firms with superior versus poor ratings on immaterial sustainability issues (Kahn et al., 2016). This highlights that commitment to CSR is not a standalone key to unlocking pathways towards superior performance. Rather, the power of pursuing more responsible business models might only be realized by grounding CSR strategy in a framework that enables leaders to identify issues most material to the corporate context, design management systems that align business goals with societal values, measure absolute progress of business activities (both positive and negative impacts) to support continued learning and adaptation, and innovation in practice. While there is no ubiquitous answer to the question of whether it pays to be responsible, research has highlighted that a proactive position catalyzes continuous innovation, new market opportunities, and diversification of wealth creation streams (Chang, 2011). A noteworthy topic for future comparative analyses involves measuring the depth and degree to which organizations can realize the business case of strategic CSR. The United Nations' SDGs framework provides an internationally transferable measurement framework for strategic CSR given their 2030 outlook. This also includes a governance transformation since the SDGs require collaboration among a tripartite of governments, private sector, and civil society members to achieve the global vision till 2030. The SDGs provide a strategic framework for sustainable business strategies given their material 17 goals, 169 targets, and unique 232 indicators. To summarize, the multi-dimensional metrics of the SDGs can provide a more robust measurement/monitoring framework and comprehensive reporting capacity, which shifts CSR from an ad hoc function into a core strategic dimension within corporate cultures.

CONCLUSION

It should be clear that corporations are among the largest contributors to issues of sustainability. Corporate Social Responsibility research and practice have made notable strides in supporting societal transitions toward more sustainable futures led by an ambitious action-oriented research agenda. However, merely adopting a long-term perspective and systems thinking is not enough. For solutions to become more actionable, a new language and broadened participation is required, engaging a range of stakeholders, across multiple levels of industry, government, and society to achieve strategic CSR. Businesses struggle with sustainability management due to the complexity of their domain, the normativity of its parameters that lacks robust measurement schemes, and finally the uncertainty given contemporary climate change risks.

It is only through the installation of appropriate strategic systems that decision-makers within firms can be aware of all risks and opportunities. Paths are not entirely set by a firm's decisions and resulting history but can also be adjusted through fast learning mechanisms, practice, making mistakes, and learning from specific experiences. To elaborate, CSR needs to become integrated with the strategy of the firm and these new or additional values need to be measured and monitored. We shed light on how the SDGs provide a better framework to manage the sustainability agenda of firms given their capacity to respond to the material issue with their 17 goals, 169 targets, and unique 232 indicators. Identifying material indicators and measuring them can solve the uncertainty challenges of CSR agendas and thus gain trust and legitimacy from stakeholders.

This chapter highlights how the SDGs helped the advancement of CSR from a functional unit into a core dimension of business strategy given their strategic outlook towards 2030. The SDGs also advanced the governance dialogues of corporate performance and risk management mechanisms through a tripartite collaboration between governments, the private sector, and civil society members. We also highlight the role of corporate culture in transforming corporate performance. Managers still need to better understand the implications of their decisions and the specific actions they can take to improve both sustainability and long-term financial performance.

To move towards a more advantageous stage of sustainability integration and to improve governance, managers must carefully measure the drivers of performance and the linkages between them. By understanding how small behavioural changes within corporations can produce larger societal changes down the road, policymakers and managers can cater to individuals, a community's, or industry's 'readiness for change'. A key take-home for readers notes that firms can contribute to sustainable development through sustainable business models, which can be achieved through mapping their visions towards achieving the SDGs. As corporate leaders and decision-makers become more familiar with the SDGs as a framework of sustainability, the better results they can achieve for their businesses, communities, and the globe.

REFERENCES

Al Mubarak, Z., Ben Hamed, A., & Al Mubarak, M. (2018). Impact of corporate social responsibility on bank's corporate image. *Social Responsibility Journal*, *15*(5), 710–722. doi:10.1108/SRJ-01-2018-0015

Angeli, W. (2017). Exploring Practitioners' Meaning of "Ethics," "Compliance," and "Corporate Social Responsibility" Practices: A Communities of Practice Perspective. *Business & Society*, *59*(3), 518–544.

Aras, G., & Crowther, D. (2008). Governance and sustainability: An investigation into the relationship between corporate governance and corporate sustainability. *Management Decision*, *46*(3), 434–448. doi:10.1108/00251740810863870

Austin, M. J., & Claassen, J. (2008). Impact of organizational change on organizational culture: Implications for introducing evidence-based practice. *Journal of Evidence-Based Social Work*, *5*(1–2), 321–359. doi:10.1300/J394v05n01_12 PMID:19064453

Banks, G. C., Pollack, J. M., Bochantin, J. E., Kirkman, B. L., Whelpley, C. E., & O'Boyle, E. H. (2016). Management's science-practice gap: A grand challenge for all stakeholders. Academy of Management Journal, 59(6).

Bansal, P., & Hoffman, A. J. (2012). *The Oxford Handbook of Business and the Natural Environment*. OUP.

Bapuji, H., Husted, B. W., Lu, J., & Mir, R. (2018). Value Creation, Appropriation, and Distribution: How Firms Contribute to Societal Economic Inequality. *Business & Society*, *57*(6), 983–109. doi:10.1177/0007650318758390

Barney, J. B. (1986). Organizational Culture: Can It Be a Source of Sustained Competitive Advantage? *Academy of Management Review*, *11*(3), 656–665. doi:10.5465/amr.1986.4306261

Baumgartner, R. J., & Ebner, D. (2010). Corporate Sustainability Strategies: Sustainability Profiles and Maturity Levels. *Sustainable Development*, *18*(2), 76–89. doi:10.1002d.447

Baumgartner, R. J., & Rauter, R. (2017). Strategic perspectives of corporate sustainability management to develop a sustainable organization. *Journal of Cleaner Production*, *140*, 81–92. doi:10.1016/j.jclepro.2016.04.146

Bednarek, A., Wyborn, T., Cvitanovic, C., Meyer, R., Colvin, R. M., Addison, P. F. E., Close, S. L., Curran, K., Farooque, M., Goldman, E., Hart, D., Mannix, H., McGreavy, B., Parris, A., Posner, S., Robinson, C., Ryan, M., & Leith, P. (2018). Boundary spanning at the science-policy interface: The practitioners' perspectives. *Sustainability Science*, *13*(4), 1175–1183. doi:10.100711625-018-0550-9 PMID:30147800

Berg, F., Koelbel, J. F., & Rigobon, R. (2020). *Aggregate Confusion: The Divergence of ESG Ratings* [MIT Sloan School Working Paper 5822-19]. MIT Sloan School of Management.

Bocken, N. M. P., Short, S. W., Rana, P., & Evans, S. (2014). A literature and practice review to develop sustainable business archetypes. *Journal of Cleaner Production*, *65*, 42–56. doi:10.1016/j.jclepro.2013.11.039

Broman, G. I., & Robert, K. H. (2017). A framework for strategic sustainable development. *Journal of Cleaner Production*, *140*, 17–31. doi:10.1016/j.jclepro.2015.10.121

Burch, S., Shaw, A., Dale, A., & Robinson, J. (2014). Triggering transformative change: A development path approach to climate change response in communities. *Climate Policy*, *14*(4), 476–487. doi:10.1080/14693062.2014.876342

Burnard, K., Bhamra, R., & Tsinopoulos, C. (2018). Building Organizational Resilience: Four Configurations. *IEEE Transactions on Engineering Management*, *65*(3), 351–362. doi:10.1109/TEM.2018.2796181

Chandler, D., & Werther, W. B. Jr. (2013). *Strategic corporate social responsibility: Stakeholders, globalization, and sustainable value creation*. Sage Publications.

Chang, C. H. (2011). The Influence of Corporate Environmental Ethics on Competitive Advantage: The Mediation Role of Green Innovation. *Journal of Business Ethics*, *104*(3), 361–370. doi:10.100710551-011-0914-x

Chang, D. S., & Kuo, L. C. R. (2008). The effects of sustainability development on firms' financial performance- an empirical approach. *Sustainable Development, 16*(6), 365–380. doi:10.1002d.351

Clément, F., & Laurent, M. (2017). *A blueprint towards accounting for the management of ecosystems.* Academic Press.

Daly, H. E. (1990). Toward some operational principles of sustainable development. *Ecological Economics, 2*(1), 1–6. doi:10.1016/0921-8009(90)90010-R

Di Fabio, A. (2017). Positive healthy organizations: Promoting well-being, meaningfulness, and sustainability in organizations. Frontiers in Psychology, 8(1938).

Donaldson, T., & Preston, L. E. (1995). The Stakeholder Theory of the Corporation: Concepts, Evidence, and Implications. *Academy of Management Review, 28*(1), 65–91. doi:10.5465/amr.1995.9503271992

Dyllick, T., & Muff, K. (2016). Clarifying the Meaning of Sustainable Business; Introducing a Typology From Business-as-Usual to True Business Sustainability. *Organization & Environment, 29*(2), 156–174. doi:10.1177/1086026615575176

Eccles, R. G., Ioannou, I., Serafeim, G., & Hall, M. (2012). *The impact of corporate sustainability on organizational processes and performance* [Working Paper 17950]. National Bureau of Economic Research. doi:10.3386/w17950

ElAlfy, A., Palaschuk, N., El-Bassiouny, D., Wilson, J., & Weber, O. (2020). Scoping the Evolution of Corporate Social Responsibility (CSR) Research in the Sustainable Development Goals (SDGs) Era. Sustainability, 12(14).

Elkington, J. (Ed.). (1997). *Cannibals with forks: the triple bottom line of 21st century business.* John Wiley & Sons, Ltd.

Feger, C., & Mermet, L. (2017, September 18). A blueprint towards accounting for the management of ecosystems. *Accounting, Auditing & Accountability Journal, 30*(7), 1511–1536. doi:10.1108/AAAJ-12-2015-2360

Folke, C., Carpenter, S., Elmqvist, T., Gunderson, L., Holling, C. S., & Walker, B. (2002). Resilience and Sustainable Development: Building Adaptive Capacity in a World of Transformations. *Ambio, 31*(5), 437-440.

Galpin, T., Whittington, J. L., & Bell, G. (2015). Is your sustainability strategy sustainable? Creating a culture of sustainability. *Corporate Governance, 15*(1), 1–17. doi:10.1108/CG-01-2013-0004

Geels, F. (2011). The multi-level perspective on sustainability transitions: Reponses to seven criticisms. *Environmental Innovation and Societal Transitions, 1*(1), 24–40. doi:10.1016/j.eist.2011.02.002

Gibbs, D., & O'Neill, K. (2017). Future green economies and regional development: A research agenda. *Regional Studies, 51*(1), 161–173. doi:10.1080/00343404.2016.1255719

Gibson, R. B. (2006). Beyond the Pillars: Sustainability Assessment as a Framework for Effective Integration of Social, Economic and Ecological Considerations in Significant Decision-Making. *Journal of Environmental Assessment Policy and Management, 8*(3), 259–280. doi:10.1142/S1464333206002517

Gladwin, T. N., Kennelly, J. J., & Krause, T. S. (1995). Shifting Paradigms for Sustainable Development: Implications for Management Theory and Research. *Academy of Management Review*, *20*(4), 874–907. doi:10.5465/amr.1995.9512280024

Gregory, B. T., Harris, S. G., Armenakis, A. A., & Shook, C. L. (2009). Organizational culture and effectiveness: A study of values, attitudes, and organizational outcomes. *Journal of Business Research*, *62*(7), 673–679. doi:10.1016/j.jbusres.2008.05.021

Griggs, D., Stafford-Smith, M., Gaffney, O., Rockström, J., Öhman, M. C., Shyamsundar, P., & Noble, I. (2013). Policy: Sustainable development goals for people and planet. *Nature*, *495*(7441), 305–307. doi:10.1038/495305a PMID:23518546

Hahn, T., Figge, F., Pinkse, J., & Preuss, L. (2010). Trade-offs in corporate sustainability: You can't have your cake and eat it. *Business Strategy and the Environment*, *19*(4), 217–229. doi:10.1002/bse.674

Hammer, J., & Pivo, G. (2017). The Triple Bottom Line and Sustainable Economic Development Theory and Practice. *Economic Development Quarterly*, *31*(1), 25–36. doi:10.1177/0891242416674808

Harris, L. C., & Crane, A. (2002). The greening of organizational culture: Management views on the depth, degree and diffusion of change. *Journal of Organizational Change Management*, *15*(3), 214–234. doi:10.1108/09534810210429273

Hoffman, A. J. (2010). Climate change as a cultural and behavioral issue. Addressing barriers and implementing solutions. *Organizational Dynamics*, *39*(4), 295–305. doi:10.1016/j.orgdyn.2010.07.005

Hoffman, A. J. (2018). The Next Phase of Business Sustainability. Stanford Social Innovation Review, 16(2).

Hofstede, G., Neuijen, B., Ohayv, D. D., & Sanders, G. (1990). Measuring organizational cultures-a qualitative and quantitative study across twenty cases. Administrative Science Quarterly, 35(2).

Horisch, J., Johnson, M. P., & Schaltegger, S. (2015). Implementation of Sustainability Management and Company Size: A Knowledge-Based View. *Business Strategy and the Environment*, *24*(8), 765–779. doi:10.1002/bse.1844

Howard-Grenville, J., Davis, G. F., Dyllick, T., Miller, C. C., Thau, S., & Tsui, A. S. (2019). Sustainable Development for a Better World: Contributions of Leadership, Management, and Organizations. *Academy of Management Discoveries*, *5*(4), 355–366. doi:10.5465/amd.2019.0275

Jamali, D., & Karam, C. (2016). Corporate Social Responsibility in Developing Countries as an Emerging Field of Study. *International Journal of Management Reviews*, *20*(1), 32–61. doi:10.1111/ijmr.12112

Kahn, M., Serafeim, G., & Yoon, A. (2016). Corporate Sustainability: First Evidence on Materiality. *The Accounting Review*, *81*(6), 1697–1724. doi:10.2308/accr-51383

Kiesnere, A. L., & Baumgartner, R. J. (2019). Sustainability management in practice: Organizational change for sustainability in smaller large-sized companies in Austria. Sustainability, 11(572).

Kolk, A. (2016). The social responsibility of international business: From ethics and the environment to CSR and sustainable development. *Journal of World Business*, *51*(1), 23–34. doi:10.1016/j.jwb.2015.08.010

Kollmuss, A., & Agyeman, J. (2002). Mind the Gap: Why do people act environmentally and what are the barriers to pro-environmental behavior? *Environmental Education Research, 8*(3), 239–260. doi:10.1080/13504620220145401

KPMG. (2020). The Time Has Come: The KPMG Survey of Sustainability Reporting 2020. KPMG Impact Report.

Kurz, T., Gardner, B., Verplanken, B., & Abraham, C. (2015). Habitual behaviors or patterns of practice? Explaining and changing repetitive climate-relevant actions. *Wiley Interdisciplinary Reviews: Climate Change*, *6*(1), 113–128. doi:10.1002/wcc.327

Laasch, O., Moosmayer, D., Antonacopoulou, E., & Schaltegger, S. (2020). Constellations of Transdisciplinary Practices: A Map and Research Agenda for the Responsible Management Learning Field. *Journal of Business Ethics*, *162*(4), 735–757. doi:10.100710551-020-04440-5

Linnenluecke, M. K., & Griffiths, A. (2010). Corporate sustainability and organizational culture. *Journal of World Business*, *45*(4), 357–366. doi:10.1016/j.jwb.2009.08.006

Lo, S. F., & Sheu, H. J. (2007). Is Corporate Sustainability a Value-Increasing Strategy for Business? *Corporate Governance*, *15*(2), 345–358. doi:10.1111/j.1467-8683.2007.00565.x

Loorbach, D., & Wijsman, K. (2018). Business transition management: Exploring a new role for business in sustainability transitions. *Journal of Cleaner Production*, *45*, 20–28. doi:10.1016/j.jclepro.2012.11.002

Lorenzoni, I., Nicholson-Cole, S., & Whitmarsh, L. (2007). Barriers perceived to engaging with climate change among the UK public and their policy implications. *Global Environmental Change, 17*(3-4), 445–459.

Lozano, R. (2012). Towards better embedding sustainability into companies' systems: An analysis of voluntary corporate initiatives. *Journal of Cleaner Production*, *25*, 14–26. doi:10.1016/j.jclepro.2011.11.060

Marcus, J., & Kurucs, E. C. (2010). Conceptions of the Business-Society-Nature Interface: Implications for Management Scholarship. *Business & Society*, *49*(3), 402–438. doi:10.1177/0007650310368827

Martinez-Ferrero, J., & Frias-Aceituno, J. V. (2015). Relationship between sustainable development and financial performance: International empirical research. *Business Strategy and the Environment, 24*(1), 20–39. doi:10.1002/bse.1803

Matute-Vallejo, J., Bravo, R., & Pina, J. M. (2011). The influence of corporate social responsibility and price fairness on customer behaviour: Evidence from the financial sector. *Corporate Social Responsibility and Environmental Management*, *18*(6), 317–331. doi:10.1002/csr.247

McKinsey. (2021). *Organizing for the future: Nine keys to becoming a future-ready company*. McKinsey & Company Insights. https://www.mckinsey.com/business-functions/organization/our-insights/organizing-for-the-future-nine-keys-to-becoming-a-future-ready-company

Meadowcroft, J. (2009). What about the politics? Sustainable development, transition management, and long-term energy transitions. *Policy Sciences*, *42*(4), 323–340. doi:10.100711077-009-9097-z

Metcalf, L., & Benn, S. (2012). The corporation is ailing social technology: Creating a "fit for purpose" design for sustainability. *Journal of Business Ethics*, *111*(2), 195–210. doi:10.100710551-012-1201-1

Nonaka, I. (1994). A Dynamic Theory of Organizational Knowledge Creation. *Organization Science*, *5*(1), 14–37. doi:10.1287/orsc.5.1.14

Ozanne, L. K., Phipps, M., Weaver, T., Carrington, M., Luchs, M., Catlin, J., Gupta, S., Santos, N., Scott, K., & Williams, J. (2016). Managing the Tensions at the Intersection of the Triple Bottom Line: A Paradox Theory Approach to Sustainability Management. *Journal of Public Policy & Marketing*, *35*(2), 249–261. doi:10.1509/jppm.15.143

Pfeffer, J. (2010). Building sustainable organizations: The human factor. *The Academy of Management Perspectives*, *24*, 34–45.

Porter, M. E., & Kramer, M. R. (2006, Dec.). Strategy and Society: The Link Between Competitive Advantage and Corporate Social Responsibility. Harvard Business Review.

Porter, M. E., & Kramer, M. R. (2011). *Creating Shared Value*. Harvard Business Review.

Portney, K. E. (2013). Local Sustainability Policies and Programs As Economic Development: Is the New Economic Development Sustainable Development? Cityscape: A Journal of Policy Development and Research, 15.

Purwanto, A., Fahlevi, M., Zuniawan, A., Kusuma, R. P., Supriatna, H., & Maryani, E. (2020). The Covid-19 pandemic impact on industries performance: An explorative study of Indonesian companies. *Journal of Critical Review*, *7*, 1965–1972.

PWC. (2018). *SDG Reporting Challenge 2017 - Exploring business communication on the global goals*. PWC.

Quinn, R. E., & Rohrbaugh, J. (1981). A Competing Values Approach to Organizational Effectiveness. *Public Productivity Review*, *5*(2), 122–140. doi:10.2307/3380029

Robinson, H. S., Anumba, C. J., Carrillo, P. M., & Al-Ghassani, A. M. (2016). STEPS: A knowledge management maturity roadmap for corporate sustainability. *Business Process Management Journal*, *12*(6), 793–808. doi:10.1108/14637150610710936

Rousseau, D. M. (2012). Organizational Behavior's Contributions to Evidence-Based Management. In The Oxford Handbook of Evidence-Based Management. doi:10.1093/oxfordhb/9780199763986.013.0004

Rynes, S. L., & Bartunek, J. M. (2017). Evidence-Based Management: Foundations, Development, Controversies and Future. *Annual Review of Organizational Psychology and Organizational Behavior*, *4*(1), 235–261. doi:10.1146/annurev-orgpsych-032516-113306

Sachs, J. D. (2012). From millennium development goals to sustainable development goals. *Lancet*, *379*(9832), 2206–2211. doi:10.1016/S0140-6736(12)60685-0 PMID:22682467

Sachs, J. D., Schmidt-Traub, G., Kroll, C., Lafortune, G., & Fuller, G. (2018). *SDG Index and Dashboards Report 2018*. New Tork: Bertelsmann Stiftung and Sustainable Development Solutions Network (SDSN).

Salzmann, O., Ionescu-Somers, A., & Steger, U. (2005). The business case for corporate sustainability: Literature review and research options. *European Management Journal*, *23*(1), 27–36. doi:10.1016/j.emj.2004.12.007

Schaltegger, S., & Burritt, R. (2018). Business cases and corporate engagement with sustainability: Differentiating ethical motivations. *Journal of Business Ethics*, *147*(2), 241–259. doi:10.100710551-015-2938-0

Schaltegger, S., Ludeke-Freund, F., & Hansen, E. G. (2012). Business cases for sustainability: The role of business model innovation for corporate sustainability. *International Journal of Innovation and Sustainable Development*, *6*(2), 95–119. doi:10.1504/IJISD.2012.046944

Schein, E. H. (2017). *Organizational Culture and Leadership* (5th ed.). Jon Wiley & Sons Inc.

Scheyvens, R., Banks, G., & Hughes, E. (2016). The Private Sector and the SDGs: The Need to Move Beyond 'Business as Usual'. *Sustainable Development*, *24*, 371–382.

Schrettle, S., Hinz, A., Scherrer-Rathje, M., & Friedli, T. (2014). Turning sustainability into action: Explaining firms' sustainability efforts and their impact on firm performance. *International Journal of Production Economics*, *147*, 73–84. doi:10.1016/j.ijpe.2013.02.030

Serafeim, G. (2020). Public Sentiment and the Price of Corporate Sustainability. *Financial Analysts Journal*, *76*(2), 26–46.

Starik, M., & Kanashiro, P. (2013). Toward a Theory of Sustainability Management: Uncovering and Integrating the Nearly Obvious. *Organization & Environment*, *26*(1), 7–30. doi:10.1177/1086026612474958

Tian, Q., & Robertson, J. L. (2019). How and When Does Perceived CSR Affect Employees' Engagement in Voluntary Pro-environmental Behavior? *Journal of Business Ethics*, *155*(2), 399–412. doi:10.100710551-017-3497-3

Truffer, B., & Coenen, L. (2012). Environmental innovation and sustainability transitions in regional studies. *Regional Studies*, *46*(1), 1–21. doi:10.1080/00343404.2012.646164

van Mossel, A., van Rijnsoever, F. J., & Hekkert, M. P. (2018). Navigators through the storm: A review of organization theories and the behavior of incumbent firms during transitions. *Environmental Innovation and Societal Transitions*, *26*, 44–63. doi:10.1016/j.eist.2017.07.001

Vermeulen, W. J. V., & Witjes, S. (2016). On addressing the dual and embedded nature of business and the route towards corporate sustainability. *Journal of Cleaner Production*, *112*, 2822–2832. doi:10.1016/j.jclepro.2015.09.132

Waddock, S. A., & Graves, S. B. (1997). The corporate social performance-financial performance link. *Strategic Management Journal*, *18*(4), 303–319. doi:10.1002/(SICI)1097-0266(199704)18:4<303::AID-SMJ869>3.0.CO;2-G

Whelan, T., & Fink, C. (2016). The comprehensive business case for sustainability. *Harvard Business Review*, *21*, 2012.

Whitmarsh, L. (2009). Behavioural responses to climate change: Asymmetry of intentions and impacts. *Journal of Environmental Psychology*, *29*(1), 13–23. doi:10.1016/j.jenvp.2008.05.003

Williams, A., Philipp, F., Kennedy, S., & Whiteman, G. (2017). Systems Thinking: A Review of Sustainability Management Research. *Journal of Cleaner Production*, *148*, 866–881. doi:10.1016/j.jclepro.2017.02.002

Williams, A., Whiteman, G., & Parker, J. N. (2019). Backstage Interorganizational Collaboration: Corporate Endorsement of the Sustainable Development Goals. *Academy of Management Discoveries*, *5*(4), 367–395. doi:10.5465/amd.2018.0154

Wolor, C., Solikah, S., Fidhyallah, N. F., & Lestari, D. P. (2020). Effectiveness of E-Training, Leadership, and Work Life Balance on Employee Performance during COVID-19. *The Journal of Asian Finance, Economics, and Business*, *7*(10), 443–450. doi:10.13106/jafeb.2020.vol7.no10.443

Wright, C., & Nyberg, D. (2017). An inconvenient truth: How organizations translate climate change into business as usual. *Academy of Management Journal*, *60*(5), 1633–1661. doi:10.5465/amj.2015.0718

Wulandari, V., Hertati, L., Antasari, R., & Nazarudin, N. (2021). The Influence of the Covid-19 Crisis Transformative Leadership Style on Job Satisfaction Implications on Company Performance. *Ilomata International Journal of Tax and Accounting*, *2*(1), 17–36. doi:10.52728/ijtc.v2i1.185

ADDITIONAL READING

ElAlfy, A., Palaschuk, N., El-Bassiouny, D., Wilson, J., & Weber, O. (2020). Scoping the Evolution of Corporate Social Responsibility (CSR) Research in the Sustainable Development Goals (SDGs) Era. Sustainability, 12(14).

Khan, M., Serfeim, G., & Yoon, A. (2016). Corporate Sustainability: First Evidence on Materiality. *The Accounting Review*, *91*(6), 1697–1724. doi:10.2308/accr-51383

Marcus, J., Kurucs, E. C., & Colbert, B. A. (2010). Conceptions of the Business-Society-Nature-Interface: Implications for Management Scholarship. *Business & Society*, *49*(3), 402–438. doi:10.1177/0007650310368827

Perez-Lopez, D., Moreno-Romero, A., & Barkemeyer, R. (2015). Exploring the relationship between sustainability reporting and sustainability management practices. *Business Strategy and the Environment*, *24*(8), 720–734. doi:10.1002/bse.1841

Rosati, F., & Faria, L. G. (2019). Addressing the SDGs in Sustainability Reports: The Relationship with Institutional Factors. *Journal of Cleaner Production*, *215*, 1312–1326. doi:10.1016/j.jclepro.2018.12.107

Scheyvens, R., Banks, G., & Hughes, E. (2016). The Private Sector and the SDGs: The Need to Move Beyond 'Business as Usual'. *Sustainable Development*, *24*(6), 371–382. doi:10.1002d.1623

Tschopp, D., & Huefner, R. J. (2014). Comparing the Evolution of CSR Reporting to that of Financial Reporting. *Journal of Business Ethics*, *127*(3), 565–577. doi:10.100710551-014-2054-6

Werther, W. B., & Chandler, D. (2010). *Strategic Corporate Social Responsibility: Stakeholders in a Global Environment*. Sage Publications, Inc.

Williams, A., Whiteman, G., & Parker, J. N. (2019). Backstage Interorganizational Collaboration: Corporate Endorsement of the Sustainable Development Goals. *Academy of Management Discoveries*, *5*(4), 367–395. doi:10.5465/amd.2018.0154

Wright, C., & Nyberg, D. (2017). An inconvenient truth: How organizations translate climate change into business as usual. *Academy of Management Journal*, *60*(5), 1633–1661. doi:10.5465/amj.2015.0718

KEY TERMS AND DEFINITIONS

Brundtland Commission: A United Nations working committee organized to unite countries to pursue sustainable development together.

Corporate Social Responsibility: A self-regulating business model that holds organizations to be accountable on all aspects of society.

Materiality: The threshold at which variables become sufficiently relevant to business activities that they should be reported.

Neo-Liberal: A business worldview that promotes economic growth, free-market capitalism, and deregulation.

Resilience: The capacity to cope with crisis and respond quickly to pre-crisis status.

Self-Concordance: A state reached when business goals are aligned with an individual's sense of self, needs, and personal values.

Sustainable Development: An organizing principle for human development that allows current generations to meet the needs of the present without compromising the ability of future generations to meet their own.

Triple-Bottom Line: a business accounting framework that measures success across three dimensions of people, planet, and profit.

Value Chain: A full set of processes and activities that a firm performs to deliver products and/or services.

ENDNOTES

1 **Triple-Bottom Line**: A corporate accounting framework that incorporates three measures of performance including social, environmental and financial dimensions. This differs from traditional reporting frameworks as it moves beyond traditional measures of return on investment and shareholder returns to include environmental and social measures. The TBL dimensions are also commonly called the three Ps: people, planet and profits (Elkington, 1997).

2 **Brundtland Commission of Sustainable Development**: Also known as the World Commission on Environment and Development (WCED), the aim of the Brundtland Commission was to help direct the nations of the world towards the goal of sustainable development. In 1987 the commission published the report titled *Our Common Future* which defined sustainable development as development which meets the needs of current generations without compromising the ability of future generations to meet their own needs (Daly, 1990).

Chapter 3
Management of the Political Enterprise in the Service of the Sustainable Development Goals (SDGs) in Cosmopolitan Society:
Integrating Ethical Values-Driven Management in the Politicization of the Corporation

Jacob Dahl Rendtorff
Roskilde University, Denmark

ABSTRACT

This chapter proposes to analyze the theory of the political enterprise with focus on the concept of ethical values-driven management in the contemporary debate on the politization of business in service of sustainability in cosmopolitan society. By service of cosmopolitan society of the political enterprise the chapter investigates the idea of the political enterprise as being a responsible political, ethical, and social agent with focus on the 17 UN Sustainable Development Goals (SDGs) that are required to justify its mission and role in society as a political actor that makes a different for its social and political community. The company is embedded in a social and political order with a diversity of political values, and the discussion about the meaning of the concept of values-driven management is therefore fundamental if one is to analyze the concept of the political enterprise in service of the Sustainable Development Goals.

INTRODUCTION

In contemporary management of business at the service of cosmopolitan society, the concept of the political enterprise with focus on sustainable development and a general politization of business activities have become central to understanding corporate public relations and the relation between business and

DOI: 10.4018/978-1-7998-8065-3.ch003

society. Politization means that there is a political and social aim of business with focus on respect for humanity and on the good and happiness in CSR and business ethics (Meyer 2015; Renouard & Ezvan 2018; Chia, Kern & Neville 2020). Referring to cosmopolitan society and cosmopolitan business ethics means that businesses must act in cosmopolitan and global context where business moves beyond local and national boundaries and addresses sustainable development from the point of view of global and cosmopolitan business ethics (Rendtorff 2017). By service of cosmopolitan society of the political enterprise we refer to the idea of the political enterprise as being a responsible political, ethical and social agent with focus on the 17 UN sustainable development goals (SDGs) that is required to justify its mission and role in society as a political actor that makes a different for its social and political community (Rendtorff 2019a). The company is embedded in a social and political order with a diversity of political values, and the discussion about the meaning of the concept of values-driven management is therefore fundamental if one is to analyze the political enterprise (Scherer & Palazzo 2007). In the political and economic sense, companies can be regarded as organizations and institutions in "turbulent and dynamic environments" and as "systems of interacting individuals with interests and preferences" (March 1962). In this perspective, the company is not only an economic entity, but the market economy is determined by the search for ethical and political objectives of business corporations, which recently has been accomplished in a centered focus on the sustainable development goals (SDGs).

This article proposes to analyze the political enterprise with focus on the concept of ethical values-driven management in the contemporary debate on the politization of business in service of sustainability in cosmopolitan society, with focus on the global responsibilities of business (Driscoll & Hoffman 2000). This debate can be seen as a confrontation between what has been called a positivistic and pragmatic concept of creating shared value (Porter 1980, Porter 1987, Porter 2008; Porter & Kramer 2003; Porter & Kramer 2006; Porter & Kramer 2011) on the one hand and the post-positivistic and deliberative and communicative concept of the political corporation on the other hand (Palazzo & Scherer 2006; Scherer & Palazzo 2007; Scherer & Palazzo 2011; Scherer, Palazzo & Seidl 2013). In their concept of the political enterprise both approaches have a general concept of value without focusing on the ethical dimensions value of the political corporation (Rendtorff 2011a). What has been missing in the debate is a deeper clarification and discussion of the concept of ethics and ethical values-driven management of the political enterprise in service of sustainable development goals (SDGs) in cosmopolitan society (Crane, Palazzo, Spence & Matten 2014). To fill this research gap, I analyze the organizational foundations for ethical values-driven management of the political enterprise which can be said to lie behind the concept of sustainable development.

As core focus of ethical values-driven management of the organization in service of sustainable development goals (SDGs) in cosmopolitan society, we can mention the basic ethical principles of respect for autonomy, dignity, integrity and vulnerability as the foundation of the democratic political values in business (Rendtorff 2009). These principles have been proposed as fundamental principles of European ethical culture (Rendtorff 2002; Rendtorff 2017). Thus, they are essential ethical values for the enterprise at the service of sustainable development goals (SDGs) in cosmopolitan society. Here, it is important to remember that the ethical principles are ideas that do not only apply at the individual level. They also get their basic significance at the organizational level (Rendtorff 2011b). This is the basis for service ethics and ethics in the enterprise in service of sustainable development goals (SDGs) in cosmopolitan society.

The theoretical framework for this research is the concept of business legitimacy with focus on the ethical dimension of legitimate business (Rendtorff 2020). Business legitimacy means that the corporation is becoming an ethical and political actor and that the social and economic activities of business are politized in a way that corporations need ethical, social and political legitimacy by citizens of society. Politization of business means that corporations are required to live up to ethical legitimacy requirements and general expectations by society (Rendtorff 2020). In a situation of a global environmental, social and political legitimation crisis of capitalism, businesses are increasingly asked to justify their economic and social activities (Habermas 1973; Habermas 1985). As basis for research in ethical values-driven management business legitimacy is defined as the requirements of social and political acceptance of business by society's expectations towards corporations. From the perspective of legitimacy and corporate citizenship, two rival approaches can be taken: the cynical one and the ethical one. If we look at the current developments of the political enterprise in service of sustainable development goals (SDGs) in cosmopolitan society, the cynical approach to values as strategic window-dressing is replaced by an ethical understanding of business legitimacy as deep commitment to fundamental ethical values.

Thus, the objective of this article is to contribute to the analysis of the ethical values of humanity of a political corporation as an institution at the service of the sustainable development goals (SDGs) in cosmopolitan society from the perspective of its dimension as a social actor requiring social and political legitimacy. The main research question of the paper is: How can we conceptualize the ethical values of the political corporation in service of sustainable development goals in cosmopolitan society in relation to different economic, social, ethical and political values? This research question can be specified in three sub questions, where the first sub question is supported by the two others: 1) What are the ethical values of the enterprise in service of sustainable development goals in cosmopolitan society 2) What is the meaning of the ethical value concept behind the debate about the enterprise in service of sustainable development goals in cosmopolitan society 3) How can we defend a humanistic ethical vision of the political enterprise in service of sustainable development goals in cosmopolitan society?

1. The Meaning of the Values of the Political Enterprise in Service of Cosmopolitan Society

Contrary to those who claim that businesses should concentrate on being neutral economic agents (The business of business is business) (Friedman 1962; Friedman [1970] 1996), the driving force of the current politization of businesses as politically and ethically responsible for society is an increasing demand from society for good, ethical and responsible management by top management and corporate boards (Good Corporate Governance). This idea lies behind the concept of creating shared value (Porter & Kramer 2011) and of the political corporation (Scherer & Palazzo 2007). But how should we understand the meaning of creating shared value and being ethically and politically responsible of the corporation? Here, it is essential to respect the idea of human autonomy, dignity, integrity and vulnerability in organizations. Management must at once increase the company's earnings, create a good brand and image and at the same time search for ethical and political legitimacy and trust and acceptance of the corporation in the public sphere (Rothenhoefer 2019). Thus, it is characteristic of the current politicization of the company that politics is not primarily understood as a politics of power but rather based on a democratic and ethical vision of the legitimate company as a good and responsible citizen respecting humanity dignity at the service of sustainable development goals (SDGs) in cosmopolitan society.

The discourse on the political enterprise is characterized by a fusion of ethics and politics in the search for a vision of corporate legitimacy, where the good citizenship of the company, its social responsibility justifies its actual existence (License to operate) (Crane, Matten, Glozer Spence & 2019). Here, economics, ethics and politics are not opposed to each other, but economics and ethics are integrated into the idea of the political corporation that needs democratic and societal legitimacy. Business ethics is not conceptualized as an oxymoron, i.e. an impossible contradiction between economic utility maximization and social responsibility but integrated into society with a democratic justification of the economy (Ulrich 2008). Both concepts of creating shared value and of the political corporation can be said to rely on the ethical concept of the values-driven company as an ethically responsible company that as a responsible political citizen works for the good of the community respecting humanity while securing an economic profit (Meyer 2015; Renouard & Ezvan 2018; Chia, Kern & Neville 2020).

The prevailing arguments for ethical values-driven management and for a more developed business ethics of the enterprise at the service of sustainable development goals (SDGs) in cosmopolitan society in order to achieve democratic business legitimacy are that in a democratic society with a strong and committed political public, there is increased external social pressure on companies (Palazzo & Scherer 2006; Scherer & Palazzo 2007; Scherer & 2011; Scherer, Palazzo & Seidl 2013). In this perspective, ethical value is a core dimension of democratic politics that cannot be reduced to power politics (Rendtorff 2010). Instead the focus on ethics means to be concerned with respect for human autonomy, dignity, integrity and vulnerability. Leading business ethicists have also argued that the leadership of a complex society risks losing contact with reality if it does not deal thoroughly with the company's ethical values and mission (Paine 1994, 1996; Driscoll & Hoffman; 2000; Hoffman, Driscoll & Painter Morland 2001). Furthermore, it is pointed out from a business ethical point of view that not everything can be accounted for in money (Paine 1997; Solomon & Flores 2001). All this can be seen as indication of the increasing politization of corporations with focus on their ethical values in complex societies.

Thus, today there is a dominant discourse of business legitimacy requiring business to justify their activities by creating ethical value in being at service for sustainable development goals (SDGs) in cosmopolitan society. Therefore, it is needed to clarify the concept of ethical value behind this vision of the political corporation. Neither Porter and Kramer (Porter & Kramer 2011) nor Scherer and Palazzo (Scherer & Palazzo 2007) are clear on this point. The reason is that the concept of ethical value as the basis for values-driven management is not unique, but it is defined in many different ways, often used interchangeably (Sen 1987; Smith 2000: 62). When discussing corporate social responsibility, different types of values collide, and values-driven management in political enterprise helps to allocate and mediate between these different types of values. Here, we can emphasize that ethical values in the political corporations are both normative and descriptive and proposed as pragmatic justification of corporate mission, visions and strategies (Putnam 2002). This perspective on values in the political corporation implies that ethical values express the basic assumptions of different worldviews and views of life that underlie ethical and political beliefs. That is why ethical values in organizations have both a descriptive or cognitive and a normative or political and ethical function. For the same reason, ethical values cannot be completely separated from facts. They are both facts and norms (Putnam 2002). They express the implicit and explicit preferences of actors that motivate these actors to pursue or act towards specific goals. Values therefore have both a cognitive and a normative influence on actors in the company.

In this way, ethical values in values-driven management have both a psychological and a sociological significance, since they serve as the basis for worldviews and beliefs in different types of cultures. Nevertheless, the core of respect for ethical values in organizations centers around respect for human rights and well-being with focus on respect for autonomy, dignity, integrity and vulnerability. At the same time, these ethical values become the basis for individuals' judgment. Here they function as normative standards that determine the behavior and behavior of individuals in organizations. Therefore, it is natural to see values as an element of organizational culture (Schein 1992). For example, they can enroll in the visible aspects of organizational culture that express themselves in "creations" and "artifacts". Values are extremely important in defining the meaning of meaning expressed in the organization's symbols and overall culture (Schein 1992).

These ethical values of respect for human autonomy, dignity, integrity and vulnerability function as cultural forms influence and create the human experience and the individual's perceptions of the corporation's political goals, since organizations are defined as the center of political conflict of interest (March 1962). Working with values-driven management of the political corporation in service of cosmopolitan society is in complex organizations and societies in a "second order", i.e. double reflective task (Frederick 1995; Thyssen 2009). The formulation of values is a conscious reflection on which stakeholders and values influence and should influence the organization's decisions and actions (Phillips & Freeman 2010). With this perspective on values, we can give meaning to "creating shared value" (Porter 2011) as respect for humanity within deliberative democracy (Scherer & Palazzo 2007). This is the basis for the application of the idea of service of sustainable development goals (SDGs) in cosmopolitan society.

2. Politics of Ethical Principles of the Enterprise Serving Cosmopolitan Society

The corporation has become a values-driven political corporation with the objective to service as a good corporate citizen in society that aims of respecting the rights and wellbeing of humanity in service of sustainable development goals (SDGs) in cosmopolitan society. This shift should not be seen in contrast to David Easton's definition of politics as an authoritative allocation of values in society (Easton 1990). Politics also include power and opportunistic politics, but there is a tendency for this policy understanding to be integrated into a moralized political view that emphasizes the importance of ethical values for legitimate political goals (Scherer, & Palazzo 2011; Rendtorff 2020). The politization of business means that its ethical values of respect for humanity should reflect the moral ideals that generally characterize a democratic public in a modern enlightened society where respect for human rights, ecological sustainability and corporate social responsibility have become fundamental values (Elkington 1997; 1998). Indeed, the political metaphor of the triple-bottom-line has replaced a traditional concept financial bottom-line as measurement of economic success of business (Wayne & MacDonald 2004).

In Europe and generally in advanced democracies, increasingly well-educated and fundamentally democratically minded consumers mean that the political consumer has become an inevitable factor in the company's marketing and communication strategy formulation. Without being particularly systematic, consumers' critical attitudes toward corporate activities typically show up in areas such as the environment, human rights, but consumers are also generally sensitive to the company's general public reputation as a service to society (Scherer, Palazzo & Seidl 2013). This is the basis for application of sustainable development goals (SDGs) in business and management. Indeed, consumers consider human rights and respect for human autonomy, dignity, integrity and vulnerability as essential for ethical business. This is also the case for the financial industry. Shareholders also demand political investment, with companies respecting general moral standards and recognizing general labor rules for their workers. Ethical investment policy also includes good corporate governance. Thus, shareholders' interest in the company is no longer strictly economical but also values-driven (ethical aspects of shareholder value), as well as other stakeholders in the company, stakeholders, have become more active in demanding that the company comply with human rights and has a sustainable environmental profile (Freeman, Harrison, Wicks, Parmar & de Colle 2010).

Ethical values-driven management with focus on respect for humanity as an element of the social responsibility of the political enterprise in service of sustainable development goals (SDGs) in cosmopolitan society is therefore generally based on a view that the company must contribute to securing and maintaining sustainability the triple bottom line of business in both economic, environmental, social and ethical sense (Elkington 1997; 1998). Here, there is a close connection between values-driven management, ethics and the comprehensive value accounts as well as the supplementary non-financial reports. Therefore, when dealing with the enterprise at the service of cosmopolitan society one cannot avoid talking about circular economy, sustainable development and "Sustainable Reporting", which involves the environment, consumer satisfaction and employees' quality of life in reporting the accounts and activities of the political corporation.

This demand for business legitimacy of the political corporation is based on the notion that states and political systems cannot stand alone when it comes to developing and sustaining the respect for human rights and humanity in welfare society. Corporate values are integrated into society's general view of ethics with focus on respect for human autonomy, dignity, integrity and vulnerability and of "the good life of and with the other human being in just institutions" (Ricoeur 1990: 202). Civil society, and especially businesses, should also contribute to the development of society. It is a key feature of the concept of corporate citizenship that the public administration needs an ethically oriented private business community to achieve common political and social goals (Matten & Crane 2005). Therefore, states seek to involve companies in the formulation of common policy goals and binding values that must be closely linked to corporate values.

This discussion of these trends in relation to the many meanings of the concept of values-driven management has documented that the politicization of the companies constitutes a sharp break with a strict separation of the economic market and the political distribution of goods where the enterprise do everything to serve to society in the best possible way (Raulet, 2011). The political corporation responds to a polyphony of voices in the public debate in order to achieve legitimacy (Andersen 2003). Relational economics means that the firm is acting in polycontextual, polyvalent and polycentric environments (Wieland 2020). This polyphonic and polycontextual condition opens for the political corporation with ethical values-driven management with focus on human autonomy, dignity, integrity and vulnerability as the core of business legitimacy.

Therefore, the emergence of ethics as an essential element of corporate politicization is not only a pointer to the company's non-economic values, but also provides a profound reflection on how different kinds of values in values-driven management can and should influence the development of the organization and how these values must be applied and implemented externally and internally. This implies "the relational view of the firm as a nexus of stakeholder interests" (Wieland 2020: 7). Here, stakeholder management contributes to value-creation in the political corporation (Harrison & Wicks 2013). The company's ability and need for reflection comes into play in value conflicts where different types of values must be prioritized in values-driven management in order to achieve business legitimacy. Thus, the focus on basic ethical principles of respect for human autonomy, dignity, integrity and vulnerability emerges a central constitutive element of ethical stakeholder management of the political corporation. From here, the enterprise enters into service of sustainable development goals (SDGs) in cosmopolitan society

3. Corporate Values of the Political Enterprise Serving Cosmopolitan Society

Looking at contemporary developments in theory and practice documents the emergence of a strong discourse of the political corporation serving cosmopolitan society as a good citizen respecting the fundamental values of human rights and humanity in service of sustainable development goals (SDGs) in cosmopolitan society. Now, we will from the point of view of complexity theory discuss the constitutive dimensions of the organization of this political corporation. Ethics is here understood here as the "second-order" reflection on the value of values-driven management, especially an assessment of the political values understood as a perception of authoritative allocation of goods in relation to stakeholders and society (Fremann 1984; March 1992, Verstraeten, 2000; Richter & Dow 2017). In this context, politics and ethics express two related, but also different ways in which corporate values are assessed: Ethics is a broader legitimacy-oriented reflection on the equitable distribution of values, while politics, in the first place, expresses a preferential distribution that is not necessarily justified by the common good.

In his analyzes of *Protestant ethics and the spirit of capitalism*, Max Weber described the close connection between capitalism and ethics by examining the role of Puritans and other Protestant groups in the rise of capitalism (Weber 1904-5). Weber understood the Protestant ethics as based on a strong professional ethics based on trust, virtue and professional vocation and responsibility. This view of the values of capitalism is also of great importance today, where most companies are initially determined by a strong and dominant work ethic. Later, Weber also described the values of the bureaucratic man (Weber 1978). In his analyzes of bureaucratic work ethic, he found that modern working man lives by a strict and objective goal rationality and perceives all other values as based on subjective mind. Modern organizational theory has, by extension, developed the concept of "Organizational Man", the conscientious office man who lives only because of the organization's instrumental rationality, i.e. "The organizational imperative of economic efficiency".

William C. Frederick has a more positive view of the company's values in its book *Values, Nature and Culture in the American Corporation* (1995) (Frederick 1995: 7). He argues that the constitutive or original values of organizations and companies can be traced back to some groups of values that concentrate on:

1. Economizing (having a good economy)
2. Power Aggrandizing (increasing power, gaining more power)
3. Ecologizing (ecologizing, relating to the outside world)

Frederick believes that these value groups express the original values that are the essentials of any business. Frederick uses both social sciences and natural sciences to justify his theory in an autopoetic, chaos and complexity theory perspective. Frederick argues that these value groups are archetypal values that can be perceived as the result of a natural evolutionary process that have given these values fundamental meanings as the social conditions that have shaped US companies (Frederick 1995: 36). The three groups of values summarize and legitimize the collection of conjectures, evaluations, conditions and assumptions that characterize the companies according to Frederick. Indeed, this model can be seen as the basis for understanding the concept of corporate sustainability behind the vision of the corporation service of sustainable development goals (SDGs) in cosmopolitan society

As the US organizational model has had a major impact on today's businesses, I believe that with some modifications, the three types of value can be considered as fundamental to all types of businesses in liberal societies, like the European where there is more focus on the corporation's impact on society including, for example, the values of political enterprise in service of sustainable development goals (SDGs) in cosmopolitan society. This becomes clearer when we look more closely at the specific content of the mentioned value groups. "Economizing" is a collective term for the values expressed in the company's economic activity (Frederick 1995: 55). A business is understood here as an organization seeking to achieve economic growth in a liberal market. The rationality of this economization is based on cost-benefit calculations, where the basic values are based on the endeavor to achieve economic profitability. Consideration of the economic bottom line is the real basis for the company's economy.

Frederick argues in this context that the company wants to find the maximum equilibrium position in relation to the economic growth of a given market. Business is a self-organizing economic growing system that strives for systemic unity in an economic market.

It is interesting that Frederick claims that profit maximization is not necessarily an original value in the business organization. Frederick therefore helps us to move beyond Friedman's provocative statement that the social responsibility of business can be reduced to making profit (Friedman 1962; Friedman [1970] 1996). Frederick argues that profit maximization is secondary to the company's financial organization. At the same time, organizational development cannot be completely understood from the point of view of economic values but involves relationships of power and interaction with the surroundings.

"Power Aggrandizing" here refers to the company's efforts to develop power (Frederick 1995: 61). There is a close correlation between this quest for power and the concept of political enterprise, since power values are about the company's involvement in the struggle for the authoritative distribution of goods in society. The group of values that deals with the company's increase in power denotes both the internal and the external pursuit of power in organizations. Power is described by Frederick as both a fact and a representation of human consciousness. For example, power is asserted in the hierarchical structure of companies, and it is reflected in the market economy's foundation in the private ownership of companies. Therefore, dominance over others is characterized as an archetypal and original feature of the values that characterize modern business organizations. Internal and external relations can help maintain this power. Desire for power determines many of the company's efforts to form organizational strategies, policy formulations, development plans, etc.

"Ecologizing" expresses the basic value (Frederick 1995: 46) that in order to survive as an organizational entity, the company wants to achieve a good relationship with the outside world. The concept of the company ecology is used here in a very broad way as an expression of the interaction between the company and its surroundings. In this context, it can be emphasized that the company acts in a unity of the ecological system and the social economy system. It is characteristic of the company that it - in its quest to survive - affects the environment, the land and the sustainability of society. At the same time, the survival of the company depends on this interaction with the surroundings.

In continuation of Frederick's conception of the companies' constitutive or original values, we can highlight Ole Thyssen's system theoretical work with values-driven management as a basis for determining the ethics of political enterprise with focus on respect for basic ethical principles of human autonomy, dignity, integrity and vulnerability as the basis for understanding the concept of values-driven management in corporation in service of sustainable development goals (SDGs) in cosmopolitan society. Value-driven management and ethics can be regarded as a political governance mechanism whereby the original values of the companies are weighted in relation to each other through the company's communication and self-reflection. Thyssen describes values-driven management as a means of improving organizations' communication and self-perception (Thyssen 2009). Businesses are systems of communication about values. Thus, politics becomes crucial to understanding the development and role of organizations in society. The political communication requires stakeholder deliberation between business and corporate stakeholders on values and their demands on businesses helps to reduce complexity and to manage the organization as a system of actions (Richter & Dow 2017).

In this perspective, the political corporation, with focus on humanity and ethical values, contributes to decision-making processes with focus on progressive business models (Rendtorff 2019b). This is the purpose of stakeholder management (Freeman 1984): The involvement of various stakeholders (employees, customers, shareholders) helps to legitimize decisions and their preconditions. Values in the political enterprise thus express a new form of leadership discourse within the enterprise, which makes up a purely hierarchical model of decision based on the absolute sovereignty of the manager (Thyssen 2009). Values-driven management, as political communication, is ideally determined by what the famous political philosopher Jürgen Habermas calls "dominance-free communication", that is, of the argument of the best argument endorsed by the participants in the discussion without coercion (Habermas 1985). It is therefore a characteristic feature of political enterprise that an ideological ideal of democratic communication and deliberative politics is a necessary alternative to traditional governance tools (Rendtorff 2013a,b,c,d).

Social, ethical and environmental accounts express one of the ways of concretizing this notion of values. Various forms of dialogue with stakeholders and user surveys also serve as means of strengthening communication and decisions about the objectives of the companies. Political communication about values clarifies the relationship between the organization's original values and creates meaning and coherence in the political message, while at the same time improving the overall image of the organization (Thyssen 2009). Political communication about the company's ethical values and service to society therefore contributes to integrating ethics with the company's original values of increasing power, economizing and interacting with the outside world.

Based on this provision of ethics as values-driven management, i.e. a "second-order" reflection on the prioritization and development of the company's original values, the company's policy can be understood as a pointer to the company's and values of increasing power and ecologizing at the expense of purely economic values. In principle, however, this intensified power-enhancing interaction with the outside world is not necessarily a break with economic and purely private values. Only when the company's politicization is given a "second-order" ethical perspective, where values are assessed in the light of the efforts to be a good citizen at the service of cosmopolitan society, can one speak of values as ethical. Faced with this, we are in front of a cynical policy understanding where the values of policing are merely instruments to strengthen the power of the company.

Thus, we face two contradictory understandings of the political enterprise in service of service of sustainable development goals (SDGs) in cosmopolitan society, both of which emphasize the increase of power and the adaptation of the world as an important element of economic markets. In the first sense, corporate politicization is an opportunistic political application of ethical values for cynical profit maximization for no other purpose than financial gain. In the second sense, which I have repeatedly emphasized as the most prevalent, corporate politicization is accompanied by ethics as a second-order reflection on how the company's original values contribute to the common good, respect for humanity and strengthen the organization's social legitimacy and good citizenship. This new vision of the enterprise in service of sustainable development goals (SDGs) in cosmopolitan society emphasizes the role of business for contribution to the common good of society

4. A Defense of the Political Enterprise in Service of Sustainable Development Goals (SDGs) in Cosmopolitan Society

With this clarification of the constitutive elements of the organizational ontology of the pragmatics of values of political corporation from the point of view of complexity theory we can now defend this view of the business organization in confrontation with the traditional concept of the business firm implying that the business of business is business (Friedman 1962; Friedman [1970] 1996) In spite of the tendency to emphasize the crucial importance of ethics in the current politicization of the market, we cannot escape the fact that there are fundamental conflicts in the tension between the different values of the company. Indeed, this is a challenge for strategic management of the political corporation (Suchman 1995). There is a constant confrontation between the cynical, power political use of corporate values and the ethical-oriented legitimacy-based course of action, in which corporate politicization must help to make society better. The potential conflict between the two forms of politization of the company is particularly visible in critical voices in the public and among skeptical consumers and employees. Among them, many probably perceive political enterprise in service of sustainable development goals (SDGs) in cosmopolitan society as a new version of economic rationality and the sensible ability of capitalism to squeeze money out of people.

Alain Etchegoyen even argued that we are living in a crisis where many private perceptions of the company's good politics and respect for humanity have replaced the need for a universal morality (Etchegoyen 1991, 135). The many programs for ethics, social responsibility and values-driven management in companies express a new restructuring of ethics at a time when morality is no longer possible as something personal and private. When society cannot respect basic ethical principles, we turn to business to find help. The current politization of the company is not a new morality, but a reappearance of a new Taylorism, where values-driven management such as ideology must make businesses function better. In short, the problem of politicization tends to turn the market's values into moral values. According to this position, it is not the task of the company, but merely the legislature, to define the ethical values of society, through the universal moral content of the law. Moreover, it is an illusion to believe that business can perceive human life as the highest value.

Therefore, in the following, I will formulate some requirements for values-driven management in the political enterprise in service of sustainable development goals (SDGs) in cosmopolitan society that strive to get beyond this harsh criticism. This is my response to the needed formulation of a vision of values-driven management as respect for humanity responding to the discourse of creating shared value in democratic community (Scherer & Palazzo 2007; Porter & Kramer 2011).

In my opinion, the starting point should be to consider values-driven management in the political enterprise in service of sustainable development goals (SDGs) in cosmopolitan society as a contribution to raising awareness of how individuals and organizations can be helped to strengthen the shared values of respect for human autonomy, dignity, integrity and vulnerability in the company and in society. It is important to integrate individual and organization in a way that is enriching for both parties (Driscoll & Hoffman 2000). Basically, there is a close connection between values and rules. However, virtue and value programs must not be reduced to mere compliance programs (Driscoll & Hoffman 2000: 21). Put another way, legal rules are only a small part of values-driven management. Ethical values express a broader, idealistic approach to leadership. There is a close connection between politics, ethics and values, although the company's politics and values-driven management do not necessarily coincide. Values-driven management is about engaging people in their organization to improve the systemic integrity of the organization and make the corporation act in service of cosmopolitan society (Pedersen & Rendtorff 2004). A well-functioning program of values-driven management in an organization thereby becomes a natural part of the culture of the organization.

In the contemporary search for ethics in values-driven management, focus on sustainability and global and cosmopolitan responsibility for sustainable development goals has become a major issue. Indeed, the movement of business for human rights integrates human autonomy, dignity, integrity and vulnerability into the conceptualization of business ethics (Rendtorff 2017). Thus, as argued we see that the enterprise in service of sustainable development goals (SDGs) in cosmopolitan society, considers the United Nations' Sustainable Development Goals (SDGs) as central dimensions of business ethics, economics and sustainability where we move from CSR and business ethics to sustainable development goals (SDGs) (Rendtorff 2019a). We are facing need for an ethical economy of sustainability in the perspective of responsible management of sustainability where the triple bottom-line (Elkington 1997; 1998) is integrated into the global management of sustainable development goals.

Thus, improvement of an organization's integrity with values-driven management programs can be implemented with various forms of credo and mission statements, ethical codes and principles that are adapted to the organization in order to respect humanity. Values-driven management can have many different structures. It can be a simple mission statement, but also a detailed set of rules and complicated accounting and reporting mechanisms. Different companies of different sizes, but also with different types of work and corporate cultures, may need different types of values-driven management (Driscoll & Hoffman 2000: 33). The initiative for values-driven management in the political enterprise can be seen as an endeavor to create a collective identity for the organization. In this way, self-awareness is formed in the organization. This creates the ethical culture of the organization. The organization's management and employees are oriented towards knowledge of the company's internal and external aspects. Against this background, the organization starts by describing the ethical problems and dilemmas it faces. Political and ethical issues should therefore be discussed at the organization's management and board meetings as it contributes to open ethical reflection at all levels of the organization.

In addition to the importance of emphasizing that ethics programs or codes of ethics can take many forms, it can be emphasized that they should be based on the commitment of employees to the values of the organization, as it increases the employees' commitment to the values in the organization (Driscoll & Hoffman 2000: 59). It is also important that values are developed in dialogue with the company's main stakeholders in the corporation in service of sustainable development goals (SDGs) in cosmopolitan society. The dialogue with stakeholders is of great importance in improving the culture of the political enterprise. This ensures respect for basic ethical principles of autonomy, dignity, integrity and vulnerability. Therefore, ethics in the organization can also help to create knowledge, reflection and understanding of the concrete development of the moral dimension of the organization. The value or virtue-based program is continued with a program to train and improve the ethical capabilities and reflection opportunities among the members of the organization.

An important result of the company's work with values-driven management - understood as a second-order reflection on what values can contribute to the company's good citizenship and enhance the viewpoint of the corporation in service of sustainable development goals in cosmopolitan society - is in particular the improvement of the ability to critically reflect and develop an ethical formulation competence. Ethical formulation competence means the capacity of the people in the corporation to reflect ethically responsibly about decisions and processes in the perspective of the interest of humanity and society. An ethical formulation competence can set focus on good solutions to difficult dilemmas, not least with a view to good corporate governance with the company's board of directors and directors, but probably with middle managers, employees and other influential stakeholders. By virtue of this ethical formulation competence, the ethical and political communication process ensures that the organization, through self-reflection and learning, forms an ethical culture in service of sustainable development goals (SDGs) in cosmopolitan society. Institutionalization of shared values makes individuals more engaged in the activities and goals of the organization. Nevertheless, creating such a learning process is not necessarily the only thing that should be done. A proper ethics program should also include procedures for evaluation, reporting and accounting. These evaluations can be considered as important as the company's financial statements. Accounting also helps to formalize the political norms and ethical culture of the company.

However, the responsibility of the political enterprise not only has a collective and organizational dimension, but also equally relates to the integrity and ability of each leader to think morally. The leader must be able to understand a given situation in the light of conditions such as respect, care, trust, commitment, shared values and shared visions. Leadership becomes a quest for ideal collaboration that must be the realized utopia of politics. Analysis of the leadership role can here combine political theory with management thinking. It is a good idea to revive the political-philosophical tradition of thinking good leadership skills and to utilize this tradition's reservoir of knowledge of leadership as the good government art. However, this must not become a charismatic worship. We should not focus on the leader without seeing him or her in close association with the other members of the organization and its structure. Here theories of judgment and idealized leadership, such as for example the legal philosopher Ronald Dworkin with his theory of the ideal judge Hercules and of "Law as Integrity" (Dworkin 1986), are of great importance. It means that a good organization maintains a strong ethical integrity in order to improve sustainability. Overall, management philosophy and organizational ethics should carefully analyze ethical judgment and personal responsibility in the organization's political environment.

Integration of ethical values in the political enterprise in service of sustainable development goals (SDGs) in cosmopolitan society thus entails a broader concept of politics, which includes both real and power politics and the ideal of politics as a pursuit of the common good (Rendtorff 2019a,b). The empirical trends document this political moralization of the companies realized in the many values that influence them in their daily activities. By examining the values of the political enterprise in service of sustainable development goals (SDGs) in cosmopolitan society, one can see that the company's original and actual values do not exclude politics understood as ethical profiling in the public debate.

However, one of the difficulties in formulating a rigorous concept of political enterprise and values-driven management is that the concept of value has many different meanings (Mattsson & Rendtorff 2006). The concept of value affects, for example, the political debate on corporate social responsibility, where it is argued that companies no longer have to take an interest in maximizing profits and meeting shareholders' demands, but also need to be more socially responsible (Van Der Linden & Freeman 2017). Nevertheless, here the question becomes, what values should really determine the company's actions to best fill its place in society? This ambiguity also affects the practical value work in companies, where they often face complicated definition problems, which, nevertheless, is the task of companies to solve through greater focus on values in management, not least in the form of high value awareness and integrity of the individual leader in daily work.

CONCLUSION

In conclusion, this article answered the research questions by discussing the role of values-driven management in the political enterprise in service of sustainable development goals (SDGs) in cosmopolitan society. The basis for was a conceptual analysis of the different dimensions of the political enterprise, politization, service value, values-driven management and corporate social responsibility. The objective was to clarify the concept of value (Porter & Kramer 2011) creating shared value within communicative and deliberative legitimacy of the political corporation (Palazzo & Scherer 2006). The focus on was basic ethical principles of respect for human autonomy, dignity, integrity and vulnerability. With this the article provided the ontological basis for a humanistic vision of value-creation of business in values-driven management for the service of cosmopolitan society. This analysis used complexity theory (Frederick 1995) and systems theory (Thyssen 2009) as basis for understanding values-driven management as a critical ability of second-order reflection on the interaction between the original values and the company's efforts to contribute to social and political development as a good citizen in the service of sustainable development goals (SDGs) in respect for humanity in cosmopolitan society. Against this background, a proposal for values-driven management in the political corporation was formulated. Values-driven management should build on well-established programs of values and ethics and focus on the good leadership role, where virtues such as integrity and judgment, understood as ethical formulation competence, become crucial elements in organizational and managerial competences for management of the political corporation in service of sustainable development goals (SDGs) in cosmopolitan society.

REFERENCES

Almond, B., & Wilson, B. (1998). *Values. A Symposium.* Humanities Press International, Atlantic Highlands.

Andersen, N. (2003). Polyphonic organizations. In T. Hernes & T. Bakken (Eds.), *Autopoietic organization theory* (pp. 151–182). CBS.

Chia, A., Kern, M. L., & Neville, B. A. (2020, July). CSR for Happiness: Corporate determinants of societal happiness as social responsibility. *Business Ethics (Oxford, England)*, *29*(3), 422–437. doi:10.1111/beer.12274

Crane, A., Matten, D., Glozer, S., & Spence, L. (2019). *Business Ethics.* Oxford University Press.

Crane, A., Palazzo, G., Spence, L. J., & Matten, D. (2014). Contesting the value of creating shared value. *California Management Review*, *56*(2), 130–153. doi:10.1525/cmr.2014.56.2.130

Driscoll, D., & Hoffman, W. M. (2000). *Ethics Matters. How to Implement Values-Driven Management.* Centre for Business Ethics, Bentley College.

Dworkin, R. (1986). *Law as Integrity.* Harvard University Press.

Easton, D. (1990). *The Analysis of Political Structure.* Routledge.

Elkington, J. (1997). *Cannibals with Forks, The Triple Bottom Line of 21st Century Business.* Capstone.

Elkington, J. (1998). Partnerships from cannibals with forks: The triple bottom line of 21st-century business. *Environmental Quality Management*, *8*(1), 37–51. doi:10.1002/tqem.3310080106

Etchegoyen, A. (1991). *La valse des ethiques*. Le Seuil.

Frederick, W. C. (1995). *Values, Nature and Culture in the American Corporation*. Academic Press.

Freeman, R. E. (1984). *Strategic Management. A Stakeholder Approach*. Pitman Publishing Inc.

Freeman, R. E., Harrison, J. S., Wicks, A. C., Parmar, B. L., & de Colle, S. (2010). *Stakeholder theory: The state of the art*. Cambridge University. Press. doi:10.1017/CBO9780511815768

Friedman, M. (1962). *Capitalism and freedom*. University of Chicago Press.

Friedman, M. (1996). The social responsibility of business is to increase its profits. (1970) Reprinted. In S. B. Rae & K. L. Wong (Eds.), *Beyond integrity. A Judeo-Christian approach to business ethics* (pp. 241–246). Zondervan Publishing House. (Original work published 1970)

Habermas, J. (1973). *Legitimation crisis*. Beacon Press.

Habermas, J., & McCarthy, T. (1985). *The theory of communicative action. Lifeworld and system: A critique of functionalist reason* (Vol. 2). Beacon Press.

Harrison, J. S., & Wicks, A. C. (2013). Stakeholder theory, value, and firm performance. *Business Ethics Quarterly*, *23*(1), 97–124. doi:10.5840/beq20132314

Hoffman, M. W., Driscoll, D., & Painter Morland, M. (2001). Integrating Ethics into organizational Cultures. In *Business Ethics: Facing up the Issues*. The Economist Books.

March, J. G. (1992). The Business Firm as a political Coalition. Journal of Politics, 24.

Matten, D., & Crane, A. (2005). Corporate citizenship: Towards an extended theoretical conceptualization. *Academy of Management Review*, *30*(1), 166–179. doi:10.5465/amr.2005.15281448

Mattsson, J., & Rendtorff, J. D. (2006). E-marketing ethics: A theory of value priorities. *International Journal of Internet Marketing and Advertising*, *3*(1), 35–47.

Meyer, M. (2015, August). Positive business: Doing good and doing well. *Business Ethics (Oxford, England)*, *24*(S2), S175–S197. doi:10.1111/beer.12105

Paine, L. S. (1994). Managing for Organizational Integrity. Harvard Business Review.

Paine, L. S. (1996). Moral Thinking in Management. An Essential Capability. *Business Ethics Quarterly*, *6*(4), 477–492. doi:10.2307/3857500

Paine, L. S. (1997). Cases in Leadership, Ethics, and Organizational Integrity. A Strategic Perspective. Academic Press.

Palazzo, G., & Scherer, A. G. (2006). Corporate legitimacy as deliberation. A communicative framework. *Journal of Business Ethics*, *66*(1), 71–88. doi:10.100710551-006-9044-2

Pedersen, J. S., & Rendtorff, J. D. (2004). Value-based Management in Local Public Organizations: A Danish Experience. *Cross Cultural Management*, *11*(2).

Phillips, R. A., & Freeman, R. E. (2010). *Stakeholders*. Edward Elgar Publishing. doi:10.4337/9781785362316

Porter, M. E. (1980). *Competitive strategy*. Free Press.

Porter, M. E. (1987). From competitive advantage to corporate strategy. *Harvard Business Review, 65*(3), 43–59. PMID:17183795

Porter, M. E. (2008). The five competitive forces that shape strategy. *Harvard Business Review, 86*(1), 79–93. PMID:18271320

Porter, M. E., & Kramer, M. R. (2003) The competitive advantage of corporate philanthropy. Reprinted In Harvard business review on corporate social responsibility. Harvard Business School Press.

Porter, M. E., & Kramer, M. R. (2006). Strategy and society: The link between competitive Advantage and corporate social responsibility. *Harvard Business Review, 84*(12), 78–92. PMID:17183795

Porter, M. E., & Kramer, M. R. (2011). Creating shared value. How to reinvent Capitalism – And unleash a wave of innovation and growth. *Harvard Business Review, 89*(1), 62–77.

Putnam, H. (2002). *The Collapse of the Fact/Value Dichotomy and Other Essays*. Harvard University Press.

Raulet, G. (2011). Legitimacy and Globalization. *Philosophy and Social Criticism, 37*(3), 313–323.

Rendtorff, J. D. (2002). Basic ethical principles in European bioethics and biolaw: Autonomy, dignity, integrity and vulnerability. towards a foundation of bioethics and biolaw. *Medicine, Health Care, and Philosophy, 5*(3), 235–244. doi:10.1023/A:1021132602330 PMID:12517031

Rendtorff, J. D. (2009). Basic ethical principles applied to service industries. *Service Industries Journal, 29*(1), 9–19. doi:10.1080/02642060802116404

Rendtorff, J. D. (2010). *Power and Principle in the Market Place: On Ethics and Economics*. Ashgate.

Rendtorff, J. D. (2011a). Institutionalization of corporate ethics and social responsibility programs in firms. I K. Buhmann, L. Roseberry, & M. Morsing (eds.), Corporate social and human rights responsibilities: global, legal and management perspectives (pp. 244-266). London: Palgrave Macmillan.

Rendtorff, J. D. (2011b). Business Ethics, Strategy and Organizational Integrity: The Importance of Integrity as a Basic Principle of Business Ethics That Contributes to Better Economic Performance. I C. Wankel, & A. Stachowicz-Stanusch (eds.), Handbook of Research on Teaching Ethics in Business and Management Education (pp. 274-288).

Rendtorff, J. D. (2013a). Basic concepts of philosophy of management and corporations. I C. Luetge (ed.), Handbook of the philosophical foundations of business ethics (pp. 1361-1386). Dordrecht, Heidelberg, New York, London: Springer Science+Business Media.

Rendtorff, J. D. (2013b). Philosophical theories of management and corporations. I C. Luetge (ed.), Handbook of the philosophical foundations of business ethics (pp. 1409-1432). Dordrecht, Heidelberg, New York, London: Springer Science+Business Media.

Rendtorff, J. D. (2013c). Recent debates in philosophy of management. I C. Luetge (ed.), Handbook of the philosophical foundations of business ethics (pp. 1433-1457). Dordrecht, Heidelberg, New York, London: Springer Science+Business Media.

Rendtorff, J. D. (2013d). The history of the philosophy of management and corporations. I C. Luetge (ed.), Handbook of the philosophical foundations of business ethics (pp. 1387-1408). Dordrecht, Heidelberg, New York, London: Springer Science+Business Media.

Rendtorff, J. D. (2017). *Cosmopolitan Business Ethics: Towards a Global Ethos of Management.* Challenges to Theory and Practice Series. Routledge. Finance, Governance and Sustainability. doi:10.4324/9781315574400

Rendtorff, J. D. (2019a). *Philosophy of Management and Sustainability: Rethinking Business Ethics and Social Responsibility in Sustainable Development.* Emerald Group Publishing.

Rendtorff, J. D. (2019b). Sustainable development goals and progressive business models for economic transformation. *Local Economy, 34*(6), 510–524.

Rendtorff, J. D. (2020). The Concept of Business Legitimacy: Learnings from Suchman. Integrating Sociological, Ethical and Critical Perspectives. In Handbook of Business Legitimacy. Springer Nature Switzerland AG.

Renouard, C., & Ezvan, C. (2018). Corporate social responsibility towards human development: A capabilities framework. *Business Ethics (Oxford, England), 27*(2), 144–155. doi:10.1111/beer.12181

Richter, U. H., & Dow, K. E. (2017). Stakeholder theory: A deliberative perspective. *Business Ethics (Oxford, England), 26*(4), 428–442. doi:10.1111/beer.12164

Ricoeur, P. (1990). *Soi-même comme un Autre.* Le Seuil.

Rothenhoefer, L. M. (2019). The impact of CSR on corporate reputation perceptions of the public—A configurational multi-time, multi-source perspective, Business Ethics. *European Review (Chichester, England), 28*(2), 141–155. doi:10.1111/beer.12207

Schein, E. (1993). *Organizational culture and leadership.* Prentice Hall.

Scherer, Palazzo, & Seidl. (2013). Managing Legitimacy in Complex and Heterogeneous Environments: Sustainable Development in a Globalized World. *Journal of Management Studies, 50*(2), 259-284.

Scherer, A. G., & Palazzo, G. (2007). „Toward a Political Conception of Corporate Responsibility: Business and Society seen from a Habermasian Perspective. *Academy of Management Review, 32*(4), 1096–1120. doi:10.5465/amr.2007.26585837

Scherer, A. G., & Palazzo, G. (2011). The new political role of business in a globalized world: A review of a new perspective on CSR and its implications for the firm, governance, and democracy. *Journal of Management Studies, 48*(4), 899–931. doi:10.1111/j.1467-6486.2010.00950.x

Sen, A. (1987). *On Ethics and Economics.* Blackwell Publishers.

Smith, T. (2000). *Viable Values. A Study of Life as the Root and Reward of Vitality.* Rowman & Littlefield Publishers.

Solomon, R. C., & Flores, F. (2001). *Building Trust in Business, Politics and Life*. Oxford University Press.

Suchman, M. C. (1995). Managing Legitimacy: Strategic and Institutional Approaches. *Academy of Management Review*, *20*(3), 571–610. doi:10.5465/amr.1995.9508080331

Thyssen, O. (2009). *Business Ethics and Organizational Values - A Systems Theoretical Analysis*. Palgrave-MacMillan.

Ulrich, P. (2008). *Integrative Economic Ethics. Foundations of a Civilized Market Economy*. Cambridge University Press. doi:10.1017/CBO9780511488658

Van Der Linden, B., & Freeman, R. E. (2017). Profit and Other Values: Thick Evaluation in Decision Making. *Business Ethics Quarterly*, *27*(3), 353–379. doi:10.1017/beq.2017.1

Verstraeten, J. (2000). *Business Ethics. Broadening the perspective*. Peters.

Wayne, N., & MacDonald, C. (2004). Getting to the bottom of the triple bottom line! *Business Ethics Quarterly*, *14*(2), 243–262. doi:10.5840/beq200414211

Weber, M. (1978). *Economy and society. An outline of interpretative sociology*. University of California Press.

Weber, M. (1904-1905). *Die Protestantische Ethik und der Geist des Kapitalismus*. Academic Press.

Wieland, J. (2020). *Relational Economics. A Political Economy. In Relational Economics and Organization Governance*. Springer. doi:10.1007/978-3-030-45112-7

Chapter 4
Socially Responsible Value Creation in the Post-COVID-19 Era:
Taking Advantage of Dynamic and Digital Capabilities

Gönenç Dalgıç Turhan
Karyatech Electrical Equipments Industry and Trade Inc. Co., Turkey

Narin Bekki
Beksan Nail and Wire Co., Turkey

Gulen Rady
Yasar University, Turkey

ABSTRACT

The unfortunate economic environment emanated from the outbreak of the coronavirus has suddenly raised business organizations' concerns over the value creation. This new era forced them to focus on dynamic and digital capabilities to cope with the adverse changes. Following the stakeholder theory and the resource-based view, this chapter attempts to specify value creation of companies to preserve strategic position while satisfying the demands and interests of their stakeholders. In this sense, corporate social responsibility (CSR) seems a viable way of providing help and support to stakeholders during the fight against the pandemic as well as a catalyzer for the integration of sustainable development goals that can bridge the widened gap in the society. Hence, this chapter seeks to present an understanding on socially responsible value creation, dynamic and digital capabilities, and implementation of sustainability-driven CSR initiatives to ensure recovery, growth, and achieve sustainable development goals.

DOI: 10.4018/978-1-7998-8065-3.ch004

INTRODUCTION

Before 2020 began, nobody was aware that a global pandemic was coming soon. The reason behind is, in the historical context, the last devastating epidemic which was known as Spanish flu and resulted in millions of people killed, occurred in 1918 (Correia et.al., 2020, p.5-6). Considering the impressive scientific developments in the pharmaceutical industry over the past century, neither business practitioners nor policy-makers could have imagined facing an infectious disease while they were determining their agenda. Unfortunately, the unexpected Covid-19 has made its way into world history by 2020 as a pandemic that brought about a global crisis. There is no government, organization or person that has not been affected more or less by the pandemic. At the organizational level, the crisis made the strategic planning that companies performed for the year of 2020 completely irrelevant. Covid-19 has tested crisis management approaches and decision-making processes. Since ad-hoc problem solving typically appears as a response to novel challenges from the environment or other relatively unpredictable events (Winter, 2003), leadership and upper-level management of many organizations had to take ad-hoc, not-well-informed decisions instead of well-informed, deliberate strategic decisions.

With the outbreak of coronavirus, most companies have shifted to the survival mode or firefighting mode and triple-bottom-line objectives were replaced immediately by a single bottom-line objective of saving the day and making profits to survive. However, the crisis is one of the driving forces for change not in the short run, but also in the long run. Under these circumstances, business organizations must rethink the entire value proposition in their strategic management framework (Kytle and Ruggie, 2005) and focus on how they can align their decisions and operations into the United Nations' (UN) Sustainable Development Goals (SDGs). As a viable tool for organizations to achieve these overarching 17 goals of the UN, corporate social responsibility (CSR) can play a leading role in decision-making processes of organizations to foster a sustainable future for societies. Adoption of responsible organizational behavior and creation of value on the basis of the triple-bottom-line approach are presumed as catalyzers to achieve SDGs amid the pandemic and afterwards.

The objective of this chapter is to discuss value creation through CSR initiatives in line with dynamic and digital capabilities and hence contribution to sustainable development goals. For this purpose, the study first provides a conceptual framework for socially responsible value creation. In the second section, drivers of value creation amid the pandemic are sought to be identified. Finally, considering the integration of various CSR practices on behalf of SDGs, the chapter specifically focuses on two of the UN's SDGs regarding good health and well being (SDG-3) and quality education (SDG-4) in order to the exemplify how CSR initiatives can be used to contribute to the sustainable development with the real-life business examples. Since the gaps on SGDs are widening due to the pandemic impacts, this theoretical study can provide an inspiring insight on socially responsible value creation and sustainability driven CSR.

CONCEPTUAL FRAMEWORK

The Concept of CSR Through the Stakeholder Perspective

The concept of CSR whose time has not yet come until the 1960s and beyond is based on the idea that a business has certain responsibilities towards society beyond profit-making motivation. Both academicians and practitioners have been struggling to establish a consensus definition of the concept since the post-World War II (Carroll, 1991; Carroll and Shabana, 2010). Due to the various conceptualizations of the role of business in society, different perspectives on CSR have developed so far (Branco and Rodrigues, 2007). For instance, during the transition from the 1960s to the 1970s, there have been thematic highlights which question the literal meaning of social responsibility and its importance to business and society, and thus contributed to the academic literature and the gradual emergence of business practices (Carroll and Shabana, 2010).

Despite the primacy of economic concerns, a broader view of responsibilities has been acknowledged and posited that a business has certain responsibilities to society in addition to its economic and legal obligations (Carroll, 1979, p.497; Carroll and Shabana, 2010). Based on the pyramid of CSR delineated by Carroll (1979, 1991), the business is required to simultaneously fulfill its economic, legal, ethical, and discretionary (philanthropic) responsibilities, that is, a company which embraces the entire range of responsibilities should struggle to "make a profit, obey the law, be ethical and be a good corporate citizen" (Carroll, 1991, p.39-42). In this context, concomitantly, Carroll (1991, p.43) accentuated the link with stakeholder theory by stating that "there is a natural fit between the idea of corporate social responsibility and an organization's stakeholders". Contrary to the general notion of the responsibility to its shareholders, the company bears a fiduciary duty to stakeholders. Stakeholders which encompass customers, suppliers, employees, stockholders, local community, and management as a representative on behalf of the company, have a stake or claim on the company. Each of these stakeholder groups must therefore get involved in determining the future direction of the company (Freeman, 1998, p.126).

Regarding the evolution of CSR from a stakeholder perspective, in the 1980s, more empirical research has been conducted while producing fewer new definitions of the CSR concept with the rise of alternative themes (Carroll and Shabana, 2010). From the 1990s onward, it has been linked to the business and society literature in line with the call of scholars for the integration of stakeholders in theories and models and hence foregrounded as a dominant paradigm in the relevant research field (Ghobadian et.al., 2015, p.276). In particular, stakeholder theory as an important theoretical framework causes significant repercussions in comparative studies of CSR in developed and developing countries. Rather than the mere satisfaction of the shareholders or owners, CSR refers to treating in a responsible manner to company's stakeholders, goes beyond understanding and satisfying the interests of only shareholders and attempts to establish balanced relations with all stakeholders of a company (Fernández-Guadaño and Sarria-Pedroza, 2018). Since organizational stability and survival are contingent not only upon the fulfilling the interests of the primary stakeholders, it must also be supported by all corporate stakeholders.

Value Creation Through CSR Perspective

Although value creation is one of the significant concepts in the management and organization literature, due to the multidisciplinary nature of the field, there is little consensus on what value creation is. Scholars from different disciplines seek to identify the concept within the targets or users for whom value can be created (Lepak et. al., 2007). In this paper, we focus on socially responsible business practices by taking the CSR initiatives as an integral part of value creation with respect to all stakeholders as stakeholder theory is founded upon the assumption that "values are necessarily and explicitly a part of doing business" (Freeman et.al, 2004, p.364). That is, it entails managers to create a shared sense of value while bringing its core stakeholders together. In this regard, the idea of creating value is directly associated with the idea of value creation for stakeholders. The deal between the company and its stakeholders in conducting business activities enables each party to win in the long run. At this point, it is worth noting that the importance of shareholders as a constituent is incontrovertible, but their profit-making concerns are the result rather than a driving force in the value creation process (Freeman et.al, 2004, pp.364-365). With this in mind, stakeholder theory can be considered as a useful approach to lead companies towards the value creation for all stakeholders (Fernández-Guadaño and Sarria-Pedroza, 2018, p.3). Therefore, while dealing with interests of total stakeholders within the organization and society, the company can use value creation in developing its strategy for CSR (Padhi and Barik, 2016, p.76).

Since the critical review of Friedman (1970), CSR has significantly evolved from profit maximization for shareholders to value creation with society (Branco and Rodrigues, 2007, p.5). Having become more prevalent in the concept of stakeholders, CSR has been identified as a value driver. Furthermore, it can be seen as a significant approach that guides companies towards value creation for primary stakeholders. In this sense, managers need to intertwine demands of stakeholders with their corporate capacities with the aim of creating value. Taken together, the theoretical perspective on CSR has evolved from philanthropy to value creation and then to the concept of shared value (Bosch-Badia et.al., 2013, pp.12-13).

DRIVERS OF VALUE CREATION DURING THE COVID-19 PANDEMIC

One of the vital tasks of organizational management is to look for the sources of value, and then to create value through bundling and orchestrating these sources rationally in order to capture the value in the long run. In this section, we have looked at creating value through the lenses of dynamic capability perspective together with digital capabilities since the outbreak of the coronavirus have led to turbulent times and unexpected events in the environment so that creating value seems to have more unforeseen constraints under these circumstances.

During their lifetime, organizations are affected by highly ambiguous situations, namely different types of organizational crisis (Pearson and Clair, 1998, p. 60) which can be defined as "*an extreme, unexpected or unpredictable event that requires an urgent response from organizations and creates challenges for them – by interfering with its operations, creating ambiguity in its decision-making processes, threatening its goals and values, damaging its public image and bottom line*" (Doern et.al., 2019, p. 401). In this regard, the Covid-19 pandemic is a fact that can be evaluated and managed within the scope of a crisis (e.g., Al-Omoush vd., 2020; Carrol and Conboy, 2020; Rai et.al., 2021) and crisis management is adopted to set on resilience and restore functionality to organizations (Kuckertz et.al., 2020), to retain or minimize the negative impacts on organizational systems and key stakeholders (Pearson and Clair, 1998), and to design a thriving response plan (Obrenovic et.al., 2020).

In times of crisis, to what extent an organization can quickly anticipate and respond to the complex and unpredictable situations of the business environment are mostly related to their capabilities. Since a capability is interpreted as an asset for organizations, the resource-based view (RBV) which emphasizes the significance of valuable organizational resources for continuous growth (Penrose, 1959) seems to take attention of policymakers whose primarily focus is protecting the present situation rather than determining the future of business following the outbreak of Covid-19 (Kuckertz et.al., 2020). Organizational resources comprise all assets, knowledge, technology, organizational capabilities, and processes (Barney, 1991, p. 101). Essentially, the roots of focusing on organizational resources stem from strategy studies that seek the roots of value and above average performance management emphasizing the dynamic relationships between the organization and its environment (Dyduch et. al., 2021). Recalling the definition by Hofer and Schendel (1978), strategy refers to "*the match an organization makes between its internal resources and skills, and the opportunities and risks created by its external environment*" (as cited in Grant, 1991, p.114). In this regard, the ongoing pandemic which can be assessed as an output of the external environment has generated drastic changes in both economic and social life. Its impacts on organizations might get an equilibrium with an emphasis on organizational resources. However, to the RBV, not all resources have the same importance for strategic position and competitive advantage of an organization. Specifically, in order to obtain positive organizational outcomes, organizations have a need for valuable, rare, and imperfectly imitable resources (Barney, 1991, pp.105-106). Hence, during the pandemic and in the post-pandemic phases, organizations might focus primarily on valuable resources that "exploit opportunities and / or neutralize threats in a firm's environment" (Barney, 1995, p. 50). In this sense, to deal with the several unexpected changes in the environment following the outbreak of the coronavirus, dynamic capabilities (Dyduch et. al., 2021) and digital capabilities (Rahul De and Pal, 2020) are addressed as significant drivers of value creation during this crisis.

Dynamic Capabilities

Dynamic capabilities ground on key resources, in other words "*internal and external firm specific competences*", to build and sustain competitive advantage in the complex environments of rapid change (Teece et. al., 1997, p. 510). They are characterized by "detailed, analytic, stable processes, with predictable outcomes" (Eisenhardt and Martin, 2000, p. 1105) and point out an organization's resource base in order "*to sense and shape opportunities and threats, to seize opportunities, and to maintain competitiveness*" (Teece, 2007, p. 1319). Although this approach was initially built on volatile industries, specifically the high technology industry, it provides an understanding for all businesses operating in a fierce competition during crises. As dynamic capabilities are concerned with change and differentiate themselves from ad hoc problem solving with being repeatable (Winter, 2003, pp. 992-993), they comprise hardly imitable managerial, organizational, technological skills, capabilities and their combinations together with research and development (R&D), human resources (HR), intellectual property, information technology and organizational learning. In this regard, developing capabilities on operations, product or service quality, technology, strategic decision-making, good relationships with networks, and intangible resources and reputation translates into value creation (Augier and Teece, 2009). Thus, encouraging dynamic capabilities become crucial for organizations as previous studies indicate that they have strategic potential that enable higher and above average organizational performance, competitive advantage, external environment – organization fit, survival of businesses, and organizational growth through facilitating flexibility, major changes and innovativeness (Dyduch et.al., 2021).

Organizational agility, one of the major dynamic capabilities, is considered as a key factor to confront difficulties of crises. Agility, in the simplest sense, refers to a capability that enables organizations to sense and detect the changes of the turbulent, complex and uncertain environments and to respond efficiently and effectively to them (Felipe et.al., 2016). Teece et.al. (2016, p.13-16) presents the linkage of agility with dynamic capabilities as a part of risk, uncertainty and strategy. For agile organizations, change is an ordinary matter of fact and those organizations' value proposition comprises generating new value through novel ideas for products, services, processes and systems repeatedly (Winby and Worley, 2014). As the ongoing pandemic is a precedent event that has generated risk, evoked uncertainty and inclined to rethink on strategy, organizations need to develop and address systems that build and strengthen agility. Agile organizations - although some of them stumbled during Covid-19- are more likely to handle challenges and uncertainty (Worley and Jules, 2020). Organizational agility which is relevant to "value-enhancing change" (Batra, 2020, p.362) has provided an effective framework for companies in the long-run and organizations that invest in dynamic capabilities may get better outcomes in times of crisis (ibid, 363).

Although the ongoing pandemic has brought uncertainty to economic and social systems, for the organizations that focus on their dynamic capabilities, this uncertainty can be seen as a challenge to investors and managers (Teece and Leih, 2016, p.5). Literature indicates that during times of crisis, dynamic capabilities facilitate the survival of companies and organization-environment fit (Dyduch et. al., 2021). In this sense, creating value in relation to dynamic capabilities can be seen as a significant tool to promote competitive advantage and over-average performance companies during the pandemic and in the post pandemic phases. For instance, when Covid-19 crisis has started, Lululemon Athletica Inc., a technical athletic apparel retailer has stood apart making short-term decisions that might damage brand positioning and drawn on innovation, omni-guest experiences and market expansion that makes up its growth strategy (Clifford, 2020) and core brand strengths in response to outbreak of the coronavirus. By the way, the company has been marked as a great retailer survivor and an outlier in the industry which reported an operating surplus in the first quarter of 2020 when apparel giants (e.g. Guess, Puma) lost their net income almost by half (Stockdill, 2020).

Digital Capabilities

Since the discovery of the coronavirus, billions of people worldwide have experienced social distancing and curfews as a part of daily life to decrease the threat of this infectious disease and its spread. The new normal conditions force organizations to focus on digitalization defined as "*the infusion of digital objects (bitstrings) into our processes, tasks, products and services*'' (Grover and Sabherwal, 2020) and lead to essential changes for organizations. Digital technologies have become remarkable for value creation, business survival and continuity during the pandemic period and are estimated to be popular in the post-Covid-19 era as well. Technological leads, i.e., IT related systems and components are related to a superior business performance (Bharadwaj, 2000), and they encourage organizations to maintain a strong competitive position (Wernerfeld, 1984, p.174). Although researchers and practitioners agree on the importance of IT facilities, there is a debate on whether IT owns the features of a rare, valuable and imperfectly imitable resource described by the RBV. The reason behind this argument is the interpretation of IT as a commodity that is shareable and replicable, and IT systems are available on the market (Carr, 2003, pp.7-8). However, several studies recognize IT and information systems (IS) as organizational capabilities and approve that they should be identified as resources in line with the considerations of the RBV. For instance, the paper by Wade and Hulland (2004) presents that the attributes of IS are intertwined with the RBV. Drawing on this assessment, IT is a valuable organizational resource that enables organizations to differentiate (Bharadwaj, 2000), enhance agility, support financial performance and competitive advantage (Altschuller, et.al., 2010). Moreover, it is observed that during the pandemic, organizations have faced with an increased demand for internet-based services (Rahul De and Pal, 2020), artificial intelligence (Papagiannidis et.al., 2020), and digital transformation (Kodama, 2020) together with changes in IS related subjects such as cybersecurity, and data privacy (Davison, 2020).

Under these circumstances, the Covid-19 outbreak has made many people wonder what the world would be like in case there was a lack of digital technology. For instance, imagine a place where there is no digital instrument under the circumstances of a global lockdown, physical and social distancing induced by coronavirus. There are two important questions on that; first, how can people buy food, medicine or other essential items to live; second, how can a company continue its business activities to make profit? If this scenario had happened, people would have died of either Covid-19 or starvation. Instead, the ongoing pandemic has triggered a "cashless society" and e-commerce purchases worldwide from online stores via web-enabled and mobile applications has grown and projected to show an upward direction by 2022. Since the early 2020, as a Covid-19 related safety precaution, consumers have tended to use cashless and contactless shopping and payment methods more than shopping in stores as it is believed that coronavirus can be transmitted through touching physical money and having a face-to-face contact with a sales person (Taskinsoy, 2020, pp.36-40). From the business side, regardless of the industry or size, digital capabilities have come into play to combat economic closure and changing consumer behavior in shopping due to the pandemics.

Compared to manufacturing, service industries which cannot continue without physical and social interaction such as restaurants, travel and leisure, or personal services like barbers, have seemed to experience more pressure of making profit with the infectious risks to their workers. Therefore, products and services have started to be offered under behavioral restrictions. For instance, after the lockdown period, restaurants have started to invite guests with masks and taking into account the distancing provisions although their major focus lies heavily on take-away menus, touchless menus on smartphones and online orders (Grover and Sabherwal, 2020). Furthermore, the education system is one of the major sectors that has been exposed to digital transformation in the first place with the pandemic and distant teaching period that has started from basic education for the young generation to higher education throughout the world. Unfortunately, not all students have equal conditions in accessing the digital technology, the internet, devices, and applications needed. Some children, for instance the ones who are being disturbed by the noise or the crowd in the class, have benefitted from distant teaching that enables quiet space for learning and independent studying. On the other hand, some children who have no access or use of digital equipment missed out on education altogether (Iivari et.al. 2020). Despite the gaps, distant and digital education is also better than a completely stopped education despite all the disadvantages and adverse impacts in times of crisis such as unprecedented Covid-19.

Therefore, it is observed that favorable steps have been achieved both at organizational and individual level through digitalism. During the period of global lockdown due to the pandemic, it has provided undeniable benefits for all. Under these circumstances, in order to enhance value proposition, many organizations have discovered online communication (e.g., tele-health services, advisory brokerage platforms) and promoted social distancing via hardware (e.g., webcams), software (e.g., Zoom, Skype, Google, augmented reality applications) or online shopping platforms (Grover and Sabherwal, 2020). Hence, building capabilities on dynamic capabilities including agility and advanced digitalization are seen as key drivers of value creation and competitive advantage in times of the pandemic and post-pandemic era.

SOCIALLY RESPONSIBLE VALUE CREATION FOR ACHIEVING SUSTAINABLE DEVELOPMENT GOALS

Socially Responsible Value Creation for Sustainable Development

In 1987, the report by the World Commission on Environment and Development (WCED) entitled "Our Common Future" and also known as "Brundtland Report" called for a new model of global economic development (WCED, 1987). The report offered what has become a conventional definition of sustainable development as development that "meets the needs of the present without compromising the ability of future generations to meet their own needs" (WCED, 1987, p: 41). Since the Brundtland Report, the target of a socially responsible value creation has become explicit. The awareness of making profit through taking into account the planet (protecting the environment, natural resources, climate, ecosystems) and people (elimination of poverty, hunger, providing gender equality, human health, and education for all) has been accepted in a widespread manner. At the organizational level, CSR can provide a viable framework for the integration of sustainability into value creation by taking the advantage of dynamic and digital capabilities. Recalling papers such as the one published by the European Union (EU) Commission in 2002 with the title "Corporate Social Responsibility: A business contribution to sustainable development" (Commission of the European Communities, 2002, p.1) improving CSR and linking it with sustainability, thus contributing to sustainable development has become essential in the 21st century business agenda.

Since the early 2000s, the business world has been strongly interested in the notion of sustainable development and sustainability, and both themes have become an integral part of all discussions about CSR (Carroll and Shabana 2010, p.88). Sustainable development which has become a well-established idea since the UN Earth Summit held in Rio de Janeiro in 1992, highlights the necessity of balancing goals in three dimensions as society, economy, and ecology (Liczma´nska-Kopcewicz et.al., 2019, p.2). Considering the profound impact of sustainable development on the implementation of CSR strategies, CSR provides a significant contribution to sustainable development since it enables businesses to act in a more socially responsible way and thus create value for a sustainable business (Liczma´nska-Kopcewicz et.al., 2019, p.2; Moon, 2007, p.296).

Sustainable development can be accomplished through a responsible approach to the external and internal environment and a continuous dialogue with all stakeholders about the actions that have been taken in order to achieve SDGs (Stankevičienė and Čepulytė, 2014, p.882). Building on a common understanding of the Organization for Economic Co-operation and Development (OECD, 2001) and European Commission (2002) about CSR, it is a contribution of business to sustainable development. It can be considered as an overarching concept in the context of CSR. Every business operating in a turbulent environment should consider the concepts of CSR and sustainable development in the value creation process. It is therefore crucial to orient the company towards sustainable development. Based on the principles of social dialogue and the search for solutions beneficial for both businesses and the entire environment, the above-presented concepts constitute a strategic and long-term approach. Integrating environmental, social, and economic issues into all aspects of the decision-making process is the key principle of sustainable development (Liczma´nska-Kopcewicz et.al., 2019, pp.6-10).

Businesses have endeavored to cope with the challenges originated from the ongoing Covid-19 pandemic in various ways including providing products, manufacturing capabilities and logistic support, community services and funding volunteering programs – as aligned with the concepts of CSR and sustainability (Marom and Lussier, 2020, p.251). Indeed, under these circumstances, adherence to CSR and sustainability practices is of paramount importance in creating business value and social impact. In this regard, CSR in its simplest sense refers to the activities of "business enterprises that have some responsibilities to society beyond that of making profits for the shareholders" (Carroll and Shabana, 2010, p.86), while sustainability reflects an organization's role to global challenges emanating from sustainable development based on three principles of economic integrity, social equity and environmental integrity (Bansal 2005; Ikram et. al., 2020). Sustainability-driven CSR is therefore deemed as a necessity for the post-pandemic period since 'CSR as usual' practices which appear to be superfluous expenses, do not contribute to the recovery and create neither value for businesses nor social impact in the society in the long-term (Delbard, 2020, p.262).

Recalling the "Black Swan Event" (Taleb, 2007), the pandemic is the time for a vast number of large organizations to make good on that commitment to the CSR initiatives towards their stakeholders and thus helping their employees, small suppliers, health care providers, communities and so on (Kramer, 2020). Fortunately, in retrospect, it has been observed that many companies have actively engaged in various CSR initiatives, notably those that can offer immediate help and assistance to the fight against the global crisis (He and Harris, 2020). Considering the business responses to the pandemic, philanthropic initiatives and transformed business models to produce high-demand products have foregrounded. Companies such as Walmart, PepsiCo, and American Airlines have engaged in mainly philanthropic responses by making financial contributions to support medical care workers, food banks and schools. On the other hand, some manufacturing companies have modified their traditional products and services in order to accommodate needs during the pandemic. For instance, giant companies in the USA including Ford, General Motors and General Electric formed various partnerships to produce ventilators and respirators with the aim of alleviating shortages while Walmart, Burger King and UPS changed their policies to eliminate signature requirements and cards on payments to decrease infection risks with transactions (Manuel and Herron, 2020). In a similar vein, some telecommunication companies (e.g., Vodafone in the UK) enabled their pay monthly customers access to the unlimited mobile data for a specified period of time (BBC, 2020a). The examples given above are indicative of the impacts of the global pandemic on the fundamental essences and developments of CSR initiatives. Amid the pandemic, it can be asserted that Covid-19 which has a profound impact on almost all aspects of economic and social life globally reconfigures the role of business in society (Brammer et al., 2020). Given that sustainability-driven CSR is one of the strong catalyst factors for sustainable development, the pandemic offers significant opportunities for businesses to shift towards more genuine and authentic CSR and create business value in this regard (He and Harris, 2020, p.4).

Sustainable Development Goals and the Impact of Covid-19 Pandemic

Starting from the late 1980s, an ongoing effort to establish the responsibility for sustainability has been witnessed globally. As part of this effort, the SDGs were adopted by the member states of the United Nations (UN) in 2015 considering the balance of economic, social and environmental sustainability by 2030 (UNDP, 2015). In this context, 17 SDGs illustrate the clear focus and dedication for the responsibility for environment and humanity.

Unfortunately, the outbreak of Covid-19 has caused many unfavorable consequences such as worldwide economic uncertainty and shutdown, increased layoffs and unemployment, rising poverty that interdependently have a domino effect on SDGs especially for developing countries (Rai et. al., 2021). The unprecedented circumstances that Covid-19 brought have impacted the SDG's and slowed down the progress achieved towards them. Thus, policy makers, practitioners and scholars seek out how to meet UN SDGs in times of pandemic under its adverse impacts. Without doubt, all 17 SDGs have been impacted by the global pandemic, especially knowing that the 2030 agenda for sustainable development is indivisible and the interconnectedness of SDGs are widely accepted (Nilsson et. al., 2016). In the similar vein, Khetrapal and Bhatia (2020) state that good health and well-being (SDG-3) is interconnected with, and grounds complementarity on Poverty (SDG-1), Zero Hunger (SDG-2), Quality Education (SDG-4), Gender Equality (SDG-5), Clean Water and Sanitation (SDG-6), Climate Action (SDG-13), Life under

Water (SDG-14), Life on Land (SDG-15) and Partnerships for Goals (SDG-17). Furthermore, SDGs are identified as a network of targets by scholars (Le Blanc, 2015) indicating that evaluating the SGDs as an ecosystem rather than in separation would be more appropriate. However, certain SDGs are immediately and dramatically impacted by the pandemic, pushing the governments and corporations to transform their 'business as usual' practices into 'future state' in a very short period. Therefore, governments had to take immediate actions to digitize their education systems impacting almost 31 million learners under the circumstances of country-wide closures (Mhlanga and Moloi, 2020; UNESCO 2021; Shulla et. Al., 2021). Besides, with the Covid-19 pandemic being a health-related crisis, countries had to adopt essential health related measures to ensure primary treatment and vaccination needs. From this point of view, in regard to cope with the dramatic effects of the pandemic and to promote global 2030 targets of sustainable development, efforts on socially responsible value creation starting from SDG-3 (Good Health and Well Being) and SDG-4 (Quality education) can be seen as an initial response during the pandemic and in the post-pandemic phase.

Impact of Covid-19 on Good Health and Well-being and Socially Responsible Value Creation

According to the World Health Organization's definition, health is "a state of complete physical, mental, and social well-being and not merely the absence of disease or infirmity". According to this definition, health is not merely a disease protection but rather an elevated state of physical, mental and social wellbeing for all at all ages. Under the UNDP, SDG-3 aspires to ensure health and well-being for all by 2030. The goal of good health and wellbeing targets healthy lives and promotes well-being for all at all ages and is a critical goal to build prosperous societies.

Till the onset of Covid-19 pandemic, substantial progress has been witnessed to improve the health of millions of people across the world (Khetrapal and Bhatia, 2020). This progress towards SDG-3 globally helped reduce child and maternal mortality, increase immunization rates and improve infectious diseases such as HIV. However, Covid-19 pandemic has changed the health priorities of most countries and placed an additional burden on the healthcare systems. Naidoo and Fisher (2020) state that Covid-19 exposed the fragility of the SDGs and to them, "every goal and target should be screened according to three points: Is this a priority, post-Covid-19; is it about development not growth; and is the pathway to it resilient to global disruptions?" (Naidoo and Fisher, 2020).

According to the UN 2020 reporting, healthcare disruptions due to Covid-19, could reverse decades of improvements such as childhood immunization rates (UN, 2020). As a matter of fact, the UN highlights the fact that the pandemic interrupted childhood immunization programs in around 70 countries and warns that broad healthcare interruptions might lead to spikes in illness and deaths. With the pandemic, limited number of health equipment, limited hospital space, inadequate number of healthcare personnel and uninsured citizens have exposed the fragility of healthcare systems worldwide (Iwuoha and Jude-Iwuoha, 2020). In addition, country-wide lockdown conditions were observed in the course of 2020 and 2021 and the negative impact of Covid-19 on the humanities health and wellbeing is likely to be long-lasting.

The identification of WHO might be more affected by Covid-19, not epidemiologically but simply by working and living in affected regions, carries important implications (Zhang et.al., 2020). A cross-sectional study measuring the impact of Covid-19 pandemic on mental health of children reveals that large proportions of children are suffering from mental health disturbances during the periods of lockdown (Yeasmin et al, 2020). Populations from more socially disadvantaged groups and those with pre-existing mental health problems likely to have worse mental health outcomes during the pandemic (O'Connor et al, 2020). As the data comes out of the evolving pandemic, it is observed that the people from Black, Asian and Minority Ethnic (BAME) backgrounds are more likely to contact the virus and become ill or die of it (Booth, 2020; Butcher and Massey, 2020).

Furthermore, poverty and inequality accelerated the negative consequences of the pandemic. Even though governments could be considered as the primary actor who should protect the health and safety of the people, businesses were observed to be a key actor during the pandemic. Business responses to pandemic have been predominantly philanthropic or transformed business models to produce high demand products (Manuel and Herron, 2020). At organizational level, companies followed their own CSR strategies and sometimes struggled to balance their stakeholders' interests. One could argue that maximizing shareholder value is the primary interest of the businesses. However, the pandemic has shown the importance of considering all stakeholders' interests and despite the economic challenges of the pandemic, not only maximizing shareholder value but also focusing on other stakeholder's interests has become a priority (Manuel and Herron, 2020). In this regard, employees can be considered as the most dominant stakeholder of companies (Chaudhary and Akhouri, 2018; Rupp and Mallory, 2015). This pandemic has elevated employee concerns about the fairness of business activities (Edelman, 2020). For example, Walmart and other retailers spent over $3 billion during the shutdown to improve cleaning, acquire testing supplies and provide sick leave pay for their employees (Pacheco, 2020). Besides, Amazon expanded its online grocery delivery service to individuals impacted by Covid-19 but at the same time faced severe worker protests claiming unsafe conditions such as lacking adequate protective health equipment (Weise and Conger, 2020). This example approves the research by Fernández-Guadaño and Sarria-Pedroza (2018) that examined whether CSR policy constitutes a factor in value creation for shareholders and certain stakeholders such as employees, creditors and the State, and indicate that distribution of value in favor of the State has a negative influence for employees.

Consequently, a high commitment to societal matters can be seen as a catalyzer to promote sustainability driven initiatives whereas orchestrating socially responsible value creation and satisfying the interests of primary stakeholders concurrently have a paramount importance.

Impact of Covid-19 on Quality Education and Socially Responsible Value Creation

According to the UN, SDG-4 aims to ensure inclusive and equitable quality education and promote lifelong learning opportunities for all. Over the past decade, major progress has been made towards this goal by increasing access to schools and improving enrollment rates to schools. However, the progress has been relatively slow as about 260 million children were still out of school in 2018 (UN, 2020).

Progress towards the SDG-4, has been severely affected by the pandemic. The most dramatic impact of the pandemic is the school closures which kept 90% of students out of school, reversing the years of progress on education (United Nations, 2020). In fact, the closure of schools and universities has influenced 1.5 billion children and young people. Despite providing remote learning to many students, children and young people, particularly those in vulnerable and disadvantaged communities do not have the same access (United Nations, 2020). The adverse impact of the digital divide in the education system has exacerbated some embedded social issues including poverty and inequality and led to discontinuity in learning, mental health problems, increased childcare burden and unemployment (He and Harris, 2020;

Kumar et al., 2020). For example, the pandemic has dramatically changed women's lives since they have to perform more childcare and are exposed to increased job insecurity (BBC, 2020b).

During the pandemic, it is observed that some businesses went above and beyond by engaging in philanthropy to support the educational needs. For instance, Best Buy offered free technology lessons for children affected by the pandemic (Best Buy, 2020). Companies across the globe donated laptops to students who had to switch to homeschooling after the pandemic. Similarly, the internet companies offered internet services to students and teachers.

Digital transformation, defined as a process with the target of improving an entity by triggering significant changes to its properties through combinations of information, computing, communication, and connectivity technologies (Vial, 2019), is a necessity to meet the needs of students and to prepare them for a more digitized future. This pandemic has suddenly forced schools to engage in digital transformation (Iivari et al., 2020) and it deepened the digital divide between the students. According to the empirical study conducted by Iivari et. al. (2020) an educational representative from Finland stated that even though the sudden lockdown caused some challenges to get all the equipment for distant teaching, the transformation was quick and smooth. On the other hand, the same empirical study reveals that the students and teachers especially from public schools in India faced numerous challenges when adopting homeschooling. Across OECD countries, about half of 15-year-old children are enrolled in schools where an effective online learning support platform is available and there is large variation within and across countries (Reimers and Schleicher, 2020).

With pandemic, companies have numerous opportunities to help tackle social issues that have been elevated by the pandemic. In addition to all the measures implemented by the respective governments, involvement of the private sector in education is a necessity to alleviate the negative effects of the pandemic.

SOLUTIONS AND RECOMMENDATIONS

According to the 2021 Edelman Trust Barometer, business is the most trusted organization in today's global world. Business is more trusted than governments, civil society and media. Hence, we can argue that business is one of the most important actors in driving sustainability. Furthermore, companies have the access to the best talent, they have the ability to impact the humanities and governments where they operate. This extended influence that the companies have on the societies indicate that companies are at the core when we are discussing diminishing the effects of the pandemic. This pandemic will increase the expectation on companies and CSR strategies can be effective tools to cope with the global problems of the pandemic, limiting the social externalities derived from the effects of Covid-19 (García-Sánchez and García-Sánchez, 2020).

CSR can facilitate positive outcomes for employees and a behavioral perspective on CSR is necessary in the context of Covid-19 pandemic (Aguinis et. al, 2020). Companies should adopt employee protecting policies and the relationship between employers and employees should be stronger than pre-Covid era (Mahmud et.al., 2021). Furthermore, as one of the key stakeholders of the companies, employees can be more engaged in CSR activities as employee engagement in CSR brings numerous benefits to both employers and employees (Xiao et. al.,2020).

Considering digital capabilities to CSR initiatives for health, well-being and education, implementing Artificial intelligence (AI) related technology and deployment of AI applications are proposed to accelerate after the pandemic. For instance, PwC has accomplished such an AI system prioritizing the health of its employees that enables tracking contact, interaction and proximity among individuals in order to reduce the risk of Covid-19 virus spreading within a company (Sipior, 2020).

In addition, the higher-level inequality caused by the pandemic can be a source of opportunities for CSR initiatives. Based on the UN call on organizations to build more inclusive and sustainable economies in the post pandemic period, they should concentrate more on struggling with social issues in the long term (He and Harris, 2020). In accordance with new and innovative ways, they should embark on CSR activities in education and training industry that can create a social impact in the society, such as developing interactive applications without limiting to virtual whiteboards, teleconference platforms and live television broadcasts and providing content of academic and professional development programs through several technologies (Ebrahim and Buheji, 2020).

At the organizational level, pandemic could offer an opportunity for companies to shift towards more genuine and authentic CSR and contribute to address urgent global social and environmental challenges (He and Harris, 2020). Given the fact that Covid-19 is still an evolving pandemic, the impact of the pandemic on populations' health, well-being and education levels and CSR strategies will continue to be a topic of increasing interest in the near future and the CSR policies of the companies can be extremely crucial for the progress towards SDGs across the globe.

FUTURE RESEARCH DIRECTIONS

The outbreak of the coronavirus has penetrated the entire world with economic, social, political and technological shockwaves it created. While many people are striving to adapt to new normal, they have had to change their priorities for the future. These complexities, impacting significantly on the business and society relationship, offer ample opportunities to people including researchers and business people (Carroll, 2021, p.12). They can therefore open up new spaces in the debate on socially responsible value creation in the post-Covid-19 era.

To begin, Carroll (2021) highlighted that the research on CSR and CSR-related topics has accelerated and flourished since the 1980s; whereas there is a need to concentrate more on its 'social impact' rather than definitions, processes, and motives. To this end, considering the current challenge facing our world, further research should go beyond a mere analysis on CSR practices, examine and measure the social impact of sustainability-driven CSR initiatives (p.16).

Moving to a second future research area, recognizing the comparative study on explicit and implicit CSR of Matten and Moon (2008), the ongoing pandemic has revealed that there are various CSR initiatives implemented in order to overcome the extant crisis; however, those CSR initiatives vary across countries, particularly for developing and developed ones, depending on their governments, culture, society, and so on. Since there is no doubt that "one size fits all model of CSR" is not valid at the global level (Carroll, 2021, p.9), new insights on different country practices can be obtained to understand how CSR-related activities are integrated into the current crisis and shaped the relationship between business and society in the post-pandemic era.

Another direction for future studies rests on an in-depth analysis of the UN SDGs. Due to the severity of the situation notably in health and education, this study has focused on SDG-3 and SDG-4. Nevertheless, further emphasis is required on other SDGs which are already interwoven and complementary in this context.

CONCLUSION

Covid-19 is the most wide-reaching public health crisis humanity has faced in the near future and has significant environmental, social and economic impacts over the course of 2020. Since the Covid-19 outbreak, a wide range of change has been witnessed. For instance, the decline in air flights and volume of motorized vehicles as well as decreasing manufacturing activities have reduced the pollution and emission of greenhouse gases globally. Although it will not be sustained in the near future (Bashir et al., 2020), restricted economic activities affect environmental sustainability in the short run. On the other hand, Covid-19 has had a catastrophic impact on economic and social matters too. Almost all business organizations have experienced intensive concerns on their bottom line in terms of loss of profit or shareholder value. In addition, difficulties in the management of risks arisen along supply chain have been observed. Both operational and disruption risks of the supply chain (Fahimnia et. al., 2018, Ivanov, 2018) need to be addressed during the Covid-19 pandemic. Changing consumer behaviors put immediate pressure on companies to manage supply in a short period of time. Due to the increasing layoffs and unemployment rate, the implications of Covid-19 on economic activities have widely spread on society. Consequently, it is witnessed once again that health disasters have both global health impacts and also cause wide ranging socioeconomic disruptions and losses as well (Ahmad et. al., 2020). For instance, the WorldBank reported that Covid-19 has pushed 100 million people to poverty. For the first time in 20 years, WorldBank estimates that the number of people in extreme poverty will increase in 2020. For 2021, the number is likely to increase.

Considering the level and magnitude of the effects emanated from the pandemic, it is highly important for the business organizations to take some invaluable lessons for the future. Building and encouraging dynamic capabilities including the development of agility and application of digital capabilities is certainly one of these lessons. Real-life business examples indicate that in times of the outbreak of the coronavirus, sensing the risks and the opportunities, and reconfiguring organizational activities on the basis of dynamic capabilities that encompass technological skills, digital transformation through information technology and systems, rather than ad-hoc decisions that might harm overall corporate strategy in the long run, combat much better to provide strengths in terms of survival, recovery, increasing financial returns and satisfying shareholder demands. Besides, this approach turns into a sustainable value when organizations take the advantage of such a policy to improve their socially responsible value creation process. In other words, the mediating role of implementation of CSR initiatives during the pandemic on achieving SDGs appears as a remarkable matter of fact. Keeping the notion of CSR as a value driver in mind, conducting business activities with the target of intertwining stakeholders' interests, providing help and assistance for the stakeholder groups who have directly and deeply impacted by the Covid-19 (i.e., employees, customers, suppliers) contributes to the "people", namely to social sustainability which is one of the three pillars of sustainable development principles. The new environment generated by the pandemic has transformed several aspects of global society including healthcare, work, education, shopping, travel and leisure. When the sustainability perspective is taken into account, among all aspects of human life, this chapter details the practices for health and well-being, and quality education which were hit immediately and dramatically by the coronavirus. Within this context, it has been highlighted that integration of CSR in the value creation process through corporate capacities and capabilities presents a significant contribution to sustainable development as this approach provides an essential tool that can bridge the widening gaps in the fields of SDGs.

ACKNOWLEDGMENT

We would like to express our sincere appreciation to Prof. Duygu Türker for sharing her invaluable comments and helpful feedback with us on writing this chapter.

REFERENCES

Aguinis, H., Villamor, I., & Gabriel, K. P. (2020). Understanding employee responses to COVID-19: a behavioral corporate social responsibility perspective. *Management Research: Journal of the Iberoamerican Academy of Management*.

Ahmad, T., Haroon, M. B., & Hui, J. (2020). Coronavirus Disease 2019 (COVID-19) Pandemic and economic impact. *Pakistan Journal of Medical Sciences, 36*(S4), S73.

Al-Omoush, K. S., Simón-Moya, V., & Sendra-García, J. (2020). The impact of social capital and collaborative knowledge creation on e-business proactiveness and organizational agility in responding to the COVID-19 crisis. *Journal of Innovation & Knowledge*, *5*(4), 279–288. doi:10.1016/j.jik.2020.10.002

Altschuller, S., Gelb, D. S., & Henry, T. F. (2010). IT as a resource for competitive agility: An analysis of firm performance during industry turbulence. *Journal of International Technology and Information Management*, *19*(1), 1.

Augier, M., & Teece, D. J. (2009). Dynamic Capabilities and the Role of Managers in Business Strategy and Economic Performance. *Organization Science*, *20*(2), 410–421. doi:10.1287/orsc.1090.0424

Bansal, P. (2005). Evolving sustainably: A longitudinal study of corporate sustainable development. *Strategic Management Journal*, *26*(3), 197–218. doi:10.1002mj.441

Barney, J. (1991). Firm resources and sustained competitive advantage. *Journal of Management*, *17*(1), 99–120. doi:10.1177/014920639101700108

Barney, J. B. (1995). Looking inside for competitive advantage. *The Academy of Management Perspectives*, *9*(4), 49–61. doi:10.5465/ame.1995.9512032192

Bashir, M. F., Benjiang, M. A., & Shahzad, L. (2020). A brief review of socio-economic and environmental impact of Covid-19. *Air Quality, Atmosphere & Health*, *13*(12), 1403–1409. doi:10.100711869-020-00894-8 PMID:32837620

Batra, D. (2020). The impact of the COVID-19 on organizational and information systems agility. *Information Systems Management*, *37*(4), 361–365. doi:10.1080/10580530.2020.1821843

BBC. (2020a). *Coronavirus: Vodafone offers 30 days free mobile data.* https://www.bbc.com/news/technology-52066048

BBC. (2020b). *How Covid-19 is changing women's lives.* https://www.bbc.com/worklife/article/20200630-how-covid-19-is-changing-womens-lives

Best Buy. (2020). https://corporate.bestbuy.com/best-buy-provides-free-tech-classes-for-kids-at-home

Bharadwaj, A. S. (2000). A resource-based perspective on information technology capability and firm performance: An empirical investigation. *Management Information Systems Quarterly*, *24*(1), 169–196. doi:10.2307/3250983

Booth, R. (2020). BAME groups hit harder by Covid-19 than white people, UK study suggests. *The Guardian*. https://www.theguardian.com/world/2020/apr/07/bame-groups-hit-harder-covid-19-thanwhite-people-uk

Bosch-Badia, M. T., Montllor-Serrats, J., & Tarrazon, M. A. (2013). Corporate Social Responsibility from Friedman to Porter and Kramer. *Theoretical Economics Letters*, *3*(3A), 11–15. doi:10.4236/tel.2013.33A003

Brammer, S., Branicki, L., & Linnenluecke, M. K. (2020). Covid-19, Societalization, and the Future of Business in Society. *The Academy of Management Perspectives*, *34*(4), 493–507. doi:10.5465/amp.2019.0053

Branco, M. C., & Rodrigues, L. L. (2007). Positioning Stakeholder Theory within the Debate on Corporate Social Responsibility. *Electronic Journal of Business Ethics and Organization Studies*, *12*(1), 5–15.

Burgess, S., & Sievertsen, H. H. (2020). *Schools, skills, and learning: The impact of COVID-19 on education*. Academic Press.

Butcher, B., & Massey, J. (2020). Are ethnic minorities being hit hardest by coronavirus? *The BBC*. https://www.bbc.co.uk/news/uk-52219070

Carr, N. G. (2003). IT doesn't matter. *EDUCAUSE Review*, *38*, 24–38. PMID:12747161

Carroll, A. B. (1979). A Three-Dimensional Conceptual Model of Corporate Social Performance. *Academy of Management Review*, *4*(4), 497–505. doi:10.5465/amr.1979.4498296

Carroll, A. B. (1991). The Pyramid of Corporate Social Responsibility: Toward the Moral Management of Organizational Stakeholders. *Business Horizons*, *34*(4), 39–48. doi:10.1016/0007-6813(91)90005-G

Carroll, A. B. (2021). Corporate Social Responsibility: Perspectives on the CSR Construct's Development and Future. *Business & Society*, *60*(6), 1–21. doi:10.1177/00076503211001765

Carroll, A. B., & Shabana, K. M. (2010). The Business Case for Corporate Social Responsibility: A Review of Concepts, Research and Practice. *International Journal of Management Reviews*, *12*(1), 85–105. doi:10.1111/j.1468-2370.2009.00275.x

Carroll, N., & Conboy, K. (2020). Normalising the "new normal": Changing tech-driven work practices under pandemic time pressure. *International Journal of Information Management*, *55*, 102186. doi:10.1016/j.ijinfomgt.2020.102186 PMID:32836643

Chaudhary, R., & Akhouri, A. (2018). Linking corporate social responsibility attributions and creativity: Modeling work engagement as a mediator. *Journal of Cleaner Production*, *190*, 809–821. doi:10.1016/j.jclepro.2018.04.187

Clifford, T. (2020). *Lululemon CEO expects digital growth momentum to continue post pandemic.* https://www.cnbc.com/2020/12/15/lululemon-ceo-expects-digital-growth-momentum-to-continue-post-pandemic.html

Commission of the European Communities. (2002). *Communication from the commission concerning corporate social responsibility: A business contribution to Sustainable Development.* https://op.europa.eu/en/publication-detail/-/publication/6e2c6d26-d1f6-48a3-9a78-f0ff2dc21aad/language-en

Correia, S., Luck, S., & Verner, E. (2020). Pandemics depress the economy, public health interventions do not: Evidence from the 1918 flu. *Health Economics eJournal.*

Davison, R. M. (2020). The transformative potential of disruptions: A viewpoint. *International Journal of Information Management*, *55*, 102149. doi:10.1016/j.ijinfomgt.2020.102149 PMID:32836628

Delbard, O. (2020). Corporate Social Responsibility beyond philanthropy? Sustainable and Responsible Business in times of Covid-19. In Managing a Post-Covid-19 Era, (pp. 258-265). ESCP.

Doern, R., Williams, N., & Vorley, T. (2019). Special issue on entrepreneurship and crises: Business as usual? An introduction and review of the literature. *Entrepreneurship and Regional Development*, *31*(5-6), 400–412. doi:10.1080/08985626.2018.1541590

Dyduch, W., Chudziński, P., Cyfert, S., & Zastempowski, M. (2021). Dynamic capabilities, value creation and value capture: Evidence from SMEs under Covid-19 lockdown in Poland. *PLoS One*, *16*(6), e0252423. doi:10.1371/journal.pone.0252423 PMID:34129597

Ebrahim, A. H., & Buheji, M. (2020). A Pursuit for a 'Holistic Social Responsibility Strategic Framework' Addressing COVID-19 Pandemic Needs. *American Journal of Economics*, *10*(5), 293–304. doi:10.5923/j.economics.20201005.04

Edelman. (2020). *Edelman trust barometer special report on COVID-19 demonstrates essential role of the private sector.* www.edelman.com/research/edelman-trustcovid-19-demonstrates-essential-role-of-private-sector

Eisenhardt, K. M., & Martin, J. A. (2000). Dynamic capabilities: What are they? *Strategic Management Journal*, *21*(10-11), 1105–1121. doi:10.1002/1097-0266(200010/11)21:10/11<1105::AID-SMJ133>3.0.CO;2-E

Fahimnia, B., Jabbarzadeh, A., & Sarkis, J. (2018). Greening versus resilience: A supply chain design perspective. *Transportation Research Part E, Logistics and Transportation Review*, *119*, 129–148. doi:10.1016/j.tre.2018.09.005

Felin, T., & Powell, T. C. (2016). Designing organizations for dynamic capabilities. *California Management Review*, *58*(4), 78–96. doi:10.1525/cmr.2016.58.4.78

Felipe, C. M., Roldán, J. L., & Leal-Rodríguez, A. L. (2016). An explanatory and predictive model for organizational agility. *Journal of Business Research*, *69*(10), 4624–4631. doi:10.1016/j.jbusres.2016.04.014

Fernández-Guadaño, J., & Sarria-Pedroza, J. (2018). Impact of Corporate Social Responsibility on Value Creation from a Stakeholder Perspective. *Sustainability*, *10*(6), 2062. doi:10.3390u10062062

Freeman, R. E. (1998). A Stakeholder Theory of the Modern Corporation. In M. B. E. Clarkson (Ed.), *The Corporation and Its Stakeholders: Classic and Contemporary Readings* (pp. 125–138). University of Toronto Press. doi:10.3138/9781442673496-009

Freeman, R. E., Wicks, A. C., & Parmar, B. (2004). Stakeholder Theory and "The Corporate Objective Revisited". *Organization Science, 15*(3), 364–369. doi:10.1287/orsc.1040.0066

Friedman, M. (1970). The Social Responsibility of Business is to Increase its Profits. *The New York Times Magazine*.

García-Sánchez, I. M., & García-Sánchez, A. (2020). Corporate social responsibility during COVID-19 pandemic. *Journal of Open Innovation, 6*(4), 126. doi:10.3390/joitmc6040126

Ghobadian, A., Money, K., & Hillenbrand, C. (2015). Corporate Responsibility Research: Past—Present—Future. *Group & Organization Management, 40*(3), 271–294. doi:10.1177/1059601115590320

Grant, R. M. (1991). The resource-based theory of competitive advantage: Implications for strategy formulation. *California Management Review, 33*(3), 114–135. doi:10.2307/41166664

Grover, V., & Sabherwal, R. (2020). Making sense of the confusing mix of digitalization, pandemics and economics. *International Journal of Information Management, 55*, 102234. doi:10.1016/j.ijinfomgt.2020.102234

He, H., & Harris, L. (2020). The Impact of Covid-19 Pandemic on Corporate Social Responsibility and Marketing Philosophy. *Journal of Business Research, 116*, 176–182. doi:10.1016/j.jbusres.2020.05.030 PMID:32457556

Idowu, S. O., Schmidpeter, R., & Zu, L. (2020). *The Future of the UN Sustainable Development Goals*. Springer International Publishing. doi:10.1007/978-3-030-21154-7

Iivari, N., Sharma, S., & Ventä-Olkkonen, L. (2020). Digital transformation of everyday life–How COVID-19 pandemic transformed the basic education of the young generation and why information management research should care? *International Journal of Information Management, 55*, 102183. doi:10.1016/j.ijinfomgt.2020.102183 PMID:32836640

Ikram, M., Zhang, Q., Sroufe, R., & Ferasso, M. (2020). The Social Dimensions of Corporate Sustainability: An Integrative Framework Including COVID-19 Insights. *Sustainability, 12*(8747), 1–29. doi:10.3390u12208747

Ivanov, D. (2018). *Structural dynamics and resilience in supply chain risk management* (Vol. 265). Springer International Publishing. doi:10.1007/978-3-319-69305-7

Iwuoha, J. C., & Jude-Iwuoha, A. U. (2020). COVID-19: Challenge to SDG and globalization. *Electronic Research Journal of Social Sciences and Humanities, 2*.

Khetrapal, S., & Bhatia, R. (2020). Impact of COVID-19 pandemic on health system & Sustainable Development Goal 3. *The Indian Journal of Medical Research, 151*(5), 395. doi:10.4103/ijmr.IJMR_1920_20 PMID:32611910

Kodama, M. (2020). Digitally transforming work styles in an era of infectious disease. *International Journal of Information Management, 55*, 102172. doi:10.1016/j.ijinfomgt.2020.102172 PMID:32836634

Kramer, M. R. (2020). Coronavirus Is Putting Corporate Social Responsibility to the Test. *Harvard Business Review*. https://hbr.org/2020/04/coronavirus-is-putting-corporate-social-responsibility-to-the-test

Kuckertz, A., Brändle, L., Gaudig, A., Hinderer, S., Reyes, C. A. M., Prochotta, A., ... Berger, E. S. (2020). Startups in times of crisis–A rapid response to the COVID-19 pandemic. *Journal of Business Venturing Insights, 13*, e00169. doi:10.1016/j.jbvi.2020.e00169

Kumar, M.S, V., M., J., P., M., P., P., J., P., S., M.B., B.A.M., & J., R. (2020). Social economic impact of COVID-19 outbreak in India. *International Journal of Pervasive Computing and Communications, 16*(4), 309–319. doi:10.1108/IJPCC-06-2020-0053

Kytle, B., & Ruggie, J. G. (2005). *Corporate social responsibility as risk management: A model for multinationals*. Academic Press.

Le Blanc, D. (2015). Towards integration at last? The sustainable development goals as a network of targets. *Sustainable Development, 23*(3), 176–187. doi:10.1002d.1582

Lepak, D. P., Smith, K. G., & Taylor, M. S. (2007). Value Creation and Value Capture: A Multilevel Perspective. *Academy of Management Review, 32*(1), 180–194. doi:10.5465/amr.2007.23464011

Liczma'nska-Kopcewicz, K., Mizera, K., & Pypłacz, P. (2019). Corporate Social Responsibility and Sustainable Development for Creating Value for FMCG Sector Enterprises. *Sustainability, 11*(20), 5808. doi:10.3390u11205808

Mahmud, A., Ding, D., & Hasan, M. M. (2021). Corporate social responsibility: Business responses to Coronavirus (COVID-19) pandemic. *SAGE Open, 11*(1). doi:10.1177/2158244020988710

Manuel, T., & Herron, T. L. (2020). An ethical perspective of business CSR and the COVID-19 pandemic. *Society and Business Review, 15*(3), 235–253. doi:10.1108/SBR-06-2020-0086

Marom, S., & Lussier, R. N. (2020). Corporate Social Responsibility during the Coronavirus Pandemic: An Interim Overview. *Business and Economic Review, 10*(2), 250–269. doi:10.5296/ber.v10i2.17046

Matten, D., & Moon, J. (2008). "Implicit" And "Explicit" CSR: A Conceptual Framework for a Comparative Understanding of Corporate Social Responsibility. *Academy of Management Review, 33*(2), 404–424. doi:10.5465/amr.2008.31193458

Mhlanga, D., & Moloi, T. (2020). COVID-19 and the digital transformation of education: What are we learning on 4IR in South Africa? *Education Sciences, 10*(7), 180. doi:10.3390/educsci10070180

Moon, J. (2007). The Contribution of Corporate Social Responsibility to Sustainable Development. *Sustainable Development, 15*(5), 296–306. doi:10.1002d.346

Naidoo, R., & Fisher, B. (2020). *Reset sustainable development goals for a pandemic world*. Academic Press.

Nilsson, M., Griggs, D., & Visbeck, M. (2016). Policy: Map the interactions between Sustainable Development Goals. *NATNews, 534*(7607), 320–322. doi:10.1038/534320a PMID:27306173

O'Connor, R. C., Wetherall, K., Cleare, S., McClelland, H., Melson, A. J., Niedzwiedz, C. L., ... Robb, K. A. (2020). Mental health and well-being during the COVID-19 pandemic: Longitudinal analyses of adults in the UK COVID-19 Mental Health & Wellbeing study. *The British Journal of Psychiatry*, 1–8. doi:10.1192/bjp.2020.212 PMID:33081860

Obrenovic, B., Du, J., Godinic, D., Tsoy, D., Khan, M. A. S., & Jakhongirov, I. (2020). Sustaining enterprise operations and productivity during the COVID-19 pandemic:"Enterprise Effectiveness and Sustainability Model. *Sustainability*, *12*(15), 5981. doi:10.3390u12155981

Organisation for Economic Co-operation and Development (OECD). (2001). *Corporate Social Responsibility: Partners for Progress*. OECD Publishing.

Pacheco, I. (2020). How much COVID-19 cost those businesses that stayed open. *The Wall Street Journal*. www.wsj.com/articles/how-much-covid-19-cost-those-businessesthat-stayed-open-11592910575

Padhi, B., & Barik, G. S. (2016). A Study on Value Creation Model in Corporate Social Responsibility. *International Journal of Research in Engineering and Science*, *4*(7), 75–82.

Papagiannidis, S., Harris, J., & Morton, D. (2020). WHO led the digital transformation of your company? A reflection of IT related challenges during the pandemic. *International Journal of Information Management*, *55*, 102166. doi:10.1016/j.ijinfomgt.2020.102166 PMID:32836631

Pearson, C. M., & Clair, J. A. (1998). Reframing crisis management. *Academy of Management Review*, *23*(1), 59–76. doi:10.5465/amr.1998.192960

Penrose, E. T. (1959). *The Theory of the Growth of the Firm*. John Wiley.

Qiu, S. C., Jiang, J., Liu, X., Chen, M. H., & Yuan, X. (2021). Can corporate social responsibility protect firm value during the COVID-19 pandemic? *International Journal of Hospitality Management*, *93*, 102759. doi:10.1016/j.ijhm.2020.102759

Rahul De, N. P., & Pal, A. (n.d.). Impact of Digital Surge during Covid-19 Pandemic: A Viewpoint on Research and Practice. *International Journal of Information Management*.

Rai, S. S., Rai, S., & Singh, N. K. (2021). Organizational resilience and social-economic sustainability: COVID-19 perspective. *Environment, Development and Sustainability*, 1–18. PMID:33519297

Reimers, F. M., & Schleicher, A. (2020). *A framework to guide an education response to the COVID-19 Pandemic of 2020*. OECD.

Rupp, D. E., & Mallory, D. B. (2015). Corporate social responsibility: Psychological, person-centric, and progressing. *Annual Review of Organizational Psychology and Organizational Behavior*, *2*(1), 211–236. doi:10.1146/annurev-orgpsych-032414-111505

Shulla, K., Voigt, B. F., Cibian, S., Scandone, G., Martinez, E., Nelkovski, F., & Salehi, P. (2021). Effects of COVID-19 on the sustainable development goals (SDGs). *Discover Sustainability*, *2*(1), 1–19. doi:10.100743621-021-00026-x

Sipior, J. C. (2020). Considerations for Development and Use of AI in Response to COVID-19. *International Journal of Information Management*, *55*, 102170. doi:10.1016/j.ijinfomgt.2020.102170 PMID:32836632

Stankevičienė, J., & Čepulytė, J. (2014). Sustainable value creation: Coherence of corporate social responsibility and performance of socially responsible investment funds. *Economic Research-Ekonomska Istraživanja*, *27*(1), 882–898. doi:10.1080/1331677X.2014.976058

Stockdill, R. (2020). *Lululemon: The great survivor of Covid-19.* Retrieved from https://insideretail.asia/2020/06/14/lululemon-the-great-survivor-of-covid-19/

Taleb, N. N. (2007). *The Black Swan.* The Random House Publishing Group.

TaskinsoyJ. (2020). A move towards a cashless society accelerates with the novel coronavirus induced global lockdown. Available at SSRN 3747750.

Teece, D., & Leih, S. (2016). Uncertainty, innovation, and dynamic capabilities: An introduction. *California Management Review*, *58*(4), 5–12. doi:10.1525/cmr.2016.58.4.5

Teece, D., Peteraf, M., & Leih, S. (2016). Dynamic capabilities and organizational agility: Risk, uncertainty, and strategy in the innovation economy. *California Management Review*, *58*(4), 13–35. doi:10.1525/cmr.2016.58.4.13

Teece, D. J. (2007). Explicating dynamic capabilities: The nature and microfoundations of (sustainable) enterprise performance. *Strategic Management Journal*, *28*(13), 1319–1350. doi:10.1002mj.640

Teece, D. J., Pisano, G., & Shuen, A. (1997). Dynamic capabilities and strategic management. *Strategic Management Journal*, *18*(7), 509–533. doi:10.1002/(SICI)1097-0266(199708)18:7<509::AID-SMJ882>3.0.CO;2-Z

Turker, D. (2008). How Corporate Social Responsibility Influences Organizational Commitment. *Journal of Business Ethics*, *89*(2), 189–204. doi:10.100710551-008-9993-8

UNESCO. (2020). https://en.unesco.org/covid19/educationresponse

United Nations (UN). (2020). *The 17 Goals.* https://sdgs.un.org/goals

Vial, G. (2019). Understanding digital transformation: A review and a research agenda. *The Journal of Strategic Information Systems*, *28*(2), 118–144. doi:10.1016/j.jsis.2019.01.003

Wade, M., & Hulland, J. (2004). The resource-based view and information systems research: Review, extension, and suggestions for future research. *Management Information Systems Quarterly*, *28*(1), 107–142. doi:10.2307/25148626

Weise, K., & Conger, K. (2020). Gaps in Amazon's response as virus spreads to more than 50 warehouses. *The New York Times.*

Wernerfelt, B. (1984). A resource-based view of the firm. *Strategic Management Journal*, *5*(2), 171–180. doi:10.1002mj.4250050207

Winby, S., & Worley, C. G. (2014). Management processes for agility, speed, and innovation. *Organizational Dynamics*, *43*(3), 225–234. doi:10.1016/j.orgdyn.2014.08.009

Winter, S. G. (2003). Understanding dynamic capabilities. *Strategic Management Journal*, *24*(10), 991–995. doi:10.1002mj.318

World Commission on Environment and Development (WCED). (1987). *Our Common Future*. Oxford University.

World Health Organization. (2020). *WHO Director-General's opening remarks at the media briefing on COVID-19*. https://www.who.int/director-general/speeches/detail/who-director-general-s-opening-remarks-at-the-media-briefing-on-covid-19---11-march-2020

Worley, C. G., & Jules, C. (2020). COVID-19's uncomfortable revelations about agile and sustainable organizations in a VUCA world. *The Journal of Applied Behavioral Science*, *56*(3), 279–283. doi:10.1177/0021886320936263

Xiao, M., Cooke, F. L., Xu, J., & Bian, H. (2020). To what extent is corporate social responsibility part of human resource management in the Chinese context? A review of literature and future research directions. *Human Resource Management Review*, *30*(4), 100726. doi:10.1016/j.hrmr.2019.100726

Yeasmin, S., Banik, R., Hossain, S., Hossain, M. N., Mahumud, R., Salma, N., & Hossain, M. M. (2020). Impact of COVID-19 pandemic on the mental health of children in Bangladesh: A cross-sectional study. *Children and Youth Services Review*, *117*, 105277. doi:10.1016/j.childyouth.2020.105277 PMID:32834275

Zhang Stephen, X., Yifei, W., Andreas, R., & Feng, W. (2020). *Unprecedented disruption of lives and work: Health, distress and life satisfaction of working adults in China one month into the COVID-19 outbreak*. https://www. ncbi. nlm. nih. gov/pmc/articles/PMC7146665/pdf/main. pdf

ADDITIONAL READING

Teece, D. J., Pisano, G., & Shuen, A. (1990). Firm capabilities, resources and the concept of strategy. Working Paper 90-9, Consortium on Competitiveness and Cooperation, Center for Research in Management, University of California, Berkeley.

Turker, D. (2018). *Managing Social Responsibility*. Springer International Publishing. doi:10.1007/978-3-319-91710-8

United Nations (UN). (2020). Sustainable Development Outlook 2020. https://sdgs.un.org/sites/default/files/2020-07/SDO2020_Book.pdf

Windsor, D. (2019). Defining corporate social responsibility for developing and developed countries: Comparing proposed approaches. In Corporate Social Responsibility: Concepts, Methodologies, Tools, and Applications (pp. 1-27). IGI Global.

KEY TERMS AND DEFINITIONS

Corporate Social Responsibility: Corporate behaviors which aim to affect stakeholders positively and go beyond its economic interest (Türker, 2008, p. 189).

Dynamic capabilities: The ability to sense and then seize new opportunities, and to reconfigure and protect knowledge assets, competencies, and complementary assets with the aim of achieving a sustained competitive advantage (Augier and Teece, 2009, p.412).

Sustainable Development Goals: (1) No poverty, (2) Zero hunger, (3) Good health and wealth being, (4) Quality education, (5) Gender equality, (6) Clean water and sanitation, (7) Affordable and clean energy, (8) Decent work and economic growth, (9) Industry innovation and infrastructure, (10) Reduced inequalities, (11) Sustainable cities and communities, (12) Responsible consumption and production, (13) Climate action, (14) Life below water, (15) Life on land, (16) Peace, justice, and strong institutions, (17) Partnerships for the goals (UN Development Program, 2015).

Chapter 5
Exploring Non-Financial Information Research:
A Literature Mapping

Estefanía Palazuelos
University of Cantabria, Spain

Paula San-Martín
University of Cantabria, Spain

Javier Montoya-del-Corte
University of Cantabria, Spain

ABSTRACT

The disclosure of non-financial information by companies in their annual reports is becoming increasingly important due to its interest for stakeholders' decision-making. This chapter aims to map research articles that have addressed the study of non-financial information in the last 20 years and have been published in journals indexed in the Web of Science (JCR) and Scopus (SJR) databases. The analyses carried out are described from a triple perspective: meta-perspective, content-based perspective, and methodological perspective. The main results obtained show the growing interest in research on non-financial information in terms of both quantity and quality of the publications. This study may be of interest to researchers, regulatory bodies, and other economic and social agents.

INTRODUCTION

In a financial environment characterized by the globalization and the increasing volatility of the stock markets, the disclosure of information in a reliable, correct, symmetrical and timely manner is an essential element to guarantee the success of companies (Larrán and García-Meca, 2004). However, for some years, there has been a consistent belief that traditional financial reports are insufficient to satisfy the information needs of companies' stakeholders (Newberry, 2015), as they do not adequately represent

DOI: 10.4018/978-1-7998-8065-3.ch005

the different dimensions of corporate activity (Simnet et al., 2009). Moreover, a study carried out by Ernst and Young (2017) highlights the importance of non-financial information for investors, as 68% of respondents stated that this information played an important role when making their investment decisions. Otherwise, the non-financial information is also relevant in the public sector, due to the discontent and distrust of citizens towards politicians and administrators of institutions. This belief has resulted in the addition of non-financial measures, trying to complete the traditional financial reports prepared by firms and public administrations (Montesinos and Brusca, 2019).

It is not until 2014 when the European Union begins to pay special attention to the disclosure of non-financial information, year in which the Directive 2014/95/EU was adopted, with the intended aim of fostering the transparency of Corporate Social Responsibility and Corporate Sustainability reporting. Specifically, information disclosure about environmental, social, employee, respect for human rights, and anti-corruption and bribery matters is pursued to be improved. Since then, more and more EU countries have decided to introduce the obligation for large companies to provide non-financial information within their financial reports or to publish specific sustainability reports (Muserra et al., 2020). Nevertheless, many more companies choose to provide narrative information on a voluntary basis as a way to improve stock liquidity, reduce the cost of capital, increase information intermediation, and improve earnings quality (Rezaee and Tuo, 2017).

In addition, other international initiatives have emerged with the aim of promoting the disclosure of this type of information. One of the most extended is the Global Reporting Initiative (GRI), whose mission is to enable organizations to be transparent and take responsibility for their impacts, enabled through the world's most widely used standards for sustainability reporting (GRI, 2021).

The increased visibility of non-financial information has heightened awareness of the importance of these reports in reflecting organizational practices (Sierra-García et al., 2018), so that researchers have increased their efforts to learn more about some aspects related to the disclosure of non-financial information. Moreover, the world is actually facing a process of global restructuring caused by the COVID-19 pandemic. That is why reviewing the research published in last years takes on special relevance, which is useful to guide future investigation in favor of true sustainable development. In this context, the objective of this Chapter is to provide a literature review based on the mapping of research articles on non-financial information published in indexed journals in the last twenty years, analysing the evolution of the field by combining quantitative and qualitative analysis.

The remainder of this paper is structured as follows. In the second section, a brief theoretical revision of non-financial information is made. In the third section, the research questions are proposed. In the fourth section, the methodology is explained. In the fifth section, the results are exposed. Finally, in the sixth section, the implications derived from the study, the limitations, and the future lines of research are set forth.

BACKGROUND

Stakeholders' interest in the disclosure that companies make of their financial information has a long tradition and is widely regulated. Nevertheless, the importance of the publishing of their non-financial information did not begin to be considered until the end of the last century (Shevlin, 1996). With the Directive 2014/95/EU (European Union, 2014), the general interest in this issue has increased notably in Europe, but also in other international countries.

The concept of non-financial information is not yet well defined (Haller et al., 2017; Tarquinio and Posadas, 2020). In a broadly sense, the Financial Accounting Standards Board (FASB, 2001) considers non-financial information as the information that is not reflected in traditional financial statements (Balance Sheet and Profit and Loss Account), being able to include: information disclosed on a mandatory basis (audit report; relevant facts) and information from voluntary nature (comments from managers).

Nevertheless, its direct relationship with Corporate Social Responsibility and Corporate Sustainability is clear, mainly in relation to social and environmental aspects (Mio and Venturelli, 2013). On the one hand, Corporate Social Responsibility can be broadly defined as "*actions that appear to further some social good, beyond the interests of the firm and that and that which is required by law*" (McWilliams and Siegel, 2001). On the other hand, Corporate Sustainability can be broadly defined as "*meeting the needs of the present without compromising the ability of future generations to meet their own needs*" (World Commission on Environment and Development, 1987).

Therefore, Corporate Social Responsibility is related to phenomena such as transparency, dialogue with stakeholders and sustainability reports, while Corporate Sustainability focuses on value creation, environmental management, environmentally friendly production systems and capital management. In general, both concepts refer to the company's voluntary activities, which demonstrate the inclusion of social and environmental concerns in business operations and in interactions with stakeholders (van Marrewijk, 2003). This also includes aspects related to employee, respect for human rights, and anti-corruption and bribery matters. In this regard, companies should report "*a description of the policies, outcomes and risks related to those matters and should be included in the management report of the undertaking concerned*" for increase investor and consumer trust (European Union, 2014).

As is the case in other many areas, the main companies affected by the mandatory disclosure of non-financial information are still only large listed companies, but many others do so on a voluntary basis and its mandatory nature is gradually being extended to them (Rezaee and Tuo, 2017). In fact, Simpson (2010) says that even in case the disclosure of non-financial information was discretionary, firms could strategically release that kind of information in order to facilitate decision making for their investors and analysts (Simpson, 2010). Consequently, the importance that non-financial information is going to have for knowing the reality and future of all companies, and for stakeholder decision-making, is going to be essential in the coming years.

It is worth mentioning that the main barrier to widespread acceptance and use of non-financial information by investors and other stakeholders is the lack of a generally accepted information framework and reporting standards. As Eccles et al. (2001) state, standards would bring consistency to reporting and permit comparison of company performance, at least within sectors, and it also would provide a benchmark against which reports could be assessed and assurance could be provided. That is why some private initiatives have arisen aimed to homogenize the disclosure of non-financial information, promoted by academic institutions, professional corporations and regulatory bodies. There are several frameworks, standards and guidelines that are generally used to elaborate reports on non-financial information (e.g., Global Reporting Initiative -GRI-, International Integrated Reporting Council -IIRC-, Sustainability Accounting Standards Board -SASB-, Climate Disclosure Standards Board –CDSB-, The United Nations Guiding Principles on Business and Human Rights -UNGPs-). However, to date, there is not a specific public regulation, either international or at a country level, that allows a true standardization of the non-financial information published by companies (Dumay et al., 2017).

Finally, it should be mentioned that integrated reporting is the latest novelty in the corporate reporting field (Vitolla et al., 2020). Integrated reporting combines both financial and non-financial (environmental, social and governance) information in a single report, becoming a tool capable of better representing the capacity of companies to create value over time (Pistoni et al., 2018).

RESEARCH QUESTIONS

In correspondence with the objective indicated in the introduction section, the following research questions are proposed to guide the subsequent analysis of the results, that is organized since three different perspectives:

Meta-perspective:
RQ1: In which years have studies on non-financial information been published?
RQ2: Which journals publish articles on non-financial information?
RQ3: What is the level of impact of journals that publish articles on non-financial information?
RQ4: What are the categories or areas of journals that publish articles on non-financial information?
RQ5: What number of authors publish each article on non-financial information?
RQ6: Which authors publish the most about non-financial information?
RQ7: From which countries are the authors who publish on non-financial information?
RQ8: In which languages are articles on non-financial information published?

Content-based perspective:
RQ9: What are the most investigated topics on non-financial information?
RQ10: In which continents have studies on non-financial information been carried out?
RQ11: In which countries have studies on non-financial information been carried out?

Methodological perspective
RQ12: What are the methodological approaches used in research on non-financial information?
RQ13: What are the methodological designs used in research on non-financial information?
RQ14: What are the data collection methods used in research on non-financial information?

METHODOLOGY

A systematic mapping study was carried out to identify and categorize existing research on non-financial information. The main goal of a systematic mapping study is to provide an overview of a research area, and identify the quantity and type of research and results available within it. A secondary goal can be to map the frequencies of publication over time to see trends and identify the journals in which research in the area has been published (Petersen et al., 2008).

For this research, a review of 116 articles related to the topic of non-financial information was carried out. For the identification and selection of relevant studies, Web of Science (JCR) and Scopus (SJR) databases were consulted. These two are the most important and widely used bibliographic databases in the field of Social Sciences.

The search criteria in the aforementioned databases were the following:

- The first filter in the search was the document type. Thus, only articles were included. This was decided because there are several authors who define the article as the knowledge transmission unit par excellence (Arguimbau-Vivó et al., 2013; Ramos and Ruiz, 2008). In addition, we consider that the inclusion of other types of publications, such as conference presentations and book Chapters, would have caused significant duplications that would distort the results.
- The second criterion was the period of time to be covered. It was decided that the review would span from 2000 to 2020. Since the analysis began in early 2021, this year was not included in the data to be as accurate as possible.
- The third and last filter was the theme. Of course, we were only interested in those articles that were related to non-financial information. For this reason, it was determined that the articles should contain the concepts "non-financial information" or "non-financial reporting" in their title. The use of keywords as a search method is quite common and has been extensively used in other reviews of the field (Erkens et al., 2015; Manes-Rossi et al., 2020). Broad keywords were introduced to be able to identify the largest possible block of literature and avoid the exclusion of important works. After conducting the search, the articles were manually reviewed to check, first, if they were all "articles"; second, if there were duplicates; and, lastly, if they actually dealt with the issue of non-financial information. The final sample obtained was made up of a total of 116 articles (the list of references for these articles has not been included due to its length, but can be requested from the authors).

Table 1 shows the process of searching and selection of the articles. As we can see, applying the filters previously described, 184 articles were obtained in the initial search, of which 88 were in the Web of Science (JCR), and 96 in the Scopus (SJR) databases. Next, the sample was refined by eliminating 11 documents that were not really "articles" (such as book Chapters or editorials) and 57 more that appeared in both databases (duplicates). Thus, 116 articles were finally obtained, of which 15 were indexed in *Emerging Sources Citation Index*.

Table 1. Searching and selection process

Stage	Description	Number of documents
Initial search	Web of Science (JCR): 88 articles Scopus (SJR): 96 articles	**184**
Dropped documents		**68**
- Other documents	Book Chapter: 10 Editorial: 1	11
- Duplicates		57
FINAL SAMPLE		**116**

For the subsequent analysis of the selected articles, a combination of qualitative and quantitative methods was used. In particular, the structure followed by Sánchez and Blanco (2014) was implemented, which consists on analysing the data from three different perspectives:

1. Meta-perspective: it refers to the quantitative analysis of the results in order to "measure" the development of a certain field of study taking into account, among others, temporal or publication criteria. This perspective includes the analysis of the number of contributions per year, the number of contributions per journal, the most prolific authors, as well as the institutions and countries where the authors belong.
2. Content-based perspective: it refers to the analysis of the studies developed in a research field in order to identify which are the recurring topics and where (continent or country) they are carried out.
3. Methodological perspective: it refers to the examination of the applied methodology of the studies found along the search.

Once the articles were identified, the content analysis was carried out. To do this, the codes collected in Table 2 were established, which aimed to answer the research questions posed in this work.

Table 2. Codebook for content analysis

Code	Definition
Year	Year in which the article was published
Journal	Scientific journal in which the article has been published
Impact	Impact factor of the journal in which the article has been published
Category	Areas of expertise in which the journals focus
Author	Name of the author(s) of the article
Origin	Country of origin of the author(s)
University	University the author(s) belong to
Language	Language in which the article is written
Topic	Main topic addressed in the article
Continent	Continent in which the study was carried out
Country	Country in which the study was carried out
Methodological approach	Whether the article follows a theoretical or empirical approach
Research design	Analysis methodology used in the article
Data collection method	Collection method used in the article

RESULTS

Literature Review From the Meta-Perspective

Table 3 shows the number of articles published by year from 2000 to 2020. It is worth mentioning that there are several years in which no article was published, and therefore they have not been included in the Table. It is observed how the trend is increasing, especially in the last five years (see Figure 1). The number of papers published in 2020 stands out above all, which represents a little more than a third part of the total and shows the growing importance of this topic at present and, probably, in the future.

Table 3. Year of publication and number of papers published

Year of publication	Number of papers
2020	40
2019	13
2018	15
2017	8
2016	8
2015	9
2014	3
2013	6
2012	1
2011	1
2010	5
2008	2
2007	2
2006	2
2003	1
TOTAL	116

Table 4 lists the outstanding journals in the field of non-financial information. It can be seen that there is not a significant concentration of articles published in one or more journals, but rather the opposite, the spectrum of journals that disseminate studies focused on non-financial information is very broad. In fact, a total of 88 journals have published any article related to non-financial information throughout the period of study (2000-2020). Of these, a total of 74 have published only one article. This may be because this topic can be investigated from multiple perspectives, sectors and areas of knowledge. However, the journals in which the publication of the greatest number of articles is concentrated are *Meditari Accountancy Research* and *Sustainability*.

Figure 1. Number of papers by year
Source: own elaboration

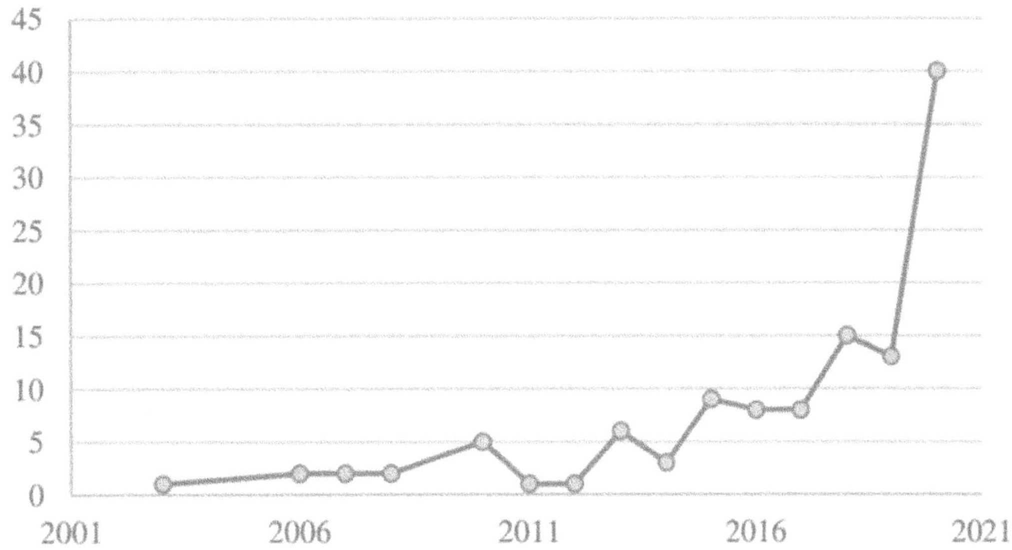

Table 4. Journal list and number of papers published

Journal	Number of papers
Meditari Accountancy Research	7
Sustainability	5
Accounting Economics and Law - A Convivium	4
Accounting and Business Research	3
Administrative Sciences	3
Amfiteatru Economic	3
Corporate Social Responsibility and Environmental Management	3
Accounting in Europe	2
Economic Annals - XXI	2
European Accounting Review	2
European Company and Financial Law Review	2
European Company Law	2
Razón Histórica - Revista Hispanoamericana de Historia de las Ideas	2
Social Responsibility Journal	2
Other journals that have published only one paper	74
TOTAL	116

Tables 5 and 6 show the impact of the journals where non-financial information related articles have been published. First of all, it should be noted that most of the research carried out on this topic has been published in journals included in the Scopus (SJR) database, not in the Web of Science (JCR) database. Specifically, in relation to the year of publication of the articles, 80.2% were published in Scopus (SJR) journals, and only 29.3% in Web of Science (JCR) journals. If the latest data available on the impact of these journals is considered, these percentages increase to 87.1% and 35.3%, respectively. This finding is indicative of a higher quality of the journals in which the results of the research on non-financial information in recent years have been published. In addition, an improvement is also observed in the impact positions of these journals. In the case of the Web of Science (JCR) database, in relation to the year of publication of the articles, of the total of 34 published works, 61.7% belong to journals with a Q1/Q2 impact factor; if the latest year available is considered, this percentage increases to 70.8% of the total of 41 articles published (see Figure 2). Regarding the Scopus (SJR) database, in relation to the year of publication of the articles, of the total of 93 published works, 67.8% belong to journals with a Q1/Q2 impact factor; if the latest year available is considered, this percentage increases to 69.3% of the total of 101 articles published (see Figure 3).

Table 5. Web of Science (JCR) journals' impact

JCR quartile publication year	Number of papers	Last JCR quartile available (2019)	Number of papers
Q1	8	Q1	9
Q2	13	Q2	20
Q3	8	Q3	6
Q4	5	Q4	6
Not JCR	82	Not JCR	75
Total	116	Total	116

Table 6. Scopus (SJR) journals' impact

SJR quartile publication year	Number of papers	Last SJR quartile available (2019)	Number of papers
Q1	18	Q1	19
Q2	45	Q2	51
Q3	21	Q3	23
Q4	9	Q4	8
Not SJR	23	Not SJR	15
Total	116	Total	116

Figure 2. JCR quartile distribution
Source: own elaboration

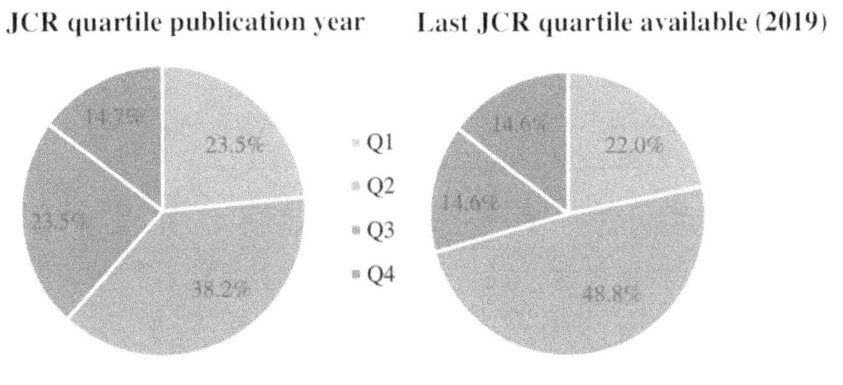

Figure 3. SJR quartile distribution
Source: own elaboration

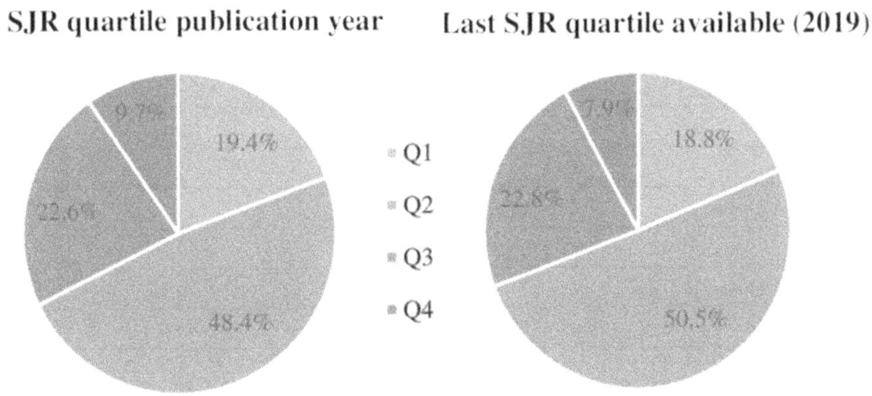

Tables 7 and 8 refer to the areas or categories covered by the journals in which articles on non-financial information have been published. It can be seen that most of them are associated with issues related to the field of economics and business. In the case of the Web of Science (JCR) database, the most frequent categories are "Business, Finance", "Management" and "Business". Regarding the Scopus (SJR) database, the areas that are repeated the most are "Accounting", "Economics, Econometrics and Finance (miscellaneous)" and "Business and International Management". However, there are other categories in which studies on non-financial information may also have a place, such as those related to the environment, law, politics or sociology.

The number of authors that non-financial information research-focused articles usually have is shown in Table 9. Most of them do not exceed four authors. In particular, articles with two authors represent a third part of the total (38 articles). Next, approximately a 25% (30 articles) have been written by three authors (see Figure 4). Moreover, 21 articles have only one author. This result is coherent, since in the field of Social Sciences the number of authors who usually sign the articles is two or three.

Table 7. Web of Science (JCR) journals' categories

JCR categories	Number of papers
Business, Finance	17
Management	15
Business	11
Environmental Studies	10
Economics	8
Green & Sustainable Science & Technology	5
Law	2
Five categories with 1 paper	5

Table 8. Scopus (SJR) journals' categories

SJR categories	Number of papers
Accounting	36
Economics, Econometrics and Finance (miscellaneous)	25
Business and International Management	19
Business, Management and Accounting (miscellaneous)	18
Finance	15
Strategy and Management	15
Management, Monitoring, Policy and Law	11
Law	11
Geography, Planning and Development	10
Economics and Econometrics	9
Sociology and Political Science	7
Environmental Science (miscellaneous)	6
Renewable Energy, Sustainability and the Environment	6
Social Sciences (miscellaneous)	6
Energy Engineering and Power Technology	5
Thirty-two categories with less than 5 papers	49

Table 9. Number of authors per paper

Number of authors	Number of papers
One author	21
Two authors	38
Three authors	30
Four authors	18
Five authors	6
Six Authors	2
Seven authors	1
TOTAL	116

Figure 4. Percentage of papers by number of authors
Source: own elaboration

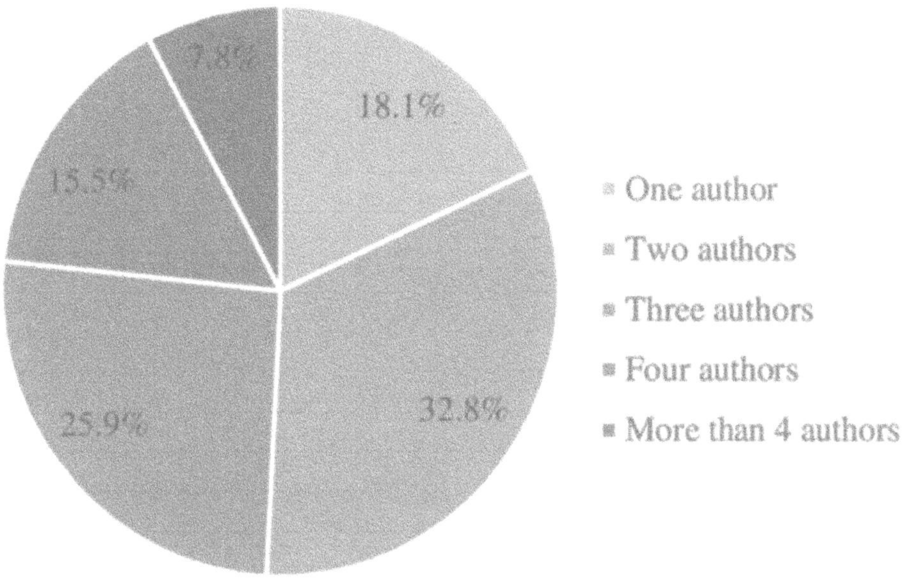

Within the 116 articles analyzed, 276 authors were identified. Table 10 shows the list of the five most prolific researchers on the subject of non-financial information. It can be seen from this table that few authors write many articles. In fact, only five authors have published more than two articles focused on this research topic (Caputo et al., 2020; Dumay et al., 2015; La Torre et al., 2018, 2020; Pizzi, 2018; Raucci and Tarquinio, 2020; Szabo and Sorensen, 2015, 2017, 2018; Tarquinio and Posadas, 2020; Venturelli et al., 2019). This may be due to the newness of non-financial information within the academic world. In addition, as previously mentioned, these articles have been published in various journals covering multiple areas of expertise, which may explain the diversity of authors that can be found. In fact, only 22 authors appear in two articles and most of them (249 authors) have collaborated on a single article.

Table 10. Most prolific co-authors

Co-authors	Number of authors
Number of authors who appear in three papers	5
Pizzi, S.	
Szabo, D.G.	
Sorensen, K.E.	
Dumay, J.	
Tarquinio, L.	
Number of authors who appear in two papers	22
Number of authors who appear in one paper	249
TOTAL	276

Table 11. Countries the authors belong to and number of universities by country

Country	Number of authors	Number of universities
Italy	28	13
Spain	28	13
Russia	27	11
Romania	23	9
Croatia	13	1
Ukraine	12	8
Germany	10	6
United Kingdom	10	9
China	9	2
Indonesia	9	4
Sweden	9	5
Poland	8	5
Australia	7	5
France	7	6
USA	7	7
Jordan	6	3
N/D	6	6
Denmark	5	2
New Zealand	5	2
Pakistan	5	3
Slovakia	5	2
Ireland	4	3
Netherlands	4	3
Czech Republic	3	3
Finland	3	2
Iran	3	1
Portugal	3	3
South Africa	3	2
Belgium	2	3
Canada	2	2
Israel	2	2
Lithuania	2	1
Taiwan	2	2
Austria	1	1
Greece	1	1
Hong Kong	1	1
Norway	1	1
TOTAL	276	155

Table 11 refers to the country of origin of the 276 authors and the number of universities per country to which these authors belong. On the one hand, if we look at the country, most of them are from European countries (78%). This reflects a greater interest in investigating this topic by authors from this continent. In fact, it can be seen that the highest concentration of authors interested in non-financial information is found in Italy, Spain, Russia and Croatia. On the other hand, in relation to the number of universities these authors belong to, in most cases, it can be seen that they are scattered in different universities, without any university as a reference centre. With the exception of the Croatian authors, who all belong to the same university, the University of Zagreb.

Finally, it should be noted that practically all the articles were written in English (Table 12). The few articles written in another language were written in Spanish, Russian, Ukrainian, French and Croatian. This is not surprising, since English is considered the vehicular language of science.

Table 12. Language of publication

Language	Number of papers
English	107
Spanish	3
Russian	3
Croatian	1
French	1
Ukrainian	1
TOTAL	116

Figure 5. Percentage of papers by language of publication
Source: own elaboration

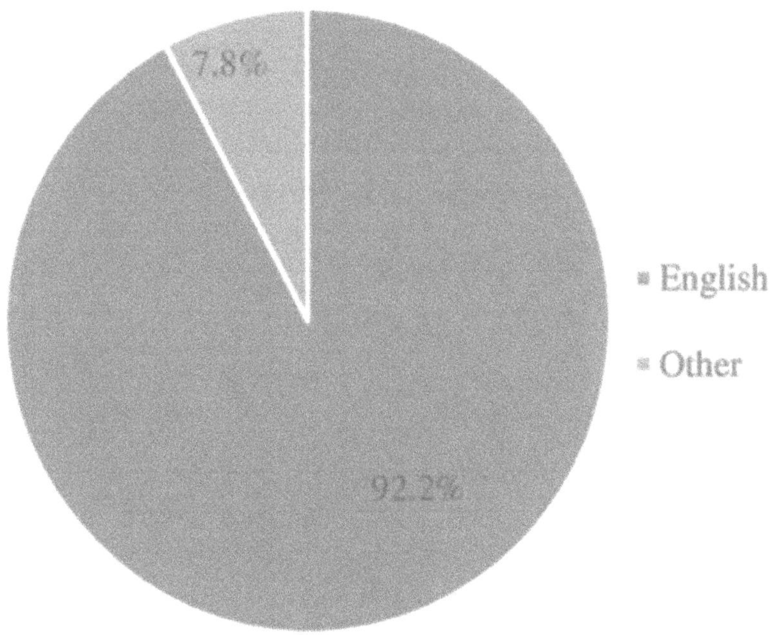

Literature Review From the Content-Based Perspective

The aim of this section is to identify which are the major topics addressed within the field of non-financial information. Knowing the trend in the field, not only enables to know what the current state of the art is, but it also facilitates the establishment of future lines of research.

Following a first reading of the 116 abstracts, 23 thematic areas were established by the authors of this Chapter. These topics are summarized in Table 13.

The most common topic among the analyzed articles was the study of the *effects/impact* that non-financial information might have on different variables (such as company creditworthiness, financial distress, corporate transparency, sustainable development or trading behavior). Specifically, 28 out of the 116 analyzed papers (24.14%) discussed this topic.

Table 13. Research topics

Topic	Number of papers
Effects/Impact	28
Evolution/current practices/initiatives	17
Content and structure	16
Determinants (for disclosure)	10
CSR	5
Quality	5
Integrated reporting	5
Determinants (for use)	4
Assurance	4
Environmental	4
SDG's	2
Intellectual capital	2
Strategy	2
Assessment model	2
Employee	2
Constraints	2
Socio-environmental	2
Intangibles	2
Terminology	2
Human rights	1
Social	1
Audit	1
Ethics	1
TOTAL	120 (*)

*The total number of papers reflected in Table 13 is 120 (and not only 116) because there are 4 articles that do not only focus on one particular topic, but on two at the same time (Content and structure & Assurance, Content and structure & Determinants (for disclosure), Determinants (for disclosure) & Constraints, Evolution/current practices/initiatives & Effects/Impact).

In second position, 17 articles talked about the evolution that non-financial information has experienced, the current practices that are nowadays being implemented, and the future trends. It should be noted that most of them had a theoretical approach, where the EU Non-Financial Reporting Directive (2014/95) played a leading role. Next, it is observed how the *content and structure* of the reports that contain financial and non-financial information is also one of the most widely analyzed topics (16 articles). The number of studies that investigate which are the most important determinants when deciding to disclose non-financial information is also notable (10 articles).

Apart from these main topics, the spectrum is very wide, being able to identify up to 19 more. On the one hand, several are directly related to the review of non-financial information, the determinants for using it or the disclosure of non-financial information in conjunction with financial information (integrated reporting). On the other hand, others focus on specific areas within the general topic of non-financial information, such as environmental, social, employee, and respect for human rights.

Once we know which topics have been the most addressed, it is interesting to know in which continents these investigations have been carried out. In this way, we can see in Table 14 that the majority of papers have been developed in a European country. Specifically, 71 articles out of 116 have focused on any country of this continent. In addition, it should be noted that, of those 71 articles, 16 focused on comparing more than one country in Europe. Moreover, although there are studies in other continents, it can be seen how the number of papers is considerably lower than in Europe. Thus, Asia, America, Oceania and Africa accumulate 12, 6, 3 and 1 article, respectively. However, it is important to note that there are 23 papers (*International* in the Table) that compare countries from different continents.

Table 14. Continent in which the research is carried out

Continent	Number of papers
Europe	71
Asia	12
America	6
Oceania	3
Africa	1
International	23
TOTAL	116

When we focus on countries (Table 15), we can see that Spain and Italy are the ones with the greatest prominence, with 9 and 8 articles respectively. Both countries are European. In the case of America, the USA is the country that gathers the highest number of studies (5 articles). Asia, otherwise, has few studies, and half of them are developed in China and Indonesia. Studies conducted in Oceania are mostly located in Australia. Finally, the only country in Africa where this type of investigation is applied is South Africa.

Table 15. Countries in which the research is carried out

Country	Number of papers
Several countries	39
Spain	9
Italy	8
Russia	6
Ukraine	6
USA	5
Romania	4
Germany	3
United Kingdom	3
China	3
Indonesia	3
Croatia	3
Belgium	2
Poland	2
Czech Republic	2
Australia	2
Pakistan	2
Countries in which only one research is carried out	14
TOTAL	116

Literature Review From the Methodological Perspective

From a methodological perspective, we first divided the sample into empirical and theoretical papers. Table 16 gathers that data, showing that there is a large percentage of empirical articles (almost 75%) compared to the theoretical ones (see Figure 6).

Once that first distribution was made, we took a second step and looked at what methodology did the articles follow, both empirical and theoretical. The results obtained are summarized in Table 17.

Table 16. Methodological approach

Approach	Number of papers
Empirical	85
Theoretical	31
TOTAL	116

Figure 6. Percentage of papers by methodological approach
Source: own elaboration

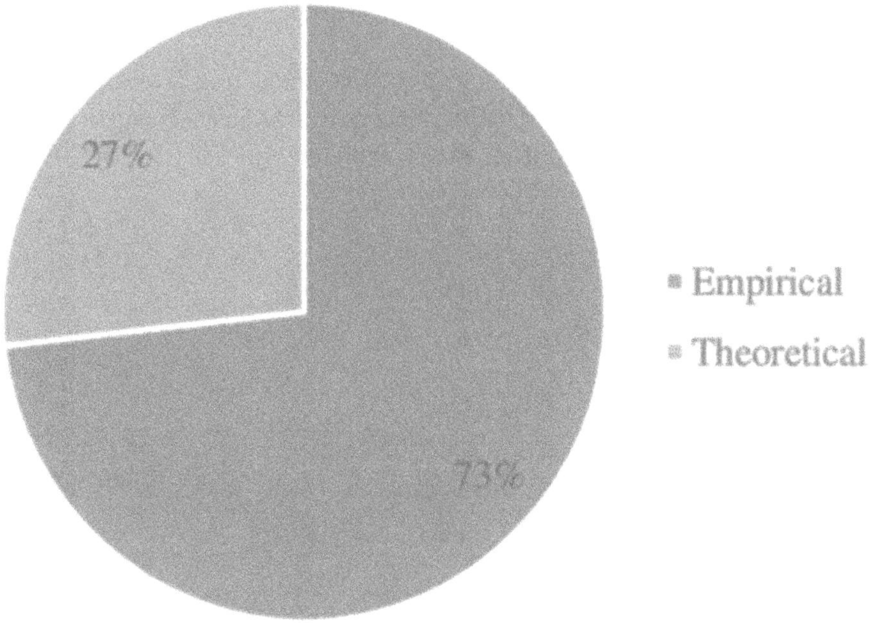

Table 17. Methodology/Research design

Methodology/Research design	Number of papers
Empirical	**85**
Exploratory study	32
Regression analysis	28
Qualitative analysis	14
Panel data analysis	3
Fuzzy logic	2
Equation modeling	2
Factorial analysis	2
N/A	2
Theoretical	**31**
Commentary/Normative/Policy	22
Literature review	5
Model/case/indicator proposal	3
Bibliometric analysis	1
TOTAL	116

The empirical papers were very different in nature and used different methodologies. Exploratory studies were the most frequent ones, followed by regression analyses and qualitative analyses (see Figure 7). However, this variety opens up a range of possibilities when it comes to delving into the investigation of non-financial information.

Theoretical articles, meanwhile, were mainly focused on commenting several aspects related to the normative or policy that affects non-financial information, as well as on analysing the evolution, current practices and future trends of this type of information (see Figure 8).

Figure 7. Percentage of empirical papers by methodology
Source: own elaboration

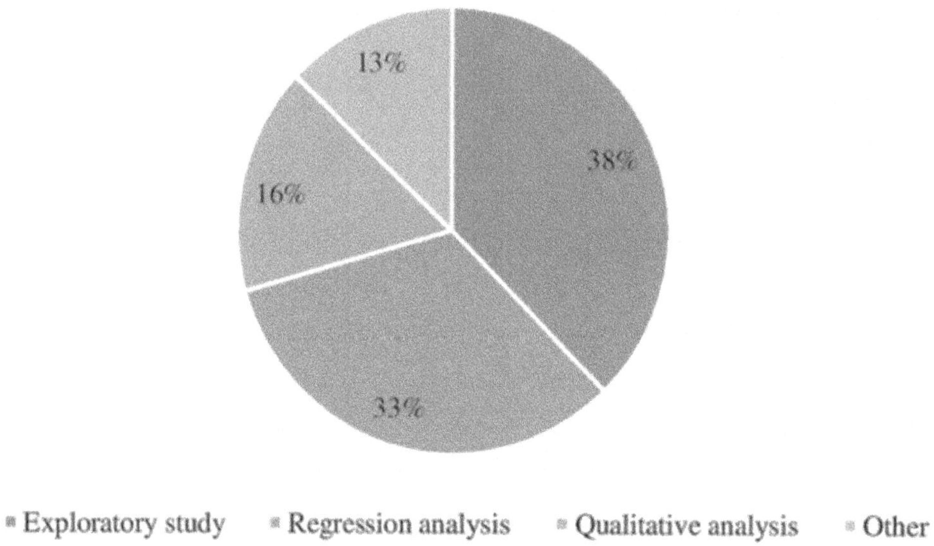

Figure 8. Percentage of theoretical papers by methodology
Source: own elaboration

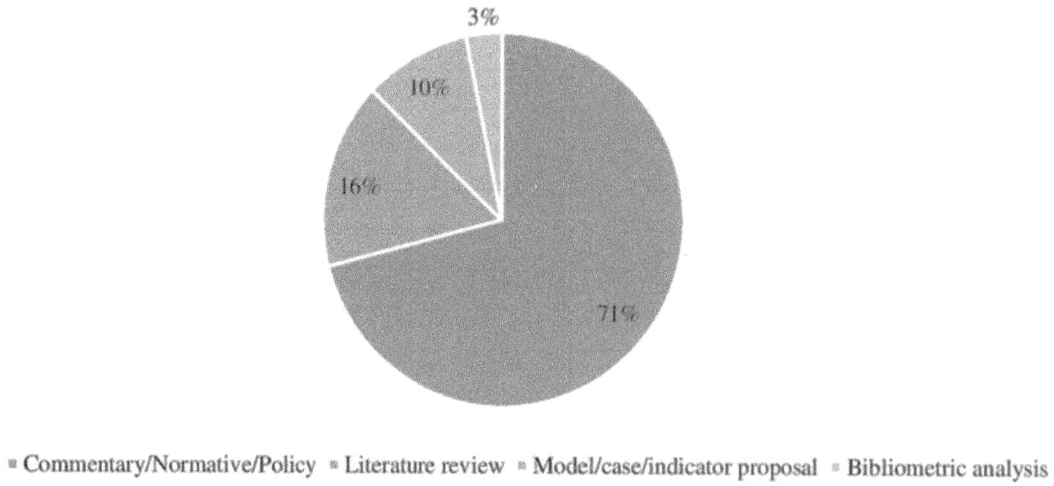

Finally, Table 18 shows the data collection technique used by the empirical articles. As we can see, report analysis was the most employed method. In fact, more than 50% of empirical papers used it. In this category, we found articles that analyzed both annual reports and sustainability reports, as well as integrated reports. This result is logical as the predominant methodology was the exploratory study, and many researchers had focused on calculating different descriptive statistics and commenting different aspects of interest about those reports. Databases and surveys were placed in the second and third positions, followed by web page analyses, case studies, interviews and experiments.

Table 18. Data collection method (empirical articles)

Data collection method	Number of papers
Report analysis	47
Database	14
Survey	14
Web page analysis	10
Case study	6
Interviews	5
Experiments	4
N/A	2
TOTAL	102*

* 11 articles obtained data from 2 different sources; 3 articles obtained data from 3 different sources

CONCLUSION

The financial information, together with the non-financial information, makes up the total information about the company's business, a concept that the FASB (2001) calls "Business Reporting". Financial information has always been relevant for decision-making. However, the importance of disclosure of non-financial information by companies has increased notably in recent decades, becoming a key factor for understanding their position and contribution to society and, therefore, for stakeholder decision-making (Miska et al., 2013). Based on articles published in journals included in Web of Science (JCR) and Scopus (SJR) databases, this Chapter offers a review of the literature on non-financial information within the 21st century, using a triple perspective: meta-perspective, content-based perspective, and methodological perspective.

From the meta-perspective, the most important conclusion is that there is a significant and progressive increase in the quantity and quality of published research in relation to non-financial information. On the one hand, the number of articles published in 2020 represents more than a third of all the papers published to date in the last twenty years. On the other hand, research on non-financial information is published in increasingly prestigious journals, if the quartile in which they are located in the main international reference databases is considered. In other words, research on non-financial information is increasingly accepted in journals included in relevant positions in the Web of Science (JCR) and Scopus (SJR) databases. All of this is indicative of the enormous relevance that the study of non-financial information has been acquiring in recent years. Furthermore, although the areas related to Business and

Economy are those that accumulate a greater number of publications, it should be noted that there are also many other categories with possibilities to carry out research on non-financial information and, therefore, there is a great diversity of journals in which the results obtained can be disclosed. Finally, it should be noted that more than half of the articles analyzed in this Chapter are signed by two or three co-authors, that researchers from European universities are those who mostly lead the research and that practically all of the published papers are written in English.

From the content-based perspective, it is found that research on non-financial information can also be carried out from a great variety of contexts, settings and points of view, and with multiple different objectives. The most common purpose, to date, is to study the effect and impact that non-financial information has on certain variables of interest to companies and other social agents, the most common practices when disclosing this type of information and the reasons that encourage companies to inform their stakeholders about the different key topics in this matter. Nevertheless, most of the articles reviewed address the study in general terms, that is, without focusing specifically on any of its particular components (environmental, social, employee, respect for human rights, and anti-corruption and bribery matters). Finally, in line with what is indicated in the previous paragraph, most of the researches are developed within the European context, comparing aspects related to non-financial information in two or more countries at the same time.

From the methodological perspective, it should be noted that most of the published papers on non-financial information are empirical in nature. For their development, the data analysis is carried out using descriptive statistics, regression analysis and qualitative information analysis. It is also important to indicate that the data collection method, in most cases, consists of collecting information from different types of reports published by companies, followed by consulting different databases, conducting surveys and browsing Web pages.

This Chapter may be of interest to different groups. Firstly, for academics and researchers, as it allows them to obtain an overview of the state of the art regarding the study of non-financial information, from which to better guide future research. Specifically, the analyzed results suggest increasing interdisciplinary collaboration for the study of non-financial information disclosed by companies, combining the field of Business and Economy with other related areas of knowledge. In addition, the scope of study should be extended to other geographical areas, such as the United States, Latin America, Asia, Africa and Australia, where research to date has been less prolific than in Europe. At the methodological level, as the availability of standardized data on non-financial information increases, empirical research can be carried out using robust statistical techniques for the study of evolution over time, such as the analysis of panel data. Secondly, for regulatory bodies, since it shows a long way to go in terms of establishing standards and recommendations for the homogeneous publication of non-financial information. The results of research published in scientific journals should be the basis for the establishment of norms that allow achieving increasingly reliable, relevant, understandable and comparable non-financial information. And, thirdly, for other economic and social agents, whose specific interests in certain matters related to non-financial information may be clarified by reading this document. In addition, they must become a key driver to promote new research that helps to shed light on the issues that most concern society.

The results analyzed in this Chapter, as well as the conclusions achieved, must be taken into consideration with certain caution, as there are a series of limitations in the review process carried out. In the first place, only articles published in the Web of Science (JCR) and Scopus (SJR) databases, between the years 2000 and 2020, whose title exactly includes the expressions "non- financial information" or "non-financial reporting" have been included. With this, it is ensured that all the selected articles meet the analyzed subject and are published in internationally recognized journals. However, other papers published in the current year and that address the study of non-financial information but do not include the term in their title, and those that were published in other media, such as the proceedings papers and book Chapters, were left out of the sample. In the second place, the keywords for the search were only considered in English, so there could be other papers of interest excluded because their title was exclusively written in another language, like Spanish, which also covers a wide range of Latin American countries. And, in the third place, the review is fundamentally based on the more generic data collected from the articles, including the abstract, but the content of the articles is not analyzed in detail, given the exploratory nature of the study carried out.

As main future lines of research, there could be included, among others, the following. First, it would be convenient to replicate, in the coming years, the study carried out to know the evolution of the main examined variables. Second, it could be interesting to go deeper into the study of the state of the question, with the elaboration of new papers that use the systematic literature review or bibliometric analysis, for example, as a research method. Third, as the regulation of non-financial information published by companies progresses and becomes standardized, more data will be available to carry out empirical papers using other research methodologies, such as panel data. Finally, it is necessary to start studying in a more rigorous way, and from all the areas of knowledge involved, specific issues that until now have only been analyzed from the point of view of financial information. For example, the materiality for the inclusion of non-financial information in the annual reports that are disclosed by companies, or the effects of the practices of manipulating this type of information on the results and growth of the companies, and on the decisions of the stakeholders.

ACKNOWLEDGMENT

This research received no specific grant from any funding agency in the public, commercial, or not-for-profit sectors. However, for its development it had the support of the Yunus Center Cantabria (https://centroyunuscantabria.unican.es) and the Cátedra Pyme of the University of Cantabria (http://www.expertoauditoria.es).

REFERENCES

Arguimbau-Vivó, L., Fuentes-Pujol, E., & Gallifa-Calatayud, M. (2013). A decade of documentary research on Scientometrics in Spain: Analysis of papers from the ISOC database (2000-2009). *Revista Espanola la de Documentacion Cientifica*, *36*(2), 1–9.

Caputo, F., Leopizzi, R., Pizzi, S., & Milone, V. (2020). The Non-Financial Reporting Harmonization in Europe: Evolutionary Pathways Related to the Transposition of the Directive 95/2014/EU within the Italian Context. *Sustainability*, *12*(1), 92–104. doi:10.3390u12010092

Dumay, J., Bernardi, C., Guthrie, J., & La Torre, M. (2017). Barriers to Implementing the International Integrated Reporting Framework: A Contemporary Academic Perspective. *Meditari Accountancy Research*, *25*(4), 461–480. doi:10.1108/MEDAR-05-2017-0150

Dumay, J., Frost, G., & Beck, C. (2015). Material legitimacy Blending organisational and stakeholder concerns through non-financial information disclosures. *Journal of Accounting and Organizational Change*, *11*(1), 2–23. doi:10.1108/JAOC-06-2013-0057

Eccles, R. G., Serafeim, G., & Krzus, M. P. (2011). Market interest in nonfinancial information. *Journal of Applied Corporate Finance*, *23*(4), 113–127. doi:10.1111/j.1745-6622.2011.00357.x

Erkens, M., Paugam, L., & Stolowy, H. (2015). Non-financial information: State of the art and research perspectives based on a bibliometric study. *Comptabilité-Contrôle-Audit*, *21*(3), 15–92. doi:10.3917/cca.213.0015

Ernst & Young. (2017). *Is Your Non-Financial Performance Revealing the True Value of Your Business to Investors?* https://assets.ey.com

European Union. (2014). *Directive 2014/95/UE of the European Parliament and of the Council of 22 October 2014 amending Directive 2013/34/UE as regards disclosure of non-financial and diversity information by certain large undertakings and groups.* https://eur-lex.europa.eu/eli/dir/2014/95/oj

Financial Accounting Standards Board (2001). *Business and financial reporting. Challenges from the new economy.* Special Report. Author.

Global Reporting Initiative. (2021). *Sustainability reporting guidelines.* https://www.globalreporting.org

Haller, A., Link, M., & Groß, T. (2017). The term 'non-financial information' – a semantic analysis of a key feature of current and future corporate reporting. *Accounting in Europe*, *14*(3), 407–429. doi:10.1080/17449480.2017.1374548

La Torre, M., Sabelfeld, S., Blomkvist, M., & Dumay, J. (2020). Rebuilding trust: Sustainability and non-financial reporting and the European Union regulation. *Meditari Accountancy Research*, *28*(5), 701–725. doi:10.1108/MEDAR-06-2020-0914

La Torre, M., Sabelfeld, S., Blomkvist, M., Tarquinio, L., & Dumay, J. (2018). Harmonising non-financial reporting regulation in Europe: Practical forces and projections for future research. *Meditari Accountancy Research*, *26*(4), 598–621. doi:10.1108/MEDAR-02-2018-0290

Larrán, M., & García-Meca, E. (2004). La relevancia de la información no-financiera en la estrategia empresarial de divulgación unitaria: Percepciones empresa-analista sobre su utilidad. *Revista Valenciana de Economía y Hacienda*, (12), 127–145.

Manes-Rossi, F., Nicolò, G., & Argento, D. (2020). Non-financial reporting formats in public sector organizations: A structured literature review. *Journal of Public Budgeting, Accounting & Financial Management*, *32*(4), 639–669. doi:10.1108/JPBAFM-03-2020-0037

McWilliams, A., & Siegel, D. (2001). Corporate Social Responsibility: A Theory of the Firm Perspective. *Academy of Management Review*, *26*(1), 117–127. doi:10.5465/amr.2001.4011987

Mio, C., & Venturelli, A. (2013). Non-financial Information About Sustainable Development and Environmental Policy in the Annual Reports of Listed Companies: Evidence from Italy and the UK. *Corporate Social Responsibility and Environmental Management*, *20*(6), 340–358. doi:10.1002/csr.1296

Miska, C., Stahl, G. K., & Mendenhall, M. E. (2013). Intercultural competencies as antecedents of responsible global leadership. *European Journal of International Management*, *7*(5), 550–569. doi:10.1504/EJIM.2013.056477

Montesinos, V., & Brusca, I. (2019). Non-financial reporting in the public sector: Alternatives, trends and opportunities. *Revista de Contabilidad*, *22*(2), 22–128. doi:10.6018/rcsar.383071

Muserra, A. L., Papa, M., & Grimaldi, F. (2020). Sustainable development and the European Union Policy on non-financial information: An Italian empirical analysis. *Corporate Social Responsibility and Environmental Management*, *27*(1), 22–31. doi:10.1002/csr.1770

Newberry, S. (2015). Public sector accounting: Shifting concepts of accountability. *Public Money & Management*, *35*(5), 371–376. doi:10.1080/09540962.2015.1061180

Petersen, K., Feldt, R., Mujtaba, S., & Mattsson, M. (2008). Systematic mapping studies in software engineering. In *12th International Conference on Evaluation and Assessment in Software Engineering (EASE) 12* (pp. 1-10). Academic Press.

Pistoni, A., Songini, L., & Bavagnoli, F. (2018). Integrated reporting quality: An empirical analysis. *Corporate Social Responsibility and Environmental Management*, *25*(4), 489–507. doi:10.1002/csr.1474

Pizzi, S. (2018). The Relationship between Non-financial Reporting, Environmental Strategies and Financial Performance. Empirical Evidence from Milano Stock Exchange. *Administrative Sciences*, *8*(4), 76–84. doi:10.3390/admsci8040076

Ramos, A. R., & Ruiz, J. (2008). Base intelectual de la investigación en creación de empresas: Un estudio biométrico. *Revista Europea de Dirección y Economía de la Empresa*, *17*(1), 13–38.

Raucci, D., & Tarquinio, L. (2020). Sustainability Performance Indicators and Non-Financial Information Reporting. Evidence from the Italian Case. *Administrative Sciences*, *10*(1), 13–29. doi:10.3390/admsci10010013

Rezaee, Z., & Tuo, L. (2017). Voluntary disclosure of non-financial information and its association with sustainability performance. *Advances in Accounting*, *39*, 47–59. doi:10.1016/j.adiac.2017.08.001

Sánchez, L., & Blanco, B. (2014). Three decades of continuous improvement. *Total Quality Management & Business Excellence*, *25*(9-10), 986–1001. doi:10.1080/14783363.2013.856547

Shevlin, T. (1996). The value-relevance of nonfinancial information: A discussion. *Journal of Accounting and Economics*, *22*(1/3), 31–42. doi:10.1016/S0165-4101(96)00441-7

Sierra-García, L., García-Benau, M. A., & Bollas-Araya, H. M. (2018). Empirical analysis of non-financial reporting by Spanish companies. *Administrative Sciences*, *8*(3), 29. doi:10.3390/admsci8030029

Simnett, R., Vanstraelen, A., & Chua, W. F. (2009). Assurance on sustainability reports: An international comparison. *The Accounting Review*, *84*(3), 937–967. doi:10.2308/accr.2009.84.3.937

Simpson, A. V. (2010). Analysts' use of non-financial information disclosures. *Contemporary Accounting Research*, *27*(1), 249–288. doi:10.1111/j.1911-3846.2010.01008.x

Szabo, D. G., & Sorensen, K. E. (2015). New EU Directive on the Disclosure of Non-Financial Information (CSR). *European Company and Financial Law Review*, *12*(3), 307–340. doi:10.1515/ecfr-2015-0307

Szabo, D. G., & Sorensen, K. E. (2017). Non-financial reporting, CSR frameworks and groups of undertakings: Application and consequences. *Journal of Corporate Law Studies*, *17*(1), 137–165. doi:10.1080/14735970.2016.1254449

Szabo, D. G., & Sorensen, K. E. (2018). Pursuing CSR Policy in Corporate Groups: Insights in the Operation of Groups from Consolidated Non-Financial Reporting. *European Company Law*, *15*(2), 51–60.

Tarquinio, L., & Posadas, S. C. (2020). Exploring the term "non-financial information": An academics' view. *Meditari Accountancy Research*, *28*(5), 727–749. doi:10.1108/MEDAR-11-2019-0602

van Marrewijk, M. (2003). Concepts and Definitions of CSR and Corporate Sustainability: Between Agency and Communion. *Journal of Business Ethics*, *44*(2), 95–105. doi:10.1023/A:1023331212247

Venturelli, A., Caputo, F., Leopizzi, R., & Pizzi, S. (2019). The state of art of corporate social disclosure before the introduction of non-financial reporting directive: A cross country analysis. *Social Responsibility Journal*, *15*(4), 409–423. doi:10.1108/SRJ-12-2017-0275

Vitolla, F., Raimo, N., & Rubino, M. (2020). Board characteristics and integrated reporting quality: An agency theory perspective. *Corporate Social Responsibility and Environmental Management*, *27*(2), 1152–1163. doi:10.1002/csr.1879

World Commission on Environment and Development. (1987). *Brundtland' Report: Our Common Future*. https://sustainabledevelopment.un.org

ADDITIONAL READING

Altman, E. I., Sabato, G., & Wilson, N. (2010). The value of non-financial information in small and medium-sized enterprise risk management. *The Journal of Credit Risk*, *6*(2), 95–127. doi:10.21314/JCR.2010.110

Cardinaels, E., & van Veen-Dirks, P. M. G. (2010). Financial versus non-financial information: The impact of information organization and presentation in a Balanced Scorecard. *Accounting, Organizations and Society*, *35*(6), 565–578. doi:10.1016/j.aos.2010.05.003

Mio, C., & Venturelli, A. (2013). Non-financial Information About Sustainable Development and Environmental Policy in the Annual Reports of Listed Companies: Evidence from Italy and the UK. *Corporate Social Responsibility and Environmental Management*, *20*(6), 340–358. doi:10.1002/csr.1296

Perrini, F. (2006). The practitioner's perspective on non-financial reporting. *California Management Review*, *48*(2), 73–103. doi:10.2307/41166339

Sierra-García, L., García-Benau, M. A., & Bollas-Araya, H. M. (2018). Empirical Analysis of Non-Financial Reporting by Spanish Companies. *Administrative Sciences*, *8*(3), 29. doi:10.3390/admsci8030029

Stolowy, H., & Paugam, L. (2018). The expansion of non-financial reporting: An exploratory study. *Accounting and Business Research*, *48*(5), 525–548. doi:10.1080/00014788.2018.1470141

Wyatt, A. (2008). What financial and non-financial information on intangibles is value-relevant? A review of the evidence. *Accounting and Business Research*, *38*(3), 217–256. doi:10.1080/00014788.2008.9663336

KEY TERMS AND DEFINITIONS

Corporate Annual Reports: Reports presented by the directors of a company to its shareholders each year, containing financial and non-financial information.

Corporate Social Responsibility: The responsibility of companies for their impacts on society, with respect for applicable legislation, and for collective agreements between social partners and with their stakeholders on issues related to integrate social, environmental, ethical, human rights and consumer concerns.

Integrated Reporting: Communication about how a company or organization's strategy, governance, performance, and prospects lead to the creation of value over the short, medium and long term.

Literature Mapping: Studies based on literature mapping review and show how literature is disseminated through scientific and academic journals, but they do not discuss the findings. It focuses on characteristics such as journals' impact, years of publication, countries considered, authors of the researches, methodologies employed, among other characteristics.

Non-Financial Information: Certain information on the way companies operate and manage social and environmental challenges, in relation to environmental protection, social responsibility and treatment of employees, respect for human rights, anti-corruption and bribery, and diversity on company boards.

Sustainability: It focuses on meeting the economic, environmental, and social needs of the present without compromising the ability of future generations to meet their own needs.

Sustainable Development: Development that meets the economic, environmental, and social needs of the present without compromising the ability of future generations to meet their own needs.

Chapter 6
Socially Responsible Attitudes and Behaviours:
How to Fulfil the Sustainable Development Goals

Dolores Gallardo Vazquez
https://orcid.org/0000-0003-4749-6034
University of Extremadura, Spain

Shafat Maqbool
Cluster University, Srinagar, India

Juan de la Cruz Sánchez-Domínguez
https://orcid.org/0000-0003-4830-193X
University of Extremadura, Spain

ABSTRACT

The 2030 Agenda implies an important commitment that should be achieved by companies, countries, and governments, and the goals set should be worked on with the aim to boost the areas they address. Corporate social responsibility is a tool for organizations to act on behalf not only of the public but also of all stakeholders, as affirmed by the stakeholders' theory. Given the interest the stakeholders have in achieving the Sustainable Development Goals, it is important to observe the attitudes and behaviors that the organizations develop to achieve their intended contribution. This chapter analyzes the companies´ attitudes and behaviors developed to fulfill five SDGs (from 1 to 5). The study is focused on the content analysis of the corporate social responsibility reports of 16 car manufacturing companies. At the end, the authors propose some future lines of research.

DOI: 10.4018/978-1-7998-8065-3.ch006

INTRODUCTION

Sustainability is a very up-to-date and necessary topic in organizations, so it has been widely researched during the last years. Companies have been working with a new orientation in which the *Triple Bottom Line* perspective (Elkington, 2000) is crucial, so the social, economic, and environmental dimensions are the areas where organizations should act if they want to achieve sustainable development (Gallardo-Vázquez, Sánchez-Hernández & Corchuelo, 2013).

The strategy being used by the organizations to achieve sustainability is Corporate Social Responsibility (CSR). The *Green Paper. Promoting a European framework for Corporate Social Responsibility* (Commission of the European Communities, 2001, p. 7) defines CSR as "a concept whereby companies integrate social and environmental concerns in their business operations and in their interaction with their stakeholders on a voluntary basis". Later, the European Commission (2011) remarked the responsibility of the organizations for their impacts on society, and they explicitly stated the need for interested parties to collaborate to "integrate social, environmental and ethical concerns, the respect of human rights and consumer concerns in their operations and basic strategy" (European Commission, 2011, p. 7).

The concern for sustainability has been a hot topic for international institutions, among them, the Global Pact for the Environment from which the Principles of the Global Pact are derived. Said principles originate from declarations of the United Nations about human rights, labour, the environment, and corruption, and have universal consensus. Later, the United Nations Programme for Development (UNPD) defined, in 2000, the Millennium Development Goals (MDGs), based on the opinions from world leaders reunited in summits. Countries assumed the compromise for a new global alliance to reduce poverty, and they established 8 goals and the limit of 2015 to reach an optimal development. After the implementation and development period, in 2015 the following improvements had been made: 1) the amount of people living in poverty had decreased by half; 2) the percentage of malnourished people in the regions in development had decreased to almost half since 1990; 3) the amount of children in primary school age who did not go to school decreased by half globally; 4) the death rate of children under 5 had decreased by more than half; 5) since 1990 the maternal mortality rate had decreased by 45% globally; and 6) infections of HIV decreased by 40% between 2000 and 2013.

As these results prove, it is evident that the efforts of governments, the international community and the private sector have decisively contributed to increase hope and opportunities worldwide. But that was considered insufficient, and in 2015 world leaders adopted another set of global goals, the so-called Sustainable Development Goals (SDGs). Again, poverty should be eradicated, the planet protected, and prosperity assured for all. 17 SDGs were proposed, with specific objectives, which should be reached during the next 15 years.

The SDGs' main achievement is a change in the attitude and behaviour of all the stakeholders of organizations. Following the stakeholders' theory, the goal each organization should achieve is the maximization of value for all the actors related to it (owners, shareholders, customers, suppliers, employees, civil society, public administrations, etc.). It is necessary that each actor creates value for the organization, while at the same time the organization influences the groups related to it. Owing to that, it is crucial to know the attitudes and behaviours of the stakeholders if we want to achieve the SDGs. Following this idea, the main purpose of this chapter is to analyze how companies fulfill SDGs 1 to 5, which form one of the *5 Ps of Sustainable Development* as defined in the 2030 Agenda for Sustainable Development, specifically the P of *People*. We consider that, in addition to being important from the point of view of the SDGs, it is also important from the perspective of stakeholder theory and legitimacy. As we have previously stated, a good approach by the companies to the SDGs will determine the satisfaction of the interest groups as well as the position of legitimacy in the market, which such brands will value for the value creation that this entails and the competitive advantages that they can achieve. In this sense, we will make special emphasis on the attitudes and behaviour of companies that develop with a view to achieving the set actions and objectives. In this sense, the research tries to cover the following research questions: Has the 2030 Agenda determined the concern in companies for the well-being of interest groups and society? Is the behaviour of the companies consistent with the achievement of the SDGs? Can this provoke an attitude of commitment, of belonging, of pride, of satisfaction in general, for the stakeholders? Does this behaviour of companies determine competitive advantage and creation of value for companies?

In this chapter, after the theoretical background, focused on CSR, the MDGs and the SDGs, the attitudes and behaviours of the stakeholders have towards the fulfilment of the SDGs will be analysed. It is a theoretical and descriptive study which will define an orientation for the organizations and its stakeholders. The methodology used will be a content analysis, and the qualitative analysis is addressed with Cmaptools software v 6.04, improving the perceptions of the actions for stakeholders and readers. 17 reports of 16 car manufacturing companies have been selected, and the level of information they give about the SDGs has been analysed. For the reports that give detailed explanations of how the companies contribute to the fulfilment of the SDGs, both the practices and the specific targets they fulfil have been studied.

BACKGROUND

Corporate Social Responsibility

Corporate social responsibility has emerged as an important concept in management literature. Earlier, the companies were only serving the interests of investors and pursued only those business activities that increased the value of the shares. In the later part of the 20th century, making profit was considered insufficient, and it became fashionable for the companies to build an inclusive corporate functioning that serves society holistically (Maqbool and Zamir, 2019). CSR in its modern sense can be traced back to the 1950s, when Howard Bowen suggested that business must function by societal norms. Bowen and Johnson (1953) affirmed that "the obligations of businessmen are to pursue those policies, to make those decisions, or to follow those lines of action which are desirable in terms of the objectives and values of our society". (p .44). This led to serious academic debates about what constitutes CSR and how it can be defined (Carroll, 1999; Carroll and Shabana, 2010). Freeman contributed to this theoretical debate by specifying the practice of CSR. Freeman (1984) defined CSR from the perspective of stakeholders. He emphasized that companies should fulfill expectations of all those "who are directly or indirectly affected by the choices and the activities of the firm" (p. 31). The pyramid of Carroll is central to the understanding of CSR. Carroll affirmed that "corporate social responsibility encompasses the economic, legal, ethical and discretionary (philanthropic) expectations that society has of organizations at a given point in time" (Carroll, 1979, p. 500). CSR is a broad term that constitutes diverse activities. Most authors define it around the five dimensions; environmental, social, economic, stakeholder and charity dimension (Dahlsrud, 2008).

With time the composition and practice of CSR changed, given that it is a socially determined practice (Deegan and Gordon, 1996). There are different debates regarding CSR theory and practice (Maqbool and Hurrah, 2020). CSR has been mainly theorized using the legitimacy and stakeholders' theories.

Stakeholder Theory

Freeman (1984) provided a solid foundation for the stakeholders' theory. Stakeholders include "any group or individual who can affect or be affected by the fulfilment of the organizations' objectives" (Freeman, 1984, p. 46). Clarkson (1995) defined stakeholders as "people or groups that have, or claim to have, ownership, rights, or interests in a corporation and its activities, past, present, or future" (p. 106). Stakeholders are an important part of the company, and their satisfaction is vital to compete in the market (Maqbool and Bakr, 2019). The survival of the organization depends on the primary stakeholders, like customers, investors, employees, and suppliers. The participation of these stakeholders is vital for the functioning of the organization and creates value for their business (Chaudhary et al., 2020).

The stakeholder theory has emerged as an essential mechanism to develop an inclusive approach to corporate functioning and include the rights and claims of non-shareholders. The stakeholder theory proposes that the corporate sector should pursue the interests of all the stakeholders who are affected by the operations of the company (Clarkson, 1995). The satisfied stakeholders are an important capital for the company, and they can impact organizations' performance and reputation in the long run (Maqbool, 2019). The stakeholders' theory incorporates the expectations of different stakeholders by making 'satisfying stakeholders' the primary objective of the business. Clarkson (1995) elucidates that the stakeholders' theory re-conceptualizes the responsibilities of the business by specifying its practices. Under this approach, the company is expected to specify the stakeholders of the company and target each group with a certain policy to ensure its responsibilities are settled. CSR helps firms in building strong ties with stakeholders, which yields several benefits such as lower risk, enhanced reputation, and competitive advantage (Schmelzer, 2013). The CSR practices directed by the stakeholders´ theory leads to the success in achieving the organizational goals. Therefore, the companies that voluntarily disclose CSR information with quantitative data while catering to stakeholders across-the-board are adopting the stakeholder theory perspective.

Legitimacy Theory

The ethical functioning of company is geared towards enhancing the company's reputation and invariably legitimizes the corporate practices. Suchman (1995) defines legitimacy as "a generalized perception or assumption that the actions of an entity are desirable, proper, or appropriate within some socially constructed system of norms, values, beliefs and definitions" (p. 574). Dowling & Pfeffer (1975) defined legitimacy as "a condition or status which exists when an entity's value system is congruent with the value system of the larger social system of which the entity is a part" (p. 122). The legitimacy for the corporate sector is buttressed by the social contract theory, which states that there is an implicit contract between society and the corporate sector. The theory postulates that company agrees to fulfill the societal expectation in return for the approval of companies' objectives and their ultimate survival. The interests of society and the corporate sector converge, and a positive relationship is beneficial for both society and the corporate sector (Maqbool and Zamir, 2019). In return for providing the basic operating structure for the corporate sector, society expects that the firm has obligations, including moral obligations to a broad range of stakeholders (Adams and Hardwick, 1998). The legitimacy theory elucidates how the company deals with the stakeholders and creates congruence between social norm and corporate functioning for the survival. The perception of society and communication with society are two important drivers of legitimacy. The companies need to continuously evolve and create different strategies to serve the expectations of society (Mobus, 2005). Patten (1992) has observed that there is positive influence of sustainable activities on the legitimacy of the company. The reporting of sustainable practices is used as a strategic instrument to bridge the legitimacy gap in the functioning of the company. Companies continuously communicate with different stakeholders to keep them informed about responsible practices and policies of the company. This communication is the bedrock for the trust between the corporate sector and society (Maqbool, 2019).

Sustainable Development Goals

The 21st century is dominated by issues related to environment and sustainable development. Sustainable development is a development that "meets the needs of the present generations without compromising the ability of future generations to meet their own needs" (United Nations General Assembly, 1987, p. 43). The key idea of sustainable development is that in the economic progress and prosperity of the world the sustainability of environment is important. It provides the "framework for the integration of the environment policies and development strategies" (United Nations General Assembly, 1987). The focus of corporate sustainability is on the survival and sustained growth over time (Garg, 2017). It can be achieved through the integration of growth, environmental, and social issues in the corporate policy.

The Brundtland report (1987) has been an important intervention in the sustainable development to focus more on the goals of "socially inclusive and environmentally sustainable economic growth". The report commissioned by the United Nations was released in 1987, and it introduced the concept of sustainable development and the way to proceed to achieve it. In 2000, the Millennium Summit of the United Nations was held to specify the targets under the Millennium Development Goals. In 2015, the UN member states agreed for 17 Sustainable Development Goals (SDGs) with the main aims of ending poverty, protecting the planet, and ensuring peace and prosperity by 2030. Under the SDGs 17 goals with 169 targets have been set to achieve the vision of the 2030 Agenda for Sustainable Development. These 17 goals are No Poverty, Zero Hunger, Good Health and Well-being, Quality Education, Gender Equality, Clean Water and Sanitation, Affordable and Clean Energy, Decent Work and Economic Growth, Industry, Innovation and Infrastructure, Reducing Inequality, Sustainable Cities and Communities, Responsible Consumption and Production, Climate Action, Life Below Water, Life on Land, Peace, Justice and Strong Institutions and Partnerships for the Goals.

The corporate sector has been actively involved in pursuing those SDG targets and reporting these activities to achieve the voluntary goals or those required by country laws (Gupta and Gupta, 2019). The corporate sector is vital to the achievement of SDGs and is increasingly included in the corporate strategies (Lloret, 2016). Corporate firms are increasingly integrating the global demands defined in SDGs-2030 and other commitment related to stakeholders. Different corporate frameworks have been developed, such as global reporting initiative and UN's global compact to integrate the agenda-2030 into the corporate functioning. It has leaded to different product and process innovations at micro-level.

Sustainable reporting has been at the core of managing the relationship with the stakeholders of the company. Reporting of non- financial information is integral part of the corporate strategy (Ghosh, 2017). The information reported in business responsibility reports, annual reports and sustainability reports is perceived as a commitment towards the SDGs and towards the primary stakeholders (Raman, 2006). The growing recognition of sustainability and its reporting gives companies strategic edge in the competitive market. It gives sense of trust and curates strong relationship with the stakeholders.

ANALYSIS OF THE SUSTAINABILITY REPORTS

Content Analysis: Companies, Sustainability Reports and SDGs Analyzed

Once the main purpose of the chapter has been established, we decided to focus on SDGs number 1 to 5, because those are the best SDGs to analyze which attitudes and behaviors companies have towards people, both in and outside the organizations. 17 sustainability reports are analyzed, corresponding to 16 car manufacturing groups. Since some of the reports not only include the car manufacturing activities, but also other activities (like motorbike manufacturing, boat engines manufacturing, steel manufacturing, etc.), the reports have been divided in two groups in Table 1: A) those of car manufacturing-only groups and B) those of industrial groups that have more than one field of activity (including either manufacturing trucks and/or buses and/or commercial vehicles and/or other products), as shown in the reports. Car parts manufacturing (like engines and transmissions, when they are manufactured in house) are included in “car manufacturing”, and the same goes for the other vehicle manufacturing activities and their parts. Financial services are included as part of the vehicle manufacturing activities (cars or others), except when explicitly included in the report as a part of the company working for not only car manufacturing, but also other organizations of the group (Table 1). In Table 2 more information about the reports and their scope is shown.

Figure 1 shows the continent of origin of the 16 groups studied. Specifically, 9 groups come from Asia, 6 from Europe and 1 from North America. It is worth noting that there are 17 reports of 16 brands because we have analyzed two different reports from the Ford Motor Company: their Sustainability Report and the United Nations SDGs Index.

Table 1. Manufacturing groups classified by their fields of activity, as shown in the reports

A) Car manufacturing-only groups	B) Groups that have more than one field of activity
BMW (although it makes motorcycles, the sustainability report is only about the car manufacturing activities of BMW, Mini and Rolls-Royce) Ferrari Mazda Mitsubishi (the report is specifically for Mitsubishi Motors Co.) Nissan Motor Co. Subaru	Daimler (manufactures cars, commercial vehicles, trucks, and buses) Fiat-Chrysler Automobiles (FCA; manufactures cars and commercial vehicles) Ford Motor Co. (manufactures cars, commercial vehicles, and trucks) Honda (manufactures cars, motorcycles, power products, aircraft, and aircraft engines) Hyundai (manufactures cars, commercial vehicles, steel, and offers construction and financial services among others) PSA (manufactures cars and commercial vehicles) Suzuki (manufactures cars, motorcycles, and outboard motors, among others) Tata Motors (manufactures cars, commercial vehicles, buses, trucks, and defense vehicles) Toyota (manufactures cars and commercial vehicles) Volkswagen (manufactures cars, motorcycles, commercial vehicles, trucks, and buses)

Source: The authors

Table 2. Information about the reports analyzed in this chapter

Brand	Year	Type of report	Information about the SDGs	Pages
BMW	2019	Sustainable Value Report	Explicit, detailed, and specific for each section of the report	142
Daimler	2019	Sustainability Report	Not explicit, SDGs only used as "important guidelines for decisions"	205
FCA	2019	Sustainability Report	Explicit, detailed, and specific for each section of the report	159
Ferrari	2019	Sustainability Report	Explicit but not detailed, sustainability approach only	136
Ford Motor Co.	2020	Sustainability Report & SDG Index	Not present in the report, but explicit, detailed, and specific in the SDG Index	54 & 14
Honda	2020	Sustainability Report	Explicit and detailed in one section of the report	183
Hyundai Group	2019	CSR Report	Explicit, detailed, and specific for each company of the group	64
Mazda	2020	Sustainability Report	Explicit and detailed in one section of the report	142
Mitsubishi Motors Co.	2020	Sustainability Report	Explicit, detailed, and specific for each section of the report	121
Nissan Motor Co.	2020	Sustainability Report	Explicit and detailed in one section of the report	255
PSA	2019	CSR Report	Explicit, detailed, and specific for each section of the report	308
Subaru	2020	CSR Report	Explicit and detailed in one section of the report	174
Suzuki	2019	CSR & Environmental Report	Explicit, detailed, and specific for each section of the report	160
Tata Motors	2019-20	CSR Report	Explicit and detailed in one section of the report	44
Toyota	2020	Environmental Report	Explicit and detailed in one section of the report	42
Volkswagen Group	2019	Sustainability Report	Not explicit, SDGs only used as guidelines for the creation of the report	100

Source: The authors

The 2030 Agenda established what we know as *the 5 Ps of Sustainable Development*. Our analysis focuses on one of the Ps, specifically on the group of SDGs destined for people, which the United Nations (2015, p. 5) defined as "The determination to end poverty and hunger, in all their forms and dimensions, and to ensure that all human beings can fulfil their potential in dignity and equality and in a healthy environment". The other four Ps, not analysed in this report, are "planet", "prosperity", "peace" and "partnerships". The SDGs that contribute towards the increase of wellbeing for people are goals 1 to 5, which are described in Table 3.

Every action or activity included in the tables below is seen as a CSR practice that the organization does to fulfil its responsibilities, in any of the dimensions of the concept (economic, social and/ or environmental). Due to the amount of information available, and to improve readability, only some examples of the actions undertaken by the organizations are shown in the tables, and the content analysis is divided by the continent of origin of the different groups. As shown in Table 2 above, Daimler and Volkswagen do not give any explicit information about their contribution to the fulfilment of the SDGs, so their reports are not included in the analysis.

Figure 1. Number of companies per continent
Source: The authors

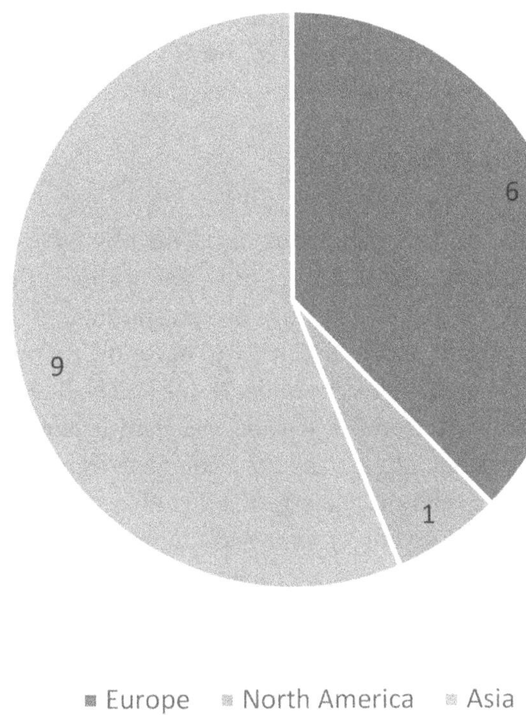

Table 3. Sustainable Development Goals analysed in this chapter

Sustainable Development Goal	Description
Goal 1	End poverty in all its forms everywhere
Goal 2	End hunger, achieve food security and improved nutrition and promote sustainable agriculture
Goal 3	Ensure healthy lives and promote wellbeing for all at all ages
Goal 4	Ensure inclusive and equitable quality education and promote lifelong learning opportunities for all
Goal 5	Achieve gender equality and empower all women and girls

Source: United Nations (2015)

Content Analysis: About the Methodology

The content analysis method is very used in literature (Krippendorf, 1980) because: (1) this is a dominant research method for collecting empirical evidence on social and environmental accounting (Adnan *et al.*, 2018), and (2) because it is a research technique for making replicable and valid inferences from data according to their context (Krippendoff, 1980). Content analysis is understood as a useful methodological technique by which a text is categorized by following a predetermined set of procedures with the aim to make valid summarization and replicable by interpreting and coding textual data. Frequently, it starts from the collecting data and then defines unit of analysis, development of categories and coding scheme, testing of coding scheme on sample text, code all text, asses coding consistency, drawing conclusion from coding data and reporting method and findings, tracking, and quantifying certain words or content to the text in order to understand the contextual use of words. This way, we developed a coding sheet and a set of rules for coding the texts. Qualitative analysis is addressed with Cmaptools software v 6.04.

Content Analysis of the Ford Motor Co.

The Ford Motor Co. believes that SDGs 1 and 2 are not fulfilled by its operations, so no information is included about them. Table 4 shows the SDGs-related CSR practices the Ford Motor Co. applies, mainly oriented to SDGs 3 to 5. To assure a healthy life and promote wellbeing (SDG 3), the Ford Motor Co. creates new technologies to improve security to halve the number of global deaths and injuries from road traffic accidents by 2020. To ensure inclusive and equitable quality education, and to promote lifelong learning opportunities for all (SDG 4), the Ford Motor Co. has established literacy programs with the aim of ensuring that all girls and boys complete free, equitable and quality primary and secondary education leading to relevant and effective learning outcomes by 2030 and to increase and improve the employment abilities of young people and adults, so that they can have decent jobs and foster entrepreneurship. Finally, to achieve gender equality and empower all women and girls, and to fight against discrimination against all women and girls everywhere, the Ford Motor Co. has signed the UN's Women Empowerment Principles and created the Ford. According to the theoretical framework established, these practices satisfy the needs of all the Ford Motor Co.'s stakeholders, in line with the stakeholders' theory affirmations, and they also increase and improve the legitimacy of the company, which could in turn cause an increase of the sales.

Table 4. SDGs-related CSR practices applied by the Ford Motor Company in its operations

	SDG 3	SDG 4	SDG 5
Ford	Good results in crash tests assessments, new technologies to enhance safety and make customers feel safe, accelerating implementation of the Automated Emergency Braking system	Filling the skills gap in the industry with initiatives such as the Ford STEAM initiative and Primary Engineer, among others, Ford Driving Dreams early reading and literacy programs, Ford Next Generation Learning	Signing of the Women's Empowerment Principles of the UN, advancing pay for women, Ford's Re-Entry Program

Source: Ford Motor Co. 2020 SDG Index

Through the Cmaptools tool, we have summarized in the following conceptual map (Figure 2), the CSR actions and the indicators that are achieved through such practices.

Figure 2. CSR actions and the indicators from Ford Motor Co
Source: The authors

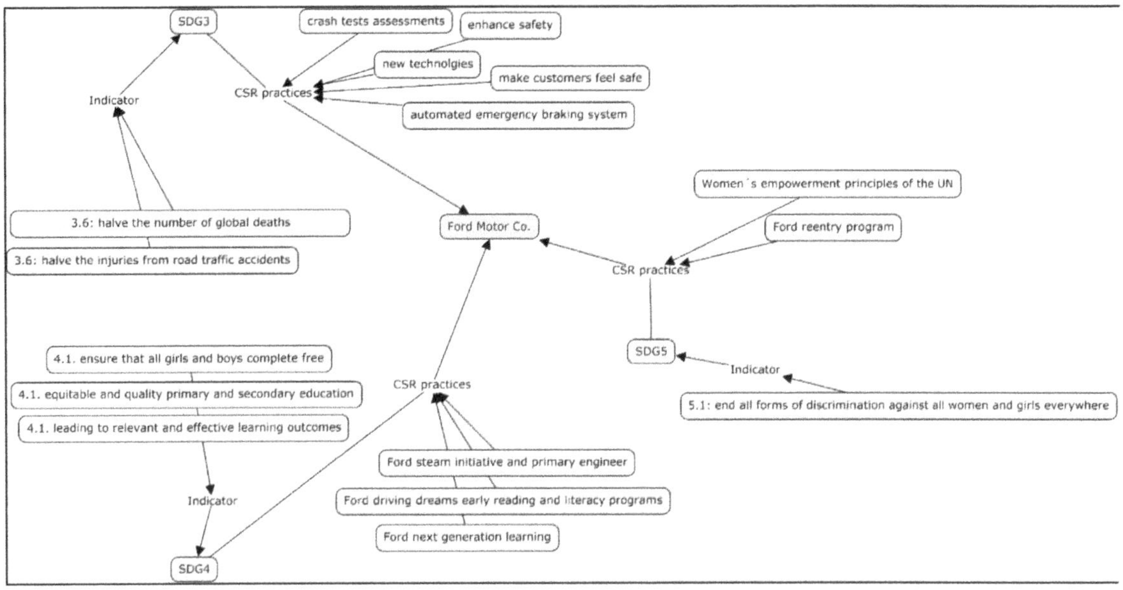

Content Analysis of the European Brands

The European brands carried out actions focused on the five SDGs. Table 5 lists the activities that this companies have developed to contribute to the fulfilment of SDGs 1 to 5. To help end poverty in all its forms everywhere (SDG 1), the analyzed European brands develop the employees' commitment by promoting volunteering actions, and they also use locally sourced raw materials for their manufacturing activities, improving the resilience of the local communities. To end hunger, achieve food security and improved nutrition and promote sustainable agriculture (SDG 2), PSA has supported the French Red Cross with a specially adapted commercial vehicle to tackle the instability caused by the lack of food. These types of initiatives can contribute to end hunger and ensure access by all people to safe, nutritious and sufficient food all year round. To fulfil the SDG number 3, ensuring healthy lives and promote wellbeing for all ages, the organizations are creating new technologies with decrease toxic gas emissions, which will cause an improvement of the employees' health. Companies have also implemented health and safety measures in their manufacturing plants, such as evaluating the risks of each manufacturing phase and process and offering preventive medical care to their employees and their families. Other aims are reducing the number of deaths caused by dangerous chemicals, achieving universal health coverage and making vaccines and basic medicines accessible to all. To ensure inclusive and equitable quality education, and to promote lifelong learning opportunities for all (SDG 4), the companies are allying with universities to combine theoretical and practical learning, improving the abilities of students, and the companies have also created scholarships, offer technical training to employees, and create associations for PhD studies programs. By 2030, companies should ensure equal access to all women and men to affordable and quality technical, vocational, and tertiary education, including universities, increase the number of youth and adults who have relevant skills, including technical and vocational skills, for employment, decent jobs and entrepreneurship, and substantially increase the supply of qualified teachers, including through international cooperation. To achieve gender equality and empower all women and men (SDG 5), the European brands are creating more diverse working forces, promoting the role of women at work, increasing the number of women in positions usually occupied by men and signing the UN's Women Empowerment Principles. Companies want to end all forms of discrimination against all women and girls everywhere, to eliminate all forms of violence against women and girls, to eliminate all harmful practices, to recognize and value unpaid care and domestic work through the provision of services, infrastructure and social protection, to ensure that women participate fully and with equal opportunities in leadership at all levels and to adopt and strengthen sound policies for promoting gender equality and the empowerment of women and girls, and by doing so, satisfying the needs of their stakeholders as the stakeholders' theory suggests. The needed fulfilment of the SDGs by the application of the practices explained above also helps increase the brands' legitimacy, which in turn helps them become more relevant.

Table 5. SDGs-related CSR practices applied by the analyzed European brands in their operations

	SDG 1	SDG 2	SDG 3	SDG 4	SDG 5
BMW	No information provided		Lowering emissions with efficient technologies, taking care of the health of employees by designing work environments appropriately	Developing potential	Having a diverse workforce, expansion of diversity campaigns, offering attractive remuneration high level of diversity in the company, encouraging work-life balance
FCA	Encouragement for employees to lead by example, combining charitable financial donations with volunteering opportunities to address community needs and foster employee engagement, with formal policies that govern employee volunteer efforts in some regions	No information provided	Implementation of health, safety and ergonomics standards, goal of achieving zero injuries, adoption of World Class Manufacturing methodologies and tools, a rigorous manufacturing methodology that involves the entire organization and all phases of production that identifies the potential unsafe acts that could happen while performing an activity, assess all potential related risks and determines proper countermeasures	Alliances with universities to bridge the gap between the classrooms and the company, designed to combine class education with hands-on, industrial experience. This gives the students the opportunity to receive instruction that caters to their career interests while nurturing the skills needed for the workforce of the future	Activities to advance the role of women in the automotive workforce, such as formal processes to ensure the application of the core equity and fairness principles to compensation levels, annual salary reviews and promotions, work-life balance arrangements and events to promote technical careers among women
Ferrari	No information provided		Offering preventive healthcare to employees and their families, free gym membership	Scholarships for junior high, high school and university students, reimbursement of employees' children's textbook costs, technical training by senior to junior employees, creation of department team leaders	Increase of the number of women working for Ferrari in all positions

continues on following page

Table 5. Continued

	SDG 1	SDG 2	SDG 3	SDG 4	SDG 5
PSA	Use of local sourcing for parts and direct materials for their manufacturing plants in Europe, Russia, Latin America, Morocco and Algeria, creation of automobile companies' clusters in Spain and Rio de Janeiro	Support of the *Red Cross on Wheels* program since 2012, using a specially adapted commercial vehicle to offer help and advice to fight against the instability that leads to, among other things, lack of food	Decrease of the emissions of all types of pollutants in all manufacturing plants (air pollutants, SO2, NO2, refrigerants and dangerous chemicals)	Creation of the *Extended University* concept, a partnership between PSA and the French Ministry of National Education which has 65 partner high schools and 600 students throughout France, and a partnership with 30 scientific and management schools for people to study for PhDs within the group.	Signatory of the UN's *Women's Empowerment Principles*, has incorporated objectives of gender balance in key positions, has a zero-tolerance policy on sexism and violence against women and was the first company to receive the *Gender Equality Label* in France in 2005

Sources: BMW Group (2019), Fiat Chrysler Automobiles (2019), Ferrari (2019), Peugeot SA (2019).

Cmaptools graphically expresses the following conceptual map (Figure 3), collecting the CSR actions and the indicators that are achieved through such practices.

Figure 3. CSR actions and the indicators from European brands
Source: The authors

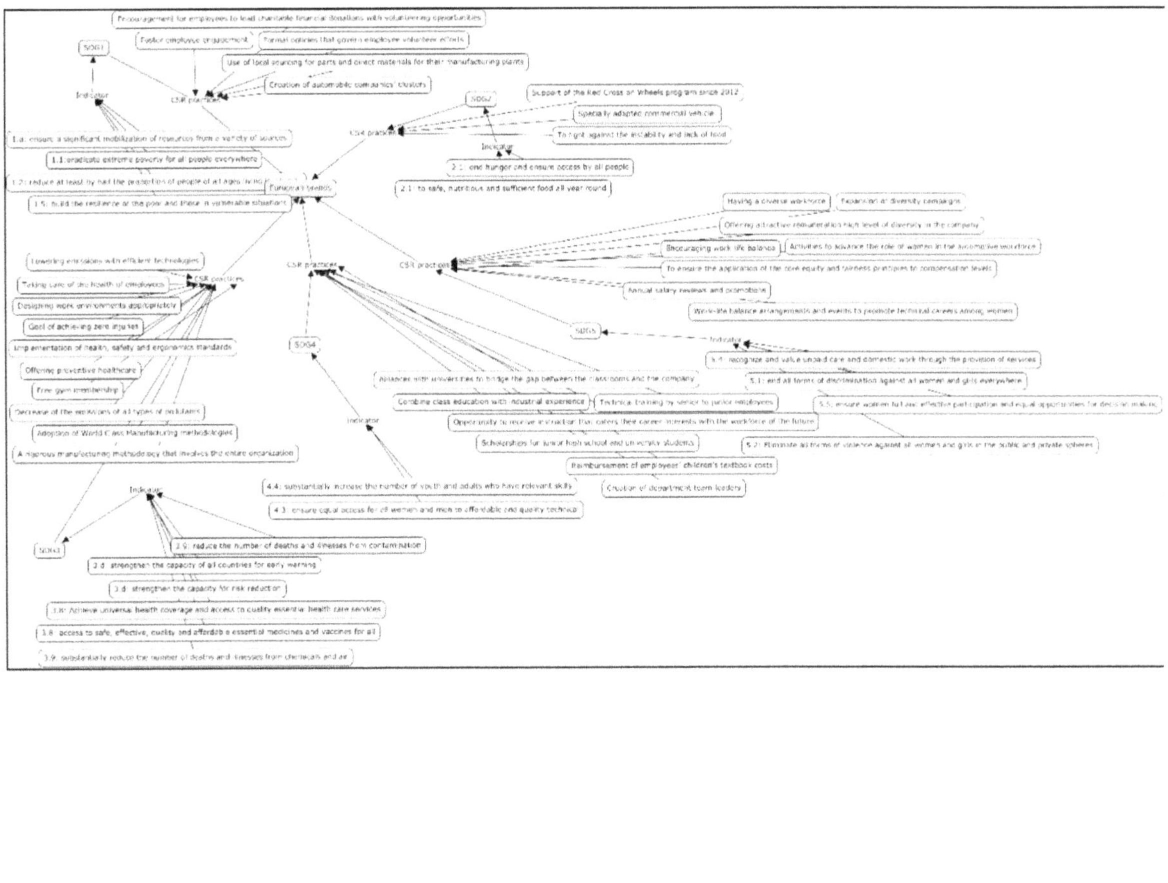

Content Analysis of the Asian Brands

Table 6 shows the SDGs-related CSR practices of the analyzed Asian brands and the indicators they contribute to fulfil. To end poverty in all its forms everywhere (SDG 1), the Asian companies offer products and services for all peoples and cultures, contributing to the economic development of developing countries, there are also projects to promote education, health care and the self-sufficiency of local communities, while orientating themselves towards the creation of a clean, safe and inclusive society with the final aims of eradicating extreme poverty for all people everywhere (measured as people living on less than \$1.25 a day), building the resilience of the poor and reducing their vulnerability to climate-related events and ensuring significant mobilization of resources from a variety of sources to provide adequate and predictable means for developing countries to implement programs and policies to end poverty in all its dimensions. To end hunger, achieve food security and improved nutrition and promote sustainable agriculture (SDG 2), brands are creating efficient mobility means to solve social problems, increasing the use of renewable energies, and the employees are also making donations to social help programs and to initiatives to decrease malnutrition. By increasing the investment in rural infrastructures, agricultural research and extension services and technology development, companies want to end all forms of malnutrition by 2030. To ensure healthy lives and promote wellbeing for all at all ages (SDG 3), the brands are eliminating toxic substances of their exhaust emissions to keep the air clean, promoting the wellbeing of all at all ages, reducing deaths and injuries caused by road accidents, even looking to achieve the goal of halving the deaths related to road traffic accidents by 2020, improving safety, quality, and fuel efficiency, complying with the environmental regulations. To ensure inclusive and equitable quality education and to promote lifelong learning opportunities for all (SDG 4), the Asian brands have implemented capacitation programs of on-the-job training, performance evaluations, provision of development opportunities based in the results of previous evaluations, promotion of the understanding of sustainability among employees and scholarships for students with less economic possibilities. With these actions and practices, the companies want to halve the number of global deaths and injuries by 2020, to increase the number of youths and adults who have relevant skills, including technical and vocational skills, for employment, decent jobs and entrepreneurship by 2030, to ensure that all learners acquire the knowledge and skills needed to promote sustainable development by 2030 and to substantially expand the number of scholarships available in developing countries by 2020. To achieve gender equality and empower all women and girls (SDG 5), the Asian brands are working to diversify their work force, promoting diversity, developing programs to help achieve work-life balance, flexible work, telework, allowing employees to show their potential and committing with women of local communities to help them get some extra income by creating agricultural programs. The Asian companies want to end all discrimination against girls and women everywhere, to ensure the full participation of women in leadership roles, promoting equality and empowering girls and women, while improving technology to help them achieve their aims.

Through the Cmaptools tool, we have summarized in the following conceptual map (Figure 4), the CSR actions and the indicators that are achieved through such practices.

Once the numerous and diverse practices carried out by the studied brands have been analyzed, we carry out a discussion of the results and present the conclusions of the chapter, while presenting future lines of research

Table 6. SDGs-related CSR activities undertook by the analysed Asian companies in their operations

	SDG 1	SDG 2	SDG 3	SDG 4	SDG 5
Honda	Contributing to the economic development of countries in development by offering products and services optimized for all people reflecting different cultures and values and diverse societies, irrespective of whether they are in developed or in development nations	Providing efficient means of mobility to resolve help social issues, such as an increase in the number of people having less mobility options and to increase the ratio of renewable energy use by connecting renewable energies with Honda products	Ensure clean air by eliminating harmful substances in exhaust emissions, change of motorcycle engines to four stroke engines, achieving a collision-free society	On-the-job training, building specialized skills and professional capabilities through direct experience, establishment of a job description and area of expertise for each job with systemized contents and levels for the knowledge and skills required	Workforce diversification as a company-wide priority task, to demonstrate the total strength of the workforce, creation of a Diversity Promotion Office, creation of a foundation to achieve a world where people can develop their careers regardless of gender
Hyundai	Creation of the *Green Light Project* in 2012 to promote education, healthcare, and self-reliance of local communities in underdeveloped countries, by first identifying the needs of citizens and then providing continuous support for the next three to five years to develop the region	The *Miracle of 1%*, started in 2012 in partnership with the Community Chest of Korea, is a social contribution program where Hyundai employees voluntarily donate 1% of their salaries to help local communities via projects chosen by the 1% Sharing Council	Since 1998 Hyundai USA, alongside its dealers, has been running the campaign *Hope on Wheels*, a campaign that supports child cancer research and that has the aim to create a future where no child suffers from cancer	Hyundai's *Traffic Safety Campaign with Robocar Poli* started in 2010 to guarantee the safety of children around the world, and developed 26 episodes of an animated series which is aired in 82 countries around the world, and 19 traffic safety experience centers have been created for hands-on experiences	Hyundai Steel supported the construction of a job training centre for women and youth in the Philippines, and through job training, training of educators and income generating activities this project is bringing about social change
Mazda	No information provided		Ensure healthy lives and promote wellbeing for all at all ages, halve the number of global deaths and injuries from road traffic accidents, reduce illnesses and deaths from hazardous chemicals and pollution, double the improvement in energy efficiency	No information provided	
Mitsubishi	No information provided		Expansion of green procurement guidelines, proper management of hazardous substances in the products, development of fuel economy improving technologies, reduce air pollutants from the plants by voluntarily enacting standards stricter than legal requirement	On and off-the-job training initiatives such as the enhancement of objective ability assessments, performance evaluations, checks of the preferred career, provision of development opportunities based on the results of previous assessments	Activities promoting LGTBQIA+ awareness, work-life balance assistance programs such as pregnancy and maternity leaves, flexible time systems, telecommuting system, accompanying leave
Nissan	Creating a cleaner, safer, and more inclusive society where everyone is given equal opportunities through community engagement activities	Providing supplies and support to the areas affected by natural disasters, ascertaining their needs	Reduce the traffic fatalities by taking measures in the areas of vehicles, individuals, and society, improving air pollution in urban areas using zero emission vehicles	Provision of educational programs that make use of the knowledge and technologies built up during business activities, promotion of the understanding of sustainability among employees, sales companies, business partners and others	Support of the advancement of women in the workplace globally through diversity, inclusion and community engagement activities, establishing an inclusive organization where individual employees with diverse backgrounds can demonstrate their potential to the fullest

continues on following page

Table 6. Continued

	SDG 1	SDG 2	SDG 3	SDG 4	SDG 5
Subaru	No information provided		Become a company that provides the utmost peace of mind to all stakeholders, by achieving the goal of zero fatal traffic accidents by 2030, by improving safety functions, by improving inspection and maintenance quality and by creating a safe workplace, among other activities	No information provided	Promotion of active roles for female employees, promotion of diverse work styles, use of diverse workforce, expansion of diverse forms of employment
Suzuki	No information provided		Improvement in fuel efficiency, development of next generation vehicles, reduction of hazardous substances and use of alternatives, seminars about traffic safety	Suzuki Foundation, Suzuki Education and Culture Foundation, educational support activities to introduce current industrial status	Actions to promote participation by women, such as reinforcing public relations for recruitment, reinforcing human resources development to support active participation by female employees and expanding the system as the base for further active participation by female employees
Tata Motors	No information provided	The health initiative focuses on addressing malnutrition on children between 0 and 6 years of age. Apart from providing a supplementary diet to malnourished children, the focus has been on working on preventive measures like enabling behavioral changes in communities, and there are also curative health care services where the communities are serviced through diagnosis, administration of generic medicines and consultations		Educational programs aimed at secondary school level that give scholarships for financially challenged students, giving support classes for difficult subjects, co-curricular activities and plugging gaps in infrastructure	Engagement with community-based groups of women and farmers, which get help earning extra income through the company's agriculture and allied programs
Toyota	No information provided		Chemical substances management implementation considering the legal trends in each region and country, promote activities to reduce waste globally, implement initiatives to reduce and recycle plastic use in packaging, compliance with environmental regulations and proactively prevent environmental risks	No information provided	

Sources: Honda (2020), Hyundai Motor Group (2019), Mazda (2020), Mitsubishi (2020), Nissan (2020), Subaru (2020), Suzuki (2019), Tata Motors (2020), Toyota (2020)

Figure 4. CSR actions and the indicators from Asian brands
Source: The authors

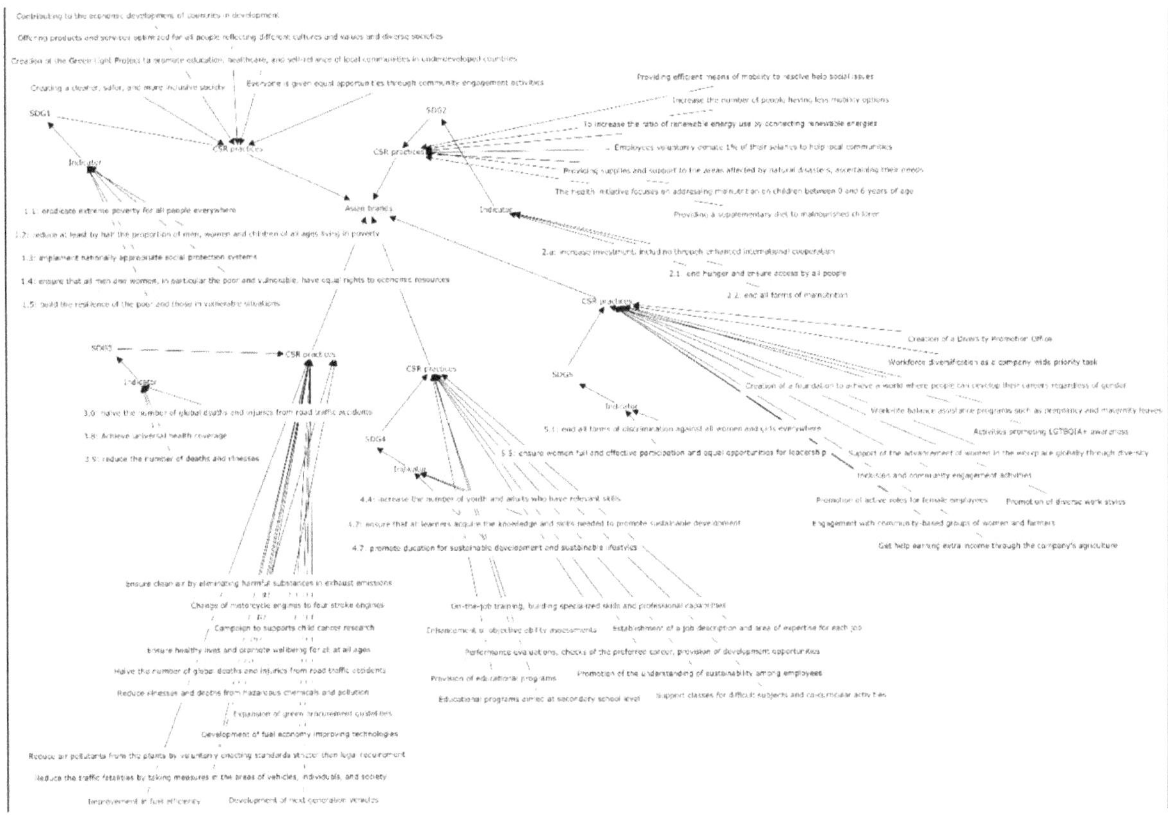

DISCUSSION

The analysis made above shows that the analyzed companies focus their actions in various targets, mainly 1) reducing the deaths in road accidents, 2) reducing the deaths caused by dangerous chemical pollutants, 3) reducing the discrimination against women and LGTBQ+ people, 4) increasing and improving the training of relevant skills for the company, both inside the organizations and in universities, 5) increase early training for children in primary and secondary schools and 6) help to reduce poverty by doing voluntary and charity work. In this sense, our research is in harmony with the results of previous works, being able to state that the literature has not stopped showing the focus of these objectives (Debnath et al., 2017; Jelonek and Urbaniec, 2019; Miotto et al., 2019; Salvioni et al., 2017; Sánchez-Medina et al., 2017). We believe that stakeholders receive focused attention in different areas, as can be seen from the approaches undertaken. Undoubtedly, the demands of numerous interest groups are attended, and behaviors which will determine their satisfaction and commitment to the organization to which they belong are implemented. Thus, the behavior of the companies in the sample follows an interest groups approach, as postulated by the stakeholder theory. Not only the needs of the customers are satisfied, but the companies also take care of their employees, suppliers and of the communities they are a part of.

By applying these practices, the organizations hope to fulfil the stakeholders' interests, and by doing so they hope to increase their reputation in the long run. Since society provides the organizations with the basic structure they need for their operations, actions like the ones studied above are needed to fulfil the expectations not only of the shareholders, but of society. As in the previous groups of brands, the actions undertook by the organizations are oriented towards the satisfaction of the needs and wellbeing of all stakeholders, as the stakeholders' theory assures. The practices being applied to fulfil the SDGs also help increase the legitimacy of the brands, improving their reputation and importance in the sector. In this sense, we find a clear link between the subject studied and the theoretical framework based on the stakeholder and legitimacy theories. A set of practices as broad as the ones we have just described show that brands pay great attention to the needs of their stakeholders, seeking to maximize their satisfaction through the implementation of actions, practices, and processes, while creating value for their business and, therefore, competitive advantage (Schmelzer, 2013; Chaudhary et al., 2020). At the same time, stakeholders feel satisfied, cared for and motivated, are proud of belonging to these companies and working for them, and that translates into gaining legitimacy in the sector in which they operate, a situation that benefits society so much. as well as the organization (Maqbool, 2019; Maqbool and Zamir, 2019).

After carrying out the study we can say that the research questions proposed at the beginning of the chapter have been answered. We can see how the 2030 Agenda has determined a clear and constant concern in these companies for the well-being of interest groups and society, even with some brands not offering specific information about the SDGs, but only using them as guidelines for preparing their reports. In this sense, the behavior of the brands has been decisive and consistent for the achievement of the SDGs. It is evident that the interest groups related to each of these brands shows commitment, belonging, satisfaction, and that this will determine the competitive advantage that will make these companies stand out, at the same time as the creation of value pursued.

CONCLUSION

This chapter focuses on sustainability, and specifically, in Sustainable Development. Based on the concept of CSR as a tool that eases the companies' path towards sustainable development, the chapter focuses on the fulfilment of 5 SDGs.

Applying CSR, voluntarily integrating actions in the economic, social and environmental dimensions is the beginning of the fulfilment of the 2030 Agenda. This document encourages countries, governments, businesses, and individuals to work together to fulfil a very heterogeneous set of goals and targets. This change is based on a change of attitude of all people and entities, and so, the postulates of the stakeholders' theory should be considered, and their needs be satisfied. It is undoubtable that, by taking stakeholders into account, the organizations will see their legitimacy increased in the context in which they exist, and the benefits of applying CSR actions will be numerous. This will also mean the survival of the stakeholders, of the public, of the planet and organizations, and value will be created.

About the practical implications of this study, we can affirm that companies by applying these actions can help achieve the reduction and ending of poverty, the deaths in road accidents, the deaths caused by the use of dangerous chemicals, the end of discrimination against women, the improvement in learning relevant abilities and competencies and a better learning for children in schools. This small sample of companies greatly helps to fulfil 5 SDGs, what we consider a very significant contribution towards the achievement of the 2030 Agenda. If every business and individual starts caring and acting, the SDGs will be fulfilled, and compliance with the agenda would be very positive and broad, an action that requires a commitment from all companies, as broad as the one we have analysed. That's what should be everyone's goal, both of organizations and of individuals, because sustainable development is of interest for all.

Related to the contributions of the study, it offers numerous results, owing to the number of SDGs being analysed and the extension of targets and topics covered. The contribution of this chapter is twofold: first, the academic literature is increased with a qualitative study, and secondly, it offers managers a clear base of actions to be undertaken if they want their organizations to contribute to sustainable development. Finally, the chapter is a guide for governments, which should design policies and orientations to ease companies' implementation of sustainable development.

The study has shown how companies act to achieve the goal of sustainable development, and attitudes that can be an example for other organizations of how actions should be undertaken to keep improving sustainability.

FUTURE RESEARCH DIRECTIONS

After analysing the actions undertaken by 16 different multinationals to reach sustainable development, the contribution of this chapter is significative. We have observed a myriad of practices, with very diverse targets, to fulfil the first five SDGs. Our research has focused on an analysis content of the sustainability reports of each group, and it can be expanded with other perspectives. For example, our analysis could be completed by research that focuses on the different stakeholders of the organizations, who could offer first-hand information about their personal and professional satisfaction, the conditions of their workplace, the achievements they see on the people they work with, their communities, the planet, the ending of poverty, etc. Thus, this study could be complemented by a qualitative study that confirms, from another point of view, the fulfilment of the SDGs. Secondly, our analysis could be complemented with a quantitative study, based on the definition and preparation of a questionnaire, which would be answered by managers and other stakeholders, to get their points of view about the topic being analysed. Thirdly, a similar analysis could be made, but focusing on another group of SDGs, so as to get a broader view of the CSR practices the companies apply. And fourthly, a bibliometric study could be made, in which the existing literature of specific SDGs in a determined period would be analysed.

REFERENCES

Adams, M., & Hardwick, P. (1998). An analysis of corporate donations: United Kingdom evidence. *Journal of Management Studies*, *35*(5), 641–654. doi:10.1111/1467-6486.00113

Adnan, S. M., Hay, D., & Staden, C. J. (2018). The Influence of Culture and Corporate Governance on Corporate Social Responsibility Disclosure: A Cross Country Analysis. *Journal of Cleaner Production*, *198*, 820–832. doi:10.1016/j.jclepro.2018.07.057

Bowen, H. R., & Johnson, F. E. (1953). *Social responsibility of the businessman*. Harper.

Brundtland, G. (1987). *Report of the World Commission on Environment and Development: Our Common Future*. Document A/42/427 of the United Nations.

Carroll, A. B. (1979). A three-dimensional conceptual model of corporate performance. *Academy of Management Review*, *4*(4), 497–505. doi:10.5465/amr.1979.4498296

Carroll, A. B. (1999). Corporate social responsibility: Evolution of a definitional construct. *Business & Society*, *38*(3), 268–295. doi:10.1177/000765039903800303

Carroll, A. B., & Shabana, K. M. (2010). The business case for corporate social responsibility: A review of concepts, research and practice. *International Journal of Management Reviews*, *12*(1), 85–105. doi:10.1111/j.1468-2370.2009.00275.x

Chaudhary, A., Hurrah, S. A., & Maqbool, S. (2020). The Influence of Corporate Social Responsibility on Actual Buying Behaviour: A Study of Indian Consumers. *Metamorphosis*, *19*(1), 21–28. doi:10.1177/0972622520931700

Clarkson, M. E. (1995). A stakeholder framework for analyzing and evaluating corporate social performance. *Academy of Management Review*, *20*(1), 92–117. doi:10.5465/amr.1995.9503271994

Commission for the European Communities. (2001). *Green Paper. Promoting a European framework for Corporate Social Responsibility*. Author.

Dahlsrud, A. (2008). How corporate social responsibility is defined: An analysis of 37 definitions. *Corporate Social Responsibility and Environmental Management*, *15*(1), 1–13. doi:10.1002/csr.132

Daimler Group. (2019). *Sustainability Report*. Author.

Debnath, A., Roy, J., Kar, S., Zavadskas, E., & Antucheviciene, J. (2017). A Hybrid MCDM Approach for Strategic Project Portfolio Selection of Agro By-Products. *Sustainability*, *9*(8), 1302. doi:10.3390u9081302

Deegan, C., & Gordon, B. (1996). A study of the environmental disclosure practices of Australian corporations. *Accounting and Business Research*, *26*(3), 187–199. doi:10.1080/00014788.1996.9729510

Dowling, J., & Pfeffer, J. (1975). Organizational legitimacy: Social values and organizational behavior. *Pacific Sociological Review*, *18*(1), 122–136. doi:10.2307/1388226

Elkington, J. (2000). Cannibals with forks: The triple bottom line of 21st century business. *Journal of Business Ethics*, *23*(2), 229–231. doi:10.1023/A:1006129603978

European Commission. (2011). *Communication from the Commission to the European Parliament, the Council, the European Economic and Social Committee and the Committee of the Regions. A renewed EU strategy 2011-2014 for Corporate Social Responsibility*. European Commission.

Ferrari N. V. (2019). *Sustainability Report*. Author.

Fiat Chrysler Automobiles. (2019). *Sustainability Report*. Author.

Ford Motor Company. (2020). *Sustainability Report*. Author.

Ford Motor Company. (2020). *United Nations Sustainable Development Goals Index*. Author.

Freeman, R. E. (1984). *Strategic management: A stakeholder approach*. Pitman.

Gallardo-Vázquez, D., Sánchez-Hernández, M. I., & Corchuelo-Martínez-Azúa, M. B. (2013). Validación de un instrumento de medida para la relación entre la orientación a la responsabilidad social corporativa y otras variables estratégicas de la empresa. *Spanish Accounting Review. Revista de Contabilidad, 16*(1), 11–23.

Garg, P. (2017). Development of sustainability reporting index (SRI) with special reference to companies in India. *Decision (Washington, D.C.), 44*(4), 259–273.

Ghosh, S. (2017). Reporting of CSR activities in India: are we still at a nascent stage even after the legal mandate? In *Corporate Social Responsibility in India* (pp. 133–147). Springer.

BMW Group. (2019). *Sustainable Value Report.* Author.

Gupta, O., & Gupta, K. (2019). CSR in India: The companies act and its implications. *Journal of Contemporary Management Research, 13*(1), 1–23.

Honda Group. (2020). *Sustainability Report.* Author.

Hyundai Motor Group. (2019). *Global Corporate Social Responsibility Report.* Author.

Jelonek, M., & Urbaniec, M. (2019). Development of Sustainability Competencies for the Labour Market: An Exploratory Qualitative Study. *Sustainability, 11*(20), 5716. https://doi.org/10.3390/su11205716

Krippendorff, K. (1980). *Content análisis: An introduction to its methodology.* Sage.

Lloret, A. (2016). Modeling corporate sustainability strategy. *Journal of Business Research, 69*(2), 418–425.

Maqbool, S. (2019). Does corporate social responsibility lead to superior financial performance? Evidence from BSE 100 index. *Decision (Washington, D.C.), 46*(3), 219–231.

Maqbool, S., & Bakr, A. (2019). The curvilinear relationship between corporate social performance and financial performance. *Journal of Global Responsibility.*

Maqbool, S., & Hurrah, S. A. (2020). Exploring the Bi-directional relationship between corporate social responsibility and financial performance in Indian context. *Social Responsibility Journal.*

Maqbool, S., & Zamir, M. N. (2019). Corporate social responsibility reporting in India: A study of SENSEX companies. *Management and Labour Studies, 44*(2), 209–223.

Mazda Motor Corporation. (2020). *Sustainability report, in-depth version.* Author.

Miotto, G., Polo López, M., & Rom Rodríguez, J. (2019). Gender Equality and UN Sustainable Development Goals: Priorities and Correlations in the Top Business Schools' Communication and Legitimation Strategies. *Sustainability, 11*(2), 302. https://doi.org/10.3390/su11020302

Mitsubishi Motors Corporation. (2020). *Sustainability Report.* Author.

Mobus, J. L. (2005). Mandatory environmental disclosures in a legitimacy theory context. *Accounting, Auditing & Accountability Journal, 18*(4), 492–517.

Nissan Motor Corporation. (2020). *Sustainability Report.* Author.

Patten, D. M. (1992). Intra-industry environmental disclosures in response to the Alaskan oil spill: A note on legitimacy theory. *Accounting, Organizations and Society*, *17*(5), 471–475.

Peugeot S. A. (2019). *Corporate Social Responsibility Report*. Author.

Raman, S. R. (2006). Corporate social reporting in India – A view from the top. *Global Business Review*, *7*(2), 313–324.

Salvioni, D. M., Franzoni, S., & Cassano, R. (2017). Sustainability in the Higher Education System: An Opportunity to Improve Quality and Image. *Sustainability*, *9*(6), 914. https://doi.org/10.3390/su9060914

Sánchez-Medina, A., Benítez-del-Rosario, J. M., & Blázquez-Santana, F. (2017). Anomia and Displacement of Responsibility as Determinants of Tourist Company Managers' Non-Involvement in Alleviating Poverty. *Sustainability*, *9*(5), 802. https://doi.org/10.3390/su9050802

Schmelzer, P. (2013). *Value relevance of corporate social responsibility reports* [Master's Thesis]. Erasmus Universiteit Rotterdam.

Subaru Corporation. (2020). *Corporate Social Responsibility Report*. Author.

Suchman, M. C. (1995). Managing legitimacy: Strategic and institutional approaches. *Academy of Management Review*, *20*(3), 571–610.

Suzuki Corporation. (2019). *Corporate Social Responsibility and Environmental Report*. Author.

Tata Motors. (2020). *Annual Corporate Social Responsibility Report*. Author.

Toyota Motor Corporation. (2020). *Environment Reporter*. Author.

United Nations. (2015). *Transforming our world: the 2030 Agenda for Sustainable Development*. Author.

United Nations. (2020). *Global indicator framework for the Sustainable Development Goals and targets of the 2030 Agenda for Sustainable Development*. 51st session of the United Nations Statistical Commission.

United Nations General Assembly. (1987). *Report of the world commission on environment and development: Our common future*. Oslo, Norway: United Nations General Assembly, Development and International Co-operation.

Volkswagen A. G. (2019). *Sustainability Report*. Author.

ADDITIONAL READING

Anna, B. (2016). Classification of the European Union member states according to the relative level of sustainable development. *Quality & Quantity*, *50*(6), 2591–2605. doi:10.100711135-015-0278-x PMID:27795586

Bal, M., Bryde, D., Fearon, D., & Ochieng, E. (2013). Stakeholder Engagement: Achieving Sustainability in the Construction Sector. *Sustainability*, *5*(2), 695–710. doi:10.3390u5020695

Bonilla, S., Silva, H., Terra da Silva, M., Franco Gonçalves, R., & Sacomano, J. (2018). Industry 4.0 and Sustainability Implications: A Scenario-Based Analysis of the Impacts and Challenges. *Sustainability, 10*(10), 3740. doi:10.3390u10103740

Bowen, F. (2019). Marking Their Own Homework: The Pragmatic and Moral Legitimacy of Industry Self-Regulation. *Journal of Business Ethics, 156*(1), 257–272. doi:10.100710551-017-3635-y

Cook, D., Saviolidis, N., Davíðsdóttir, B., Jóhannsdóttir, L., & Ólafsson, S. (2019). Synergies and Trade-Offs in the Sustainable Development Goals—The Implications of the Icelandic Tourism Sector. *Sustainability, 11*(15), 4223. doi:10.3390u11154223

ElAlfy, A., Palaschuk, N., El-Bassiouny, D., Wilson, J., & Weber, O. (2020). Scoping the Evolution of Corporate Social Responsibility (CSR) Research in the Sustainable Development Goals (SDGs) Era. *Sustainability, 12*(14), 5544. doi:10.3390u12145544

Haseeb, M., Hussain, H. I., Kot, S., Androniceanu, A., & Jermsittiparsert, K. (2019). Role of Social and Technological Challenges in Achieving a Sustainable Competitive Advantage and Sustainable Business Performance. *Sustainability, 11*(14), 3811. doi:10.3390u11143811

Leal Filho, W., Shiel, C., Paço, A., Mifsud, M., Ávila, L. V., Brandli, L. L., Molthan-Hill, P., Pace, P., Azeiteiro, U. M., Vargas, V. R., & Caeiro, S. (2019). Sustainable Development Goals and sustainability teaching at universities: Falling behind or getting ahead of the pack? *Journal of Cleaner Production, 232*, 285–294. doi:10.1016/j.jclepro.2019.05.309

Lu, I.-Y., Kuo, T., Lin, T.-S., Tzeng, G.-H., & Huang, S.-L. (2016). Multicriteria Decision Analysis to Develop Effective Sustainable Development Strategies for Enhancing Competitive Advantages: Case of the TFT-LCD Industry in Taiwan. *Sustainability, 8*(7), 646. doi:10.3390u8070646

MacGregor Pelikánová, R. (2019). Corporate Social Responsibility Information in Annual Reports in the EU—A Czech Case Study. *Sustainability, 11*(1), 237. doi:10.3390u11010237

KEY TERMS AND DEFINITIONS

Agenda 2030: Document that includes the 17 Sustainable Development Goals. It brings together the commitments of 193 countries that pursue its fulfillment by the year 2030. The objectives pursue equality among people, protect the planet and ensure prosperity.

Corporate Social Responsibility: Voluntary integration by the organizations of social and environmental concerns in its business operations and the relationships with their interlocutors.

Organizational Legitimacy: Social acceptance of organizations, which means that they should develop a collection of actions that are appropriate for communities because they are adjusted to a set of regulations, values and beliefs that determine their behavior and legitimate them in their market, sector and with the society they are set into.

Stakeholders: People, individuals, and groups of people that affect, can affect and can be affected by the activities of an organization. They are considered to be an essential element on the strategic planning of the organizations.

Sustainable Development: Development that satisfies present needs without compromising the capacity of future generations, guaranteeing the balance between economic development, taking care of the environment and social wellbeing.

Sustainable Development Goals: Goals adopted by the United Nations Member States, set by the 2030 Agenda, aimed at achieving peace and prosperity for people and the planet, now and in the future. They constitute an urgent call to action by all countries, developed and developing, in a global partnership.

Triple Bottom Line Perspective: Accounting framework with three parts (social, environmental, and financial). Some organizations have adopted this framework in order to evaluate their performance in a broader perspective to create greater business value.

Chapter 7
How Luxury Fashion Brands Contribute Efficiently to Sustainable Development

Belen Lopez
ESIC University, Madrid, Spain

Celia Rangel
https://orcid.org/0000-0002-5692-2915
Complutense University of Madrid, Spain

ABSTRACT

This chapter explores how luxury fashion and accessories firms are adapting their CSR strategies to be more sustainable considering that the firms have been impacted by the COVID-19 pandemic. In this context, the authors explore how companies are communicating their efforts and how they engage consumers according to sustainable development. The methodology followed in this study is based on case studies analyzing the activities of luxury fashion and accessories brands operating in different countries, such as LVMH, Kering, Richemont, Chanel, EssilorLuxottica, Chow Tai Fook, PVH, and Swatch Group. The results show that almost all luxury fashion and accessories firms include the SDGs in their CSR/sustainability strategies and communicate how their efforts contribute to achieving the 17 SDGs. Nearly all these companies set long-term objectives including areas, such as 1) environmental protection as a key axis of their strategy, 2) support for the communities where they operate, and 3) promotion of equality and inclusion of their employees.

INTRODUCTION

In recent years, sustainability has become an essential area for companies in all industries. Specifically, the current global context is also characterized by profound changes since the global pandemic caused by COVID-19, accelerating the need to know how companies contribute in a positive way through their activities (Barnett et al., 2020) and how firms create value for their stakeholders (Porter & Kramer, 2011;

DOI: 10.4018/978-1-7998-8065-3.ch007

Carroll & Buchholtz, 2014). Furthermore, researchers identify consumer demands as the key driver of sustainability (Belz & Schmidt-Riediger, 2010) by requesting sustainable solutions from brands (Charter et al., 2006). Moreover, luxury brands face pressure to make their business more sustainable today (Karaosman et al., 2019; Li & Leonas, 2019). Thus, scholars also found the need for luxury brands to become more sustainable (Thomas, 2018) when considering consumer expectations (Cervellon, 2013). Today, luxury is associated with sustainability since luxury brands can positively impact society and the environment (Gardetti & Justo, 2017). Likewise, luxury focuses on obtaining transparency by including new sustainable trends in its Corporate Social Responsibility (CSR) strategies and according to the consumer expectations.

The luxury industry has been hit by COVID-19 with sales falling by around 20% in 2020, going back to 2015 levels (Bain & Co, 2020). Although the luxury fashion sector is expected to recover by the end of 2023 (McKinsey & Company, 2020), a radical change is expected in the luxury industry in 2030 accelerated by COVID-19, to meet the 2030 agenda targets and remain relevant to the new generations who are expected to make 180% of global purchases and who are interested in diversity and inclusion, in addition to sustainability and environmental issues (Bain & Co, 2020). The mobility restrictions that will remain in place because of COVID-19 have made luxury brands want to attract the local shopper and other stakeholders who are also concerned about issues such as social justice, dignity, and the working conditions of luxury fashion brand workers (McKinsey & Company, 2020).

The current study on sustainable luxury focuses on some aspects, which also analyze its effect on consumer behaviour (Kunz et al., 2020). Consequently, luxury brands work towards a more ethical luxury (Deloitte, 2020) following the United Nations Agenda 2030 and considering the new expectations of consumers. These firms communicate their activities and impacts on SDGs in CSR/Sustainability reports and on corporate websites showing how luxury fashion and accessories companies are accelerating towards more sustainable business. However, there is scarce literature that explores the contribution of luxury brands to sustainable development and how this affects their relationship with consumers, who demand information on the social and environmental commitments of these brands.

The purpose of this chapter is to analyze how luxury fashion and accessories brands contribute better to sustainable development through their CSR strategies considering the global challenges for business caused by COVID-19. Moreover, the pandemic crisis could act as an accelerator for brands adopting strategies of value creation with sustainable activities in the luxury fashion industry and considering that the fashion industry is the second largest cause of pollution worldwide (Woodside & Fine, 2019). As a consequence, luxury companies are reporting their medium-term sustainability strategies, reducing their environmental impact and making a positive contribution to society in different areas of their business.

The objectives set out in this chapter concerning CSR and the sustainability of luxury fashion and accessories brands are to analyze how firms become sustainable and how they measure and report their results following the sustainable development goals promoted by the United Nations; all this considering that luxury brands in the fashion industry have a big opportunity to attend to consumers' demands for responsible and sustainable brands.

In all cases, we analyze how these firms integrate sustainable activities in accordance with their CSR strategy and considering the interest of consumers concerned about some elements, such as materials, supply chain, emissions, among others. In addition, these companies communicate the impacts in different annual reports providing information about their commitments with society in the long term and in the fight against climate change.

BACKGROUND

What We Know About Corporate Social Responsibility in Luxury Brands

Corporate Social Responsibility is a field widely studied in the academic literature, especially in the last 20 years. Although CSR refers to the responsibility of companies and their voluntary contribution and positive impact on the environment and society, the current global context is characterized by profound changes since the global pandemic caused by COVID-19. Thus, this situation gives a new meaning to CSR (Carroll, 2021), where more sustainable actions are demanded from companies, as well as the measurement of impacts to better know their contributions to society (Barnett et al., 2020).

As we know, CSR activities can improve society creating value for all stakeholders (Porter & Kramer, 2011; Carroll & Buchholtz, 2014), more engagement and stronger relationships. Some scholars argue that sustainability focuses on the long-term competitive advantage because consumers request the companies to deal with it to understand sustainability and its implications (Claro et al., 2013). Thus, researchers identify consumer demand as the key driver for sustainability (Belz & Schmidt-Riediger, 2010) demanding sustainable solutions from brands (Charter et al., 2006).

Recently, some authors have investigated CSR and sustainability in the luxury sector linking theory and practice (Amatulli et al., 2017a; Gardetti, 2017). Also, luxury brands are facing pressure to make their businesses more sustainable (Li & Leonas, 2019). Some scholars argue that different luxury brands are reacting to sustainability trends taking an active stance on customers' expressed desire for sustainability (Khan & Ahmed, 2017). In fact, other scholars also found the need for luxury brands to become more sustainable (Thomas, 2018) when considering the expectations of consumers (Cervellon, 2013). Though luxury has always been focused on scarcity, what would be most desirable nowadays is a healthy planet in which future generations could live in a healthy environment (Gardetti & Girón, 2014). Today, luxury is associated with sustainability, since luxury brands can transcend in society by leading and empowering respect both for the environment, social development and culture and also by protecting local craftsmanship (Gardetti & Justo, 2017). Luxury firms have the ambition to increase transparency including the new sustainable trends in their CSR strategies.

On the other hand, different researchers found that circular economy and sustainability are new cultural macro-trends providing opportunities for brands (Todeschini et al., 2017; Kapferer, 2018; Olšanová, et al., 2018). Moreover, luxury brands often act as industry models (Choi, 2014). Nowadays, research on sustainable luxury focuses on some aspects, such as supply chain, communication and product innovation, among others, analyzing the effect of these activities on consumer behaviour (Kunz et al., 2020). Consequently, best practices are being included in luxury brands towards a more ethical luxury (Deloitte, 2020) following the United Nations Agenda 2030 and considering the expectations of consumers, especially millennials and Generation Z. These generations are expected by 2025 to account for half of all global personal luxury goods sales and they are very aware of the sustainability and environmental impact affecting their purchasing decisions (Deloitte, 2020).

The Agenda 2030 has been approved by the United Nations in 2015 and signed by more than 190 countries. It promotes sustainability and invites companies worldwide to boost growth by being respectful of the environment and society. Thus, companies can provide solutions to the global challenges defined in the 17 sustainable development goals (SDGs) in several ways (SDG 1, no poverty; SDG 2, zero hunger; SDG 3, good health and wellbeing; SDG 4, quality education; SDG 5, gender equality; SDG 6, clean water and sanitation; SDG 7, affordable and clean energy; SDG 8, decent work and economic growth;

SDG 9, industry, innovation and infrastructure; SDG 10, reduced inequality; SDG 11, sustainable cities and communities; SDG 12, responsible consumption and production; SDG 13, climate action; SDG 14, life below water; SDG 15, life on land; SDG 16, peace, justice and strong institutions; SDG 17, partnerships to achieve the goals) (UN, 2015).

As a consequence, in the era of COVID-19, luxury fashion brands are working in different areas, such as circular design for circular economy (SDG 8, SDG 12), technological and innovative materials (SDG 9, SDG 11, SDG 12), cleaner production and sustainable consumption (SDG 3, SDG 6, SDG 7, SDG 8, SDG 9, SDG 12) and also transparency (SDG 4, SDG 8, SDG 10, SDG 12, SDG 16) (Unlocking responsible luxury, 2019). All these areas are communicated on CSR/Sustainability reports including their impacts on SDGs and showing how luxury fashion companies are accelerating their business transformation including sustainability in their CSR strategy (SDGs for better fashion, UN).

Why CSR Communication and Consumer Engagement Matters

CSR communication is an important aspect of CSR strategies of companies. In general, communication is how firms inform about their sustainable commitments, results and impacts on their CSR activities. In this sense, the communication strategy is an opportunity to create an engagement and dialogue to benefit their relationships (Villagra et al., 2015) using different channels and tools, such as CSR/Sustainable and/or integrated report, corporate website and social media (YouTube, Twitter, Facebook, Instagram, etc.). CSR communication is how companies communicate the corporate purpose and values (Morsing & Schultz, 2006; Du et al., 2010) connecting their activities in a responsible manner, creating value and explaining their contribution to society (Peloza & Shang, 2011; Lopez & Monfort, 2017). As a consequence, companies can increase their transparency (Colleoni, 2013) and legitimacy.

Furthermore, CSR communication has some barriers and opportunities, especially in social media (Monfort & Mas, 2021). These authors argue that although companies can engage their stakeholders through communication, some studies show that communication channels are not used to generate dialogue between the company and stakeholders in social media (Abitbol et al, 2019). As a consequence, companies are not creating dialogue and, therefore, are not encouraging the participation of their stakeholders in social networks (Monfort et al., 2019). Moreover, creating a dialogue depends on the participation and influence of the stakeholders in the organization (Saxton et al., 2020). In addition, CSR communication based on the values of companies should differentiate from competitors. However, the messages are similar and the firms do not take advantage of their strategy to identify them against other firms (Paliwoda-Matiolanska et al., 2020). Therefore, companies should explore the interests of their stakeholders and generate engagement through specific content on social networks that captures their attention (Okazaki et al., 2020) and thus increases the interaction with the companies (Hartmann et al., 2020).

Regarding the opportunities that CSR communication offers to companies, despite the fact that the literature indicates some positive characteristics, companies are nevertheless not taking advantage of communication for this purpose. Some authors have pointed out that a presence in social networks can serve to generate conversation about the interests of the public and the company in CSR matters (Barbeito-Caamaño & Chalmeta, 2020), where the content and the platform are strategic for firms in order to facilitate the interaction of users and engagement (Llao & Mak, 2019).

Some scholars have studied the consequences of engagement on CSR and sustainability in luxury firms (Cheah et al., 2016; Amatulli et al., 2018) and confirm a positive impact of sustainable practices on the consumers' perception. However, other scholars provide results suggesting that CSR and sustainable activities do not positively influence consumers' responses and negative consequences in terms of brand attitude and perception of credibility (Jin et al., 2017). However, in some cases, luxury buyers that care about sustainability declared the intention to recommend a luxury brand they perceive as sustainable (Hepner, 2020).

Whether a company intends to communicate its social and environmental commitments, it should communicate some values, such as authenticity, legitimacy, and transparency to the stakeholders (Freire, 2014; Gardetti, 2016; Ivan et al., 2016). Although transparency is presumably inherent to the companies, research suggests that sharing both positive and less favourable information can lend credibility to a company's message. Besides the annual report, firms could communicate across consumer channels to reaffirm their commitment, annual objectives and progress on sustainability (Cavender, 2018). As a consequence, communication strategy is a key aspect for luxury firms, especially to engage younger generations in their social and environmental commitments.

LUXURY BRANDS AND SUSTAINABILITY

The Leading Luxury Firms Worldwide

The methodology followed in this study is based on case studies analyzing the activities linked to SDGs of the leading luxury fashion and accessories groups of brands operating with the highest sales globally and which account for half of worldwide luxury sales. According to Deloitte (2020), these companies are (Table 1): LVMH, Kering, Richemont, Chanel, EssilorLuxottica, Chow Tai Fook, PVH and Swatch Group. The Estée Lauder company and L'Oréal, which have been ranked 3 and 5 respectively by Deloitte, have not been considered in this analysis because, although they are in the luxury sector, they are considered as beauty companies. The sample is taken from Deloitte's annual report on the 100 largest luxury companies by sales. According to the latest available report, which does not yet assess the full impact of COVID-19, the 100 luxury brand companies generated revenues of $281 billion in 2019 (down 9.6% from the previous year).

In order to carry out the research, the information provided by the companies in the sample on their websites and their respective sustainability reports were consulted. To this end, their CSR/sustainability strategy and their key areas of work were analyzed in relation to the different SDGs. Regarding the sustainable development goals, specific actions of each objective were provided, as well as specific goals that each company analyzed has set for the coming years.

The Contribution of Luxury Fashion Firms to Sustainable Development

The luxury fashion and accessories companies analyzed are contributing to sustainable development in different ways and they communicate their information related to the 17 SDGs in their reports and corporate websites. The analysis of each of the companies in the sample is presented below in different tables explaining the SDG they are working on, an example of their major contribution and a key target.

Table 1. Leading luxury fashion and accessories companies by sales

Ranking	Name of the company	Country of origin	Main fashion and accessories brands
1	LVMH (Louis Vuitton Moët Hennessy)	France	Louis Vuitton, Fendi, Christian Dior, Givenchy, Marc Jacobs, Kenzo, Loewe, Emilio Pucci, Loro Piana, Celine, Berluti, Bulgary, Tiffany & Co, Tag Heuer.
2	Kering	France	Gucci, Saint Laurent, Bottega Veneta, Balenciaga, Alexander McQueen, Brioni, Boucheron
4	Richemont	Switzerland	Buccellati, Cartier, Van Cleef & Arpels, A. Lange & Söhne, Baume & Mercier, JWC, Jaeger-LeCoultre, Panerai, Piaget, Roger Dubuis.
6	Chanel	France	Chanel
7	EssilorLuxottica	Italy	Giorgio Armani, Ferrari, Dolce & Gabbana, Ralph Lauren, Valentino, Versace, Michael Kors.
8	Chow Tai Fook Jewellery Group	China/Hong Kong	Enzo, Hearts on fire, T Mark, Soinlove, Monologue
9	PVH (Phillips-Van Heusen)	United States	Calvin Klein, Tommy Hilfiger, Van Heusen, Izod, Arrow, Geoffrey Beene.
10	Swatch Group	Switzerland	Breguet, Harry Winston, Blancpain, Omega, Glashütte, Jaquet Droz, Longines

Source: own elaboration based on Deloitte (2020), LVMH (2021a), Kering (2021a), Richemont (2021a), Chanel (2021a), EssilorLuxottica (2021a), Chow Tai Fook Jewellery Group (2021a), PVH (2021a) and The Swatch Group (2021a).

1. LVMH

LVMH considers sustainability as a strategic pillar of the company and a long-term commitment to society. The company believes that environmental protection generates more competitiveness. For LVMH, such protection is more than an obligation if the company wants to be successful in the long term, as many products depend directly on the protection and respect of raw materials that come from nature. Respect for people, their individuality and integrity is another of the cornerstones of its sustainability policy, as well as social and professional inclusion and promoting a positive impact in all the countries where LVMH operates. In the words of Bernard Arnault, Chairman and Chief Executive Officer of LVMH, "Our position as a leader entails social and environmental responsibilities. We need to go further than simply meeting standards." (LVMH, 2021b).

Concerning the SDGs, the company has an account to show how its CSR strategy helps to achieve the 17 SDGs. LVMH highlights its efforts to minimize inequalities, work to leave a better planet for future generations, fight climate change, and work for peace and prosperity worldwide (LVMH, 2020b). Although LVMH claims to work on all the SDGs, the analysis shows how they orient their work under four pillars related to climate change, resource management and optimization, circular economy and people (internal talent and social justice).

Table 2. LVMH's contribution to the SDGs

SDG	Example of a major contribution	Key target
Goal 1 – No poverty	Supporting vulnerable populations.	LVMH provides support for numerous institutions recognized for their work with children, the elderly and people with disabilities, as well as their efforts to combat suffering and exclusion.
Goal 2 – Zero hunger	Standardizing eco-design.	Improve the Environmental Performance Index (EPI) for Perfumes & Cosmetics and Wines & Spirits packaging by 10%.
Goal 3 – Good health and wellbeing	Protecting the wellbeing of employees.	Their Environment Academy will provide fundamental training on environmental issues to all employees from any department.
Goal 4 – Quality education	Safeguarding the future of tradition by recruiting talent.	LVMH has supported a broad cultural program for youth, art education and encouraging young artists for more than 25 years.
Goal 5 – Gender equality	Improving equality and promoting career development for women.	LVMH is aiming to achieve gender equality in key positions by 2025.
Goal 6 – Clean water and sanitation	Saving water.	Improve sites' key environmental efficiency indicators (water consumption, energy consumption and waste production) by at least 10%.
Goal 7 – Affordable and clean energy	Optimizing the carbon footprint generated by transport and raw materials.	LVMH wants to ensure that the strictest standards are rolled out covering their procurement of supplies of strategic raw materials and their suppliers across 100% of the supply chain by 2025.
Goal 8 – Decent work and economic growth	Develop talents and social responsibility.	LVMH is also striving to reduce its environmental impact and boost the livelihoods of local populations.
Goal 9 – Industry, innovation and infrastructure	Designing long-lasting products.	Reduce CO^2 emissions related to energy consumption by 25%.
Goal 10 – Reduced inequalities	Supporting people with disabilities into work.	Louis Vuitton aims to promote circular creativity by committing to sustainable design for all their products by 2025.
Goal 11 – Sustainable cities and communities	Playing an active role in the communities in which LVMH operates.	Ensure respect and support for local communities while preserving the environment and its biodiversity throughout the different stages of each of the animal-based supply chains.
Goal 12 – Responsible consumption and production	Combining economic growth and respect for sustainability criteria.	
Goal 13 – Climate action	Reducing energy consumption.	Louis Vuitton wants to map out a climate trajectory approved by the Science Based Targets initiative by 2025.
Goal 14 – Life below water	Championing products that fully respect biodiversity.	Ensure visibility along the whole sourcing channel to achieve traceability of origin and in-depth knowledge of the supply chains.
Goal 15 – Life on land	Working for increasingly stringent standards.	Obtain concrete guarantees related to animal welfare by adopting the most demanding certification systems and end supplies from value chains that have not demonstrated willingness to improve welfare practices.
Goal 16 – Peace, justice and strong institutions	Encouraging dialogue.	Ensure the traceability of sourcing channels, improving the living and farming conditions for animals, as well as respecting local populations, the environment and biodiversity.
Goal 17 – Partnerships	Creating employment opportunities and economic momentum.	LVMH encourages innovation and the search for new solutions through special partnerships.

Source: own elaboration based on LVMH (2020a & b; 2021b & c).

2. Kering

The three pillars that shape Kering's 2025 Sustainability Strategy are "care, collaborate and create" to develop a more sustainable and responsible luxury industry in a world where reducing resource consumption and respecting people is necessary. Those pillars embody and drive their ambition: "to craft tomorrow's luxury" (Kering, 2021b). According to François-Henri Pinault, Kering CEO, "We are redesigning our business to continue to thrive and prosper sustainably into the future, while at the same time helping to transform the luxury sector and contributing to meet the significant social and environmental challenges of our generation" (Kering, 2021c). Table 3 below summarises the main contributions that the Kering Group makes to achieving 7 SDGs.

Table 3. Kering's contribution to the SDGs

SDG	Example of a major contribution	Key target
Goal 3 – Good health and wellbeing	No person shall be employed under the age of 15 or under the age for completion of compulsory education, whichever is higher.	To partner with schools around the world to promote education for sustainability.
Goal 5 – Gender equality	Kering's ambition is to become an exemplary luxury industry employer.	Implement a sponsorship program for training and coaching women managers and roll out mentoring programs in all countries. Promote the development of innovative career paths and ensure all genders are always considered for new opportunities.
Goal 6 – Clean water and sanitation	Reduction of water consumption	Implement advanced water and energy-efficient water-based techniques.
Goal 8 – Decent work and economic growth	No use of forced labour.	Kering is focusing on developing a working environment and working relationships that ensure wellbeing at work, in order to promote the development of all employees and contribute to the welfare of all their employees.
Goal 12 – Responsible consumption and production	Innovation and knowledge sharing.	Kering's aim is for 100% of its supply chain to be transparent by 2025.
Goal 13 – Climate action	Climate change.	Kering is targeting a 50% reduction in its carbon emissions by 2025.
Goal 15 – Life on land	Biodiversity.	By 2025, in order to have a net positive impact on biodiversity, Kering will restore and regenerate a million hectares for its supply chain and protect one million hectares of critical, irreplaceable habitat.

Source: own elaboration based on Kering (2019 & 2021b, c, d).

At the strategic level, Kering highlights which SDGs they work on according to the five stages of value creation they have identified for all its brands (Kering, 2021c). In the first stage of creation, they consider that they work on SDGs 12 and 13; in the development stage they contribute to SDGs 13 and 15; in the production stage they support SDGs 6, 8 and 13; in the sales and marketing stage they work on SDGs 5 and 13; and in the fifth and final stage of customer experience they have more influence on SDG 3. Therefore, Kering focuses on two main areas in its sustainability strategy: the fight against climate change and better use of resources; and people management, both by taking care of its employees and those who live where the company operates.

3. Richemont

In order to develop its sustainability strategy, Richemont conducted prior research that included the expectations of its main stakeholders, so that their interests are at the heart of the change to be pursued. For Richemont, in terms of sustainable innovation, they include the improvement of its products and processes, but also the development of its employees. Within its governance, Richemont includes strategic and operational risks related to sustainability. In this respect, Burkhart Grund, Richemont CFO, says "Our Group has a long-standing commitment to doing business responsibly. We know that there is always more to do regarding such corporate and industry-wide sustainability efforts and strive to improve each year" (Richemont, 2021b).

The following table shows how the sustainability strategy translates into support for 5 SDGs.

Table 4. Richemont's contribution to the SDGs

SDG	Example of a major contribution	Key target
Goal 5 – Gender equality	Diversity and inclusion.	Richemont has expanded its benefits program for childcare services, including parental leave.
Goal 8 – Decent work and economic growth	Promote inclusive and sustainable economic growth.	To preserve craftsmanship and employability throughout retail academies in different countries.
Goal 12 – Responsible consumption and production	Ensure sustainable consumption.	Richemont has committed to reaching 100% renewable electricity worldwide by 2025.
Goal 13 – Climate action	Take urgent action to combat climate change and its impacts.	They have committed to lower their carbon emissions from business travel and to source 100% renewable electricity by 2025.
Goal 17 – Partnerships	To build capacity beyond their operations as they promote dialogue and multi-lateral partnerships.	Create a visible leadership platform on specific societal or environmental issues, convening opinion formers and external stakeholders to drive best practices by 2025.

Source: own elaboration based on Richemont (2021c)

Richemont's strategy is embodied in what they have called the 'Movement for Better Luxury' which focuses on four areas: People, Sourcing, Environment and Communities. This focus coincides with the five SDGs with the highest relevance for Richemont; these SDGs are 5, 8, 12, 13 and 17, with specific targets that the group aims to achieve by 2025. Therefore, it can be concluded that its sustainability strategy and its commitment to the SDGs are aligned. Furthermore, in their Sustainability Report (Richemont, 2021c), they point out that their activity contributes to working on most of the SDGs.

4. Chanel

Chanel (2020a) says climate change is one of the major challenges facing our society. Chanel wants to be among the top companies that have taken the most ambitious steps to fight climate change. In addition to investing in climate change research, new technologies and start-ups related to raw materials and packaging, Chanel has four concrete commitments in relation to climate change: reducing Chanel's carbon footprint across its own operations and its entire supply chain to meet Science-Based Targets; shifting to 100% renewable electricity on a worldwide basis by 2025; balancing their residual carbon emissions; and financing climate change adaptation (Chanel, 2020). Chanel's commitment to climate change is also reflected in its contribution to the five SDGs, as shown in Table 5 below.

Table 5. Chanel's contribution to the SDGs

SDG	Example of a major contribution	Key target
Goal 5 – Gender equality	Empower women with regard to climate change	Gender, Climate and Environment are the key thematic areas of work for the Foundation Chanel.
Goal 7 – Affordable and clean energy	Access to clean energy	Shift to 100% renewable electricity in their operations by 2025.
Goal 13 – Climate action	Accelerate the speed of transition to lower carbon and a more resilient world.	Chanel aims to decrease their own carbon footprint by 50% by 2030.
Goal 15 – Life on land	Enable communities and landscapes to adapt to climate change.	By 2024, Chanel will invest more than $55m in projects that protect and preserve the natural world. This includes helping to protect and restore 9,000km^2 of land.
Goal 17 – Partnerships	Collaboration with the fashion industry	They support several cross-sector or multi-sector partnerships that aim to deliver change.

Source: own elaboration based on Chanel (2020).

Chanel wants to play a part in protecting the planet on which our society depends. To this end, in March 2020, Chanel launched their 'Mission 1.5°' to reduce their carbon emissions across their value chain and accelerate the achievement of the 2015 Paris Summit targets (Chanel 2020b). Their Mission 1.5° contributes to SDGs 5, 7, 13, 15 and 17. As for the last SDG, Chanel points out that the fight against climate change must involve all players in the fashion industry, which is why they are also one of the signatories of The Fashion Pact (2020).

5. EssilorLuxottica

The EssilorLuxottica group was founded in 2018 and defined its sustainability strategy considering the international context, the 2030 Agenda with the SDGs and the Paris Climate Change Conference (EssilorLuxottica, 2021b). Although they have a common vision, they continue with the effort of each of the companies to support the SDGs, as reflected in Table 6 (Luxottica) and Table 7 (Essilor).

The pillars of EssilorLuxottica's sustainability strategy are based on three axes: people, environment and society; these axes correspond to its commitment to the SDGs related to climate change, social justice and human dignity, as well as natural resource management. According to their vision, value creation and sustainability go hand-in-hand to promote the wellbeing of employees and sustainable impact wherever it operates. Hence, the importance of stakeholder management for EssilorLuxottica, whether in the consultation process for business decisions or risk management, in the reporting process or in joint collaboration on specific projects (EssilorLuxottica, 2021b).

Table 6. Luxottica's contribution to the SDGs

SDG	Example of a major contribution	Key target
Goal 3 – Good health and wellbeing	The Safety Culture.	Luxottica adopts all necessary measures to maintain a safe working environment and prevent risky situations.
Goal 4 – Quality education	Talent management.	Luxottica University provides on-the-job training for specific retail competencies, from selling techniques to soft skills on how to better serve their customers.
Goal 5 – Gender equality	Equal opportunities.	Beyond gender equality, Luxottica's inclusion efforts include equal opportunities for all their employees regardless of their gender, age, religion, marital status, sexual or political orientation, or disability.
Goal 6 – Clean water and sanitation	Optimize the use of natural resources.	Requirements related to energy consumption, water use, waste generation and valorization are integral to Luxottica's innovation process so as to minimize the environmental impact of the product and process from an early stage.
Goal 7 – Affordable and clean energy	Improving energy efficiency.	By 2021, the company will develop further on renewable energy sourcing along with an effort to increase its renewable shares in its energy mix.
Goal 8 – Decent work and economic growth	Protecting intellectual property and the struggle against counterfeiting.	Luxottica collaborates with local institutions and authorities around the world to intercept counterfeit products and combat the entire illegal production chain as best permitted by law.
Goal 9 – Industry, innovation and infrastructure	Eyecare.	Luxottica has taken a leading role in the industry's efforts to raise awareness around the need for quality eye care.
Goal 10 – Reduced inequalities	Value creation and long-term sustainable growth.	Luxottica pursues its commitment towards the local communities and territories where it operates, supporting social, sport and cultural initiatives.
Goal 12 – Responsible consumption and production	Sustainable product development.	All materials undergo rigorous checks on their chemical composition as well as on their physical and mechanical properties to guarantee compliance with strict quality standards and safety requirements.
Goal 16 – Peace, justice and strong institutions	Luxottica interprets and values different cultures and the particular features of diverse markets and consumers.	The desire to truly understand Chinese culture, constant and valuable interaction with institutions and the community enabled Luxottica to integrate and become a local manufacturer while contributing to the social and economic development in the region.

Source: own elaboration based on Luxottica (2021).

Due to COVID-19, Essilor (2021) postponed meeting its targets by the end of 2021, while working on the 2025 goals. Their main areas of sustainability work are threefold: reaching out to people in a tangible way, contributing to SDGs 1, 3, 10 and 17; optimising their environmental footprint by working on SDGs 6, 7 and 13; caring for their employees through SDGs 4 and 8, and working with society by committing to SDGs 12 and 16. For its part, Luxottica's four strategic pillars seek to contribute to ten SDGs: commitment to excellence with a focus on SDG 16; visual wellbeing which seeks to work in favour of SDGs 8, 9 and 12; social impact which contributes to SDGs 3, 4, 5, 8 and 10; while protecting the environment aims at SDGs 6, 7, 8, 9 and 12 (Luxottica, 2021).

Table 7. Essilor's contribution to the SDGs

SDG	Example of a major contribution	Key target
Goal 1 – No poverty	Bring tangible social and economic benefits to individuals and their communities.	Improve the lives of 50 million individuals "at the base of the pyramid" by 2021. Create 25,000 primary care providers by 2021. Invest €30 million in philanthropic visual health programs by 2021.
Goal 3 – Good health and wellbeing		
Goal 10 – Reduced inequalities		
Goal 17 – Partnerships		
Goal 6 – Clean water and sanitation	Climate change.	Reduce water intensity by 20% by 2021. Lower energy intensity by 15% by 2021.
Goal 7 – Affordable and clean energy		
Goal 13 – Climate action		
Goal 4 – Quality education	Engage employees in sustainable growth.	Decrease by 30% the work-related injury frequency rate towards a zero-accident goal by 2021. 100% of employees have access to the online training platform at Essilor University in 2021. 35% of employees as shareholders by 2021.
Goal 8 – Decent work and economic growth		
Goal 12 – Responsible consumption and production	Lead sustainable business practices in the industry.	100% of strategic suppliers undertake CSR assessments by 2021. 100% of preferred suppliers acknowledge Essilor's Supplier Charter by 2021.
Goal 16 – Peace, justice and strong institutions		

Source: own elaboration based on Essilor (2021).

6. Chow Tai Fook

According to Chow Tai Fook Jewellery Group's mission, in terms of sustainability, they want to "Unlock future possibilities with sustainable practices" (2021b). In their latest CSR report, Chow Tai Fook Jewellery Group (2020) has reviewed its sustainability strategy with a view to marking the company's century-long existence in 2029. In the revision of the new sustainability strategy, the effort to incorporate the insights of the company's different stakeholders has been reinforced. In the words of Suen Chi-Keung, Executive Director and Chairman of Sustainability Committee at Chow Tai Fook Jewellery Group, "In the next decade, our society and surrounding environment will continue to change, which may lead to various challenges ahead. As a leader in the industry, we should work collaboratively on our ten-year action plans" (Chow Tai Fook Jewellery Group, 2020).

To respond to the industry's main challenges, such as resource scarcity, technological breakthroughs, climate change, demographic and social change, the new priority areas of Chow Tai Fook Jewellery Group (2020) are related to the SDGs, such as, responsible sourcing contributing to SDGs 12 and 17; craftsmanship, innovation & technology which are related to SDGs 9 and 17; resource efficiency & carbon reduction to work on SDGs 12 and 13; and people-focused contributing to SDGs 8 and 17. It can therefore be concluded that broadly speaking its efforts are focused on improving people's lives and protecting the planet.

Table 8. Chow Tai Fook's contribution to the SDGs

SDG	Example of a major contribution	Key target
Goal 8 – Decent work and economic growth	Cultivating a decent people-centric workplace and nurturing wellbeing in their community.	Volunteer service hours by employees increased by 30% by 2029.
Goal 17 – Partnerships		
Goal 9 – Industry, innovation and infrastructure	Preserving traditional craftsmanship while fostering future technology and innovation.	To promote cross-generational craftsmanship, innovation, and technology in the industry and to cultivate the artisanal spirit of perseverance with 10 million people through mass engagement initiatives and in-depth experiential programs, by 2029.
Goal 17 – Partnerships		
Goal 12 – Responsible consumption and production	Driving higher social and environmental standards in their supply chain.	To achieve full compliance with Chow Tai Fook's "Best Practice Principles" by all long-term key suppliers by 2029.
Goal 17 – Partnerships		
Goal 12 – Responsible consumption and production	Pursuing a sustainable operation pattern to protect the planet.	To achieve a reduction of at least 15% in their ecological footprint, namely greenhouse gas intensity and water consumption intensity of the group, and waste generation intensity at our production hubs by 2029.
Goal 13 – Climate action		

Source: own elaboration based on Chow Tai Fook (2020).

7. PVH

PVH states that the *momentum* created by younger generations, investors, NGOs and different movements have made sustainable development an obligation for companies (PHV, 2020). For the company, these demands from society reinforce their efforts in this area, which recognises their responsibility by focusing on three areas: contributing to reducing the negative environmental impact of their activity, increasing their positive impacts and improving the lives of people throughout its value chain (PVH, 2021). In fact, "Forward Fashion" represents PVH's sustainable strategy "to transform how clothes are made and (re)used, and the actions we are taking to move our business and the fashion industry toward a more innovative and responsible future" (PVH, 2021b).

The company works on all the SDGs to materialise its *Forward Fashion (for good)* strategy and thus align its efforts with the global goals, as can be seen in the Table 9.

In its commitment to the sustainability of the fashion industry and its business, PVH works to contribute to all SDGs with a special focus on a cleaner, fairer and healthier world (PHV, 2020). PVH promotes industry-wide collaboration for the development of people and promotes social justice, the circular economy, and the fight against climate change.

8. Swatch Group

The pillars of Swatch Group's sustainability strategy are the protection of life, quality of life, safety and health, as well as environmental protection (Swatch Group, 2021b). Since 2001, the Group has been implementing various measures and targets to protect the environment (Swatch Group, 2020).

Table 9. PVH's contribution to the SDGs

SDG	Example of a major contribution	Key target
Goal 1 – No poverty	Advance living wages.	100% of their key suppliers in key production countries proactively support industry-wide collective bargaining to achieve living wages (two countries by 2025 and four by 2030)
Goal 2 – Zero hunger	Educate the future.	Reach 135,000 individuals worldwide through early education and childcare services, teacher training, parenting resources and training, and youth employability training services by 2030.
Goal 3 – Good health and wellbeing	Promote safe workplaces.	100% of their suppliers will promote and maintain safe and healthy work environments by 2030.
Goal 4 – Quality education	Develop talent.	Expand professional skills development and digital literacy programs through PVH University to reach all 38,000+ PVH associates globally by 2023.
Goal 5 – Gender equality	Empower women.	Professional and life skills development programs and services will be made available to 500,000 women across the PVH supply chain by 2030.
Goal 6 – Clean water and sanitation	Eliminate water pollution from wet processors.	Water leaving wet processors will have zero hazardous chemicals and be filtered for harmful microfibers by 2025.
Goal 7 – Affordable and clean energy	Protect the global climate by reducing energy use.	PVH offices, warehouses and stores will be powered by 100% renewable electricity by 2030.
Goal 8 – Decent work and economic growth	Amplify worker voices.	100% of workers employed by key suppliers will have their voices heard through representative workplace committees by 2025.
Goal 9 – Industry, innovation and infrastructure	Innovate for circularity.	Three of PVH's most commonly purchased products will be completely circular including the full traceability of key raw materials by 2025.
Goal 10 – Reduced inequalities	Recruit ethically.	100% of migrant workers at their Level 1 and key Level 2 suppliers will not pay recruitment fees by 2025.
Goal 11 – Sustainable cities and communities	Regenerate materials.	100% sustainable sourcing of PVH's cotton, viscose and polyester (cotton and viscose by 2025, polyester by 2030)
Goal 12 – Responsible consumption and production	Eliminate hazardous chemicals & microfibers.	To manage wastewater in a way that will remove hazardous chemicals from the supply chain, they encourage suppliers to go beyond legal requirements, for example, application of the ZDHC (Zero Discharge of Hazardous Chemicals) Wastewater Guidelines and more advanced wastewater treatment technologies.
Goal 13 – Climate action	Eliminate carbon emissions.	Protect the global climate by reducing energy use and powering their business through renewable sources
Goal 14 – Life below water	Provide access to water.	PVH will drive a 30% reduction in their supply chain emissions by 2030.
Goal 15 – Life on land	End waste.	All PVH offices, distribution centers and stores will achieve zero waste and eliminate single-use plastics by 2030.
Goal 16 – Peace, justice and strong institutions	Source ethically.	100% of PVH suppliers will meet or exceed all of their social and environmental standards by 2030.
Goal 17 – Partnerships	Partnerships and collaborations.	For every priority, PVH partners with their peers, NGOs and other stakeholders in their supply chain regularly.

Source: own elaboration based on PHV (2020).

Swatch Group is the only company that does not explicitly mention the SDGs on its website (Swatch Group, 2021b) or in its latest published sustainability report (Swatch Group, 2020). This report reviews their sustainability commitments in terms of environment, sourcing, health and safety, and talent. In terms of specific targets for the coming years, the report highlights two targets for 2030 and 2050, both related to reducing emissions into the atmosphere, so it can be deduced that they work to contribute to SDGs 6, 7 and 13 (Impakter, 2021)

Among the main results of the analysis of the sample of the world's leading luxury fashion and accessories brands, the most notable is their support for the SDGs, given that all the companies analyzed, except Swatch Group, show how they contribute to achieving the SDGs. In general, most of the companies analyzed focus their efforts on the SDGs most relevant to their sustainability strategy and their core business, although other companies show how their direct or indirect efforts contribute to achieving the 17 SDGs. All companies set medium- and long-term objectives, with 2025 being the most frequently repeated year for the achievement of their targets. Regarding the sustainability strategies of the companies analyzed, all of them consider environmental protection as a key axis of their strategy given its impact on the business; the two other axes that are most mentioned are support for the communities where they operate and the promotion of equality and inclusion of their employees.

Table 10. Synthesis of the SDGs which the world's leading luxury fashion brands are working on

Company/ SDG	1	2	3	4	5	6	7	8	9	10	11	12	13	14	15	16	17
LVMH	x	x	x	x	x	x	x	x	x	x	x	x	x	x	x	x	x
Kering			x		x	x		x				x	x		x		
Richemont					x			x				x	x				x
Chanel					x		x						x		x		x
EssilorLuxottica	x		x	x	x	x	x	x	x	x		x	x			x	x
Chow Tai Fook								x	x			x	x				x
PVH	x	x	x	x	x	x	x	x	x	x	x	x	x	x	x	x	x
Swatch Group						x	x						x				

The SDG that receives the most attention from the luxury industry is SDG 13 (Climate action), given that it is an SDG in which all the analyzed brands are active, where best practices and ambitious targets are focused on reducing energy and water consumption, reducing carbon emissions, and using renewable energies. That focus on climate change is followed by SDGs 5 (Gender Equality), 8 (Decent work and economic growth), 12 (Responsible consumption and production) and 17 (Partnerships). On the other hand, the SDGs least worked on are 2 (Zero Hunger), 11 (Sustainable cities and communities) and 14 (Life below water); in fact, only two major groups consider them in their strategy, i.e. LVMH and PVH.

Hence, we can conclude that in terms of the sustainability strategies of the companies analyzed, all consider environmental protection as a key axis of their strategy given its impact on the business; the other three axes on which the industry is working the most are responsible consumption and production, support for the communities where they operate and the promotion of equality and inclusion of the people who make up their companies.

FUTURE RESEARCH DIRECTIONS

This chapter explores how luxury fashion and accessories brands contribute to sustainable development. These firms are facing pressure to make their businesses more sustainable (Thomas, 2018; Li & Leonas, 2019) due to consumer expectations (Cervellon, 2013). In addition, luxury brands can transcend society by leading and promoting respect for the environment and social development (Gardetti & Justo, 2017). All the companies analyzed (LVMH, Kering, Richemont, Chanel, EssilorLuxottica, Chow Tai Fook and PVH) report information on their activities and their involvement with the SDGs, except Swatch Group. We can affirm that luxury firms are committed to society, as reflected in the different tables of the analysis by firms.

According to the analysis, one way a brand demonstrating its international commitment to sustainability is through the implementation and monitoring of concrete targets to meet the SDGs. Although the commitment to the SDGs is a long-term commitment by all the luxury brands analyzed, in a year marked by COVID-19 and where the vulnerability of people to global external effects has been highlighted, all the companies say they have maintained their commitment to their CSR strategy (Table 10), especially the LVMH and PVH groups as they affirm they are working on all the SDGs. Climate change (SDG 13) is the SDG that most influences luxury fashion brands when it comes to the companies' sustainability strategy, given the impact it has on the sourcing of raw materials and their processing when manufacturing products, something that is closely related to SDG 12 (Responsible consumption and production). On the other hand, given the visibility that the fashion industry has globally, the other two SDGs most worked on are SDG 5 (Gender Equality) and SDG 8 (Decent work and economic growth)

In a unique historical moment, experienced due to COVID-19, where the luxury industry has experienced great economic losses, it has been an opportunity to be relevant to consumers and stakeholders concerned about sustainability, the environment, inclusion, diversity, social justice and human dignity (Bain & Co, 2020: McKinsey & Company, 2020). In this way, luxury fashion and accessories brands are contributing to these challenges and consumer demands to promote sustainable development through their CSR strategies and their commitment to the SDGs mainly related to climate change, circular economy, people's development and wellbeing, and proper management of natural resources.

Regarding the opportunities that CSR communication offers to companies, these firms are not taking advantage of communication for this purpose. Some authors have pointed out that a presence in social networks can serve to generate a dialogue about the interests of stakeholders in CSR matters (Barbeito-Caamaño & Chalmeta, 2020), where the content and the platform are strategic for companies in order to facilitate the interaction and engagement (Llao & Mak, 2019). Further, some academics have studied the consequences of commitment on CSR and sustainability in luxury firms (Cheah et al., 2016; Amatulli et al., 2018) and confirm a positive impact of sustainable practices on consumer perception. Moreover, when companies communicate their commitments, people perceive them as responsible and authentic.

For future lines of research, it would be interesting to compare the sustainability measures being taken by fashion and accessories companies in the Fast-Moving Consumer Goods (FMCG) sector with those in the luxury sector, as well as their commitment to the SDGs. Another line of future research could be related to the communication strategy of luxury firms in different social networks to find out if they are generating a real interaction with consumers in relation to the firms' social commitments.

CONCLUSION

While luxury fashion and accessories brands are convinced of the strategic focus of sustainability on their business, the SDGs are enabling a more concrete realisation of their efforts, priorities and targets for the coming years. As a result of the momentum of the conversation around climate change and social justice, many fashion, retail, luxury and lifestyle companies decided to come together and shape The Fashion Pact (2020) initiative to demonstrate the change that needs to be made in the industry and amplify the actions that have been taken to protect the planet and its diversity.

Beyond fine words, today's stakeholders demand a real commitment to society's problems, to fight against climate change, to protect the planet's resources, to give fair and receive equal treatment of people or to improve the lives of people around the world. This is something that the fashion and accessory luxury industry are aware of, as their business depends on the existence of raw materials and the know-how of people who are able to create unique products.

We can conclude that luxury companies make a real contribution to society from their CSR / sustainability strategies and reporting SDGs impacts; luxury firms are proactive and respond to consumer demands in the current post-pandemic context in a responsible manner. Thus, this chapter reflects that these firms take sustainability into account in their core business. In addition, adequate communication could serve as an element of engagement, considering the current demands of consumers and other stakeholders. Today, companies have to make and communicate their commitments to sustainability, and this work shows what some of the world's leading luxury firms are doing and how they are doing it.

This study makes some contributions to the literature based on the analysis of luxury firms: i) on the one hand, it is argued that luxury companies make a real contribution to society from their CSR / sustainability strategies; ii) in addition, those sustainable development objectives related to luxury fashion and accessories brands are identified, based on specific activities that these firms carry out; iii) on the other hand, the authors explain what and how luxury fashion and accessories brands communicate their sustainable contributions. In the end, the chapter shows how luxury firms respond in the current post-pandemic context to consumer demands in the area of sustainability.

REFERENCES

Abitbol, A., Meeks, J., & Cummins, R. G. (2019). Does oil and goodwill mix? Examining the oil and gas industry's impact on stakeholder engagement on Facebook. *Environmental Communication*, *13*(2), 192–208. doi:10.1080/17524032.2018.1546751

Amatulli, C., De Angelis, M., Costabile, M., & Guido, G. (2017a). *Sustainable luxury brands: Evidence from research and implications for managers*. Springer. doi:10.1057/978-1-137-60159-9

Amatulli, C., De Angelis, M., Korschun, D., & Romani, S. (2018). Consumers' perceptions of luxury brands' CSR initiatives: An investigation of the role of status and conspicuous consumption. *Journal of Cleaner Production*, *194*, 277–287. doi:10.1016/j.jclepro.2018.05.111

Bain & Co. (2020). *The future of Luxury: Bouncing Back from Covid-19*. Retrieved from https://cutt.ly/hmd5Imn

Barbeito-Caamaño, A., & Chalmeta, R. (2020). Using big data to evaluate corporate social responsibility and sustainable development practices. *Corporate Social Responsibility and Environmental Management*, *27*(6), 2831–2848. doi:10.1002/csr.2006

Barnett, M. L., Henriques, I., & Husted, B. W. (2020). Beyond good intentions: Designing CSR initiatives for greater social impact. *Journal of Management*, *46*(6), 937–964. doi:10.1177/0149206319900539

Belz, F. M., & Schmidt-Riediger, B. (2010). Marketing strategies in the age of sustainable development: Evidence from the food industry. *Business Strategy and the Environment*, *19*(7), 401–416.

Carroll, A. B. (2021). Corporate Social Responsibility: Perspectives on the CSR Construct's Development and Future. *Business & Society*.

Carroll, A. B., & Buchholtz, A. K. (2014). *Business and Society: Ethics*. Sustainability, and Stakeholder Management, Nelson Education.

Cavender, R. (2018). The Marketing of Sustainability and CSR Initiatives by Luxury Brands: Cultural Indicators, Call to Action, and Framework. In *Sustainability in Luxury Fashion Business* (pp. 29–49). Springer. doi:10.1007/978-981-10-8878-0_3

Cervellon, M. C. (2013). Conspicuous conservation: Using semiotics to understand sustainable luxury. *International Journal of Market Research*, *5*(5), 695–717. doi:10.2501/IJMR-2013-030

Chanel. (2020a). *Chanel announces climate commitments.* Retrieved from https://cutt.ly/lbbWChJ

Chanel. (2020b). *Channel. Mission 1.5º*. Retrieved from https://cutt.ly/ubbW5Hs

Chanel. (2021a). Retrieved from https://www.Chanel.com/

Chanel. (2021b). *Informe climático. Nuestro viaje hace un futuro bajo en carbono*. Retrieved from https://www.Chanel.com/es/informe-climatico/

Charter, M., Peattie, K., Ottman, J., & Polonsky, M. J. (2006). *Marketing and Sustainability*. Centre for Business Relationships, Accountability, Sustainability and Society (BRASS). Available at: http://www.cfsd.org.uk/smart-know-net/links/smart-know-net.pdf

Cheah, I., Zainol, Z., & Phau, I. (2016). Conceptualizing country-of-ingredient authenticity of luxury brands. *Journal of Business Research*, *69*(12), 5819–5826. doi:10.1016/j.jbusres.2016.04.179

Choi, T. M. (2014). Luxury fashion branding: Literature review, research trends, and research agenda. In T.-M. Choi (Ed.), *Fashion branding and consumer behaviours, International series on consumer science* (pp. 7–16). Springer. doi:10.1007/978-1-4939-0277-4_2

Chow Tai Fook Jewellery Group. (2020). *Sustainable Report 2020*. https://www.ctfjewellerygroup.com/file/Sustainability/reports/csr-report.pdf

Chow Tai Fook Jewellery Group. (2021a). *Brands*. Retrieved from https://www.ctfjewellerygroup.com/en/brands/our-brands.html

Chow Tai Fook Jewellery Group. (2021b). *Vision, mission & values*. Retrieved from https://www.ctfjewellerygroup.com/en/group/vision.html

Claro, D. P., Laban Neto, S. A., & De Oliveira Claro, P. B. (2013). Sustainability drivers in food retail. *Journal of Retailing and Consumer Services, 29*(3), 365–371. doi:10.1016/j.jretconser.2013.02.003

Colleoni, E. (2013). CSR communication strategies for organizational legitimacy in social media. *Corporate Communications, 18*(2), 228–248. doi:10.1108/13563281311319508

Deloitte. (2020). *Global Powers of Luxury Goods 2020. The new age of fashion and luxury.* Available https://www2.deloitte.com/content/dam/Deloitte/global/Documents/Consumer-Business/gx-consumer-business-gplg-2020-report.pdf

Du, S., Bhattacharya, C. B., & Sen, S. (2010). Maximizing business returns to corporate social responsibility (CSR): The role of CSR communication. *International Journal of Management Reviews, 12*(1), 8–19. doi:10.1111/j.1468-2370.2009.00276.x

Essilor. (2021). *Our commitments.* Retrieved from https://www.essilor.com/en/sustainability/commitments/

EssilorLuxottica. (2021a). *Brands.* Retrieved from https://www.essilorluxottica.com/brands

EssilorLuxottica. (2021b). *Sustainability.* Retrieved from https://www.essilorluxottica.com/sustainability

Freire, N. A. (2014). When luxury advertising adds the identitary values of luxury: A semiotic analysis. *Journal of Business Research, 67*(12), 2666–2675. doi:10.1016/j.jbusres.2014.04.004

Gardetti, M. A. (2016). Loewe: Luxury and sustainable management. Handbook of Sustainable Luxury Textiles and Fashion, 2, 1–16.

Gardetti, M. A. (2017). *Sustainable management of luxury. Springer book series on environmental footprints and eco-design of products and processes.* Springer.

Gardetti, M. A., & Girón, M. E. (Eds.). (2014). *Sustainable luxury and social entrepreneurship: Stories from the pioneers.* Greenleaf Publishing.

Gardetti, M. A., & Justo, R. (2017). Sustainable luxury fashion: The entrepreneurs' vision. In M. A. Gardetti (Ed.), *Sustainable Management of Luxury* (pp. 347–360). Springer Singapore. doi:10.1007/978-981-10-2917-2_16

Hartmann, P., Fernández, P., Apaolaza, V., Eisend, M., & D'Souza, C. (2020). Explaining Viral CSR Message Propagation in Social Media: The Role of Normative Influences. *Journal of Business Ethics,* 1–21. doi:10.100710551-020-04540-2

Hepner, J., Chandon, J. L., & Bakardzhieva, D. (2020). Competitive advantage from marketing the SDGs: A luxury perspective. *Marketing Intelligence & Planning, 39*(2), 284–299. doi:10.1108/MIP-07-2018-0298

Impakter. (2021). *Swatch Group.* Retrieved from https://index.impakter.com/swatch/

Ivan, C. M., Mukta, R., Sudeep, C., & Burak, C. (2016). Long-term sustainable sustainability in luxury. Where else? In *Handbook of Sustainable Luxury Textiles and Fashion* (pp. 17–34). Springer Singapore. doi:10.1007/978-981-287-742-0_2

Jin, Y.-J., Park, S.-C., & Yoo, J.-W. (2017). Effects of corporate social responsibility on consumer credibility perception and attitude toward luxury brands. *Social Behavior and Personality*, *45*(5), 795–808. doi:10.2224bp.5897

Kapferer, J. N. (2018). Second-hand luxury: Should personal luxury brands sell pre-owned products? *European Business Review*, (November-December), 59–65.

Karaosman. (2019). *'Unlocking Responsible Luxury: The Manifesto 2019*. Politecnico di Milano School of Management & Mazars.

Kering. (2019). *Kering standards for raw materials and manufacturing processes*. Retrieved from https://cutt.ly/hbEVLeA

Kering. (2021a). *Houses*. Retrieved from https://www.kering.com/en/houses/

Kering. (2021b). *Sustainability*. Retrieved from https://www.kering.com/en/sustainability/

Kering. (2021c). *Press. Sustainability*. Retrieved from https://www.kering.com/en/special-reports/sustainability

Kering. (2021d). *Our value chain: from creation to the customer experience*. Retrieved from https://www.kering.com/integrated-report-2020/en/chaine-de-valeur/#block-88

Khan, S., & Ahmed, M. (2017). Who are the consumers for sustainable luxury? In *2017 Global Fashion Management Conference at Vienna* (pp. 181-182). 10.15444/GFMC2017.03.02.03

Kunz, J., May, S., & Schmidt, H. J. (2020). Sustainable luxury: current status and perspectives for future research. *Business Research*, 1-61.

Li, J., & Leonas, K. K. (2019). Trends of Sustainable Development Among Luxury Industry. In M. Gardetti & S. Muthu (Eds.), *Sustainable luxury. Environmental footprints and eco-design of products and processes* (pp. 107–126). Springer. doi:10.1007/978-981-13-0623-5_6

Liao, M. Q., & Mak, A. K. (2019). "Comments are disabled for this video": A technological affordances approach understanding source credibility assessment of CSR information on YouTube. *Public Relations Review*, *45*(5), 101840. doi:10.1016/j.pubrev.2019.101840

López, B., & Monfort, A. (2017). Creating shared value in the context of sustainability: The communication strategy of MNCs. *Corporate Governance and Strategic Decision Making*, 119-135.

Luxottica. (2021). *Sustainable Development Goals*. Retrieved from https://www.luxottica.com/en/sustainable-development-goals

LVMH. (2020a). *2019 Environmental Responsibility Report*. Retrieved from https://cutt.ly/7bEKbB5

LVMH. (2020b). *2019 Social Responsibility Report*. Retrieved from https://cutt.ly/GbbQtjF

LVMH. (2021a). *Houses*. Retrieved from https://www.lvmh.com/houses/

LVMH. (2021b). *Social & environmental responsibility*. Retrieved from https://cutt.ly/Ubbm7Vg

LVMH. (2021c). *2020 Annual Report. Passionate about creativity*. Retrieved from https://cutt.ly/ubbm6iI

McKinsey & Company. (2020). *The State of Fashion 2021*. Retrieved from https://cutt.ly/smd530p

Monfort, A., & Iglesias, J. M. M. (2021). Communicating CSR in social media: Challenges and opportunities. *Comunicación y Hombre*, (17), 349–361. doi:10.32466/eufv-cyh.2021.17.645.349-361

Monfort, A., Villagra, N., & López, B. (2019). Exploring stakeholders' dialogue and corporate social responsibility (CSR) on Twitter. *El Profesional de la Información*, *28*(5). Advance online publication. doi:10.3145/epi.2019.sep.13

Morsing, M., & Schultz, M. (2006). Corporate social responsibility communication: Stakeholder information, response and involvement strategies. *Business Ethics (Oxford, England)*, *15*(4), 323–339. doi:10.1111/j.1467-8608.2006.00460.x

Okazaki, S., Plangger, K., West, D., & Menéndez, H. D. (2020). Exploring digital corporate social responsibility communications on Twitter. *Journal of Business Research*, *117*, 675–682. doi:10.1016/j.jbusres.2019.09.006

Olšanová, K., Gook, G., & Zlatić, M. (2018). Influence of luxury companies' corporate social responsibility activities on consumer purchase intention: Development of a theoretical framework. *Central European Business Review*, *7*(3), 1–25. doi:10.18267/j.cebr.200

Paliwoda-Matiolanska, A., Smolak-Lozano, E., & Nakayama, A. (2020). Corporate image or social engagement: Twitter discourse on corporate social responsibility (CSR) in public relations strategies in the energy sector. *El Profesional de la Información*, *29*(3).

Peloza, J., & Shang, J. (2011). How can corporate social responsibility activities create value for stakeholders? A systematic review. *Journal of the Academy of Marketing Science*, *39*(1), 117–135. doi:10.100711747-010-0213-6

Porter, M. E., & Kramer, M. R. (2011). Creating shared value. *Harvard Business Review*, *89*(1-2).

PVH. (2020). *2019 CR Report*. Retrieved from https://www.pvh.com/-/media/Files/pvh/responsibility/PVH-CR-Report-2019.pdf

PVH. (2021a). *Brands*. Retrieved from https://www.pvh.com/brands

PVH. (2021b). *Responsibility*. Retrieved from https://www.pvh.com/responsibility

Richemont. (2021a). Retrieved from https://www.richemont.com/en/home/

Richemont. (2021b). *Sustainability. Our approach*. Retrieved from https://www.richemont.com/en/home/sustainability/our-approach/

Richemont. (2021c). *Sustainability Report 2020*. Retrieved from https://www.richemont.com/media/4ksenvnu/sustainability_report_2020.pdf

Saxton, G. D., Ren, C., & Guo, C. (2020). Responding to Diffused Stakeholders on Social Media: Connective Power and Firm Reactions to CSR-Related Twitter Messages. *Journal of Business Ethics*, •••, 1–24.

SDGs for better fashion. (n.d.). *United Nations*. Available at: https://sustainabledevelopment.un.org/partnership/?p=28041

Swatch Group. (2020). *2020 CR Report.* Retrieved from https://www.swatchgroup.com/en/services/archive/2020/half-year-report-2020

Swatch Group. (2021a). *Brands & Companies.* Retrieved from https://www.swatchgroup.com/en/brands-companies

Swatch Group. (2021b). *Sustainability report & social policy.* Retrieved from https://www.swatchgroup.com/en/brands-companies

The Fashion Pact. (2020). *First steps to transform our industry.* Retrieved from https://cutt.ly/ybbvtee

Thomas, S. (2018). Peace of mind: The quintessential luxury. Journal of Design. *Business & Society, 4*(2), 151–169.

Todeschini, B. V., Cortimiglia, M. N., Callegaro-de-Menezes, D., & Ghezzi, A. (2017). Innovative and sustainable business models in the fashion industry: Entrepreneurial drivers, opportunities, and challenges. *Business Horizons, 60*(6), 759–770. doi:10.1016/j.bushor.2017.07.003

United Nations. (2015). *Transforming our world. The Agenda 2030 for sustainable development.* Available at: https://sdgs.un.org/sites/default/files/publications/21252030%20Agenda%20for%20Sustainable%20Development%20web.pdf

Villagra, N., López, B., & Monfort, A. (2015). The management of intangibles and corporate branding: Has anything changed in the relationship between business and society? *Revista Latina de Comunicación Social*, (70), 793. doi:10.4185/RLCS-2015-1072en

Woodside, A. G., & Fine, M. B. (2019). Sustainable fashion themes in luxury brand storytelling: The sustainability fashion research grid. *Journal of Global Fashion Marketing, 10*(2), 111–128. doi:10.1080/20932685.2019.1573699

KEY TERMS AND DEFINITIONS

Agenda 2030: This Agenda is a global plan of action for people, the planet and prosperity for all the countries and acting in collaborative partnership through 17 Sustainable Development Goals and 169 targets that involve the society as a whole.

Corporate Purpose: The purpose is a guide that gives meaning to the organization's activity by creating ethical, social, environmental and economic value, through shared beliefs and the generation of unity among stakeholders.

Corporate Social Responsibility: A term that refers to the responsibility of companies and their voluntary contribution and positive impact on the environment and society and considering the expectation of stakeholders.

CSR Communication: It is the strategy of an organization to provide true information of its business operations, social and environmental concerns, and interactions with stakeholders in online/offline channels.

Customer Engagement: It is the interaction of brands with their customers using a variety of channels to help brands build and strengthen a connection with them in the long term.

Ethical Luxury Fashion Brands: These brands are environmentally conscious and offer a high-quality product that is sustainably and ethically made.

Sustainable Consumption: It is the use of material products that minimize impacts on the environment. It is also about decoupling economic growth from environmental degradation and promoting sustainable lifestyles.

Chapter 8
How Green Is Their Latte Now?
Corporate Sustainability Effort of Starbucks During COVID-19

M. Banu Durukan
https://orcid.org/0000-0002-3619-2732
Dokuz Eylül University, Turkey

Semen Son-Turan
https://orcid.org/0000-0002-7457-8417
MEF University, Turkey

ABSTRACT

This chapter investigates whether sustainability practices of one of the leaders of the coffee industry, Starbucks, have changed during the COVID-19 pandemic as compared to the period before the virus outbreak. In particular, the authors ask which dimensions, or sub-dimensions, of sustainability in particular have been cut off first. Secondary data in the form of industry and company reports, websites, as well as research articles has been used. The findings of this study are particularly important for practitioners and researchers interested in changes in the coffee market, corporate sustainability, and consumer behavior, particularly during a systemic crisis, such as the COVID-19 pandemic. The topic is very current, and high-quality interdisciplinary research on a continuously deepening crisis with an unknown expiration date promises value-added potential, much more than "filling a gap" in the literature.

INTRODUCTION

The global economy with all its sectors has been shaken to varying degrees since the start of the pandemic in the early months of 2020. Wide-ranging lockdowns have led to increased digitization efforts to enable effective remote working structures.

DOI: 10.4018/978-1-7998-8065-3.ch008

As the Covid-19 has sparked a new health crisis, it is not surprising that consumers not only demand companies to care beyond profit-making but also expect brands to protect the health and wellbeing of their workforce and simultaneously help local communities to make the world cleaner, healthier, more resilient and equitable (Euromonitor International, 2021).

Businesses have gone bankrupt due to weakened demand for particular types of non-essential services and goods as well as due to the aggravated risk perceptions of consumers. Education, the foundation of society, and universities, the bedrocks of sustainable development, were forced to swiftly redefine their value propositions to adapt to the transformed industry conditions in a much tighter job market. Thousands of households have been left to their own devices, especially in developing and less developed countries where governmental emergency funds occasionally came solely in the form of consumer credit expansions. Similarly, financial markets have suffered unprecedented turmoil with investors frantically trying to rebalance portfolios in a quest for high-yield investments.

In midst of this chaos, the corporate world has been heavily engaged in juggling a wide range of novel priorities: Accommodating the changed needs of their employees and their families and keeping up with their day-to-day operations while coping with falling revenues, increased expenses, lay-offs and litigations. Moreover, the trust that was lost in the financial system more than a decade ago, extended to form an all-encompassing body of fear, at both the individual and collective levels: the fear of what is to come, the fear of getting sick, the fear of people, and the fear of never being able to return to the "old" normal. In this backdrop it would not be misleading to presume that budget cuts for sustainability activities might have followed or that sustainability-related activities have become to be less prioritized for a multitude of reasons.

Has this really been the case? Has there indeed been a noticeable slowdown in social and environmental efforts by businesses during the pandemic compared to those practiced in the "old" normal times? And, if so, which dimensions, or sub-dimensions, of sustainability in particular have been cut off first? These are some of the questions tackled in the present study. Furthermore, this chapter discusses how a leading business operating in a sector that has particularly been hit by lockdowns and social distancing measures has tackled the "sustainability challenge" in the face of the Covid-19 pandemic: Starbucks.

Of the liquid beverage equivalents, coffee is among the most consumed beverages worldwide with roughly 42.6 liters per person and year (12.6 liters of roast coffee and 30 liters of instant coffee) (Statista Outlook, 2021) at home as well as at numerous coffee shops. The rationale for choosing Starbucks is that the brand ranks first in the coffee shop market (Shim et al., 2021) and, particularly, its ethical sourcing approach to buying coffee which has been translated into the Coffee and Farmer Equity (C.A.F.E.) practices, one of the coffee industry's first set of ethical sourcing standards when it launched in 2004 (Starbucks Stories and News, 2020).

At the outset, the chapter briefly introduces the coffee market and provides a short history of common sustainability practices followed by a short account of the relatively scarce literature on sustainability in the coffee market. Additionally, several market statistics are presented. The rationale for selecting Starbucks as a case for this particular study (based on market share, customer reach (international, number of stores, etc.) and various other indicators (such as its popular commitment to sustainability) is explained. Secondary data in the form of industry and company reports, websites as well as research articles has been used.

The rest of the chapter is dedicated towards an analysis of the company's website, its press releases, published financial and non-financial (social impact) reports as well as media coverages on various platforms. The results are analyzed by two researchers and presented in a well-structured and thorough discussion centered around the main topic of how the company has fared on its commitments to support environmental and social sustainability during the pandemic.

The findings of this study are particularly important for practitioners and researchers interested in changes in the coffee market, corporate sustainability, and consumer behavior, particularly during a systemic crisis, such as the Covid-19pandemic. The topic is very current and high-quality interdisciplinary research on a continuously deepening crisis with an unknown expiration date promises value-added potential, much more than "filling a gap" in the literature

BACKGROUND

According to The Global Risks Report (WEF, 2021), global risk trends and their imminence have changed with Covid-19: Unquestionably, infectious diseases and their impact have the greatest impact next to existing environmental risks such as climate action failure, biodiversity loss, natural resource crises, and human environmental damage. According to the report, an emerging, yet, powerful risk that is triggered by job loss and widening inequality is livelihood crises and the erosion of social cohesion, particularly among the young generation with gloomy job prospects and deteriorating mental health. Clearly, many of these risks had been foreseen by the members of the UN and outlined in Agenda 2030.

However, progress on the SDGs has been rather slow for many countries and industries, and with the pandemic, sustainable development is more at risk than ever. The UN Secretary General's annual report on progress stresses that ending poverty by 2030, is out of reach due to the "triple threat of Covid-19, conflict and climate change," and that the pandemic might have pushed an additional 83-132 million into chronic hunger in 2020, and multiple forms of malnutrition are a problem in countries around the world. SDG 3 (good health and wellbeing), the report finds that essential health services are still disrupted in 90% of countries. SDG 4 (quality education), the report describes Covid-19 as a "generational catastrophe" for children's learning and wellbeing (UN, 2021).

According to The Coffee Barometer, written by a group of global non-governmental organizations (NGOs), Voluntary Sustainability Standards (VSS) in the coffee sector are key elements of corporate sustainability and CSR strategies across the coffee industry. However, as the name suggests, these reporting standards are of voluntary nature, and, thus, many sustainability practices in the coffee industry lack a common ground for comparability, and are to a large extend non-transparent except for large coffee roasters and procurers such as Nestle, JDE Peet's, Lavazza, and Starbucks, among others. Unknown for the most part, is how individual companies contribute towards achieving the SDGs, and there is, as of yet, no generally agreed upon measurement tool in the coffee industry with respect to the SDGs (Coffee Barometer, 2020).

The Coffee Market and Sustainability Practices

In line with the aforementioned discussion, the coffee market and the related sustainability practices are worth noting in order to put sustainability practices carried out by Starbucks into perspective.

Evolution

America is continuously ranked as the top coffee-producing region producing more than 80000 60-kg bags for the past three years. On the consumption side, Europe is the largest consumer followed by North America. The leading coffee market chains, by number of outlets, in the United States are Starbucks, Dunkin and JAB owned brands (Statista, 2021). Revenue in the coffee segment is expected to reach US$436,632m in 2021. The expected growth of the market per annum is 8.3% (CAGR 2021-2025). The market's largest segment will be the roast coffee segment with a market volume of US$319,871m in 2021 (Statista Outlook, 2021).

So, while it is quite ironic that the world coffee market evolved by a great extent through slavery practices in the 19th century (Vegro and de Almeida, 2020), companies in the coffee market have made a great deal of progress towards sustainability. Millard (2017) provides a detailed history of sustainability practices in the coffee market. According to the author, the 1990s witnessed a spark of initiatives including The Fair Labor Association, Social Accountability International, and Ethical Trading Initiative, which began providing guidelines and frameworks for participating companies to promote good labor practices in their supply chains. Accordingly, in 1997 The Global Reporting Initiative was launched promoting good practice in company reporting on sustainability followed by the Sustainable Agriculture Initiative (SAI) Platform launched in 2002, by companies including Nestlé, Kraft and Unilever, to guide food and drink companies to good practice in sustainable agriculture. In parallel, history witnessed the launch of other organizations, that shaped approaches to sustainable coffee production such as The World Business Council for Sustainable Development (WBCSD) founded in 1995, the UN Global Compact established in 2000 and, particularly the United Nations Sustainable Development Goals agreed upon by all member states of the United Nations in 2015. Backed by an increasing consumer sentiment with respect to buying coffee and other products sourced from farms under sustainable management systems (Potts et al., 2014), the market approach to sustainable coffee was established (Millard, 2017).

Although there are several certifications for coffee production, in 2017, the Sustainable Coffee Challenge and Global Coffee Platform signed a Memorandum of Understanding to move forward collaboratively towards a shared vision for 2020 (Millard, 2017). This had also important implications for retail, as by now it is very well known, that, for instance similar to fair-trade labelling, which is a market-based policy instrument that aims to reduce poverty (Fairtrade International 2019), sustainability-certifications immensely increase consumers' willingness to pay a premium for such products (Durevall, 2020).

Fairtrade, USDA Organic, Rainforest Alliance, Bird Friendly and UTZ are the main sustainable coffee standards. While Fairtrade, the oldest of them, started off by supporting small producers, Rainforest Alliance and USDA Organic have focused on protecting ecosystems and biodiversity, whereas UTZ has concentrated on sustainability. Additionally, there are corporate programs from Starbucks (Coffee and Farmer Equity Practices, CAFÉ) and Nestlé (AAA Nespresso), and 4C, the Common Code for the Coffee Community that identifies coffee that is compliant with its Code (Kolk, 2012). Nespresso has available a sustainability report published in 2017 GRI G4 Guidelines, whereas Starbucks reports its sustainability practice through non-GRI reports available from 2002-2019 on the Global Reporting Initiative (GRI)'s database (GRI, 2021).

The International Coffee Organization (ICO, 2020) expects that the Covid-19 pandemic is likely to significantly affect the global coffee sector, including production, consumption and international trade. According to the organization's analysis based on a sample of the top-20 coffee-consuming countries, which represent 71% of global demand, covering the period 1990-2018, a one percentage point drop in

GDP growth is associated with a reduction in the growth of global demand for coffee of 0.95 percentage points or 1.6 million 60-kg bags. Furthermore, according to ICO the continuous downward trend in coffee prices since 2016 has negatively affected many of the 25 million farmers globally. As a consequence, farm incomes decline and the lack of modernization of farms in adaptation to the effects of climate change represents a serious risk to the sustainability of the sector and the future supply of coffee.

Apart from the production side, retailers in general exert influence upon the earth, the environment, the people, their communities and the economic systems in several ways and coffee retailers are by no means an exception.

Vadakkepatt et al. (2020) offer a framework for achieving sustainable supply chain management in retail. Therein innovations in product, package, price, place, and promotions applicable to the coffee market may include offering durable products from recycled material, offer discounts or return deposits for collected recyclables, and communicate correct recycling policies as well as promoting reusables, and communicating practice through certifications on the consumer side. Whereas on the supplier side innovating product design to reduce packaging, using recycled materials, encouraging suppliers to use recycling labels, and paying fair wages to laborers are some of the measures identified.

A Short Account of Recent Literature on Sustainability in the Coffee Market

Similar to corporate sustainability reporting practice, which is mainly voluntary in nature, most of the coffee market has been an early adopter of Voluntary Sustainability Standards (VSS) and continues to be a leader of sustainability initiatives that transcend into the agricultural industries and their supply chain (Samper and Quinones-Ruiz, 2017).

Bager and Lambin (2020) determine that a third of 513 companies in their random sample that includes companies specialized in the supply chain function and those that undertake roasting and functions as café, show no commitment to sustainability, whereas another third report vague commitment. The final third of companies report tangible commitments to sustainability. The authors observe market differentiation through sustainability with progressive companies adopting sustainability strategies that align with their stakeholders, depending on value chain characteristics and point to the notable reliance on internal sustainability practices. Their results suggest that for common coffee sustainability indicators are relevant for all actors along the value chain, which are consistent with the Sustainable Development Goals, and a transparent, mandatory reporting framework.

Dietz et al. (2018) contribute to the existing, but highly fragmented, impact literature on topics relating to sustainability improvements in global coffee production through VSS. The authors thereby draw attention that almost no rigorous impact studies have so far assessed the impacts of industry- and company-led certification programs such as 4C, Nespresso AAA or Starbucks C.A.F.E Practices. Furthermore, they underline that existing studies fall short of providing a clear picture about the effects of VSS in various ways. Some studies are said to show positive effects for at least some environmental, social or economic suitability indicators, other studies find no or even negative impacts while assessing the same VSS. The authors quote DeFries (2017, p.8), who recently noted: "Comparison across certification programs is hampered by lack of cases that cover the range of commodities and outcome categories required for a valid comparison. [...] Many more studies are needed to confidently assess whether these different programs have led to varying outcomes" (Dietz et al., 2018).

Similarly, Vanderhaegen (2018) underscores how unclear the sustainability impact of standards is since research focuses on either economic or environmental implications. The author asserts furthermore that combining different standards in multiple certification is counterproductive; he suggests that the design of standards could improve to mitigate observed trade-offs between economic and environmental outcomes pointing out this requires increased productivity within ecological boundaries, rather than a price premium and added control mechanisms through multiple certification.

In spite of the contradictory findings, there is a large literature on the effects of sustainability labels. Moreover, interest in environmental and social production externalities is increasing along similar lines with the market share of products with sustainability labels (Wuepper et al., 2019).

How Companies Create Impact through Corporate Communication Tools

According to Biloslavo and Trnavčevič (2009), simply being green is not sufficient and a green reputation may be strongly influenced by different means of communication (i.e. advertising, public relations, etc.) and the change of identity of an object (the change of the product, the business policy, marketing strategy, etc.). As a result, conveying sustainability-related information through the corporate website and receiving feedback can be an effective tool for communication, and legitimation of the company's activities.

Similarly, Seele and Lock (2015) posit that rather simply providing information, regardless of the medium, a two-way communication which enables a dialogue where the stakeholders can voice their opinion on the company's activities, is necessary. The authors, further provide a typology of corporate social responsibility communication tools whereby they differentiate between instrumental and deliberative tools like a specially-dedicated website, reports, a handbook and brochures and a weblog, social media, stakeholder roundables, stakeholder dialogues, and advocacy groups.

Consumer Sentiment and Covid-19

According to the Euromonitor International Lifestyles Survey (Euromonitor International Consumer Trends, 2021) Consumer Sentiment on Sustainability before Covid-19 prior to the outbreak of the pandemic concentrated on issues such as reduced plastic use, worries about climate change, reduction in food waste, recycling, sustainable packaging, among others. Accordingly, during lockdowns consumers pay closer attention to companies' actions and therefore brand activism gained a new sense of social purpose. The pandemic also accelerated digital adoption particularly by younger customers as opposed to older ones, the latter preferring customer services. The response by corporation to the pandemic has followed suit. Additionally, 73% of the corporations believe that sustainability initiatives are critical for success while 69% expect customers to be more concerned about sustainability. Hence, utilizing various corporate social responsibility communication tools to achieve green reputation has gained even more importance.

MAIN FOCUS OF CHAPTER

Starbucks and its Sustainability Practices

Starbucks, as one of the front runners in its sustainability initiatives in the coffee market, has been chosen as the focus of the present study to investigate how the sustainability related activities have been influenced by the Covid-19 pandemic in the coffee market. Within this context the research questions of the study are determined to be as:

RQ1: Have sustainability-related activities slowed down during the Covid-19 pandemic?
RQ2: Has there been a slowdown in social and environmental efforts by businesses during the pandemic compared to those practiced in the "old" normal times?
RQ3: Which dimensions, or sub-dimensions, of sustainability in particular have been cut off first?

As per the company, Starbucks, sustainability has been at the core of their operations since the company's inception in 1971.

In 2002, Starbucks became the premier international company to develop a supplier system for green coffee purchasing. In their pursuit of ensuring quality coffee and compliance with their rigid standards, the company controls its coffee sourcing, roasting, and distribution (Atzori et al., 2018).

The company prides itself in its sustainability practice and underscores its wide-ranging efforts in its diverse reports and on its website. It has 18,354 stores in the Americas and 14,306 stores internationally. Among the international stores, Korea, the UK and Turkey have the highest number. The retail mix by product type for company operated-stores is 75% beverages and 20% food (Starbucks Annual Report 2020). In its 2020 annual report, a long explanation as to why the company's financial condition and results of operations have been and are expected to continue to be adversely affected by the Covid-19 pandemic, is provided, particularly stressing the high uncertainty regarding future developments (Starbucks Annual Report 2020, p. 10-18). The company's revenue as of September 2020 is USD 23.5 billion and has decreased for the past two years from USD 24.7 billion and USD 26.5 billion for 2018 and 2019, respectively (Starbucks Annual Report 2020, p. 22). The global coffee market is projected to reach USD 436.6 billion in 2021 (Statista Outlook, 2021).

According to the company's Global Social Impact Report (2019) from the start of the pandemic, it has taken quick measures to address people and planet priorities. For instance, Starbucks has committed to a first-of-its-kind $ 10 million emergency relief fund for partners in both company-operated and licensed retail store markets around the world. Moreover, In the U.S. and Canada, the company has provided temporary benefits for partners, more support for food banks and free coffee for first responders and frontline healthcare workers. A pause in the usage of their reusable cups due to sanitary reasons and the continued investments of The Starbucks Foundation supporting organizations towards recovery and resilience, is mentioned in the report. The company claims to be a resource-positive organization and has announced target reductions in carbon, waste and water by 2030. Currently 99% of their coffee and tea is ethically sourced (the target is to achieve 100% in both products), 160,000 farmers are trained (the goal is to reach 200,000 by the end of 2020). Furthermore, 40 million coffee trees have been distributed to farmers so far (the goal is to provide them 100 million by 2025), 66,000 women have been empowered (the target is to reach at least 250,000 women and families in coffee, tea and cocoa growing communities by 2025). Several statistics and targets are further given relating to recycling reusability rates, farmer loans, emergency funds, strawless lids, greener retail, renewable energy usage, and greener apron partners in addition to a Civil Rights Assessment published in 2019 (p.8). The strengthened communities and partners through the company's practices are also covered (p.9).

On their website the company explains their response to Covid-19, detailed measures ranging from mandatory facial coverings and social distancing protocols, enhanced cleaning measures, product ordering and pick up arrangements facilitated through the company's app, as well as community engagements like catastrophe pay, extending their employees (they call "partners") Covid-19 related leave of absences while continuing their fringe benefits, hardship grants, vaccination guidance childcare help and their continued support for local as well as the national community is listed (Stories, 2021).

Methodology and Analysis of Starbucks' Sustainability Practices

Starbucks' sustainability practices have been systematically analyzed by categorizing them based on the three pillars of sustainability put forth by Purvis et al. (2019), and then further broken down based on the 5P's of sustainability to tie them to the SDG's to answer the research questions of the study. The three pillars of sustainability were used as a common view (Purvis et al., 2019), first, to categorize the company's activities as social, environmental, and economic during the 1985-2020 period. The aim was to investigate the distribution of the sustainability practices of the company to get a general view of Starbucks' sustainability focus as well as to determine the shift between different pillars during the Covid-19 pandemic. Some of the practices did not fall only in one category but multiple categories. This exercise also proved that these pillars are not distinct and one activity can serve more than one purpose. Hence, some activities are categorized as environmental-social, environmental-economic, environmental-social, and economic social. The below paragraph details the used methodology: The activities between 1985 and 2020, and official press releases (Starbucks Stories, 2021) between 2018 and 2021 were analyzed by two researchers independently and all entries were divided into sustainability-related and other activities. The researchers compiled the information on these activities provided by Starbucks through different corporate social responsibility communication tools as listed by Seele and Lock (2015). The procedure for determining which activities were sustainability-related is straightforward: Beneath every heading there is a text explaining the details of that particular activity. In most cases, just looking at the heading sufficed to determine whether or not the activity was sustainability-related, in cases where the heading was not clear, the researchers directly analyzed the text of the press release. For instance, the press release dated 09.12.2020 and entitled "Starbucks Announces the Appointment of Mellody Hobson as Non-Executive Chair of the Board" is clearly not sustainability-related, whereas the sustainability practice dated 13.11.2019 with the heading "TATA Starbucks Achieves 100% Pay Equity" needed to be analyzed more closely to understand that it was about Tata Starbucks creating opportunities for women through flexible employment programs as part of ongoing commitment to diversity, equity and inclusion. Secondly, sustainability-related activities were sub-categorized into the three pillars of sustainability: social, environmental, and economic (Purvis et al., 2019). The detailed text below each heading for that particular press release was meticulously analyzed independently by both researchers who then verified the correct sub-categorization. For instance, the press release dated 26.11.2019 entitled "Starbucks Eliminates Plastic Straws in Japan Beginning January 2020" was first categorized as Environmental (En), where highlight of the text beneath include explanations such as "Change will eliminate 200 million single-use plastic straws per year from nearly 1,500 stores across Japan", which verified the correct categorization. In retrospect, the researchers together, decided that in some instances, the activity the press release was referring to related to more than one sub-category, and, hence, additional sub-categories such as Economic/Social (Ec/S), or Environmental/ Social (En/S), were created. For example, on 15.04.2019 the press release entitled "Starbucks and Cypress Creek Solar Farms Team Up to Power 360 Stores in Texas" upon first reading seemed to belong to the Environmental (En) category, however, upon analyzing the main text and highlights such as "Starbucks new approach to renewable energy investments directly benefits local community", the researchers categorized this activity as Environmental/ Social

(En/S).Consequently, the yearly distribution of the Starbucks' sustainability activities from 1985 to 2020 categorized as explained is determined and exhibited at Table 1 and Figure 1.

Table 1. Distribution of Starbucks' sustainability practices categorized based on the 3 pillars by year

Year	Total	S	En	Ec	Ec/S	En/S	En/Ec
1985	1		100%				
1992	1					100%	
1995	1		100%				
1996	1		100%				
1997	2	50%					50%
1998	1					100%	
2001	3		33%			67%	
2004	2		100%				
2005	2		50%			50%	
2006	2		50%				50%
2008	4		25%	25%		25%	25%
2009	4		75%			25%	
2010	1		100%				
2011	1					100%	
2012	5		60%			40%	
2013	2		50%	50%			
2014	3		100%				
2015	7		43%			29%	29%
2016	5	20%	40%	20%		20%	
2017	13		85%	8%		8%	
2018	16	13%	56%			25%	6%
2019	22	36%	41%	9%			14%
2020	12	50%	42%			8%	

Source: Compiled by the authors from Starbucks' website
En: Environmental sustainability; S: Social sustainability; Ec: Economic sustainability

In the initial years, Starbucks carried out activities mainly focusing on environmental sustainability. Over the years, the activities were designed to serve both environmental and social sustainability. Their focus was on developing coffee production and cooperating with the farmers to achieve sustainable production. To serve this purpose, Starbucks provided farmer support in terms of ethical sourcing, providing trees, serving farmer communities, roasting procedures. Moreover, Starbucks aimed to improve its waste management and recycling activities by working on cups, strawless lids as well as giving out coffee grounds as fertilizers. In the recent years, Starbucks focused more on how the stores are run. Renewable energy usage, programs designed for greener operations and stores were in the forefront of Starbucks activities. Employment strategies designed to provide equal opportunities were followed. As the Covid-19 period hit, even though the sustainability activities went down in terms of numbers, the focus shifted more towards social sustainability and providing relief to communities. Starbucks has put environmental and social sustainability in the heart of its sustainability practices targeted to a wide range of stakeholders from the farmers to the communities it serves.

Figure 1. Categorization of activities and press releases based on the 3 pillars of sustainability by year

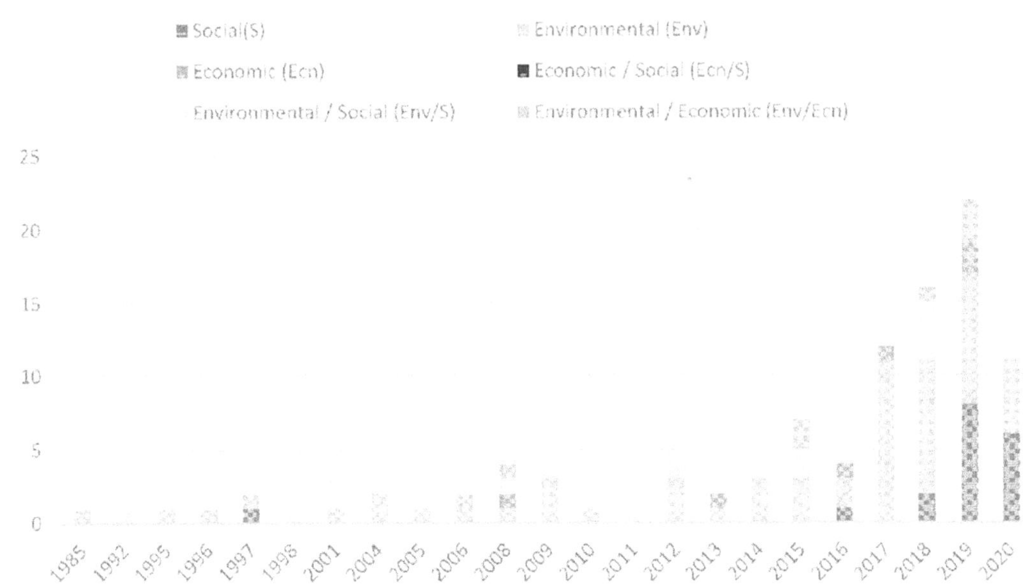

Subsequently, another categorization was made according to the 5P's that are the critical dimensions at the heart of the 2030 Agenda: people, prosperity, planet, partnership, and peace. (2030 Agenda for Sustainable Development, 2021). The rationale for applying the 5P framework was to understand how the company's sustainability practices tie into the SDGs since, as put forth by the United Nations, all P's comprise of one or more SDGs. To put it succinctly, "Peace" relates to SDG 16 (Peace, Justice and Strong Institutions), "Planet" corresponds to SDGs 6 (Clean Water and Sanitation), 7 (Affordable and Clean Energy), 12 (Responsible Consumption and Production), and 13 (Climate Action), Partnership relates to SDGs 3 (Good Health and Well-Being), 4 (Quality Education), 9 (Industry, Innovation, and Infrastructure), and 17 (Partnerships for the Goals), "People" relating to SDGs 5 (Gender Equality) and 10 (Reduced Inequalities), and "Prosperity" comprising of SDGs 1 (No Poverty) and 8 (Decent Work and Economic Growth).

During the categorization procedure, similar to the first categorization (the rationale of which was described above), the authors have determined overlapping categories like activities that serve multiple dimensions like people, prosperity, and planet or prosperity, peace and people, and, thus, for succinctness, have decided to limit the dimensions to a maximum of two by only accounting for the major purposes and not the minor purposes, which may have turned out to be indirect consequences. For instance, contributing to disaster relief may serve multiple purposes like people, planet, peace but the authors decided that it is mainly about prosperity.

Table 2. Distribution of Starbucks' sustainability practices categorized based on the 5P Framework by year

Year	Total	Planet	People	Profit	Prosperity	Peace	Planet/ People	Planet/ Profit	Planet/ Peace	Planet/ Profit/ Peace	People/ Prosperity	Profit/ People
1985	1	100%										
1992	1						100%					
1995	1	100%										
1996	1	100%										
1997	2		50%					50%				
1998	1								100%			
2001	3	33%							67%			
2004	2	100%										
2005	2	50%						50%				
2006	2	50%						50%				
2008	4	25%		25%			25%			25%		
2009	4	75%					25%					
2010	1	100%										
2011	1						100%					
2012	5	60%					40%					
2013	2	50%		50%								
2014	3	100%										
2015	7	43%					14%	29%	14%			
2016	5	40%		20%	20%		20%					
2017	3	33%		33%			33%					
2018	16	56%	13%				25%	6%				
2019	22	41%	9%	9%	18%			14%				9%
2020	12	42%	17%		25%		8%				8%	

Source: Compiled by the authors from Starbucks' website

Furthermore, in retrospect, the authors determined that, although there are items where for instance, the wording of the press release also signals "sustainability purpose", upon further analysis, the goal seemed to be more economic that could not be categorized as one of the 5 Ps. Therefore, a sixth P (Profit) dimension was added by the authors, which originally comes from the idea of the triple bottom line (Elkington, 1994). As an example, heritage site preservation that seems to serve community development has also economic advantages that is why the authors decided to group it under the dimension "profit/people".

Table 2 and Figure 2 provide the distribution of Starbucks' sustainability practices categorized based on 5P Framework over the years. The sustainability practices concentrated on planet and people. Even the profit-oriented practices also had a planet or people perspective. During the pandemic, Starbucks' sustainability practices were geared towards serving the planet, prosperity and peace. These findings also support the conclusion derived from the categorization based on the 3 pillars. Starbucks being sensitive to needs of its stakeholders have focused on their needs in times of hardship during the Covid-19 period. Hence, even though the number of activities went down, the magnitude and the impact of the activities were aimed to be much bigger.

Figure 2. Categorization of activities and press releases based on the 5P Framework by year

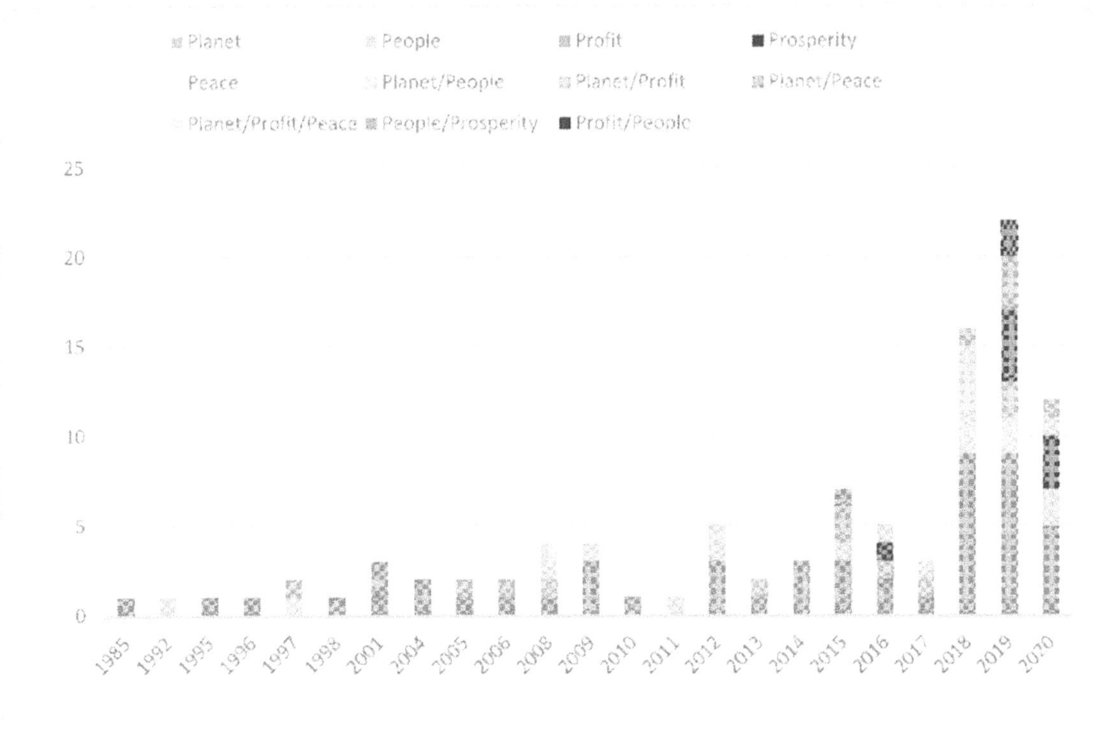

The limitation of this analysis is that, as mentioned above, the news items being of qualitative nature, necessitated a subjective evaluation and hence may be affected by researcher bias. To minimize this shortcoming, a parallel evaluation has been made independently by two researchers and results have been compared subsequently.

Another limitation of the analysis to be worth noting is that the magnitude, the impact and the budget of the sustainability practices are not considered due to data unavailability. Some practices being more strategy oriented or some emphasizing community or supplier development may require higher budgets and their impact might be greater. Thus, the number of activities may be lower but the required budget might be higher. On the other hand, some activities related to the same goal, such as developing straw-less lids or cups, are counted multiple times.

To further understand the sustainability activities of Starbucks around the pandemic, a second analysis of the official press releases available at the company's website were analyzed. This analysis shows that out of 72 official press releases between September 2018 and April 2021, 26 are about sustainability (36%). There are no press releases after 26.01.2021. For the Covid-19 period starting 1.04.2020 the number of Sustainability-related releases is 8 out of a total of 15 (53%) for a one-year period with the majority addressing Economic/Social Aspects of sustainability. Table 3 summarizes the sustainability-related activities.

Table 3. Sustainability-related press releases (September 2018 - April 2021)

Date	News Headline	Category
12.01.2021	Starbucks expands initiatives to advance opportunity, equity and inclusion in the communities it serves	Ec/S
10.09.2020	Starbucks Strawless Lids Now Available Across the U.S. and Canada	En
19.08.2020	The Starbucks Foundation and Alshaya Group Donate $200,000 to Lebanon Disaster Relief Efforts	Ec/S
8.04.2020	Starbucks commits $10M USD in Covid-19 relief for partners around the world	Ec/S
1.04.2020	The Starbucks Foundation Donates More Than $3M to Global Covid-19 Relief Efforts	Ec/S
18.03.2020	Starbucks Hosts Virtual Annual Meeting of Shareholders Rooted in Caring for People and Growing its Business Responsibly	S
16.03.2020	Starbucks Transforms Mental Health Benefit for U.S. Employees	S
21.01.2020	Starbucks Commits to a Resource-Positive Future	En
16.01.2020	Starbucks Expands Commitment in Underserved Communities Across the U.S.	S
26.11.2019	Starbucks Eliminates Plastic Straws in Japan Beginning January 2020	En
13.11.2019	TATA Starbucks Achieves 100% Pay Equity	Ec/S
29.10.2019	Starbucks invests $10 million in small business in Chicago	Ec/S
10.10.2019	Starbucks announces Community Store expansion in South Korea in 2020	Ec/S
29.08.2019	Starbucks Preserves Heritage Site in China to Open Flagship Location in Tianjin	
19.08.2019	Starbucks, United Way, Mary's Place and Wellspring welcome UW to coalition supporting local unsheltered families	Ec/S
13.05.2019	Starbucks Completes Issuance of Third and Largest Sustainability Bond	Ec
15.04.2019	Starbucks and Cypress Creek Solar Farms Team Up to Power 360 Stores in Texas	En/S
20.03.2019	Starbucks commits $100 million as cornerstone investor in Valor Siren Ventures I	Ec
20.03.2019	Greener cups, fewer straws and tracing your coffee's journey via app	En
27.02.2019	Closed Loop Partners Announces 12 Winners of the NextGen Cup Challenge	En
04.02.2019	Starbucks Canada Announces a Commitment to Rescue 100 Percent of Food Available for Donation	S
17.01.2019	Starbucks Mexico opens its second store operated exclusively by older citizens	Ec/S
29.11.2018	Starbucks Opens New Community Store in Dallas Oak Cliff Area	S
23.10.2018	Starbucks Deepens its Commitment to China by Creating Pathways in Yunnan Coffee Farming Communities	S
25.09.2018	Starbucks Commits $20M for Emergency Relief to Farmers Impacted by Coffee Price in Central America	En/S
24.09.2018	Starbucks Recognized as Employer of Choice for its Unique Family Culture in China	S

Source: Compiled by the authors from Starbucks' website

Explanations: En: Environmental sustainability; S: Social sustainability; Ec: Economic sustainability

SOLUTIONS AND RECOMMENDATIONS

Based on the authors' analysis, Starbucks as one of the big players in the coffee-industry, has engaged sustainability-related activities that fall under all three pillars (Purvis et al., 2019) as well as all five P's (2030 Agenda for Sustainable Development, 2021) of sustainability early on. With the break out of the pandemic, measures have intensified towards both, help to communities, but also in the form of mental benefits and increased safety precautions for its employees.

Even though the number of sustainability-related activities went down as suggested by the first research question, the focus of the activities shifted more towards the social dimension. Hence, the findings also show that the number of social and environmental activities went down as suggested by the second research question. However, as the research question 3 suggests, the number of activities solely focusing on the environment went down further during the Covid-19 pandemic but persisted. Hence the shift has been towards social efforts. It should also be noted that the findings of the study are based on the number of activities not the budget. The final analysis and Table 3 suggest that these activities may require a higher budget. In conclusion, the answers to the research questions suggest that the sustainability related activities went down during the Covid-19 pandemic in quantity and the efforts have shifted more towards the social dimension which focused on providing relief to stakeholders. These efforts may be less in numbers but may require a higher budget.

What is also striking is that the company, which has frequently issued press releases in the past, has stopped doing so on its website since February 2021. However, this does not necessarily mean that it halted its efforts to inform its stakeholders about its performance and progress. On the contrary, on another section on its website, an interesting development about its plan to start sustainability reporting in line with SASB practices is announced. Beginning in 2021, the company has committed to incorporate The Sustainability Accounting Standards Board (SASB) ESG reporting standards into its annual Global Environmental and Social Impact Report. Accordingly, the company continues its commitment of proactively publishing annual updates on their performance against key ESG factors, a practice that had started in 2001 This development is in line with Seele and Lock (2015), who recommend multiple tools of sustainability practice communication that serve towards enhancing stakeholder dialogue.

FUTURE RESEARCH DIRECTIONS

The key performance indicators of sustainability-related activities, their measurement, reporting frameworks, and auditing aspects are still grey areas. Reporting standards are to a large extend voluntary, which leads only certain sectors in the economy to engage is such "costly" efforts. Furthermore, there are no unanimously agreed upon reporting standards. As a result, there is a lot of room for diverse research opportunities regarding various aspects of sustainability across the whole supply chain from sourcing, transportation and production to marketing, sales and customer relationship management. Furthermore, compared to the coffee market, there are other industries and sectors that have received less attention, or stakeholder pressure, which also deserve scrutiny like insurance, construction or the film industry. Additionally, the value of sustainability efforts is for the most part unknown, and voluntary activities, if practiced at all, are a result of public and consumer awareness or competitive pressure rather than altruistic reasons. For that reason, research portraying the medium-to-long run relationship between sustainability and financial performance as well as the value of companies may be fruitful, both as a contribution to academic, but also for motivating the industry.

The communication of the sustainability-related efforts utilizing different corporate social responsibility communication tools and their impact may also lead to communication strategies for companies in establishing their reputation for being sustainable and creating a shared value (Biloslavo and Trnavčevič, 2009; Porter and Kramer, 2011).

DISCUSSION AND CONCLUSION

This paper aimed at understanding, in light of the current extraordinary, pandemic-related circumstances, whether or not sustainability-related activities have become to be less prioritized for Starbucks. The paper analyzed pre- and mid-Covid 19 press releases announced on the website of the company to further determine which dimensions, or sub-dimensions, of sustainability in particular might have potentially been neglected.

To that end, this study has summarized Starbucks' sustainability-related activities with the intention to pinpoint how or whether they have changed with the start of the Covid-19 pandemic.

Clearly, the company, as a leader in innovative practices along its whole supply chain, has not shied away from continuing to care about economic, environmental, and social sustainability as evidenced in Tables 1- 3. Its support to all its stakeholders has been explained in detail in the previous sections, and has neither changed with the start of the pandemic nor have any sustainability dimensions (economic, social, environmental) been neglected. This determination is consistent with its track record in various aspects. For instance, going back to their ethical sourcing approach to buying coffee is Coffee and Farmer Equity (C.A.F.E.) Practices, which was one of the coffee industry's first set of ethical sourcing standards when it launched in 2004, Starbucks coffee, since 2015, has been verified as 99 percent ethically sourced and we are the largest coffee retailer to achieve this milestone Clearly, the company has continued these efforts.

Renewable energy, farmer support, disaster relief, addressing problems of underrepresented communities and groups, social development programs, donations, grants, funds and support for good causes, the development of environmental-friendly services and products, as well as various employee support programs are recurring activities the company prides itself in.

Also, Starbucks has set a track record of being one of the first responders to national and global disasters. It has also reacted swiftly with the outbreak of the pandemic. On 01.04.2020, The Starbucks Foundation donated more than $3M to global Covid -19 relief efforts, and on 08.04.2020 announced its commitment of $10M USD in Covid-19 relief for partners around the world. In August of the same year, the Starbucks Foundation and Alshaya Group have committed matching donations of $100,000 each to support disaster relief and rebuilding efforts on the ground for Lebanon following the catastrophic explosions in Beirut Port in the same month. Moreover, the pandemic did not stop the company to continue caring for the environment, as evidenced by the company's efforts to phase out plastic straws worldwide, a recyclable, strawless lid is the new standard for iced beverages in Starbucks stores, and, the community, evidence by its announcement in January 2021, to expand initiatives advancing opportunity, equity and inclusion in the community it serves. Succinctly put, the company commits to invest $100 million to create the Starbucks Community Resilience Fund focused on advancing racial equity and environmental resilience by supporting small business growth and community development projects in honor of Dr. Martin Luther King Jr.'s legacy

This paper has demonstrated that Starbucks, a major player in the coffee market, from sourcing its raw materials to caring for its employees, has shown utmost interest in pursuing its sustainability practice throughout the pandemic. Even though the number of activities declined, the focus has shifted more towards the social dimension, which may require higher budgets. Moreover, the social efforts are more visible and impact the lives of people directly. Hence, such efforts, especially during times of hardship such as the Covid-19 pandemic, may have more impact and create a "shared value" (Porter and Kramer, 2011) as people become more sensitive.

As addressed in the sub-section "How Companies Create Impact through Corporate Communication Tools", companies, to legitimize their sustainability practices and create "shared value" based on value principles (Porter and Kramer, 2011), simply posting news on their sustainability practices in a one-way communication manner is not enough. Starbucks, sets an example of creating shared value by engaging in an open public dialogue through its social media accounts like Twitter, voluntarily and transparently publishes its sustainability impact through platforms like the GRI database (GRI, 2021) as mentioned in the text, and the company for many years, has been named one of the best companies to work for due to factors such as its work-life balance, perks and benefits, best company for women according to various news agencies (Brown, 2019).

As a result, other companies can adopt similar practices, forge alliances with non-profit organizations, not only care for direct stakeholders, the local community but also afar countries that are plagued by natural disaster and other perils. The company's location selections for new venues also sets an example for preserving natural treasuries and shows its respect for honoring cultural values in respective markets it has entered during the course of its expansion.

This research received no specific grant from any funding agency in the public, commercial, or not-for-profit sectors.

REFERENCES

Agenda for Sustainable Development. (2021). Accessed at: https://www.unssc.org/sites/unssc.org/files/2030_agenda_for_sustainable_development_kcsd_primer_en.pdf

Akiyama, T. (2001). Coffee market liberalization since 1990. *Commodity market reforms: Lessons of two decades*, 83-120.

Atzori, R., Shapoval, V., & Murphy, K. S. (2018). Measuring Generation Y consumers' perceptions of green practices at Starbucks: An IPA analysis. *Journal of Foodservice Business Research*, *21*(1), 1–21.

Bager, S. L., & Lambin, E. F. (2020). Sustainability strategies by companies in the global coffee sector. *Business Strategy and the Environment*, *29*(8), 3555–3570.

Biloslavo, R., & Trnavčevič, A. (2009). Web sites as tools of communication of a "green" company. *Management Decision*, *47*(8), 1158–1173.

Brown, D. (2019). Google, Microsoft and Starbucks are some of the best places to work in the US, workers say. *USA Today*. Accessed at: https://www.usatoday.com/story/money/2019/03/28/google-among-best-companies-work-us-ranked-region/3276066002/

Coffee Barometer. (2020). Accessed at: https://coffeebarometer.org/

Dietz, T., Auffenberg, J., Chong, A. E., Grabs, J., & Kilian, B. (2018A). The voluntary coffee standard index (VOCSI). Developing a composite index to assess and compare the strength of mainstream voluntary sustainability standards in the global coffee industry. *Ecological Economics*, *150*, 72–87.

Durevall, D. (2020). Fairtrade and Market Efficiency: Fairtrade-Labeled Coffee in the Swedish Coffee Market. *Economies*, *8*(2), 30.

Elkington, J. (1994). Towards the sustainable corporation: Win-win-win business strategies for sustainable development. *California Management Review*, *36*(2), 90–100.

Euromonitor International. (2021). *Reimagining Consumer Markets*. Accessed at https://www.euromonitor.com/

Euromonitor International Consumer Trends. (2021). *Top 10 Global Consumer Trends 2021*. Accessed at: https://blog.euromonitor.com/?_gl=1%2A3ehags%2A_ga%2AODI2OTY0ODY4LjE2MTI4NjQ4MDc.%2A_ga_6D3QFKH8G9%2AMTYxMjg2NDgwNi4xLjAuMTYxMjg2NDgwNi4w

Fairtrade International. (2019). *What Is Fairtrade?* Available at: http://www.fairtrade.net/what-is-fairtrade.html

GRI. (2021). *Global Reporting Initiative Database*. Available at: https://database.globalreporting.org/search/

Kolk, A. (2012). Towards a sustainable coffee market: Paradoxes faced by a multinational company. *Corporate Social Responsibility and Environmental Management*, *19*(2), 79–89.

Millard, E. (2017). Still brewing: Fostering sustainable coffee production. *World Development Perspectives*, *7*, 32–42.

Porter, M., & Kramer, M. R. (2011, January-February). Creating shared value. *Harvard Business Review*, 1–17.

Potts, J., Lynch, M., Wilkings, A., Huppé, G. A., Cunningham, M., & Voora, V. A. (2014). *The state of sustainability initiatives review 2014: Standards and the green economy*. International Institute for Sustainable Development.

Purvis, B., Mao, Y., & Robinson, D. (2019). Three pillars of sustainability: In search of conceptual origins. *Sustainability Science*, *14*, 681–695.

Samper, L. F., & Quiñones-Ruiz, X. F. (2017). Towards a balanced sustainability vision for the coffee industry. *Resources*, *6*(2), 17.

Seele, P., & Lock, I. (2015). Instrumental and/or deliberative? A typology of CSR communication tools. *Journal of Business Ethics*, *131*(2), 401–414.

Shim, J., Moon, J., Song, M., & Lee, W. S. (2021). Antecedents of Purchase Intention at Starbucks in the Context of Covid-19 Pandemic. *Sustainability*, *13*(4), 1758.

Starbucks Social Impact Report. (2019). Accessed at: https://www.starbucks.com/responsibility/global-report

Starbucks Stories. (2021). Accessed at: https://stories.starbucks.com/press/2021/starbucks-commitment-to-environmental-social-and-governance-disclosures/

Starbucks Stories and News. (2020). *C.A.F.E. Practices: Starbucks Approach to Ethically Sourcing Coffee.* Accessed at: https://stories.starbucks.com/press/2020/cafe-practices-starbucks-approach-to-ethically-sourcing-coffee/

Statista. (2021). *Market Share of Selected Leading Coffee Chains in the United States as of October 2019, by number of outlets.* Accessed at: https://www.statista.com/statistics/250166/market-share-of-major-us-coffee-shops/

Statista Outlook. (2021). *Coffee Worldwide.* Accessed at: https://www.statista.com/outlook/30010000/100/coffee/worldwide

Tan, B. C., & Yeap, P. F. (2012). What drives green restaurant patronage intention? *International Journal of Business and Management*, *7*(2), 215.

UN. (2021). *UN Secretary-General's annual report on SDG progress.* Accessed at: https://sdg.iisd.org/news/secretary-generals-sdg-progress-report-recaps-pandemic-impacts-on-17-global-goals/

Vadakkepatt, G. G., Winterich, K. P., Mittal, V., Zinn, W., Beitelspacher, L., Aloysius, J., ... Reilman, J. (2020). Sustainable Retailing. *Journal of Retailing*.

Vegro, C. L. R., & de Almeida, L. F. (2020). Global coffee market: Socio-economic and cultural dynamics. In *Coffee Consumption and Industry Strategies in Brazil* (pp. 3–19). Woodhead Publishing.

WEF. (2021). *The Global Risks Report.* Accessed at: http://www3.weforum.org/docs/WEF_The_Global_Risks_Report_2021.pdf

Wuepper, D., Clemm, A., & Wree, P. (2019). The preference for sustainable coffee and a new approach for dealing with hypothetical bias. *Journal of Economic Behavior & Organization*, *158*, 475–486.

ADDITIONAL READING

Ballou, B., Heitger, D., & Landes, C. (2006). The rise of corporate sustainability reporting: A rapidly growing assurance opportunity. *Journal of Accountancy*, *202*(6), 65–74.

Campbell, K., & Helleloid, D. (2016). Starbucks: Social responsibility and tax avoidance. *Journal of Accounting Education*, *37*, 38–60. doi:10.1016/j.jaccedu.2016.09.001

De Luca, P., & Pegan, G. (2014). The coffee shop and customer experience: A study of the US market. In *Handbook of research on retailer-consumer relationship development* (pp. 173–196). IGI Global. doi:10.4018/978-1-4666-6074-8.ch010

Goodman, M., Rolland, D., & Bazzoni, J. O. K. (2009). Greening corporate identity: CSR online corporate identity reporting. *Corporate Communications*.

Macdonald, K. (2007). Globalising justice within coffee supply chains? Fair Trade, Starbucks and the transformation of supply chain governance. *Third World Quarterly*, *28*(4), 793–812. doi:10.1080/01436590701336663

Murthy, P. S., & Naidu, M. M. (2012). Sustainable management of coffee industry by-products and value addition—A review. *Resources, Conservation and Recycling*, *66*, 45–58. doi:10.1016/j.resconrec.2012.06.005

Reinecke, J., Manning, S., & Von Hagen, O. (2012). The emergence of a standards market: Multiplicity of sustainability standards in the global coffee industry. *Organization Studies*, *33*(5-6), 791–814. doi:10.1177/0170840612443629

Taecharungroj, V. (2017). Starbucks' marketing communications strategy on Twitter. *Journal of Marketing Communications*, *23*(6), 552–571. doi:10.1080/13527266.2016.1138139

KEY TERMS AND DEFINITIONS

5 Ps: Refers to the five pillars (people, planet, prosperity, peace, and partnership) for achieving sustainability as defined by the United Nations Agenda 2030.

COVID-19 Pandemic: The pandemic caused by the novel coronavirus disease that spread around the world in the first quarter of 2020.

Lockdown: A state of isolation that many countries have fully or partially instituted during the pandemic.

Profit: The remainder of revenue (sales) after all costs and expenses are deducted.

Revenue: Income gained by selling a product or a service.

Sustainability: The global capacity to endure in a relatively stable manner across various domains of life.

Three Pillars of Sustainability: The three aspects of sustainability are social, environmental, and economic.

Chapter 9
Health Schools in Spain:
Health Promotion at the Regional Level to Advance Sustainable Development Goal 3

María Luisa Gracia-Pérez
Universidad de Zaragoza, Spain

Marta Gil-Lacruz
Universidad de Zaragoza, Spain

Arelys López-Concepción
Universidad de Zaragoza, Spain

Victor Bazán-Monasterio
Universidad de Zaragoza, Spain

Isabel Saz-Gil
Universidad de Zaragoza, Spain

Ana I. Gil-Lacruz
Universidad de Zaragoza, Spain

ABSTRACT

In 2015, the United Nations adopted 17 major Sustainable Development Goals (SDGs) to address current economic, social, and environmental challenges. Governments play a key role in achieving the SDGs through advocacy, awareness, and regulation. In this work, the authors focus on SDG 3, "Guarantee a Healthy Life and Promote Well-Being for All Ages." Specifically, the articulation of citizen participation for health promotion in health schools is reviewed. They have been selected by choosing four schools and a Spanish entity that show how health education can facilitate the development of citizen participation in the field of health. The health schools and their corresponding training programs show the multiplicity of ways that citizens acquire access to the health field, ranging from information to decision-making in the system.

1. INTRODUCTION

The formulation of SDG 3 ("Guarantee a healthy life and promote well-being for all at all ages") expresses that health is a good that must be achieved because of the value it represents in itself. However, the Agenda reminds us that health is also a mean to achieve other goals and a reliable indicator of global progress towards sustainable development (World Health Organization, 2015). Health is one of the pil-

DOI: 10.4018/978-1-7998-8065-3.ch009

lars of the 2030 Agenda for Sustainable Development. Therefore, promoting health is essential for the achievement of the SDGs. In November 2016, the Ninth World Conference on Health Promotion was held in Shanghai, organized by the Government of China and the World Health Organization, culminating in the Shanghai Declaration on Health Promotion in the 2030 Agenda. for Sustainable Development. The Conference showed the close link between health and sustainable development with the aim of sensitizing national governments, municipal leaders and other social agents about the enormous potential to promote health in all sectors of society. The Shanghai Declaration emphasizes the need to implement local health policies that promote social inclusion, the integration of health into municipal policies, as well as promoting community collaboration to promote health and reorient municipal health and social services towards equity and universal health coverage.

According to the World Health Organization, health promotion allows people to have greater control of their own development. It encompasses a wide range of social and environmental interventions aimed at benefiting and protecting individual health and quality of life by preventing and solving the root causes of health problems without focusing solely on treatment and cure (Camarelles, 2020). Health promotion has three essential components:

- Good health governance, requires that policy makers in all government departments make health a central aspect of their policy. This means that they must consider health implications in all their decisions, and prioritize policies that prevent people from getting sick or injured.
- Health education is as a fundamental element, since it facilitates the participation of people not only to acquire knowledge, skills and information, but also attitudes, behavior and ethics values that allow them to choose healthy options and to be patient autonomous (León Correa, 2008). Indeed, the inclusion of a basic training subject in Health Education in the curriculum of the Degree in Early Childhood Education has contributed to a better perception of the knowledge and skills necessary to develop Health Promotion and Education strategies at school (Torres-García and Santana-Hernández, 2017). However, some researchers highlights that health education as a cross-cutting theme in the Spanish educational curriculum requires efforts from families, caregivers and social agents to turn into an efficient Health Promotion tool. Therefore, to be systematically and widely integrated into the curricular projects of all schools requires including effective practices, through innovation and investigation activities (Gavó et al., 2008; Gavidia, 2009).
- Healthy cities, the local level plays a leading role in promoting good health. This model has emphasized public policies and transcends community activities and isolated intersectoral projects, beyond the state or government focus, differing with other models and theories such as Franco highlights (Franco, 2006). Specifically, individual and neighborhoods socio-economic status, which are explained through theories like Pierre Bourdieu's capital interaction theory (Frohlich and Abel, 2014) or others Health Theories such as Life Course Theory, Link and Phelan Fundamental Cause Theory, Social Capital or Health Lifestyle Theory (these last two highly related to the previous paragraph) (Cockerham, Hamby and Oates, 2017), are factors to understand the environment in where Health Promotion Schools will develop their activities. For example, "local health professionals are more likely to achieve success in addressing the social determinants of health as they bring public health administration, community leaders, funding organizations, and other stakeholders to the table and demonstrate to them the opportunities to reduce health disparities and improve health across all sectors of society by focusing on social determinants" (Hunter, Neiger, and West, 2011, p. 527).

Considering these components, Ramirez et al., (2020), identify: gender, social and environmental determinants of health, climate change, non-communicable diseases and mental health, as priorities to consider for the fulfillment of the SDGs and its effective implementation in Health in all policies in Spain. This transversal approach requires the effective coordination of the different agents of the health system and a determined effort to improve our awareness and social sensitization about the role of participation in improving our health.

This chapter reviews the articulation of citizen participation for education and health promotion in Spain, delving into the institutional antecedents. The Health Schools in various Autonomous Communities are presented as an example. The five selected entities show important institutional differences and very varied activities that show the multiplicity of ways of citizen participation in the health field.

2. BACKGROUND

2.1 Spanish Health System Description

Not only Spanish health system is complex and practically universal coverage, but also is provided with scarce resources funded with taxes and inside a technological transition period in which costs related to technology are more and more expensive (Macia-Soler and Moncho-Vasallo, 2007; Valls-Martínez and Abad Segura, 2018). In this sense, Spanish health system has some characteristics in this manuscript remarkably.

Firstly, its financed with very limited resources linked to the annual evolution of Spanish tax revenue, as a consequence of its financed mechanism inside of the general system (Cantanero, 2006); Secondly, this mechanism has been triggering territorial's inequalities as well as the equity ones between Autonomous Comunities, especially since the 2008 economic crisis (Cantarero, 2008; Martín, 2016); Thirdly, and as a consequence of this economic crisis, with resources cut back, some authors highlight the need to promote participatory processes that involve all social actors and, above all, citizens, considered not as recipients and users, but also as active and collaborative agents (Cía et al., 2018); Finally, this health promotion participatory process adheres mainly to intrapersonal models, focusing on helping people become empowered by increasing awareness of the risks and benefits of behavior change, and guiding them in implementing healthy behavior (Gil-Girbau, et al., 2021).

A practical example is the actual COVID-19 pandemic crisis. Some researchers recommend educational interventions should focus on helping the population to understand the benefits of compliance with preventive behaviors and the harms of unhealthy behaviors. mitigating practices that are constructed as moral imperatives, required to prevent harm to oneself and others through hand-washing, social distancing, or social isolating (Kamran and Naeim, 2020; Prosser et al., 2020). This actual pandemic crisis has caused both a reorganization of services and more costs of protection material (funded by Central Administration and, in the end, taxes) (Ares-Blanco et al., 2021).

According to the ownership of Spanish health services organizations, private and public centers (in different areas – physiotherapy, psychiatric, hospitals, etc.) coexists. For example, the *Servicio Andaluz de Salud* guarantees the right to choose between public and private hospitals for surgical interventions based on a maximum waiting time (120 days), which under these circumstances it allows to speak of mixed markets with "implicit bonds" (Miragaya, 2008). In this sense, it is necessary keep in mind the decentralization of health system. For instance, comparing the global activity (hospital assistance) of the centers between autonomous communities without taking into account the type of care provided (acute, chronic or psychiatric care) can lead to a significant distortion in the activity indices (mainly average stay and turnover), depending on how it is distributed the weight of the activity of each healthcare purpose and its financing, between the different territories, as this situation may vary in each autonomous community (Gisper and Giné, 2006).

Since the beginning of the 2008 economic crisis, the problems of rural regions have been accentuated because of increase in unemployment and the poverty rate, reduction and suppression of public and private services, equipment and investments, etc (Sanz Tolosana, 2018). Also, there are differences of health habits between districts –rural or urban residents- and gender – female or male – and generational cohorts in Spain. For instance, overweight and obesity occur to a greater extent among men and in rural areas (Hernán, Fernández, and Ramos, 2004). Another example is the gap between health education practices in the nutritional area (mainly influenced by material resources available and cultural factor) and the incorporation of messages into the practices of older people living in rural areas (Rivero-Jiménez, Conde-Caballero and Mariano-Juárez, 2016).

2.2 Background on the Importance of Participation and Health Education for the Health System

The improvement of our well-being and quality of life have to do with social achievements such as the increase in life expectancy and the development of health care, but it also presents numerous social and health challenges such as population aging, multiple pathologies and the chronification of diseases. Lifestyle and socioeconomic determinants of health are key factors when it comes to predicting our well-being and, as such, are indicators collected in numerous health surveys (Oliver and González, 2020).

Therefore, increasingly, it is necessary for citizens to be aware of their health status and take responsibility for caring for them throughout their life cycle (Augsburger and Fondato, 2020). The concept of "expert patient" has to do with the acquisition of knowledge, skills, attitudes and values of the citizen about his health (González Mestre, 2012)

Faced with the previous healthcare model in which the patient was characterized by his passivity, from the current impulse towards the biopsychosocial model of health, the patient must adopt an active and integrated role in making decisions about his health. Faced with the contemporary risks of medicalization, commercialism and technology, primary care and the health system as a whole must provide a democratizing and humanizing coping response (García Aguayo, 2021). In this point, it is essential to indicate some theories and models related to Health Promotion. According to Grech and Grech (2021) and Heard et al. (2020), some theories and models that are related with health promotion are:

- Health Belief Model: to clarify why people may or may not adopt certain health behaviours and use health services through four core constructs identified, which determine a subject's behaviour: 'perceived susceptibility', 'perceived severity', 'perceived barriers', and 'perceived costs of adhering to the proposed intervention'.
- Transtheoretical (stages of change) Model: to suggest that the willingness and readiness of people to modify a health related behavior change between individuals and within individuals over time.
- Theory of Planned Behavior: to display that behavioral intention is dependent on a person's perceived control of opportunities, resources and the skills needed to perform such behavior.

- Theory of Reasoned Action: to show that individual's behavior is determined by his or her intrinsic behavioral intentions, which are based on his or her 'attitude' towards the behavior in question and beliefs on whether other people ('subjective norms') would support such behavior
- Social Learning Theory or Social Cognitive Theory: to indicate that behavior is shaped though observation and imitation as well as by positive reinforcement, through six constructs: 'reciprocal determinism', 'behavioural capability', 'expectations', 'self-efficacy', 'observational learning', and 'reinforcements'.
- Social Ecological Model: to describe that an individual's biological makeup and physiology are continuously shaped by the immediate physical and social environments.
- Intersectionality theory (applied to health promotion): to reveal and explore implications for individuals and groups who sit at unique, intersecting social positions striving to understand how interactions between societal and individual factors play out in diverse, localized contexts.

Hence, at present, the patient's opinion is no longer simply a question of value, it is now a relevant indicator of results measurement of the quality of the Health Administration (eg, European Foundation Quality Management Model, Gracia-Pérez, 2015).

The P4 medicine (Sobradillo, Pozo and Agustí, 2010) constitutes an interesting example of this change. Leroy Hood coined this term to integrate into the same model of health intervention: personalization, prevention, prediction and participation. The decisions shared between the patient and the doctor have to do not only with making decisions about his health status, but also with his responsibility in the rational use of resources, the prioritization of preventive plans and the evaluation of the system.

These issues require training. You learn to participate and the health system should take responsibility for this training (Ruiz-Azarola and Perestelo-Pérez, 2012). The way in which training for participation in health has been articulated has evolved over time.

For decades, in health care we have witnessed the synergy of emerging and complementary issues such as cultural sensitivity and health literacy (Gracia and Gil-Lacruz, 2019). When health literacy is promoted, the benefits are observable on several fronts: the improvement of self-esteem and responsibility towards one's own health, the development of healthy habits, the better control over the state of health, the reduction in the number of consultations, emergencies and health complications, building trust in the healthcare professional, etc.

One of the first scientific findings of these improvements was obtained through the pioneering Chronic Disease Self-Management Program (CDSMP) promoted by Stanford University in the 1980s). Later, in the 90s of the last century, the American Group Health Research Institute promoted the Chronic Care Model (CCM), which had important repercussions on the initiatives to promote participation in Spanish health.

The CCM prioritizes among other issues: the community, self-management, clinical information systems, without neglecting satisfaction with the system and saving costs. The positive results of the implementation of this program were observed in 35% fewer days of hospitalization in patients with diabetes, asthma, and congestive heart failure.

These types of programs have also been designed and implemented from Europe. According to Nuño, Rodríguez, Piñera, Zaballa and Bikandi (2013: 333) would highlight the complementary government initiatives launched in England since 2002. "The Expert Patients Program", with the aim of providing and evaluating support for self-management on a large scale also English project, Co-Creating Health, which combines the delivery of self-management courses for patients, specific training for doctors and service improvement processes.

2.3 Participation for Health in Spain: Institutional Background

Citizen participation in the field of health has acquired special relevance in recent years in Spain. Proof of this prominence is found in the legal regulation to which it has been subjected. We can go back to the 1986 General Health Law as the frame of reference for the development of citizen participation in health through the Health Councils of the Autonomous Communities. In the Health Councils, this participation intervenes both in the formulation of health policy and in the control of its execution (Moreno, 2021).

In addition to the important role of Health Councils, other institutional tools provide resources for citizens to empower themselves and to exercise such participation in the health system with the relevant information and training.

For example, patient associations constitute a key part of health participation today. However, according to Arrighi, Blancafort and Novell (2010), the segmentation of the central theme (different diseases) that brings together the associates entails representation difficulties and limits their ability to work in common interests. In order to join associative efforts, the Spanish Patient Forum was created. In fact, its 2006 Political Agenda (Arrghi et al, 2010) defends the importance of integrating patient representatives in the decision-making and democratization of healthcare processes.

In parallel, the Expert Patient Programs and Patient Schools emerge as an institutional response and from the support of the international trajectory of reorientation of the CCM, Stanford University and the English experience. The Expert Patient Programs of the Catalan Health Institute and of the Education, Health and Society Foundation of Murcia in 2006 would be the pioneers.

Subsequently, in 2008, the Andalusian School of Patients attached to the Andalusian Regional Government Health Council (with its own method) and the University of the patients of the Josep Laporte Foundation and the Autonomous University of Barcelona would join. These were followed in 2009 by the Escola Galega de Saúde para Ciudadáns del Servicio Gallego de Saúde (SERGAS). Finally, in 2010, Paziente Bizia-Active Patient from Osakidetza of the Basque Country and the School of Health and Care of Castilla-La Mancha, linked to the Health Service of Castilla-La Mancha (SESCAM), are presented. In the case of Aragon, the participation program was based on the initiative of the Aragonese Institute of Health Sciences (IACS), in collaboration with Patient Associations.

The empowerment of citizens through health training in these schools is achieved through various informational and training formats, combining face-to-face classes with the use of technology (Ossebaard and Seydel, 2012). Thanks to social networks, the exchange of experiences, connection and solidarity links between professionals, patients, family members and users in general are facilitated (eg School of Patients 2.0 of the Junta de Andalucía). These initiatives are a sample of the new responses and trends that are being forged in our health system in relation to citizen participation.

2.4 Health Schools in the Autonomous Communities

For this chapter, five Spanish entities have been selected that show important institutional differences and very varied activities. All of them show the multiplicity of ways that citizens acquire access to the field of health from the decentralization of health competence and taking into account the diversity of the territory. In this way, the following initiatives are analyzed: 1) University of Patients of Catalonia, 2) School of Patients of Andalusia, 3) PyDeSalud of the Canary Islands, 4) Conference of Patients and Health CIBA, and, 5) School of Health of Aragon.

3. METHODOLOGY

To facilitate the work of this analysis, a series of variables have been defined:

- **Institutional dependence:** As Spanish health system allow public and private providers, as well as institutional and political and administrative divisions (see Spanish health system description subsection), it is a require variable to know the type of management it carries out.
- **Rationale:** The mission of the Health Promotion School.
- **Goals:** It is point out the fundamental objectives of the initiatives.
- **Recipients:** It is sum up who is going to receive the Health Promotion School activities / services.
- **Collaborators:** Public or private institutions that share resources (time, knowledge, others) with the institutions.
- **Activities:** The services Health Schools provide to the recipients.
- **Methodology:** The "pillar" of the grounds (rationale), goals and activities.
- **Results:** The indicators Health Schools have accomplished.
- **Impact:** It means what the Health Schools have achieved.

Table 1 summarizes the main comparative criteria. The foremost characteristics are described in the text:

3.1. University of Patients of Catalonia

Catalonia acceded to the healthcare competition in 1981. It was the first Autonomous Community (CA) that began to manage its own healthcare system. This date marked the beginning of a process of health transfers from the State to the Autonomous Communities that ended in 2002, in which all the Autonomous Entities had recognized this competence.

The University of Patients was created in 2006, it constitutes a specific and monographic university dedicated to patients, relatives, caregivers, volunteers and citizens in general, interested in health and sanitation issues.

It aims to contribute to the promotion of equal opportunities in education and access to quality care by patients and users of health services, allocating its actions to patients, family members, caregivers, volunteers and citizens, in general. The Department of Health of the Generalitat of Catalonia also contributes as a collaborator and sponsor the Esteve Laboratories and the Grunenthal Foundation

Among its activities, the "Expert Patient" Program in collaboration with the "Josep Laporte" Foundation stands out. This program is the result of the application of the model proposed by Stanford University, promoting the role of the patient, the family member and the caregiver as the main responsible for self-care of their health and facilitates the acquisition of the necessary skills to manage the symptoms of chronic disease.

Over the course of six sessions, patients set acceptable health goals, learn to manage pain, solve problems, control their diet, increase physical activity, and control their mood and the way in which the disease influences your personal relationships. The results show improvements in aspects related to the health and quality of life of patients, as well as a reduction in the use of health resources and services.

3.2 Andalusian School of Patients

Andalusia acceded to competition in health matters in 1984, but it would not be until 2008 when the Andalusian School of Patients was created. The Ministry of Health of the Junta de Andalucía is the responsible entity and coordinates with the Andalusian School of Public Health.

It is committed to the application of the deliberative model in health that prioritizes self-care training for patients with chronic diseases and their caregivers, although it is also open to associations and the general public who participate in its training activities to learn and teach the best ways of caring and take care of yourself.

They collaborate with groups of experts and professional experts of the Andalusian Public Health System for the elaboration of the contents of each one of the diseases that are treated. A "peer-to-peer" learning method is used and there is expert support from SSPA professionals. The School for Patients has its own didactic material, prepared by experts in different topics: guides, manuals and audiovisual resources, among others. The material is accessible on the web (www.escueladepacientes.es).

Among the results referring to 2015, the diversity and extension of its audience stands out: 44 patient training workshops, with a degree of satisfaction by the participants of 9.2 out of 10. 2,272 patients trained. More than 600 professionals involved in 250 clinical management units. III Congress of the School of Patients with the participation of 300 people. III Summer Camp attended by 22 boys and girls with chronic health problems.

The intense work of dissemination through social networks also stands out. In 2015, the Twitter account of the School of Patients (@escpacientes) reached 18,500 followers, with a total of 3,975 new followers. The Facebook account records about 1,000 daily interactions. There have also been 14 video-chats between patients and experts on certain diseases, 14 Blogs, where patients share advice and experiences and the development of mobile applications with the aim of bringing patients and their caregivers closer to training, information and exchange between equals.

Similarly, the School for Patients has had a great impact on the media during 2015, with a total of 152 news items (written and digital) in local and national media.

Concluded the research project: "Evaluation of results of the training of patients in health, quality of life and use of health services", (Health Department) with a sample of 700 patients and the application of a questionnaire before and after training, the results couldn't be more promising. The influence of training on improving the quality of life, on self-efficacy in managing the disease, and on reducing visits to the family doctor and attendance at emergency services has been confirmed.

3.3 PyDeSalud Canarias

PyDeSalud is the acronym for "participate and decide on your health". It is a project that was created recently, in 2016. It is based on a web platform (open and free) of integrated services to promote knowledge, autonomy and active participation of people about their health problems.

The Canarian Health Service, the Canarian Health Research Foundation, the Research Network in Health Services in Chronic Diseases, Projections and transnational studies, participate in its organization. It facilitates the integration of different entities to share and transfer experience and knowledge regarding participation in health. Its main objective is to promote the knowledge, autonomy and active participation of people about their health problems.

Its recipients are patients, caregivers, family members and health professionals from Spain, Hispano America and other Spanish-speaking areas. They collaborate with associations and hospital services of different Autonomous Communities on cancer, depression and diabetes.

Regarding the work methodology, the use of various types of strategies stands out:

- Patient experiences: from a qualitative methodological perspective, an inductive analysis is carried out based on first-person accounts of the experience of the disease. A semi-structured interview is conducted at the home. The selection of patients tries to represent the greatest diversity of profiles and experiences. It aims to know their family and social context, the process and experience of each patient's disease, as well as the strategies they have put in place to deal with it.
- Shared decision making: it is a form of joint work between the patient and the healthcare professional to choose between two or more diagnostic or therapeutic options about which there may be uncertainty. "Help tools for shared decision making" consists of: brochures, booklets, audiovisuals, web pages and interactive programs.
- Research needs: The Delphi Method is applied to obtain the most consensual opinion possible from patients and professionals.
- Information and support resources: guides, videos, associations, events, etc.

Through the selection of a committee of experts for each line of work, a specific pathology is addressed. They are professionals, scientists and members of Patient Associations whose work is to advise, propose, extract results, etc., but also study on the subject, translating this work into research projects of the European Union and publications (articles, books).

3.4 Autonomous Community of Aragon: Two Types of Actions Stand Out

1) The Patient and Health Conference: Forums at the CIBA Organized by Health

It consists of a series of conferences that arises at the initiative of the Aragonese Institute of Health Sciences (IACS) in order to create a shared space for information, training and debate, in which patients and professionals meet through their concerns, experiences, new therapeutic treatments, recent research, etc. It is a channel of collaboration between public institutions and patient associations for future training and empowerment actions and patient self-responsibility, understanding that knowledge is the starting point of any improvement initiative. Collaborating: Patient Associations, Company and Aragonese Health Service.

The sessions are held at the Center for Biomedical Research of Aragon (CIBA), headquarters of the IACS, from 4:45 pm to 8:00 pm. The format of all of them was as follows:

- 16:45 - 17:00. Presentation by institutional representatives (Public Organizations and Patient Association) demonstrating the commitment and collaboration between both.
- 17:00 - 18:30. Three or four presentations by health professionals addressing aspects of interest of the subject matter.
- 18:30 - 20:00 Participation forum and questions from the assistants to the speakers.

Each day is designed and organized by the IACS and the corresponding patient association according to the subject matter. Topics and speakers are agreed upon between the IACS and the Patient Association in close collaboration.

The assessment of the training impact is very positive. At least in Aragon there has not been such a close and generalized collaboration initiative between public institutions and patient associations, considering them as a group representing patients and within a project that covers a varied set of pathologies and not something specific and punctual.

The project uses the technical means available to the CIBA and new technologies to bring the conference closer to everyone regardless of where they live. Anyone with a mobile device can access live viewing of the day.

All the conferences have been recorded and can be accessed later both individually and collectively, being able to serve as reflection and group analysis within the Association or other groups.

There is no doubt that the participation of the Associations has meant that the social impact is much greater than if the initiative started solely from the IACS. Added to this is the fact that all the associations respond affirmatively to the proposal made by the Institute and the collaboration with them is considered very successful and rewarding by both parties. In fact, attendance data and attendee feedback on evaluation surveys indicate a high level of satisfaction. It has been proven, both by the interest of the media, and by the number of attendees, that the conference had a growing social impact.

2) Aragon School of Health

The Aragon Health School is organized by the General Directorate of Rights and Guarantees of Users of the Department of Health of the Government of Aragon. It began its journey in 2016, with the detection and analysis of the situation and the activities of the Associations of Patients and HEALTH Executives through a survey. 146 associations and 56 managers were surveyed. Among the needs detected, the need to coordinate the actions of the associations among themselves and their work with the Public Administration stands out.

Given this lack, one of the priorities of the School of Health of Aragon is based on coordination between the actions of the health system and civil society, the sustainability of the health system, and the basic principles of the social health model. It is based on the previous experience of other Autonomous Communities and on transparency policies. It is not a School for Patients, but a School of Health based on the rights of patients and citizens.

Hence, its objectives include: promoting the exercise of the rights and duties of users; inform about the resources and operation of the health system; plan training actions with patients, caregivers and citizens; support representative organizations of patients, professionals and citizens; generate knowledge and experiences of collaboration between professionals and patients; serve as a platform to disseminate existing information and resources considered useful by patients or users to citizens; the exchange of experiences with other networks or schools.

Its work methodology is fundamentally interactive, creating its own interdisciplinary and intersectoral promoter group. It promotes its presence in all Aragonese municipalities and regions and its dissemination and information work is carried out in associations, schools, professional associations, public administration, universities, and other entities.

4. DISCUSSION AND CONCLUSIONS

It should be noted that from the study carried out it can be concluded that citizen participation in the field of health has acquired special relevance over recent years in Spain and progress has been made in achieving SDG 3, progressing in all three essential components of health promotion:

- Good health governance, the consequences of health system decisions are taken into account, and preventive policies are prioritized. In this sense, the Health Schools add value to the importance of the evaluation of health programs. In its evolution, there is a change from one healthcare model to another whose commitment is the comprehensive treatment of the biopsychosocial and the promotion of health
- Health education openly encourages people to have the opportunity to choose and enjoy a healthy environment. Health education is undoubtedly one of the most important resources that a society has for the development of values and attitudes needed to allow their citizens to choose healthy options and to be autonomous patient, which is highly desired to prevent harm to oneself and others in pandemic crisis as COVID-19 one. The Health Schools endorse these premises from very different training strategies.
- The local sphere and cities play a major role in promoting well-being and quality of life. The Health Schools present a local vocation and their health promotion strategies are proposed in a community territory (Autonomous Community). They also articulate various territorial spheres of both primary care and specialized care. At the national level they are coordinated in the National Network of Health Schools for Citizenship. The establishment of networks and the effort to improve communication between the different health agents involved, places participation at one of its highest links: shared decision-making.

Furthermore, joint conclusions can be drawn on the five projects studied. For this, Table 1, summary, has been made, in which the variables selected in relation to each of the experiences appear, giving rise to the following questions and conclusions:

1. All the initiatives support its mission, vision and values in the development of the democratic model based in turn on the bioethical value of the patient's autonomy. In this way, these entities respond to the new needs posed not only by the patient but by the general public as a whole and that the previous structures (Health Councils) did not meet.
2. Organizational dependency: it is observed that the entity responsible and organizing the activity is diverse. In most cases, it is the Public Administration that supports the experience, but in the case of Catalonia it is the Autonomous University that owns the entity. The most recent experiences show new forms of collaborative management between various public and private organizations.
3. Rationale for the project: in general, they all respond to compliance with the new bioethical values. Bioethical values should be taught at schools (León Correa, 2008) as learning processes which reinforce the acquisition of skills that allow discovering the ethical conflicts that beat in the daily life of the health professions, and also, the ethically consistent decisions, in the case of medical experts (Urionabarrenetxea, 2011).
4. Objectives: the definition of the objectives depends on the breadth of the strategy of each project. In the case of PyDeSalud de Canarias or Paciente Expert de Catalunya, they focus on very specific

objectives such as training and research. In other cases, they refer to more general objectives, which, as confirmed by the activities carried out, obey areas related to the promotion of rights and duties and even the accreditation of activities of other centers.

5. Recipients: all agree in this section referring to Patients, family members, caregivers, professionals and citizens. The issue that makes a difference is that they refer to their autonomous areas except in the Canarian project that is intended for all Spanish-language speakers.
6. Collaborators: consensus is given regarding the participation of Patient Associations. From there, there are notable differences. Entities that are oriented to the transfer of knowledge and research include among their collaborators groups of experts, professionals and health and research organizations. The pharmaceutical company also appears as a participant in these projects. From which it is clear, that they are initiatives open to the broad social fabric.
7. Activities: closely related to the objectives. They present diversity, although they all coincide in being aimed at responding to a set of pathologies.
8. Methodology: the way that is offered to the patient and citizen to access the services and activities offered by the entities and programs is in any case interactive and dynamic. It obeys the mission of the deliberative model that is being developed. The incorporation of the Delphi Method in the Canarian project stands out.
9. Results: the results to which you have access differ depending on the type of experience. In some cases, very concrete results are presented, as a consequence of an evaluation of activities, as is the case of the Andalusian School of Patients or the Aragón Patient Conference. Very concise results are also shown on the PyDeSalud website that refer to the publications with an impact factor that have resulted from their research. In the case of the Aragón School of Health, being a project in the production phase, it refers to the results of its creation process.
10. Impact: it is about assessing the effects that these projects produce in the social and health fields. As they are exposed in them, they are related, on the one hand, with the improvement of the quality of life, according to the results of Stanford University. On the other hand, reference is made to the impact of the initiatives in the media and on social networks. Undoubtedly, its impact transcends purely healthcare information and its informative work aims to pivot on the promotion of health and citizen participation.

Finally, this work is not exempt from weaknesses, which in turn represent a valid starting point for future work. The main limitation of this research is that we restraint empirical approach to the analysis of secondary data (regional reports on Health Schools). As a future research we propose compiling quantitative and qualitative data from primary resources. These new sources of information will allow to identify similarities and differences among regional Health Schools along the same time horizon, that is, it will be possible to transcend the descriptive analysis with statistical tests of main theoretical hypotheses.

Table 1. Main comparative criteria of variables summarized

Variables	University of Patients (*Cataluña*)	*Patients school (Andalucía)*	*PyDeSalud (Canarias)*	CIBA Patient Conferences (Aragón)	Health School (*Aragón*) – production
Institutional (organic) dependency	*Universidad Autónoma de Barcelona* (UAB)	Regional Government Health Department of *Junta de Andalucía*	Cluster (Health Services of *Canarias*, FUNCIS, REDISSEC, PROYECTFAN)	Aragon Institute of Health (Health Department – Government of Aragon)	General management and user guarantees. Health Department of Government of Aragon)
Grounds (rationale - basis)	Promotion of equal opportunities education Quality of health service	Application of the democratic model, deliberative in health	Health knowledge transfer and participation	Shared space for information, training and debate	Expressed need Public Administrations (civil service). Empowerment. Sustainability. Coordination Socio-Sant.
Goals	Accreditation, democratization, social responsibility of the UAB, patient activities	Training in self-care of chronic patients and caregivers.	Promote knowledge, autonomy and active participation	Patient-system approach. Sanitary system. Admon. + AAPP collaboration.	Promover derechos y deberes pacientes. Informar y formar. Intercambio. Acreditación
Recipients	Patients, relatives, caregivers, volunteers, citizens	Patients, caregivers, family, associations and citizens	Patients, caregivers, family, Spanish-speaking professionals	Patients, caregivers, family, associations and citizens	Patients, family members, caregivers, professionals and citizens
Collaborators	Health Department of *Cataluña*, Grunenthal Foundation, Lab. Esteve	Health professional expert groups	Public Administrations and Hospital Services of the Autonomous Communities	Public Administrations, Enterprise, Health	Public Administrations, Health System, Professional Associations, FAMCP, University of Zaragoza
Activities	Self-care program, training of trainers	Courses, information, resources by disease	Classified by diseases. Patient experiences, TDC, Research	18 Conference on different pathologies	Information, training, programs and events
Methodology	Interactive: role play, brainstorming, etc.	Between peers	Interactive, cte. Experts and patients	Informative and interactive	Interactive web, presence of municipalities and Public Administrations
Results	Refers to Stanford University	44 workshops, 2,272 students, 600 professionals involved. Social Networks (blogs)	Research projects, publications	10,803 followers. 98.8% utility	Promoter group, collaborators quarry, 16 activities (590 attendees), web design, accreditation
Impact	Health and quality of life improvement.	Media, APP innovations, research	Improves health, quality of life. Scientific dissemination and recognition	Innovation and social impact	Media dissemination, presence of the Public Administrations and municipalities

REFERENCES

Ares-Blanco, S., Astier-Peña, M. P., Gómez-Bravo, R., Fernández-García, M., & Bueno-Ortiz, J. M. (2021). Gestión de los recursos humanos y estrategias de vacunación en atención primaria en Europa en la pandemia COVID-19. *Atencion Primaria*, *53*(10), 102132. Advance online publication. doi:10.1016/j.aprim.2021.102132 PMID:34256236

Arrighi, E., Blancafort, S., & Novell, A. (2010). *Manual para formadores en autocuidado y control de la diabetes tipo 2. Universidad de los Pacientes*. Fundación Joseph Laporte.

Augsburger, A. C., & Fondato, M. (2020). Salud y participación social. Las y los jóvenes en las estrategias de promoción de la salud. *Kairos, Revista de temas sociales*, (45). https://www.revistakairos.org/salud-y-participacion-social-las-y-los-jovenes-en-las-estrategias-de-promocion-de-la-salud/

Camarelles, F. (2020). La prevención y la promoción de la salud en tiempos de cambio. *Atencion Primaria*, *52*(2), 1–2. doi:10.1016/j.aprim.2020.09.006

Cantanero, D. (2006). Descentralización y financiación autonómica del sistema sanitario español. *Economistas*, *24*(108), 201–205.

Cantarero, D. (2008). Desigualdades territoriales y equidad en el sistema sanitario español. *Cuadernos económicos de ICE*, (75), 141-166.

Cía, N. M., Pérez, M. P., Heras-Mosteiro, J., Ávila, G. G., Díaz-Olalla, J. M., & Aguilar, J. L. R. G. (2018). Encuentros y desencuentros entre salud comunitaria y sistema sanitario español. *Informe SESPAS 2018. Gaceta Sanitaria*, *32*, 17–21. doi:10.1016/j.gaceta.2018.06.004

Cockerham, W. C., Hamby, B. W., & Oates, G. R. (2017). The social determinants of chronic disease. *American Journal of Preventive Medicine*, *52*(1), S5–S12. doi:10.1016/j.amepre.2016.09.010 PMID:27989293

Danet, A., Prieto, M. A., Garrido, F., López, M., Luque, N., & March, J. C. (2017). Cronicidad y uso de servicios sanitarios: La formación entre iguales de la Escuela de Pacientes. *Revista da Escola de Enfermagem da U S P.*, *USP51*. Advance online publication. doi:10.1590/S1980-220X2017004203280

Davó, M. C., Gil-González, D., Vives-Cases, C., Álvarez-Dardet, C., & La Parra, D. (2008). Las investigaciones sobre promoción y educación para la salud en las etapas de infantil y primaria de la escuela española: Una revisión de los estudios publicados entre 1995 y 2005. *Gaceta Sanitaria*, *22*(1), 58–64. doi:10.1157/13115112 PMID:18261445

Decreto 53/2013, de 2 de abril, del Gobierno de Aragón, por el que se regula el Consejo de Salud de Aragón. BOA de 11 de abril de 2013.

Departamento de Sanidad del Gobierno de Aragón. (n.d.). *Salud Informa-Inicio*. https://www.saludinforma.es

Escuela Andaluza de Salud Pública. (n.d.). *Escuela de Pacientes: Inicio*. Consejería de Salud y Familias de la Junta de Andalucía. http://www.escueladepacientes.es

Franco, Á. (2006). Tendencias y teorías en salud pública. *Revista Facultad Nacional de Salud Pública*, *24*(2), 119–130.

Frohlich, K. L., & Abel, T. (2014). Environmental justice and health practices: Understanding how health inequities arise at the local level. *Sociology of Health & Illness*, *36*(2), 199–212. doi:10.1111/1467-9566.12126 PMID:24372359

García Aguayo, F. J. (2021). La crisis de la medicina: sus males y sus posibles remedios. Razón y fe. *Revista Hispanoamericana de Cultura, 283*(1451), 283-290. https://revistas.comillas.edu/index.php/razonyfe/article/view/16610

Gavidia, V. (2009). El profesorado ante la educación y promoción de la salud en la escuela. *Didáctica de las Ciencias Experimentales y Sociales*, (23), 171–180.

Gil-Girbau, M., Pons-Vigués, M., Rubio-Valera, M., Murrugarra, G., Masluk, B., Rodríguez-Martín, B., García Pineda, A., Vidal Thomás, C., Conejo-Cerón, S., Recio, J. I., Martínez, C., Pujol-Ribera, E., & Berenguera, A. (2021). Modelos teóricos de promoción de la salud en la práctica habitual en atención primaria de salud. *Gaceta Sanitaria*, *35*(1), 48–59. doi:10.1016/j.gaceta.2019.06.011 PMID:31753510

Gispert, R., & Giné, J. M. (2006). Diferencias entre público y privado en la asistencia hospitalaria en España: ¿realidad asistencial o falacia numérica? *Gaceta Sanitaria*, *20*(2), 149–152. doi:10.1157/13087327 PMID:16753092

González, A. (2012). *Programa Paciente Experto Catalunya: una estrategia para potenciar la autorresponsabilidad del paciente y el fomento del autocuidado*. Departamento de Salut. Generalitat de Catalunya.

Gracia-Pérez, M. L. (2015). *Evaluación del impacto formativo: dimensiones y modelos. Una experiencia en la sanidad de Aragón* [Tesis doctoral, Universidad de Zaragoza]. https://zaguan.unizar.es/record/64481?ln=es

Gracia-Pérez, M. L., & Gil-Lacruz, M. (2019). Participación y Salud: Nuevas iniciativas en España. *Acciones e Investigaciones Sociales*, (39), 111–131. doi:10.26754/ojs_ais/ais.2018393234

Grech, P., & Grech, R. (2021). The role of health promotion theories in Stroke Awareness and Education. *Applied Nursing Research*, *58*, 151415. doi:10.1016/j.apnr.2021.151415 PMID:33745555

Group Health Research Institute. (n.d.). *Improving Chronic Health*. http://www.improvingchroniccare.org

Heard, E., Fitzgerald, L., Wigginton, B., & Mutch, A. (2020). Applying intersectionality theory in health promotion research and practice. *Health Promotion International*, *35*(4), 866–876. doi:10.1093/heapro/daz080 PMID:31390472

Hernán, M., Fernández, A., & Ramos, M. (2004). La salud de los jóvenes. *Gaceta Sanitaria*, *18*(Supl.1), 47–55. doi:10.1157/13062251 PMID:15171858

Hood, L. (2006). Chalmers, J. Lyons memorial lecture: Health Care of the 21st Century: Predective, Preventive, Personlized and Partipatory (P4) Medicine. *Journal of Oral and Maxillofacial Surgery*, *64*(9), 14. doi:10.1016/j.joms.2006.06.302

Hunter, B. D., Neiger, B., & West, J. (2011). The importance of addressing social determinants of health at the local level: The case for social capital. *Health & Social Care in the Community*, *19*(5), 522–530. doi:10.1111/j.1365-2524.2011.00999.x PMID:21595772

Instituto Aragonés de Ciencias de la Salud. (n.d.). *Plataforma de Formación del IACS*. Gobierno de Aragón. http://www.iacs.aragon.es

Kamran, A., & Naeim, M. (2020). Behavioural change theories: A necessity for managing COVID-19. *Public Health*. Advance online publication. doi:10.1016/j.puhe.2020.10.010 PMID:33468323

León Correa, F. J. (2008). Salud escolar y educación para la salud: Principios y valores desde la bioética. *Revista Hacia la Promoción de la Salud*, *13*, 25–41.

Ley 14/1986, de 25 de abril, General de Sanidad. BOE núm. 102, de 29 de abril de 1986.

Macia-Soler, M., & Moncho-Vasallo, J. (2007). Sistema Nacional de Salud Español. Características y análisis. *Enfermeria global, 6*(1).

Martín, J. J. M. (2016). El sistema nacional de salud español ante la gran recesión. *Cuadernos de relaciones laborales, 34*(2), 315-334. doi:10.5209/CRLA.53459

Ministerio de Sanidad del Gobierno de España. (n.d.). *PyDeSalud: Participa y Decide sobre tu Salud.* http://www.pydesalud.com/

Miragaya, L. C. (2008). Sistemas nacionales de salud en proceso de reforma: Hacia fórmulas mixtas entre lo público y lo privado. *Panorama Social*, (7), 8–20.

Moreno, S. (2021). La participación en salud: los Consejos de Salud. *Ocronos, 4*(2). https://revistamedica.com/participacion-consejos-salud/

Nuño, R., Rodríguez, C., Piñera, K., Zaballa, I., & Bikandi, J. (2013). Panorama de las iniciativas de educación para el cuidado en España. *Gaceta Sanitaria, 27*(4), 332–337. doi:10.1016/j.gaceta.2013.01.008 PMID:23465729

Oliver, A., & González, A. (2020). Facilitando la salud comunitaria. Indicadores básicos de salud por área básica de salud en Cataluña. *Gaceta Sanitaria, 34*(2), 204–207. doi:10.1016/j.gaceta.2019.05.012 PMID:31488325

Organización Mundial de la Salud. (n.d.). https://www.who.int/healthpromotion/conferences/9gchp/about/es/

Ossebaard, H., Seydel, E., & van Gemert-Pijnen, L. (2012). Online usability and patients with long-term conditions: A mixed-methods approach. *Review International Journal of Medical Informatics, 81*(6), 374–387. doi:10.1016/j.ijmedinf.2011.12.010 PMID:22261086

Prosser, A. M., Judge, M., Bolderdijk, J. W., Blackwood, L., & Kurz, T. (2020). 'Distancers' and 'non-distancers'? The potential social psychological impact of moralizing COVID-19 mitigating practices on sustained behaviour change. *British Journal of Social Psychology, 59*(3), 653–662. doi:10.1111/bjso.12399 PMID:32584437

Ramirez, O., Carrasco, J.M., González, R., & Fanjul, G. (2020). Resumen de ODS3+ del concepto a la implementación de la "Salud en todas las políticas" en España. *Revista Diecisite: Investigación interdisciplinar para los Objetivos del Desarrollo Sostenible,* (3), 25-42. doi:10.36852/2695-4427_2020_03.02

Rivero-Jiménez, B. R., Conde-Caballero, D., & Mariano-Juárez, L. (2020). Educación para la salud y alimentación en personas mayores. Tradición, cultura y autoridad en Las Hurdes (Extremadura-España). *Educación (Lima)*, (3), 18–25.

Ruiz-Azarola, A., & Perestelo-Pérez, L. (2012). Participación ciudadana en salud: Formación y toma de decisiones compartida. Informe SESPAS 2012. *Gaceta Sanitaria, 26,* 158–161. doi:10.1016/j.gaceta.2011.10.005 PMID:22265652

Sanz-Tolosana, E. (2018). Crisis, austeridad y áreas rurales: Estudio cualitativo de las percepciones sobre los impactos en el sistema sanitario y la salud en Navarra, España. *Saúde e Sociedade, 27*(3), 898–908. doi:10.15900104-12902018170745

Self-Management Resource Center. (n.d.). https://www.selfmanagementresource.com/

Sobradillo, P., Pozo, F., & Álvar, A. (2011). Medicina P4: El futuro a la vuelta de la esquina. *Archivos de Bronconeumologia*, *47*(1), 35–40. doi:10.1016/j.arbres.2010.09.009 PMID:21190770

Torres-García, M., & Santana-Hernández, H. (2017). La Educación para la Salud en la formación de maestros desde el Espacio Europeo de Educación Superior. *Revista Complutense de Educación*, *28*(4), 1083–1011. doi:10.5209/RCED.51536

Universidad de los Pacientes. (n.d.). *Universidad de los Pacientes*. https://www.universidadpacientes.org/

Urionabarrenetxea, K. M. (2011). La educación en bioética, camino para la profesionalidad. *Revista de Calidad Asistencial*, *26*(1), 62–66. doi:10.1016/j.cali.2010.11.007 PMID:21256065

Valls-Martínez, M. C., & Abad-Segura, E. (2018, December). Satisfacción del paciente en el Sistema Nacional de Salud español. *Anales del Sistema Sanitario de Navarra*, *41*(3), 309–320. doi:10.23938/ASSN.0315 PMID:30277227

Woeld Health Organization. (2015). *Garantizar una vida sana y promover el bienestar para todos en todas las edades*. https://www.who.int/es/news/item/25-09-2015-ensure-healthy-lives-and-promote-well-being-for-all-at-all-ages

Chapter 10
B Corp Certification Effects: Design and Validation of a Questionnaire Applying Delphi Method

Elsa Diez-Busto
https://orcid.org/0000-0002-1631-3189
University of Cantabria, Spain

Ana Fernandez-Laviada
https://orcid.org/0000-0002-4517-1124
University of Cantabria, Spain

Lidia Sanchez-Ruiz
University of Cantabria, Spain

ABSTRACT

Compliance with the Sustainable Development Goals (SDGs) and the 2030 Agenda represents a large investment that cannot be obtained solely through public resources. Therefore, it is necessary for the private sector to align itself with the SDGs and integrate them into its business model. In an attempt to align private interests with the SDGs, various impact measurement initiatives have emerged in recent years. However, none of them have been universally accepted, in part, because they still have weaknesses. As an alternative, some companies have chosen to become certified. The figures show that the B Corp certification is one of the most important ones internationally, since it has been growing at a rapid pace since its creation. In fact, there are currently almost 4,000 certified companies throughout the world. Despite this fact, there are very few studies which analyze the main effects of this certification yet. Therefore, the objective of this chapter is to validate a questionnaire that collects these effects through a Delphi study, formed by a panel of experts in the B Corp movement.

DOI: 10.4018/978-1-7998-8065-3.ch010

INTRODUCTION

In 2015, the United Nations (UN) approved the 2030 Agenda on Sustainable Development, which includes 17 Sustainable Development Goals (SDGs), which range from the elimination of poverty to the fight against climate change, education, equality of women, the defense of the environment or the design of cities among others (United Nations, 2021). In order to meet the 17 goals in 2030, the involvement and channeling of resources from multiple agents from various fields, such as government organizations, the private sector, civil society and individual citizens is needed (Avrampou et al., 2019; Bebbington & Unerman, 2018). In fact, the private sector is so important that many experts consider that it is not possible to meet the SDGs without the contribution of companies (Van Zanten, J.A.; van Tulder, 2018).

This is the reason why B Corps play a fundamental role in the achievement of the SDGs, since they are companies that balance social purpose and economic benefits (*B Corp Spain*, 2020; B Lab Spain, 2018; B the change, 2017, 2019). Specifically, B Certified companies or B Corps are a model of companies that meet the highest standards of social and environmental performance, public transparency and corporate responsibility to balance profit with purpose (*B Corp Spain*, 2020). These companies, and the entire B Corp community, work to solve society's problems such as inequality, poverty or caring for the environment. In other words, they use their profits to generate a positive impact for their employees, the communities where they work in and the local and global environment.

Companies must meet three requirements to obtain the certification (*B Corp Spain*, 2020). In the first place, they must comply with the performance requirements. They refer to completing the Impact Evaluation, which evaluates the interaction of the company with workers, customers, community, governance and environment. Companies must obtain at least 80 points out of 200. Secondly, they must comply with the legal requirements, among which the need to incorporate all stakeholders in the bylaws so that they have a relevant role in the decision-making process stands out. Finally, they must sign the B Lab term sheet and the Declaration of Interdependence, as well as pay the annual fee.

Taken into account the areas of the B Impact Assessment, it can be said that the B Corp movement is aligned with the Stakeholder theory. This theory spotlight the importance of maintaining productive relationships with all types of stakeholders as a means of attaining both business success and societal benefits (Cao & Gehman, 2021). Some authors have included Stakeholder theory as a conceptual framework for their research focused on the B Corp movement (Paelman et al., 2020; Poponi et al., 2019; Villela et al., 2019; Waddock & McIntosh, 2011; Winkler et al., 2019).

Furthermore, this movement is becoming increasingly important, a fact that is evident in various changes that are taking place in the market. In the first place, there is a considerable increase in socially responsible investment, as indicated by the Global Sustainable Investment Review (2018), which shows that this type of investment has grown by 34% between 2016 and 2018 in the five main global markets (Europe, United States, Japan, Canada and Australia-New Zealand). Second, there is a clear preference on the part of consumers towards companies that have a social and environmental commitment. Thus, as observed in the B Lab Spain Annual Report (2018), 66% of consumers will pay more for goods and services that are sustainable. Therefore, the consumer has become aware and concerned about what is happening in the world and no longer hesitate to mobilize for social injustices, human rights and the health of their planet (B Lab Spain, 2018). Finally, global action to address the climate emergency and the SDGs is increasingly important. In addition, more and more companies are joining this recent and rapid movement. Worldwide. In 2017, there were 2,300 certified companies from 50 countries and 130 sectors (B the change, 2017), while in 2019 there were 3,100 companies from 70 countries and 150 sectors (B the change, 2019), that is, in just two years the number of certified companies has grown by 34.78%. In the year 2020, the number of certified companies rises to 3,500, which again shows the rapid growth of the B Corp movement.

All the foregoing has also been reflected in the academic literature. Based on a literature review conducted on the two main academic databases of the area (Web of Science and Scopus), it was concluded that the first paper related to B Corp was published in 2009, three years after the movement began. From them onwards, the number of papers about this topic has dramatically increased. In fact, 70% of the publications about this certification appeared in the period 2018-2020 (Diez-Busto et al., 2021). Despite this impressive growth, absolute numbers (50 articles were found for the period 2009-2020 in both databases) show that we are still dealing with an incipient field of research with high potential.

In their work, Diez-Busto, Sanchez-Ruiz and Fernandez-Laviada (2021) also concluded that the vast majority of papers fall within the stakeholder theory and have an empirical orientation. Many of those studies conduct surveys while others use publicly available databases, such as B Lab, to develop their analysis. Concerning the methodologies applied, content analysis and regression analysis are the two most common ones among the identified papers. Finally, with regard to the geographical scope, there is a clear predominance of studies based on the United States, probably due to the fact that it is the country where the movement appeared.

Despite the growth in the number of certified companies, more studies on B Corp companies should be developed (Alonso-Martínez et al., 2019; Bianchi et al., 2020; Gamble et al., 2019; Gazzola et al., 2019; Nigri & Del Baldo, 2018; Stubbs, 2017a, 2017b; Tabares, 2021). It seems appropriate to do more research on the B Corp certification process and its critical success factors (Kim et al., 2016). These kinds of studies, which is widely common when doing research about different certifications (EFQM) or improvement initiatives (Chesbrough, 2010; Gómez-López et al., 2017; Mariotti et al., 2014; Sanchez-Ruiz et al., 2019, 2020; Sánchez-Ruiz et al., 2019) is virtually non-existent when talking about B Corp certification. In fact, just a few authors have analyzed these topics. This is the case of Kim et al. (2016) who analyze the motivations of companies to achieve the certification and conclude that their main motivation is to publicly claim an identity as an organization interested in the success of shareholders and other stakeholders, in order to distinguish themselves from traditional companies. Concerning the results companies obtain from certification, the work of Romi et al. (2018) might be highlighted. In this case, the authors analyse the main economic and social effects companies obtained once they have been certified, being greater sales growth one of them. Conversely, Parker et al. (2019) identified a slowdown in revenue and company growth.

Overall, taking the above-mentioned ideas into consideration, the authors want to develop a new research line focused on the analysis of the main effects or results of the B Corp certification. In order to do it, it will be necessary to know the specific experience of companies that have gone through the certification process; therefore, developing a questionnaire is the first step and the main aim of this contribution. Specifically, the objective of this study is to design and validate a questionnaire built on the basis of previous literature to analyse the main effects of the B Corp certification and how they are related based on Delphi methodology.

BACKGROUND

B Corps

Certified B Corporations are a new type of for-profit organizations that balance purpose and profit, as they are formally committed to creating social and environmental benefits in addition to their traditional profit motives (B Corporation, 2021; Bianchi et al., 2020; X. Chen & Kelly, 2015; Hiller, 2013; Stubbs, 2017a).

To become certified, companies have to achieve a verified minimum score of 80 points out of 200 on the B Impact Assessment tool, that is a rigorous assessment of a company's impact on its workers, customers, governance, the community, and the environment (B Corporation, 2021), as can be show in Table 1.

Table 1. B Impact Assessment areas

Impact area	Description
Governance	It evaluates how the company is structured to pursue and achieve its mission, ethics, responsibility and transparency. It measures whether the company has adopted a social or environmental mission and how it engages its employees, board members and the community. It also assesses employee access to financial information, opportunities for clients to provide feedback and diversity of the company´s governing bodies.
Workers	It evaluates the positive material impact of the company on its workers. It measures how the company treats its workers through compensation, benefits, training and opportunities. It also focuses on the work environment within the company, evaluating communication between management and workers, work flexibility, corporate culture and health and safety practices.
Community	It evaluates the positive material impact of the company on the communities which it is part of. It measures practices and policies around community services and charitable donations, including whether a company product or service is designed to solve a social problem, such as access to basic services, health or education.
Environment	It evaluates the impact and ecological footprint of facilities, materials, emissions, resources and energy use. Its transport and distribution channels and the environmental impact of its supply chain are taken into account. It also measures whether the company's products or services are designed to solve an environmental problem, including products that help provide renewable energy, preserve resources, reduce waste, promote land conservation, prevent toxic or dangerous substances, as well as educate, measure or consult to solve environmental problems.
Customers	It evaluates the positive material impact of the company through the offer of products and services to its clients or beneficiaries. It focuses on whether the business sells products or services that promote public benefit and whether those products or services are intended to serve underserved populations. It also measures whether the product or service is designed to solve a social or environmental problem.
Source: (B Corporation, 2020)	

The certification is issued by the independent non-profit organization B Lab, which was founded in the United States in 2006, and whose objectives are (Paelman et al., 2020):

- Building a community of Certified B Corporations
- Promoting legislation creating a new corporate form that meets higher standards of purpose, accountability, and transparency
- Accelerating the growth of "impact investing" through the use of B Lab's impact investment rating system

- Galvanizing support for the movement by sharing the stories of Certified B Corporations.

Studies of the B Corp movement indicate that it is an incipient field of research and that it is gaining increasing importance (Diez-Busto et al., 2021). In addition, the number of certified companies does not stop growing, with almost 4000 B Corps currently.

Effects Derived From the B Corp Certification

Since it is a recent field of research, there are currently very few studies on the effects related to the B Corp certification. However, it is a type of study that is very common when researching in other certifications (ISO, EFQM) or improvement initiatives (Chesbrough, 2010; Gómez-López et al., 2017; Mariotti et al., 2014; Sanchez-Ruiz et al., 2019, 2020; Sánchez-Ruiz et al., 2019).

In order to identify the effects that might occur after obtaining the certification two parallel strategies were followed. On one side, the papers identified by previous literature reviews on the B Corp movement (Diez-Busto et al., 2021) were carefully analysed. Among them, only five studies were specifically focused on the results obtained by companies after achieving certification. Their results, sometimes opposed, show that more research on this topic is needed. Thus, three of the studies established a positive relationship between being certified and some of the most common business management indicators. This is the case of Chen et al. (2015) who concluded that B Corps obtain a higher revenue growth rate. Similarly, Romi et al. (2018) analyze the main economic and social effects that companies obtain once certified, being the highest growth in sales one of the main important ones. Equally, Gazzola et al. (2019) verified the relationship between the scores obtained from the B Impact Assessment and the net profit for year. In the opposite corner, the works of Parket et al. (2019) and Gamble et al (2019). According to these authors, B Corp companies registered a slowdown in revenue and company growth.

On the other side, and due to the scarce number of studies identified, the literature focused on other business certifications, such as ISO, was also reviewed. It should not be forgotten that, although it is true that each certification has its own characteristics, all of them have aspects in common and are aimed at improving how companies manage their resources and processes. Therefore, taking into consideration that this literature review will be the base for designing a new questionnaire about this topic, it is important to identify as many effects as possible so the decision seems approppriate.

Finally, 12 effects were identified. They are all summarised in Table 2.

METHODOLOGY

Study Design

The aim of this study is to design and validate a questionnaire concerning the effects obtained by B Corp certified companies by applying the Delphi method. However, this is the first stage of a wider project. Thus, before describing the Delphi methodology in detail, a general overview of the whole project will be given.

The ultimate goal of our research is to analyse the effects companies obtain when becoming B Corps. As an example, we would like to answer these questions: What are the main effects? Could they be classified into different typologies? Are those effects equally important for all companies or do differences exist based on companies' sector or size? Answering all those questions, among others, implies the creation of a measurement instrument, in this case, a questionnaire/survey which has to be later validate.

Table 2. Potential effects derived from the B Corp Certification

Effects	References
Work absenteeism	(Middel et al., 2007)
Employee working conditions	(Wu & Chen, 2011)
Employee satisfaction	(*Mathews et al*>, 2001; Douglas>*et al*>, 2003)
Sales / revenue / customers	(Hammer, 2007; Hendricks & Singhal, 1996; Ittner & Larcker, 1997; Kohlbacher, 2010; Saizarbitoria Iñaki et al., 2006)
Customer loyalty	(Wu & Chen, 2011)
Customer satisfaction	(*Sun et al*>, 1992; Mathews>*et al*>, 2001)
Competitiveness of the company	(Küng & Hagen, 2007)
Transparency	(Kohlbacher, 2010)
Market share	(Zairi y Sinclair, 1995; Mat*hews et al*>, 2001; Saizarbitoria Iñaki, Arana Landín y Casadesús Fa, 2006)
Internal communication	(Mathews *et al*>, 2001; Douglas>*et al*>, 2003)
Social commitment of the company	(Wu & Chen, 2011)
Efficiency in the use of resources	(Wu & Chen, 2011)

Overall, the different stages that will be pursued along the project are briefly described in the following lines. It is important to highlight that this chapter exclusively refers to phases 1 and 2.

- **Phase 1. Literature review**: this is an essential phase when designing a new questionnaire as it helps to identify the potential items to be included on it based on what has been previously written by other authors. In this case, results on the literature review have been described in this chapter's *background* section.
- **Phase 2. Survey design and validation**: once an initial draft of the survey has been created, it has to be validated. It is at this point where the Delphi method is proposed to be applied. After going through the different phases, which will be explained in detailed in the following section (*Delphi method*), a final design of the survey is obtained.
- **Phase 3. Data collection**: the final survey is distributed among the target population, in our case, companies that have obtained the B Corp certification.
- **Phase 4. Data analysis**: based on the obtained responses, data will be analysed and results will be obtained. At this point different methodologies, commonly applied in this kind of research papers, are planned to be used, for instance: factorial analysis, Rasch Measurement Theory and Structural Equation Model (SEM).

Delphi Method

In order to validate the questionnaire, a two-round Delphi study was carried out, in which a total of 20 experts participated (Mira, Padrón y Mengual-Andrés, 2010; Bringhenti, Zandonade y Günther, 2011; Mengual-Andrés, 2011; *Soon et al>*, 2012; Taheri>*et al>*, 2018).

The Delphi method is a structured process whose aim is to gather information from a group of experts. It uses a series of 'rounds' which are repeated until 'group' consensus is reached (Beretta, 1996; Green et al., 1999; Hasson et al., 2000; Keeney et al., 2006; Powell, 2003)(Beretta, 1996; Green et al., 1999; Hasson et al., 2000; Keeney et al., 2006; Powell, 2003). To form the group, people who have experience in the subject under investigation are recruited (Keeney et al., 2006).

Specifically, four aspects characterize this qualitative methodology (Futures, 1969):

a) Iterative process. The experts participating in the process must express their opinion or answers on more than one occasion, through several rounds that lead to stabilizing opinions. With this sequence, the experts have the possibility to reflect or reconsider their opinions, in the light of their own or other experts' approaches.
b) Anonymity. No member of the group knows who a particular answer corresponds to. Among the advantages of anonymity is avoiding negative influences from dominant group members or inhibiting a participant. Control of communication is in the hands of the coordinating group and direct participation is never established between the experts involved.
c) Feedback or controlled feedback. Before the start of each round, the coordinating group transmits the position of the experts as a whole regarding the problem or situation being analyzed, highlighting the significant contributions of an expert, the discordant positions or additional information requested by an expert. In this way, the feedback through the analysis of the driving group of the method allows the circulation of information among the experts and facilitates the establishment of a common language.
d) Statistical response of the group. In case the group has been asked for a numerical estimate, the median of the individual responses is used. With this, the inclusion of individual responses in the final result of the group is achieved.

The procedure used throughout this Delphi study follows the criteria applied by other authors in their research (Bravo Estévez & Arrieta Gallastegui, 2005; Cruz, 2009; Santiago Mengual-Andrés et al., 2016; Mira et al., 2010), so that it is composed of three fundamental stages: Preliminary, Exploratory and Final (Figure 1).

In the **preliminary stage**, the group of study researchers is constituted and, using the existing literature, the first version of the questionnaire is carried out. Likewise, the panel of experts is designed taking into account the defined criteria.

Second, in the **exploratory stage**, the questionnaire is sent to the experts so that they can assess the items. Once the evaluations have been collected, a statistical analysis is carried out and the comments, improvements and items proposed by the experts are introduced, until the second version of the questionnaire is formed.

In the **final stage**, a statistical analysis of the evaluations is performed again and those items that do not meet the established criteria are eliminated, so that the definitive questionnaire is obtained.

Figure 1. Stages of the study

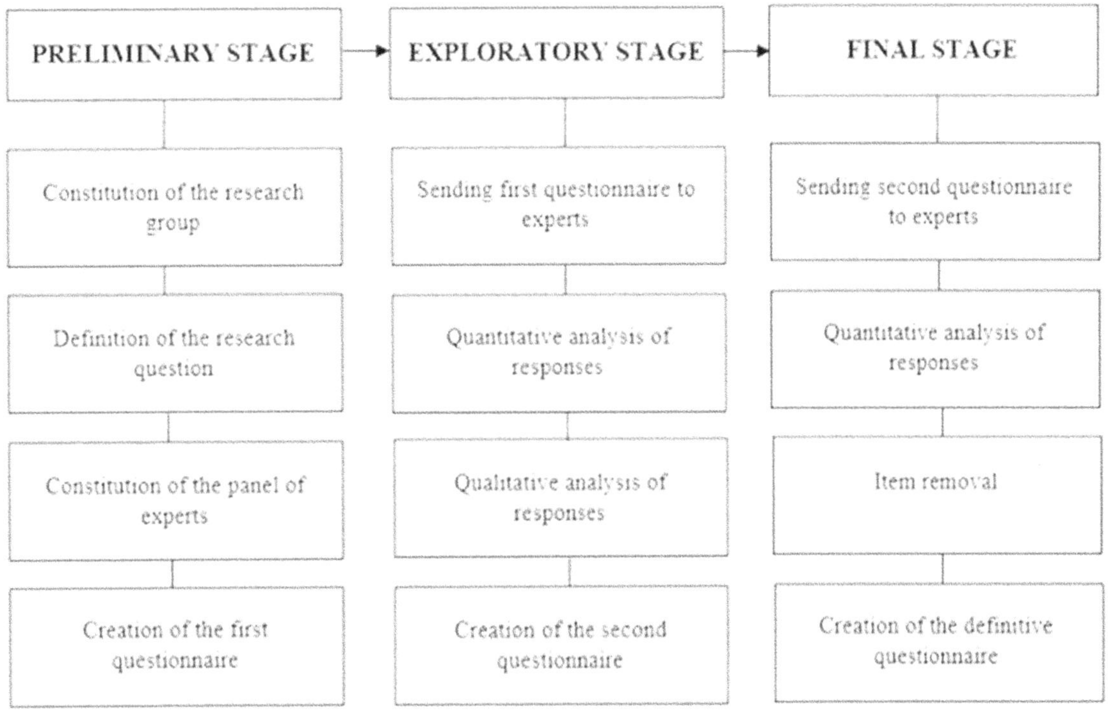

RESULTS

Preliminary Stage

As above mentioned, the construction of the questionnaire was carried out in three different stages (Bravo Estévez & Arrieta Gallastegui, 2005), the first being the preliminary stage. During this stage, the researchers involved in the project build a first version of the questionnaire.

In the present case, the proposed question will be as follows: Which effects did you obtain after certifying as a B Corp company? Value each option according to the following scale: -2 (very negative effect), 0 (neutral) or 2 (very positive effect).

Concerning the items integrating the question, 20 effects have been initially defined (Table 3). Some of them are based on the literature review; others have been proposed by the authors in response to the scarcity of papers dealing with this specific topic. The suggestion of the authors is based on their experience on the B Corp certification (principles and requirements of the certification itself) together with their experience on other business certificates.

The panel of experts who have participated in this study is made up of people from different fields. On the one hand, the B multipliers who have collaborated closely with different companies on numerous occasions and are aware of the main problems and advantages of the process, have also been invited to take part in this study. On the other hand, some managers or people in charge of the certification of companies that are already certified as B Corp and who have experienced the whole process very closely have been part of the panel. In order not to give up the more technical aspect, some members of

Table 3. Effects derived from the B Corp Certification

Code	Effects	Based on:
E1	Work absenteeism	Literature review
E2	Employee working conditions	
E3	Employee satisfaction	
E4	Sales / revenue / customers	
E5	Customer loyalty	
E6	Customer satisfaction	
E7	Competitiveness of the company	
E8	Transparency	
E9	Market share	
E10	Internal communication	
E11	Social commitment of the company	
E12	Efficiency in the use of resources	
E13	Employee engagement	Author's proposal
E14	Interaction with clients	
E15	Access to new sources of financing	
E16	Stakeholder participation in decision-making	
E17	Effect on the carbon footprint	
E18	Company visibility	
E19	The company is a social benchmark in its environment	
E20	Stakeholder awareness of the Sustainable Development Goals	

B Academics have also been part of the group of experts. They can contribute with their research vision. Some researchers with great experience in the field of B Corp also participated. Finally, to complete the group, an expert in other certifications has participated in the following stages of the Delphi method. We consider this last person could provide a more objective and general vision.

Despite the close relationship between all of them due to the commitment and unity of the movement, none of them has had access to the names of the rest of the panel, in order to maintain anonymity. Finally, the panel was constituted by a total of 15 experts: 3 B Multipliers, 6 B Corp Directors, 3 B Academics members, 2 Researchers and 1 Certification Expert (Table 4).

Table 4. Expert panel

Group	Number
B Multiplier	3
B Corp Director	6
B Academics Member	3
Researcher	2
Certification expert	1

Exploratory Stage

The questionnaire which contained the objective of the research, the instructions for the study and a link to the questionnaire was sent by email. Specifically, it was decided to use LimeSurvey platform for the electronic questionnaire. It was considered that this mean would facilitate the work of all the experts, as well as the subsequent collection of data.

In this first round experts have to evaluate whether the proposed items (see table 3) were appropriate. The specific question launched to the experts was: *According to your experience, value if companies get the following effects after becoming B Corps.*

Thus, the experts must score each of the items on a 7-point Likert scale (1: it is not a main effect to 7: it is one of the main effects), depending on the importance they believe they are and if they are relevant in the B Corp certification.

In addition, they have a blank box to be able to add everything they want, such as an element not previously identified that they consider relevant.

In the first round of responses, 20 experts participated in the study, so their responses were used to prepare the second version of the questionnaire. On the one hand, a quantitative analysis was carried out, in which three statistics were used: mean, median and standard deviation, so that an overall view of the results obtained in each item is obtained. The mean and median show the central tendency of the set of the experts' responses, while the standard deviation indicates the degree of dispersion of the responses.

On the other hand, a qualitative analysis was made with the answers that the experts presented in the open questions. In this way, a new item was introduced:

"Access to a new provider network / Access to a new global network of B Corps"

After both analysis, a questionnaire for the second round was designed. On this occasion, the questionnaire was designed ad hoc for each expert, indicating their initial assessment and the mean of the group of experts. The experts, by comparing their answers with the average of the group, could decide to maintain their previous answer or change it if it did not coincide with the rest of the panel of experts. Below is an example of how this second questionnaire is presented (Table 5).

Final Stage

In the second round of the questionnaire, the complete questionnaire was sent to the experts by email. In contrast to what it was done in the first round, this time experts received a personalized document following the structure described in Table 5.

Table 5. Example of the second questionnaire

Effects			
	Individual value 1st round	**Mean panel of experts**	**Individual value second round (1 a 7)**
Employee satisfaction	7	6	

At this stage of the study, responses were obtained from 15 experts, which represents a response rate of 75%. A statistical analysis was performed again to determine if the items were valid and if they should remain in the questionnaire or, on the contrary, they should be removed. To decide which items were removed, 75% of the mean of the scores was used as the cut-off score (Abad et al., 2011; Enrique et al., 2018; García-Ruiz & Lena-Acebo, 2018). That is, the criteria for maintaining an item is that it exceeds 75% of the average according to the experts' evaluations, which in a scale of 1 to 7 represents an index of 5.25. Therefore, those items with an average score lower than 5.25 are eliminated from the questionnaire (Table 6). Therefore, items E2, E3, E8, E9, E10 and E13 are eliminated from the questionnaire. This is the last round as a reasonable consensus has been reached among the experts.

Table 6. Statistical results of the responses of the second round

Code	Effects	Mean	Median	SD	Permanence
E13	Employee engagement	5,93	6,00	0,59	Yes
E1	Work absenteeism	3,73	4,00	1,53	No
E2	Employee working conditions	5,20	5,00	1,42	No
E3	Employee satisfaction	5,93	6,00	0,88	Yes
E4	Sales / revenue / customers	4,80	5,00	1,21	No
E5	Customer loyalty	5,80	6,00	0,68	Yes
E6	Customer satisfaction	5,73	6,00	0,59	Yes
E14	Interaction with clients	5,20	5,00	0,68	No
E15	Access to new sources of financing	4,40	5,00	1,45	No
E16	Stakeholder participation in decision-making	5,00	5,00	1,36	No
E7	Competitiveness of the company	5,60	6,00	1,55	Yes
E8	Transparency	6,27	6,00	0,59	Yes
E9	Market share	4,87	5,00	1,19	No
E10	Internal communication	5,73	6,00	0,88	Yes
E11	Social commitment of the company	6,87	7,00	0,35	Yes
E17	Effect on the carbon footprint	5,67	6,00	1,05	Yes
E12	Efficiency in the use of resources	5,53	6,00	1,19	Yes
E18	Company visibility	6,20	6,00	0,56	Yes
E19	The company is a social benchmark in its environment	6,33	6,00	0,62	Yes
E20	Stakeholder awareness of the Sustainable Development Goals	5,40	5,00	0,83	Yes
E21	Access to a new provider network / Access to a new global network of B Corps	5,79	6,00	0,89	Yes

Once the modifications had been made, a final questionnaire was obtained, made up of suitable items.

CONCLUSION AND FUTURE RESEARCH DIRECTIONS

The purpose of this chapter was to validate a questionnaire that pointed out the main effects observed by B Corp companies after obtaining certification. To develop the questionnaire and determine the effects to be added, a literature review was carried out, which is a theoretical contribution in itself.

After developing the analysis, a new and valid questionnaire integrated by 14 effects (items) has been obtained. This study is one more example that demonstrates the usefulness of the Delphi method as a validation tool for cases like this, in which the degree of development of the research topic is incipient, making it necessary to resort to the opinion of experts.

Likewise, as part of the contribution of the chapter, the questionnaire may be used in the future by different researchers, so that a homogeneous measurement instrument is used, allowing comparison between the results obtained. Likewise, it can be useful for those companies and consultants interested in movement B and in knowing the effects that companies achieve when obtaining the B Corp certification.

Once this first analysis has been finished, the data collection phase might begin. First of all, the final version of the questionnaire will be sent to the University Ethics Committee. This board is responsible to guarantee that the research respects the research ethical principles. Once their approval is received, the questionnaire will be sent to Spanish B Corp companies. At the moment when this document is written, there are 100 certified B Corps.

As a complement of the Delphi study presented in this paper, which is a qualitative methodology, additional methodologies such as exploratory and confirmatory factor analysis will be applied. They will help us to validate the level of consistency and reliability of the questionnaire. Another possible line of future research would be the validation of the questionnaire in other settings, that is, with a panel of experts from other countries.

Regarding the limitations of the study, it should be noted that the Delphi method itself has some of the limitations, since it is a qualitative method, which may lead to greater subjectivity in the analysis. However, as above-mentioned, this gap might be at least reduced when applying other qualitative methodologies.

ACKNOWLEDGMENT

The authors would like to thank the University of Cantabria (PhD Fellowhip) for funding this research.

REFERENCES

Abad, F. J., Olea, J., Ponsoda, V., & García, C. (2011). *Medición en ciencias sociales y de la salud*. M. Síntesis, Ed..

Alonso-Martínez, D., De Marchi, V., & Di Maria, E. (2019). Which country characteristics support corporate social performance? *Sustainable Development*. Advance online publication. doi:10.1002d.2018

Avrampou, A., Skouloudis, A., Iliopoulos, G., & Khan, N. (2019). Advancing the Sustainable Development Goals: Evidence from leading European banks. *Sustainable Development*, *27*(4), 743–757. doi:10.1002d.1938

B Corp Spain. (2020). https://www.bcorpspain.es/

B Corporation. (2018). *Global Sustainable Investment Review*. http://www.gsi-alliance.org/wp-content/uploads/2019/03/gsir_review2018.3.28.pdf

B Corporation. (2021). *Certified B Corporation*. https://bcorporation.net/

B Lab Spain. (2018). *Annual Report 2018*. https://issuu.com/bcorpspain/docs/memoria_anaul_b_lab_spain_2018

B the change. (2017). *Year in Review: The B Corp Impact in 2017*. https://bthechange.com/year-in-review-the-b-corp-impact-in-2017-f529a229921f

B the change. (2019). *A Year of Business as a Force for Good: 2019 in Review*. https://bthechange.com/a-year-of-business-as-a-force-for-good-2019-in-review-8e744ed4d620

Bebbington, J., & Unerman, J. (2018). Achieving the United Nations sustainable development goals. In *Auditing & Accounting*. https://www.emerald.com/insight/content/doi/10.1108/AAAJ-05-2017-2929/full/html

Beretta, R. (1996). A critical review of the Delphi technique. *Nurse Researcher*. https://europepmc.org/article/med/27285530

Bianchi, C., Reyes, V., & Devenin, V. (2020). Consumer motivations to purchase from benefit corporations (B Corps). *Corporate Social Responsibility and Environmental Management*, *27*(3), 1445–1453. doi:10.1002/csr.1897

Bravo Estévez, M., & Arrieta Gallastegui, J. J. (2005). El método Delphi. Su implementación en una estrategia didáctica para la enseñanza de las demostraciones geométricas. *Revista Iberoamericana de Educación*, *36*(7), 1–10. doi:10.35362/rie3672962

Bringhenti, J., Zandonade, E., & Günther, W. (2011). Selection and validation of indicators for programs selective collection evaluation with social inclusion. *Conservation and Recycling*. https://www.sciencedirect.com/science/article/pii/S0921344911000668

Cao, K., & Gehman, J. (2021). Certified B Corporations and Benefit Corporations. *Oxford Bibliographies in Management*. https://papers.ssrn.com/sol3/papers.cfm?abstract_id=3772009

Chen, X., & Kelly, T. F. (2015). B-Corps—A Growing Form of Social Enterprise: Tracing Their Progress and Assessing Their Performance. *Journal of Leadership & Organizational Studies*, *22*(1), 102–114. doi:10.1177/1548051814532529

Chen, X., & Kelly, T. F. (2015). B-Corps-A Growing Form of Social Enterprise: Tracing Their Progress and Assessing Their Performance. *Journal of Leadership & Organizational Studies*, *22*(1), 102–114. doi:10.1177/1548051814532529

Chesbrough, H. (2010). Business model innovation: opportunities and barriers. *Long Range Planning*. https://www.sciencedirect.com/science/article/pii/S0024630109000569

B Corporation. (2020). *The Complete Guide to B Corp Certification for Small to Medium-Sized Enterprises Join the Global Movement of People Using Business as a Force for Good*. Author.

Cruz, M. (2009). *El método Delphi en las investigaciones educacionales*. Editorial Academia.

Diez-Busto, E., Sanchez-Ruiz, L., & Fernandez-Laviada, A. (2021, March 1). The B Corp movement: A systematic literature review. *Sustainability*, *13*(5), 1–17. doi:10.3390u13052508

Douglas, A., & George, C. (2003). Implementing the EFQM excellence model in a local authority. *Managerial Auditing Journal*, *18*(2), 122–127. doi:10.1108/02686900310455100

Enrique, C., Reyes, G., & Liñan, L. T. (2018). Aplicación del Método Delphi Modificado para la Validación de un Cuestionario de Incorporación de las TIC en la Práctica Docente Application of the Modified Delphi Method for the Validation of a Questionnaire on the Incorporation of ICT in Teaching Practice. *Revista Iberoamericana de Evaluación Educativa*, *11*(1), 113–135. doi:10.15366/riee2018.11.1.007

Futures, N. D. (1969). *An experimental study of group opinion: the Delphi method*. Elsevier. https://www.sciencedirect.com/science/article/pii/S001632876980025X

Gamble, E. N., Parker, S. C., & Moroz, P. W. (2019). Measuring the Integration of Social and Environmental Missions in Hybrid Organizations. *Journal of Business Ethics*. Advance online publication. doi:10.100710551-019-04146-3

García-Ruiz, E., & Lena-Acebo, F. J. (2018). Aplicación del metodo delphi en el diseño de una investigación cuantitativa sobre el fenómeno FABLAB. *Revista de Metodología de Ciencias Sociales*, 129–166. https://www.fablabs.io/labs

Gazzola, P., Grechi, D., Ossola, P., & Pavione, E. (2019). Certified Benefit Corporations as a new way to make sustainable business: The Italian example. *Corporate Social Responsibility and Environmental Management*, *26*(6), 1435–1445. doi:10.1002/csr.1758

Gómez-López, R., López-Fernández, M. C., & Serrano-Bedia, A. M. (2017). Implementation barriers of the EFQM excellence model within the Spanish private firms. *Total Quality Management & Business Excellence*, *28*(7–8), 695–711. doi:10.1080/14783363.2015.1106314

Green, B., Jones, M., Hughes, D., & Williams, A. (1999). Applying the Delphi technique in a study of GPs' information requirements. *Health & Social Care in the Community*, *7*(3), 198–205. doi:10.1046/j.1365-2524.1999.00176.x PMID:11560634

Hammer, M. (2007). The Process Audit. *Harvard Business Review*. www.hbrreprints.org

Hasson, F., Keeney, S., & McKenna, H. (2000). Research guidelines for the Delphi survey technique. *Journal of Advanced Nursing*, *32*(4), 1008–1015. doi:10.1046/j.1365-2648.2000.t01-1-01567.x PMID:11095242

Hendricks, K. B., & Singhal, V. R. (1996). Quality awards and the market value of the firm: An empirical investigation. *Management Science*, *42*(3), 415–436. doi:10.1287/mnsc.42.3.415

Hiller, J. S. (2013). The Benefit Corporation and Corporate Social Responsibility. *Journal of Business Ethics*, *118*(2), 287–301. doi:10.100710551-012-1580-3

Ittner, C. D., & Larcker, D. F. (1997). The performance effects of process management techniques. *Management Science*, *43*(4), 522–534. doi:10.1287/mnsc.43.4.522

Keeney, S., Hasson, F., & McKenna, H. (2006). Consulting the oracle: Ten lessons from using the Delphi technique in nursing research. *Journal of Advanced Nursing*, *53*(2), 205–212. doi:10.1111/j.1365-2648.2006.03716.x PMID:16422719

Kim, S., Karlesky, M. J., Myers, C. G., & Schifeling, T. (2016). Social Responsibility: Why Companies Are Becoming B Corporations. *Harvard Business Review*, 2–5. https://www.christophergmyers.net/hbr2016_bcorporations.pdf

Kohlbacher, M. (2010). The effects of process orientation: A literature review. *Business Process Management Journal*, *16*(1), 135–152. doi:10.1108/14637151011017985

Küng, P., & Hagen, C. (2007). The fruits of Business Process Management: An experience report from a Swiss bank. *Business Process Management Journal*, *13*(4), 477–487. doi:10.1108/14637150710763522

Mariotti, F., Kadasah, N., & Abdulghaffar, N. (2014). Motivations and barriers affecting the implementation of ISO 14001 in Saudi Arabia: An empirical investigation. *Total Quality Management & Business Excellence*, *25*(11–12), 1352–1364. doi:10.1080/14783363.2014.912038

Mathews, B. P., Ueno, A., Periera, Z. L., Silva, G., Kekal, T., & Repka, M. (2001). Quality training: Findings from a European survey. *The TQM Magazine*, *13*(1), 61–68. doi:10.1108/09544780110360615

Mengual-Andrés, S. (2011). *La importancia percibida por el profesorado y el alumnado sobre la inclusión de la competencia digital en Educación Superior: Un análisis en Ciencias de la*. https://dialnet.unirioja.es/servlet/tesis?codigo=59631

Mengual-Andrés, S., Roig-Vila, R., & Mira, J. B. (2016). Delphi study for the design and validation of a questionnaire about digital competences in higher education. *International Journal of Educational Technology in Higher Education*, *13*(1), 12. Advance online publication. doi:10.118641239-016-0009-y

Middel, R., Op De Weegh, S., & Gieskes, J. (2007). Continuous Improvement in the Netherlands: A Survey-Based Study into Current Practices. *International Journal of Technology Management, 37*. doi:10.1504/IJTM.2007.012262

Mira, J. B., Padrón, A. L., & Mengual-Andrés, S. (2010). Validación mediante el metodo Delphi de un cuestionario para conocer las experiencias e interés hacia las actividades acuáticas con especial atención al Winsurf. *AGORA*. https://cerro64.cpd.uva.es/handle/10324/23693

Nigri, G., & Del Baldo, M. (2018). Sustainability Reporting and Performance Measurement Systems: How do Small- and Medium-Sized Benefit Corporations Manage Integration? *Sustainability*, *10*(12), 4499. Advance online publication. doi:10.3390u10124499

Paelman, V., Van Cauwenberge, P., & Vander Bauwhede, H. (2020). Effect of B corp certification on short-term growth: European evidence. *Sustainability (Switzerland)*, *12*(20), 1–18. doi:10.3390u12208459

Parker, S. C., Gamble, E. N., Moroz, P. W., & Branzei, O. (2019). The impact of B lab certification on firm growth. *Academy of Management Discoveries*, *5*(1), 57–77. doi:10.5465/amd.2017.0068

Poponi, S., Colantoni, A., Cividino, S. R. S., & Mosconi, E. M. (2019). The Stakeholders' perspective within the B corp certification for a circular approach. *Sustainability (Switzerland)*, *11*(6), 1584. Advance online publication. doi:10.3390u11061584

Powell, C. (2003). The Delphi technique: Myths and realities. Journal of Advanced Nursing, 41(4), 376–382. doi:10.1046/j.1365-2648.2003.02537.x

Romi, A., Cook, K. A., & Dixon-Fowler, H. R. (2018). The influence of social responsibility on employee productivity and sales growth: Evidence from certified B corps. *Sustainability Accounting. Management and Policy Journal*, *9*(4), 392–421. doi:10.1108/SAMPJ-12-2016-0097

Saizarbitoria Iñaki, H., Arana Landín, G., & Casadesús Fa, M. (2006). A Delphi study on motivation for ISO 9000 and EFQM. *International Journal of Quality & Reliability Management*, *23*(7), 807–827. doi:10.1108/02656710610679824

Sanchez-Ruiz, L., Blanco, B., & Diaz, E. (2019). Difficulty in implementing continuous improvement – Rasch measurement analysis. *Business Process Management Journal*, *25*(6), 1228–1250. doi:10.1108/BPMJ-05-2017-0125

Sánchez-Ruiz, L., Blanco, B., & Gómez-López, R. (2019). Continuous improvement enablers: Defining a new construct. *Journal of Industrial Engineering and Management JIEM*, *12*(1), 51. doi:10.3926/jiem.2743

Sanchez-Ruiz, L., Gomez-Lopez, R., & Blanco, B. (2020). Barriers to effectively implementing continuous improvement in Spanish firms. *Total Quality Management & Business Excellence*, *31*(13–14), 1409–1426. doi:10.1080/14783363.2019.1699783

Soon, J., Davies, W., Chadd, S., & Baines, R. (2012). A Delphi-based approach to developing and validating a farm food safety risk assessment tool by experts. *Expert Systems*. https://www.sciencedirect.com/science/article/pii/S0957417412002175

Stubbs, W. (2017a). Characterising B Corps as a sustainable business model: An exploratory study of B Corps in Australia. *Journal of Cleaner Production*, *144*, 299–312. doi:10.1016/j.jclepro.2016.12.093

Stubbs, W. (2017b). Sustainable Entrepreneurship and B Corps. *Business Strategy and the Environment*, *26*(3), 331–344. doi:10.1002/bse.1920

Sun, H., Li, S., Ho, K., Gertsen, F., Hansen, P., & Frick, J. (1992). The trajectory of implementing ISO 9000 standards versus total quality management in Western Europe. *International Journal of Quality & Reliability Management*, *21*(2), 131–153. doi:10.1108/02656710410516952

Tabares, S. (2021). Do hybrid organizations contribute to Sustainable Development Goals? Evidence from B Corps in Colombia. *Journal of Cleaner Production*, *280*, 124615. doi:10.1016/j.jclepro.2020.124615

Taheri, B., Gannon, M. J., Cordina, R., & Lochrie, S. (2018). Measuring host sincerity: Scale development and validation. *International Journal of Contemporary Hospitality Management*, *30*(8), 2752–2772. doi:10.1108/IJCHM-08-2017-0535

United Nations. (2021). *United Nations*. https://www.un.org/en/

Van Zanten, J. A., & van Tulder, R. (2018). Article. *Journal of International Business Policy*, *1*(3–4), 208–233. doi:10.105742214-018-0008-x

Villela, M., Bulgacov, S., & Morgan, G. (2019). B Corp Certification and Its Impact on Organizations Over Time. *Journal of Business Ethics*. Advance online publication. doi:10.100710551-019-04372-9

Waddock, S., & McIntosh, M. (2011). Business unusual: Corporate responsibility in a 2.0 World. *Business and Society Review*, *116*(3), 303–330. doi:10.1111/j.1467-8594.2011.00387.x

Winkler, A.-L. P., Brown, J. A., & Finegold, D. L. (2019). Employees as Conduits for Effective Stakeholder Engagement: An Example from B Corporations. *Journal of Business Ethics*, *160*(4), 913–936. doi:10.100710551-018-3924-0

Wu, S., & Chen, J. (2011). Comparison between manufacturing companies that are ISO certified and those that are not certified using performance measurement model. *Total Quality Management & Business Excellence*, *22*(8), 869–890. doi:10.1080/14783363.2011.593860

Zairi, M., & Sinclair, D. (1995). Business process re-engineering and process management. *Management Decision*. https://www.emerald.com/insight/content/doi/10.1108/00251749510085021/full/html

ADDITIONAL READING

Grimes, M. G., Gehman, J., & Cao, K. (2018). Positively deviant: Identity work through B Corporation certification. *Journal of Business Venturing*, *33*(2), 130–148. doi:10.1016/j.jbusvent.2017.12.001

Harjoto, M., Laksmana, I., & Yang, Y.-W. (2019). Why do companies obtain the B corporation certification? *Social Responsibility Journal*, *15*(5), 621–639. doi:10.1108/SRJ-07-2018-0170

Poponi, S., Colantoni, A., Cividino, S. R. S., & Mosconi, E. M. (2019). The Stakeholders' perspective within the B corp certification for a circular approach. *Sustain.*, *11*(6), 1584. Advance online publication. doi:10.3390u11061584

Putnam Rankin, C., & Matthews, T. L. (2020). Patterns of B Corps Certification: The Role of Institutional, Economic, and Political Resources. *Societies (Basel, Switzerland)*, *10*(3), 72. doi:10.3390oc10030072

Saiz-Álvarez, J. M., Vega-Muñoz, A., Acevedo-Duque, Á., & Castillo, D. (2020). B Corps: A Socioeconomic Approach for the COVID-19 Post-crisis. *Frontiers in Psychology*, *11*(July), 1–8. doi:10.3389/fpsyg.2020.01867 PMID:32849095

Stubbs, W. (2018). Examining the Interplay of Social and Market Logics in Hybrid Business Models: A Case Study of Australian B Corps. In L. Moratis, F. Melissen, & S. O. Idowu (Eds.), *Sustainable Business Models: Principles, Promise, And Practice. (CSR Sustainability Ethics and Governance)* (pp. 63–84)., doi:10.1007/978-3-319-73503-0_4

Wilburn, K., & Wilburn, R. (2014). The double bottom line: Profit and social benefit. *Business Horizons*, *57*(1), 11–20. doi:10.1016/j.bushor.2013.10.001

KEY TERMS AND DEFINITIONS

B Academics: A network of educators and researchers from around the world who are committed to accelerating the sustainable business movement by studying the global movement of B Corporation certification and benefit corporations.

B Corporations (B Corps): A model of companies that meet the highest standards of social and environmental performance, public transparency, and corporate responsibility to balance profit with purpose.

B Impact Assessment: It is a free tool aimed at helping companies to measure and manage their impact on five areas: workers, community, customers, and environment. It focuses on both the day-to-day operations and the business model. As a final outcome, companies obtain a score which ranges from 0 to 200. A minimum score of 80 is needed in order to start the B Corp certification process.

B Lab: A non-profit organization serving this global movement and is uniquely positioned to accelerate this cultural change in a meaningful and lasting way.

B Multipliers: Drivers and agents of change that are helping in the necessary but complex transition of large, medium, and small companies towards new business models of impact.

Delphi Method: It is a qualitative methodology aimed to gather information about a specific topic from experts of the field. The experts participate in several rounds of questionnaires. After each round, their responses are aggregated and shared with the group in order to receive more feedback. This is an iterative process which finishes once a consensus is reach.

Effect: Result of consequence of a fact.

Expert: A person who has a great deal of knowledge or experience in a particular topic.

Sustainable Development Goals: A collection of 17 interlinked global goals proposed by United Nations in 2015 and designed to end poverty, protect the planet, and ensure that all people enjoy peace and prosperity by 2030.

Chapter 11
CSR and SDGs in Early-Stage Entrepreneurship:
A Startup Perspective of Sustainability

Sofía Louise Martínez-Martínez
https://orcid.org/0000-0002-5093-9177
University of Málaga, Spain

Rafael Ventura Fernández
University of Málaga, Spain

Clara Plata Ríos
University of Málaga, Spain

ABSTRACT

Entrepreneurship conditions the sustainable development of a society by the economic, social, and environmental impact of new ventures. Specifically, startups, due to their high level of innovation and scalability, have an important role in fostering and accelerating the implementation of sustainable practices. An empirical analysis is carried out through data collected in the framework of the GEM project to define the extent in which startups innovation impact SDGs. The results highlight that the most frequently addressed goals belong to the economic sphere (e.g., SDG 8 and SDG 9), while environmental and social aspects are scarcely considered. More than half of the SDGs are addressed by less than 10% of the startups. A change in policies to promote SDGs is needed to foster the implementation of CSR strategies from early entrepreneurial stages, increase startups awareness, and face the lack of attention that some SDGs are receiving from the currently emerging innovation.

DOI: 10.4018/978-1-7998-8065-3.ch011

INTRODUCTION

Entrepreneurship leverages the potential of existing resources by creating new outputs that meet the demands of society (Cuervo et al., 2007). In this area, startups stand out as examples of innovative entrepreneurship, as their business models involve innovation and are characterized by replicability and scalability (Blank, 2010; Skala, 2019). In this sense, through the detection of opportunities and disruptive thinking, startups satisfy needs in a novel way by creating value through products, services and business models (Hsieh & Wu, 2018). This value is not only economic but can also have an impact on social and environmental dimensions. Through Corporate Social Responsibility (CSR), companies in general, and startups in particular, can maximize this social and environmental impact by contributing to the sustainable development of society.

In this sense, startups must be aware of their potential incorporating a systemic thinking into their business models from initial phases, favoring the impact on real and viable sustainable objectives through their innovative proposals. Previous studies show that entrepreneurial initiatives give less weight to CSR compared to established companies and large corporations (e.g., Gartner & Carter, 2003). This is mainly due to the scarcity of initial resources, a short-term vision and the prioritization of economic and financial issues that ensure business survival (Luetkenhorst, 2004). Even so, incorporating sustainability strategies from the outset can be crucial for business success, as it favors the establishment of partnerships and the development of competitive advantages and business reputation in the eyes of investors and other stakeholders (De Lange, 2017; Murillo & Lozano, 2006).

To achieve this goal, a growing number of studies highlight the key role of the Sustainable Development Goals (SDGs). Specifically, ElAlfy et al. (2020) state the importance of considering the SDGs into CSR strategies because of their numerous benefits for the company, its stakeholders and society in general. These goals help startups to understand their potential social and environmental impact, as well as to focus their innovative actions on specific areas. The SDGs are therefore defined as a facilitating tool and a precursor for startups' sustainability. However, a company cannot influence through their activity all of the SDGs, but its consideration must be based on real impact possibilities and environmental needs, which can be grouped in different SDG dimensions. In this sense, the present study highlights the SDG classification "The Wedding Cake", developed by the Stockholm Resilience Centre (2016). It is a grouping that not only differentiates three dimensions (biosphere, society and economy), but also establishes premises on the mainstreaming of these goals. In addition, it emphasizes the relevance of generating partnerships (SDG 17) as a way to maximize the potential economic, social and environmental impact.

Although both CSR and SDGs are fields of research that are currently receiving a great deal of interest, there is little research that focuses on the relationship between these two areas with a view on startups (Retolaza et al., 2009). In this sense, this study fills an important gap by analyzing the impact of startup innovation on the SDGs through one general and two specific objectives. In general terms, the aim is to determine what SDGs does startup innovation impact on, i.e., to analyze which SDGs are most and least related to startups activities, in order to discover whether there are predominant goals and if there are SDGs on which startup innovation has little impact.

The specific research objectives are, firstly, to identify the SDGs addressed by startups according to a framework of needs based on the Wedding Cake Model (Stockholm Resilience Centre, 2016), differentiating the three dimensions: biosphere, society and economy. Secondly, to determine the extent to which startups impact SDG 17 through their business strategy.

In this way, the present study promotes further research along the above-mentioned fields, contributing to build knowledge on the process of impacting the SDGs in nascent, especially innovative, entrepreneurship. This in order to favor a greater business commitment to social and environmental aspects and to promote the relevance and presence of SDGs in entrepreneurial ecosystems (Liguori, & Bendickson, 2020).

The chapter takes the first step with a theoretical review of startups, CSR and SDGs, followed by the formulation of the methodology and empirical testing. The results and findings are then analyzed and discussed. Finally, the theoretical and practical contributions are presented together with the future lines of research.

BACKGROUND

Entrepreneurship and Startups as Vehicles of Social Impact

The socioeconomic development of a country or region is conditioned by a large number of factors, among which innovation and entrepreneurship stand out. Innovation brings new ways of responding to societal challenges, through the advancement of knowledge and technology. New tools, products and services cover previously unsatisfied or poorly satisfied needs; at the same time, they foster the emergence of new needs that must be addressed by scientific and technical advances. Entrepreneurship serves as a vehicle for innovation, returning the value to society (Martínez-Martínez, 2020). Already in the first half of the 20th century, innovation through entrepreneurship occupied a key place in the development of society. Schumpeter (1934) emphasized its role as a factor that boosted economic and social changes allowing progress of institutions and the civilization as a whole. In the same vein, the promotion of entrepreneurial human capital through economic and educational initiatives is key to employability, competitiveness and societal development (Galvão et al., 2017; Martínez-Martínez & Ventura, 2020) In this sense, during the last decades it has been stated that the driving force of the economy is entrepreneurship (Mazzarol et al.,1999; Ribeiro-Soriano, 2017; Sanyang & Huang, 2009).

Entrepreneurship is understood as "a creation of a new enterprise" (Low & McMillan, 1988, p. 141), the activity that harnesses the potential of existing resources in the economic system and the wider environment to generate new outputs that address societal needs (Cuervo et al., 2007). Entrepreneurship involves recognizing and seizing opportunities, creating value through the development of new products, services, processes or business models, and encompasses the process of designing, launching and managing a new business (Hsieh & Wu, 2018). Nevertheless, it is important to point out that entrepreneurship does not always imply innovation, since on numerous occasions businesses are started by offering products or services that already exist in the market or by responding to the needs of clients and users in a similar way to the competitors (Autio et al. 2014).

In this context, the term startup (also spelt start-up) takes on special relevance as it refers to business initiatives that involve innovation and whose business models are characterized by replicability and scalability (Blank, 2010). Skala (2019) performs a conceptualization work of this term and emphasize the relationship of this type of companies with innovation. In this sense, she specifies its formation as a result of innovative entrepreneurship. This implies that the main characteristic that differentiates startups from other entrepreneurial initiatives is the novel nature of their products or services. For this author, startups "are a manifestation of the digital revolution and an economy based on innovation in the broadly understood use of information and communication technologies (ICT)" (Skala, 2019, p.13). Figueredo et al. (2019) refer to the uncertainty faced by these companies and define them as nascent companies that are seeking a feasible value proposition through innovation in products, services and models that potentially offers high return and impact. In this sense, they play a key role in the development of countries and regions by enriching the socioeconomic fabric and by being drivers of innovation (Colombo & Piva, 2008). This great potential impact of startups should not be understood solely in economic terms but must be approached from a holistic perspective. Startups can also positively influence their environment in social and environmental terms if they incorporate these goals into their objectives and include strategies that address their commitment to society in their business model design. In this respect, CSR and SDGs are of particular relevance.

CSR in Startup Companies

CSR is understood as the voluntary integration of social and environmental concerns into company strategy and into transactions with stakeholders (European Commission, 2001). Research in this field has been carried out since the middle of the last century. As early as 1953, Bowen defined corporate responsibility beyond the economic sphere as: 'obligations of businessmen to pursue those policies, to make those decisions, or to follow those lines of action which are desirable in terms of the objectives and values of our society.'' (p.6). Thus, through CSR, companies engage with society to improve areas such as health and wellbeing, urban and rural development, education, culture and arts, social integration and the improvement of the quality of life of disadvantaged groups or those at risk of social exclusion. Carroll (1979, 1991) defined CSR and grouped these concerns into four areas to be covered by any company, representing four types of expectations: economic, legal, ethical and philanthropic. In the same line, Dahlsrud (2008) differentiated five dimensions of action: environmental, social, economic, stakeholder and charity. These actions are normally materialized through volunteering, donations, awareness campaigns or activities organized in relation to other companies, governments, public entities, educational institutions or civil society (Carroll & Buchholtz, 2015; Castillo-Villar, 2020).

CSR has been widely studied in relation to large companies (e.g., Bowen, 1953; Carroll, 1979; Kreps, 1940; Snider et al., 2003) and, in recent decades, this research has also been extended to the field of SMEs (e.g., Jenkins, 2004; Morsing & Perrini, 2009; Russo & Perrini, 2009; Vázquez-Carrasco & López-Pérez, 2013), which has been noted in a growing increase of initiatives to promote CSR in this type of companies (Zadek, 2002), responding to society's increasing demand in this regard (Carroll, 2000) and the importance of SMEs for the advancement of innovation and the development of the society (Campos et al., 2021). There is also a growing body of research that looks at CSR from a comparative perspective, considering both large corporations and SMEs (e.g., Perrini et al., 2007, Russo & Perrini, 2009; Russo & Tencati, 2009). Even so, this issue is less developed in the field of startups. These strategies are not as well developed in nascent companies and new business[1], since the main resources of entrepreneurs are allocated to the activities defined by Lichtenstein et al. (2007) as "organizing activities". These activities are related to the definition and launch of the business model and are usually associated to scarce resources. Especially in the early stages of business development, startups tend to have a lack of tangible and intangible resources (Wymer & Regan, 2005). During this period, the main concerns of the entrepreneurs are based on activities such as the team formation, the search for financing, the establishment of relationships with suppliers or the search for clients (Gartner & Carter, 2003). For that reason, CSR strategies are usually addressed by entrepreneurs at later stages of business development.

Even so, it is understood that CSR is fundamental to all types of entrepreneurial initiatives. In the words of Maignan et al. (1999, p. 457), CSR is "the way in which a company faces the economic, legal, ethical and discretionary responsibilities placed on them by their various stakeholders". In this regard, it is worth noting that a lack of these strategies can have a negative impact on the business development, since "the presence or absence of one activity can impact the potential or the effectiveness of another" (Lichtenstein et al., 2007, p. 239).

Research on CSR in SMEs also highlights the low presence of social or environmental strategies in this type of companies, particularly during their first years of life. In this regard, Luetkenhorst (2004) identifies several factors that, by their nature, can be extrapolated to the startups' reality. This author indicates that the lack of integration of social and environmental responsibility strategies is explained by the short-term focus, a relatively small network of access to resources as well as the efforts put on those that facilitate business survival. It is also conditioned by a generally limited influence and negotiating power with suppliers and authorities, that requires a greater investment in terms of time and money to achieve the business objectives. Also based on previous research carried out in the field of SMEs and extrapolated to the reality that concerns the present study, it is important to point out that, although CSR is less present in this type of companies than in large corporations, there are numerous cases of good practices and research interest on this subject. In this sense, Murillo & Lozano (2006) state that currently the incorporation of CSR strategies in entrepreneurial projects is mainly due to ethical concerns and the social or environmental values of the entrepreneurs themselves. At the same time, the incorporation of this kind of strategies is also determined by the motivations and values of the clients/users and stakeholders or by the actions developed by other companies in the sector in which they operate, either to implement similar strategies or to obtain a competitive advantage through differentiation (Ditlev-Simonsen & Wenstøp 2013). Still, regardless of the reason for its implementation, the incorporation of CSR strategies enhances the success and survival of the firm. Thus, through its alignment "with market drivers and stakeholder demands, CSR practices have become due diligence for preserving the firm's license to operate, avoiding reputational damages, building loyalty, and maintaining competitive positioning" (ElAlfy et al., 2020, p.2).

Retolaza et al. (2009), who developed a specific study of CSR regarding startups, stated that they obtain large benefits from integrating a social and environmental mission into their business model. Startups that address CSR strategy from the outset have a competitive advantage, both financially and in terms of environmental relations (Murillo & Lozano, 2006). Business commitment to society boosts resource mobilization as well as the establishment of alliances, favoring visibility, business survival and growth. The engagement in social and environmental issues also increase the startups legitimacy towards investors and other third parties (De Lange, 2017). Thus, defining a good CSR strategy translates into reputational terms. Nowadays, the social and environmental awareness of customers and stakeholders, largely boosted by the increasing visibility of social inequalities and environmental degradation in the media and social networks, places greater demands on companies (Barrena et al., 2016). Startups that not only respond to these issues by developing their activity based on legal requirements, but also make a greater effort to have a positive impact on their environment and respond to global problems, will be better positioned (Zyglidopoulos, 2003). In relation to this, the communication of the social and environmental commitment is a decisive aspect of the CSR strategy.

The importance of CSR for startups is also based on their dynamic nature. If a startup is understood as a "process of becoming rather than state of being" (Bygrave, 1989, p. 21), the business model has to integrate not only the present objectives of the company, but also its desirable future impact on society.

In this sense, the way of planning and ensuring that this future impact is aligned with the startup's mission is the CSR strategy and its definition at early business stage is a great challenge (Porter & Kramer, 2006). The identification of the main social and/or environmental issues or aspects that the business activity can influence both directly and indirectly will increase the creativity and the chances of detecting business opportunities and generating value (Lefebvre & Lefebvre, 2012). Even if this can be a difficult task at the beginning while defining the value proposition, this effort to integrate a systemic approach is worthwhile, as including a holistic view from the formation of the business model contributes to improving the product or service offered and the relationships with stakeholders, developing a greater competitive advantage by increasing "awareness of different and new ways of doing business and making profits" (Lefebvre and Lefebvre, 2012, p. 22). In this process of identifying areas of impact or action, the SDGs play a key role.

The Role of SDGs in Defining a Sustainable Strategy

In 1972, the United Nations (UN) first introduced the concept of sustainable development, referring to the balance between economic growth, social welfare, and conservation and preservation of the environment (Ngan et al., 2019). Specifically, the World Commission on Environment and Development defines sustainable development "as development in which the needs of the present generation are met without compromising the ability of future generations" (WCED, 1987, p.43). The challenges of global sustainability have evolved over the years from the Brundtland Report (WCED, 1987), through the eight Millennium Development Goals (United Nations, 2000) to the current vision that summarizes the global challenges in 17 broad areas. Thus, today's prevailing conception of global sustainability is reflected in the 17 UN Sustainable Development Goals (SDGs) adopted by the United Nations General Assembly in September 2015 and included in Agenda 2030, understood as "an interconnected strategy for the promotion of sustainable practices and solutions that addresses the main issues faced by our society" (Dantas et al., 2021).

The SDGs represent an "universal set of goals to develop a global vision for sustainable development by balancing economic growth, social development, and environmental protection" (United Nations, 2015). These objectives are particularly useful because they outline a common framework recognized by the civil society, governments and public and private entities around the world. Although they cover a wide range of spectrums and fields of action and represent the systemic nature and complexity of sustainable development, their concretization into specific targets helps their materialization and the design of actions that respond to the needs of specific individuals or groups (Schönherr et al., 2017).

Within this framework, a growing number of studies are emerging that link entrepreneurship and sustainable development, establishing a "win-win" relationship between business, society and environment (Scheyvens et al., 2016). Business creation allows the development of solutions that improve society in a sustainable way over time (Youssef et al., 2017). In this sense, "businesses are critical stakeholders capable of accelerating the implementation of sustainable practices" (Dantas et al., 2021). Thus, the inclusion of SDGs in startups' design processes encourages the consideration of social and environmental aspects from the business model generation phase, fostering the transfer of business value to society. The vehicle for this inclusion is the CSR strategy, as it is understood as the company's way to plan and act towards sustainability (Kotler & Lee, 2005; Mackey et al., 2007).

Based on the importance to link SDGs to CSR strategies in order to meet the contemporary global challenges, ElAlfy et al. developed a theoretical study that determines that the 2030 agenda and its goals have a high potential to impact positively on business social and environmental performance, influencing "corporate strategy, CSR agendas, reporting practices, disclosure mechanisms, stakeholder expectations, and regulatory requirement" (ElAlfy et al., 2020, p.2). These authors recognize the integration of the SDGs into CSR as an opportunity for innovation and stakeholder engagement, that can even reduce business risk by the diversification of the value proposition through redirecting investments to social and environmental aspects. Nevertheless, more research is needed around this issue as there is still a lack of knowledge in the way in which companies actually address the SDGs. "While there is growing recognition regarding the potential for the SDGs to drive global-scale transformations towards more sustainable futures, the role of corporations in supporting the process and how the SDGs inform business models lacks clarity" (ElAlfy et al., 2020, p.4).

In the process of assessing the SDGs and their integration into business models, it is important to consider that not all goals can be directly addressed by a company and their generality and long-term focus can be overwhelming for young business (Pedersen, 2018). In this sense, startups must prioritize the impact in those areas that are most aligned with its mission and value proposition. Given the wide variety and heterogeneity of the SDGs, which were created to respond to a broad spectrum of global challenges, two key aspects for startups' treatment of the SDGs are discussed below: the SDGs' classification according to types of needs and the importance of SDG 17 - partnerships for the goals.

A Classification of the SDGs based on the Planet's Needs

The SDGs refer to a broad spectrum of global needs. These needs can be classified in a pyramidal fashion, taking Maslow's Need Hierarchy Theory (1943, 1954) as a reference point. This well-known theory organizes human needs by levels of satisfaction, pointing out that lower need must be met before facing the fulfillment of the higher level. In this sense, SDGs can be categorized according to three types of needs: environment or biosphere, society or human and economy, and in that order. Based on Maslow's logic, biosphere issues should be prioritized (SDGs 6, 13, 14 and 15), followed by society issues (SDGs 1, 2, 3, 4, 5, 7, 11 and 16) and economic needs (SDGs 8, 9, 10 and 12), as currently "the focus is shifting from the environment as externality to the biosphere as precondition for social justice, economic development and sustainability" (Folke et al., 2016). This approach to the SDGs is considered suitable for CSR strategies, as it helps to identify needs, determine the SDGs' potential impact and, most importantly, to prioritize them. Based in this logic, the hierarchy of SDGs is represented graphically by the Stockholm Resilience Centre (2016) on an integrated framework or model called "The Wedding Cake" (Figure 1).

Maximizing Impact through SDG 17

A wide range of actors are involved in meeting economic, social and environmental objectives. The SDGs help to identify these actors and promote their collaboration, so that challenges are not addressed in isolation, but in a shared and joint manner. "SDGs have recognized the essential role of the main social actors such as businesses, government, civil society, and universities working together to reach a sustainable development" (Castillo-Villar, 2020). Thus, the complexity of the global problems requires the involvement and cooperation of all those stakeholders (MacDonald et al., 2018). In this scenario, SDG 17 is particularly relevant, as it recognizes the importance of partnerships and collaborative engagement and promotes cross-sectoral and multidisciplinary relationships as a means to achieve other SDGs.

Figure 1. SDGs integrated framework: The Wedding Cake Model
Source: Stockholm Resilience Centre (2016)

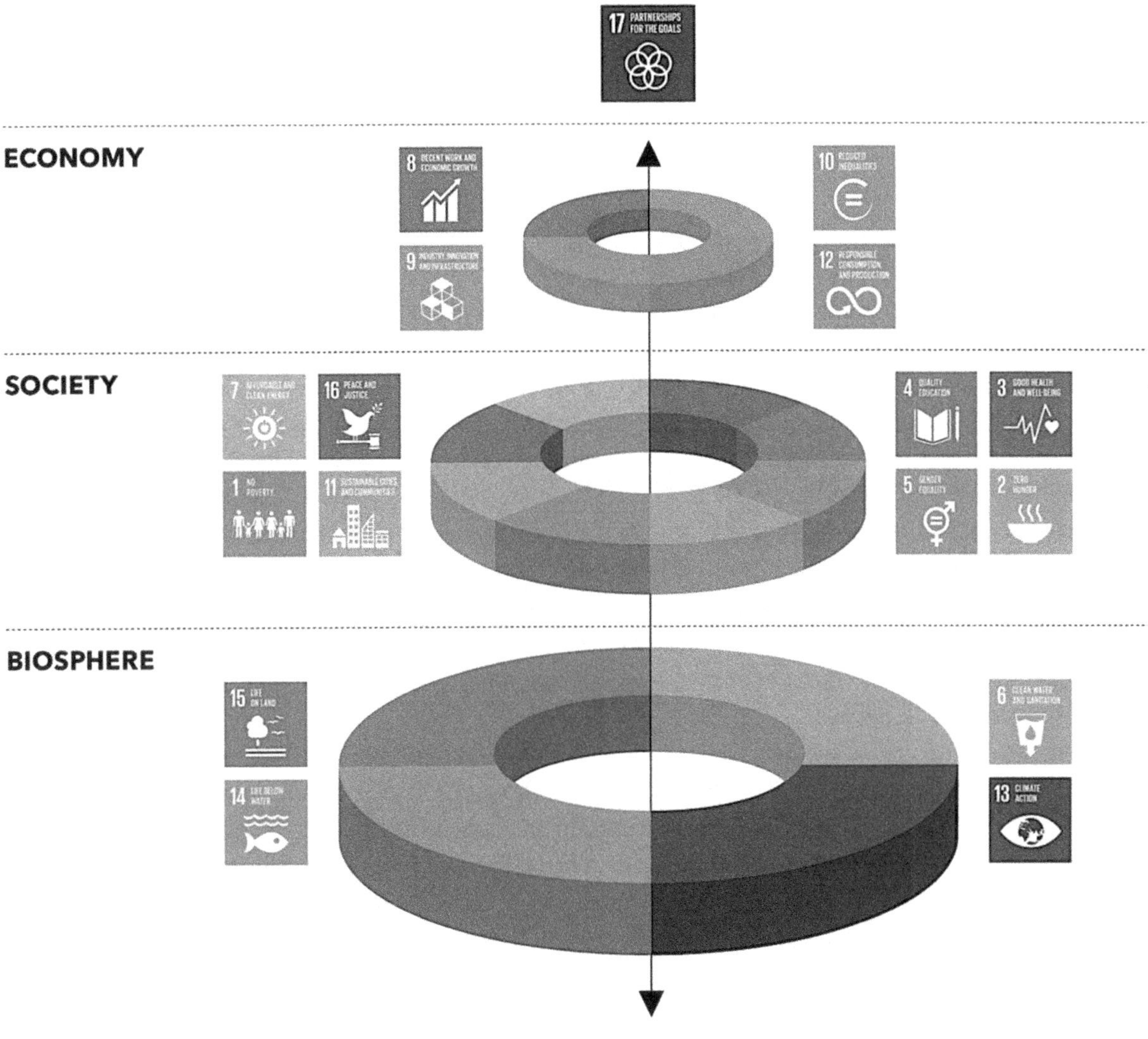

SDG 17 calls for a multistakeholder partnership, i.e., the creation of alliances between different business and non-business actors in order to maximize the positive impact on the environment (Franco & Abe, 2020). It is closely related to the company's CSR, as it aims to involve both shareholders and stakeholders in the achievement of the global goals and responds to the relevance of social capital in this type of practices (Russo & Perrini, 2010). In this sense, a startup cannot encompass all the SDGs in its strategy, but through the promotion of SDG 17, i.e., with the establishment of partnerships with various and committed actors, the company can expand its framework of action. Specifically, fostering a wider range of initiatives in a collaborative manner, joining activities already initiated by other actors, supporting them or simply engaging in their dissemination; as these are also ways of integrating the SDGs into the business strategy. In the same way, the company can also encourage the engagement of its partners in the realization of actions that favors the development of SDGs. SDG 17 enhance the "capacity of businesses to contribute to a sustainable society through the creation of partnerships where they can add their expertise, knowledge and resources" (Castillo-Villar, 2020). Therefore, it is concluded that, through SDG 17 a startup can increase its potential of action, influence and impact on global challenges (Van Hille et al., 2020). Furthermore, Kask & Linton (2013) state that the establishment of partnerships is a priority for the success of startups. It is therefore argued that SDG 17 should always be considered in any company's CSR strategy, in addition to the SDGs that can be specifically related to the company's mission and value proposition.

METHODOLOGY

A descriptive quantitative analysis is carried out based on primary data gathered in Malaga (Spain). The collection has been carried out through an online semi-structured questionnaire developed within the framework of Global Entrepreneurship Monitor (GEM) Malaga 2019/2020 Report (Ventura & Martínez-Martínez, 2020). This instrument collects information of 101 startup projects incubated in 9 incubators of Malaga in the last quarter of 2020. The questionnaire is answered directly by the founding partners of the startups. It covers the following questions relevant to this study: business activity, sector, number of team members, economic and social nature of the projects, social impact and SDGs considered in the business model. The variable on SDGs is the most relevant for the analysis and is collected through the following question: Indicate which SDGs are related to the startup's innovative activity. In this sense, companies could indicate all the SDGs related to their company, with a maximum of 6. This limit was established to obtain a higher level of concreteness and relationship between the SDGs indicated and the real purpose of the business.

The name of the incubators and the number of startups is the following: BIC Euronova (35), CADE Málaga-PTA (12); Costa del Sol Tourism Hub (3); Demium (3); Go2Work EOI (5); La Farola (23); Link by UMA-Atech (14); Promálaga (6). In order to obtain an image in accordance with Malaga's reality, the study includes all of the city's business incubators. The entrepreneurial initiatives of each incubator were selected by the managers, experts in entrepreneurship, of each of the incubation spaces. The indications for the selection were: newly created companies that could be considered as startups, with less than three years of life with a solid and viable business project. No selection biases have been introduced by sector or nature of entrepreneurial activity. Therefore, the sample reflects a great entrepreneurial heterogeneity in accordance with the reality of Malaga's entrepreneurial ecosystem.

To show this heterogeneity and in order to provide a description of the main areas in which the startups under analysis operate, a word cloud has been developed, using software Atlas.ti v. 9.0.7, based on the keywords and descriptions provided by the companies about their field of activity (Figure 2). The size of the words reflects the weight of each field in the total sample.

As shown in Figure 2, industry is the main sector in which the analyzed startups develop their business activities. The service sector in general, and consulting and training in particular, are also relevant areas for these companies. Other sectors in which Malaga startups develop their business activities are tourism, technology, software development, e-health, smart retail and vehicles, the latest related to the development of automation and connectivity solutions. To a lesser but also relevant extent, startups develop products and services in the audiovisual sector, telecommunication and ITC. The smart city concept also has an important presence in the entrepreneurial activity of the analyzed startups.

Figure 2. Main areas of business activity of the startups analyzed in Malaga
Source: Author's own elaboration

Other descriptive information about the sample is that the number of members of the analyzed startups ranges from 1 to 19 (mean: 4.43; standard deviation: 2.94). Differentiating by groups, the proportion of number of team members in the sample is the following: 1 founder: 17%; 2-4 team members: 47%; 5-8 team members: 35%; more than 8 team members: 11%). With regard to the gender role in the management of these business projects, 72% are founded by men and 28% by women. Regarding the nature of the companies analyzed, 50% state that their business model is solely economic, while 48% indicate that they combine both economic and social goals. Only 2% have a purely social nature.

The analysis of the SDGs addressed by each of the startups is developed using Stata 14.0.

Results

The results of this research are intended to shed light on the impact of emerging innovation developed by startups on the SDGs. Figure 3 shows the result of the frequency analysis, indicating the proportion in which each of the SDGs is related to the entrepreneurial initiatives. It is important to emphasize that most of the companies indicate between one and three SDGs in their responses. Only 8% of the companies analyzed consider that their innovative proposal is related to four SDGs, 4% consider that they address five SDGs and only 1% respond that the business model influences six SDGs.

Figure 3 shows an initial overview of the SDGs related to the startup's business projects. It is possible to observe a great predominance of SDGs 9 and 8 over the rest. These are the two objectives most associated with the economic sphere (Industry, innovation and infrastructure and Decent work and economic growth). Figure 3 also shows a number of SDGs that are less developed but still taken into account by the innovative proposal of a considerable number of companies (SDGs: 11, 3, 17, 12 and 4). Then, there is an even larger number of SDGs that are contemplated by a very small number of startups. More than half of the sustainable development goals have hardly any presence in innovative entrepreneurial activity.

These results are analyzed in more detail in Table 1, which presents a ranking of the SDGs most and least addressed, ordered by percentage and presented together with the scope of action and its description.

Figure 3. Proportion of SDGs related to the emerging innovation developed by Malaga startups (%)
Source: Author's own elaboration

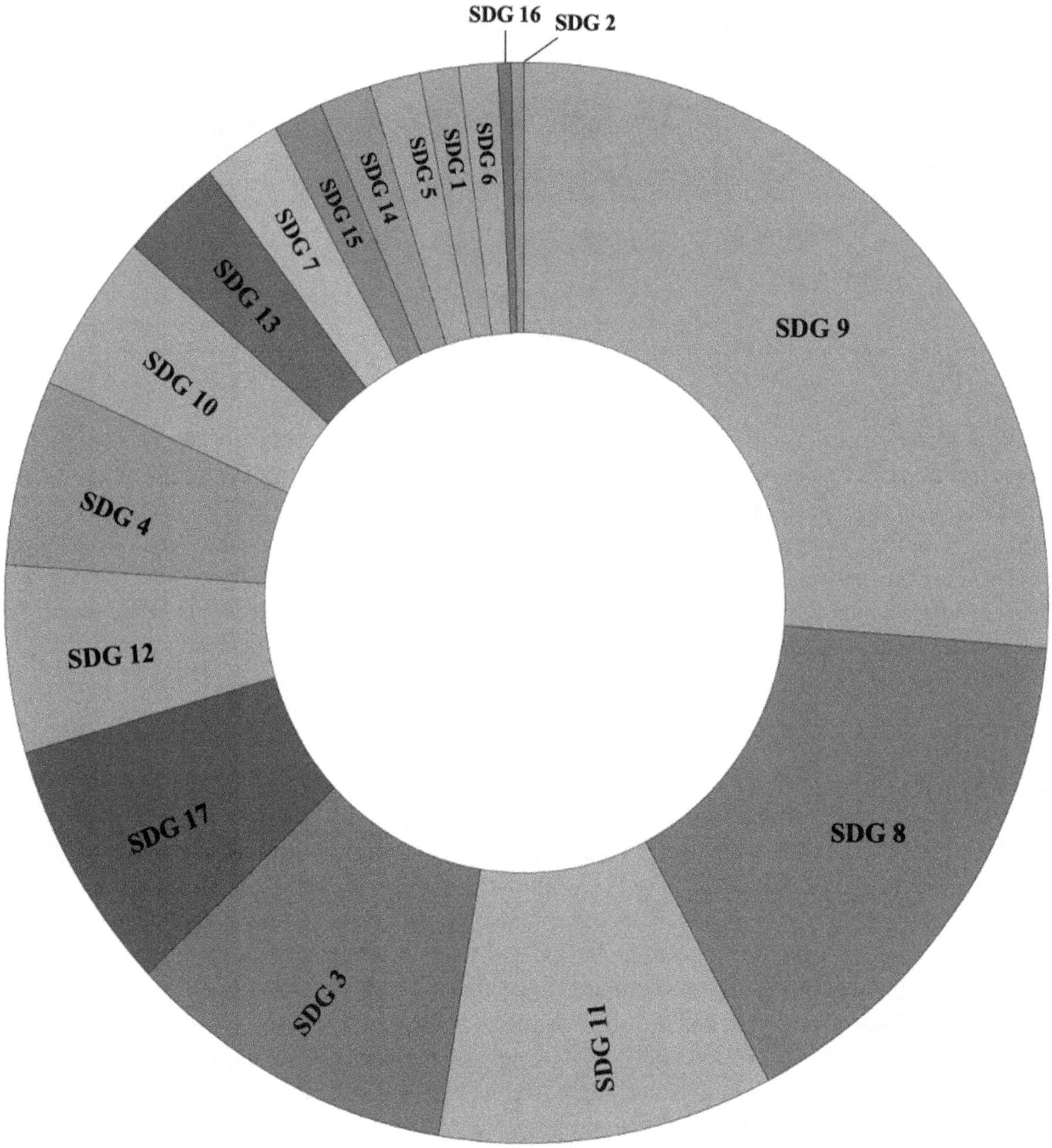

Table 1 shows that there is one SDG that stands out above the rest. This is the case of SDG 9, which refers to the development of industrialization through infrastructure and sustainable innovation. More than half of the startups in Malaga indicate that their business project contributes to this objective (65%). The second SDG that is most addressed is related to the labor market and the progress of the economy as a whole. More than a third of startups consider that their company favors decent work and economic growth (40%). In addition to these outstanding SDGs, Table 1 shows that there are two others to which a considerable number of companies contribute through their innovation. Around a quarter of the startups analyzed (26%) indicate that their innovative proposal promotes sustainability in cities and communities or brings improvements to the field of health and wellbeing.

Table 1. Ranking of SDGs related to the innovation of Malaga startups, scope of action and description

%	SDG	
	Nº and name	**Description**
65%	9. Industry, innovation and infraestructure	Build resilient infrastructure, promote inclusive and sustainable industrialization and foster innovation
40%	8. Decent work and economic growth	Promote sustained, inclusive and sustainable economic growth, full and productive employment and decent work for all
26%	3. Good health and well-being	Ensure healthy lives and promote well-being for all at all ages
26%	11. Sustainable cities and communities	Make cities and human settlements inclusive, safe, resilient and sustainable
19%	17. Partnerships for the goals	Strengthen the means of implementation and revitalize the global partnership for sustainable development
14%	4. Quality education	Ensure inclusive and equitable quality education and promote lifelong learning opportunities for all
14%	12. Responsable consumption and production	Ensure sustainable consumption and production patterns
12%	10. Reduced inequalities	Reduce inequality within and among countries
8%	13. Climate action	Take urgent action to combat climate change and its impacts
6%	7. Affordable and clean energy	Ensure access to affordable, reliable, sustainable and modern energy for all
4%	14. Life below water	Conserve and sustainably use the oceans, seas and marine resources for sustainable development
4%	15. Life on land	Protect, restore and promote sustainable use of terrestrial ecosystems, sustainably manage forests, combat desertification, and halt and reverse land degradation and halt biodiversity loss
4%	5. Gender equality	Achieve gender equality and empower all women and girls
3%	6. Clean water and sanitation	Ensure availability and sustainable management of water and sanitation for all
3%	1. No poverty	End poverty in all its forms everywhere
1%	2. Zero hunger	End hunger, achieve food security and improved nutrition and promote sustainable agriculture
1%	16. Peace, justice and strong institutions	Promote peaceful and inclusive societies for sustainable development, provide access to justice for all and build effective, accountable and inclusive institutions at all levels

Source: Author's own elaboration from collected data and UN information[2]

The remaining SDGs are selected by less than 20% of the startups. To facilitate the interpretation, they are divided in three groups: SDGs addressed by between 20% and 10% of startups, SDGs considered by between 10% and 3% of startups and goals related to 3% or less of startups.

In the first group, SDG 17 stands out. This objective is related to the generation of partnerships for the achievement of the global challenges and related to the entrepreneurial initiative of 19% of the startups. The rest of the goals in this group are considered by less than 15% of the companies analyzed. 14% place value on inclusive and quality education, as well as on the promotion of lifelong learning opportunities. The same percentage of startups is committed to responsible consumption and production. Finally, 12% consider that they contribute to the reduction of inequalities through their innovative business project.

The second group is characterized by goals related to the protection, conservation and restoration of the environment, in both marine and terrestrial ecosystems. In other words, it includes objectives that allude to the protection of the planet. 8% of the startups carry out innovative actions to fight climate change, 6% support solutions that promote renewable and sustainable energy through products or services. This also includes energy accessibility, since the aim of this goal is also to make energy available to everyone in an affordable way. 4% of startups promote, through their innovative proposal, the protection of both marine and terrestrial ecosystems. Likewise, in this range is the sustainable objective that refers to gender equality. In this sense, 4% of startups consider that they contribute to reduce gender inequalities through their business activity.

The last group includes the SDGs that are less related to startup innovation. These are goals associated with social welfare and basic needs. Only 3% of startups refer to the sustainable management of water and sanitation and the fight against poverty. The problem of world hunger is even less addressed. Only 1% of startups develop activities that have an impact on the elimination of hunger or the promotion of secure and sustainable nutrition and food production. Similarly, only 1% of the companies analyzed consider their business activity to be linked to the promotion of peace, justice and strong and inclusive institutions.

The impact of startups innovation on SDGs is related to the three dimensions differentiated by the Wedding Cake Model (Stockholm Resilience Centre, 2016) outlined in the theoretical review. It is important to note that even if the SDGs address a general global goal, which is to promote the sustainable development of the planet as a whole, they allude to specific challenges that can be grouped, differentiating goals connected with the biosphere, the society or the economy. Figure 4 presents the integration of these dimensions in the analysis, showing their relevance in the innovative activity of the startups.

The first dimension, biosphere, is hardly addressed by the startups. The circle sizes shows that the innovation developed by startups hardly respond to these global environmental challenges. The one that receives the most prominence is SDG 13, which refers to the fight against climate change. Even so, in comparative terms with the other dimensions, the size indicates that it is poorly addressed. Secondly, an analysis of the social dimension shows that startups respond mainly to SDGs 3 and 11, while the rest are addressed slightly. In this sense, the business projects do not meet the majority of the social needs established as global challenges. In this regard, SDGs 5, 1, 2 and 16, which refer respectively to gender equality, end of poverty, elimination of hunger and promotion of peace, justice and strong institutions, stand out because of their scant consideration in the innovation of startups.

Thirdly, the SDGs most frequently mentioned by the analyzed companies are to be found in the economic dimension. Even so, the four goals that compose this group are not equally important. SDGs 9 and 8 predominate, while the other two dimensions receive much less consideration. This indicates that, in the economic sphere, startup innovation impact more on the development of industry, innovation, infrastructure, decent work and global economic growth than on the sustainability of consumption and production processes and the reduction of inequalities.

Figure 4. Startup's impact on SDGs by Biosphere, Society and Economy dimensions
Source: Author's own elaboration based on the Wedding Cake Model (Stockholm Resilience Centre, 2016). Color and number of circles: SDG. Size of circles: Proportion of the impact of startups innovation on SDG

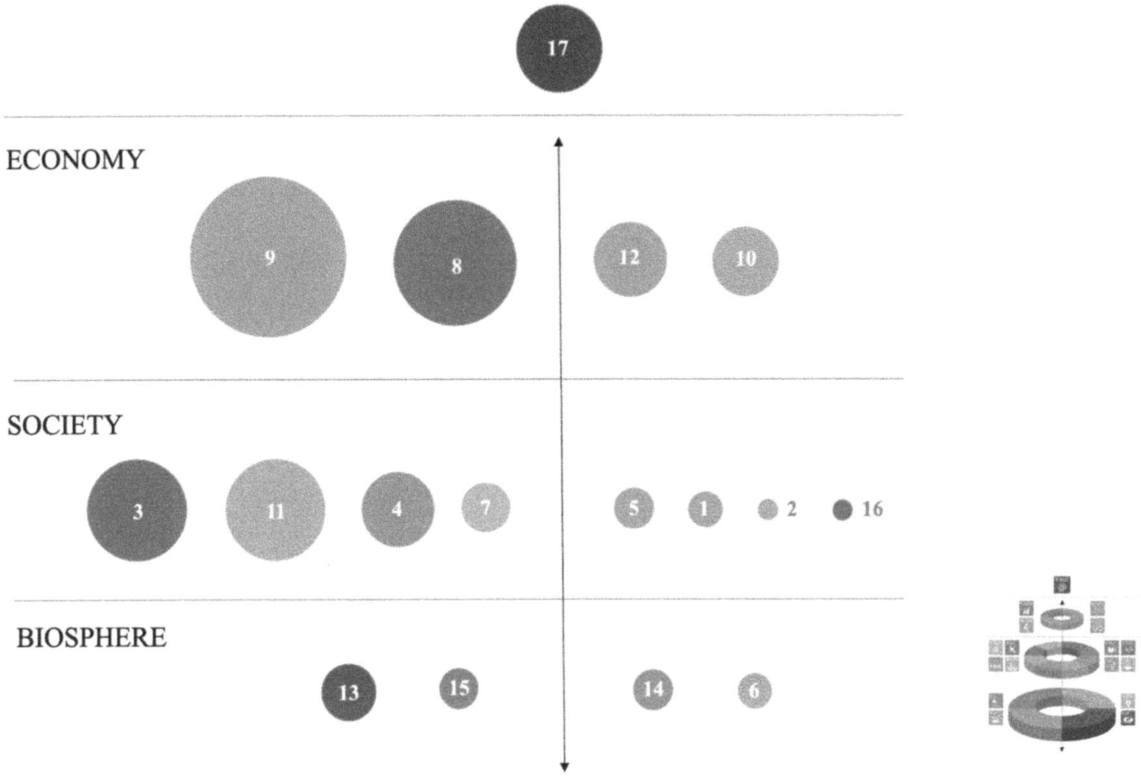

CONCLUSION

The theoretical review developed shows that the consideration of SDGs is beneficial to promote CSR strategies from early business stages and that, specifically, startups have a great potential of generating employment and economic and social development (Retolaza et al., 2009). Even so, the analysis shows an unequal impact of the innovation of startups on the SDGs. Only some aspects are being addressed by startups, leaving ample room for improvement in terms of the economic, social and environmental impact. The promotion of a broader consideration of the SDGs in innovative proposals is discussed in more detail below and recommendations are made.

SDGs 9 and 8 stand out notably above the rest. A large proportion of startups contribute to these goals through their innovative business activity, which is very positive. This may be due to the startup nature, since by definition they are companies that are committed to innovation and the development of disruptive solutions that favor business scalability (Blank, 2010). The analysis of the word cloud shows that the business activities are mainly developed in the industrial sector, which explains the predominance of SDG 9, based on industry progress and innovation. Most companies integrate technological components into their business models, for example through ICTs, software development or other technologies that favor automation and connectivity.

This technological nature, linked to innovation, also boosts economic growth in general (SDG 8), through the introduction of new solutions in the market that dynamize the economy and increase productivity and competitiveness, even enhancing the generation of new business opportunities (Carlaw & Lipsey, 2003). Starting a company also implies in most cases the hiring of personnel. Startups are extensively recognized to be important drivers of long-run job creation (Haltiwanger, et al., 2013; Sedláček & Sterk, 2017). Based on the collected information it was found that 83% of the companies have more than one person involved in the entrepreneurial activity and 46% of the startups have 5 or more members. Some of them even have more than 10 employees in their first years of life. This means that they generate employment, which explains why many of them consider that they contribute to promoting SDG 8 (decent work).

Although the very nature of startups promotes the contribution to these two SDGs, it is important to foster impact on the rest of the goals through innovation. Following the grouping shown in Table 1, in addition to the two main SDGs mentioned above, two others stand out as being addressed by a quarter of the startups analyzed (SDGs 3 and 11). In this line, improving people's health and well-being and the sustainability of cities and communities are concerns that are gaining importance in society (Shamsrizi, et al., 2020; Vaidya & Chatterji, 2020). Startups focused on SDG 3 develop mostly e-health solutions, some created from the socio-health crisis resulting from Covid-19 (Shamsrizi, et al., 2020). SDG 11 is addressed by companies involved in the development of smart cities. In this area most operate in the automotive sector, developing technology to improve vehicle automation and connectivity (Figure 2). Startups with a special focus on services for more sustainable tourism also contribute to this SDG.

In contrast, aspects such as poverty, hunger or water sanitation are problems hardly covered by the emerging innovation promoted by startups. The SDGs most often addressed are those that are clearly market-oriented, or whose solutions may have a market opportunity (Pedersen, 2018). These results are in line with previous research on entrepreneurial impact on SDGs in other contexts (Horne et al., 2020). In this respect, in order to enter the market and grow, startups recognize opportunities in solving more advanced needs regarding health, wellness and sustainability. Thus, the rest of the SDGs are covered by less than 20% of startups, which is worrying, since nascent entrepreneurship should be one of the main ways of tackling global problems (Colombo & Piva, 2008). The analysis shows that some startups integrate education and technology to offer training solutions especially in the field of job qualification and continuous training, which is why SDG 4 is mentioned by 14% of the companies. On the other hand, 14% of startups also contribute through its innovation to responsible production and consumption (SDG 12). This group is dominated by those dedicated to the smart retail and the trade sector (Figure 2). The need to impact on this goal in a transversal way is highlighted, not only in those startups dedicated to trade, but also in industry in general. In this regard, given the nature of the startups analyzed, it is important to emphasize that the impact on this SDG should be much greater as "businesses play a pivotal role in society's shift towards sustainable consumption and production" (Batalhone & Clement, 2018). Any startup with a product development phase or a production process has the possibility of integrating a sustainable logic, maximizing the use of resources and avoiding waste. In the same way, any startup, whether it is based on product or service, can address consumer sustainability through its relational and marketing strategies (Palakshappa & Dodds, 2020).

Finally, it is essential to emphasize that nine SDGs, out of the total of 17, have been mentioned by less than 10% of the startups analyzed. All of these SDGs are found in the first two dimensions identified by Stockholm Resilience Centre (2016) in The Wedding Cake Model (biosphere and society). This contradicts the recommendations of previous research, which indicate that the SDGs should be addressed starting with the biosphere, in order to face the needs of the other two dimensions in a real and effective way (Folke et al., 2016). After addressing the environmental sphere, it is recommended to undertake the social dimension, responding to human needs. Based on this logic, the SDGs related to the economy should be attended after having ensured the previous ones, since the real sustainability of this dimension can only be effectively achieved if the two previous spheres are sufficiently developed (Folke et al., 2016). In this regard, the present study shows that the economic SDGs prevails in startups strategies.

As exposed in the theoretical review, the goal number 17 is fundamental for startups to expand their scope of action and influence on sustainable development. This SDG is placed in the Stockholm Resilience Centre (2016) model, at the top of the "cake", with the aim of showing its outstanding relevance and influence on the rest of the goals. "Partnership for the goals", as its own description indicates "strengthen the means of implementation and revitalize the global partnership for sustainable development" (United Nations, 2021). By integrating this SDG into the business strategy, startups expand their resources and acquired social capital, promoting sustainable development in a broader range of areas through their collaboration with other stakeholders committed to sustainability. By means of their business relationships they can also encourage the involvement of new public and private actors to maximize the positive impact on their environment (Franco & Abe, 2020; Van Hille et al., 2020). The present chapter detects the need to increase the commitment to this SDG, since only 19% of startups consider the establishment of partnerships for the goals as a relevant issue. The enhancement of this SDG involves an important source of resources and reputation that can be decisive for business success (Kask & Linton, 2013).

In relation to the importance of SDG 17, it is also interesting to note that while previously the UN placed greater emphasis on governments for the achievement of global challenges, the SDGs are also linked to business (Pedersen, 2018). Through SDG 17, companies have a key role in supporting the accomplishment of the other objectives, acting sustainably in their specific areas and promoting sustainability among the actors of the business ecosystems (Buhmann, 2018). And this is not only a challenge for consolidated companies but also for startups, which must take advantage of the characteristics of their own nature, especially innovation, dynamism and flexibility, to achieve this end.

Finally, in order to offer a comparative perspective, the results of this study show some similarities with the analysis developed in 2016 by the Spanish Global Pact Network - Red Española del Pacto Mundial (Pacto Mundial, 2017), which, based on an analysis of sustainability reports, extracts the impact of large corporations and SMEs on the SDGs. The results agree on the relevance of decent work and economic growth (SDG 8), especially for SMEs. This goal is the most addressed by this type of companies and the second most relevant for large corporations; in the case of startups it also ranks second. SDG 3 (health and well-being) and SDG 4 (quality education) are also relevant for all three types of companies. However, while there are commonalities, certain dissimilarities can also be observed, especially in relation to startups. The most notable is the place occupied by SDG 9. While for startups it is by far the most frequently addressed goal, for both large companies and SMEs it is located in seventh place. This difference could be explained by startups' innovative nature. SDG 17, ranked fifth by startups, is in tenth and eighth place in the studies on large corporations and SMEs. In contrast, climate action (SDG 13) and responsible production and consumption (SDG 12) are more prominent among large corporations and SMEs than among startups. The less addressed goals show similar results, so it can be concluded that there is some homogeneity in the business sector in terms of impact on ending poverty (SDG 1) and achieving zero hunger (SDG 2) (Pacto Mundial, 2017). This comparison shows that, even if there are similarities in the approach to the SDGs, startups impact differently on many of the global challenges. This supports the importance of studying them in depth as a business typology with its own nature, considering these characteristics in the improvement of the design and implementation of policies that promote business impact on SDGs.

Theoretical and Practical Contributions

This study has both theoretical and practical contributions. It completes the existent literature on CSR highlighting the role of SDGs particularly in startups, a business typology in which these issues are less addressed (Retolaza et al., 2009). It also enriches the startup literature from a sustainable perspective. There are few studies that analyze the impact of startups on SDGs and the relation between the goals and the type of activities developed by entrepreneurial initiatives. At the same time, by the introduction of the Wedding Cake Model (Stockholm Resilience Centre, 2016), the study is adding value from a startup perspective to a theoretical model already developed and tested in a general scope.

In relation to the applied contributions of the study, first, it highlights the need to promote a greater awareness about CSR in early entrepreneurship, as the social and environmental contributions of the companies are considered by many to be as important as the economic profitability derived from corporate actions (Joyner & Payne 2002). Second, it encourages the development of strategies to increase the impact of startups on the SDGs, as companies have an important role as promoters of these goals (Buhmann et al., 2019; Kolstad, 2012). In this sense, a great effort is currently being made by national and international public and private institutions to promote the relevance of the SDGs globally. The UN is doing an important job of fostering, developing and implementing multi-stakeholder partnerships strategies (Hazlewood, 2015) to involve the maximum number of actors in working towards these goals. Even so, these efforts are not having the expected results in the field of startups.

The results of this study show that, even if startup innovation has a key role to play in generating new solutions, improving society and tackling grand challenges, we cannot expect startups to contribute in a similar way to all SDGs, since the emerging innovation only responds to a few global challenges. This vision is key for public policy makers as the orientation of innovation to these SDGs will not occur naturally, it needs to be incentivized. Therefore, some SDGs must receive greater attention from governments and leading institutions in order to encourage meaningful progress on all global challenges. In this sense, it is important to further explore this issue to determine the causes of this situation. Is it a problem of incentivizing certain types of startups? of relocating public funding? of integrating the SDGs into the designing of programs to promote entrepreneurship? of awareness? or of lack of knowledge about the impact that startup innovation can have on the SDGs? In this sense, the present study encourages the review and adaptation of existing SDG supporting strategies, policies and programs to the startup reality. Namely, emphasis should be placed on the importance of innovation for SDGs in initiatives aimed at promoting startup creation and consolidation (e.g., business creation programs, training of entrepreneurs, mentoring initiatives or startups investment forums). Furthermore, for policies to be effective, it is also necessary to ensure that stakeholders are aware of the meaning and details of each of the SDGs, as the complexity of the challenges requires the consciousness and cooperation of all actors in the entrepreneurial ecosystem (MacDonald et al., 2018).

Lastly, the present study also helps to increase the awareness of governments and other actors that promote SDGs, highlighting the key role of startups. In this sense, it is possible to identify implications for the Sustainable Development Agenda, focusing on the important role of entrepreneurship for the success of SDGs. Currently, extensive work is being carried out to promote SDGs at the institutional level. A wide range of actors are involved in their promotion; the United Nations through various agencies, NGOs, NGDOs, governments, private institutions and universities (United Nations 2015, 2021). At the same time, entrepreneurship occupies a key place for economic growth and is increasingly gaining prominence in political agendas (Álvarez et al., 2011; Thurik & Wennekers, 2004). Even so, this study shows that in the field of startups, although some SDGs especially belonging to the economic dimension (SDG 8 and SDG 9) are addressed by a large number of startups, the rest are poorly attended. Therefore, this study encourages the integration of CSR plans with an SDGs approach in startups, due to its benefits for the company, the stakeholders and the society as whole (ElAlfy et al., 2020). This requires policies and programs focused on increasing the awareness of the entrepreneurial ecosystem actors, especially potential and current entrepreneurs and mentors who support the creation of startups (Pacto Mundial, 2017). In this regard, the promotion of SDGs must be carried out with a sufficient degree of concreteness and from an applied point of view to enable a real commitment of startups to the sustainable development of the environment, the society and the economy.

FUTURE RESEARCH DIRECTIONS

The results of the present study show that there is a wide field for further investigation. It is relevant to deepen the research on CSR in startups, due to the lack of studies on this topic, to complete the existing literature that focus on corporates and SMEs. Similarly, it is considered important to delve into the relationship between startups and SDGs, given the key role of this type of companies for innovation and economic growth, and the demonstrated scarce impact of startup innovation on SDGs (Retolaza et al., 2009). The following are a series of proposals for future research in this field.

Firstly, it would be interesting to develop a longitudinal analysis of startups impact on SDGs, in order to identify the existence of key milestones that determine a growth or decrease in the impact of startups innovation on certain goals throughout the evolution of the company. Secondly, an analysis of successful policies that foster commitment with SDGs or startups good practices regarding their impact on sustainable goals, could help to improve the design of further policies that increase CSR plans in this type of companies. It may also be of interest to analyze the relationship of this commitment to sustainability with aspects such as business success, access to finance or the implementation of circular economy strategies. Recent research on circular economy shows its usefulness to achieve SDGs, as it provides sustainable solutions, solves environmental challenges and reduces excessive consumption of resources both at global and local level (Schroeder et al., 2018).

Finally, regarding the sample, it is proposed to replicate the study in other contexts (nationally or internationally) to determine, from a comparative perspective, the influence of contextual or cultural issues. The increase of the sample would also allow a more in-depth analysis by differentiating sectors. Both of these proposals would add value to the field, since they are important aspects in the study of innovation and entrepreneurship (Autio et al., 2014).

ACKNOWLEDGMENT

The authors gratefully acknowledge the collaboration and interest of the incubators in the city of Malaga that made possible the data collection (BIC Euronova, CADE Málaga-PTA, Costa del Sol Tourism Hub, Demium, Go2Work EOI, La Farola, Link by UMA-Atech and Promálaga), as well as the participation of the startups for their diligent responses to the questionnaire.

This research was supported by the Chair "Cátedra de Emprendimiento Sostenible" of the University of Malaga, financed by the city council of Malaga through the municipal company Promálaga [2020-2021].

REFERENCES

Autio, E., Kenney, M., Mustar, P., Siegel, D., & Wright, M. (2014). Entrepreneurial innovation: The importance of context. *Research Policy*, *43*(7), 1097–1108. doi:10.1016/j.respol.2014.01.015

Barrena, J., López, M., & Romero, P. (2016). Corporate social responsibility: Evolution through institutional and stakeholder perspectives. *European Journal of Management and Business Economics*, *25*(1), 8–14. doi:10.1016/j.redee.2015.11.002

Batalhone, A. P., & Clement, D. (2018). How sustainability standards contribute to SDG 12. *International Trade Forum*, *3*(3), 14–15. doi:10.18356/15645304-2018-3-6

Ben Youssef, A., Boubaker, S., & Omri, A. (2018). Entrepreneurship and sustainability: The need for innovative and institutional solutions. *Technological Forecasting and Social Change*, *129*, 232–241. doi:10.1016/j.techfore.2017.11.003

Blank, S. (2010, April 12). *Why startups are agile and opportunistic – pivoting the business model*. https://steveblank.com/2010/04/12/why-startups-are-agile-and-opportunistic-–-pivoting-the-business-model/

Bowen, H. P. (1953). *Social Responsibilities of the Businessman*. Harper.

Buhmann, K. (2018). Future perspectives: doing good but avoiding SDG-washing: creating relevant societal value without causing harm. In H. Mulder & S. V. Voort (Eds.), *OECD Guidelines for Multinational Enterprises: A Glass Half Full* (pp. 127–134). OECD and Nyenrode Business University.

Buhmann, K., Jonsson, J., & Fisker, M. (2019). Do no harm and do more good too: Connecting the SDGs with business and human rights and political CSR theory. *Corporate Governance*, *19*(3), 389–403. doi:10.1108/CG-01-2018-0030

Bygrave, W. D. (1989). The entrepreneurship paradigm: A philosophical look at research methodologies. *Entrepreneurship Theory and Practice*, *14*(1), 7–26. doi:10.1177/104225878901400102

Campos, M., Martínez-Martínez, S. L., & Diéguez-Soto, J. (2021). Financial Literacy and Innovation Performance in SMEs. In *Financial Management and Risk Analysis Strategies for Business Sustainability* (pp. 58–81). IGI Global. doi:10.4018/978-1-7998-7634-2.ch004

Carlaw, K. I., & Lipsey, R. G. (2003). Productivity, Technology and Economic Growth: What is the Relationship? *Journal of Economic Surveys*, *17*(3), 457–495. doi:10.1111/1467-6419.00201

Carroll, A. B. (1979). A three-dimensional conceptual model of corporate performance. *Academy of Management Review*, *4*(4), 497–505. doi:10.5465/amr.1979.4498296

Carroll, A. B. (1991). The pyramid of corporate social responsibility: Toward the moral management of organizational stakeholders. *Business Horizons*, *34*(4), 39–48. doi:10.1016/0007-6813(91)90005-G

Carroll, A. B. (2000). Ethical Challenges for Business in the New Millennium: Corporate Social Responsibility and Models of Management Morality. *Business Ethics Quarterly*, *10*(1), 33–42. doi:10.2307/3857692

Carroll, A. B., & Buchholtz, A. K. (2015). *Business & society: Ethics, sustainability, and stakeholder management* (9th ed.). Cengage Learning.

Castillo-Villar, R. G. (2020). Identifying determinants of CSR implementation on SDG 17 partnerships for the goals. *Cogent Business & Management*, *7*(1), 1847989. doi:10.1080/23311975.2020.1847989

Colombo, M. G., & Piva, E. (2008). Strengths and Weaknesses of Academic Startups: A Conceptual Model. *IEEE Transactions on Engineering Management*, *55*(1), 37–49. doi:10.1109/TEM.2007.912807

Cuervo, Á., Ribeiro, D., & Roig, S. (2007). Entrepreneurship: concepts, theory and perspective. Introduction. In Á. Cuervo, D. Ribeiro, & S. Roig (Eds.), *Entrepreneurship* (pp. 1–20). Springer., doi:10.1007/978-3-540-48543-8_1

Dahlsrud, A. (2008). How corporate social responsibility is defined: An analysis of 37 definitions. *Corporate Social Responsibility and Environmental Management*, *15*(1), 1–13. doi:10.1002/csr.132

Dantas, T. E. T., De-Souza, E. D., Destro, I. D., Hammes, G., Rodriguez, C. M. T., & Soares, S. R. (2021). How the combination of Circular Economy and Industry 4.0 can contribute towards achieving the Sustainable Development Goals. *Sustainable Production and Consumption*, *26*, 213–227. doi:10.1016/j.spc.2020.10.005

De Lange, D. E. (2017). Start-ups sustainability: An insurmountable cost or a life-giving investment? *Journal of Cleaner Production*, *156*, 838–854. doi:10.1016/j.jclepro.2017.04.108

Ditlev-Simonsen, C. D., & Wenstøp, F. (2013). How stakeholders view stakeholders as CSR motivators. *Social Responsibility Journal*, *9*(1), 137–147. doi:10.1108/17471111311307868

ElAlfy, A., Palaschuk, N., El-Bassiouny, D., Wilson, J., & Weber, O. (2020). Scoping the evolution of corporate social responsibility (CSR) research in the sustainable development goals (SDGs) era. *Sustainability*, *12*(14), 5544. doi:10.3390u12145544

European Commission. (2001, July 19). *Green Paper Promoting a European Framework for Corporate Social Responsibility*. https://ec.europa.eu/commission/presscorner/detail/en/DOC_01_9

Figueredo, C., Falcão, D., & Olavo, C. (2019). Startups and the innovation ecosystem in Industry 4.0. *Technology Analysis and Strategic Management*, *31*(12), 1474–1487. doi:10.1080/09537325.2019.1628938

Folke, C., Biggs, R., Norström, A. V., Reyers, B., & Rockström, J. (2016). Social-ecological resilience and biosphere-based sustainability science. *Ecology and Society*, *21*(3), art41. Advance online publication. doi:10.5751/ES-08748-210341

Franco, I. B., & Abe, M. (2020). SDG 17 Partnerships for the Goals. In I. Franco, T. Chatterji, E. Derbyshire & J. Tracey (Eds.), Actioning the Global Goals for Local Impact. Science for Sustainable Societies. Springer. doi:10.1007/978-981-32-9927-6_18

Galvão, A., Ferreira, J. J., & Marques, C. (2017). Entrepreneurship education and training as facilitators of regional development. *Journal of Small Business and Enterprise Development*, *25*(1), 17–40. doi:10.1108/JSBED-05-2017-0178

Gartner, W. B., & Carter, N. M. (2003). Entrepreneurial behavior and firm organizing processes. In Z. J. Acs & D. B. Audretsch (Eds.), *Handbook of entrepreneurship research* (pp. 195–221). Springer., doi:10.1007/0-387-24519-7_9

Haltiwanger, J., Jarmin, R., & Miranda, J. (2013). Who Creates Jobs? Small vs. Large vs. Young. *The Review of Economics and Statistics*, *45*(2), 347–361. doi:10.1162/REST_a_00288

Hazlewood, P. (2015). *Global Multi-stakeholder Partnerships: Scaling up public-private collective impact for the SDGs*. Independent Research Forum.

Hsieh, Y. J., & Wu, Y. (2018). Entrepreneurship through the platform strategy in the digital era: Insights and research opportunities. *Computers in Human Behavior*, *95*, 315–323. doi:10.1016/j.chb.2018.03.033

Jenkins, H. (2004). A Critique of Conventional CSR Theory: An SME Perspective. *Journal of General Management*, *29*(4), 37–57. doi:10.1177/030630700402900403

Joyner, B. E., & Payne, D. (2002). Evolution and implementation: A study of values, business ethics and corporate social responsibility. *Journal of Business Ethics*, *41*(4), 297–311. doi:10.1023/A:1021237420663

Kask, J., & Linton, G. (2013). Business mating: When start-ups get it right. *Journal of Small Business and Entrepreneurship*, *26*(5), 511–536. doi:10.1080/08276331.2013.876765

Kolstad, I. (2012). Human rights and positive corporate duties: The importance of corporate–state interaction. *Business Ethics (Oxford, England)*, *21*(3), 276–285. doi:10.1111/j.1467-8608.2012.01654.x

Kotler, P., & Lee, N. (2005). *Corporate Social Responsibility: Doing the Most Good for Your Company and Your Cause*. Wiley.

Kreps, T. J. (1940). *Measurement of the Social Performance of Business*. Government Printing Office.

Lefebvre, V., & Lefebvre, M. R. (2012). Integrating Corporate Social Responsibility at the Start-up Level: Constraint or Catalyst for Opportunity Identification? *International Business Research*, *5*(7). Advance online publication. doi:10.5539/ibr.v5n7p17

Lichtenstein, B. B., Carter, N. M., Dooley, K. J., & Gartner, W. B. (2007). Complexity dynamics of nascent Entrepreneurship. *Journal of Business Venturing*, *22*(2), 236–261. doi:10.1016/j.jbusvent.2006.06.001

Liguori, E., & Bendickson, J. S. (2020). Rising to the challenge: Entrepreneurship ecosystems and SDG success. *Journal of the International Council for Small Business*, *1*(3-4), 118–125. doi:10.1080/26437015.2020.1827900

Low, M. B., & MacMillan, I. C. (1988). Entrepreneurship: Past research and future challenges. *Journal of Management*, *14*(2), 139–161. doi:10.1177/014920638801400202

Luetkenhorst, W. (2004). Corporate social responsibility and the development agenda. *Inter Economics*, *39*(3), 157–166. doi:10.1007/BF02933583

MacDonald, A., Clarke, A., Huang, L., Roseland, M., & Seitanidi, M. M. (2018). Multi-stakeholder partnerships (SDG #17) as a means of achieving sustainable communities and cities (SDG #11). In W. Leal Filho (Ed.), *Handbook of sustainability science and research* (pp. 193–209). Springer. doi:10.1007/978-3-319-63007-6_12

Mackey, A., Mackey, T. B., & Barney, J. B. (2007). Corporate social responsibility and firm performance: Investor preferences and corporate strategies. *Academy of Management Review*, *32*(3), 817–835. doi:10.5465/amr.2007.25275676

Maignan, I., Ferrell, O. C., & Hult, G. T. M. (1999). Corporate Citizenship: Cultural Antecedents and Business Benefits. *Journal of the Academy of Marketing Science*, *27*(4), 455–469. doi:10.1177/0092070399274005

Martínez-Martínez, S. L. (2020). El Rol de la digitalización en el emprendimiento internacional: El modelo "Born Global". In J. C. Álvarez. & F. Vila (Eds.), Nuevas tecnologías y mercado de trabajo: una aproximación multidisciplinar (pp. 41-60). Laborum.

Martínez-Martínez, S. L., & Ventura, R. (2020). Entrepreneurial Profiles at the University: A Competence Approach. *Frontiers in Psychology*, *11*(612796), 1–20. doi:10.3389/fpsyg.2020.612796 PMID:33391131

Maslow, A. H. (1943). A theory of human motivation. *Psychological Review*, *50*(4), 370–396. doi:10.1037/h0054346

Maslow, A. H. (1954). *Motivation and personality*. Harper and Row.

Mazzarol, T., Volery, T., Doss, N., & Thein, V. (1999). Factors influencing small business start-ups. *International Journal of Entrepreneurial Behaviour & Research*, *5*(2), 48–63. doi:10.1108/13552559910274499

Morsing, M., & Perrini, F. (2009). CSR in SMEs: Do SMEs matter for the CSR agenda? *Business Ethics (Oxford, England)*, *18*(1), 1–6. doi:10.1111/j.1467-8608.2009.01544.x

Murillo, D., & Lozano, J. M. (2006). SMEs and CSR: An approach to CSR in their own words. *Journal of Business Ethics*, *67*(3), 227–240. doi:10.100710551-006-9181-7

Ngan, S. L., How, B. S., Teng, S. Y., Promentilla, M. A. B., Yatim, P., Er, A. C., & Lam, H. L. (2019). Prioritization of sustainability indicators for promoting the circular economy: The case of developing countries. *Renewable & Sustainable Energy Reviews*, *111*, 314–331. doi:10.1016/j.rser.2019.05.001

Pacto Mundial. (2017). *Empresas españolas y ODS: Oportunidades y desafíos*. Red Española del Pacto Mundial. https://www.pactomundial.org/sdm_downloads/empresas-espanolas-ods-oportunidades-desafios/

Palakshappa, N., & Dodds, S. (2020). Mobilising SDG 12: Co-creating sustainability through brands. *Marketing Intelligence & Planning*, *39*(2), 265–283. doi:10.1108/MIP-08-2018-0360

Perrini, F., Russo, A., & Tencati, A. (2007). CSR Strategies of SMEs and Large Firms. Evidence from Italy. *Journal of Business Ethics*, *74*(3), 285–300. doi:10.100710551-006-9235-x

Porter, M. E., & Kramer, M. R. (2006). The link between competitive advantage and corporate social responsibility. *Harvard Business Review*, *84*(12), 78–92. doi:10.1108d.2007.05623ead.006 PMID:17183795

Retolaza, J. L., Ruiz, M., & San-Jose, L. (2009). CSR in business start-ups: An application method for stakeholder engagement. *Corporate Social Responsibility and Environmental Management*, *16*(6), 324–336. doi:10.1002/csr.191

Ribeiro-Soriano, D. (2017). Small business and entrepreneurship: Their role in economic and social development. *Entrepreneurship and Regional Development*, *29*(1-2), 1–3. doi:10.1080/08985626.2016.1255438

Russo, A., & Perrini, F. (2009). Investigating Stakeholder Theory and Social Capital: CSR in Large Firms and SMEs. *Journal of Business Ethics*, *91*(2), 207–221. doi:10.100710551-009-0079-z

Russo, A., & Tencati, A. (2008). Formal vs. Informal CSR Strategies: Evidence from Italian Micro, Small, Medium-sized, and Large Firms. *Journal of Business Ethics*, *85*(S2), 339–353. doi:10.100710551-008-9736-x

Sanyang, S. E., & Huang, W. C. (2009). Entrepreneurship and economic development: The EMPRETEC showcase. *The International Entrepreneurship and Management Journal*, *6*(3), 317–329. doi:10.100711365-008-0106-z

Scheyvens, R., Banks, G., & Hughes, E. (2016). The Private Sector and the SDGs: The Need to Move Beyond 'Business as Usual'. *Sustainable Development*, *24*(6), 371–382. doi:10.1002d.1623

Schroeder, P., Anggraeni, K., & Weber, U. (2018). The Relevance of Circular Economy Practices to the Sustainable Development Goals. *Journal of Industrial Ecology*, *23*(1), 77–95. doi:10.1111/jiec.12732

Schumpeter, J. A. (1934). *The theory of economic development: An inquiry into profits, capital, credit, interest, and the business cycle*. Transaction Publishers.

Sedláček, P., & Sterk, V. (2017). The Growth Potential of Startups over the Business Cycle. *The American Economic Review*, *107*(10), 3182–3210. doi:10.1257/aer.20141280

Shamsrizi, M., Pakura, A., Wiechers, J., Pakura, S., & Dauster, D. V. (2021). Digital Entrepreneurship for the "Decade of Action". In M. Soltanifar, M. Hughes, & L. Göcke (Eds.), *Digital Entrepreneurship. Future of Business and Finance* (pp. 303–327). Springer. doi:10.1007/978-3-030-53914-6_15

Skala, A. (2019). The Startup as a Result of Innovative Entrepreneurship. In A. Skala (Ed.), *Digital Startups in Transition Economies* (pp. 1–40). Palgrave Pivot. doi:10.1007/978-3-030-01500-8_1

Snider, J., Hill, R., & Martin, D. (2003). Corporate Social Responsibility in the 21st century: A view from the world's most successful firms. *Journal of Business Ethics*, *48*(2), 175–187. doi:10.1023/B:BUSI.0000004606.29523.db

Stockholm Resilience Centre. (2016, June 14). *How food connects all the SDGs*. https://www.stockholmresilience.org/research/research-news/2016-06-14-how-food-connects-all-the-sdgs.html

Thurik, R., & Wennekers, S. (2004). Entrepreneurship, small business and economic growth. *Journal of Small Business and Enterprise Development*, *11*(1), 140–149. doi:10.1108/14626000410519173

United Nations. (2000). *United Nations Millennium Declaration. New York* (A/RES/55/2). https://documents-dds-ny.un.org/doc/UNDOC/GEN/N00/559/54/PDF/N0055954.pdf?OpenElement

United Nations. (2015). *Transforming our world: the 2030 Agenda for Sustainable Development.* United Nations, A/RES/70/1, Agenda items 15 and 116, 1–35. https://sustainabledevelopment.un.org/post2015/transformingourworld

United Nations. (2021). *Transforming our world: The 2030 Agenda for Sustainable Development.* Sustainable Development Knowledge Platform. https://sustainabledevelopment.un.org/post2015/transformingourworld

Vaidya, H., & Chatterji, T. (2020). SDG 11 Sustainable Cities and Communities. In I. Franco, T. Chatterji, E. Derbyshire, & J. Tracey (Eds), Actioning the Global Goals for Local Impact. Science for Sustainable Societies (pp. 73–185). Springer. doi:10.1007/978-981-32-9927-6_12

Van Hille, I., De Bakker, F. G. A., Ferguson, J. E., & Groenewegen, P. (2020). Cross-Sector Partnerships for Sustainability: How Mission-Driven Conveners Drive Change in National Coffee Platforms. *Sustainability, 12*(7), 2846. doi:10.3390u12072846

Vázquez-Carrasco, R., & López-Pérez, M. E. (2013). Small and medium-sized enterprises and Corporate Social Responsibility: A systematic review of the literature. *Quality & Quantity, 47*(6), 3205–3218. doi:10.100711135-012-9713-4

Ventura, R., & Martínez-Martínez, S. L. (2020). *Global Entrepreneurship Monitor. Informe GEM Málaga 2019/20.* UMA Editorial.

World Commission on Environment and Development (WCED). (1987). *Our common future.* Oxford university Press.

Wymer, S., & Regan, E. (2005). Factors Influencing e-commerce Adoption and Use by Small and Medium Businesses. *Electronic Markets, 15*(4), 438–453. doi:10.1080/10196780500303151

Zadek, S. (2002). Mapping Instruments for Corporate Social Responsibility. Directorate General for Employment and Social Affairs. European Commission.

Zyglidopoulos, S. C. (2003). The issue life-cycle: Implications for reputation for social performance and organizational legitimacy. *Corporate Reputation Review, 6*(1), 70–81. doi:10.1057/palgrave.crr.1540191

ADDITIONAL READING

Horne, J., Recker, M., Michelfelder, I., Jay, J., & Kratzer, J. (2020). Exploring entrepreneurship related to the sustainable development goals-mapping new venture activities with semi-automated content analysis. *Journal of Cleaner Production, 242*, 118052. doi:10.1016/j.jclepro.2019.118052

Iqbal, J., & Kousar, S. (2020). Sustainopreneurship: A New World Order. In P. Ordoñez de Pablos, X. Zhang, & K. T. Chui (Eds.), *Handbook of Research on Managerial Practices and Disruptive Innovation in Asia* (pp. 322–350). IGI Global., doi:10.4018/978-1-7998-0357-7.ch018

Montenegro, E. A. T. (2021). Sustainability and Economy: A Paradigm for Managing Entrepreneurship Towards Sustainable Development. In R. I. Perez-Uribe, C. Largacha-Martínez, & D. Ocampo-Guzman (Eds.), *Handbook of Research on International Business and Models for Global Purpose-Driven Companies* (pp. 289–309). IGI Global., doi:10.4018/978-1-7998-4909-4.ch016

Perry, A., Rahim, E., & Davis, B. (2018). Startup Success Trends in Small Business Beyond Five-Years: A Qualitative Research Study. *International Journal of Sustainable Entrepreneurship and Corporate Social Responsibility*, *3*(1), 1–16. doi:10.4018/IJSECSR.2018010101

Rendtorff, J. D. (2019). *Philosophy of Management and Sustainability: Rethinking Business Ethics and Social Responsibility in Sustainable Development*. Emerald Group Publishing., doi:10.1108/9781789734539

Schönherr, N., Findler, F., & Martinuzzi, A. (2017). Exploring the interface of CSR and the sustainable development goals. *Transnational Corporations*, *24*(3), 33–47. doi:10.18356/cfb5b8b6-en

Shepherd, D. A., & Patzelt, H. (2011). The new field of sustainable entrepreneurship: Studying entrepreneurial action linking "what is to be sustained" with "what is to be developed". *Entrepreneurship Theory and Practice*, *35*(1), 137–163. doi:10.1111/j.1540-6520.2010.00426.x

Von Geibler, J., Piwowar, J., & Greven, A. (2019). The SDG-Check: Guiding Open Innovation towards Sustainable Development Goals. *Technology Innovation Management Review*, *9*(3), 20–37. doi:10.22215/timreview/1222

KEY TERMS AND DEFINITIONS

CSR: Corporate Social Responsibility. Responsible policies, decisions and actions of a company that take into consideration stakeholders and society as a whole, focusing on social and environmental justice and value creation.

Entrepreneurship: Value creation through the development of new products, services, processes or business models that contribute to satisfying the needs of society, boosting its progress and that of the economy as a whole.

Partnerships: Collaborative relationships between different actors (public or non-public) based on a mutual agreement to achieve common purposes, sharing both responsibilities and benefits.

SDGs: Sustainable Development Goals. Seventeen key objectives adopted by United Nations in 2015 that represent a global agreement and commitment to world's challenges. They constitute a framework to face sustainable development from a systemic perspective.

Stakeholders: Individuals or organizations, both public and private, related to and affected by the decisions and activities of a given entity.

Startup: Newly created company based on innovation with a high technology component, a clear growth orientation and a global-market focus, normally operating in fast-moving industries.

Sustainability: Developmental characteristic that ensure the fulfillment of the present economic, societal, and environmental needs without compromising the resources of the future, ensuring balanced global progress.

ENDNOTES

1. It is possible to measure the level of entrepreneurship of a region through the Total Entrepreneurial Activity rate or TEA, defined by the Global Entrepreneurship Monitor (GEM) methodology (Reynolds, et al., 2005). This indicator includes the nascent companies (less than 3 months old) and the new business (from 3 to 42 months old).
2. Description of SDGs extracted from Sustainable Development Goals Knowledge Platform (UN): https://sustainabledevelopment.un.org/topics/sustainabledevelopmentgoals (retriewed 20 april 2021).

Chapter 12
Social Entrepreneurship Typologies:
Mapping the Territory

Andrea Pérez
https://orcid.org/0000-0003-3521-1783
University of Cantabria, Spain

Carlos López-Gutiérrez
University of Cantabria, Spain

Ana Fernández-Laviada
https://orcid.org/0000-0002-4517-1124
University of Cantabria, Spain

ABSTRACT

Despite the increasing research in the field of social entrepreneurship (SE), unfortunately there is not yet consensus on its conceptualization. The main points of disagreement are related to the business mission and to the source of income. Based on these two dimensions and a bottom-up approach, this chapter contributes to previous literature by proposing and empirically exploring a categorization of three types of social entrepreneurs—socially responsible entrepreneur (SRE), social enterprise entrepreneur (SEE), and social initiative entrepreneur (SIE)—which is applied empirically to explore the social entrepreneurs' personal characteristics (gender, age, and education), similarities, and differences. Multinomial logistic regressions are applied on an international sample of GEM data that includes 11,280 commercial entrepreneurs and 3,373 social entrepreneurs. The findings of the study will permit researchers and practitioners to understand previous empirical findings on social entrepreneurship more clearly and to advance in the study of this evolving phenomenon.

DOI: 10.4018/978-1-7998-8065-3.ch012

INTRODUCTION

Within the entrepreneurship field, certain areas have been gaining prominence in recent years, because they have particularities that require the development of new lines of research. This is especially the case of social entrepreneurship (SE) (Lepoutre et al., 2013), for which there is an exponentially growing number of papers that discuss the institutionalization of SE, the emergence of thematic clusters within the area and several methodological issues that require further attention (Sassmannshausen & Volkmann, 2018). Along this line, SE is currently a field of study in its own right and it has a powerful identity that has to be approached scientifically (Choi & Majumdar, 2014). It seems that the novelty along this line of research lies more on the label that is given to the phenomenon of "social entrepreneurship" than on the phenomenon itself (Dees, 2001). Apart from isolated early research on the topic, the term SE only emerged in the academic world in the late 1990s (Boschee, 1995; Leadbeater, 1997). Since then, research has proliferated in searching for a unified definition of what should be understood by SE, social entrepreneur and social enterprise (Bacq & Janssen, 2011; Bedi & Yadav, 2019; Brouard & Larivet, 2010; Cagarman et al., 2020; Defourny & Nyssens, 2017; Doherty et al., 2014; Kraus et al., 2014; Rey-Martí et al., 2016; Short et al., 2009). Researchers have also devoted numerous efforts to differentiating social entrepreneurship from traditional, regular or commercial entrepreneurship (Austin et al., 2006).

In these advances, one of the major foundations of SE research has found that it still lacks a clear conceptualization of the construct (Mort et al., 2003) and that its meaning is not widely understood across disciplines, countries and researchers (Lepoutre et al., 2013). However, as Cukier et al. (2011) state, almost all previous studies acknowledge three different levels of comprehension: a micro-level, where the focus is on individual entrepreneurs; a meso level, where the focus is on organizations; and, a macro level, which focuses on an overall perspective of the economic and social context.

Whereas numerous researchers advocate a very narrow definition of the concept, only acknowledging earned-income non-profit organizations in support of its charitable missions (Boschee & McClurg, 2003), other scholars argue that the definition has become so inclusive that it now has an immense tent into which all manner of socially beneficial activities fit (Martin & Osberg, 2007). Therefore, the looseness of the definition has resulted in different studies applying it in different ways, which complicates the possibility of developing further solid research based on a consensus on how to apply the definition adequately for research purposes (Lyon et al., 2010). Lack of clarity around what is and is not SE may also lead to exaggerated claims about its positive attributes and policies merely based on expectation rather than evidence (Teasdale, 2010).

Additionally, it is unfortunate that, from an academic point of view, research in the field of SE has only remained theoretical or, at most, descriptive but partisan (Bacq & Janssen, 2011; Dacin et al., 2010; García-Jurado et al., 2021; Gupta et al., 2020). Very few conceptual constructions have been tested against or derived from, empirical evidence (Defourny & Nyssens, 2017). What is more, most empirical studies follow the case study methodology or are based on stories of successful social entrepreneurs, which prevents in-depth knowledge of these types of entrepreneurs (Lepoutre et al., 2013; Nicolás & Rubio, 2012). Missing from current scholarly work on SE are studies that can test the scope and generalizability of theoretical propositions, discover antecedents and consequences of social entrepreneurial activity, and statistically analyze differences among various social entrepreneurs through a large-scale quantitative dataset (Lepoutre et al., 2013).

Based on the limited scope of previous research on SE, this study aims to contribute to this line of research by feeding previous theoretical conceptualization efforts with a new contribution starting from a bottom-up approach built upon the 'the impossibility of a unified definition' hypothesis (Defourny & Nyssens, 2017). This being accepted, the authors provide a new feasible perspective to deal with the huge diversity of SE conceptualizations that exists in previous literature, by trying to achieve groupings or categories of social firms on various grounds and exploring their characteristics, similarities and differences empirically through the application of a quantitative research method. More precisely, the authors will explore whether individual factors related to social entrepreneurs (such as age, gender and education) affect each category of entrepreneurs differently. In addition, the authors will study the effect of the development level of the country, distinguishing between innovation-driven economies and factor/efficiency-driven economies. In doing so, the present study can contribute to previous academic literature significantly because it assists in developing a consistent body of knowledge to adequately operationalize the SE construct and better capture its role in current international economies.

The chapter is structured in four additional sections. First, the authors make a review of the previous theoretical and empirical literature on SE to provide the reader with an adequate background on the definition, typologies and individual/country factors that determine the behaviour of social entrepreneurs. Second, the authors describe the methodology they have implemented to empirically describe the diverse types of social entrepreneurs previously suggested theoretically in their literature review section. In doing so, the sample and estimation strategy used for the empirical analysis are described. Third, the authors discuss the main findings of the study in light of previous academic literature. Finally, the chapter concludes by presenting the main implications derived from the study, along with the limitations and future lines of research that may derive from it.

BACKGROUND

Social Entrepreneurship Definition

Roughly speaking, SE refers to entrepreneurship leading to the establishment of new social enterprises and businesses and the continued innovation in existing ones (Mort et al., 2003). Common across all definitions of SE is the fact that the underlying drive is to create social value, rather than personal and shareholder wealth, and that the activity is characterized by innovation, or the creation of something new rather than simply the replication of existing enterprises or practices (Austin et al., 2006; Brouard & Larivet, 2010; Martin & Osberg, 2007).

Nonetheless, there is little consensus on the definition of the concept beyond these two generalizations (Bravo, 2018; Dacin et al., 2010). For example, some scholars define SE as a process demonstrated when government or NGOs operate using business principles (Austin et al., 2006; Mort et al., 2003). Others see it as the activities of conventional entrepreneurs who practice corporate social responsibility or as outcomes of organized philanthropy (Baron, 2007). As suggested by Nicolás & Rubio (2012), the conceptual framework of SE is very broad and covers different types of initiatives and legal forms. SE has thus developed within academia as an 'umbrella' construct, with wide scope and ambiguous boundaries (Battilana & Lee, 2014).

The main points of disagreement are related to the varying importance authors assign to the business' mission (social mission vs. financial mission) and the source of income of the social business venture (created by the business through the sale of a product or service or donations and grants) (Bravo, 2018; Dees, 2001). The most restrictive definitions of SE defend that businesses can only be considered social if they prioritize social over financial while selling products and services in a market economy (Battilana & Lee, 2014; Boschee & McClurg, 2003; Defourny & Nyssens, 2017; López-Arceiz et al., 2016). Broader definitions allow the possibility that purely altruistic non-profit organizations that do not participate in a market, or traditional for-profit businesses that incorporate corporate social responsibility into their value scheme, are also understood as social enterprises (Austin et al., 2006; Dees, 2001; Lepoutre et al., 2013; Martin & Osberg, 2007). Similarly, Defourny & Nyssens (2017) suggest that three dimensions –namely the nature of the social mission or social aims, the type of economic model and the governance structure– particularly inform the diversity of social enterprises and SE definitions that exist nowadays. Moreover, the EMES (Emergence des Enterprises Sociales en Europe) Network approach (Defourny, 1994) relies on the hypothesis that these three major dimensions are deeply interdependent: the kind of social mission is likely to shape the type of business model and governance structure; conversely, the chosen economic model is likely to influence how the social mission is pursued and/or evolves, and the primacy of the latter may be better ensured by some forms of governance (Defourny & Nyssens, 2017).

Along this line, Choi & Majumdar (2014) define SE as an essentially contested concept based on the theory of W. B. Gallie (Gallie, 1956). This means that a universal definition, which would be accepted among the different users, is hardly possible. Responding to this concern, they propose the conceptualization of SE as a cluster concept, a conglomerate of certain concepts that they call sub-concepts, which can occur in varying degrees and various combinations in different instantiations of the concept. According to these authors, SE can be viewed as a conglomerate of the following sub-concepts: (1) social value creation, (2) the social entrepreneur, (3) the social entrepreneurship organization, (4) market orientation and (5) social innovation.

Table 1 reflects a compilation of the most representative definitions of SE provided in previous literature, which makes evidence of the current state of conceptual confusion that serves as a barrier to cross-disciplinary dialogue and theory- and empirical-based advances in the field.

Table 1. Social entrepreneurship definitions

Authors	Definition
Dees (2001)	Social entrepreneurship combines the passion of a social mission with an image of business-like discipline, innovation and determination.
Mort et al. (2003)	The entrepreneurship leading to the establishment of new social enterprises/organizations and the continued innovation in existing ones (...) Multidimensional construct involving the expression of entrepreneurially virtuous behaviour to achieve the social mission, a coherent unity of purpose and action in the face of moral complexity, the ability to recognize social value-creating opportunities and key decision-making characteristics of innovativeness, proactiveness and risk-taking.
Hibbert et al. (2005)	The use of entrepreneurial behaviour for social ends rather than for-profit objectives or that the profits generated are used for the benefit of a specific disadvantaged group.
Roberts & Woods (2005)	The construction, evaluation, and pursuit of opportunities for transformative social change are carried out by visionary, passionately dedicated individuals.
Seelos & Mair (2005)	Social entrepreneurship creates new models for the provision of products and services that cater directly to basic human needs that remain unsatisfied by current economic or social institutions. It combines the resourcefulness of traditional entrepreneurship with a mission to change society.
Mair & Martí (2006)	A process involving the innovative use and combination of resources to pursue opportunities to catalyze social change and address important social needs in a way that is not dominated by direct financial benefits for the entrepreneurs.

continues on following page

Table 1. Continued

Authors	Definition
Austin et al. (2006)	Innovative, social value-creating activity that can occur within or across the non-profit, business, or government sectors.
Nicholls (2006)	Innovative and effective activities that focus strategically on resolving social market failures and creating new opportunities to add social value systematically by using a range of resources and organizational formats to maximize social impacts and bring about changes.
Peredo & McLean (2006)	Social entrepreneurship is exercised where a person or group aims at creating social value, shows a capacity to recognize and take advantage of opportunities, employs innovation, accepts an above-average degree of risk and is unusually resourceful in pursuing their social venture.
Zahra et al. (2009)	Social entrepreneurship is the art of simultaneously pursuing both a financial and a social return on investment (the double bottom line).
Martin & Osberg (2007)	Social entrepreneurship has three components: (1) identifying a stable but inherently unjust equilibrium that causes the exclusion, marginalization, or suffering of a segment of humanity that lacks the financial means or political clout to achieve any transformative benefit of its own; (2) identifying an opportunity in this unjust equilibrium, developing a social value proposition, and bringing to bear inspiration, creativity, direct action, courage, and fortitude, thereby challenging the stable state's hegemony; and (3) forging a new, stable equilibrium that releases trapped potential or alleviates the suffering of the targeted group, and through imitation and the creation of a stable ecosystem around the new equilibrium ensuring a better future for the targeted group and even society at large.
Ormiston & Seymour (2011)	A social entrepreneur seeks to generate change (creating social, cultural or natural value), through the creation or expansion of economic activity, by identifying and exploiting new products, processes or markets.
European Commission (2014)	The combination of social and entrepreneurial organizations that aim to achieve social, environmental, and community objectives. However, the enterprise must meet five criteria: engage in continuous economic activity, have a primary social objective, have limits on the distribution of profits, must be an independent organization from the state or other for-profit organizations, and must have inclusive governance characterized by the democratic decision making process.
GEM (2015)	(broad definition) Any kind of activity, organization, or initiative that has a particular social, environmental or community objective. (narrow definition) The organization is driven by (social) value creation, rather than value capture; and the organization is market-based, rather than nonmarket-based.
Sengupta & Sahay (2017)	Social entrepreneurship is a process of using entrepreneurial and business skills to create innovative approaches to social problems. These non-profit and for-profit ventures pursue the double bottom line of social impact and financial self-sustainability or profitability.
Terziev & Arabska (2017)	Social entrepreneurship is the field in which entrepreneurs tailor their activities to be directly tied with the ultimate goal of creating social value.
Iyigun (2018)	Social entrepreneurship is a professional, innovative and sustainable approach to systematic change that resolves social market failures and grasps opportunities.

Source: Compiled by the authors

Social Entrepreneurship Typologies

Based on the confronting opinions around SE across the world, some scholars have started to defend that the arena of conceptualization efforts should now be fed with more contributions starting from bottom-up approaches built upon a hypothesis that could be termed 'the impossibility of a unified definition' (Defourny & Nyssens, 2017). For instance, empirical papers would notably benefit from clearer applications of SE definitions, which would allow researchers and practitioners to understand better what is included or excluded from empirical studies (Lyon et al., 2010).

Along this line, and in an attempt to offer some more conceptual clarity, several authors have already called to provide typologies of SE conceptions to overcome the limitations imposed by the lack of consensus of previous conceptual research (Alter, 2007; Brouard & Larivet, 2010; López-Arceiz et al., 2016; Mair et al., 2012; Margiono et al., 2018). A synthesis of the previous categorizations of social entrepreneurship made by these scholars is provided in table 2.

Table 2. Categorizations of social entrepreneurship typologies in academic literature

Authors	Classification Criteria	SE Typologies
Alter (2007)	Mission orientation	• Mission-centric social enterprise • Mission-related social enterprise • Social enterprise unrelated to the mission
	Business/Program integration	• Embedded social enterprise • Integrated social enterprise • External social enterprise
Brouard & Larivet (2010)	Fields of activity & Social mission & Target group & Legislative support & Governance model	• Co-operative • Non-profit organization • Community development/interest organizations • First Nation business • Business with a social mission
Mair et al. (2012)	Capital leverage	• Political capital • Human capital • Economic capital • Social capital
López-Arceiz et al. (2016)	Financial management	• Socially-responsible enterprise • Social enterprise (SEO) • Market-oriented nonprofit • Conventional nonprofit
Margiono et al. (2018)	Funding & External control	• Novelty-centred business model • Lock-in centred business model • Efficiencycentered business model • Non-existent category (public funding + public control)

Source: Compiled by the authors

Nevertheless, these previous attempts to categorize SE take very different criteria to classify businesses (e.g., legal form, capital leverage, external control, etc) but they do not specifically focus on the two most conflictive dimensions of the definition previously described in this study (i.e., social-financial mission and (non-)market-based approach to earn income). However, a categorization based on the relevance of the social-financial mission and the use of market-based approaches to generate income would allow researchers and practitioners not only to categorize SE initiatives but also to establish clearer comparisons among them and also with conventional commercial companies.

Based on this idea, we follow the suggestion of Margiono et al. (2018) and provide a proposal that is aligned with the EMES school of thought to provide a clear framework of SE that allows us to categorize social initiatives along with the two most disputed areas of the SE definition. In doing so, the study aims to identify the different types of SE organizations that may exist in the galaxy of institutions that range from the stricter to the wider definitions of SE and to apply this categorization to the detailed study of the similarities and differences among them in terms of the personal characteristic as gender, age and education.

To do so, the categorization of entrepreneurship initiatives proposed in this study aligns with recent calls to avoid the classical consideration of commercial and social entrepreneurship as separated realities located opposite from each other in a dichotomous scale (Austin et al., 2006; Brouard & Larivet, 2010; Defourny & Nyssens, 2017; López-Arceiz et al., 2016; Margiono et al., 2018). It is evident that, for most of the twentieth century, commercial businesses, public organizations and private charities comprised distinct forms associated, respectively, with the private, public, and non-profit sectors. Over the last three decades, however, the boundaries between these forms and their corresponding sectors have become increasingly blurred, which is epitomized by the rise of hybrid organizations that combine aspects of multiple organizational forms (Battilana & Lee, 2014). Recent literature proposes that this combination of organizational forms is central to organizational innovation and, in particular, to the creation of new forms of SE (Battilana & Lee, 2014). Therefore, it seems necessary that researchers and practitioners do not consider the distinction between commercial and social entrepreneurship dichotomous, but they rather more accurately conceptualize it as a continuum ranging from purely economic to purely social (Alter, 2007; Austin et al., 2006; Brozek, 2009). Even at the extremes, however, there are still elements of both realities. That is, economic activity must still generate social value, while charitable activity must still reflect economic realities, as for-profit companies increasingly engage in social responsibility related activities, and non-profits increasingly engage in commercial activities to complement their primary, philanthropic sources of funding (Battilana & Lee, 2014).

Based on these ideas and an extensive literature review, the authors classify entrepreneurship (from purely commercial to purely social) initiatives into the following categories:

- **Commercial Entrepreneurship (CE):** Also known as traditional or regular entrepreneurship (Austin et al., 2006), CE is subject to market discipline, which determines in large part whether entrepreneurs are creating value. Thus, wealth creation and profit-making are common ways of measuring value creation for CE (Dees, 2001). If CE does not shift resources to more economically productive uses, commercial entrepreneurs tend to be driven out of business. Therefore, commercial entrepreneurs are mostly oriented by purely profit-making goals.
- **Social Entrepreneurship (SE):** ranging from the hybrid spectrum, which combines profit-making with social goals, to purely social goals, SE can be divided into three categories of entrepreneurship:
    - **Socially Responsible Entrepreneurship (SRE):** SRE are hybrid enterprises that relate to profit-making entrepreneurs, mainly focused on wealth creation (i.e., financial mission), but who implement corporate social responsibility (CSR) initiatives that generate social value for stakeholders and society (Defourny & Nyssens, 2010). This category of SE was first discussed in the course of the 1990s when diverse authors began to consider CSR as part of the spectrum of SE (Boschee, 1995). As defined by Lepoutre et al. (2013), this category would be an extreme form of hybridization, which occurs when an organization self-identify as a social organization but indicates that it aims to realize its social objective primarily by paying attention to the economic bottom line.
    - **Social Enterprise Entrepreneurship (SEE):** Hybrid enterprises can either consider economic objectives numerically more important than social and environmental objectives (i.e., SRE) or they can be organizations for which the reverse is true (Lepoutre et al., 2013). In this case, they are usually defined as socially-oriented hybrids, which include the specific case of social businesses as defended by Prof. Muhammad Yunus. These entrepreneurs apply inno-

vative means in solving problems and, to varying degrees, they understand that they cannot accomplish their goals without money. Therefore, they balance social activism with some degree of business savvy (Vega & Kidwell, 2007), by operating in the market through the commercialization of products and services that represent one of the main sources of funding for their social activities (Defourny & Nyssens, 2017).

- **Social Initiative Entrepreneurship (SIE):** Finally, this fourth type of SE includes organizations focused on their social mission (social value creation) but that do not operate in the market by selling products or services, that is, they receive economic support for their social activities from different sources of funding that are not market-based. This being so, the main world of SIE is the voluntary sector (Thompson, 2002), which represents some of the most loosely structured social initiatives aimed at social change, such as activist movements or purely social non-governmental organizations (NGOs) (Mair & Martí, 2006).

Figure 1 synthesizes this spectrum of entrepreneurs graphically.

Figure 1. Classification of entrepreneurs

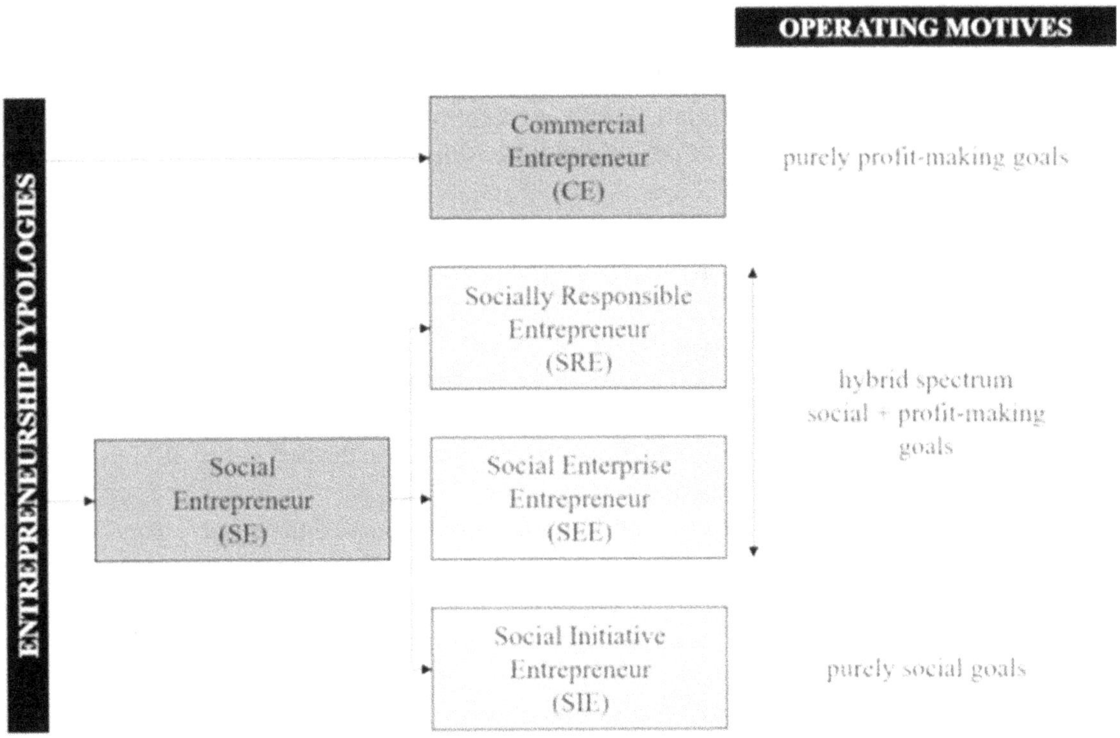

Individual and Country Level Factors

Because previous literature does not agree about which variables could affect individuals to have more or less social orientation, consistent with previous GEM research (Brieger et al., 2020; Fernández-

Laviada et al., 2020a, 2020b; Marín et al., 2019; Nicolás et al., 2018; Terjesen et al., 2012), in this study individual- and country-level variables are explored.

At the individual level, the authors consider age, gender and education. Despite recent research shows that an entrepreneur's social orientation is stronger for women, more educated and older people (Marín et al., 2019), prior research provides different and complementary results.

Regarding age, so far, the evidence found is not yet conclusive. On the one hand, as occurs with commercial entrepreneurs (Arenius & Minniti, 2005; Langowitz & Minniti, 2007), empirical evidence indicates that younger individuals may be more inclined to engage in SE (Harding & Cowling, 2006; Lepoutre et al., 2013; Nga & Shamuganathan, 2010; Stephan et al., 2015). In this sense, proposals exist, such as the one by Hoogendoorn (2016), that find that young people value non-materialistic goals more and, therefore, choose the creation of social enterprises. On the other hand, it can be found that an entrepreneur is more likely to be social in the intermediate years, but not in the youngest and oldest age groups (Levie & Hart, 2011). Finally, more recently Brieger et al. (2020) confirm that there is a U-shaped relationship between an entrepreneur's age and his/her social value creation in doing business.

Gender is another key factor studied in the literature (Gupta et al., 2009). While there is a broad consensus on the greater propensity of males in commercial entrepreneurship literature (Langowitz & Minniti, 2007; Minniti, 2010; Minniti et al., 2006; Themudo, 2009), this difference is not as high in SE (Fernández-Laviada et al., 2020a; Marín et al., 2019).

Furthermore, education also conditions the decision to start a business. Several studies demonstrate that it is positively related to entrepreneurs' social value creation goals (Bosma, 2013; Brieger et al., 2020; Estrin et al., 2013, 2016; Levie & Hart, 2011; Pathak & Muralidharan, 2016; Vuorio, 2017). Higher education implies greater training and security to create a business and less difficulty to access resources. Besides, the effect can even be intensified, as the social entrepreneur faces more insecure environments with possible financial problems that higher education could help to cope with successfully.

At the country level, the economic development of the country is considered (Sengupta et al., 2018). GEM data highlight differences in the number of SE across countries and different studies evidence that the country's economic development has a positive effect on the entrepreneur's social orientation (Fernández-Laviada et al., 2020b; Marín et al., 2019). Hoogendoorn (2016) reveals that SE is a phenomenon strongly driven by the wealth level of a country and suggest an inverted U shape because although the demand for SE activities may be lower in the wealthiest countries, the prevalence of SE is positively affected by the level of economic development.

Moreover, Marín et al. (2019) results show how the development of the country plays a decisive moderating role among social orientation gender and educational level. Fernández-Laviada et al. (2020a) find this moderation effect on gender and other cognitive variables modifying their influence and conclude that when this influence is not controlled, the results can present relevant biases which can lead to inaccurate conclusions.

Table 3 provides the definitions and references for all the variables considered in our study.

Table 3. Variables

Dimension	Variable	Definition	Authors
INDIVIDUAL-LEVEL FACTORS	GENDER	Differentiation between men and women	Bacq et al., 2016; Brieger et al., 2020; Estrin et al., 2013, 2016; Hechavarria et al., 2012; Levie & Hart, 2011; Marín et al., 2019; Muralidharan & Pathak, 2018; Nicolás et al., 2018; Nicolás & Rubio, 2012; Pathak & Muralidharan, 2016; Stephan et al., 2015; van Ryzin et al., 2009
	AGE	Age under 34, between 34 and 54 and over 54	Bacq et al., 2016; Brieger et al., 2020; Estrin et al., 2013, 2016; Hechavarria et al., 2012; Hechavarría et al., 2017; Levie & Hart, 2011; Marín et al., 2019; Muralidharan & Pathak, 2018; Nicolás et al., 2018; Nicolás & Rubio, 2012; Pathak & Muralidharan, 2016; Stephan et al., 2015; van Ryzin et al., 2009
	EDUC	Primary, secondary or higher education	Bacq et al., 2016; Brieger et al., 2020; Estrin et al., 2013, 2016; Harding, 2007; Hechavarría, 2016; Hechavarria et al., 2012; Hechavarría et al., 2017; Levie & Hart, 2011; Marín et al., 2019; Muralidharan & Pathak, 2018; Nicolás et al., 2018; Nicolás & Rubio, 2012; Pathak & Muralidharan, 2016; Stephan et al., 2015
COUNTRY-LEVEL FACTORS	IDE	Level of economic development of countries	Brieger et al., 2020; Fernández-Laviada et al., 2020a; Lepoutre et al., 2013; Marín et al., 2019; Nicolás et al., 2018

Source: based on Fernández-Laviada et al. (2020a)

EMPIRICAL ANALYSIS

Sample

The source of data used for the empirical analysis is the Global Entrepreneurship Monitor (GEM). Specifically, the authors used the 2015 Adult Population Survey (APS), since in that year the survey included a specific section related to SE.

To categorize the entrepreneurs, the authors applied a three steps procedure. The first step is to differentiate commercial and social entrepreneurs. In this first step, the authors follow the broad definition proposed by GEM methodology (Bosma et al., 2015), identifying as a social entrepreneur an individual who is initiating or running any kind of activity, organization or initiative that has a social, environmental or community objective. The rest of the entrepreneurial population was identified as Commercial Entrepreneurs (CE). The second step is to consider, among the social entrepreneurs, those who consider that for their organization generating value to society and the environment is more important than generating financial value for the company. By doing this, the authors identified the second group, the social entrepreneurs that are more focused on financial than social value creation, named Socially Responsible Entrepreneurs (SRE). The third, and last step, is focused on social entrepreneurs focused on social value creation. In this case, the authors distinguish between those whose organization operates in the market by producing goods and services, Social Enterprises Entrepreneurs (SEE), and those that are not focused in the market by selling products or services, Social Initiative Entrepreneurs (SIE). This classification derived from GEM data is under the theoretical categorization of entrepreneurs provided in the literature review section and synthesized in Figure 1 above.

The composition of the sample is shown in table 4, which reflects the number of entrepreneurs included in the analysis according to the level of development of their countries. The level of development of the countries is established according to the Global Competitiveness Index (GCI) of the World Economic

Forum (WEF), distinguishing two different groups of countries. On the one hand, there are innovation-driven economies, which include more developed countries, with economies based on innovation; on the other hand, there are countries with a lower level of development, with economies based on factors or efficiency (factor/efficiency-driven economies).

Table 4. Sample composition

	Factor/efficiency driven economies (22 countries)		Innovation driven economies (14 countries)		Total economies (36 countries)	
	N	%	N	%	N	%
Commercial Entrepreneurs (CE)	8,087	79.5	3,193	71.3	11,280	77.0
Socially Responsible Entrepreneurs (SRE)	430	4.2	294	6.6	724	4.9
Social Enterprises Entrepreneurs (SEE)	1,131	11.1	596	13.3	1,727	11.8
Social Initiative Entrepreneurs (SIE)	528	5.2	394	8.8	922	6.3
Total	**10,176**	**100.0**	**4,477**	**100.0**	**14,653**	**100.0**

Estimation Strategy

The empirical analysis is carried out applying multinomial logistic regressions, where the dependent variable is a categorical variable representing different states of nature (in our case, the four different groups of entrepreneurs). The functional form of this model is as follows:

$$Pr\left(y=j/x\right)=\frac{\exp\left(x'Bj\right)}{\sum_{j=0}^{3}\exp(x'Bj)}$$

where:

yj - Dependent variable that can take the value 0, 1, 2 or 3 in the case of “Commercial Entrepreneurs (CE)”, “Socially Responsible Entrepreneurs (SRE)”, “Social Enterprises Entrepreneurs (SEE)” and “Social Initiative Entrepreneurs (SIE)”.

x - Vector of independent variables.

Bj - Coefficients for the independent variables.

$$x'Bj=\beta_0+\beta_1 GENDER_i+\sum_{k=1}^{3}\gamma_k AGE_i+\sum_{z=1}^{3}\gamma_z EDUC_i+\beta_2 IDE_i$$

The βj parameters allow us to evaluate the influence of each independent variable on the probability that these four described situations occur. In the interpretation of the results, the relative risk ratio (RRR) is used (Carriles-Alberdi et al., 2021; Klyver & Grant, 2010). In multinomial models the categories of response are independent and not ordered, that is why risk ratios are used rather than odds ratios (Hilbe, 2009). The relative risk ratio is the likelihood of the occurrence of an event after exposure to a risk variable compared with the likelihood of its occurrence in the reference group. The use of the relative risk ratio (RRR), in addition to facilitating interpretation, allows comparing the magnitude of the relationships.

As explanatory variables, the personal characteristics of the entrepreneur are included. The authors include three different explanatory variables. Firstly, the gender of the individual (GENDER) is considered, measured as a dummy variable that takes value 1 in the case of women and zero for men. Secondly, the authors consider the age, including three levels: under 34 years, between 34-54 years and over 54 years. Each of them is considered as a different variable in the model, defined under the same designation of the joint variable "AGE". To control the effect of multicollinearity, the last two levels are incorporated into the model (individuals under 34 are the base level). Finally, the educational level is also considered, which is also grouped into three different levels: primary, secondary, and higher education. Again, the last two groups are introduced in the model, being the base category, in this case, those whose educational level is "primary".

Additionally, the authors include the level of development of the country (IDE) as a control variable in the study. This is a dummy variable that takes value 1 for the category of "Innovation-driven economies" and zero otherwise.

FINDINGS AND DISCUSSION

Table 5 shows the results of the multinomial logistic regression. For each category of social entrepreneurs, the table shows the relative risk ratio (RRR) and the p-value to test the level of significance of each independent variable, being the reference group of the commercial entrepreneurs. In the case of multinomial logit, the RRR is used because in standard logit regressions it is assumed that the binary responses are ordered and not independent, but this hypothesis is not valid for multinomial regressions (Hilbe, 2009). Using the relative risk ratio, the analyzed effect is on a multiplicative scale. The RRR of the dichotomous variables shows how much more likely it is belonging to the group compared to commercial entrepreneurs when the independent variable takes the value 1 (when the RRR takes values greater than 1, the influence on the probability is positive; when the values are less than 1, the influence is negative). Additionally, the difference between the relative risk ratios as a percentage of the previous category and the level of significance of the differences are included. Finally, the number of observations, the pseudo R2 and the mean of the variance inflation factor (VIF) are detailed in the lower part of the table. The authors calculate the variance inflation factor (VIF) to confirm that multicollinearity does not bias our results. A value of 1 of the VIF is a characteristic of an orthogonal system and a value of less than 10 would indicate a non-collinear or stable system (Chatterjee & Haidi, 2012). The results confirm that analyses are robust to multicollinearity problems since the mean VIF is 1.68.

In the case of the AGE, a common pattern is observed, as evidenced by the previous literature, where commercial entrepreneurship (CE) predominates in young people (Arenius & Minniti, 2005; Langowitz & Minniti, 2007) since it has a significantly positive relationship after 34 (Levie & Hart, 2011), which is even greater after 54. This finding corroborates in part the U-shaped relationship identified by Brieger et al (2020). However, the magnitude of this general pattern presents differences among the different categories of social entrepreneurs, which justifies that the results previously obtained in academic literature were not conclusive. Firstly, compared to commercial entrepreneurs, the results show that there are 18.2% more probabilities of being Socially Responsible Entrepreneurs (SRE) for those between 34 & 54 (RRR=1.182, $p<0.05$), and this difference rises to 69% for those over 54 years old (RRR=1.69, p<0.01). For Social Enterprises Entrepreneurs (SEE) the effect for those between 34 & 54 is similar, but the difference is much bigger for those over 54 since they show more than 2.5 times probability (RRR=2.561, p<0.01). Finally, in the case of Social Initiative Entrepreneurs (SIE), the situation is slightly different, since there are no differences for those under 54, but there is still a greater probability for those over 54 (RRR=2.359, p<0.01).

Table 5. Multinomial logistic regression results

	SRE	Sig.	SEE	Sig.	Dif. (SEE vs. SRE)	Sig.	SIE	Sig.	Dif. (SIE vs. SEE)	Sig.
GENDER	0.857	**	0.981		14.4%		1.195	***	21.9%	**
AGE										
Under 34	Base		Base				Base			
Between 34 & 54	1.182	**	1.203	***	1.8%		1.005		-16.5%	*
Over 54	1.690	***	2.561	***	51.6%	***	2.359	***	-7.9%	
EDUCATION										
Primary	Base		Base				Base			
Secondary	1.306	**	1.691	***	29.4%		2.412	***	42.7%	*
Higher	1.580	***	3.012	***	90.6%	***	4.695	***	55.9%	**
IDE	1.596	***	1.126	**	-29.4%	***	1.592	***	41.4%	***
CONSTANT	0.038	***	0.061	***	61.6%		0.020	***	-67.8%	
Observations	14653									
Pseudo R2	0.0271									
Mean VIF	1.68									

Sig: level of significance: *** 0.01; ** 0.05; * 0.1.
SRE: Socially Responsible Entrepreneurs; SEE: Social Enterprises Entrepreneurs; SIE: Social Initiative Entrepreneurs.
GENDER: male or female; AGE: age intervals; EDUCATION: education level; IDE: innovation-driven economies; Dif: percentage difference over the previous category.

Regarding GENDER, the results show significant differences between the different categories of entrepreneurs. On the one hand, compared to commercial entrepreneurs (CE), there is a lower probability of being Socially Responsible Entrepreneurs (SRE) for females (Langowitz & Minniti, 2007; Minniti, 2010; Themudo, 2009), so males are even more predominant for this category of social entrepreneurs (women have almost 15% less probability, RRR=0.857, p<0.05). However, in the case of Social Enterprises Entrepreneurs (SEE), the difference disappears, and males and females show the same probability of being in this category (RRR is not significantly different from one). Finally, for Social Initiative Entrepreneurs (SIE) there is around 20% of probability for females (RRR=1.195, p<0.01). The results in gender show a non-linear pattern since, in the case of Socially Responsible Entrepreneurs (SRE), who are more focused on financial value creation, males play a more significant role, but the gender difference disappears for Social Enterprises Entrepreneurs (SEE) and females are predominant in Social Initiative Entrepreneurship (SIE). Therefore, it is observed that, as the orientation towards social goals increases, female entrepreneurship prevails (Fernández-Laviada et al., 2020a; Marín et al., 2019).

Finally, EDUCATION also shows a general pattern according to previous studies (Bosma, 2013; Brieger et al., 2020; Estrin et al., 2013, 2016; Levie & Hart, 2011; Pathak & Muralidharan, 2016; Vuorio, 2017), with a positive relationship of the level of education with all categories of SE (the greater the level of education the greater the probability of an entrepreneur to be social). However, the different categories of social entrepreneurs do have not homogeneous behaviour since there are differences between them. In the case of Socially Responsible Entrepreneurs (SRE) those with secondary education show a probability more than 30% greater compared to commercial entrepreneurs (RRR=1.306, p<0.05), and this difference is even greater for those with higher education (RRR=1.580, p<0.01). For Social Enterprises Entrepreneurs (SEE) the effect for those with secondary education is similar, but the difference is much bigger for those with higher education, who have a probability more than 3 times greater (RRR=3.012, p<0.01). Finally, the influence of the level of education is even more relevant in the case of Social Initiative Entrepreneurs (SIE), where the results show a probability more than 2.4 times greater for those with secondary education (RRR=2.412, p<0.01), difference than rises to more than 4.6 times in the case of higher education (RRR=4.695, p<0.01). In other words, as the social focus increases, the educational level of entrepreneurs increases as well, as previous studies have also evidenced (Bosma, 2013; Brieger et al., 2020; Estrin et al., 2013, 2016; Levie & Hart, 2011; Pathak & Muralidharan, 2016; Vuorio, 2017)

Finally, as Hoogendoorn (2016) revealed, the degree of development of the country (IDE) exerts a positive influence on the probability of being a social entrepreneur but, again, the effect is not the same in all the categories. The results show that there is a difference around 60% in this case of Socially Responsible Entrepreneurs (SRE) and Social Initiative Entrepreneurs (SIE) (RRR=1.596, p<0.01 and RRR=1.592, p<0.01 respectively), but this difference is reduced to more than 12% for Social Enterprises Entrepreneurs (SEE) (RRR=1.126, p<0.05).

CONCLUSION

The lack of consensus on the definition of SE (Lepoutre et al., 2013) and the recently defended hypothesis labelled "the impossibility of a unified definition" (Defourny & Nyssens, 2017) -because SE is a contested concept (Choi & Majumdar, 2014)- have motivated that several authors provide typologies of SE (Alter, 2007; Brouard & Larivet, 2010; López-Arceiz et al., 2016; Mair et al., 2012; Margiono et al., 2018), although these classifications have been scarcely tested and proved empirically.

Following this idea, the authors propose a new typology using GEM data based on the two most conflictive dimensions of SE: the social-financial mission orientation and the use of market-based approaches to generate income. With these premises in mind, the authors classify SE into three categories, (1) "socially responsible entrepreneurship" (SRE), (2) "social enterprise entrepreneurship" (SEE) and (3) "social initiative entrepreneurship" (SIE).

Using multinomial logistic regressions on a sample of 36 different countries that include 11,280 commercial entrepreneurs and 3,373 social entrepreneurs -taken from GEM data-, the results show significant differences between the diverse categories defined previously. In this chapter, the authors focus the study on personal characteristics: gender, age and education, and the level of development of the country. In all these cases, a common pattern is observed, which confirms that each typology of SE has its characteristics and should be studied separately. Specifically, as the orientation towards a social mission increases, the presence of women (Fernández-Laviada et al., 2020a; Marín et al., 2019) and the level of education increases too (Bosma, 2013; Brieger et al., 2020; Estrin et al., 2013, 2016; Levie

& Hart, 2011; Pathak & Muralidharan, 2016; Vuorio, 2017). In the case of age, the same pattern is observed when considering the difference between "socially responsible entrepreneurship" and "social enterprise entrepreneurship" (Levie & Hart, 2011). In the case of "social initiative entrepreneurship", the entrepreneur's age plays a relevant role too, but its influence is only observed for entrepreneurs over 54. This finding confirms in part the U-shaped relationship identified by Brieger et al. (2020). Finally, the degree of economic development is also considered an important factor to be taken into account, not only due to its moderator role on other cognitive variables (Fernández-Laviada et al., 2020a). As the findings of Fernández-Laviada et al. (2020b) and Marín et al. (2019), the results in this research demonstrate that there is a positive effect of the degree of the country's economic development and the entrepreneur's social orientation.

This classification offers a solution to the definitional problem by identifying three types of SE whose study will contribute to a better understanding of this field. Not all social entrepreneurs are the same and they should not be considered and treated as if they were. This typology will contribute to developing a systematic SE research despite the contested nature of this concept. Additionally, the study is also relevant for policymakers (Cagarman et al., 2020), who will be able to map the SE phenomenon better at the time that they can also design public policies that are more effective to promote social business creation. Nongovernmental private social organizations can also benefit from the findings of the study as they will be able to place themselves in the SE field more clearly and evaluate their strategies and activities in comparison with other social initiatives.

In the future, the authors will continue to analyze different factors that previous literature has shown to affect social entrepreneurial intentions. For instance, the authors will study the role of entrepreneurs' cognitive variables such as having an entrepreneurial network, the perception of opportunities in the environment, having the skills and abilities to start a business and/or fear of failure.

Finally, this study is not without limitations, some of them related to the sample used. In this regard, the use of GEM data has many advantages but also presents some limitations. For instance, the number of countries analyzed is conditioned by their participation in the project. Additionally, GEM is based on surveys of individuals, which is especially relevant since there is no consensus about what is understood by SE. Based on these limitations, some interesting future lines of research could contribute to further advance our empirical knowledge on social entrepreneurship categories. For instance, it is suggested that future researchers focus more specifically on the diverse typologies of SE that exist and develop new methodological tools to explore their characteristics, beliefs, attitudes and behaviours. GEM is a nice starting point, but it is important to notice that it is not specifically focused on social entrepreneurship and, therefore, further questionnaires and methods to explore data should be developed. The creation of social entrepreneurship national databases across countries could be an interesting way to start this process, as they would grant access to a proven catalogue of social entrepreneurs that are internationally comparable.

REFERENCES

Alter, K. (2007). *Social enterprise typology*. Academic Press.

Arenius, P., & Minniti, M. (2005). Perceptual variables and nascent entrepreneurship. *Small Business Economics*, *24*(3), 233–247. doi:10.100711187-005-1984-x

Austin, J., Stevenson, H., & Wei-Skillern, J. (2006). Social and commercial entrepreneurship: Same, different, or both? *Entrepreneurship Theory and Practice*, *30*(1), 1–22. doi:10.1111/j.1540-6520.2006.00107.x

Bacq, S., Hartog, C., & Hoogendoorn, B. (2016). Beyond the moral portrayal of social entrepreneurs: An empirical approach to who they are and what drives them. *Journal of Business Ethics*, *133*(4), 703–718. doi:10.100710551-014-2446-7

Bacq, S., & Janssen, F. (2011). Structuring the field of social entrepreneurship: A transatlantic comparative approach. In O. J. Borch, A. Fayolle, P. Kyro, & E. Ljunggren (Eds.), *The Entrepreneurship Research in Europe: Evolving Concepts and Processes*. Edward-Elgar Publications. doi:10.4337/9780857931757.00017

Baron, D. P. (2007). Corporate social responsibility and social entrepreneurship. *Journal of Economics & Management Strategy*, *16*(3), 683–717. doi:10.1111/j.1530-9134.2007.00154.x

Battilana, J., & Lee, M. (2014). Advancing research on hybrid organizing - Insights from the study of social enterprises. *The Academy of Management Annals*, *8*(1), 397–441. doi:10.5465/19416520.2014.893615

Bedi, H. S., & Yadav, N. (2019). Social entrepreneurship: A conceptual clarity. *Our Heritage*, *67*(10), 1006–1016.

Boschee, J. (1995). Social entrepreneurship: Some non-profits are not only thinking about the unthinkable, they're doing it – Running a profit. *The Conference Board Magazine*, *32*(3), 20–25.

Boschee, J., & McClurg, J. (2003). *Towards a better understanding of social entrepreneurship. Some important distinctions*. Academic Press.

Bosma, N. (2013). The Global Entrepreneurship Monitor (GEM) and its impact on entrepreneurship research. *Foundations and Trends in Entrepreneurship*, *9*(2), 143–248. doi:10.1561/0300000033

Bosma, N., Schøtt, T., Terjesen, S., & Kew, P. (2015). Social Entrepreneurship. In Global Entrepreneurship Monitor Special Topic Report. Academic Press.

Bravo, C. (2018). *Identifying cross-country key drivers of social entrepreneurial activity*. University of San Diego. doi:10.22371/05.2018.014

Brieger, S. A., Bäro, A., Criaco, G., & Terjesen, S. A. (2020). Entrepreneurs' age, institutions, and social value creation goals: A multi-country study. *Small Business Economics*. . doi:10.1007/s11187-020-00317-z

Brouard, F., & Larivet, S. (2010). Essay of clarifications and definitions of the related concepts of social enterprise, social entrepreneur and social entrepreneurship. In A. Fayolle & H. Matlay (Eds.), Handbook of Research on Social Entrepreneurship. Edward Elgar Ed. doi:10.4337/9781849804684.00008

Brozek, K. O. (2009). Exploring the continuum of social and financial returns: When does a nonprofit become a social enterprise? *Community Development Investment Review*, *5*(2), 7–17.

Cagarman, K., Kratzer, J., von Arnim, L. H., Fajga, K., & Gieseke, M. J. (2020). Social entrepreneurship on its way to significance: The case of Germany. *Sustainability*, *12*(21), 1–13. doi:10.3390u12218954

Carriles-Alberdi, M., López-Gutiérrez, C., & Fernández-Laviada, A. (2021). The influence of the ecosystem on the motivation of social entrepreneurs. *Sustainability*, *13*(2), 1–17. doi:10.3390u13020922 PMID:34123411

Chatterjee, S., & Haidi, A. S. (2012). *Regression analysis by example*. John Wiley & Sons.

Choi, N., & Majumdar, S. (2014). Social entrepreneurship as an essentially contested concept: Opening a new avenue for systematic future research. *Journal of Business Venturing*, *29*(3), 363–376. doi:10.1016/j.jbusvent.2013.05.001

Cukier, W., Trenholm, S., Carl, D., & Gekas, G. (2011). Social entrepreneurship: A content analysis. *Journal of Strategic Innovation and Sustainability*, *7*(1), 99–119.

Dacin, P. A., Dacin, M. T., & Matear, M. (2010). Social entrepreneurship: Why we don't need a new theory and how we move forward from here. *The Academy of Management Perspectives*, *24*(3), 36–56. doi:10.5465/amp.24.3.37

Dees, J. G. (2001). *The meaning of "Social Entrepreneur"*. Academic Press.

Defourny, J. (1994). *Développer l'enterprise sociale*. Foundation Roi Baudouin.

Defourny, J., & Nyssens, M. (2010). Conceptions of social enterprise and social entrepreneurship in Europe and the United States: Convergences and divergences. *Journal of Social Entrepreneurship*, *1*(1), 32–53. doi:10.1080/19420670903442053

Defourny, J., & Nyssens, M. (2017). Fundamentals for an international typology of social enterprise models. *Voluntas*, *28*(6), 2469–2497. doi:10.100711266-017-9884-7

Doherty, B., Haugh, H., & Lyon, F. (2014). Social enterprises as hybrid organizations: A review and research agenda. *International Journal of Management Reviews*, *16*(4), 417–436. doi:10.1111/ijmr.12028

Estrin, S., Mickiewicz, T., & Stephan, U. (2013). Entrepreneurship, social capital, and institutions: Social and commercial entrepreneurship across nations. *Entrepreneurship: Theory and Practice Theory and Practice*, *37*(3), 479–504. doi:10.1111/etap.12019

Estrin, S., Mickiewicz, T., & Stephan, U. (2016). Human capital in social and commercial entrepreneurship. *Journal of Business Venturing*, *31*(4), 449–467. doi:10.1016/j.jbusvent.2016.05.003

European Commission. (2014). *A map of social enterprises and their eco-systems in Europe*. https://ec.europa.eu/social/BlobServlet?docId=12987&langId=en

Fernández-Laviada, A., López-Gutiérrez, C., & Pérez, A. (2020a). How does the development of the social enterprise sector affect entrepreneurial behavior? An empirical analysis. *Sustainability*, *12*(3), 1–15. doi:10.3390u12030826

Fernández-Laviada, A., López-Gutiérrez, C., & San-Martín, P. (2020b). The moderating effect of countries' development on the characterization of the social entrepreneur: An empirical analysis with GEM data. *Voluntas*, *31*(3), 563–580. doi:10.100711266-020-00216-7

Gallie, W. B. (1956). Art as an essentially contested concept. *The Philosophical Quarterly*, *6*(23), 97–114. doi:10.2307/2217217

García-Jurado, A., Pérez-Barea, J. J., & Nova, R. J. (2021). A new approach to social entrepreneurship: A systematic review and meta-analysis. *Sustainability*, *13*(5), 1–16. doi:10.3390u13052754

GEM. (2015). *2015 Report on Social Entrepreneurship.* Special Topic Report. GEM.

Gupta, P., Chauhan, S., Paul, J., & Jaiswal, M. P. (2020). Social entrepreneurship research: A review and future research agenda. *Journal of Business Research, 113*, 209–229. doi:10.1016/j.jbusres.2020.03.032

Gupta, V. K., Turban, D. B., Wasti, S. A., & Sikdar, A. (2009). The role of gender stereotypes in perceptions of entrepreneurs and intentions to become an entrepreneur. *Entrepreneurship Theory and Practice, 33*(2), 397–417. doi:10.1111/j.1540-6520.2009.00296.x

Harding, R. (2007). Understanding social entrepreneurship. *Industry and Higher Education, 21*(1), 73–84. doi:10.5367/000000007780222723

Harding, R., & Cowling, M. (2006). *Social Entrepreneurship Monitor United Kingdom 2006.* Academic Press.

Hechavarría, D. M. (2016). The impact of culture on national prevalence rates of social and commercial entrepreneurship. *The International Entrepreneurship and Management Journal, 12*(4), 1025–1052. doi:10.100711365-015-0376-1

Hechavarria, D. M., Ingram, A., Justo, R., & Terjesen, S. (2012). Are women more likely to pursue social and environmental entrepreneurship? In K. D. Hughes & J. E. Jennings (Eds.), *Global Women's Entrepreneurship Research: Diverse Settings, Questions and Approaches* (pp. 135–151). Edward Elgar Publishing. doi:10.4337/9781849804752.00016

Hechavarría, D. M., Terjesen, S. A., Ingram, A. E., Renko, M., Justo, R., & Elam, A. (2017). Taking care of business: The impact of culture and gender on entrepreneurs' blended value creation goals. *Small Business Economics, 48*(1), 225–257. doi:10.100711187-016-9747-4

Hibbert, S. A., Hogg, G., & Quinn, T. (2005). Social entrepreneurship: Understanding consumer motives for buying The Big Issue. *Journal of Consumer Behaviour, 4*(3), 159–172. doi:10.1002/cb.6

Hilbe, J. M. (2009). *Logistic regression models.* Chapman & Hall/CRC. doi:10.1201/9781420075779

Hoogendoorn, B. (2016). The prevalence and determinants of social entrepreneurship at the macro level. *Journal of Small Business Management, 54*(S1), 278–296. doi:10.1111/jsbm.12301

Iyigun, N. O. (2018). *Creating business value and competitive advantage with social entrepreneurship.* IGI Global.

Klyver, K., & Grant, S. (2010). Gender differences in entrepreneurial networking and participation. *International Journal of Gender and Entrepreneurship, 2*(3), 213–227. doi:10.1108/17566261011079215

Kraus, S., Filser, M., O'Dwyer, M., & Shaw, E. (2014). Social entrepreneurship: An exploratory citation analysis. *Review of Managerial Science, 8*(2), 275–292. doi:10.100711846-013-0104-6

Langowitz, N., & Minniti, M. (2007). The entrepreneurial propensity of women. *Entrepreneurship Theory and Practice, 31*(3), 341–364. doi:10.1111/j.1540-6520.2007.00177.x

Leadbeater, C. (1997). The rise of the social entrepreneur. *Demos (Mexico City, Mexico).*

Lepoutre, J., Justo, R., Terjesen, S., & Bosma, N. (2013). Designing a global standardized methodology for measuring social entrepreneurship activity: The Global Entrepreneurship Monitor social entrepreneurship study. *Small Business Economics, 40*(3), 693–714. doi:10.100711187-011-9398-4

Levie, J., & Hart, M. (2011). Business and social entrepreneurs in the UK: Gender, context and commitment. *International Journal of Gender and Entrepreneurship, 3*(3), 200–217. doi:10.1108/17566261111169304

López-Arceiz, F. J., Bellostas, A. J., & Rivera, M. P. (2016). The effects of resources on social activity and economic performance in social economy organizations. *Nonprofit Management & Leadership, 20*(4), 83–96. doi:10.1002/nml.21204

Lyon, F., Teasdale, S., & Baldock, R. (2010). *Approaches to measuring the scale of the social enterprise sector in the UK.* Working Paper (Vol. 43).

Mair, J., Battilana, J., & Cardenas, J. (2012). Organizing for society: A typology of social entrepreneuring models. *Journal of Business Ethics, 111*(3), 353–373. doi:10.100710551-012-1414-3

Mair, J., & Martí, I. (2006). Social entrepreneurship research: A source of explanation, prediction, and delight. *Journal of World Business, 41*(1), 36–44. doi:10.1016/j.jwb.2005.09.002

Margiono, A., Zolin, R., & Chang, A. (2018). A typology of social venture business model configurations. *International Journal of Entrepreneurial Behaviour & Research, 24*(3), 626–650. doi:10.1108/IJEBR-09-2016-0316

Marín, L., Nicolás, C., & Rubio, A. (2019). How gender, age and education influence the entrepreneur's social orientation: The moderating effect of economic development. *Sustainability, 11*(17), 1–16. doi:10.3390u11174514

Martin, R. L., & Osberg, S. (2007). Social entrepreneurship: The case for definintion. *Stanford Social Innovation Review*, (Spring), 28–39.

Minniti, M. (2010). Female entrepreneurship and economic activity. *European Journal of Development Research, 22*(3), 294–312. doi:10.1057/ejdr.2010.18

Minniti, M., Arenius, P., & Langowitz, N. (2006). *The 2005 Global Entrepreneurship Monitor special topic report: Women in entrepreneurship*. Academic Press.

Mort, G. S., Weerawardena, J., & Carnegie, K. (2003). Social entrepreneurship: Towards conceptualisation. *International Journal of Nonprofit and Voluntary Sector Marketing, 8*(1), 76–88. doi:10.1002/nvsm.202

Muralidharan, E., & Pathak, S. (2018). Sustainability, transformational leadership, and social entrepreneurship. *Sustainability, 10*(2), 1–22. doi:10.3390u10020567

Nga, J. K. H., & Shamuganathan, G. (2010). The influence of personality traits and demographic factors on social entrepreneurship start up intentions. *Journal of Business Ethics, 95*(2), 259–282. doi:10.100710551-009-0358-8

Nicholls, A. (2006). *Social Entrepreneurship. New Models of Sustainable Change*. Oxford University Press.

Nicolás, C., & Rubio, A. (2012). El emprendimiento social: Una comparativa entre España y países sudamericanos. *Faedpyme International Review, 1*(1), 38–49.

Nicolás, C., Rubio, A., & Fernández-Laviada, A. (2018). Cognitive determinants of social entrepreneurship: Variations according to the degree of economic development. *Journal of Social Entrepreneurship, 9*(2), 154–168. doi:10.1080/19420676.2018.1452280

Ormiston, J., & Seymour, R. (2011). Understanding value creation in social entrepreneurship: The importance of aligning mission, strategy and impact measurement. *Journal of Social Entrepreneurship, 2*(2), 125–150. doi:10.1080/19420676.2011.606331

Pathak, S., & Muralidharan, E. (2016). Informal institutions and their comparative influences on social and commercial entrepreneurship: The role of in-group collectivism and interpersonal trust. *Journal of Small Business Management, 54*(S1), 168–188. doi:10.1111/jsbm.12289

Peredo, A. M., & McLean, M. (2006). Social entrepreneurship: A critical review of the concept. *Journal of World Business, 41*(1), 56–65. doi:10.1016/j.jwb.2005.10.007

Rey-Martí, A., Ribeiro-Soriano, D., & Palacios-Marqués, D. (2016). A bibliometric analysis of social entrepreneurship. *Journal of Business Research, 69*(5), 1651–1655. doi:10.1016/j.jbusres.2015.10.033

Roberts, D., & Woods, C. (2005). Changing the world on a shoestring: The concept of social entrepreneurship. *University of Auckland Business Review, 7*(1), 45–51.

Sassmannshausen, S. P., & Volkmann, C. (2018). The scientometrics of social entrepreneurship and its establishment as an academic field. *Journal of Small Business Management, 56*(2), 251–273. doi:10.1111/jsbm.12254

Seelos, C., & Mair, J. (2005). Social entrepreneurship: Creating new business models to serve the poor. *Business Horizons, 48*(3), 241–246. doi:10.1016/j.bushor.2004.11.006

Sengupta, S., & Sahay, A. (2017). Social entrepreneurship research in Asia-Pacific: Perspectives and opportunities. *Social Enterprise Journal, 13*(1), 17–37. doi:10.1108/SEJ-11-2016-0050

Sengupta, S., Sahay, A., & Croce, F. (2018). Conceptualizing social entrepreneurship in the context of emerging economies: An integrative review of past research from BRIICS. *The International Entrepreneurship and Management Journal, 14*(5), 771–803. doi:10.100711365-017-0483-2

Short, J. C., Moss, T. W., & Lumpkin, G. T. (2009). Research in social entrepreneurship: Past contributions and future opportunities. *Strategic Entrepreneurship Journal, 3*(2), 161–194. doi:10.1002ej.69

Stephan, U., Uhlaner, L. M., & Stride, C. (2015). Institutions and social entrepreneurship: The role of institutional voids, institutional support, and institutional configurations. *Journal of International Business Studies, 46*(3), 308–331. doi:10.1057/jibs.2014.38

Teasdale, S. (2010). Can social enterprise address disadvantage? Evidence from an inner city community. *Nonprofit and Public Sector Marketing, 22*(2), 89–107. doi:10.1080/10495141003601278

Terjesen, S., Lepoutre, J., Justo, R., & Bosma, N. (2012). *2009 Report on Social Entrepreneurship*. Academic Press.

Terziev, V., & Arabska, E. (2017). Social entrepreneurship, social values and social impact. *International Journal of Research in Management, Economics and Commerce, 7*(4), 41–46. doi:10.2139srn.3142936

Themudo, N. S. (2009). Gender and the nonprofit sector. *Nonprofit and Voluntary Sector Quarterly*, *38*(4), 663–683. doi:10.1177/0899764009333957

Thompson, J. L. (2002). The world of the social entrepreneur. *International Journal of Public Sector Management*, *15*(5), 412–431. doi:10.1108/09513550210435746

van Ryzin, G. G., Grossman, S., DiPadova-Stocks, L., & Bergrud, E. (2009). Portrait of the social entrepreneur: Statistical evidence from a US panel. *Voluntas*, *20*(2), 129–140. doi:10.100711266-009-9081-4

Vega, G., & Kidwell, R. E. (2007). Toward a typology of new venture creators: Similarities and contrasts between business and social entrepreneurs. *New England Journal of Entrepreneurship*, *10*(2), 15–28. doi:10.1108/NEJE-10-02-2007-B002

Vuorio, A. (2017). Young adults and sustainable enterpreneurship: The role of culture and demographic factors. *Journal of International Business and Entrepreneurship Development*, *10*(3), 209–230. doi:10.1504/JIBED.2017.085499

Zahra, S. A., Gedajlovic, E., Neubaum, D. O., & Shulman, J. M. (2009). A typology of social entrepreneurs: Motives, search processes and ethical challenges. *Journal of Business Venturing*, *24*(5), 519–532. doi:10.1016/j.jbusvent.2008.04.007

ADDITIONAL READING

André, K., & Pache, A. C. (2016). From caring entrepreneur to caring enterprise: Addressing the ethical challenges of scaling up social enterprises. *Journal of Business Ethics*, *133*(4), 659–675. doi:10.100710551-014-2445-8

Bull, M. (2018). Reconceptualising social enterprise in the UK through an appreciation of legal identities. *International Journal of Entrepreneurial Behaviour & Research*, *24*(3), 587–605. doi:10.1108/IJEBR-11-2017-0470

Bygrave, W., & Minniti, M. (2000). The social dynamics of entrepreneurship. *Entrepreneurship Theory and Practice*, *24*(3), 25–36. doi:10.1177/104225870002400302

Corner, P. D., & Ho, M. (2010). How opportunities develop in social entrepreneurship. *Entrepreneurship Theory and Practice*, *34*(4), 635–659. doi:10.1111/j.1540-6520.2010.00382.x

Hockerts, K. (2017). Determinants of social entrepreneurial intentions. *Entrepreneurship Theory and Practice*, *41*(1), 105–130. doi:10.1111/etap.12171

Kerlin, J. A. (2006). Social enterprise in the United States and Europe: Understanding and learning from the differences. *Voluntas*, *17*(3), 247–263. doi:10.100711266-006-9016-2

Littlewood, D., & Holt, D. (2018). Social entrepreneurship in South Africa: Exploring the influence of environment. *Business & Society*, *57*(3), 525–561. doi:10.1177/0007650315613293

Lumpkin, G. T., Moss, T. W., Gras, D. M., Kato, S., & Amezcua, A. S. (2013). Entrepreneurial processes in social contexts: How are they different, if at all? *Small Business Economics*, *40*(3), 761–783. doi:10.100711187-011-9399-3

Weerawardena, J., & Sullivan Mort, G. (2006). Investigating social entrepreneurship: A multidimensional model. *Journal of World Business*, *41*(1), 21–35. doi:10.1016/j.jwb.2005.09.001

Yunus, M. (2008). Creating a world without poverty: Social business and the future of capitalism. *Global Urban Development Magazine*, *4*(2), 16–41.

KEY TERMS AND DEFINITIONS

Global Entrepreneurship Monitor (GEM): A networked consortium of national country teams primarily associated with top academic institutions. GEM carries out survey-based research on entrepreneurship and entrepreneurship ecosystems around the world. GEM is the only global research source that collects data on entrepreneurship directly from individual entrepreneurs.

Social Business: A very specific type of business – a non-dividend company with a social objective. A social business may pursue goals similar to those sought by some social entrepreneurs, but the specific business structure of social business makes it distinctive and unique.

Social Business Entrepreneur: An entrepreneur engaged in social business.

Social Enterprise: Initiative that solves some social or environmental problems. It may not be a business at all. It may be a non-business initiative of a person to help society overcome some problem. It ranges from non-business to business making an attractive profit. A social enterprise may be a charity organization and/or it can be a profit-making business producing both personal profits and social benefits.

Social Entrepreneur: An entrepreneur engaged in social entrepreneurship.

Social Entrepreneurship: An initiative of social consequences created by an entrepreneur with a social vision. This initiative may be non-economic, a charity initiative, or a business initiative with or without personal profit. Some social entrepreneurs house their projects within the traditional non-governmental organizations (NGOs), while others are involved in for-profit activities.

Chapter 13
The Antecedents of Consumer Engagement in CSR Communication in Social Media:
A Study on Omani University Students

Mansour Alraja
Dhofar University, Oman

Mohamed Hamdoun
Dhofar University, Oman

ABSTRACT

This study aims to explore the ways in which targeted consumers engage with corporate social responsibility (CSR) activities on social media platforms, specifically when discussing their opinions and experiences regarding the CSR activities of their favorite brands. Therefore, the variable moral norms were integrated in the theory of reasoned action. The study data about consumers' engagement (CE) in corporate social responsibility communication (CSRC) over social media (SM) platforms—electronic word of mouth, or e-WoM—was collected from 290 actual engaged consumers in online ordering and involved in social media groups. The findings confirmed that the antecedent factors (consumers' attitudes, subjective norms, and moral norms) have a positive influence on consumers' intention to use e-WoM, while no effect was found on CE in CSRC in SM. Furthermore, e-WoM was found to have direct significant impact on CE in CSRC in SM as it mediates the relationship between the antecedent factors and CE in CSRC in SM.

INTRODUCTION

Social media platforms are increasingly becoming an important part of our life for all generations, particularly young people. In the near future, young consumers are expected to be the most important and influential consumer group (Schmeltz, 2017). Firms from all industries engaging in actions of corporate

DOI: 10.4018/978-1-7998-8065-3.ch013

social responsibility (CSR) has increased drastically (refer to appendix A: all used abbreviations). In addition, companies occupying a range of industries have significantly expanded their CSR deployment (Ettinger, Grabner-Kräuter, & Terlutter, 2018). In summary, "CSR encompasses the economic, legal, ethical, and discretionary (philanthropic) expectations that society has of organisations at a given point in time" (Carroll, 1979, 1991). According to the European Commission, the definition of CSR has been simplified as "the responsibility of enterprises for their impacts on society and … what an enterprise should do to meet that responsibility" (The European Commission, 2011). Therefore, to garner maximum benefits from CSR, businesses should communicate their initiatives with all stakeholders (Maignan & Ferrell, 2004). Customers - as one of the most important stakeholders - are increasingly more socially aware and exigent for CSR adoption (De Grosbois, 2012). Therefore, they should be engaged in such initiatives and CSR activities (Ettinger et al., 2018). The dissemination of information pertaining to CSR can be achieved through a variety of channels and platforms. As a result, communication of CSR online possesses huge scope in its multifaceted engagement with consumers through (Du & Vieira, 2012) corporate websites and social media platforms (Mkono & Tribe, 2017; Wong, Leung, & Law, 2015).

WoM communication, which typically refers to the notion of person-to-person conversation among consumers (Sen & Lerman, 2007), has been recognised as affecting and shaping consumer attitudes and behavioural intentions (Jalilvand & Samiei, 2012). Word of mouth communication is also regarded as more effective, and as providing more reliable information compared with other methods of communication (Park & Lee, 2009). However, the huge advance and spread of information and communication technology (ICT) over the globe has reduced the occurrence of direct in-person communication, and increased drastically the indirect personal form of WoM communication: electronic word-of-mouth (e-WoM) communication. This advance in ICT, and more specifically, the advance in social media and the availability of many different social media platforms, has become an important environment for such communications (Li & Du, 2011), through which everyone can share, read, and discuss their opinions and experiences with others, regardless of social background, geographical location, and potential anonymity (Duan, Gu, & Whinston, 2008). Therefore, e-WoM has recently been considered a significant factor that influences consumer behaviour (Farzin & Fattahi, 2018). E-WoM on social media, through consumers' comments on products and companies, directly exposes their opinion, and as a result holds greater influence among other consumers as a non-bias, trustworthy source (Sen & Lerman, 2007; Zhou, Zhang, Tan, Tseng, & Zhang, 2020). Moreover, social media plays a vital role in the communication and transmission of information, and further facilitates consumer engagement in brand-related e-WoM (Lin & Wang, 2020), which has recently become an incredibly important tool to engage targeted consumers in different company activities, as well as in shaping and influencing their attitudes and behaviours (Ahmad & Laroche, 2017).

Engaging consumers is a mechanism by which companies directly or indirectly add value (Pansari & Kumar, 2017). This engagement has shifted to social media through viewing, reacting to, creating, and sharing information about the CSR activities of a company or one of its brands. CSR positively increases consumer trust in a company or brand, and thereby strengthens their relationship (Giakoumaki & Krepapa, 2020).

As a result of the preeminence of social media platforms as a mechanism by which companies directly engage with consumers, companies are facing increasing legal and societal pressure to communicate their CSR commitments (Schmeltz, 2017). In this regard, few research works have studied the antecedents of consumers' engagement in CSR communication in social media (CE in CSRC in SM) (e.g. (Chu, Chen, & Gan, 2020)). Recent research also demonstrates that the e-WoM is a very important tool used by consumers to communicate with peers and businesses (D'Acunto, Tuan, Dalli, Viglia, & Okumus, 2020). Despite this, only a few researchers have investigated whether e-WoM can be considered a tool for CSR communication, and provide feedback about CSR activities (D'Acunto et al., 2020; Ettinger et al., 2018). However, companies have realised the increase of awareness level about CSR activities, which reflects the importance of these activities (Randle, Kemperman, & Dolnicar, 2019). E-WOM, through social media, is a source that can be used to appraise companies' engagement in CSR activities (Procter, Angus, Blaszczynski, & Gainsbury, 2019). Consumers can use social media platforms not only to read others' comments, opinions and experiences, but also share their own experiences about the CSR activities of the companies that produce their favorite brands (Bialkova & Te Paske, 2020). Therefore, measuring consumer engagement is vital when taking into consideration its positive influence on customers' satisfaction, which in turn affects consumer behaviour (Kim, 2017).

This study will expose, through social media platforms, how consumers engage with the CSR activities of companies that produce their favourite brands. More specifically, this study represents the first empirical investigation embedding moral norms within the theory of reasoned action, in the context of CE in CSRC on SM. This study suggests e-WoM as a mediator between consumers' attitude, subjective norms, moral norms, and CE in CSRC on SM. This study will further determine whether e-WoM predicts CE in CSRC on SM. For this purpose, this study will employ data collected from consumers who use social media to pay for products or services online.

This research encompasses original theoretical contributions compared to previous works. First, this research provides new practical evidence about CE in CSRC over SM platforms (e-WoM) by collecting data from consumers currently engaged in online ordering, and involved in social media groups. Second, this study will enhance the limited literature pertaining to the field of CSR from a consumer perspective, in comparison with companies-oriented CSR literature. Third, this study looks at consumers' attitude, subjective norms and moral norms and how these factors influence their involvement in spreading e-WoM, especially when they are exposed to CSR related posts over social media. Consequently, understanding which of those factors are related to e-WoM, this study can propose methods to enhance the use of the e-WoM, which in turn helps increase CE in CSRC in SM. Fourth, to the best of our knowledge, the theory of reasoned action and moral norms have not been used to explain the CE in CSRC in SM. Fifth, the central question still concerns the particular of youth people in developing countries, whose dependence upon social media could provide an opportunity to raise CSR awareness.

Furthermore, this study's outcome offers companies increased understanding of consumers' attention towards companies' CSR activities. Therefore, this study offers immediate actions, such as improving the reporting of CSR activities in a way that promotes company conduct, with an emphasis on social media outreach through e-WoM.

THEORETICAL FRAMEWORK AND HYPOTHESES DEVELOPMENT

Theory of Reasoned Action

Information systems research utilized many different theories such as the Theory of Planned Behavior, theory of the diffusion of innovation, theory of the rational choice, the Unified Theory of Acceptance and Use of Technology, and theory of the value-belief-norm...etc. Those theories uesed a foundation to interpret individuals behavioral intention, and the current study is anchored on the Theory of Reasoned

Action (TRA) (Fishbein and Azjen, 1975). This theory is based on a individuals's attitude toward an object, or behavior is based on a set of beliefs that the individual considers about the results of engaging with that object. In the area of information systems, scholars put emphasis on determining salient variables that are enabling in understanding the phenomenon under research not just relying on underpinning theory. Therefore, researchers in the field of information systems investigated different variables may affect consumers' behavior during the decision process to buy or adopt object (Featherman, Jia, Califf, & Hajli, 2021; Hong, Chan, Thong, Chasalow, & Dhillon, 2013). In addition, many other reasons account for our dependence on TRA as our theoretical framework. **First**, the main goal of our study is to investigate consumers' engagement in CSR communication in social media therefore social influences is one of the most influential factors. Thus, compared with other underpinning theories, TRA is appropriate due to its focus on measuring the strength of social effect (Subjective norms) affecting consumers' behavior toward adopting an object, or behavior. **Second,** recently, many scholars adopted TRA as an underlying framework for individuals' behavioral intention(Chang, Wang, & Wills, 2020; Featherman et al., 2021; Jain, Paul, & Shrivastava, 2021; Kong & Wang, 2021; Wu, 2020). Therefore, the current study pursues previous research to investigate how consumers' engage in CSR communication in social media. **Third,** as a general framework, TRA allows researchers add other related constructs to develop customized research models to more carefully understand the phenomenon under investigation(Featherman et al., 2021; Jain et al., 2021; Kong & Wang, 2021; Wu, 2020). **Fourth,** among other theories that have good explanation power, TRA considered a good model predicting goals and activities (Chang et al., 2020; Kong & Wang, 2021).

The Theory of Reasoned Action (TRA) developed by Fishbein & Ajzen (1975) has significantly influenced the literature on attitudes and behavior (Rutter & Bunce, 1989). The predictive utility of this model has been investigated through meta-analysis (Sheppard, Hartwick, & Warshaw, 1988). The Theory of Reasoned Action is a cognitive theory that provides a conceptual framework to understand human behavior in particular contexts (LaCaille, 2013). In summary, there is a casual chain formed by beliefs, attitudes, intentions and behavior (Rutter & Bunce, 1989). If people consider a behavior as positive, they will consequently regard it as important for their surroundings and the society. It is therefore more likely to for people to adopt that behavior (LaCaille, 2013). This theory supposes that people believe that they can adopt the behavior whenever they want (Staats, 2004).

The TRA framework relates beliefs, attitudes, intentions and behaviors (Fishbein & Ajzen, 1975b). For these authors, people form beliefs about objects based on direct information and observation from external sources or through inference processes. Next, beliefs determine the attitude of an individual towards the object. Attitude is a learned predisposition to respond in a consistent manner favorably or unfavorably towards a specific object. Therefore, this attitude leads to intentions that reflect a specific amount of effect towards this object. Finally, each intention is related to a specific behaviour. The performance of a particular behavior may modify the existing belief about the object.

Fishbein (2008) described the steps of application of the Theory of Reasoned Action. First, it requires the identification of the behaviour or behavious that an individual wishes to understand, predict, change, or reinforce. Next, the selection of the population must be considered. Based on measures of the central variables of the theory from beliefs to behaviors, the Theory of Reasoned Action is deployed to understand why members of the population adopt a certain behaviour, whilst others do not. In fact, the principle of correspondence or compatibility is critical to ensure an accurate prediction and total understanding of a particular behavior (Fishbein, 2008).

Attitude

There is a person's beliefs about the ramifications of the behaviour based on the appraisal of the importance of those ramifications (Ajzen, 1991). i.e. it is a whole evaluation of a specific result as negative or positive, and the expected probability of this result (Eagly & Chaiken, 1993; Hutchings & Michailova, 2004). Branley and Covey (2018) measured attitude towards specific behavior by identifying the personal benefit or risk an individual may perceive (Branley & Covey, 2018). In terms of behavioural intention toward green purchase, the attitude of Chinese consumers plays the most important role in predicting this behaviour (Liu, Liu, & Mo, 2020). The favourable or unfavourable attitude toward specific behaviour will estimate the intention to behave in a similar way (Liu, Hsueh, & Chen, 2018; Verma, Chandra, & Kumar, 2019). For instance, if students have a favourable attitude toward knowledge dissemination and sharing, this will increase the intention to do such dissemination (Arpaci & Baloğlu, 2016).

Based on the TRA, the behavioral intention is the main antecedent of this behavior and that intention is affected by attitude toward this same behavior which result in actual behavior (Fishbein & Ajzen, 1975a), e.g. with clear CSR messages, attitude predicted the intention to purchase from a brand (Kang & Hustvedt, 2014; Yan, Ogle, & Hyllegard, 2010). Furthermore, from psychological perspective, Attitude is identified to be an important latent factor affecting the behavioral intention (Lien, Cao, & Zhou, 2017). Consumers' attitude considered to be among the most siginficant factors in predicting their response (Lien & Cao, 2014). Consumers attitude towards media may identify how the e-WoM could be an effective communication tool to response to consumers concerns about product or service (Gan & Wang, 2017). Attitude positively predicted the behavior of social media users e-WoM engagement (Chu & Kim, 2011). Chu, Chen, and Gan (2020) found that Chinese consumers' attitude has a direct effect on their intention to engage with corporate social responsibility (CSR) in social media while it has no effect from American consumers' perspective, therefore the level of interdependent cultural orientation may have its effect in forming those attitude. Moreover, attitude toward using WeChat did not have effect on e-WoM engagement (Pang, 2021). However, in contemporaneous study, if the consumer believes that the result of specific behaviour will be negative, then they will hold an unfavourable attitude towards the behaviour, and vice versa. Therefore, this study hypothesises:

Hypothesis one: Attitude influences significantly the intention to use e-WoM over social media platforms.
Hypothesis four: Attitude influences significantly the CE in CSRC in SM.

Subjective Norms

Subjective norms represent the extent to which the reference groups (e.g. important people such as family members, friends, colleagues) are important, and create social pressure on individuals to engage in a specific behaviour (Ajzen, 1991; Ajzen & Fishbein, 2005; Sia & Jose, 2019). Subjective norms are expected to have a significant influence on behavioural intention (Ajzen, 1991). Furthermore, many studies support that subjective norms hold a significant effect on an individual's intention to act in a specific manner (Sia & Jose, 2019), e.g. consumers intention toward green purchase significantly affected by their subjective norms (Liu et al., 2020), purchasing organic food products (Basha & Lal, 2019), intention to purchase energy-saving devices (Zhao, Zhang, & Wang, 2019), and intention to bicycle-share for low carbon commuting (Cai et al., 2019). Subjective norm deemed to be vital factor in predicting pro-environmental behavioral intentions (Choi & Johnson, 2019), as well as it has significant effect on users' intention toward using sustainable bikes (Si, Shi, Tang, Wu, & Lan, 2020) and the intention toward environmentally friendly behavior (Chen & Tung, 2014). Further, subjective norm accepted to be effective in determining young consumers' intention toward buying green products (Yadav & Pathak, 2016). On other hand, the subjective norm did not has direct or indirect role in predicting pro-environmental behavioral intentions (Ateş, 2020). Moreover, neither direct nor indirect effect found on ecologically conscious consumer behavior (Taufique & Vaithianathan, 2018). However, in current study consumers who perceive more favorable the subjective norms will have a stronger intention to use e-WoM over social media. Accordingly, the study hypothesises:

Hypothesis two: Subjective norms influences significantly the intention to use e-WoM over social media platforms.
Hypothesis five: Subjective norms influences significantly the CE in CSRC in SM.

Moral Norms

This refers to "one's own socially determined and socially validated values attached to a particular behaviour" (Conner & Armitage, 1998). Also, it may be defined as "perceived moral obligation or personal norm" (Rivis, Sheeran, & Armitage, 2009). Moral norms were used interchangeably with personal norms in the literature (Botetzagias, Dima, & Malesios, 2015). Moral obligations may determine intentions, attitudes, subjective norms and perceptions of behavioural control (Ajzen, 1991). "Moral norms represent our learned expectations regarding the treatment of other individuals in interaction settings; i.e., they govern behaviour which has consequences for the welfare of others" (Liere & Dunlap, 1978). They occupy a special position among the predictors of behaviour (Botetzagias et al., 2015), and may be considered an additional form of normative pressure (Conner & Armitage, 1998). They raised the variance explained in intentions while controlling the Theory of Planned Behavior factors (Rivis et al., 2009). In contrast, another study found that moral norms do not contribute to this theory in understanding intentions (Kaiser & Scheuthle, 2003).

However, the impact of moral norms on behavior depends upon the definition adopted by the individual in the moral choice situation (Schwartz, 1968). When an individual makes a moral choice decision, their moral norms inform and influence their behaviour, these norms should be activated to determine individual behaviors. Two conditions should be satisfied to activate moral norms when an individual confronts a decision: first, the individual considers that their potential actions may influence the welfare of others. Secondly, the individual must attribute some responsibility for these actions and their effects to himself. Furthermore, Conner and Armitage (1998) found that moral norms are significant predictors of intentions. However, Ajzen (1991) assumed that, in addition to the pressure from the important references, the moral obligation towards specific behaviours should be considered in certain situations. Hence, Conner and Armitage (1998) suggested that moral norms, along with subjective norms and attitude, have the same influence on behaviour, especially in certain situations where the ethical or moral considerations are involved. Moreover, the predictive power of subjective norms itself is relatively weak in estimating behavioural intention (Bagozzi, Wong, Abe, & Bergami, 2000). Thus, moral norms are included to strengthen the predictive ability of subjective norms and attitude (Thogersen & Olander, 2006). Consequently, many scholars include moral norms in their models, in addition to subjective norms and attitude, and found they are a significant estimator of recycling (Chan & Bishop, 2013), purchasing organic food (Arvola et al., 2008), saving energy (Chen, 2016), visiting green hotels (Chen

& Tung, 2014), and consumers' intention to purchase green products (Liu et al., 2020). Thus, this study investigates the direct effect of moral norms on intention to use e-WoM over social media. Therefore, the following hypotheses are suggested:

Hypothesis three: Moral norms influences significantly the intention to use e-WoM over social media platforms.
Hypothesis six: Moral norms influences significantly the CE in CSRC in SM.

E-WoM and Consumer Engagement in CSR on Social Media

Companies considered word of mouth (WoM) to be an incredibly significant form of communication that affects consumers' behaviour (Reimer & Benkenstein, 2018), In comparison to traditional advertisements methods, WoM has the highest degree of persuasiveness and credibility (Wirtz & Chew, 2002), as the communication between consumer-to-consumer possesses both of these characteristics (Trusov, Bucklin, & Pauwels, 2009). This strong and important method pushed companies to search for establishing tools and technological methods to transform this interaction between consumers to internet platforms, that provide a wide range, involving more consumers in the discussion, and providing their opinions in review forms, which in turn is considered a creditable and low cost method (Ahrens, Coyle, & Strahilevitz, 2013; Reimer & Benkenstein, 2018). Furthermore, advances in technology, and increased consumer consumption of social media, has instigated a shift to online purchasing (Alraja & Said Kashoob, 2019). Therefore, this creditable and low cost method, known as electronic word of mouth (e-WoM) has been widely implemented. Through which, consumers (potential, actual, and/or former) write any negative or positive statement about a company's product, and is made available online for others to read. Current advances in technology make it easy to attract consumers, to establish a virtual social community, and to bond with peers with no centralised control to discuss all related issues (Fatma, Ruiz, Khan, & Rahman, 2020). However, attraction became a fact with the intensive use of social media which is an appropriate tool for e-WoM (Kim, Sung, & Kang, 2014; Srivastava & Sharma, 2017), enabling the ubiquitous dissemination of e-WoM information among consumers (Sohn, 2014). These social media platforms allow, on a daily basis, conversations in forms of written texts, reviews, votes, videos, and pictures between consumers as well as opinion leaders. Such conversation will build an informative profile about products and services related to a specific brand (Erkan & Evans, 2016). Furthermore, as ease of use is considered one of the important factors that affects people adopting new technology (Davis, 1989), e-WoM over social media can be done only by liking, voting, forwarding, and/or sharing opinions with which consumers agree (Chu & Kim, 2011). This ease pushed consumers to stick to social media platforms in order to obtain the benefit of crowdsourcing, and gain information about the targeted brand (Barreda, Bilgihan, Nusair, & Okumus, 2015).

Empirical studies on e-WoM have a strong effect on purchasing decision as it save consumers time and to some extent it reduces the accompanied risk (Hennig-Thurau & Walsh, 2003). Communicating e-WoM has a significant influence on this decision, for example by recommending trialed products (Christodoulides, Michaelidou, & Argyriou, 2012; Jalilvand & Samiei, 2012; Samson, 2010), and provides supporting evidence for offline advocacy (Graham & Havlena, 2007), especially that e-WoM over social media has an effective role in shorting the sales cycle (Spekman & Dotson, 2009). It has recommended that the corporate brand profile over social media have a positive effect on brand image

(Bruhn, Schoenmueller, & Schäfer, 2012). Therefore, corporates may increase consumer involvement by providing more information about their products and activities (Sharma & Srivastava, 2017).

However, engaging consumers in e-WoM over social media may be affected by many different factors, for instance their attitude which represent the over-all effect of e-WoM communication in terms of goodness and badness (Ayeh, 2015; Fu, Ju, & Hsu, 2015). This study adopts three main factors as antecedents for e-WoM - attitude, subjective norms, and moral norms - which are expected to determine how consumers react to certain ideas discussed on social media in our case CSR activities.

The engagement forms a relationship with the stimulus as a result of their emotional reaction to that stimulus (Kapoor & Kulshrestha, 2011). Hence, implementing this concept on consumer engagement from corporate's perspective reflects consumers' behaviour toward the company (CSR activities), which may affect the company from different aspects not only purchasing its products (van Doorn et al., 2010). From the e-WoM perspective, consumers' behaviour towards firms may be seen in the form of writing reviews, sharing positive or negative experiences and opinions, recommendations, and co-creation in brand communities (Hollebeek, Glynn, & Brodie, 2014).

However, the current study aims to investigate the influence of e-WoM on CE in CSR activities on social media. Therefore, considering consumers' engagement in e-WoM communications, and understanding the main drivers of such engagement, we can determine consumers' willingness to share or request information with/from other consumers on social media in form of e-WoM. Previous studies have demonstrated that the consumer tendency toward purchasing intention will be increased upon their engagement in e-WOM communication (Baber et al., 2016; Yusuf, Che Hussin, & Busalim, 2018). Thus, in this study consumers who engage more in e-WOM communication on social media are expected to develop a higher engagement in the communication of CSR activities.

Consumer behaviour, in terms of decision-making process regarding CSR, is affected by consumers' awareness of companies' CSR activities, evaluation of the influencing factors and their antecedents like attitude, intention to purchase from firms that engaged in CSR activities, experience (good/bad), and product disposal (Beckmann, 2007).

Therefore, communicating CSR activities to consumers has significant effects that fall in the following areas: purchasing behaviour, response and attitude toward CSR, credibility, and overcoming skepticism. In this context, previous studies showed CSR communication has a positive effect on consumer's buying behaviour; for example, if consumers hold positive beliefs about companies' CSR activities, this will increase the potentiality of the intended behaviour, which in turn will be reflected on consumers brand loyalty (Bhattacharya, Korschun, & Sen, 2009; Du, Bhattacharya, & Sen, 2007; Schmeltz, 2012).

Technology has completely transformed business, changing the ways in which companies communicate with consumers, placing a greater emphasis on online, live brand experiences (Khan, Rahman, & Fatma, 2016; Loureiro, Gorgus, & Kaufmann, 2017; Morgan-Thomas & Veloutsou, 2013). In addition, consumers should be involved in any development activity which in turn should be communicated with them (Tuškej & Podnar, 2018). Therefore, an interactive approach with consumers has been adopted as a base for consumer brand engagement (Brodie, Hollebeek, Jurić, & Ilić, 2011), which is beyond the traditional method of consumer involvement to the intensive participation in companies activities and initiatives (Vivek, Beatty, & Morgan, 2012). In this context, previous research has shed light on the CE in brand activities on social media (Brodie, Ilic, Juric, & Hollebeek, 2013; Martínek, 2021; Tuškej & Podnar, 2018; Vernuccio, 2014). Drawing on the above-mentioned literature when studying active engagement, e-WoM on social media should be considered an antecedent of consumer engagement in CSR activities. Accordingly, the following is hypothesised:

Hypothesis seven: E-WoM over social media platforms influences significantly CE in CSRC in SM.

Previous research proved that e-WoM predicted by many factors such as performance value, social value and user satisfaction. On other hand many other factors were not able to do so such as emotional value, and value for money (Alrwashdeh, Jahmani, Ibrahim, & Aljuhmani, 2020). Furthermore, positive and negative e-WoM have a direct effect on consumer ethnocentrism towards two different brands. While only positive e-WOM was able to predict brand equity but the negative e-WOM was not (Sun, Gonzalez-Jimenez, & Wang, 2020). As well as it fully mediates the relation between website quality and trust (Al-Debei, Akroush, & Ashouri, 2015) and partially this relation (Septiari, 2018). WoM mediated the relationship between customer loyalty and marketing (Ngoma & Ntale, 2019). E-WOM adoption partially mediates the relation between purchase intention and eWOM credibility, while it fully mediates the relation between purchase intention and eWOM usefulness (Tien, Amaya Rivas, & Liao, 2019). Moreover, e-WoM mediated the relation between green purchasing intentions and the content marketing (Al-Gasawneh & Al-Adamat, 2020). Notwithstanding, e-WoM negatively affected the relation between online purchases and usefulness (Malik & Hadi, 2019). However, a review study conducted on the green purchase intention using factors of source credibility as antecedents, this review investigated whether e-WoM could play a mediation role between those factors which is proved by the result of the above-mentioned study(Rahim, Sulaiman, Chin, Baharun, & Muharam, 2016).

On the other hand, previous studies have demonstrated that e-WoM ply a significant mediation role in predicting the consumers intention towards engagement with CSR activities in social media. i.e. it mediates the relation between peer communication with weak ties, peer communication with strong ties, opinion leader, opinion seeker, and attitude toward CSR in social media (independent variables) and the consumers' engagement with CSR communication in social media (dependent variables)(Chu et al., 2020). Furthermore, e-WoM can play a moderating role between personal norms and behavioural intention (Han, 2015; Jaini, Quoquab, Mohammad, & Hussin, 2019; Moser, 2016). Moreover, e-WoM was found to play a significant role between consumer satisfaction and electronic purchasing (Kuo, Hu, & Yang, 2013), but no single study has investigated the mediation role of e-WoM between attitude, subjective norms, and moral norms. Therefore, this study considers incorporating e-WoM as a mediator in the relationship between the aforementioned variables, which is a relatively new relation in the literature. Thereby, the following hypothesis is proposed:

Hypothesis eight: E-WoM mediates the relationship between attitude and CE in CSRC in SM.
Hypothesis nine: E-WoM mediates the relationship between subjective norms and CE in CSRC in SM.
Hypothesis ten: E-WoM mediates the relationship between moral norms and CE in CSRC in SM.

RESEARCH METHODOLOGY

The main aim of this study is to empirically investigate the antecedents of CE in CSRC in SM post crisis (COVID-19) and e-WoM, as well as the link between the two latter constructs. This investigation will reflect the university students in a developing country (i.e. Oman)

Figure 1. Proposed framework

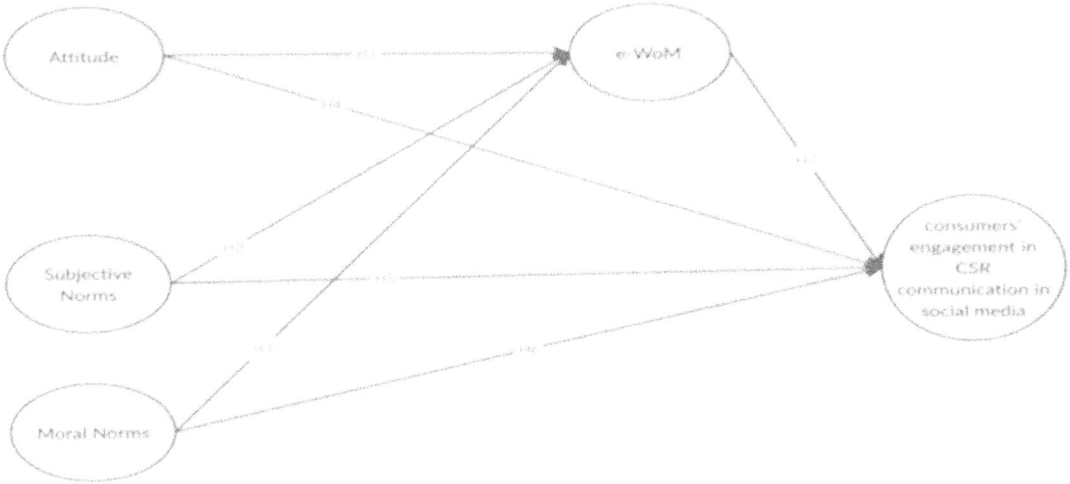

Population

The targeted population of this study will be University students in Oman who are active on social media, and have used online food delivery services at least once during the last year.

Sampling and Data Collection

In this study, the purposive sampling approach will be implemented which fits with both qualitative and quantitative techniques (Tongco, 2007). The following criteria were applied in the selection of the participants. They have to be: (1) University students (2) active on social media; and (3) concerned about corporate social responsibility. The research model was tested using data collected between February and March of 2021. Even though the data collected from one University but students are belong to all Oman's states which ensure good diversity in the research sample.

The data was collected from the targeted respondents using online questionnaire-based survey, because of the pandemic COVID 19. Explanation and guidance regarding ways to answer the questions were provided along with the study purpose. The confidentiality, anonymity of respondents was assured, and their data are not divulged to any third-party. Thereby, respondents were encouraged to provide accurate, honest, and trustful answers.

67.6% (n=196) of the respondents are female and 32.4% are male (n=94). The distribution in terms of age is as follows: 18-24 years (n=188), 25-34 years (n=71), 35-44 years (n=29), 45-59 years (n=2) and no one is older than 60. In terms of education, 2.4% (n=7) have reached the secondary level or below, 64.5% (n=187) undergraduate level, 4.1% (n=12) graduate level and 29% (n=84) postgraduate level. Almost two-third (65.5%) of interviewed respondents do not work and the remaining are distributed as follows: 1-3 years (9.3%), 4-6 years (6.2%), 7-9 years (8.3%) and 10 years and more (10.7%). Table 1 portrays the consumption of food delivery service.

Table 1. Consumer experience with OFD

	n	Frequency
Frequency of using Social Media		
0 to less than 1 hour	9	3.1%
1 to less than 2 hours	42	14.5%
2 to less than 4 hours	99	34.1%
4 to less than 6 hours	68	23.4%
6 to less than 8 hours	47	16.2%
8 hours and more	25	8.6%
Frequency of using OFD during the last year		
1 - 5 times	129	44.5&
6 - 10 times	35	12.1%
More than 10 times	126	43.4%
Total	290	100%

Measurements

The survey is based on brands of Food Delivery Service that are operating in the Omani market. The research questionnaire comprises items already developed and validated by previous research. Close-ended questions based on the Likert scale from "Strongly Disagree" (1) to "Strongly Agree" (5) were used to measure the other constructs. CE in CSRC in SM was measured by the items developed by (Chu et al., 2020). To assess environmental norms, the scale of (Bakti et al., 2020) was adopted. The (Razali, Daud, Weng-Wai, & Jiram, 2020) measurement was used to measure moral norms. Subjective norms were measured on the basis of the works (Ahmmadi, Rahimian, & Movahed, 2021; Bakti et al., 2020; Kim & Hwang, 2020; Razali et al., 2020). Finally, the measure of attitude is based on the works of, (Ahmmadi et al., 2021; Bakti et al., 2020; Cheow, Yeo, Goh, & Rezaei, 2017; Razali et al., 2020).

However, the items were adapted according to the current context i.e. university students in developing country by making few amendments. A group of three researchers related to our study area, and two experts from the industry, were asked to review the questionnaire to ensure that the questions are appropriate, readable and understandable in the context of the study. Arabic language will be utilized in the distribution questionnaire. Therefore, the questionnaire was reviewed by at least two bilingual faculty members.

Statistical Analysis Procedure

The collected quantitative data will be first scanned using the statistical analysis software SPSS 23. Then will be analysed using the Smart PLS 3.3.2. However, for measurement and model validity the following tests will be implemented: multi-collinearity, normality, common method bias, reliability, convergent validity and discriminant validity. For testing our proposed hypotheses, the study is based on Partial Least Squares-Structural Equation Modeling (PLS-SEM).

Data Analysis and Results

Measurement Model

First, there is no multi-collinearity as the variance inflation factor (VIF) varies between 1.305 and 2.576, which are under the tolerance limits set up by (Hair, Anderson, Tatham, & Black, 2010). The normality verified as skewness varies between -3 and 3, and kurtosis varies between -10 and 10 (Brown, 2015). To calculate common method bias, Harman's single-factor method is used. The single factor explains 30.6% of total variance. Thus, there is no common method bias as the total variance is less than 50%.

A confirmatory factor analysis was conducted to test the internal consistency, reliability and validity of the measurement model using the maximum likelihood estimation. All of the model fit indices were acceptable. Cronbach's Alpha is greater than the threshold of 0.6 for all constructs. In addition, the reliability is verified through the values of the composite reliability (CR) which exceed the cap of 0.7 for all constructs (Table 2). The average variance extracted (AVE) and factor loadings served to evaluate the convergent validity. All AVE are above the 0.5 and factor loadings exceed 0.5 and are significant at the 1% level leading to the assertion of the convergent validity (Table 2). To examine the discriminant validity, the square root of the AVE of each construct was compared to the correlation between constructs. Table 3 confirms the discriminant validity.

Table 2. Internal consistency, reliability and convergent validity

Construct	Cronbach's Alpha	CR	AVE
Attitude	0.811	0.869	0.573
Subjective Norms	0.868	0.901	0.602
Moral Norms	0.792	0.861	0.560
E-wow	0.828	0.875	0.539
CE in CSRC in SM	0.902	0.919	0.534

Table 3. Discriminant validity

Construct	Attitude	Subjective Norms	Moral Norms	E-WoM	CE in CSRC in SM
Attitude	0.757				
Subjective Norms	0.662	0.776			
Moral Norms	0.226	0.387	0.749		
E-WoM	0.434	0.486	0.493	0.734	
CE in CSRC in SM	0.335	0.413	0.410	0.639	0.730

Furthermore, as this study used PLS-SEM to test its hypotheses. One of benefits and attraction to PLS-SEM is that it tolerates unevenly distributed data, and the measurement quality of the inner model could be ensured with good reliability scores and validity scores, which has already been proven with scores that surpass 0.7 for reliability and validity scores that exceed 0.5. Furthermore, the results also show that the value of RMS theta is less than the threshold value (i.e. <0.14) (Henseler et al., 2014). Moreover, the calculated goodness of fit (GoF) is about 0.23 which falls in acceptable rang (even though it is small but very close to medium) (Henseler & Sarstedt, 2013).

Hypotheses Test

The findings reveal that attitude, subjective norms and moral norms positively influence e-WoM. Therefore, the hypotheses H1 (β=0.219; $p<0.01$), H3 (β=0.200; $p<0.01$), and H5 (β=0.367; $p<0.01$) are supported.

Furthermore, the results show that attitude, subjective norms and moral norms do not exert any significant effect on CE in CSRC in SM. Therefore, the hypotheses H2 (β=0.009; $p>0.01$), H4 (β=0.109; $p>0.01$) and H6 (β=0.103; $p>0.01$) are not supported. Also, e-WoM is positively related to CE in CSRC in SM supporting H7 (β=0.532; $p<0.01$).

Finally, the results demonstrate the significant mediation roles of e-WoM in the links between antecedents and CE in CSRC in SM. Hence, the hypotheses H8 (β=0.116; $p<0.01$), H9 (β=0.106; $p<0.01$) and H10 (β=0.195; $p<0.01$) are supported. All findings are presented in Table 4.

Table 4. Results of hypotheses testing

	Path	β	T Statistics	P-value	Result
H1	Attitude - e-wow	0.219	3.459	0.001	Supported
H2	Attitude - CE in CSRC in SM	0.009	0.155	0.877	Not Supported
H3	Subjective Norms - e-wow	0.200	2.822	0.005	Supported
H4	Subjective Norms - CE in CSRC in SM	0.109	1.550	0.121	Not Supported
H5	Moral Norms - e-wow	0.367	7.231	0.000	Supported
H6	Moral Norms - CE in CSRC in SM	0.103	1.676	0.094	Not Supported
H7	E-WoM - CE in CSRC in SM	0.532	9.283	0.000	Supported
H8	Attitude - e-wow - CE in CSRC in SM	0.116	3.301	0.001	Supported
H9	Subjective Norms - e-wow - CE in CSRC in SM	0.106	2.699	0.007	Supported
H10	Moral Norms - e-wow - CE in CSRC in SM	0.195	5.679	0.000	Supported

DISCUSSION

The COVID-19 pandemic has negatively impacted individuals and businesses globally. The main aim of this study is to empirically investigate the antecedents of CE in CSRC in SM post crisis (COVID-19) and e-WoM as well as the link between the two latter constructs. This investigation reflects the university students in a developing country, Oman.

To the best of the researchers' knowledge, this study could be considered one of the few pieces of pioneering research conducted during the COVID-19 pandemic, which developed a holistic model (framework) of CE in CSRC in SM, by incorporating moral norms with the Theory of Reasoned Action (TRA) as our theoretical underpinning. This incorporation aims to measure CE in CSRC in SM through e-WoM in a Middle Eastern developing country - Oman. The results of this study have demonstrated the importance of moral norms for the e-WoM as it has the highest impact level comparing to other influencing factors. The result is in alignment with sources (Chen, 2016; Chen & Tung, 2014; Liu et al., 2020). Moreover, the main adopted factors from the theory of reasoned action (i.e. Attitude, and Subjective Norms respectively) have a significant effect on e-WoM. This finding is in consistent with (Arpaci & Baloğlu, 2016; Basha & Lal, 2019; Liu et al., 2018, 2020; Verma et al., 2019).

These findings prove that consumers ensure buying the right brands through intensive reading of written reviews by group members on related social networks. In addition, they visit the written reviews about the products by other members on related social networks. Moreover, they do not hesitate to share the information they have about products and brands over the same social networks, which affected others' opinion towards a specific product or brand. Consumers are also willing and ready to share effectively their experience with a specific brand or product with members of social networks upon request. It can be assumed that it is essential to invest in social media and use it as a communication tool with consumers to inform, explain, and clarify all the firms' activities such as CSR activities, especially during crisis, more specifically during health crisis (COVID-19 pandemic) because the movement of consumers is restricted.

On the other hand, all our independent factors (moral norms, subjective norms, and attitude) show no direct impact on CE in CSRC in SM post crisis (COVID-19). This result agreed with (Chu et al., 2020) study, that found no direct relation between consumers attitudes and their engagement in CSR communication over social media, while the indirect relationship was significant.

Furthermore, our findings show a positive significant relationship between e-WoM and CE in CSRC in SM, supporting the finding of (Chu et al., 2020) study. However, the direct effect of attitude, subjective norm, and moral norm on the CE in CSRC in SM were not significant. This insignificant linkage here could possibly be attributable to the fact that users may less aware about CSR activities and their vital role in community. This may ensured by their focus on using social media application either to purchase or share their experience about specific brand . Another explanation may be that the investigated applications (Talabet and Tasleem) may focus more on responding consumers orders rather than collecting and providing information about the CSR activities of the purchased items' company. In addition, consumers may still have doubt whether their feedback about any CSR activities of any company will be conveyed to the respective company or not.

Whereas, the direct effect of attitude, subjective norm, and moral norm on e-WoM were positive. Consequently, as the e-WoM was found to have a positive effect on CE in CSRC in SM. Therefore, it is expected to enhance the relationship between the attitude, subjective norms, and moral norms and the CE in CSRC in SM. This finding may indicate that consumers are interested in discussing information about CSR activities, but they need a proper platform to express and share their experiences and perspectives.

THEORETICAL IMPLICATIONS

Based on our findings, the study contributes to the theoretical framework as follows: first, to the best of our knowledge, the theory of reasoned action and moral norms were not used to explain the CE in CSRC in SM. Therefore, the variable moral norms were integrated in the theory of reasoned action, and it was in line with this theory and supported its assumption. This considered a new extension of the above-mentioned model, specifically in terms of engaging in e-WoM to communicate CSR activities from educated people perspective under specific circumstance i.e. the COVID-19 pandemic. Second, this study looks at consumers' attitude, subjective norms and moral norms and how these factors influence their involvement in spreading e-WoM, especially when they were exposed to CSR related posts over social media. Consequently, understanding which of those factors are related to e-WoM, could propose methods to enhance the use of the e-WoM, which in turn could help increase CE in CSRC in SM. Furthermore, the extended model suggests that attitude, subjective norms and moral norms possess no direct effect on CE in CSRC in SM post crisis (COVID-19), and all those factors have an indirect effect on CE in CSRC in SM post crisis (COVID-19) through their engagement in e-WoM. Third, the results of this study practically evidenced CE in CSRC over SM platforms (e-WoM) through data collected from actual engaged consumers in online ordering and involved in social media groups. Fourth, enhanced the literature related to the field of CSR from a consumer perspective, which is partially covered by limited research comparing with companies-oriented CSR literature. Fifth, the central question still concerns the particular demographic of young (specifically University students) people in developing countries, whose dependence on social media could provide a platform for increasing CSR awareness.

PRACTICAL AND EDUCATIONAL IMPLICATIONS

If the senior management of corporations care about their society, and invest more time and effort in serving their community, they are more likely to adopt new social media technology and use it as communication medium. Therefore, the study's outcome offers managers opportunities to understand their consumers' attention toward companies CSR activities. Thus, proper action is needed, for example improving their companies CSR activities, reporting those activities in a proper way and increasing awareness about those activities especially over social media using e-WoM method.

The results of this study inspires firms' managers and decision makers to give more attention to the consumer's attitude, subjective norms and moral norms and, e-WoM factors during the crisis (COVID-19). Our findings also suggest that variables such as attitude, subjective norms, and moral norms have an indirect influence on the CE in CSRC in SM through e-WoM. Therefore, firms' top management and decision makers, especially in times of the crisis, would engage more with consumers and provide awareness sessions about the importance of their WoM, which expected to lead to: 1) sharing experiences, photos, videos, memes or gifs, thoughts about CSR activities of the selected brand company; 2) following and liking the product/brand of the company that offers CSR activities; 3) receiving and forwarding information from the selected brand regarding its CSR activities; 4) attending, gathering, creating groups over social media, and joining groups related to the product/brand of the company that offers CSR activities.

Furthermore, firms are highly requested to create their social media accounts as well as be active over social media networks and communicate with customers about firms' different activities especially those related to CSR, and motivate consumers to participate and share their experience and opinions on that platform. However, firms are highly advised to use different motivational strategies to increase the mentioned participation.

Moreover, the absence of empirical evidence, and best practices relating to the e-WoM and CE in CSRC in SM will make this study a strong target for educational institutions. Teaching CSR especially in times of crisis where practical case studies in academies are limited. Additionally, our theoretical framework and the discussed findings can offer valuable knowledge for academic staff when developing the curricula and teaching plans of modules.

CONCLUSION

People are increasingly and extensively using social media for personal as well as professional reasons. Marketers started to carefully consider the implication of consumer in CSR communication on Social media platforms. The current study explored the effect of environmental norms, subjective norms, moral norms, and attitude on consumers' engagement in CSR communication in social media, through the mediation role of e-WoM. These links were investigated on the basis of the theory of reasoned action and moral norm. The results show that all predictors affect positively e-WoM, which influences positively and significantly CE in CSRC in SM. This research comprises some contributions to the current literature. First, it contributes to the limited extant research, which treated the antecedents of consumers' engagement in CSR communication in social media CE in CSRC in SM. Secondly, the study was conducted among university students, in contrast to previous studies that investigated other categories predominantly in developed countries. In addition, it comprises a set of practical implications. The university students, particularly young people, form a considerable part of developing countries populations, and CSR in these contexts remains in its infancy. Therefore, marketers may better understand the mechanisms behind the commitment of this social category in CSR communication through social media. It is an interesting opportunity to spread awareness among this category of people which, in contrast to their predecessors, may create a new wave of CSR interest through social media platforms.

This research, however has some limitations. First, only two theories, namely theory of reasoned actions and moral norms were employed to investigate the antecedents of CE in CSRC in SM. The results are not generalisable as they are validated in the particular university context in Oman. The study does not explore the benefits of the dependent variable because the commitment of university students in CSR communication in social media may be inefficient or require other pre-existing conditions. This work provides some opportunities for further research. Other mediator and moderator constructs may be integrated in the theoretical model. Furthermore, other theories may serve as a solid theoretical basis to understand the predictors of CE in CSRC in SM. Therefore, it is interesting to investigate other contexts and categories.

REFERENCES

Ahmad, S. N., & Laroche, M. (2017). Analyzing electronic word of mouth: A social commerce construct. *International Journal of Information Management*, *37*(3), 202–213. doi:10.1016/j.ijinfomgt.2016.08.004

Ahmmadi, P., Rahimian, M., & Movahed, R. G. (2021). Theory of planned behavior to predict consumer behavior in using products irrigated with purified wastewater in Iran consumer. *Journal of Cleaner Production*, *296*, 126359. doi:10.1016/j.jclepro.2021.126359

Ahrens, J., Coyle, J. R., & Strahilevitz, M. A. (2013). Electronic word of mouth: The effects of incentives on e-referrals by senders and receivers. *European Journal of Marketing*, *47*(7), 1034–1051. doi:10.1108/03090561311324192

Ajzen, I. (1991). The theory of planned behavior. *Organizational Behavior and Human Decision Processes*, *50*(2), 179–211. doi:10.1016/0749-5978(91)90020-T

Ajzen, I., & Fishbein, M. (2005). The Influence of Attitudes on Behavior. In D. Albarracín, B. T. Johnson, & M. P. Zanna (Eds.), *The handbook of attitudes* (1st ed., pp. 173–221). Lawrence Erlbaum Associates Publishers. Retrieved from https://psycnet.apa.org/record/2005-04648-005?utm_source=mp-fotoscapes

Al-Debei, M. M., Akroush, M. N., & Ashouri, M. I. (2015). Consumer attitudes towards online shopping: The effects of trust, perceived benefits, and perceived web quality. *Internet Research, 25*(5), 707–733. doi:10.1108/IntR-05-2014-0146

Al-Gasawneh, J. A., & Al-Adamat, A. M. (2020). The mediating role of e-word of mouth on the relationship between content marketing and green purchase intention. *Management Science Letters, 10*(8), 1701–1708. doi:10.5267/j.msl.2020.1.010

Alraja, M. N., & Said Kashoob, M. A. (2019). Transformation to electronic purchasing: An empirical investigation. *TELKOMNIKA, 17*(3), 1209. doi:10.12928/telkomnika.v17i3.9390

Alrwashdeh, M., Jahmani, A., Ibrahim, B., & Aljuhmani, H. Y. (2020). Data to model the effects of perceived telecommunication service quality and value on the degree of user satisfaction and e-WOM among telecommunications users in North Cyprus. *Data in Brief, 28*, 104981. doi:10.1016/j.dib.2019.104981 PMID:31890816

Arpaci, I., & Baloğlu, M. (2016). The impact of cultural collectivism on knowledge sharing among information technology majoring undergraduates. *Computers in Human Behavior, 56*, 65–71. doi:10.1016/j.chb.2015.11.031

Arvola, A., Vassallo, M., Dean, M., Lampila, P., Saba, A., Lähteenmäki, L., & Shepherd, R. (2008). Predicting intentions to purchase organic food: The role of affective and moral attitudes in the Theory of Planned Behaviour. *Appetite, 50*(2–3), 443–454. doi:10.1016/j.appet.2007.09.010 PMID:18036702

Ateş, H. (2020). Merging Theory of Planned Behavior and Value Identity Personal norm model to explain pro-environmental behaviors. *Sustainable Production and Consumption, 24*, 169–180. doi:10.1016/j.spc.2020.07.006

Ayeh, J. K. (2015). Travellers' acceptance of consumer-generated media: An integrated model of technology acceptance and source credibility theories. *Computers in Human Behavior, 48*, 173–180. doi:10.1016/j.chb.2014.12.049

Baber, A., Thurasamy, R., Malik, M. I., Sadiq, B., Islam, S., & Sajjad, M. (2016). Online word-of-mouth antecedents, attitude and intention-to-purchase electronic products in Pakistan. *Telematics and Informatics, 33*(2), 388–400. doi:10.1016/j.tele.2015.09.004

Bagozzi, R. P., Wong, N., Abe, S., & Bergami, M. (2000). Cultural and situational contingencies and the theory of reasoned action: Application to fast food restaurant consumption. *Journal of Consumer Psychology, 9*(2), 97–106. doi:10.1207/S15327663JCP0902_4

Bakti, I. G. M. Y., Rakhmawati, T., Sumaedi, S., Widianti, T., Yarmen, M., & Astrini, N. J. (2020). Public transport users' WOM: an integration model of the theory of planned behavior, customer satisfaction theory, and personal norm theory. *World Conference on Transport Research - WCTR 2019, 48*, 3365–3379. 10.1016/j.trpro.2020.08.117

Barreda, A. A., Bilgihan, A., Nusair, K., & Okumus, F. (2015). Generating brand awareness in Online Social Networks. *Computers in Human Behavior*, *50*, 600–609. doi:10.1016/j.chb.2015.03.023

Basha, M. B., & Lal, D. (2019). Indian consumers' attitudes towards purchasing organically produced foods: An empirical study. *Journal of Cleaner Production*, *215*, 99–111. doi:10.1016/j.jclepro.2018.12.098

Beckmann, S. C. (2007). Consumers and Corporate Social Responsibility: Matching the Unmatchable? *Australasian Marketing Journal*, *15*(1), 27–36. doi:10.1016/S1441-3582(07)70026-5

Bhattacharya, C. B., Korschun, D., & Sen, S. (2009). Strengthening stakeholder-company relationships through mutually beneficial corporate social responsibility initiatives. *Journal of Business Ethics*, *85*(S2, SUPPL. 2), 257–272. doi:10.100710551-008-9730-3

Bialkova, S., & Te Paske, S. (2020). Campaign participation, spreading electronic word of mouth, purchase: How to optimise corporate social responsibility, CSR, effectiveness via social media? *European Journal of Management and Business Economics*, *30*(1), 108–126. doi:10.1108/EJMBE-08-2020-0244

Botetzagias, I., Dima, A. F., & Malesios, C. (2015). Extending the Theory of Planned Behavior in the context of recycling: The role of moral norms and of demographic predictors. *Resources, Conservation and Recycling*, *95*, 58–67. doi:10.1016/j.resconrec.2014.12.004

Branley, D. B., & Covey, J. (2018). Risky behavior via social media: The role of reasoned and social reactive pathways. *Computers in Human Behavior*, *78*, 183–191. doi:10.1016/j.chb.2017.09.036

Brodie, R. J., Hollebeek, L. D., Jurić, B., & Ilić, A. (2011). Customer Engagement: Conceptual Domain, Fundamental Propositions, and Implications for Research. *Journal of Service Research*, *14*(3), 252–271. doi:10.1177/1094670511411703

Brodie, R. J., Ilic, A., Juric, B., & Hollebeek, L. (2013). Consumer engagement in a virtual brand community: An exploratory analysis. *Journal of Business Research*, *66*(1), 105–114. doi:10.1016/j.jbusres.2011.07.029

Brown, T. A. (2015). *Confirmatory Factor Analysis for Applied Research* (2nd ed.). Guilford Press.

Bruhn, M., Schoenmueller, V., & Schäfer, D. B. (2012). Are social media replacing traditional media in terms of brand equity creation? *Management Research Review*, *35*(9), 770–790. doi:10.1108/01409171211255948

Cai, S., Long, X., Li, L., Liang, H., Wang, Q., & Ding, X. (2019). Determinants of intention and behavior of low carbon commuting through bicycle-sharing in China. *Journal of Cleaner Production*, *212*, 602–609. doi:10.1016/j.jclepro.2018.12.072

Carroll, A. B. (1979). A Three-Dimensional Conceptual Model of Corporate Performance. *Academy of Management Review*, *4*(4), 505. doi:10.5465/amr.1979.4498296

Carroll, A. B. (1991). The pyramid of corporate social responsibility: Toward the moral management of organizational stakeholders. *Business Horizons*, *34*(4), 39–48. doi:10.1016/0007-6813(91)90005-G

Chan, L., & Bishop, B. (2013). A moral basis for recycling: Extending the theory of planned behaviour. *Journal of Environmental Psychology*, *36*, 96–102. doi:10.1016/j.jenvp.2013.07.010

Chang, V., Wang, Y., & Wills, G. (2020). Research investigations on the use or non-use of hearing aids in the smart cities. *Technological Forecasting and Social Change, 153*, 119231. doi:10.1016/j.techfore.2018.03.002

Chen, M. F. (2016). Extending the theory of planned behavior model to explain people's energy savings and carbon reduction behavioral intentions to mitigate climate change in Taiwan-moral obligation matters. *Journal of Cleaner Production, 112*, 1746–1753. doi:10.1016/j.jclepro.2015.07.043

Chen, M. F., & Tung, P. J. (2014). Developing an extended Theory of Planned Behavior model to predict consumers' intention to visit green hotels. *International Journal of Hospitality Management, 36*, 221–230. doi:10.1016/j.ijhm.2013.09.006

Cheow, V., Yeo, S., Goh, S.-K., & Rezaei, S. (2017). Consumer experiences, attitude and behavioral intention toward online food delivery (OFD) services. *Journal of Retailing and Consumer Services, 35*, 150–162. doi:10.1016/j.jretconser.2016.12.013

Choi, D., & Johnson, K. K. P. (2019). Influences of environmental and hedonic motivations on intention to purchase green products: An extension of the theory of planned behavior. *Sustainable Production and Consumption, 18*, 145–155. doi:10.1016/j.spc.2019.02.001

Christodoulides, G., Michaelidou, N., & Argyriou, E. (2012). Cross-national differences in e-WOM influence. *European Journal of Marketing, 46*(11), 1689–1707. doi:10.1108/03090561211260040

Chu, S. C., Chen, H. T., & Gan, C. (2020). Consumers' engagement with corporate social responsibility (CSR) communication in social media: Evidence from China and the United States. *Journal of Business Research, 110*, 260–271. doi:10.1016/j.jbusres.2020.01.036

Chu & Kim, Y. (2011). Determinants of consumer engagement in electronic Word-Of-Mouth (eWOM) in social networking sites. *International Journal of Advertising, 30*(1). doi:10.2501/IJA-30-1-047-075

Conner, M., & Armitage, C. J. (1998). Extending the Theory of Planned Behavior: A Review and Avenues for Further Research. *Journal of Applied Social Psychology, 28*(15), 1429–1464. doi:10.1111/j.1559-1816.1998.tb01685.x

D'Acunto, D., Tuan, A., Dalli, D., Viglia, G., & Okumus, F. (2020). Do consumers care about CSR in their online reviews? An empirical analysis. *International Journal of Hospitality Management, 85*, 102342. doi:10.1016/j.ijhm.2019.102342

Davis, F. D. (1989). Perceived Usefulness, Perceived Ease of Use, and User Acceptance of Information Technology. *Management Information Systems Quarterly, 13*(3), 319. doi:10.2307/249008

De Grosbois, D. (2012). Corporate social responsibility reporting by the global hotel industry: Commitment, initiatives and performance. *International Journal of Hospitality Management, 31*(3), 896–905. doi:10.1016/j.ijhm.2011.10.008

Du, S., Bhattacharya, C. B., & Sen, S. (2007). Reaping relational rewards from corporate social responsibility: The role of competitive positioning. *International Journal of Research in Marketing, 24*(3), 224–241. doi:10.1016/j.ijresmar.2007.01.001

Du, S., & Vieira, E. T. Jr. (2012). Striving for Legitimacy Through Corporate Social Responsibility: Insights from Oil Companies. *Journal of Business Ethics, 110*(4), 413–427. doi:10.100710551-012-1490-4

Duan, W., Gu, B., & Whinston, A. B. (2008). Do online reviews matter? - An empirical investigation of panel data. *Decision Support Systems, 45*(4), 1007–1016. doi:10.1016/j.dss.2008.04.001

Eagly, A. H., & Chaiken, S. (1993). *The psychology of attitudes* (1st ed.). Harcourt Brace Jovanovich College Publishers. Retrieved from https://psycnet.apa.org/record/1992-98849-000

Erkan, I., & Evans, C. (2016). The influence of eWOM in social media on consumers' purchase intentions: An extended approach to information adoption. *Computers in Human Behavior, 61*, 47–55. doi:10.1016/j.chb.2016.03.003

Ettinger, A., Grabner-Kräuter, S., & Terlutter, R. (2018). Online CSR communication in the hotel industry: Evidence from small hotels. *International Journal of Hospitality Management, 68*, 94–104. doi:10.1016/j.ijhm.2017.09.002

Farzin, M., & Fattahi, M. (2018). eWOM through social networking sites and impact on purchase intention and brand image in Iran. *Journal of Advances in Management Research, 15*(2), 161–183. doi:10.1108/JAMR-05-2017-0062

Fatma, M., Ruiz, A. P., Khan, I., & Rahman, Z. (2020). The effect of CSR engagement on eWOM on social media. *The International Journal of Organizational Analysis, 28*(4), 941–956. doi:10.1108/IJOA-10-2019-1895

Featherman, M., Jia, S., Califf, C. B., & Hajli, N. (2021). The impact of new technologies on consumers beliefs: Reducing the perceived risks of electric vehicle adoption. *Technological Forecasting and Social Change, 169*, 120847. doi:10.1016/j.techfore.2021.120847

Fishbein, M. (2008). Reasoned Action, Theory of. In *The International Encyclopedia of Communication*. John Wiley & Sons, Ltd., doi:10.1002/9781405186407.wbiecr017

Fishbein, M., & Ajzen, I. (1975a). *Belief, Attitude, Intention, and Behavior: An Introduction to Theory and Research* (I. Ajzen, Ed.). Addison-Wesley Pub. Co.

Fishbein, M., & Ajzen, I. (1975b). *Belief, attitude, intention and behaviour: An introduction to theory and research*. Addison-Wesley. Retrieved from https://www.researchgate.net/publication/233897090_Belief_attitude_intention_and_behaviour_An_introduction_to_theory_and_research

Fu, J. R., Ju, P. H., & Hsu, C. W. (2015). Understanding why consumers engage in electronic word-of-mouth communication: Perspectives from theory of planned behavior and justice theory. *Electronic Commerce Research and Applications, 14*(6), 616–630. doi:10.1016/j.elerap.2015.09.003

Gan, C., & Wang, W. (2017). The influence of perceived value on purchase intention in social commerce context. *Internet Research, 27*(4), 772–785. doi:10.1108/IntR-06-2016-0164

Giakoumaki, C., & Krepapa, A. (2020). Brand engagement in self-concept and consumer engagement in social media: The role of the source. *Psychology and Marketing, 37*(3), 457–465. doi:10.1002/mar.21312

Graham, J., & Havlena, W. (2007). Finding the "missing link": Advertising's impact on word of mouth, web searches and site visits. *Journal of Advertising Research, 47*(4), 427–435. doi:10.2501/S0021849907070444

Hair, J. F., Anderson, R. E., Tatham, R. L., & Black, W. C. (2010). *Multivariate data analysis* (7th ed.). Prentice-Hall, Inc. Retrieved from https://dl.acm.org/citation.cfm?id=207590

Han, H. (2015). Travelers' pro-environmental behavior in a green lodging context: Converging value-belief-norm theory and the theory of planned behavior. *Tourism Management, 47*, 164–177. doi:10.1016/j.tourman.2014.09.014

Hennig-Thurau, T., Walsh, G., & Walsh, G. (2003). Electronic word-of-mouth: Motives for and consequences of reading customer articulations on the internet. *International Journal of Electronic Commerce, 8*(2), 51–74. doi:10.1080/10864415.2003.11044293

Henseler, J., Dijkstra, T. K., Sarstedt, M., Ringle, C. M., Diamantopoulos, A., Straub, D. W., Ketchen, D. J. Jr, Hair, J. F., Hult, G. T. M., & Calantone, R. J. (2014). Common Beliefs and Reality About PLS. *Organizational Research Methods, 17*(2), 182–209. doi:10.1177/1094428114526928

Henseler, J., & Sarstedt, M. (2013). Goodness-of-fit indices for partial least squares path modeling. *Computational Statistics, 28*(2), 565–580. doi:10.100700180-012-0317-1

Hollebeek, L. D., Glynn, M. S., & Brodie, R. J. (2014). Consumer brand engagement in social media: Conceptualization, scale development and validation. *Journal of Interactive Marketing, 28*(2), 149–165. doi:10.1016/j.intmar.2013.12.002

Hong, W., Chan, F. K. Y., Thong, J. Y. L., Chasalow, L. C., & Dhillon, G. (2013). *A Framework and Guidelines for Context-Specific Theorizing in Information Systems Research.* doi:10.1287/isre.2013.0501

Hutchings, K., & Michailova, S. (2004). Facilitating knowledge sharing in Russian and Chinese subsidiaries: The role of personal networks and group membership. *Journal of Knowledge Management, 8*(2), 84–94. doi:10.1108/13673270410529136

Jain, G., Paul, J., & Shrivastava, A. (2021). Hyper-personalization, co-creation, digital clienteling and transformation. *Journal of Business Research, 124*, 12–23. doi:10.1016/j.jbusres.2020.11.034

Jaini, A., Quoquab, F., Mohammad, J., & Hussin, N. (2019). "I buy green products, do you…?": The moderating effect of eWOM on green purchase behavior in Malaysian cosmetics industry. *International Journal of Pharmaceutical and Healthcare Marketing, 14*(1), 89–112. doi:10.1108/IJPHM-02-2019-0017

Jalilvand, M. R., & Samiei, N. (2012). The effect of electronic word of mouth on brand image and purchase intention: An empirical study in the automobile industry in Iran. *Marketing Intelligence & Planning, 30*(4), 460–476. doi:10.1108/02634501211231946

Kaiser, F. G., & Scheuthle, H. (2003). Two challenges to a moral extension of the theory of planned behavior: Moral norms and just world beliefs in conservationism. *Personality and Individual Differences, 35*(5), 1033–1048. doi:10.1016/S0191-8869(02)00316-1

Kang, J., & Hustvedt, G. (2014). Building Trust Between Consumers and Corporations: The Role of Consumer Perceptions of Transparency and Social Responsibility. *Journal of Business Ethics*, *125*(2), 253–265. doi:10.100710551-013-1916-7

Kapoor, A., & Kulshrestha, C. (2011). Branding and sustainable competitive advantage: Building virtual presence. In *Branding and Sustainable Competitive Advantage: Building Virtual Presence*. IGI Global. doi:10.4018/978-1-61350-171-9

Khan, I., Rahman, Z., & Fatma, M. (2016). The concept of online corporate brand experience: An empirical assessment. *Marketing Intelligence & Planning*, *34*(5), 711–730. doi:10.1108/MIP-01-2016-0007

Kim, S., Sung, Y., & Kang, H. (2014). Brand followers' retweeting behavior on Twitter: How brand relationships influence brand electronic word-of-mouth. *Computers in Human Behavior*, *37*, 18–25. doi:10.1016/j.chb.2014.04.020

Kim & Hwang, J. (2020). Merging the norm activation model and the theory of planned behavior in the context of drone food delivery services: Does the level of product knowledge really matter? *Journal of Hospitality and Tourism Management, 42*, 1–11. doi:10.1016/j.jhtm.2019.11.002

Kim. (2017). Consumer Responses to the Food Industry's Proactive and Passive Environmental CSR, Factoring in Price as CSR Tradeoff. *Journal of Business Ethics, 140*(2), 307–321. doi:10.1007/s10551-015-2671-8

Kong, S.-C., & Wang, Y.-Q. (2021). Investigating primary school principals' programming perception and support from the perspective of reasoned action: A mixed methods approach. *Computers & Education, 172*, 104267. doi:10.1016/j.compedu.2021.104267

Kuo, Y. F., Hu, T. L., & Yang, S. C. (2013). Effects of inertia and satisfaction in female online shoppers on repeat-purchase intention: The moderating roles of word-of-mouth and alternative attraction. *Managing Service Quality*, *23*(3), 168–187. doi:10.1108/09604521311312219

LaCaille, L. (2013). Theory of Reasoned Action. In *Encyclopedia of Behavioral Medicine* (pp. 1964–1967). Springer. doi:10.1007/978-1-4419-1005-9_1619

Li, F., & Du, T. C. (2011). Who is talking? An ontology-based opinion leader identification framework for word-of-mouth marketing in online social blogs. *Decision Support Systems*, *51*(1), 190–197. doi:10.1016/j.dss.2010.12.007

Lien, C. H., & Cao, Y. (2014). Examining WeChat users' motivations, trust, attitudes, and positive word-of-mouth: Evidence from China. *Computers in Human Behavior*, *41*, 104–111. doi:10.1016/j.chb.2014.08.013

Lien, C. H., Cao, Y., & Zhou, X. (2017). Service quality, satisfaction, stickiness, and usage intentions: An exploratory evaluation in the context of WeChat services. *Computers in Human Behavior*, *68*, 403–410. doi:10.1016/j.chb.2016.11.061

Liere, K. D., & Dunlap, R. E. (1978). Moral Norms and Environmental Behavior: An Application of Schwartz's Norm-Activation Model to Yard Burning1. *Journal of Applied Social Psychology*, *8*(2), 174–188. doi:10.1111/j.1559-1816.1978.tb00775.x

Lin, X., & Wang, X. (2020). Examining gender differences in people's information-sharing decisions on social networking sites. *International Journal of Information Management*, *50*, 45–56. doi:10.1016/j.ijinfomgt.2019.05.004

Liu, K. S., Hsueh, S. L., & Chen, H. Y. (2018). Relationships between environmental education, environmental attitudes, and behavioral intentions toward ecolodging. *Open House International*, *43*(2), 5–12. doi:10.1108/OHI-02-2018-B0002

Liu, L., Liu, Y., & Mo, Z. (2020). Moral norm is the key: An extension of the theory of planned behaviour (TPB) on Chinese consumers' green purchase intention. *Asia Pacific Journal of Marketing and Logistics*, *32*(8), 1823–1841. doi:10.1108/APJML-05-2019-0285

Loureiro, S. M. C., Gorgus, T., & Kaufmann, H. R. (2017). Antecedents and outcomes of online brand engagement: The role of brand love on enhancing electronic-word-of-mouth. *Online Information Review*, *41*(7), 985–1005. doi:10.1108/OIR-08-2016-0236

Maignan, I., & Ferrell, O. C. (2004). Corporate Social Responsibility and Marketing: An Integrative Framework. *Journal of the Academy of Marketing Science*, *32*(1), 3–19. doi:10.1177/0092070303258971

Malik, I. A., & Hadi, N. U. (2019). Inspirational Factors of Electronic Word of Mouth: A Case of Social Networking Sites. *Journal of Managerial Sciences*, *13*(2), 253–265. https://www.researchgate.net/publication/336651644_Inspirational_Factors_of_Electronic_Word_of_Mouth_A_Case_of_Social_Networking_Sites

Martínek, P. A. (2021). Mapping methods of research on consumer engagement with brands on social media: A literature review. *Methodological Innovations*, *14*(1). doi:10.1177/2059799120985384

Mkono, M., & Tribe, J. (2017). Beyond Reviewing: Uncovering the Multiple Roles of Tourism Social Media Users. *Journal of Travel Research*, *56*(3), 287–298. doi:10.1177/0047287516636236

Morgan-Thomas, A., & Veloutsou, C. (2013). Beyond technology acceptance: Brand relationships and online brand experience. *Journal of Business Research*, *66*(1), 21–27. doi:10.1016/j.jbusres.2011.07.019

Moser, A. K. (2016). Consumers' purchasing decisions regarding environmentally friendly products: An empirical analysis of German consumers. *Journal of Retailing and Consumer Services*, *31*, 389–397. doi:10.1016/j.jretconser.2016.05.006

Ngoma, M., & Ntale, P. D. (2019). *Word of mouth communication: A mediator of relationship marketing and customer loyalty*. doi:10.1080/23311975.2019.1580123

Pang, H. (2021). Identifying associations between mobile social media users' perceived values, attitude, satisfaction, and eWOM engagement: The moderating role of affective factors. *Telematics and Informatics*, *59*, 101561. doi:10.1016/j.tele.2020.101561

Pansari, A., & Kumar, V. (2017). Customer engagement: The construct, antecedents, and consequences. *Journal of the Academy of Marketing Science*, *45*(3), 294–311. doi:10.100711747-016-0485-6

Park, C., & Lee, T. M. (2009). Information direction, website reputation and eWOM effect: A moderating role of product type. *Journal of Business Research*, *62*(1), 61–67. doi:10.1016/j.jbusres.2007.11.017

Procter, L., Angus, D. J., Blaszczynski, A., & Gainsbury, S. M. (2019). Understanding use of consumer protection tools among Internet gambling customers: Utility of the Theory of Planned Behavior and Theory of Reasoned Action. *Addictive Behaviors*, *99*, 106050. doi:10.1016/j.addbeh.2019.106050 PMID:31522130

Rahim, R. A., Sulaiman, Z., Chin, T. A., Baharun, R., & Muharam, F. M. (2016). Measuring electronic word of mouth review adoption on green purchase intention using source credibility theory. *Advanced Science Letters*, *22*(12), 4283–4287. doi:10.1166/asl.2016.8129

Randle, M., Kemperman, A., & Dolnicar, S. (2019). Making cause-related corporate social responsibility (CSR)count in holiday accommodation choice. *Tourism Management*, *75*, 66–77. doi:10.1016/j.tourman.2019.05.002

Razali, F., Daud, D., Weng-Wai, C., & Jiram, W. R. A. (2020). Waste separation at source behaviour among Malaysian households: The Theory of Planned Behaviour with moral norm. *Journal of Cleaner Production*, *271*, 122025. doi:10.1016/j.jclepro.2020.122025

Reimer, T., & Benkenstein, M. (2018). Not just for the recommender: How eWOM incentives influence the recommendation audience. *Journal of Business Research*, *86*, 11–21. doi:10.1016/j.jbusres.2018.01.041

Rivis, A., Sheeran, P., & Armitage, C. J. (2009). Expanding the Affective and Normative Components of the Theory of Planned Behavior: A Meta-Analysis of Anticipated Affect and Moral Norms. *Journal of Applied Social Psychology*, *39*(12), 2985–3019. doi:10.1111/j.1559-1816.2009.00558.x

Rutter, D. R., & Bunce, D. J. (1989). The theory of reasoned action of Fishbein and Ajzen: A test of Towriss's amended procedure for measuring beliefs. *British Journal of Social Psychology*, *28*(1), 39–46. doi:10.1111/j.2044-8309.1989.tb00844.x

Samson, A. (2010). Product Usage and Firm-Generated Word of Mouth: Some Results from FMCG Product Trials. *International Journal of Market Research*, *52*(4), 459–482. doi:10.2501/S1470785309201405

Schmeltz, L. (2012). Consumer-oriented CSR communication: Focusing on ability or morality? *Corporate Communications*, *17*(1), 29–49. doi:10.1108/13563281211196344

Schmeltz, L. (2017). Getting CSR communication fit: A study of strategically fitting cause, consumers and company in corporate CSR communication. *Public Relations Inquiry*, *6*(1), 47–72. doi:10.1177/2046147X16666731

Schwartz, S. H. (1968). Awareness of Consequences and the Influence of Moral Norms on Interpersonal Behavior. *Sociometry*, *31*(4), 355. doi:10.2307/2786399

Sen, S., & Lerman, D. (2007). Why are you telling me this? An examination into negative consumer reviews on the web. *Journal of Interactive Marketing*, *21*(4), 76–94. doi:10.1002/dir.20090

Septiari, E. D. (2018). The Effect of eWOM as Mediation of Website Quality and Trust. *KINERJA Journal of Business and Economics, 22*(2), 142–155. Retrieved from https://ojs.uajy.ac.id/index.php/kinerja/article/view/1810

Sharma, R. W., & Srivastava, D. (2017). Measuring Customer Response to Word-of-mouth Messages on Social Media: Development of a Multi-item Scale. *Journal of Creative Communications, 12*(3), 185–204. doi:10.1177/0973258617722004

Sheppard, B. H., Hartwick, J., & Warshaw, P. R. (1988). The Theory of Reasoned Action: A Meta-Analysis of Past Research with Recommendations for Modifications and Future Research. *The Journal of Consumer Research, 15*(3), 325. doi:10.1086/209170

Si, H., Shi, J., Tang, D., Wu, G., & Lan, J. (2020). Understanding intention and behavior toward sustainable usage of bike sharing by extending the theory of planned behavior. *Resources, Conservation and Recycling, 152*, 104513. doi:10.1016/j.resconrec.2019.104513

Sia, S. K., & Jose, A. (2019). Attitude and subjective norm as personal moral obligation mediated predictors of intention to build eco-friendly house. *Management of Environmental Quality, 30*(4), 678–694. doi:10.1108/MEQ-02-2019-0038

Sohn, D. (2014). Coping with information in social media: The effects of network structure and knowledge on perception of information value. *Computers in Human Behavior, 32*, 145–151. doi:10.1016/j.chb.2013.12.006

Spekman, R. E., & Dotson, E. (2009). *Using Social Media in the B2B Context*. Academic Press.

Srivastava, D., & Sharma, R. W. (2017). Developing a Model for Studying the Antecedents and Effects of Word of Mouth (WoM) and e-WoM Marketing Based on Literature Review. *Jindal Journal of Business Research, 6*(1), 25–43. doi:10.1177/2278682117700307

Staats, H. (2004). Proenvironmental attitudes and behavioral change. In C. D. Spielberger (Ed.), Encyclopedia of Applied Psychology (vol. 3). Elsevier.

Sun, Y., Gonzalez-Jimenez, H., & Wang, S. (2020). Examining the relationships between e-WOM, consumer ethnocentrism and brand equity. *Journal of Business Research*. Advance online publication. doi:10.1016/j.jbusres.2019.09.040

Taufique, K. M. R., & Vaithianathan, S. (2018). A fresh look at understanding Green consumer behavior among young urban Indian consumers through the lens of Theory of Planned Behavior. *Journal of Cleaner Production, 183*, 46–55. doi:10.1016/j.jclepro.2018.02.097

The European Commission. (2011, October 25). *Corporate Social Responsibility: a new definition, a new agenda for action.* Retrieved April 2, 2021, from MEMO/11/730 website: https://ec.europa.eu/commission/presscorner/detail/en/MEMO_11_730

Thogersen, J., & Olander, F. (2006). The Dynamic Interaction of Personal Norms and Environment-Friendly Buying Behavior: A Panel Study1. *Journal of Applied Social Psychology, 36*(7), 1758–1780. doi:10.1111/j.0021-9029.2006.00080.x

Tien, D. H., Amaya Rivas, A. A., & Liao, Y. K. (2019). Examining the influence of customer-to-customer electronic word-of-mouth on purchase intention in social networking sites. *Asia Pacific Management Review, 24*(3), 238–249. doi:10.1016/j.apmrv.2018.06.003

Tongco, M. D. C. (2007). Purposive sampling as a tool for informant selection. *Ethnobotany Research and Applications, 5*, 147–158. doi:10.17348/era.5.0.147-158

Trusov, M., Bucklin, R. E., & Pauwels, K. (2009). Effects of Word-of-Mouth versus Traditional Marketing: Findings from an Internet Social Networking Site. *Journal of Marketing, 73*(5), 90–102. doi:10.1509/jmkg.73.5.90

Tuškej, U., & Podnar, K. (2018). Consumers' identification with corporate brands: Brand prestige, anthropomorphism and engagement in social media. *Journal of Product and Brand Management, 27*(1), 3–17. doi:10.1108/JPBM-05-2016-1199

van Doorn, J., Lemon, K. N., Mittal, V., Nass, S., Pick, D., Pirner, P., & Verhoef, P. C. (2010). Customer Engagement Behavior: Theoretical Foundations and Research Directions. *Journal of Service Research, 13*(3), 253–266. doi:10.1177/1094670510375599

Verma, V. K., Chandra, B., & Kumar, S. (2019). Values and ascribed responsibility to predict consumers' attitude and concern towards green hotel visit intention. *Journal of Business Research, 96*, 206–216. doi:10.1016/j.jbusres.2018.11.021

Vernuccio, M. (2014). Communicating Corporate Brands Through Social Media: An Exploratory Study. *International Journal of Business Communication, 51*(3), 211–233. doi:10.1177/2329488414525400

Vivek, S. D., Beatty, S. E., & Morgan, R. M. (2012). Customer engagement: Exploring customer relationships beyond purchase. *Journal of Marketing Theory and Practice, 20*(2), 122–146. doi:10.2753/MTP1069-6679200201

Wirtz, J., & Chew, P. (2002). The effects of incentives, deal proneness, satisfaction and tie strength on word-of-mouth behaviour. *International Journal of Service Industry Management, 13*(2), 141–162. doi:10.1108/09564230210425340

Wong, E., Leung, R., & Law, R. (2015). How Effective Are Asian Hotels in Communicating CSR Efforts Through the Property Websites? The Case of Hong Kong. In Information and Communication Technologies in Tourism 2015 (pp. 651–663). Springer International Publishing. doi:10.1007/978-3-319-14343-9_47

Wu, D. (2020). Empirical study of knowledge withholding in cyberspace: Integrating protection motivation theory and theory of reasoned behavior. *Computers in Human Behavior, 105*, 106229. doi:10.1016/j.chb.2019.106229

Yadav, R., & Pathak, G. S. (2016). Young consumers' intention towards buying green products in a developing nation: Extending the theory of planned behavior. *Journal of Cleaner Production, 135*, 732–739. doi:10.1016/j.jclepro.2016.06.120

Yan, R.-N., Ogle, J. P., & Hyllegard, K. H. (2010). *The impact of message appeal and message source on Gen Y consumers' attitudes and purchase intentions toward American Apparel*. doi:10.1080/13527260902863221

Yusuf, A. S., Che Hussin, A. R., & Busalim, A. H. (2018). Influence of e-WOM engagement on consumer purchase intention in social commerce. *Journal of Services Marketing*, *32*(4), 493–504. doi:10.1108/JSM-01-2017-0031

Zhao, C., Zhang, M., & Wang, W. (2019). Exploring the influence of severe haze pollution on residents' intention to purchase energy-saving appliances. *Journal of Cleaner Production*, *212*, 1536–1543. doi:10.1016/j.jclepro.2018.12.134

Zhou, J., Zhang, B., Tan, R., Tseng, M.-L., & Zhang, Y. (2020). Exploring the Systematic Attributes Influencing Gerontechnology Adoption for Elderly Users Using a Meta-Analysis. *Sustainability*, *12*(7), 2864. doi:10.3390u12072864

APPENDIX A: ABBREVIATIONS

Abbreviations	Concept
CSR	Corporate Social Responsibility
CE	Consumers' Engagement
CSRC	Corporate Social Responsibility Communication
SM	Social Media
WoM	Word of Mouth
e-WoM	Electronic Word of Mouth
CE in CSRC in SM	Consumers' Engagement in Corporate Social Responsibility Communication in Social Media
TRA	Theory of Reasoned Action

APPENDIX B: MEASURES

Attitude towards OFD services
Att1: Purchasing food through OFD services is wise
Att2: Purchasing food through OFD services is good
Att3: Purchasing food through OFD services is sensible
Att4: Purchasing food through OFD services is rewarding
Att5: I am interested in purchasing food through OFD services
Subjective norm
SN1: My family thinks that I should purchase food through OFD services
SN2: My friends think that purchasing food through OFD services is a good thing to do.
SN3: My colleagues think that I should purchase food through OFD services
SN4: My community thinks that I should purchase food through OFD services
SN5: Individuals whose opinions are valuable to me, they confirmed the purchasing food through OFD services.
SN6: If I purchase food through OFD services, important people approve this behavior.
Moral norm
MN1: I feel shameful if I do not purchase food through OFD services even if nobody is aware of my action
MN2: I feel guilty when I don't purchase food through OFD services
MN3: I hope I can be thought as a person that purchase food through OFD services
MN4: I feel an obligation to choose an environmentally friendly way, such as purchasing food through OFD services when ordering food.
MN5: Regardless of what other people do, because of my own values/principles, I feel that I should behave in an environmentally friendly way when ordering food.
MN6: I feel it is important that consumers behave in a sustainable way when ordering food.
MN7: The society needs to prioritize using the OFD services than the traditional method (in person)
e-WOM Intention
e-WoMI1: I will invite friends to learn more about [Brand]'s CSR on social media
e-WoMI2: I will recommend [Brand]'s CSR on social media to my friends
e-WoMI3: I will talk about [Brand]'s CSR on social media
e-WoMI4: I will talk positively about [Brand]'s CSR on social media
Consumers' Engagement with CSR Communication in Social Media
CSR1: Posting personal experiences related to [Brand]'s CSR activities
CSR2: Friending, liking or following [Brand]'s CSR activities
CSR3: Posting or sharing thoughts about [Brand]'s CSR activities
CSR4: Posting or sharing photos, videos, memes or gifs created by others that relate to [Brand]'s CSR5 activities
CSR6: Posting or sharing photos, videos, memes or gifs created by you that relate to [Brand]'s CSR activities
CSR7: Receiving messages or information from [Brand] regarding its CSR activities
CSR8: Forwarding someone else's discussion on [Brand]'s CSR activities to other people
CSR9: Joining groups dedicated to [Brand]'s CSR activities
CSR10: Creating a group dedicated to [Brand]'s CSR activities
CSR11: Attending a gathering regarding [Brand]'s CSR activities that you learned about through social media.

Compilation of References

Agenda for Sustainable Development. (2021). Accessed at: https://www.unssc.org/sites/unssc.org/files/2030_agenda_for_sustainable_development_kcsd_primer_en.pdf

Abad, F. J., Olea, J., Ponsoda, V., & García, C. (2011). *Medición en ciencias sociales y de la salud.* M. Síntesis, Ed..

Abitbol, A., Meeks, J., & Cummins, R. G. (2019). Does oil and goodwill mix? Examining the oil and gas industry's impact on stakeholder engagement on Facebook. *Environmental Communication, 13*(2), 192–208. doi:10.1080/17524032.2018.1546751

Accenture. (2019). *The decade to deliver a call to business action. The United Nations Global Compact - Accenture Strategy CEO study on sustainability 2019* [Report]. Accenture.

Adams, C. (2017). Conceptualising the contemporary corporate value creation processes. *Accounting, Auditing & Accountability Journal, 30*(4), 906–931. doi:10.1108/AAAJ-04-2016-2529

Adams, M., & Hardwick, P. (1998). An analysis of corporate donations: United Kingdom evidence. *Journal of Management Studies, 35*(5), 641–654. doi:10.1111/1467-6486.00113

Adnan, S. M., Hay, D., & Staden, C. J. (2018). The Influence of Culture and Corporate Governance on Corporate Social Responsibility Disclosure: A Cross Country Analysis. *Journal of Cleaner Production, 198*, 820–832. doi:10.1016/j.jclepro.2018.07.057

Aguinis, H., Villamor, I., & Gabriel, K. P. (2020). Understanding employee responses to COVID-19: a behavioral corporate social responsibility perspective. *Management Research: Journal of the Iberoamerican Academy of Management.*

Ahmad, T., Haroon, M. B., & Hui, J. (2020). Coronavirus Disease 2019 (COVID-19) Pandemic and economic impact. *Pakistan Journal of Medical Sciences, 36*(S4), S73.

Ahmad, S. N., & Laroche, M. (2017). Analyzing electronic word of mouth: A social commerce construct. *International Journal of Information Management, 37*(3), 202–213. doi:10.1016/j.ijinfomgt.2016.08.004

Ahmed, H., Mohieldin, M., Verbeek, J., & Aboulmagd, F. (2015, May). *On the Sustainable Development Goals and the role of Islamic finance* [Working paper]. Policy Research World Bank Group.

Ahmmadi, P., Rahimian, M., & Movahed, R. G. (2021). Theory of planned behavior to predict consumer behavior in using products irrigated with purified wastewater in Iran consumer. *Journal of Cleaner Production, 296*, 126359. doi:10.1016/j.jclepro.2021.126359

Ahrens, J., Coyle, J. R., & Strahilevitz, M. A. (2013). Electronic word of mouth: The effects of incentives on e-referrals by senders and receivers. *European Journal of Marketing, 47*(7), 1034–1051. doi:10.1108/03090561311324192

Ajzen, I. (1991). The theory of planned behavior. *Organizational Behavior and Human Decision Processes, 50*(2), 179–211. doi:10.1016/0749-5978(91)90020-T

Ajzen, I., & Fishbein, M. (2005). The Influence of Attitudes on Behavior. In D. Albarracín, B. T. Johnson, & M. P. Zanna (Eds.), *The handbook of attitudes* (1st ed., pp. 173–221). Lawrence Erlbaum Associates Publishers. Retrieved from https://psycnet.apa.org/record/2005-04648-005?utm_source=mp-fotoscapes

Akiyama, T. (2001). Coffee market liberalization since 1990. *Commodity market reforms: Lessons of two decades*, 83-120.

Al Mubarak, Z., Ben Hamed, A., & Al Mubarak, M. (2018). Impact of corporate social responsibility on bank's corporate image. *Social Responsibility Journal, 15*(5), 710–722. doi:10.1108/SRJ-01-2018-0015

Al-Debei, M. M., Akroush, M. N., & Ashouri, M. I. (2015). Consumer attitudes towards online shopping: The effects of trust, perceived benefits, and perceived web quality. *Internet Research, 25*(5), 707–733. doi:10.1108/IntR-05-2014-0146

Al-Gasawneh, J. A., & Al-Adamat, A. M. (2020). The mediating role of e-word of mouth on the relationship between content marketing and green purchase intention. *Management Science Letters, 10*(8), 1701–1708. doi:10.5267/j.msl.2020.1.010

Almond, B., & Wilson, B. (1998). *Values. A Symposium*. Humanities Press International, Atlantic Highlands.

Al-Omoush, K. S., Simón-Moya, V., & Sendra-García, J. (2020). The impact of social capital and collaborative knowledge creation on e-business proactiveness and organizational agility in responding to the COVID-19 crisis. *Journal of Innovation & Knowledge, 5*(4), 279–288. doi:10.1016/j.jik.2020.10.002

Alonso-Martínez, D., De Marchi, V., & Di Maria, E. (2019). Which country characteristics support corporate social performance? *Sustainable Development*. Advance online publication. doi:10.1002d.2018

Alraja, M. N., & Said Kashoob, M. A. (2019). Transformation to electronic purchasing: An empirical investigation. *TELKOMNIKA, 17*(3), 1209. doi:10.12928/telkomnika.v17i3.9390

Alrwashdeh, M., Jahmani, A., Ibrahim, B., & Aljuhmani, H. Y. (2020). Data to model the effects of perceived telecommunication service quality and value on the degree of user satisfaction and e-WOM among telecommunications users in North Cyprus. *Data in Brief, 28*, 104981. doi:10.1016/j.dib.2019.104981 PMID:31890816

Alt, E., & Craig, J. B. (2016). Selling issues with solutions: Igniting social intrapreneurship in for-profit organizations. *Journal of Management Studies, 53*(5), 794–820. doi:10.1111/joms.12200

Alter, K. (2007). *Social enterprise typology*. Academic Press.

Altschuller, S., Gelb, D. S., & Henry, T. F. (2010). IT as a resource for competitive agility: An analysis of firm performance during industry turbulence. *Journal of International Technology and Information Management, 19*(1), 1.

Amatulli, C., De Angelis, M., Costabile, M., & Guido, G. (2017a). *Sustainable luxury brands: Evidence from research and implications for managers*. Springer. doi:10.1057/978-1-137-60159-9

Amatulli, C., De Angelis, M., Korschun, D., & Romani, S. (2018). Consumers' perceptions of luxury brands' CSR initiatives: An investigation of the role of status and conspicuous consumption. *Journal of Cleaner Production, 194*, 277–287. doi:10.1016/j.jclepro.2018.05.111

Andersen, N. (2003). Polyphonic organizations. In T. Hernes & T. Bakken (Eds.), *Autopoietic organization theory* (pp. 151–182). CBS.

Angeli, W. (2017). Exploring Practitioners' Meaning of "Ethics," "Compliance," and "Corporate Social Responsibility" Practices: A Communities of Practice Perspective. *Business & Society, 59*(3), 518–544.

Aras, G., & Crowther, D. (2008). Governance and sustainability: An investigation into the relationship between corporate governance and corporate sustainability. *Management Decision, 46*(3), 434–448. doi:10.1108/00251740810863870

Arenius, P., & Minniti, M. (2005). Perceptual variables and nascent entrepreneurship. *Small Business Economics, 24*(3), 233–247. doi:10.100711187-005-1984-x

Ares-Blanco, S., Astier-Peña, M. P., Gómez-Bravo, R., Fernández-García, M., & Bueno-Ortiz, J. M. (2021). Gestión de los recursos humanos y estrategias de vacunación en atención primaria en Europa en la pandemia COVID-19. *Atencion Primaria, 53*(10), 102132. Advance online publication. doi:10.1016/j.aprim.2021.102132 PMID:34256236

Arguimbau-Vivó, L., Fuentes-Pujol, E., & Gallifa-Calatayud, M. (2013). A decade of documentary research on Scientometrics in Spain: Analysis of papers from the ISOC database (2000-2009). *Revista Espanola la de Documentacion Cientifica, 36*(2), 1–9.

Arpaci, I., & Baloğlu, M. (2016). The impact of cultural collectivism on knowledge sharing among information technology majoring undergraduates. *Computers in Human Behavior, 56*, 65–71. doi:10.1016/j.chb.2015.11.031

Arrighi, E., Blancafort, S., & Novell, A. (2010). *Manual para formadores en autocuidado y control de la diabetes tipo 2. Universidad de los Pacientes*. Fundación Joseph Laporte.

Arvola, A., Vassallo, M., Dean, M., Lampila, P., Saba, A., Lähteenmäki, L., & Shepherd, R. (2008). Predicting intentions to purchase organic food: The role of affective and moral attitudes in the Theory of Planned Behaviour. *Appetite, 50*(2–3), 443–454. doi:10.1016/j.appet.2007.09.010 PMID:18036702

Ateş, H. (2020). Merging Theory of Planned Behavior and Value Identity Personal norm model to explain pro-environmental behaviors. *Sustainable Production and Consumption, 24*, 169–180. doi:10.1016/j.spc.2020.07.006

Atzori, R., Shapoval, V., & Murphy, K. S. (2018). Measuring Generation Y consumers' perceptions of green practices at Starbucks: An IPA analysis. *Journal of Foodservice Business Research, 21*(1), 1–21.

Augier, M., & Teece, D. J. (2009). Dynamic Capabilities and the Role of Managers in Business Strategy and Economic Performance. *Organization Science, 20*(2), 410–421. doi:10.1287/orsc.1090.0424

Augsburger, A. C., & Fondato, M. (2020). Salud y participación social. Las y los jóvenes en las estrategias de promoción de la salud. *Kairos, Revista de temas sociales*, (45). https://www.revistakairos.org/salud-y-participacion-social-las-y-los-jovenes-en-las-estrategias-de-promocion-de-la-salud/

Austin, J., Stevenson, H., & Wei-Skillern, J. (2006). Social and commercial entrepreneurship: Same, different, or both? *Entrepreneurship Theory and Practice, 30*(1), 1–22. doi:10.1111/j.1540-6520.2006.00107.x

Austin, M. J., & Claassen, J. (2008). Impact of organizational change on organizational culture: Implications for introducing evidence-based practice. *Journal of Evidence-Based Social Work, 5*(1–2), 321–359. doi:10.1300/J394v05n01_12 PMID:19064453

Autio, E., Kenney, M., Mustar, P., Siegel, D., & Wright, M. (2014). Entrepreneurial innovation: The importance of context. *Research Policy, 43*(7), 1097–1108. doi:10.1016/j.respol.2014.01.015

Avrampou, A., Skouloudis, A., Iliopoulos, G., & Khan, N. (2019). Advancing the Sustainable Development Goals: Evidence from leading European banks. *Sustainable Development, 27*, 743–757. doi:10.1002d.1938

Ayeh, J. K. (2015). Travellers' acceptance of consumer-generated media: An integrated model of technology acceptance and source credibility theories. *Computers in Human Behavior, 48*, 173–180. doi:10.1016/j.chb.2014.12.049

B Corp Spain. (2020). https://www.bcorpspain.es/

B Corporation. (2018). *Global Sustainable Investment Review*. http://www.gsi-alliance.org/wp-content/uploads/2019/03/gsir_review2018.3.28.pdf

B Corporation. (2020). *The Complete Guide to B Corp Certification for Small to Medium-Sized Enterprises Join the Global Movement of People Using Business as a Force for Good.* Author.

B Corporation. (2021). *Certified B Corporation.* https://bcorporation.net/

B Lab Spain. (2018). *Annual Report 2018.* https://issuu.com/bcorpspain/docs/memoria_anaul_b_lab_spain_2018

B the change. (2017). *Year in Review: The B Corp Impact in 2017.* https://bthechange.com/year-in-review-the-b-corp-impact-in-2017-f529a229921f

B the change. (2019). *A Year of Business as a Force for Good: 2019 in Review.* https://bthechange.com/a-year-of-business-as-a-force-for-good-2019-in-review-8e744ed4d620

Baber, A., Thurasamy, R., Malik, M. I., Sadiq, B., Islam, S., & Sajjad, M. (2016). Online word-of-mouth antecedents, attitude and intention-to-purchase electronic products in Pakistan. *Telematics and Informatics, 33*(2), 388–400. doi:10.1016/j.tele.2015.09.004

Bacq, S., Hartog, C., & Hoogendoorn, B. (2016). Beyond the moral portrayal of social entrepreneurs: An empirical approach to who they are and what drives them. *Journal of Business Ethics, 133*(4), 703–718. doi:10.100710551-014-2446-7

Bacq, S., & Janssen, F. (2011). Structuring the field of social entrepreneurship: A transatlantic comparative approach. In O. J. Borch, A. Fayolle, P. Kyrö, & E. Ljunggren (Eds.), *Entrepreneurship research in Europe: Evolving concepts and processes* (pp. 153–188). Edward Elgar Publishing Limited. doi:10.4337/9780857931757.00017

Bager, S. L., & Lambin, E. F. (2020). Sustainability strategies by companies in the global coffee sector. *Business Strategy and the Environment, 29*(8), 3555–3570.

Bagozzi, R. P., Wong, N., Abe, S., & Bergami, M. (2000). Cultural and situational contingencies and the theory of reasoned action: Application to fast food restaurant consumption. *Journal of Consumer Psychology, 9*(2), 97–106. doi:10.1207/S15327663JCP0902_4

Bain & Co. (2020). *The future of Luxury: Bouncing Back from Covid-19.* Retrieved from https://cutt.ly/hmd5Imn

Bakti, I. G. M. Y., Rakhmawati, T., Sumaedi, S., Widianti, T., Yarmen, M., & Astrini, N. J. (2020). Public transport users' WOM: an integration model of the theory of planned behavior, customer satisfaction theory, and personal norm theory. *World Conference on Transport Research - WCTR 2019, 48*, 3365–3379. 10.1016/j.trpro.2020.08.117

Banks, G. C., Pollack, J. M., Bochantin, J. E., Kirkman, B. L., Whelpley, C. E., & O'Boyle, E. H. (2016). Management's science-practice gap: A grand challenge for all stakeholders. Academy of Management Journal, 59(6).

Bansal, P. (2005). Evolving sustainably: A longitudinal study of corporate sustainable development. *Strategic Management Journal, 26*(3), 197–218. doi:10.1002mj.441

Bansal, P., & Hoffman, A. J. (2012). *The Oxford Handbook of Business and the Natural Environment.* OUP.

Bapuji, H., Husted, B. W., Lu, J., & Mir, R. (2018). Value Creation, Appropriation, and Distribution: How Firms Contribute to Societal Economic Inequality. *Business & Society, 57*(6), 983–109. doi:10.1177/0007650318758390

Baraibar-Diez, E., Luna, M., Odriozola, M. D., & Llorente, I. (2020). Mapping social impact: A bibliometric analysis. *Sustainability, 12*(22), 1–20. doi:10.3390u12229389

Barbeito-Caamaño, A., & Chalmeta, R. (2020). Using big data to evaluate corporate social responsibility and sustainable development practices. *Corporate Social Responsibility and Environmental Management, 27*(6), 2831–2848. doi:10.1002/csr.2006

Barnett, M. L., Henriques, I., & Husted, B. W. (2020). Beyond good intentions: Designing CSR initiatives for greater social impact. *Journal of Management, 46*(6), 937–964. doi:10.1177/0149206319900539

Barney, J. (1991). Firm resources and sustained competitive advantage. *Journal of Management, 17*(1), 99–120. doi:10.1177/014920639101700108

Barney, J. B. (1986). Organizational Culture: Can It Be a Source of Sustained Competitive Advantage? *Academy of Management Review, 11*(3), 656–665. doi:10.5465/amr.1986.4306261

Barney, J. B. (1995). Looking inside for competitive advantage. *The Academy of Management Perspectives, 9*(4), 49–61. doi:10.5465/ame.1995.9512032192

Baron, D. P. (2007). Corporate social responsibility and social entrepreneurship. *Journal of Economics & Management Strategy, 16*(3), 683–717. doi:10.1111/j.1530-9134.2007.00154.x

Barreda, A. A., Bilgihan, A., Nusair, K., & Okumus, F. (2015). Generating brand awareness in Online Social Networks. *Computers in Human Behavior, 50*, 600–609. doi:10.1016/j.chb.2015.03.023

Barrena, J., López, M., & Romero, P. (2016). Corporate social responsibility: Evolution through institutional and stakeholder perspectives. *European Journal of Management and Business Economics, 25*(1), 8–14. doi:10.1016/j.redee.2015.11.002

Basha, M. B., & Lal, D. (2019). Indian consumers' attitudes towards purchasing organically produced foods: An empirical study. *Journal of Cleaner Production, 215*, 99–111. doi:10.1016/j.jclepro.2018.12.098

Bashir, M. F., Benjiang, M. A., & Shahzad, L. (2020). A brief review of socio-economic and environmental impact of Covid-19. *Air Quality, Atmosphere & Health, 13*(12), 1403–1409. doi:10.100711869-020-00894-8 PMID:32837620

Batalhone, A. P., & Clement, D. (2018). How sustainability standards contribute to SDG 12. *International Trade Forum, 3*(3), 14–15. doi:10.18356/15645304-2018-3-6

Batra, D. (2020). The impact of the COVID-19 on organizational and information systems agility. *Information Systems Management, 37*(4), 361–365. doi:10.1080/10580530.2020.1821843

Battilana, J., & Lee, M. (2014). Advancing research on hybrid organizing - Insights from the study of social enterprises. *The Academy of Management Annals, 8*(1), 397–441. doi:10.5465/19416520.2014.893615

Baumgartner, R. J., & Ebner, D. (2010). Corporate Sustainability Strategies: Sustainability Profiles and Maturity Levels. *Sustainable Development, 18*(2), 76–89. doi:10.1002d.447

Baumgartner, R. J., & Rauter, R. (2017). Strategic perspectives of corporate sustainability management to develop a sustainable organization. *Journal of Cleaner Production, 140*, 81–92. doi:10.1016/j.jclepro.2016.04.146

BBC. (2020a). *Coronavirus: Vodafone offers 30 days free mobile data*. https://www.bbc.com/news/technology-52066048

BBC. (2020b). *How Covid-19 is changing women's lives*. https://www.bbc.com/worklife/article/20200630-how-covid-19-is-changing-womens-lives

Bebbington, J., & Unerman, J. (2018). Achieving the United Nations sustainable development goals. In *Auditing & Accounting*. https://www.emerald.com/insight/content/doi/10.1108/AAAJ-05-2017-2929/full/html

Bebbington, J., & Unerman, J. (2018). Achieving the United Nations Sustainable Development Goals: An enabling role for accounting research. *Accounting, Auditing & Accountability Journal, 31*(1), 2–24. doi:10.1108/AAAJ-05-2017-2929

Beckmann, S. C. (2007). Consumers and Corporate Social Responsibility: Matching the Unmatchable? *Australasian Marketing Journal, 15*(1), 27–36. doi:10.1016/S1441-3582(07)70026-5

Bedi, H. S., & Yadav, N. (2019). Social entrepreneurship: A conceptual clarity. *Our Heritage*, *67*(10), 1006–1016.

Bednarek, A., Wyborn, T., Cvitanovic, C., Meyer, R., Colvin, R. M., Addison, P. F. E., Close, S. L., Curran, K., Farooque, M., Goldman, E., Hart, D., Mannix, H., McGreavy, B., Parris, A., Posner, S., Robinson, C., Ryan, M., & Leith, P. (2018). Boundary spanning at the science-policy interface: The practitioners' perspectives. *Sustainability Science*, *13*(4), 1175–1183. doi:10.100711625-018-0550-9 PMID:30147800

Belz, F. M., & Schmidt-Riediger, B. (2010). Marketing strategies in the age of sustainable development: Evidence from the food industry. *Business Strategy and the Environment*, *19*(7), 401–416.

Ben Youssef, A., Boubaker, S., & Omri, A. (2018). Entrepreneurship and sustainability: The need for innovative and institutional solutions. *Technological Forecasting and Social Change*, *129*, 232–241. doi:10.1016/j.techfore.2017.11.003

Beretta, R. (1996). A critical review of the Delphi technique. *Nurse Researcher*. https://europepmc.org/article/med/27285530

Berg, F., Koelbel, J. F., & Rigobon, R. (2020). *Aggregate Confusion: The Divergence of ESG Ratings* [MIT Sloan School Working Paper 5822-19]. MIT Sloan School of Management.

Best Buy. (2020). https://corporate.bestbuy.com/best-buy-provides-free-tech-classes-for-kids-at-home

Bharadwaj, A. S. (2000). A resource-based perspective on information technology capability and firm performance: An empirical investigation. *Management Information Systems Quarterly*, *24*(1), 169–196. doi:10.2307/3250983

Bhattacharya, C. B., Korschun, D., & Sen, S. (2009). Strengthening stakeholder-company relationships through mutually beneficial corporate social responsibility initiatives. *Journal of Business Ethics*, *85*(S2, SUPPL. 2), 257–272. doi:10.100710551-008-9730-3

Bialkova, S., & Te Paske, S. (2020). Campaign participation, spreading electronic word of mouth, purchase: How to optimise corporate social responsibility, CSR, effectiveness via social media? *European Journal of Management and Business Economics*, *30*(1), 108–126. doi:10.1108/EJMBE-08-2020-0244

Bianchi, C., Reyes, V., & Devenin, V. (2020). Consumer motivations to purchase from benefit corporations (B Corps). *Corporate Social Responsibility and Environmental Management*, *27*(3), 1445–1453. doi:10.1002/csr.1897

Biloslavo, R., & Trnavčevič, A. (2009). Web sites as tools of communication of a "green" company. *Management Decision*, *47*(8), 1158–1173.

Blank, S. (2010, April 12). *Why startups are agile and opportunistic – pivoting the business model*. https://steveblank.com/2010/04/12/why-startups-are-agile-and-opportunistic-—-pivoting-the-business-model/

Blowfield, M. (2012). Business and development: Making sense of business as a development agent. *Corporate Governance: The International Journal of Business in Society*, *12*(4), 414–426. doi:10.1108/14720701211267775

BMW Group. (2019). *Sustainable Value Report*. Author.

Bocken, N. M. P., Short, S. W., Rana, P., & Evans, S. (2014). A literature and practice review to develop sustainable business archetypes. *Journal of Cleaner Production*, *65*, 42–56. doi:10.1016/j.jclepro.2013.11.039

Bonfanti, A., Battisti, E., & Pasqualino, L. (2016). Social entrepreneurship and corporate architecture: Evidence from Italy. *Management Decision*, *54*(2), 390–417. doi:10.1108/MD-08-2014-0532

Booth, R. (2020). BAME groups hit harder by Covid-19 than white people, UK study suggests. *The Guardian*. https://www.theguardian.com/world/2020/apr/07/bame-groups-hit-harder-covid-19-thanwhite-people-uk

Bosch-Badia, M. T., Montllor-Serrats, J., & Tarrazon, M. A. (2013). Corporate Social Responsibility from Friedman to Porter and Kramer. *Theoretical Economics Letters*, *3*(3A), 11–15. doi:10.4236/tel.2013.33A003

Boschee, J., & McClurg, J. (2003). *Towards a better understanding of social entrepreneurship. Some important distinctions*. Academic Press.

Boschee, J. (1995). Social entrepreneurship: Some non-profits are not only thinking about the unthinkable, they're doing it – Running a profit. *The Conference Board Magazine*, *32*(3), 20–25.

Bosma, N., Schøtt, T., Terjesen, S., & Kew, P. (2015). Social Entrepreneurship. In Global Entrepreneurship Monitor Special Topic Report. Academic Press.

Bosma, N. (2013). The Global Entrepreneurship Monitor (GEM) and its impact on entrepreneurship research. *Foundations and Trends in Entrepreneurship*, *9*(2), 143–248. doi:10.1561/0300000033

Botetzagias, I., Dima, A. F., & Malesios, C. (2015). Extending the Theory of Planned Behavior in the context of recycling: The role of moral norms and of demographic predictors. *Resources, Conservation and Recycling*, *95*, 58–67. doi:10.1016/j.resconrec.2014.12.004

Boto-Álvarez, A., & García-Fernández, R. (2020). Implementation of the 2030 Agenda Sustainable Development Goals in Spain. *Sustainability*, *12*(2546), 1–31. doi:10.3390u12062546

Bowen, H. P. (1953). *Social Responsibilities of the Businessman*. Harper.

Bowen, H. R., & Johnson, F. E. (1953). *Social responsibility of the businessman*. Harper.

Brammer, S., Branicki, L., & Linnenluecke, M. K. (2020). Covid-19, Societalization, and the Future of Business in Society. *The Academy of Management Perspectives*, *34*(4), 493–507. doi:10.5465/amp.2019.0053

Branco, M. C., & Rodrigues, L. L. (2007). Positioning Stakeholder Theory within the Debate on Corporate Social Responsibility. *Electronic Journal of Business Ethics and Organization Studies*, *12*(1), 5–15.

Branley, D. B., & Covey, J. (2018). Risky behavior via social media: The role of reasoned and social reactive pathways. *Computers in Human Behavior*, *78*, 183–191. doi:10.1016/j.chb.2017.09.036

Bravo Estévez, M., & Arrieta Gallastegui, J. J. (2005). El método Delphi. Su implementación en una estrategia didáctica para la enseñanza de las demostraciones geométricas. *Revista Iberoamericana de Educación*, *36*(7), 1–10. doi:10.35362/rie3672962

Bravo, C. (2018). *Identifying cross-country key drivers of social entrepreneurial activity*. University of San Diego. doi:10.22371/05.2018.014

Brieger, S. A., Bäro, A., Criaco, G., & Terjesen, S. A. (2020). Entrepreneurs' age, institutions, and social value creation goals: A multi-country study. *Small Business Economics*. . doi:10.1007/s11187-020-00317-z

Bringhenti, J., Zandonade, E., & Günther, W. (2011). Selection and validation of indicators for programs selective collection evaluation with social inclusion. *Conservation and Recycling*. https://www.sciencedirect.com/science/article/pii/S0921344911000668

Brock, D. D., & Steiner, S. (2009). *Social entrepreneurship education: Is it achieving the desired aims?* [Working paper]. Policy Research World Bank Group.

Brodie, R. J., Hollebeek, L. D., Jurić, B., & Ilić, A. (2011). Customer Engagement: Conceptual Domain, Fundamental Propositions, and Implications for Research. *Journal of Service Research*, *14*(3), 252–271. doi:10.1177/1094670511411703

Brodie, R. J., Ilic, A., Juric, B., & Hollebeek, L. (2013). Consumer engagement in a virtual brand community: An exploratory analysis. *Journal of Business Research, 66*(1), 105–114. doi:10.1016/j.jbusres.2011.07.029

Broman, G. I., & Robert, K. H. (2017). A framework for strategic sustainable development. *Journal of Cleaner Production, 140*, 17–31. doi:10.1016/j.jclepro.2015.10.121

Brouard, F., & Larivet, S. (2010). Essay of clarifications and definitions of the related concepts of social enterprise, social entrepreneur and social entrepreneurship. In A. Fayolle & H. Matlay (Eds.), Handbook of Research on Social Entrepreneurship. Edward Elgar Ed. doi:10.4337/9781849804684.00008

Brown, D. (2019). Google, Microsoft and Starbucks are some of the best places to work in the US, workers say. *USA Today*. Accessed at: https://www.usatoday.com/story/money/2019/03/28/google-among-best-companies-work-us-ranked-region/3276066002/

Brown, T. A. (2015). *Confirmatory Factor Analysis for Applied Research* (2nd ed.). Guilford Press.

Brozek, K. O. (2009). Exploring the continuum of social and financial returns: When does a nonprofit become a social enterprise? *Community Development Investment Review, 5*(2), 7–17.

Bruhn, M., Schoenmueller, V., & Schäfer, D. B. (2012). Are social media replacing traditional media in terms of brand equity creation? *Management Research Review, 35*(9), 770–790. doi:10.1108/01409171211255948

Brundtland, G. (1987). *Report of the World Commission on Environment and Development: Our Common Future*. Document A/42/427 of the United Nations.

Buhmann, K. (2018). Future perspectives: doing good but avoiding SDG-washing: creating relevant societal value without causing harm. In H. Mulder & S. V. Voort (Eds.), *OECD Guidelines for Multinational Enterprises: A Glass Half Full* (pp. 127–134). OECD and Nyenrode Business University.

Buhmann, K., Jonsson, J., & Fisker, M. (2019). Do no harm and do more good too: Connecting the SDGs with business and human rights and political CSR theory. *Corporate Governance, 19*(3), 389–403. doi:10.1108/CG-01-2018-0030

Buijink, W. F. J., Sellhorn, T., & Wagenhofer, A. (2019). Special issue: Regulation of corporate disclosure. *Schmalenbach Business Review, 71*(2), 131–136. doi:10.100741464-019-00075-w

Burch, S., Shaw, A., Dale, A., & Robinson, J. (2014). Triggering transformative change: A development path approach to climate change response in communities. *Climate Policy, 14*(4), 476–487. doi:10.1080/14693062.2014.876342

Burgess, S., & Sievertsen, H. H. (2020). *Schools, skills, and learning: The impact of COVID-19 on education*. Academic Press.

Burnard, K., Bhamra, R., & Tsinopoulos, C. (2018). Building Organizational Resilience: Four Configurations. *IEEE Transactions on Engineering Management, 65*(3), 351–362. doi:10.1109/TEM.2018.2796181

Busco, C., Fiori, G., Frigo, M. L., & Riccaboni, A. (2017). Sustainable Development Goals: Integrating sustainability initiatives with long-term value creation. *Strategic Finance*, (September), 28–37.

Butcher, B., & Massey, J. (2020). Are ethnic minorities being hit hardest by coronavirus? *The BBC*. https://www.bbc.co.uk/news/uk-52219070

Bygrave, W. D. (1989). The entrepreneurship paradigm: A philosophical look at research methodologies. *Entrepreneurship Theory and Practice, 14*(1), 7–26. doi:10.1177/104225878901400102

Byun, S. K., & Oh, J. (2018). Local Corporate Social Responsibility, media coverage, and shareholder. *Journal of Banking & Finance, 87*, 68–86. doi:10.1016/j.jbankfin.2017.09.010

Cagarman, K., Kratzer, J., von Arnim, L. H., Fajga, K., & Gieseke, M. J. (2020). Social entrepreneurship on its way to significance: The case of Germany. *Sustainability*, *12*(21), 1–13. doi:10.3390u12218954

Cai, S., Long, X., Li, L., Liang, H., Wang, Q., & Ding, X. (2019). Determinants of intention and behavior of low carbon commuting through bicycle-sharing in China. *Journal of Cleaner Production*, *212*, 602–609. doi:10.1016/j.jclepro.2018.12.072

Camarelles, F. (2020). La prevención y la promoción de la salud en tiempos de cambio. *Atencion Primaria*, *52*(2), 1–2. doi:10.1016/j.aprim.2020.09.006

Campos, M., Martínez-Martínez, S. L., & Diéguez-Soto, J. (2021). Financial Literacy and Innovation Performance in SMEs. In *Financial Management and Risk Analysis Strategies for Business Sustainability* (pp. 58–81). IGI Global. doi:10.4018/978-1-7998-7634-2.ch004

Cantanero, D. (2006). Descentralización y financiación autonómica del sistema sanitario español. *Economistas*, *24*(108), 201–205.

Cantarero, D. (2008). Desigualdades territoriales y equidad en el sistema sanitario español. *Cuadernos económicos de ICE*, (75), 141-166.

Cao, K., & Gehman, J. (2021). Certified B Corporations and Benefit Corporations. *Oxford Bibliographies in Management*. https://papers.ssrn.com/sol3/papers.cfm?abstract_id=3772009

Caputo, F., Leopizzi, R., Pizzi, S., & Milone, V. (2020). The Non-Financial Reporting Harmonization in Europe: Evolutionary Pathways Related to the Transposition of the Directive 95/2014/EU within the Italian Context. *Sustainability*, *12*(1), 92–104. doi:10.3390u12010092

Carlaw, K. I., & Lipsey, R. G. (2003). Productivity, Technology and Economic Growth: What is the Relationship? *Journal of Economic Surveys*, *17*(3), 457–495. doi:10.1111/1467-6419.00201

Carriles-Alberdi, M., López-Gutiérrez, C., & Fernández-Laviada, A. (2021). The influence of the ecosystem on the motivation of social entrepreneurs. *Sustainability*, *13*(922), 1–17.

Carr, N. G. (2003). IT doesn't matter. *EDUCAUSE Review*, *38*, 24–38. PMID:12747161

Carroll, A. B. (1979). A three-dimensional conceptual model of corporate performance. *Academy of Management Review*, *4*(4), 497–505. doi:10.5465/amr.1979.4498296

Carroll, A. B. (1991). The Pyramid of Corporate Social Responsibility: Toward the Moral Management of Organizational Stakeholders. *Business Horizons*, *34*(4), 39–48. doi:10.1016/0007-6813(91)90005-G

Carroll, A. B. (1999). Corporate social responsibility: Evolution of a definitional construct. *Business & Society*, *38*(3), 268–295. doi:10.1177/000765039903800303

Carroll, A. B. (2000). Ethical Challenges for Business in the New Millennium: Corporate Social Responsibility and Models of Management Morality. *Business Ethics Quarterly*, *10*(1), 33–42. doi:10.2307/3857692

Carroll, A. B. (2021). Corporate Social Responsibility: Perspectives on the CSR Construct's Development and Future. *Business & Society*, *60*(6), 1–21. doi:10.1177/00076503211001765

Carroll, A. B., & Buchholtz, A. K. (2014). *Business and Society: Ethics*. Sustainability, and Stakeholder Management, Nelson Education.

Carroll, A. B., & Buchholtz, A. K. (2015). *Business & society: Ethics, sustainability, and stakeholder management* (9th ed.). Cengage Learning.

Carroll, A. B., & Shabana, K. M. (2010). The Business Case for Corporate Social Responsibility: A Review of Concepts, Research and Practice. *International Journal of Management Reviews*, *12*(1), 85–105. doi:10.1111/j.1468-2370.2009.00275.x

Carroll, N., & Conboy, K. (2020). Normalising the "new normal": Changing tech-driven work practices under pandemic time pressure. *International Journal of Information Management*, *55*, 102186. doi:10.1016/j.ijinfomgt.2020.102186 PMID:32836643

Castillo-Villar, R. G. (2020). Identifying determinants of CSR implementation on SDG 17 partnerships for the goals. *Cogent Business & Management*, *7*(1), 1847989. doi:10.1080/23311975.2020.1847989

Cavender, R. (2018). The Marketing of Sustainability and CSR Initiatives by Luxury Brands: Cultural Indicators, Call to Action, and Framework. In *Sustainability in Luxury Fashion Business* (pp. 29–49). Springer. doi:10.1007/978-981-10-8878-0_3

Cervellon, M. C. (2013). Conspicuous conservation: Using semiotics to understand sustainable luxury. *International Journal of Market Research*, *5*(5), 695–717. doi:10.2501/IJMR-2013-030

Chandler, D., & Werther, W. B. Jr. (2013). *Strategic corporate social responsibility: Stakeholders, globalization, and sustainable value creation*. Sage Publications.

Chanel. (2020a). *Chanel announces climate commitments*. Retrieved from https://cutt.ly/lbbWChJ

Chanel. (2020b). *Channel. Mission 1.5º*. Retrieved from https://cutt.ly/ubbW5Hs

Chanel. (2021a). Retrieved from https://www.Chanel.com/

Chanel. (2021b). *Informe climático. Nuestro viaje hace un futuro bajo en carbono*. Retrieved from https://www.Chanel.com/es/informe-climatico/

Chang, C. H. (2011). The Influence of Corporate Environmental Ethics on Competitive Advantage: The Mediation Role of Green Innovation. *Journal of Business Ethics*, *104*(3), 361–370. doi:10.100710551-011-0914-x

Chang, D. S., & Kuo, L. C. R. (2008). The effects of sustainability development on firms' financial performance- an empirical approach. *Sustainable Development*, *16*(6), 365–380. doi:10.1002d.351

Chang, V., Wang, Y., & Wills, G. (2020). Research investigations on the use or non-use of hearing aids in the smart cities. *Technological Forecasting and Social Change*, *153*, 119231. doi:10.1016/j.techfore.2018.03.002

Chan, L., & Bishop, B. (2013). A moral basis for recycling: Extending the theory of planned behaviour. *Journal of Environmental Psychology*, *36*, 96–102. doi:10.1016/j.jenvp.2013.07.010

Charter, M., Peattie, K., Ottman, J., & Polonsky, M. J. (2006). *Marketing and Sustainability*. Centre for Business Relationships, Accountability, Sustainability and Society (BRASS). Available at: http://www.cfsd.org.uk/smart-know-net/links/smart-know-net.pdf

Chatterjee, S., & Haidi, A. S. (2012). *Regression analysis by example*. John Wiley & Sons.

Chaudhary, A., Hurrah, S. A., & Maqbool, S. (2020). The Influence of Corporate Social Responsibility on Actual Buying Behaviour: A Study of Indian Consumers. *Metamorphosis*, *19*(1), 21–28. doi:10.1177/0972622520931700

Chaudhary, R., & Akhouri, A. (2018). Linking corporate social responsibility attributions and creativity: Modeling work engagement as a mediator. *Journal of Cleaner Production*, *190*, 809–821. doi:10.1016/j.jclepro.2018.04.187

Cheah, I., Zainol, Z., & Phau, I. (2016). Conceptualizing country-of-ingredient authenticity of luxury brands. *Journal of Business Research*, *69*(12), 5819–5826. doi:10.1016/j.jbusres.2016.04.179

Chen, M. F. (2016). Extending the theory of planned behavior model to explain people's energy savings and carbon reduction behavioral intentions to mitigate climate change in Taiwan-moral obligation matters. *Journal of Cleaner Production, 112*, 1746–1753. doi:10.1016/j.jclepro.2015.07.043

Chen, M. F., & Tung, P. J. (2014). Developing an extended Theory of Planned Behavior model to predict consumers' intention to visit green hotels. *International Journal of Hospitality Management, 36*, 221–230. doi:10.1016/j.ijhm.2013.09.006

Chen, X., & Kelly, T. F. (2015). B-Corps—A Growing Form of Social Enterprise: Tracing Their Progress and Assessing Their Performance. *Journal of Leadership & Organizational Studies, 22*(1), 102–114. doi:10.1177/1548051814532529

Cheow, V., Yeo, S., Goh, S.-K., & Rezaei, S. (2017). Consumer experiences, attitude and behavioral intention toward online food delivery (OFD) services. *Journal of Retailing and Consumer Services, 35*, 150–162. doi:10.1016/j.jretconser.2016.12.013

Chesbrough, H. (2010). Business model innovation: opportunities and barriers. *Long Range Planning*. https://www.sciencedirect.com/science/article/pii/S0024630109000569

Chia, A., Kern, M. L., & Neville, B. A. (2020, July). CSR for Happiness: Corporate determinants of societal happiness as social responsibility. *Business Ethics (Oxford, England), 29*(3), 422–437. doi:10.1111/beer.12274

Choi, D., & Johnson, K. K. P. (2019). Influences of environmental and hedonic motivations on intention to purchase green products: An extension of the theory of planned behavior. *Sustainable Production and Consumption, 18*, 145–155. doi:10.1016/j.spc.2019.02.001

Choi, N., & Majumdar, S. (2014). Social entrepreneurship as an essentially contested concept: Opening a new avenue for systematic future research. *Journal of Business Venturing, 29*(3), 363–376. doi:10.1016/j.jbusvent.2013.05.001

Choi, T. M. (2014). Luxury fashion branding: Literature review, research trends, and research agenda. In T.-M. Choi (Ed.), *Fashion branding and consumer behaviours, International series on consumer science* (pp. 7–16). Springer. doi:10.1007/978-1-4939-0277-4_2

Chow Tai Fook Jewellery Group. (2020). *Sustainable Report 2020*. https://www.ctfjewellerygroup.com/file/Sustainability/reports/csr-report.pdf

Chow Tai Fook Jewellery Group. (2021a). *Brands*. Retrieved from https://www.ctfjewellerygroup.com/en/brands/our-brands.html

Chow Tai Fook Jewellery Group. (2021b). *Vision, mission & values*. Retrieved from https://www.ctfjewellerygroup.com/en/group/vision.html

Christodoulides, G., Michaelidou, N., & Argyriou, E. (2012). Cross-national differences in e-WOM influence. *European Journal of Marketing, 46*(11), 1689–1707. doi:10.1108/03090561211260040

Chu & Kim, Y. (2011). Determinants of consumer engagement in electronic Word-Of-Mouth (eWOM) in social networking sites. *International Journal of Advertising, 30*(1). doi:10.2501/IJA-30-1-047-075

Chu, S. C., Chen, H. T., & Gan, C. (2020). Consumers' engagement with corporate social responsibility (CSR) communication in social media: Evidence from China and the United States. *Journal of Business Research, 110*, 260–271. doi:10.1016/j.jbusres.2020.01.036

Cía, N. M., Pérez, M. P., Heras-Mosteiro, J., Ávila, G. G., Díaz-Olalla, J. M., & Aguilar, J. L. R. G. (2018). Encuentros y desencuentros entre salud comunitaria y sistema sanitario español. *Informe SESPAS 2018. Gaceta Sanitaria, 32*, 17–21. doi:10.1016/j.gaceta.2018.06.004

Clark, C., Rosenzweig, W., Long, D., & Olsen, S. (2004). *Double bottom line project report: Assessing social impact in double bottom line ventures. Methods catalog*ue [Working paper]. UC Berkeley Working Paper Series.

Clarkson, M. E. (1995). A stakeholder framework for analyzing and evaluating corporate social performance. *Academy of Management Review*, *20*(1), 92–117. doi:10.5465/amr.1995.9503271994

Claro, D. P., Laban Neto, S. A., & De Oliveira Claro, P. B. (2013). Sustainability drivers in food retail. *Journal of Retailing and Consumer Services*, *29*(3), 365–371. doi:10.1016/j.jretconser.2013.02.003

Clément, F., & Laurent, M. (2017). *A blueprint towards accounting for the management of ecosystems*. Academic Press.

Clifford, T. (2020). *Lululemon CEO expects digital growth momentum to continue post pandemic*. https://www.cnbc.com/2020/12/15/lululemon-ceo-expects-digital-growth-momentum-to-continue-post-pandemic.html

Cockerham, W. C., Hamby, B. W., & Oates, G. R. (2017). The social determinants of chronic disease. *American Journal of Preventive Medicine*, *52*(1), S5–S12. doi:10.1016/j.amepre.2016.09.010 PMID:27989293

Coffee Barometer. (2020). Accessed at: https://coffeebarometer.org/

Colleoni, E. (2013). CSR communication strategies for organizational legitimacy in social media. *Corporate Communications*, *18*(2), 228–248. doi:10.1108/13563281311319508

Colombo, M. G., & Piva, E. (2008). Strengths and Weaknesses of Academic Startups: A Conceptual Model. *IEEE Transactions on Engineering Management*, *55*(1), 37–49. doi:10.1109/TEM.2007.912807

Commission for the European Communities. (2001). *Green Paper. Promoting a European framework for Corporate Social Responsibility*. Author.

Commission of the European Communities. (2002). *Communication from the commission concerning corporate social responsibility: A business contribution to Sustainable Development*. https://op.europa.eu/en/publication-detail/-/publication/6e2c6d26-d1f6-48a3-9a78-f0ff2dc21aad/language-en

Conner, M., & Armitage, C. J. (1998). Extending the Theory of Planned Behavior: A Review and Avenues for Further Research. *Journal of Applied Social Psychology*, *28*(15), 1429–1464. doi:10.1111/j.1559-1816.1998.tb01685.x

Correia, S., Luck, S., & Verner, E. (2020). Pandemics depress the economy, public health interventions do not: Evidence from the 1918 flu. *Health Economics eJournal*.

Crane, A., Matten, D., Glozer, S., & Spence, L. (2019). *Business Ethics*. Oxford University Press.

Crane, A., Palazzo, G., Spence, L. J., & Matten, D. (2014). Contesting the value of creating shared value. *California Management Review*, *56*(2), 130–153. doi:10.1525/cmr.2014.56.2.130

Cruz, M. (2009). *El método Delphi en las investigaciones educacionales*. Editorial Academia.

Cuervo, Á., Ribeiro, D., & Roig, S. (2007). Entrepreneurship: concepts, theory and perspective. Introduction. In Á. Cuervo, D. Ribeiro, & S. Roig (Eds.), *Entrepreneurship* (pp. 1–20). Springer., doi:10.1007/978-3-540-48543-8_1

Cukier, W., Trenholm, S., Carl, D., & Gekas, G. (2011). Social entrepreneurship: A content analysis. *Journal of Strategic Innovation and Sustainability*, *7*(1), 99–119.

D'Acunto, D., Tuan, A., Dalli, D., Viglia, G., & Okumus, F. (2020). Do consumers care about CSR in their online reviews? An empirical analysis. *International Journal of Hospitality Management*, *85*, 102342. doi:10.1016/j.ijhm.2019.102342

Dacin, P. A., Dacin, M. T., & Matear, M. (2010). Social entrepreneurship: Why we don't need a new theory and how we move forward from here. *The Academy of Management Perspectives*, *24*(3), 37–57.

Dahlsrud, A. (2008). How corporate social responsibility is defined: An analysis of 37 definitions. *Corporate Social Responsibility and Environmental Management, 15*(1), 1–13. doi:10.1002/csr.132

Daimler Group. (2019). *Sustainability Report.* Author.

Daly, H. E. (1990). Toward some operational principles of sustainable development. *Ecological Economics, 2*(1), 1–6. doi:10.1016/0921-8009(90)90010-R

Danet, A., Prieto, M. A., Garrido, F., López, M., Luque, N., & March, J. C. (2017). Cronicidad y uso de servicios sanitarios: La formación entre iguales de la Escuela de Pacientes. *Revista da Escola de Enfermagem da U S P., USP51.* Advance online publication. doi:10.1590/S1980-220X2017004203280

Dantas, T. E. T., De-Souza, E. D., Destro, I. D., Hammes, G., Rodriguez, C. M. T., & Soares, S. R. (2021). How the combination of Circular Economy and Industry 4.0 can contribute towards achieving the Sustainable Development Goals. *Sustainable Production and Consumption, 26*, 213–227. doi:10.1016/j.spc.2020.10.005

Davis, F. D. (1989). Perceived Usefulness, Perceived Ease of Use, and User Acceptance of Information Technology. *Management Information Systems Quarterly, 13*(3), 319. doi:10.2307/249008

Davison, R. M. (2020). The transformative potential of disruptions: A viewpoint. *International Journal of Information Management, 55*, 102149. doi:10.1016/j.ijinfomgt.2020.102149 PMID:32836628

Davó, M. C., Gil-González, D., Vives-Cases, C., Álvarez-Dardet, C., & La Parra, D. (2008). Las investigaciones sobre promoción y educación para la salud en las etapas de infantil y primaria de la escuela española: Una revisión de los estudios publicados entre 1995 y 2005. *Gaceta Sanitaria, 22*(1), 58–64. doi:10.1157/13115112 PMID:18261445

Daye, M., & Gill, K. (2017). Social enterprise evaluation: Implications for tourism development. In P. J. Sheldon & R. Daniele (Eds.), *Social entrepreneurship and tourism. Philosophy and practice* (pp. 173–192). Springer International Publishing. doi:10.1007/978-3-319-46518-0_10

De Grosbois, D. (2012). Corporate social responsibility reporting by the global hotel industry: Commitment, initiatives and performance. *International Journal of Hospitality Management, 31*(3), 896–905. doi:10.1016/j.ijhm.2011.10.008

De Lange, D. E. (2017). Start-ups sustainability: An insurmountable cost or a life-giving investment? *Journal of Cleaner Production, 156*, 838–854. doi:10.1016/j.jclepro.2017.04.108

Debnath, A., Roy, J., Kar, S., Zavadskas, E., & Antucheviciene, J. (2017). A Hybrid MCDM Approach for Strategic Project Portfolio Selection of Agro By-Products. *Sustainability, 9*(8), 1302. doi:10.3390u9081302

Decreto 53/2013, de 2 de abril, del Gobierno de Aragón, por el que se regula el Consejo de Salud de Aragón. BOA de 11 de abril de 2013.

Deegan, C., & Gordon, B. (1996). A study of the environmental disclosure practices of Australian corporations. *Accounting and Business Research, 26*(3), 187–199. doi:10.1080/00014788.1996.9729510

Dees, J. G. (2001). *The meaning of "Social Entrepreneur".* Academic Press.

Defourny, J. (1994). *Développer l'enterprise sociale.* Foundation Roi Baudouin.

Defourny, J., & Nyssens, M. (2010). Conceptions of social enterprise and social entrepreneurship in Europe and the United States: Convergences and divergences. *Journal of Social Entrepreneurship, 1*(1), 32–53. doi:10.1080/19420670903442053

Defourny, J., & Nyssens, M. (2017). Fundamentals for an international typology of social enterprise models. *Voluntas, 28*(6), 2469–2497. doi:10.100711266-017-9884-7

Delbard, O. (2020). Corporate Social Responsibility beyond philanthropy? Sustainable and Responsible Business in times of Covid-19. In Managing a Post-Covid-19 Era, (pp. 258-265). ESCP.

Delmas, M. A., & Burbano, V. C. (2011). The drivers of greenwashing. *California Management Review*, *54*(1), 64–87. doi:10.1525/cmr.2011.54.1.64

Deloitte. (2020). *Global Powers of Luxury Goods 2020. The new age of fashion and luxury*. Available https://www2.deloitte.com/content/dam/Deloitte/global/Documents/Consumer-Business/gx-consumer-business-gplg-2020-report.pdf

Departamento de Sanidad del Gobierno de Aragón. (n.d.). *Salud Informa-Inicio*. https://www.saludinforma.es

Di Fabio, A. (2017). Positive healthy organizations: Promoting well-being, meaningfulness, and sustainability in organizations. Frontiers in Psychology, 8(1938).

Dietz, T. (1987). Theory and method in social impact assessment. *Sociological Inquiry*, *57*(1), 54–69. doi:10.1111/j.1475-682X.1987.tb01180.x

Dietz, T., Auffenberg, J., Chong, A. E., Grabs, J., & Kilian, B. (2018A). The voluntary coffee standard index (VOCSI). Developing a composite index to assess and compare the strength of mainstream voluntary sustainability standards in the global coffee industry. *Ecological Economics*, *150*, 72–87.

Diez-Busto, E., Sanchez-Ruiz, L., & Fernandez-Laviada, A. (2021, March 1). The B Corp movement: A systematic literature review. *Sustainability*, *13*(5), 1–17. doi:10.3390u13052508

Ditlev-Simonsen, C. D., & Wenstøp, F. (2013). How stakeholders view stakeholders as CSR motivators. *Social Responsibility Journal*, *9*(1), 137–147. doi:10.1108/17471111311307868

Doern, R., Williams, N., & Vorley, T. (2019). Special issue on entrepreneurship and crises: Business as usual? An introduction and review of the literature. *Entrepreneurship and Regional Development*, *31*(5-6), 400–412. doi:10.1080/08985626.2018.1541590

Doherty, B., Haugh, H., & Lyon, F. (2014). Social enterprises as hybrid organizations: A review and research agenda. *International Journal of Management Reviews*, *16*(4), 417–436. doi:10.1111/ijmr.12028

Donaldson, T., & Preston, L. E. (1995). The Stakeholder Theory of the Corporation: Concepts, Evidence, and Implications. *Academy of Management Review*, *28*(1), 65–91. doi:10.5465/amr.1995.9503271992

Dorado, S. (2006). Social entrepreneurial ventures: Different values so different process of creation, no? *Journal of Developmental Entrepreneurship*, *11*(04), 319–343. doi:10.1142/S1084946706000453

Douglas, A., & George, C. (2003). Implementing the EFQM excellence model in a local authority. *Managerial Auditing Journal*, *18*(2), 122–127. doi:10.1108/02686900310455100

Dowling, J., & Pfeffer, J. (1975). Organizational legitimacy: Social values and organizational behavior. *Pacific Sociological Review*, *18*(1), 122–136. doi:10.2307/1388226

Driscoll, D., & Hoffman, W. M. (2000). *Ethics Matters. How to Implement Values-Driven Management*. Centre for Business Ethics, Bentley College.

Duan, W., Gu, B., & Whinston, A. B. (2008). Do online reviews matter? - An empirical investigation of panel data. *Decision Support Systems*, *45*(4), 1007–1016. doi:10.1016/j.dss.2008.04.001

Dumay, J., Bernardi, C., Guthrie, J., & La Torre, M. (2017). Barriers to Implementing the International Integrated Reporting Framework: A Contemporary Academic Perspective. *Meditari Accountancy Research*, *25*(4), 461–480. doi:10.1108/MEDAR-05-2017-0150

Dumay, J., Frost, G., & Beck, C. (2015). Material legitimacy Blending organisational and stakeholder concerns through non-financial information disclosures. *Journal of Accounting and Organizational Change*, *11*(1), 2–23. doi:10.1108/JAOC-06-2013-0057

Durevall, D. (2020). Fairtrade and Market Efficiency: Fairtrade-Labeled Coffee in the Swedish Coffee Market. *Economies*, *8*(2), 30.

Du, S., Bhattacharya, C. B., & Sen, S. (2007). Reaping relational rewards from corporate social responsibility: The role of competitive positioning. *International Journal of Research in Marketing*, *24*(3), 224–241. doi:10.1016/j.ijresmar.2007.01.001

Du, S., Bhattacharya, C. B., & Sen, S. (2010). Maximizing business returns to corporate social responsibility (CSR): The role of CSR communication. *International Journal of Management Reviews*, *12*(1), 8–19. doi:10.1111/j.1468-2370.2009.00276.x

Du, S., & Vieira, E. T. Jr. (2012). Striving for Legitimacy Through Corporate Social Responsibility: Insights from Oil Companies. *Journal of Business Ethics*, *110*(4), 413–427. doi:10.100710551-012-1490-4

Dworkin, R. (1986). *Law as Integrity*. Harvard University Press.

Dyduch, W., Chudziński, P., Cyfert, S., & Zastempowski, M. (2021). Dynamic capabilities, value creation and value capture: Evidence from SMEs under Covid-19 lockdown in Poland. *PLoS One*, *16*(6), e0252423. doi:10.1371/journal.pone.0252423 PMID:34129597

Dyllick, T., & Muff, K. (2016). Clarifying the Meaning of Sustainable Business; Introducing a Typology From Business-as-Usual to True Business Sustainability. *Organization & Environment*, *29*(2), 156–174. doi:10.1177/1086026615575176

Eagly, A. H., & Chaiken, S. (1993). *The psychology of attitudes* (1st ed.). Harcourt Brace Jovanovich College Publishers. Retrieved from https://psycnet.apa.org/record/1992-98849-000

Easton, D. (1990). *The Analysis of Political Structure*. Routledge.

Ebrahim, A. H., & Buheji, M. (2020). A Pursuit for a 'Holistic Social Responsibility Strategic Framework' Addressing COVID-19 Pandemic Needs. *American Journal of Economics*, *10*(5), 293–304. doi:10.5923/j.economics.20201005.04

Eccles, R. G., Ioannou, I., Serafeim, G., & Hall, M. (2012). *The impact of corporate sustainability on organizational processes and performance* [Working Paper 17950]. National Bureau of Economic Research. doi:10.3386/w17950

Eccles, R. G., Serafeim, G., & Krzus, M. P. (2011). Market interest in nonfinancial information. *Journal of Applied Corporate Finance*, *23*(4), 113–127. doi:10.1111/j.1745-6622.2011.00357.x

Edelman. (2020). *Edelman trust barometer special report on COVID-19 demonstrates essential role of the private sector*. www.edelman.com/research/edelman-trustcovid-19-demonstrates-essential-role-of-private-sector

Eisenhardt, K. M., & Martin, J. A. (2000). Dynamic capabilities: What are they? *Strategic Management Journal*, *21*(10-11), 1105–1121. doi:10.1002/1097-0266(200010/11)21:10/11<1105::AID-SMJ133>3.0.CO;2-E

El Ghoul, S., Guedhami, O., & Kim, Y. (2017). Country-level institutions, firm value, and the role of Corporate Social Responsibility initiatives. *Journal of International Business Studies*, *48*(3), 360–385. doi:10.1057/jibs.2016.4

ElAlfy, A., Palaschuk, N., El-Bassiouny, D., Wilson, J., & Weber, O. (2020). Scoping the Evolution of Corporate Social Responsibility (CSR) Research in the Sustainable Development Goals (SDGs) Era. Sustainability, 12(14).

ElAlfy, A., Darwish, K. M., & Weber, O. (2020a). Corporations and Sustainable Development Goals communication on social media: Corporate social responsibility or just another buzzword? *Sustainable Development, 28*(5), 1418–1430. doi:10.1002d.2095

ElAlfy, A., Palaschuk, N., El-Bassiouny, D., Wilson, J., & Weber, O. (2020b). Scoping the evolution of Corporate Social Responsibility (CSR) research in the Sustainable Development Goals (SDGs) era. *Sustainability, 12*(5544), 1–21. doi:10.3390u12145544

Elkington, J. (1994). Towards the sustainable corporation: Win-win-win business strategies for sustainable development. *California Management Review, 36*(2), 90–100.

Elkington, J. (1997). *Cannibals with Forks, The Triple Bottom Line of 21st Century Business.* Capstone.

Elkington, J. (1998). Partnerships from cannibals with forks: The triple bottom line of 21st-century business. *Environmental Quality Management, 8*(1), 37–51. doi:10.1002/tqem.3310080106

Elkington, J. (2000). Cannibals with forks: The triple bottom line of 21st century business. *Journal of Business Ethics, 23*(2), 229–231. doi:10.1023/A:1006129603978

Elkington, J. (Ed.). (1997). *Cannibals with forks: the triple bottom line of 21st century business.* John Wiley & Sons, Ltd.

Enrique, C., Reyes, G., & Liñan, L. T. (2018). Aplicación del Método Delphi Modificado para la Validación de un Cuestionario de Incorporación de las TIC en la Práctica Docente Application of the Modified Delphi Method for the Validation of a Questionnaire on the Incorporation of ICT in Teaching Practice. *Revista Iberoamericana de Evaluación Educativa, 11*(1), 113–135. doi:10.15366/riee2018.11.1.007

Epstein, M. J., & Yuthas, K. (2014). *Measuring and improving social impacts. A guide for nonprofits, companies, and impact investors.* Berrett-Koehler Publishers.

Erkan, I., & Evans, C. (2016). The influence of eWOM in social media on consumers' purchase intentions: An extended approach to information adoption. *Computers in Human Behavior, 61*, 47–55. doi:10.1016/j.chb.2016.03.003

Erkens, M., Paugam, L., & Stolowy, H. (2015). Non-financial information: State of the art and research perspectives based on a bibliometric study. *Comptabilité-Contrôle-Audit, 21*(3), 15–92. doi:10.3917/cca.213.0015

Ernst & Young. (2017). *Is Your Non-Financial Performance Revealing the True Value of Your Business to Investors?* https://assets.ey.com

Escuela Andaluza de Salud Pública. (n.d.). *Escuela de Pacientes: Inicio.* Consejería de Salud y Familias de la Junta de Andalucía. http://www.escueladepacientes.es

Essilor. (2021). *Our commitments.* Retrieved from https://www.essilor.com/en/sustainability/commitments/

EssilorLuxottica. (2021a). *Brands.* Retrieved from https://www.essilorluxottica.com/brands

EssilorLuxottica. (2021b). *Sustainability.* Retrieved from https://www.essilorluxottica.com/sustainability

Estrin, S., Mickiewicz, T., & Stephan, U. (2013). Entrepreneurship, social capital, and institutions: Social and commercial entrepreneurship across nations. *Entrepreneurship Theory and Practice, 37*(3), 479–504. doi:10.1111/etap.12019

Estrin, S., Mickiewicz, T., & Stephan, U. (2016). Human capital in social and commercial entrepreneurship. *Journal of Business Venturing, 31*(4), 449–467. doi:10.1016/j.jbusvent.2016.05.003

Etchegoyen, A. (1991). *La valse des ethiques.* Le Seuil.

Ettinger, A., Grabner-Kräuter, S., & Terlutter, R. (2018). Online CSR communication in the hotel industry: Evidence from small hotels. *International Journal of Hospitality Management, 68*, 94–104. doi:10.1016/j.ijhm.2017.09.002

Euromonitor International Consumer Trends. (2021). *Top 10 Global Consumer Trends 2021.* Accessed at: https://blog.euromonitor.com/?_gl=1%2A3ehags%2A_ga%2AODI2OTY0ODY4LjE2MTI4NjQ4MDc.%2A_ga_6D3QFKH8G9%2AMTYxMjg2NDgwNi4xLjAuMTYxMjg2NDgwNi4w

Euromonitor International. (2021). *Reimagining Consumer Markets.* Accessed at https://www.euromonitor.com/

European Commission. (2001, July 19). *Green Paper Promoting a European Framework for Corporate Social Responsibility.* https://ec.europa.eu/commission/presscorner/detail/en/DOC_01_9

European Commission. (2011). *Communication from the Commission to the European Parliament, the Council, the European Economic and Social Committee and the Committee of the Regions. A renewed EU strategy 2011-2014 for Corporate Social Responsibility.* European Commission.

European Commission. (2014). *A map of social enterprises and their eco-systems in Europe.* https://ec.europa.eu/social/BlobServlet?docId=12987&langId=en

European Union. (2014). *Directive 2014/95/UE of the European Parliament and of the Council of 22 October 2014 amending Directive 2013/34/UE as regards disclosure of non-financial and diversity information by certain large undertakings and groups.* https://eur-lex.europa.eu/eli/dir/2014/95/oj

Fahimnia, B., Jabbarzadeh, A., & Sarkis, J. (2018). Greening versus resilience: A supply chain design perspective. *Transportation Research Part E, Logistics and Transportation Review, 119*, 129–148. doi:10.1016/j.tre.2018.09.005

Fairtrade International. (2019). *What Is Fairtrade?* Available at: http://www.fairtrade.net/what-is-fairtrade.html

Farzin, M., & Fattahi, M. (2018). eWOM through social networking sites and impact on purchase intention and brand image in Iran. *Journal of Advances in Management Research, 15*(2), 161–183. doi:10.1108/JAMR-05-2017-0062

Fatma, M., Ruiz, A. P., Khan, I., & Rahman, Z. (2020). The effect of CSR engagement on eWOM on social media. *The International Journal of Organizational Analysis, 28*(4), 941–956. doi:10.1108/IJOA-10-2019-1895

Featherman, M., Jia, S., Califf, C. B., & Hajli, N. (2021). The impact of new technologies on consumers beliefs: Reducing the perceived risks of electric vehicle adoption. *Technological Forecasting and Social Change, 169*, 120847. doi:10.1016/j.techfore.2021.120847

Feger, C., & Mermet, L. (2017, September 18). A blueprint towards accounting for the management of ecosystems. *Accounting, Auditing & Accountability Journal, 30*(7), 1511–1536. doi:10.1108/AAAJ-12-2015-2360

Felin, T., & Powell, T. C. (2016). Designing organizations for dynamic capabilities. *California Management Review, 58*(4), 78–96. doi:10.1525/cmr.2016.58.4.78

Felipe, C. M., Roldán, J. L., & Leal-Rodríguez, A. L. (2016). An explanatory and predictive model for organizational agility. *Journal of Business Research, 69*(10), 4624–4631. doi:10.1016/j.jbusres.2016.04.014

Feng, Z., Chen, C. R., & Tseng, Y. J. (2018). Do capital markets value corporate social responsibility? Evidence from seasoned equity offerings. *Journal of Banking & Finance, 94*, 54–74. doi:10.1016/j.jbankfin.2018.06.015

Fernández-Guadaño, J., & Sarria-Pedroza, J. (2018). Impact of Corporate Social Responsibility on Value Creation from a Stakeholder Perspective. *Sustainability, 10*(6), 2062. doi:10.3390u10062062

Fernández-Laviada, A., López-Gutiérrez, C., & Pérez, A. (2020a). How does the development of the social enterprise sector affect entrepreneurial behavior? An empirical analysis. *Sustainability, 12*(3), 1–15. doi:10.3390u12030826

Fernández-Laviada, A., López-Gutiérrez, C., & San-Martín, P. (2020b). The moderating effect of countries' development on the characterization of the social entrepreneur: An empirical analysis with GEM data. *Voluntas, 31*(3), 563–580. doi:10.100711266-020-00216-7

Ferrari N. V. (2019). *Sustainability Report.* Author.

Fiat Chrysler Automobiles. (2019). *Sustainability Report.* Author.

Figueredo, C., Falcão, D., & Olavo, C. (2019). Startups and the innovation ecosystem in Industry 4.0. *Technology Analysis and Strategic Management, 31*(12), 1474–1487. doi:10.1080/09537325.2019.1628938

Financial Accounting Standards Board (2001). *Business and financial reporting. Challenges from the new economy.* Special Report. Author.

Fishbein, M. (2008). Reasoned Action, Theory of. In *The International Encyclopedia of Communication.* John Wiley & Sons, Ltd., doi:10.1002/9781405186407.wbiecr017

Fishbein, M., & Ajzen, I. (1975a). *Belief, Attitude, Intention, and Behavior: An Introduction to Theory and Research* (I. Ajzen, Ed.). Addison-Wesley Pub. Co.

Fishbein, M., & Ajzen, I. (1975b). *Belief, attitude, intention and behaviour: An introduction to theory and research.* Addison-Wesley. Retrieved from https://www.researchgate.net/publication/233897090_Belief_attitude_intention_and_behaviour_An_introduction_to_theory_and_research

Flammer, C. (2013). Corporate social responsibility and shareholder reaction: The environmental awareness of investors. *Academy of Management Journal, 56*(3), 758–781. doi:10.5465/amj.2011.0744

Folke, C., Carpenter, S., Elmqvist, T., Gunderson, L., Holling, C. S., & Walker, B. (2002). Resilience and Sustainable Development: Building Adaptive Capacity in a World of Transformations. *Ambio, 31*(5), 437-440.

Folke, C., Biggs, R., Norström, A. V., Reyers, B., & Rockström, J. (2016). Social-ecological resilience and biosphere-based sustainability science. *Ecology and Society, 21*(3), art41. Advance online publication. doi:10.5751/ES-08748-210341

Ford Motor Company. (2020). *Sustainability Report.* Author.

Ford Motor Company. (2020). *United Nations Sustainable Development Goals Index.* Author.

Franco, I. B., & Abe, M. (2020). SDG 17 Partnerships for the Goals. In I. Franco, T. Chatterji, E. Derbyshire & J. Tracey (Eds.), Actioning the Global Goals for Local Impact. Science for Sustainable Societies. Springer. doi:10.1007/978-981-32-9927-6_18

Franco, Á. (2006). Tendencias y teorías en salud pública. *Revista Facultad Nacional de Salud Pública, 24*(2), 119–130.

Frederick, W. C. (1995). *Values, Nature and Culture in the American Corporation.* Academic Press.

Freeman, R. E. (1984). *Strategic Management. A Stakeholder Approach.* Pitman Publishing Inc.

Freeman, R. E. (1984). *Strategic management: A stakeholder approach.* Pitman.

Freeman, R. E. (1998). A Stakeholder Theory of the Modern Corporation. In M. B. E. Clarkson (Ed.), *The Corporation and Its Stakeholders: Classic and Contemporary Readings* (pp. 125–138). University of Toronto Press. doi:10.3138/9781442673496-009

Freeman, R. E., Harrison, J. S., Wicks, A. C., Parmar, B. L., & de Colle, S. (2010). *Stakeholder theory: The state of the art.* Cambridge University. Press. doi:10.1017/CBO9780511815768

Freeman, R. E., Wicks, A. C., & Parmar, B. (2004). Stakeholder Theory and "The Corporate Objective Revisited". *Organization Science*, *15*(3), 364–369. doi:10.1287/orsc.1040.0066

Freire, N. A. (2014). When luxury advertising adds the identitary values of luxury: A semiotic analysis. *Journal of Business Research*, *67*(12), 2666–2675. doi:10.1016/j.jbusres.2014.04.004

Friedman, M. (1970). The Social Responsibility of Business is to Increase its Profits. *The New York Times Magazine*.

Friedman, M. (1962). *Capitalism and freedom*. University of Chicago Press.

Friedman, M. (1996). The social responsibility of business is to increase its profits. (1970) Reprinted. In S. B. Rae & K. L. Wong (Eds.), *Beyond integrity. A Judeo-Christian approach to business ethics* (pp. 241–246). Zondervan Publishing House. (Original work published 1970)

Frohlich, K. L., & Abel, T. (2014). Environmental justice and health practices: Understanding how health inequities arise at the local level. *Sociology of Health & Illness*, *36*(2), 199–212. doi:10.1111/1467-9566.12126 PMID:24372359

Fu, J. R., Ju, P. H., & Hsu, C. W. (2015). Understanding why consumers engage in electronic word-of-mouth communication: Perspectives from theory of planned behavior and justice theory. *Electronic Commerce Research and Applications*, *14*(6), 616–630. doi:10.1016/j.elerap.2015.09.003

Futures, N. D. (1969). *An experimental study of group opinion: the Delphi method.* Elsevier. https://www.sciencedirect.com/science/article/pii/S001632876980025X

Gallardo-Vázquez, D., Hourneaux, F., da Silva, M. L., & Valdez-Juárez, L. E. (2021). On earth as in heaven: Proxy measurements to assess the Sustainable Development Goals at the company's level through CSR indicators. *Sustainability*, *13*(2), 1–16. doi:10.3390u13020914

Gallardo-Vázquez, D., Sánchez-Hernández, M. I., & Corchuelo-Martínez-Azúa, M. B. (2013). Validación de un instrumento de medida para la relación entre la orientación a la responsabilidad social corporativa y otras variables estratégicas de la empresa. *Spanish Accounting Review. Revista de Contabilidad*, *16*(1), 11–23.

Gallie, W. B. (1956). Art as an essentially contested concept. *The Philosophical Quarterly*, *6*(23), 97–114. doi:10.2307/2217217

Galpin, T., Whittington, J. L., & Bell, G. (2015). Is your sustainability strategy sustainable? Creating a culture of sustainability. *Corporate Governance*, *15*(1), 1–17. doi:10.1108/CG-01-2013-0004

Galvão, A., Ferreira, J. J., & Marques, C. (2017). Entrepreneurship education and training as facilitators of regional development. *Journal of Small Business and Enterprise Development*, *25*(1), 17–40. doi:10.1108/JSBED-05-2017-0178

Gamble, E. N., Parker, S. C., & Moroz, P. W. (2019). Measuring the Integration of Social and Environmental Missions in Hybrid Organizations. *Journal of Business Ethics*. Advance online publication. doi:10.100710551-019-04146-3

Gan, C., & Wang, W. (2017). The influence of perceived value on purchase intention in social commerce context. *Internet Research*, *27*(4), 772–785. doi:10.1108/IntR-06-2016-0164

Gao, F., Dong, Y., Ni, C., & Fu, R. (2016). Determinants and economic consequences of non-financial disclosure quality. *European Accounting Review*, *25*(2), 287–317. doi:10.1080/09638180.2015.1013049

García Aguayo, F. J. (2021). La crisis de la medicina: sus males y sus posibles remedios. Razón y fe. *Revista Hispanoamericana de Cultura, 283*(1451), 283-290. https://revistas.comillas.edu/index.php/razonyfe/article/view/16610

García-Jurado, A., Pérez-Barea, J. J., & Nova, R. J. (2021). A new approach to social entrepreneurship: A systematic review and meta-analysis. *Sustainability*, *13*(5), 1–16. doi:10.3390u13052754

García-Ruiz, E., & Lena-Acebo, F. J. (2018). Aplicación del metodo delphi en el diseño de una investigación cuantitativa sobre el fenómeno FABLAB. *Revista de Metodología de Ciencias Sociales*, 129–166. https://www.fablabs.io/labs

García-Sánchez, I. M., & García-Sánchez, A. (2020). Corporate social responsibility during COVID-19 pandemic. *Journal of Open Innovation*, *6*(4), 126. doi:10.3390/joitmc6040126

Gardetti, M. A. (2016). Loewe: Luxury and sustainable management. Handbook of Sustainable Luxury Textiles and Fashion, 2, 1–16.

Gardetti, M. A. (2017). *Sustainable management of luxury. Springer book series on environmental footprints and eco-design of products and processes*. Springer.

Gardetti, M. A., & Girón, M. E. (Eds.). (2014). *Sustainable luxury and social entrepreneurship: Stories from the pioneers*. Greenleaf Publishing.

Gardetti, M. A., & Justo, R. (2017). Sustainable luxury fashion: The entrepreneurs' vision. In M. A. Gardetti (Ed.), *Sustainable Management of Luxury* (pp. 347–360). Springer Singapore. doi:10.1007/978-981-10-2917-2_16

Garg, P. (2017). Development of sustainability reporting index (SRI) with special reference to companies in India. *Decision (Washington, D.C.)*, *44*(4), 259–273.

Gartner, W. B., & Carter, N. M. (2003). Entrepreneurial behavior and firm organizing processes. In Z. J. Acs & D. B. Audretsch (Eds.), *Handbook of entrepreneurship research* (pp. 195–221). Springer., doi:10.1007/0-387-24519-7_9

Gavidia, V. (2009). El profesorado ante la educación y promoción de la salud en la escuela. *Didáctica de las Ciencias Experimentales y Sociales*, (23), 171–180.

Gazzola, P., Grechi, D., Ossola, P., & Pavione, E. (2019). Certified Benefit Corporations as a new way to make sustainable business: The Italian example. *Corporate Social Responsibility and Environmental Management*, *26*(6), 1435–1445. doi:10.1002/csr.1758

Geels, F. (2011). The multi-level perspective on sustainability transitions: Reponses to seven criticisms. *Environmental Innovation and Societal Transitions*, *1*(1), 24–40. doi:10.1016/j.eist.2011.02.002

GEM. (2015). *2015 Report on Social Entrepreneurship*. Special Topic Report. GEM.

Ghobadian, A., Money, K., & Hillenbrand, C. (2015). Corporate Responsibility Research: Past—Present—Future. *Group & Organization Management*, *40*(3), 271–294. doi:10.1177/1059601115590320

Ghosh, S. (2017). Reporting of CSR activities in India: are we still at a nascent stage even after the legal mandate? In *Corporate Social Responsibility in India* (pp. 133–147). Springer.

Giakoumaki, C., & Krepapa, A. (2020). Brand engagement in self-concept and consumer engagement in social media: The role of the source. *Psychology and Marketing*, *37*(3), 457–465. doi:10.1002/mar.21312

Gibbs, D., & O'Neill, K. (2017). Future green economies and regional development: A research agenda. *Regional Studies*, *51*(1), 161–173. doi:10.1080/00343404.2016.1255719

Gibson, R. B. (2006). Beyond the Pillars: Sustainability Assessment as a Framework for Effective Integration of Social, Economic and Ecological Considerations in Significant Decision-Making. *Journal of Environmental Assessment Policy and Management*, *8*(3), 259–280. doi:10.1142/S1464333206002517

Gil-Girbau, M., Pons-Vigués, M., Rubio-Valera, M., Murrugarra, G., Masluk, B., Rodríguez-Martín, B., García Pineda, A., Vidal Thomás, C., Conejo-Cerón, S., Recio, J. I., Martínez, C., Pujol-Ribera, E., & Berenguera, A. (2021). Modelos teóricos de promoción de la salud en la práctica habitual en atención primaria de salud. *Gaceta Sanitaria*, *35*(1), 48–59. doi:10.1016/j.gaceta.2019.06.011 PMID:31753510

Gispert, R., & Giné, J. M. (2006). Diferencias entre público y privado en la asistencia hospitalaria en España: ¿realidad asistencial o falacia numérica? *Gaceta Sanitaria*, *20*(2), 149–152. doi:10.1157/13087327 PMID:16753092

Gladwin, T. N., Kennelly, J. J., & Krause, T. S. (1995). Shifting Paradigms for Sustainable Development: Implications for Management Theory and Research. *Academy of Management Review*, *20*(4), 874–907. doi:10.5465/amr.1995.9512280024

Global Reporting Initiative. (2021). *Sustainability reporting guidelines*. https://www.globalreporting.org

Gómez-López, R., López-Fernández, M. C., & Serrano-Bedia, A. M. (2017). Implementation barriers of the EFQM excellence model within the Spanish private firms. *Total Quality Management & Business Excellence*, *28*(7–8), 695–711. doi:10.1080/14783363.2015.1106314

González, A. (2012). *Programa Paciente Experto Catalunya: una estrategia para potenciar la autorresponsabilidad del paciente y el fomento del autocuidado*. Departamento de Salut. Generalitat de Catalunya.

Gracia-Pérez, M. L. (2015). *Evaluación del impacto formativo: dimensiones y modelos. Una experiencia en la sanidad de Aragón* [Tesis doctoral, Universidad de Zaragoza]. https://zaguan.unizar.es/record/64481?ln=es

Gracia-Pérez, M. L., & Gil-Lacruz, M. (2019). Participación y Salud: Nuevas iniciativas en España. *Acciones e Investigaciones Sociales*, (39), 111–131. doi:10.26754/ojs_ais/ais.2018393234

Graham, J., & Havlena, W. (2007). Finding the "missing link": Advertising's impact on word of mouth, web searches and site visits. *Journal of Advertising Research*, *47*(4), 427–435. doi:10.2501/S0021849907070444

Grant, R. M. (1991). The resource-based theory of competitive advantage: Implications for strategy formulation. *California Management Review*, *33*(3), 114–135. doi:10.2307/41166664

Grech, P., & Grech, R. (2021). The role of health promotion theories in Stroke Awareness and Education. *Applied Nursing Research*, *58*, 151415. doi:10.1016/j.apnr.2021.151415 PMID:33745555

Green, B., Jones, M., Hughes, D., & Williams, A. (1999). Applying the Delphi technique in a study of GPs' information requirements. *Health & Social Care in the Community*, *7*(3), 198–205. doi:10.1046/j.1365-2524.1999.00176.x PMID:11560634

Gregory, B. T., Harris, S. G., Armenakis, A. A., & Shook, C. L. (2009). Organizational culture and effectiveness: A study of values, attitudes, and organizational outcomes. *Journal of Business Research*, *62*(7), 673–679. doi:10.1016/j.jbusres.2008.05.021

GRI. (2021). *Global Reporting Initiative Database*. Available at: https://database.globalreporting.org/search/

Griggs, D., Stafford-Smith, M., Gaffney, O., Rockström, J., Öhman, M. C., Shyamsundar, P., & Noble, I. (2013). Policy: Sustainable development goals for people and planet. *Nature*, *495*(7441), 305–307. doi:10.1038/495305a PMID:23518546

Group Health Research Institute. (n.d.). *Improving Chronic Health*. http://www.improvingchroniccare.org

Grover, V., & Sabherwal, R. (2020). Making sense of the confusing mix of digitalization, pandemics and economics. *International Journal of Information Management*, *55*, 102234. doi:10.1016/j.ijinfomgt.2020.102234

Gupta, O., & Gupta, K. (2019). CSR in India: The companies act and its implications. *Journal of Contemporary Management Research*, *13*(1), 1–23.

Gupta, P., Chauhan, S., Paul, J., & Jaiswal, M. P. (2020). Social entrepreneurship research: A review and future research agenda. *Journal of Business Research, 113*, 209–229. doi:10.1016/j.jbusres.2020.03.032

Gupta, V. K., Turban, D. B., Wasti, S. A., & Sikdar, A. (2009). The role of gender stereotypes in perceptions of entrepreneurs and intentions to become an entrepreneur. *Entrepreneurship Theory and Practice, 33*(2), 397–417. doi:10.1111/j.1540-6520.2009.00296.x

Habermas, J. (1973). *Legitimation crisis*. Beacon Press.

Habermas, J., & McCarthy, T. (1985). *The theory of communicative action. Lifeworld and system: A critique of functionalist reason* (Vol. 2). Beacon Press.

Hadad, S., & Gauca, O. D. (2014). Social impact measurement in social entrepreneurial organizations. *Management & Marketing, 9*, 119–136.

Hahn, T., Figge, F., Pinkse, J., & Preuss, L. (2010). Trade-offs in corporate sustainability: You can't have your cake and eat it. *Business Strategy and the Environment, 19*(4), 217–229. doi:10.1002/bse.674

Hair, J. F., Anderson, R. E., Tatham, R. L., & Black, W. C. (2010). *Multivariate data analysis* (7th ed.). Prentice-Hall, Inc. Retrieved from https://dl.acm.org/citation.cfm?id=207590

Haller, A., Link, M., & Groß, T. (2017). The term 'non-financial information' – a semantic analysis of a key feature of current and future corporate reporting. *Accounting in Europe, 14*(3), 407–429. doi:10.1080/17449480.2017.1374548

Hall, M., Millo, Y., & Barman, E. (2015). Who and what really counts? Stakeholder prioritization and accounting for social value. *Journal of Management Studies, 52*(7), 907–934. doi:10.1111/joms.12146

Halme, M., Lindeman, S., & Linna, P. (2012). Innovation for inclusive business: Intrapreneurial bricolage in multinational corporations. *Journal of Management Studies, 49*(4), 743–784. doi:10.1111/j.1467-6486.2012.01045.x

Haltiwanger, J., Jarmin, R., & Miranda, J. (2013). Who Creates Jobs? Small vs. Large vs. Young. *The Review of Economics and Statistics, 45*(2), 347–361. doi:10.1162/REST_a_00288

Hammer, M. (2007). The Process Audit. *Harvard Business Review*. www.hbrreprints.org

Hammer, J., & Pivo, G. (2017). The Triple Bottom Line and Sustainable Economic Development Theory and Practice. *Economic Development Quarterly, 31*(1), 25–36. doi:10.1177/0891242416674808

Han, H. (2015). Travelers' pro-environmental behavior in a green lodging context: Converging value-belief-norm theory and the theory of planned behavior. *Tourism Management, 47*, 164–177. doi:10.1016/j.tourman.2014.09.014

Harding, R., & Cowling, M. (2006). *Social Entrepreneurship Monitor United Kingdom 2006*. Academic Press.

Harding, R. (2007). Understanding social entrepreneurship. *Industry and Higher Education, 21*(1), 73–84. doi:10.5367/000000007780222723

Harris, L. C., & Crane, A. (2002). The greening of organizational culture: Management views on the depth, degree and diffusion of change. *Journal of Organizational Change Management, 15*(3), 214–234. doi:10.1108/09534810210429273

Harrison, J. S., & Wicks, A. C. (2013). Stakeholder theory, value, and firm performance. *Business Ethics Quarterly, 23*(1), 97–124. doi:10.5840/beq20132314

Hartmann, P., Fernández, P., Apaolaza, V., Eisend, M., & D'Souza, C. (2020). Explaining Viral CSR Message Propagation in Social Media: The Role of Normative Influences. *Journal of Business Ethics*, 1–21. doi:10.100710551-020-04540-2

Hasson, F., Keeney, S., & McKenna, H. (2000). Research guidelines for the Delphi survey technique. *Journal of Advanced Nursing, 32*(4), 1008–1015. doi:10.1046/j.1365-2648.2000.t01-1-01567.x PMID:11095242

Hazlewood, P. (2015). *Global Multi-stakeholder Partnerships: Scaling up public-private collective impact for the SDGs.* Independent Research Forum.

Heard, E., Fitzgerald, L., Wigginton, B., & Mutch, A. (2020). Applying intersectionality theory in health promotion research and practice. *Health Promotion International, 35*(4), 866–876. doi:10.1093/heapro/daz080 PMID:31390472

Hechavarría, D. M. (2016). The impact of culture on national prevalence rates of social and commercial entrepreneurship. *The International Entrepreneurship and Management Journal, 12*(4), 1025–1052. doi:10.100711365-015-0376-1

Hechavarria, D. M., Ingram, A., Justo, R., & Terjesen, S. (2012). Are women more likely to pursue social and environmental entrepreneurship? In K. D. Hughes & J. E. Jennings (Eds.), *Global Women's Entrepreneurship Research: Diverse Settings, Questions and Approaches* (pp. 135–151). Edward Elgar Publishing. doi:10.4337/9781849804752.00016

Hechavarría, D. M., Terjesen, S. A., Ingram, A. E., Renko, M., Justo, R., & Elam, A. (2017). Taking care of business: The impact of culture and gender on entrepreneurs' blended value creation goals. *Small Business Economics, 48*(1), 225–257. doi:10.100711187-016-9747-4

He, H., & Harris, L. (2020). The impact of Covid-19 pandemic on corporate social responsibility and marketing philosophy. *Journal of Business Research, 116*, 176–182. doi:10.1016/j.jbusres.2020.05.030 PMID:32457556

Hendarto, K. A., & Purwanto, B. M. (2012). Market reactions of mandatory implementation of corporate social responsibility: Indonesia context. *Asia Pacific Management Review, 17*(4), 379–402.

Hendricks, K. B., & Singhal, V. R. (1996). Quality awards and the market value of the firm: An empirical investigation. *Management Science, 42*(3), 415–436. doi:10.1287/mnsc.42.3.415

Hennig-Thurau, T., Walsh, G., & Walsh, G. (2003). Electronic word-of-mouth: Motives for and consequences of reading customer articulations on the internet. *International Journal of Electronic Commerce, 8*(2), 51–74. doi:10.1080/10864415.2003.11044293

Henseler, J., Dijkstra, T. K., Sarstedt, M., Ringle, C. M., Diamantopoulos, A., Straub, D. W., Ketchen, D. J. Jr, Hair, J. F., Hult, G. T. M., & Calantone, R. J. (2014). Common Beliefs and Reality About PLS. *Organizational Research Methods, 17*(2), 182–209. doi:10.1177/1094428114526928

Henseler, J., & Sarstedt, M. (2013). Goodness-of-fit indices for partial least squares path modeling. *Computational Statistics, 28*(2), 565–580. doi:10.100700180-012-0317-1

Hepner, J., Chandon, J. L., & Bakardzhieva, D. (2020). Competitive advantage from marketing the SDGs: A luxury perspective. *Marketing Intelligence & Planning, 39*(2), 284–299. doi:10.1108/MIP-07-2018-0298

Hernán, M., Fernández, A., & Ramos, M. (2004). La salud de los jóvenes. *Gaceta Sanitaria, 18*(Supl.1), 47–55. doi:10.1157/13062251 PMID:15171858

Hibbert, S. A., Hogg, G., & Quinn, T. (2005). Social entrepreneurship: Understanding consumer motives for buying The Big Issue. *Journal of Consumer Behaviour, 4*(3), 159–172. doi:10.1002/cb.6

Hilbe, J. M. (2009). *Logistic regression models.* Chapman & Hall/CRC. doi:10.1201/9781420075779

Hiller, J. S. (2013). The Benefit Corporation and Corporate Social Responsibility. *Journal of Business Ethics, 118*(2), 287–301. doi:10.100710551-012-1580-3

Hoffman, A. J. (2018). The Next Phase of Business Sustainability. Stanford Social Innovation Review, 16(2).

Hoffman, M. W., Driscoll, D., & Painter Morland, M. (2001). Integrating Ethics into organizational Cultures. In *Business Ethics: Facing up the Issues.* The Economist Books.

Hoffman, A. J. (2010). Climate change as a cultural and behavioral issue. Addressing barriers and implementing solutions. *Organizational Dynamics, 39*(4), 295–305. doi:10.1016/j.orgdyn.2010.07.005

Hofstede, G., Neuijen, B., Ohayv, D. D., & Sanders, G. (1990). Measuring organizational cultures-a qualitative and quantitative study across twenty cases. Administrative Science Quarterly, 35(2).

Hollebeek, L. D., Glynn, M. S., & Brodie, R. J. (2014). Consumer brand engagement in social media: Conceptualization, scale development and validation. *Journal of Interactive Marketing, 28*(2), 149–165. doi:10.1016/j.intmar.2013.12.002

Honda Group. (2020). *Sustainability Report.* Author.

Hong, W., Chan, F. K. Y., Thong, J. Y. L., Chasalow, L. C., & Dhillon, G. (2013). *A Framework and Guidelines for Context-Specific Theorizing in Information Systems Research.* doi:10.1287/isre.2013.0501

Hood, L. (2006). Chalmers, J. Lyons memorial lecture: Health Care of the 21st Century: Predective, Preventive, Personlized and Partipatory (P4) Medicine. *Journal of Oral and Maxillofacial Surgery, 64*(9), 14. doi:10.1016/j.joms.2006.06.302

Hoogendoorn, B. (2016). The prevalence and determinants of social entrepreneurship at the macro level. *Journal of Small Business Management, 54*(S1), 278–296. doi:10.1111/jsbm.12301

Horisch, J., Johnson, M. P., & Schaltegger, S. (2015). Implementation of Sustainability Management and Company Size: A Knowledge-Based View. *Business Strategy and the Environment, 24*(8), 765–779. doi:10.1002/bse.1844

Howard-Grenville, J., Davis, G. F., Dyllick, T., Miller, C. C., Thau, S., & Tsui, A. S. (2019). Sustainable Development for a Better World: Contributions of Leadership, Management, and Organizations. *Academy of Management Discoveries, 5*(4), 355–366. doi:10.5465/amd.2019.0275

Hsieh, Y. J., & Wu, Y. (2018). Entrepreneurship through the platform strategy in the digital era: Insights and research opportunities. *Computers in Human Behavior, 95*, 315–323. doi:10.1016/j.chb.2018.03.033

Hunter, B. D., Neiger, B., & West, J. (2011). The importance of addressing social determinants of health at the local level: The case for social capital. *Health & Social Care in the Community, 19*(5), 522–530. doi:10.1111/j.1365-2524.2011.00999.x PMID:21595772

Hutchings, K., & Michailova, S. (2004). Facilitating knowledge sharing in Russian and Chinese subsidiaries: The role of personal networks and group membership. *Journal of Knowledge Management, 8*(2), 84–94. doi:10.1108/13673270410529136

Hyundai Motor Group. (2019). *Global Corporate Social Responsibility Report.* Author.

Idowu, S. O., Schmidpeter, R., & Zu, L. (2020). *The Future of the UN Sustainable Development Goals.* Springer International Publishing. doi:10.1007/978-3-030-21154-7

Iivari, N., Sharma, S., & Ventä-Olkkonen, L. (2020). Digital transformation of everyday life–How COVID-19 pandemic transformed the basic education of the young generation and why information management research should care? *International Journal of Information Management, 55*, 102183. doi:10.1016/j.ijinfomgt.2020.102183 PMID:32836640

Ikram, M., Zhang, Q., Sroufe, R., & Ferasso, M. (2020). The Social Dimensions of Corporate Sustainability: An Integrative Framework Including COVID-19 Insights. *Sustainability, 12*(8747), 1–29. doi:10.3390u12208747

Impakter. (2021). *Swatch Group.* Retrieved from https://index.impakter.com/swatch/

Instituto Aragonés de Ciencias de la Salud. (n.d.). *Plataforma de Formación del IACS*. Gobierno de Aragón. http://www.iacs.aragon.es

Ittner, C. D., & Larcker, D. F. (1997). The performance effects of process management techniques. *Management Science*, *43*(4), 522–534. doi:10.1287/mnsc.43.4.522

Ivan, C. M., Mukta, R., Sudeep, C., & Burak, C. (2016). Long-term sustainable sustainability in luxury. Where else? In *Handbook of Sustainable Luxury Textiles and Fashion* (pp. 17–34). Springer Singapore. doi:10.1007/978-981-287-742-0_2

Ivanov, D. (2018). *Structural dynamics and resilience in supply chain risk management* (Vol. 265). Springer International Publishing. doi:10.1007/978-3-319-69305-7

Iwuoha, J. C., & Jude-Iwuoha, A. U. (2020). COVID-19: Challenge to SDG and globalization. *Electronic Research Journal of Social Sciences and Humanities, 2*.

Iyigun, N. O. (2018). *Creating business value and competitive advantage with social entrepreneurship*. IGI Global.

Izzo, M. F., Ciaburri, M., & Tiscini, R. (2020). The challenge of Sustainable Development Goal reporting: The first evidence from Italian listed companies. *Sustainability*, *12*(3494), 1–18. doi:10.3390u12083494

Jain, G., Paul, J., & Shrivastava, A. (2021). Hyper-personalization, co-creation, digital clienteling and transformation. *Journal of Business Research*, *124*, 12–23. doi:10.1016/j.jbusres.2020.11.034

Jaini, A., Quoquab, F., Mohammad, J., & Hussin, N. (2019). "I buy green products, do you…?": The moderating effect of eWOM on green purchase behavior in Malaysian cosmetics industry. *International Journal of Pharmaceutical and Healthcare Marketing*, *14*(1), 89–112. doi:10.1108/IJPHM-02-2019-0017

Jalilvand, M. R., & Samiei, N. (2012). The effect of electronic word of mouth on brand image and purchase intention: An empirical study in the automobile industry in Iran. *Marketing Intelligence & Planning*, *30*(4), 460–476. doi:10.1108/02634501211231946

Jamali, D., & Karam, C. (2016). Corporate Social Responsibility in Developing Countries as an Emerging Field of Study. *International Journal of Management Reviews*, *20*(1), 32–61. doi:10.1111/ijmr.12112

Jelonek, M., & Urbaniec, M. (2019). Development of Sustainability Competencies for the Labour Market: An Exploratory Qualitative Study. *Sustainability*, *11*(20), 5716. https://doi.org/10.3390/su11205716

Jenkins, H. (2004). A Critique of Conventional CSR Theory: An SME Perspective. *Journal of General Management*, *29*(4), 37–57. doi:10.1177/030630700402900403

Jin, Y.-J., Park, S.-C., & Yoo, J.-W. (2017). Effects of corporate social responsibility on consumer credibility perception and attitude toward luxury brands. *Social Behavior and Personality*, *45*(5), 795–808. doi:10.2224bp.5897

Joyner, B. E., & Payne, D. (2002). Evolution and implementation: A study of values, business ethics and corporate social responsibility. *Journal of Business Ethics*, *41*(4), 297–311. doi:10.1023/A:1021237420663

Kahn, M., Serafeim, G., & Yoon, A. (2016). Corporate Sustainability: First Evidence on Materiality. *The Accounting Review*, *81*(6), 1697–1724. doi:10.2308/accr-51383

Kaiser, F. G., & Scheuthle, H. (2003). Two challenges to a moral extension of the theory of planned behavior: Moral norms and just world beliefs in conservationism. *Personality and Individual Differences*, *35*(5), 1033–1048. doi:10.1016/S0191-8869(02)00316-1

Kamran, A., & Naeim, M. (2020). Behavioural change theories: A necessity for managing COVID-19. *Public Health*. Advance online publication. doi:10.1016/j.puhe.2020.10.010 PMID:33468323

Kang, J., & Hustvedt, G. (2014). Building Trust Between Consumers and Corporations: The Role of Consumer Perceptions of Transparency and Social Responsibility. *Journal of Business Ethics*, *125*(2), 253–265. doi:10.100710551-013-1916-7

Kapferer, J. N. (2018). Second-hand luxury: Should personal luxury brands sell pre-owned products? *European Business Review*, (November-December), 59–65.

Kapoor, A., & Kulshrestha, C. (2011). Branding and sustainable competitive advantage: Building virtual presence. In *Branding and Sustainable Competitive Advantage: Building Virtual Presence*. IGI Global. doi:10.4018/978-1-61350-171-9

Karaosman. (2019). *'Unlocking Responsible Luxury: The Manifesto 2019*. Politecnico di Milano School of Management & Mazars.

Kask, J., & Linton, G. (2013). Business mating: When start-ups get it right. *Journal of Small Business and Entrepreneurship*, *26*(5), 511–536. doi:10.1080/08276331.2013.876765

Keeney, S., Hasson, F., & McKenna, H. (2006). Consulting the oracle: Ten lessons from using the Delphi technique in nursing research. *Journal of Advanced Nursing*, *53*(2), 205–212. doi:10.1111/j.1365-2648.2006.03716.x PMID:16422719

Kering. (2019). *Kering standards for raw materials and manufacturing processes*. Retrieved from https://cutt.ly/hbEVLeA

Kering. (2021a). *Houses*. Retrieved from https://www.kering.com/en/houses/

Kering. (2021b). *Sustainability*. Retrieved from https://www.kering.com/en/sustainability/

Kering. (2021c). *Press. Sustainability*. Retrieved from https://www.kering.com/en/special-reports/sustainability

Kering. (2021d). *Our value chain: from creation to the customer experience*. Retrieved from https://www.kering.com/integrated-report-2020/en/chaine-de-valeur/#block-88

Khan, I., Rahman, Z., & Fatma, M. (2016). The concept of online corporate brand experience: An empirical assessment. *Marketing Intelligence & Planning*, *34*(5), 711–730. doi:10.1108/MIP-01-2016-0007

Khan, S., & Ahmed, M. (2017). Who are the consumers for sustainable luxury? In *2017 Global Fashion Management Conference at Vienna* (pp. 181-182). 10.15444/GFMC2017.03.02.03

Kharas, H., & Zhang, C. (2014). New agenda, new narrative: What happens after 2015? *SAIS Review (Paul H. Nitze School of Advanced International Studies)*, *34*(2), 25–35. doi:10.1353ais.2014.0019

Khetrapal, S., & Bhatia, R. (2020). Impact of COVID-19 pandemic on health system & Sustainable Development Goal 3. *The Indian Journal of Medical Research*, *151*(5), 395. doi:10.4103/ijmr.IJMR_1920_20 PMID:32611910

Kiesnere, A. L., & Baumgartner, R. J. (2019). Sustainability management in practice: Organizational change for sustainability in smaller large-sized companies in Austria. Sustainability, 11(572).

Kim & Hwang, J. (2020). Merging the norm activation model and the theory of planned behavior in the context of drone food delivery services: Does the level of product knowledge really matter? *Journal of Hospitality and Tourism Management, 42*, 1–11. doi:10.1016/j.jhtm.2019.11.002

Kim. (2017). Consumer Responses to the Food Industry's Proactive and Passive Environmental CSR, Factoring in Price as CSR Tradeoff. *Journal of Business Ethics, 140*(2), 307–321. doi:10.1007/s10551-015-2671-8

Kim, S., Karlesky, M. J., Myers, C. G., & Schifeling, T. (2016). Social Responsibility: Why Companies Are Becoming B Corporations. *Harvard Business Review*, 2–5. https://www.christophergmyers.net/hbr2016_bcorporations.pdf

Kim, S., & Park, H. (2011). Corporate Social Responsibility as an organizational attractiveness for prospective public relations practitioners. *Journal of Business Ethics*, *103*(4), 639–653. doi:10.100710551-011-0886-x

Kim, S., Sung, Y., & Kang, H. (2014). Brand followers' retweeting behavior on Twitter: How brand relationships influence brand electronic word-of-mouth. *Computers in Human Behavior*, *37*, 18–25. doi:10.1016/j.chb.2014.04.020

Klyver, K., & Grant, S. (2010). Gender differences in entrepreneurial networking and participation. *International Journal of Gender and Entrepreneurship*, *2*(3), 213–227. doi:10.1108/17566261011079215

Kodama, M. (2020). Digitally transforming work styles in an era of infectious disease. *International Journal of Information Management*, *55*, 102172. doi:10.1016/j.ijinfomgt.2020.102172 PMID:32836634

Kohlbacher, M. (2010). The effects of process orientation: A literature review. *Business Process Management Journal*, *16*(1), 135–152. doi:10.1108/14637151011017985

Kolk, A. (2012). Towards a sustainable coffee market: Paradoxes faced by a multinational company. *Corporate Social Responsibility and Environmental Management*, *19*(2), 79–89.

Kolk, A. (2016). The social responsibility of international business: From ethics and the environment to CSR and sustainable development. *Journal of World Business*, *51*(1), 1–38. doi:10.1016/j.jwb.2015.08.010

Kolk, A., Rivera-Santos, M., & Rufín, C. (2018). Multinationals, international business, and poverty: A cross-disciplinary research overview and conceptual framework. *Journal of International Business Policy*, *1*(1), 92–115. doi:10.105742214-018-0004-1

Kollmuss, A., & Agyeman, J. (2002). Mind the Gap: Why do people act environmentally and what are the barriers to pro-environmental behavior? *Environmental Education Research*, *8*(3), 239–260. doi:10.1080/13504620220145401

Kolstad, I. (2012). Human rights and positive corporate duties: The importance of corporate–state interaction. *Business Ethics (Oxford, England)*, *21*(3), 276–285. doi:10.1111/j.1467-8608.2012.01654.x

Kong, S.-C., & Wang, Y.-Q. (2021). Investigating primary school principals' programming perception and support from the perspective of reasoned action: A mixed methods approach. *Computers & Education*, *172*, 104267. doi:10.1016/j.compedu.2021.104267

Kotler, P., & Lee, N. (2005). *Corporate Social Responsibility: Doing the Most Good for Your Company and Your Cause*. Wiley.

KPMG. (2020). The Time Has Come: The KPMG Survey of Sustainability Reporting 2020. KPMG Impact Report.

Kramer, M. R. (2020). Coronavirus Is Putting Corporate Social Responsibility to the Test. *Harvard Business Review*. https://hbr.org/2020/04/coronavirus-is-putting-corporate-social-responsibility-to-the-test

Kraus, S., Filser, M., O'Dwyer, M., & Shaw, E. (2014). Social entrepreneurship: An exploratory citation analysis. *Review of Managerial Science*, *8*(2), 275–292. doi:10.100711846-013-0104-6

Kreps, T. J. (1940). *Measurement of the Social Performance of Business*. Government Printing Office.

Krippendorff, K. (1980). *Content análisis: An introduction to its methodology*. Sage.

Kuckertz, A., Brändle, L., Gaudig, A., Hinderer, S., Reyes, C. A. M., Prochotta, A., ... Berger, E. S. (2020). Startups in times of crisis–A rapid response to the COVID-19 pandemic. *Journal of Business Venturing Insights*, *13*, e00169. doi:10.1016/j.jbvi.2020.e00169

Kumar, M.S, V., M., J., P., M., P., P., J., P., S., M.B., B.A.M., & J., R. (2020). Social economic impact of COVID-19 outbreak in India. *International Journal of Pervasive Computing and Communications*, *16*(4), 309–319. doi:10.1108/IJPCC-06-2020-0053

Kumar, S., Kumar, N., & Vivekadhish, S. (2016). Millennium Development Goals (MDGs) to Sustainable Development Goals (SDGs): Addressing unfinished agenda and strengthening sustainable development and partnership. *Indian Journal of Community Medicine*, *41*(1), 1–4. doi:10.4103/0970-0218.170955 PMID:26917865

Küng, P., & Hagen, C. (2007). The fruits of Business Process Management: An experience report from a Swiss bank. *Business Process Management Journal*, *13*(4), 477–487. doi:10.1108/14637150710763522

Kunz, J., May, S., & Schmidt, H. J. (2020). Sustainable luxury: current status and perspectives for future research. *Business Research*, 1-61.

Kuo, Y. F., Hu, T. L., & Yang, S. C. (2013). Effects of inertia and satisfaction in female online shoppers on repeat-purchase intention: The moderating roles of word-of-mouth and alternative attraction. *Managing Service Quality*, *23*(3), 168–187. doi:10.1108/09604521311312219

Kurz, T., Gardner, B., Verplanken, B., & Abraham, C. (2015). Habitual behaviors or patterns of practice? Explaining and changing repetitive climate-relevant actions. *Wiley Interdisciplinary Reviews: Climate Change*, *6*(1), 113–128. doi:10.1002/wcc.327

Kytle, B., & Ruggie, J. G. (2005). *Corporate social responsibility as risk management: A model for multinationals*. Academic Press.

La Torre, M., Sabelfeld, S., Blomkvist, M., & Dumay, J. (2020). Rebuilding trust: Sustainability and non-financial reporting and the European Union regulation. *Meditari Accountancy Research*, *28*(5), 701–725. doi:10.1108/MEDAR-06-2020-0914

La Torre, M., Sabelfeld, S., Blomkvist, M., Tarquinio, L., & Dumay, J. (2018). Harmonising non-financial reporting regulation in Europe: Practical forces and projections for future research. *Meditari Accountancy Research*, *26*(4), 598–621. doi:10.1108/MEDAR-02-2018-0290

Laasch, O., Moosmayer, D., Antonacopoulou, E., & Schaltegger, S. (2020). Constellations of Transdisciplinary Practices: A Map and Research Agenda for the Responsible Management Learning Field. *Journal of Business Ethics*, *162*(4), 735–757. doi:10.100710551-020-04440-5

Lab, B. (2020). *Certified B corporation*. https://bcorporation.net/

LaCaille, L. (2013). Theory of Reasoned Action. In *Encyclopedia of Behavioral Medicine* (pp. 1964–1967). Springer. doi:10.1007/978-1-4419-1005-9_1619

Langowitz, N., & Minniti, M. (2007). The entrepreneurial propensity of women. *Entrepreneurship Theory and Practice*, *31*(3), 341–364. doi:10.1111/j.1540-6520.2007.00177.x

Larrán, M., & García-Meca, E. (2004). La relevancia de la información no-financiera en la estrategia empresarial de divulgación unitaria: Percepciones empresa-analista sobre su utilidad. *Revista Valenciana de Economía y Hacienda*, (12), 127–145.

Le Blanc, D. (2015). Towards integration at last? The Sustainable Development Goals as a network of targets. *Sustainable Development*, *23*(3), 176–187. doi:10.1002d.1582

Leadbeater, C. (1997). The rise of the social entrepreneur. *Demos (Mexico City, Mexico)*.

Leal Filho, W., Tripathi, S. K., de Andrade Guerra, J. B. S. O., Giné-Garriga, R., Orlovic Lovren, V., & Willats, J. (2019). Using the sustainable development goals towards a better understanding of sustainability challenges. *International Journal of Sustainable Development and World Ecology*, *26*(2), 179–190. doi:10.1080/13504509.2018.1505674

Lefebvre, V., & Lefebvre, M. R. (2012). Integrating Corporate Social Responsibility at the Start-up Level: Constraint or Catalyst for Opportunity Identification? *International Business Research*, *5*(7). Advance online publication. doi:10.5539/ibr.v5n7p17

León Correa, F. J. (2008). Salud escolar y educación para la salud: Principios y valores desde la bioética. *Revista Hacia la Promoción de la Salud*, *13*, 25–41.

Lepak, D. P., Smith, K. G., & Taylor, M. S. (2007). Value Creation and Value Capture: A Multilevel Perspective. *Academy of Management Review*, *32*(1), 180–194. doi:10.5465/amr.2007.23464011

Lepoutre, J., Justo, R., Terjesen, S., & Bosma, N. (2013). Designing a global standardized methodology for measuring social entrepreneurship activity: The Global Entrepreneurship Monitor social entrepreneurship study. *Small Business Economics*, *40*(3), 693–714. doi:10.100711187-011-9398-4

Levie, J., & Hart, M. (2011). Business and social entrepreneurs in the UK: Gender, context and commitment. *International Journal of Gender and Entrepreneurship*, *3*(3), 200–217. doi:10.1108/17566261111169304

Ley 14/1986, de 25 de abril, General de Sanidad. BOE núm. 102, de 29 de abril de 1986.

Liao, M. Q., & Mak, A. K. (2019). "Comments are disabled for this video": A technological affordances approach understanding source credibility assessment of CSR information on YouTube. *Public Relations Review*, *45*(5), 101840. doi:10.1016/j.pubrev.2019.101840

Lichtenstein, B. B., Carter, N. M., Dooley, K. J., & Gartner, W. B. (2007). Complexity dynamics of nascent Entrepreneurship. *Journal of Business Venturing*, *22*(2), 236–261. doi:10.1016/j.jbusvent.2006.06.001

Liczma'nska-Kopcewicz, K., Mizera, K., & Pypłacz, P. (2019). Corporate Social Responsibility and Sustainable Development for Creating Value for FMCG Sector Enterprises. *Sustainability*, *11*(20), 5808. doi:10.3390u11205808

Lien, C. H., & Cao, Y. (2014). Examining WeChat users' motivations, trust, attitudes, and positive word-of-mouth: Evidence from China. *Computers in Human Behavior*, *41*, 104–111. doi:10.1016/j.chb.2014.08.013

Lien, C. H., Cao, Y., & Zhou, X. (2017). Service quality, satisfaction, stickiness, and usage intentions: An exploratory evaluation in the context of WeChat services. *Computers in Human Behavior*, *68*, 403–410. doi:10.1016/j.chb.2016.11.061

Liere, K. D., & Dunlap, R. E. (1978). Moral Norms and Environmental Behavior: An Application of Schwartz's Norm-Activation Model to Yard Burning1. *Journal of Applied Social Psychology*, *8*(2), 174–188. doi:10.1111/j.1559-1816.1978.tb00775.x

Li, F., & Du, T. C. (2011). Who is talking? An ontology-based opinion leader identification framework for word-of-mouth marketing in online social blogs. *Decision Support Systems*, *51*(1), 190–197. doi:10.1016/j.dss.2010.12.007

Liguori, E., & Bendickson, J. S. (2020). Rising to the challenge: Entrepreneurship ecosystems and SDG success. *Journal of the International Council for Small Business*, *1*(3-4), 118–125. doi:10.1080/26437015.2020.1827900

Li, J., & Leonas, K. K. (2019). Trends of Sustainable Development Among Luxury Industry. In M. Gardetti & S. Muthu (Eds.), *Sustainable luxury. Environmental footprints and eco-design of products and processes* (pp. 107–126). Springer. doi:10.1007/978-981-13-0623-5_6

Lin, C., Chen, S., Chiu, C., & Lee, W. (2011). Understanding purchase intention during product-harm crises: Moderating effects of perceived corporate ability and Corporate Social Responsibility. *Journal of Business Ethics*, *102*(3), 455–471. doi:10.100710551-011-0824-y

Linnenluecke, M. K., & Griffiths, A. (2010). Corporate sustainability and organizational culture. *Journal of World Business*, *45*(4), 357–366. doi:10.1016/j.jwb.2009.08.006

Lin, X., & Wang, X. (2020). Examining gender differences in people's information-sharing decisions on social networking sites. *International Journal of Information Management*, *50*, 45–56. doi:10.1016/j.ijinfomgt.2019.05.004

Littlewood, D., & Holt, D. (2018). How social enterprises can contribute to the Sustainable Development Goals (SDGs) – A conceptual framework. In Entrepreneurship and the Sustainable Development Goals (pp. 33-46). Emerald Publishing Limited.

Liu, K. S., Hsueh, S. L., & Chen, H. Y. (2018). Relationships between environmental education, environmental attitudes, and behavioral intentions toward ecolodging. *Open House International*, *43*(2), 5–12. doi:10.1108/OHI-02-2018-B0002

Liu, L., Liu, Y., & Mo, Z. (2020). Moral norm is the key: An extension of the theory of planned behaviour (TPB) on Chinese consumers' green purchase intention. *Asia Pacific Journal of Marketing and Logistics*, *32*(8), 1823–1841. doi:10.1108/APJML-05-2019-0285

Lloret, A. (2016). Modeling corporate sustainability strategy. *Journal of Business Research*, *69*(2), 418–425.

Loorbach, D., & Wijsman, K. (2018). Business transition management: Exploring a new role for business in sustainability transitions. *Journal of Cleaner Production*, *45*, 20–28. doi:10.1016/j.jclepro.2012.11.002

López, B., & Monfort, A. (2017). Creating shared value in the context of sustainability: The communication strategy of MNCs. *Corporate Governance and Strategic Decision Making*, 119-135.

López-Arceiz, F. J., Bellostas, A. J., & Rivera, M. P. (2016). The effects of resources on social activity and economic performance in social economy organizations. *Nonprofit Management & Leadership*, *20*(4), 83–96. doi:10.1002/nml.21204

Lorenzoni, I., Nicholson-Cole, S., & Whitmarsh, L. (2007). Barriers perceived to engaging with climate change among the UK public and their policy implications. *Global Environmental Change, 17*(3-4), 445–459.

Lo, S. F., & Sheu, H. J. (2007). Is Corporate Sustainability a Value-Increasing Strategy for Business? *Corporate Governance*, *15*(2), 345–358. doi:10.1111/j.1467-8683.2007.00565.x

Loureiro, S. M. C., Gorgus, T., & Kaufmann, H. R. (2017). Antecedents and outcomes of online brand engagement: The role of brand love on enhancing electronic-word-of-mouth. *Online Information Review*, *41*(7), 985–1005. doi:10.1108/OIR-08-2016-0236

Low, M. B., & MacMillan, I. C. (1988). Entrepreneurship: Past research and future challenges. *Journal of Management*, *14*(2), 139–161. doi:10.1177/014920638801400202

Lozano, R. (2012). Towards better embedding sustainability into companies' systems: An analysis of voluntary corporate initiatives. *Journal of Cleaner Production*, *25*, 14–26. doi:10.1016/j.jclepro.2011.11.060

Luetkenhorst, W. (2004). Corporate social responsibility and the development agenda. *Inter Economics*, *39*(3), 157–166. doi:10.1007/BF02933583

Lu, J., Liang, M., Zhang, C., Rong, D., Guan, H., Mazeikaite, K., & Streimikis, J. (2021). Assessment of corporate social responsibility by addressing sustainable development goals. *Corporate Social Responsibility and Environmental Management*, *28*(2), 686–703. doi:10.1002/csr.2081

Luxottica. (2021). *Sustainable Development Goals*. Retrieved from https://www.luxottica.com/en/sustainable-development-goals

LVMH. (2020a). *2019 Environmental Responsibility Report*. Retrieved from https://cutt.ly/7bEKbB5

LVMH. (2020b). *2019 Social Responsibility Report*. Retrieved from https://cutt.ly/GbbQtjF

LVMH. (2021a). *Houses*. Retrieved from https://www.lvmh.com/houses/

LVMH. (2021b). *Social & environmental responsibility*. Retrieved from https://cutt.ly/Ubbm7Vg

LVMH. (2021c). *2020 Annual Report. Passionate about creativity*. Retrieved from https://cutt.ly/ubbm6iI

Lyon, F., Teasdale, S., & Baldock, R. (2010). *Approaches to measuring the scale of the social enterprise sector in the UK*. Working Paper (Vol. 43).

MacDonald, A., Clarke, A., Huang, L., Roseland, M., & Seitanidi, M. M. (2018). Multi-stakeholder partnerships (SDG #17) as a means of achieving sustainable communities and cities (SDG #11). In W. Leal Filho (Ed.), *Handbook of sustainability science and research* (pp. 193–209). Springer. doi:10.1007/978-3-319-63007-6_12

Macia-Soler, M., & Moncho-Vasallo, J. (2007). Sistema Nacional de Salud Español. Características y análisis. *Enfermeria global, 6*(1).

Mackey, A., Mackey, T. B., & Barney, J. B. (2007). Corporate social responsibility and firm performance: Investor preferences and corporate strategies. *Academy of Management Review, 32*(3), 817–835. doi:10.5465/amr.2007.25275676

Mahmud, A., Ding, D., & Hasan, M. M. (2021). Corporate social responsibility: Business responses to Coronavirus (COVID-19) pandemic. *SAGE Open, 11*(1). doi:10.1177/2158244020988710

Maignan, I., & Ferrell, O. C. (2001). Antecedents and benefits of corporate citizenship: An investigation of French businesses. *Journal of Business Ethics, 23*(3), 283–294. doi:10.1023/A:1006262325211

Maignan, I., & Ferrell, O. C. (2004). Corporate social responsibility and marketing: An integrative framework. *Journal of the Academy of Marketing Science, 32*(1), 3–19. doi:10.1177/0092070303258971

Maignan, I., Ferrell, O. C., & Hult, G. T. M. (1999). Corporate Citizenship: Cultural Antecedents and Business Benefits. *Journal of the Academy of Marketing Science, 27*(4), 455–469. doi:10.1177/0092070399274005

Mair, J., Battilana, J., & Cardenas, J. (2012). Organizing for society: A typology of social entrepreneuring models. *Journal of Business Ethics, 111*(3), 353–373. doi:10.100710551-012-1414-3

Mair, J., & Marti, I. (2006). Social entrepreneurship research: A source of explanation, prediction, and delight. *Journal of World Business, 41*(1), 36–44. doi:10.1016/j.jwb.2005.09.002

Malik, I. A., & Hadi, N. U. (2019). Inspirational Factors of Electronic Word of Mouth: A Case of Social Networking Sites. *Journal of Managerial Sciences, 13*(2), 253–265. https://www.researchgate.net/publication/336651644_Inspirational_Factors_of_Electronic_Word_of_Mouth_A_Case_of_Social_Networking_Sites

Manes-Rossi, F., Nicolò, G., & Argento, D. (2020). Non-financial reporting formats in public sector organizations: A structured literature review. *Journal of Public Budgeting, Accounting & Financial Management, 32*(4), 639–669. doi:10.1108/JPBAFM-03-2020-0037

Manuel, T., & Herron, T. L. (2020). An ethical perspective of business CSR and the COVID-19 pandemic. *Society and Business Review, 15*(3), 235–253. doi:10.1108/SBR-06-2020-0086

Maqbool, S. (2019). Does corporate social responsibility lead to superior financial performance? Evidence from BSE 100 index. *Decision (Washington, D.C.), 46*(3), 219–231.

Maqbool, S., & Bakr, A. (2019). The curvilinear relationship between corporate social performance and financial performance. *Journal of Global Responsibility*.

Maqbool, S., & Hurrah, S. A. (2020). Exploring the Bi-directional relationship between corporate social responsibility and financial performance in Indian context. *Social Responsibility Journal.*

Maqbool, S., & Zamir, M. N. (2019). Corporate social responsibility reporting in India: A study of SENSEX companies. *Management and Labour Studies, 44*(2), 209–223.

March, J. G. (1992). The Business Firm as a political Coalition. Journal of Politics, 24.

Marcus, J., & Kurucs, E. C. (2010). Conceptions of the Business-Society-Nature Interface: Implications for Management Scholarship. *Business & Society, 49*(3), 402–438. doi:10.1177/0007650310368827

Margiono, A., Zolin, R., & Chang, A. (2018). A typology of social venture business model configurations. *International Journal of Entrepreneurial Behaviour & Research, 24*(3), 626–650. doi:10.1108/IJEBR-09-2016-0316

Marín, L., Nicolás, C., & Rubio, A. (2019). How gender, age and education influence the entrepreneur's social orientation: The moderating effect of economic development. *Sustainability, 11*(17), 1–16. doi:10.3390u11174514

Mariotti, F., Kadasah, N., & Abdulghaffar, N. (2014). Motivations and barriers affecting the implementation of ISO 14001 in Saudi Arabia: An empirical investigation. *Total Quality Management & Business Excellence, 25*(11–12), 1352–1364. doi:10.1080/14783363.2014.912038

Marom, S., & Lussier, R. N. (2020). Corporate Social Responsibility during the Coronavirus Pandemic: An Interim Overview. *Business and Economic Review, 10*(2), 250–269. doi:10.5296/ber.v10i2.17046

Martín, J. J. M. (2016). El sistema nacional de salud español ante la gran recesión. *Cuadernos de relaciones laborales, 34*(2), 315-334. doi:10.5209/CRLA.53459

Martínek, P. A. (2021). Mapping methods of research on consumer engagement with brands on social media: A literature review. *Methodological Innovations, 14*(1). doi:10.1177/2059799120985384

Martinez-Ferrero, J., & Frias-Aceituno, J. V. (2015). Relationship between sustainable development and financial performance: International empirical research. *Business Strategy and the Environment, 24*(1), 20–39. doi:10.1002/bse.1803

Martínez-Martínez, S. L. (2020). El Rol de la digitalización en el emprendimiento internacional: El modelo "Born Global". In J. C. Álvarez. & F. Vila (Eds.), Nuevas tecnologías y mercado de trabajo: una aproximación multidisciplinar (pp. 41-60). Laborum.

Martínez-Martínez, S. L., & Ventura, R. (2020). Entrepreneurial Profiles at the University: A Competence Approach. *Frontiers in Psychology, 11*(612796), 1–20. doi:10.3389/fpsyg.2020.612796 PMID:33391131

Martin, R. L., & Osberg, S. (2007). Social entrepreneurship: The case for definintion. *Stanford Social Innovation Review,* (Spring), 28–39.

Maslow, A. H. (1943). A theory of human motivation. *Psychological Review, 50*(4), 370–396. doi:10.1037/h0054346

Maslow, A. H. (1954). *Motivation and personality.* Harper and Row.

Mathews, B. P., Ueno, A., Periera, Z. L., Silva, G., Kekal, T., & Repka, M. (2001). Quality training: Findings from a European survey. *The TQM Magazine, 13*(1), 61–68. doi:10.1108/09544780110360615

Matten, D., & Crane, A. (2005). Corporate citizenship: Towards an extended theoretical conceptualization. *Academy of Management Review, 30*(1), 166–179. doi:10.5465/amr.2005.15281448

Matten, D., & Moon, J. (2008). "Implicit" And "Explicit" CSR: A Conceptual Framework for a Comparative Understanding of Corporate Social Responsibility. *Academy of Management Review, 33*(2), 404–424. doi:10.5465/amr.2008.31193458

Mattsson, J., & Rendtorff, J. D. (2006). E-marketing ethics: A theory of value priorities. *International Journal of Internet Marketing and Advertising*, *3*(1), 35–47.

Matute-Vallejo, J., Bravo, R., & Pina, J. M. (2011). The influence of corporate social responsibility and price fairness on customer behaviour: Evidence from the financial sector. *Corporate Social Responsibility and Environmental Management*, *18*(6), 317–331. doi:10.1002/csr.247

Mazda Motor Corporation. (2020). *Sustainability report, in-depth version*. Author.

Mazzarol, T., Volery, T., Doss, N., & Thein, V. (1999). Factors influencing small business start-ups. *International Journal of Entrepreneurial Behaviour & Research*, *5*(2), 48–63. doi:10.1108/13552559910274499

McKinsey & Company. (2020). *The State of Fashion 2021*. Retrieved from https://cutt.ly/smd530p

McKinsey. (2021). *Organizing for the future: Nine keys to becoming a future-ready company*. McKinsey & Company Insights. https://www.mckinsey.com/business-functions/organization/our-insights/organizing-for-the-future-nine-keys-to-becoming-a-future-ready-company

McWilliams, A., & Siegel, D. (1997). Event studies in management research: Theoretical and empirical issues. *Academy of Management Journal*, *40*(3), 626–657.

McWilliams, A., & Siegel, D. (2001). Corporate Social Responsibility: A Theory of the Firm Perspective. *Academy of Management Review*, *26*(1), 117–127. doi:10.5465/amr.2001.4011987

Meadowcroft, J. (2009). What about the politics? Sustainable development, transition management, and long-term energy transitions. *Policy Sciences*, *42*(4), 323–340. doi:10.100711077-009-9097-z

Mengual-Andrés, S. (2011). *La importancia percibida por el profesorado y el alumnado sobre la inclusión de la competencia digital en Educación Superior: Un análisis en Ciencias de la*. https://dialnet.unirioja.es/servlet/tesis?codigo=59631

Mengual-Andrés, S., Roig-Vila, R., & Mira, J. B. (2016). Delphi study for the design and validation of a questionnaire about digital competences in higher education. *International Journal of Educational Technology in Higher Education*, *13*(1), 12. Advance online publication. doi:10.118641239-016-0009-y

Metcalf, L., & Benn, S. (2012). The corporation is ailing social technology: Creating a "fit for purpose" design for sustainability. *Journal of Business Ethics*, *111*(2), 195–210. doi:10.100710551-012-1201-1

Meyer, M. (2015, August). Positive business: Doing good and doing well. *Business Ethics (Oxford, England)*, *24*(S2), S175–S197. doi:10.1111/beer.12105

Mhlanga, D., & Moloi, T. (2020). COVID-19 and the digital transformation of education: What are we learning on 4IR in South Africa? *Education Sciences*, *10*(7), 180. doi:10.3390/educsci10070180

Middel, R., Op De Weegh, S., & Gieskes, J. (2007). Continuous Improvement in the Netherlands: A Survey-Based Study into Current Practices. *International Journal of Technology Management*, *37*. doi:10.1504/IJTM.2007.012262

Millard, E. (2017). Still brewing: Fostering sustainable coffee production. *World Development Perspectives*, *7*, 32–42.

Ministerio de Sanidad del Gobierno de España. (n.d.). *PyDeSalud: Participa y Decide sobre tu Salud*. http://www.pydesalud.com/

Minniti, M., Arenius, P., & Langowitz, N. (2006). *The 2005 Global Entrepreneurship Monitor special topic report: Women in entrepreneurship*. Academic Press.

Minniti, M. (2010). Female entrepreneurship and economic activity. *European Journal of Development Research, 22*(3), 294–312. doi:10.1057/ejdr.2010.18

Mio, C., & Venturelli, A. (2013). Non-financial Information About Sustainable Development and Environmental Policy in the Annual Reports of Listed Companies: Evidence from Italy and the UK. *Corporate Social Responsibility and Environmental Management, 20*(6), 340–358. doi:10.1002/csr.1296

Miotto, G., Polo López, M., & Rom Rodríguez, J. (2019). Gender Equality and UN Sustainable Development Goals: Priorities and Correlations in the Top Business Schools' Communication and Legitimation Strategies. *Sustainability, 11*(2), 302. https://doi.org/10.3390/su11020302

Mira, J. B., Padrón, A. L., & Mengual-Andrés, S. (2010). Validación mediante el metodo Delphi de un cuestionario para conocer las experiencias e interés hacia las actividades acuáticas con especial atención al Winsurf. *AGORA*. https://cerro64.cpd.uva.es/handle/10324/23693

Miragaya, L. C. (2008). Sistemas nacionales de salud en proceso de reforma: Hacia fórmulas mixtas entre lo público y lo privado. *Panorama Social*, (7), 8–20.

Miska, C., Stahl, G. K., & Mendenhall, M. E. (2013). Intercultural competencies as antecedents of responsible global leadership. *European Journal of International Management, 7*(5), 550–569. doi:10.1504/EJIM.2013.056477

Mitsubishi Motors Corporation. (2020). *Sustainability Report*. Author.

Mkono, M., & Tribe, J. (2017). Beyond Reviewing: Uncovering the Multiple Roles of Tourism Social Media Users. *Journal of Travel Research, 56*(3), 287–298. doi:10.1177/0047287516636236

Mobus, J. L. (2005). Mandatory environmental disclosures in a legitimacy theory context. *Accounting, Auditing & Accountability Journal, 18*(4), 492–517.

Monfort, A., & Iglesias, J. M. M. (2021). Communicating CSR in social media: Challenges and opportunities. *Comunicación y Hombre*, (17), 349–361. doi:10.32466/eufv-cyh.2021.17.645.349-361

Monfort, A., Villagra, N., & López, B. (2019). Exploring stakeholders' dialogue and corporate social responsibility (CSR) on Twitter. *El Profesional de la Información, 28*(5). Advance online publication. doi:10.3145/epi.2019.sep.13

Montesinos, V., & Brusca, I. (2019). Non-financial reporting in the public sector: Alternatives, trends and opportunities. *Revista de Contabilidad, 22*(2), 22–128. doi:10.6018/rcsar.383071

Moon, J. (2007). The Contribution of Corporate Social Responsibility to Sustainable Development. *Sustainable Development, 15*(5), 296–306. doi:10.1002d.346

Moreno, S. (2021). La participación en salud: los Consejos de Salud. *Ocronos, 4*(2). https://revistamedica.com/participacion-consejos-salud/

Morgan-Thomas, A., & Veloutsou, C. (2013). Beyond technology acceptance: Brand relationships and online brand experience. *Journal of Business Research, 66*(1), 21–27. doi:10.1016/j.jbusres.2011.07.019

Morsing, M., & Perrini, F. (2009). CSR in SMEs: Do SMEs matter for the CSR agenda? *Business Ethics (Oxford, England), 18*(1), 1–6. doi:10.1111/j.1467-8608.2009.01544.x

Morsing, M., & Schultz, M. (2006). Corporate social responsibility communication: Stakeholder information, response and involvement strategies. *Business Ethics (Oxford, England), 15*(4), 323–339. doi:10.1111/j.1467-8608.2006.00460.x

Mort, G. S., Weerawardena, J., & Carnegie, K. (2003). Social entrepreneurship: Towards conceptualisation. *International Journal of Nonprofit and Voluntary Sector Marketing, 8*(1), 76–88. doi:10.1002/nvsm.202

Moser, A. K. (2016). Consumers' purchasing decisions regarding environmentally friendly products: An empirical analysis of German consumers. *Journal of Retailing and Consumer Services*, *31*, 389–397. doi:10.1016/j.jretconser.2016.05.006

Muralidharan, E., & Pathak, S. (2018). Sustainability, transformational leadership, and social entrepreneurship. *Sustainability*, *10*(2), 1–22. doi:10.3390u10020567

Murillo, D., & Lozano, J. M. (2006). SMEs and CSR: An approach to CSR in their own words. *Journal of Business Ethics*, *67*(3), 227–240. doi:10.100710551-006-9181-7

Muserra, A. L., Papa, M., & Grimaldi, F. (2020). Sustainable development and the European Union Policy on non-financial information: An Italian empirical analysis. *Corporate Social Responsibility and Environmental Management*, *27*(1), 22–31. doi:10.1002/csr.1770

Naidoo, R., & Fisher, B. (2020). *Reset sustainable development goals for a pandemic world*. Academic Press.

Nandan, M., London, M., & Bent-Goodley, T. (2014). Social workers as social change agents: Social innovation, social intrapreneurship, and social entrepreneurship. *Faculty Publications*, *3770*, 1–34.

Newberry, S. (2015). Public sector accounting: Shifting concepts of accountability. *Public Money & Management*, *35*(5), 371–376. doi:10.1080/09540962.2015.1061180

Nga, J. K. H., & Shamuganathan, G. (2010). The influence of personality traits and demographic factors on social entrepreneurship start up intentions. *Journal of Business Ethics*, *95*(2), 259–282. doi:10.100710551-009-0358-8

Ngan, S. L., How, B. S., Teng, S. Y., Promentilla, M. A. B., Yatim, P., Er, A. C., & Lam, H. L. (2019). Prioritization of sustainability indicators for promoting the circular economy: The case of developing countries. *Renewable & Sustainable Energy Reviews*, *111*, 314–331. doi:10.1016/j.rser.2019.05.001

Ngoma, M., & Ntale, P. D. (2019). *Word of mouth communication: A mediator of relationship marketing and customer loyalty*. doi:10.1080/23311975.2019.1580123

Nicholls, A. (2006). *Social Entrepreneurship. New Models of Sustainable Change*. Oxford University Press.

Nicolás, C., & Rubio, A. (2012). El emprendimiento social: Una comparativa entre España y países sudamericanos. *Faedpyme International Review*, *1*(1), 38–49.

Nicolás, C., Rubio, A., & Fernández-Laviada, A. (2018). Cognitive determinants of social entrepreneurship: Variations according to the degree of economic development. *Journal of Social Entrepreneurship*, *9*(2), 154–168. doi:10.1080/19420676.2018.1452280

Nigri, G., & Del Baldo, M. (2018). Sustainability Reporting and Performance Measurement Systems: How do Small- and Medium-Sized Benefit Corporations Manage Integration? *Sustainability*, *10*(12), 4499. Advance online publication. doi:10.3390u10124499

Nilsson, M., Griggs, D., & Visbeck, M. (2016). Policy: Map the interactions between Sustainable Development Goals. *NATNews*, *534*(7607), 320–322. doi:10.1038/534320a PMID:27306173

Nissan Motor Corporation. (2020). *Sustainability Report*. Author.

Nonaka, I. (1994). A Dynamic Theory of Organizational Knowledge Creation. *Organization Science*, *5*(1), 14–37. doi:10.1287/orsc.5.1.14

Nuño, R., Rodríguez, C., Piñera, K., Zaballa, I., & Bikandi, J. (2013). Panorama de las iniciativas de educación para el cuidado en España. *Gaceta Sanitaria*, *27*(4), 332–337. doi:10.1016/j.gaceta.2013.01.008 PMID:23465729

O'Connor, R. C., Wetherall, K., Cleare, S., McClelland, H., Melson, A. J., Niedzwiedz, C. L., ... Robb, K. A. (2020). Mental health and well-being during the COVID-19 pandemic: Longitudinal analyses of adults in the UK COVID-19 Mental Health & Wellbeing study. *The British Journal of Psychiatry*, 1–8. doi:10.1192/bjp.2020.212 PMID:33081860

Obrenovic, B., Du, J., Godinic, D., Tsoy, D., Khan, M. A. S., & Jakhongirov, I. (2020). Sustaining enterprise operations and productivity during the COVID-19 pandemic:"Enterprise Effectiveness and Sustainability Model. *Sustainability*, *12*(15), 5981. doi:10.3390u12155981

Okazaki, S., Plangger, K., West, D., & Menéndez, H. D. (2020). Exploring digital corporate social responsibility communications on Twitter. *Journal of Business Research*, *117*, 675–682. doi:10.1016/j.jbusres.2019.09.006

Oliver, A., & González, A. (2020). Facilitando la salud comunitaria. Indicadores básicos de salud por área básica de salud en Cataluña. *Gaceta Sanitaria*, *34*(2), 204–207. doi:10.1016/j.gaceta.2019.05.012 PMID:31488325

Olšanová, K., Gook, G., & Zlatić, M. (2018). Influence of luxury companies' corporate social responsibility activities on consumer purchase intention: Development of a theoretical framework. *Central European Business Review*, *7*(3), 1–25. doi:10.18267/j.cebr.200

Organisation for Economic Co-operation and Development (OECD). (2001). *Corporate Social Responsibility: Partners for Progress*. OECD Publishing.

Organización Mundial de la Salud. (n.d.). https://www.who.int/healthpromotion/conferences/9gchp/about/es/

Ormiston, J., & Seymour, R. (2011). Understanding value creation in social entrepreneurship: The importance of aligning mission, strategy and impact measurement. *Journal of Social Entrepreneurship*, *2*(2), 125–150. doi:10.1080/19420676.2011.606331

Ossebaard, H., Seydel, E., & van Gemert-Pijnen, L. (2012). Online usability and patients with long-term conditions: A mixed-methods approach. *Review International Journal of Medical Informatics*, *81*(6), 374–387. doi:10.1016/j.ijmedinf.2011.12.010 PMID:22261086

Ozanne, L. K., Phipps, M., Weaver, T., Carrington, M., Luchs, M., Catlin, J., Gupta, S., Santos, N., Scott, K., & Williams, J. (2016). Managing the Tensions at the Intersection of the Triple Bottom Line: A Paradox Theory Approach to Sustainability Management. *Journal of Public Policy & Marketing*, *35*(2), 249–261. doi:10.1509/jppm.15.143

Pacheco, I. (2020). How much COVID-19 cost those businesses that stayed open. *The Wall Street Journal*. www.wsj.com/articles/how-much-covid-19-cost-those-businessesthat-stayed-open-11592910575

Pacto Mundial. (2017). *Empresas españolas y ODS: Oportunidades y desafíos*. Red Española del Pacto Mundial. https://www.pactomundial.org/sdm_downloads/empresas-espanolas-ods-oportunidades-desafios/

Padhi, B., & Barik, G. S. (2016). A Study on Value Creation Model in Corporate Social Responsibility. *International Journal of Research in Engineering and Science*, *4*(7), 75–82.

Paelman, V., Van Cauwenberge, P., & Vander Bauwhede, H. (2020). Effect of B corp certification on short-term growth: European evidence. *Sustainability (Switzerland)*, *12*(20), 1–18. doi:10.3390u12208459

Paine, L. S. (1994). Managing for Organizational Integrity. Harvard Business Review.

Paine, L. S. (1997). Cases in Leadership, Ethics, and Organizational Integrity. A Strategic Perspective. Academic Press.

Paine, L. S. (1996). Moral Thinking in Management. An Essential Capability. *Business Ethics Quarterly*, *6*(4), 477–492. doi:10.2307/3857500

Palakshappa, N., & Dodds, S. (2020). Mobilising SDG 12: Co-creating sustainability through brands. *Marketing Intelligence & Planning*, *39*(2), 265–283. doi:10.1108/MIP-08-2018-0360

Palazzo, G., & Scherer, A. G. (2006). Corporate legitimacy as deliberation. A communicative framework. *Journal of Business Ethics*, *66*(1), 71–88. doi:10.100710551-006-9044-2

Paliwoda-Matiolanska, A., Smolak-Lozano, E., & Nakayama, A. (2020). Corporate image or social engagement: Twitter discourse on corporate social responsibility (CSR) in public relations strategies in the energy sector. *El Profesional de la Información*, *29*(3).

Panapanaan, V. M., Linnanen, L., Karvonen, M., & Phan, V. T. (2003). Roadmapping corporate social responsibility in Finnish companies. *Journal of Business Ethics*, *44*(2-3), 133–148. doi:10.1023/A:1023391530903

Pang, H. (2021). Identifying associations between mobile social media users' perceived values, attitude, satisfaction, and eWOM engagement: The moderating role of affective factors. *Telematics and Informatics*, *59*, 101561. doi:10.1016/j.tele.2020.101561

Pansari, A., & Kumar, V. (2017). Customer engagement: The construct, antecedents, and consequences. *Journal of the Academy of Marketing Science*, *45*(3), 294–311. doi:10.100711747-016-0485-6

Papagiannidis, S., Harris, J., & Morton, D. (2020). WHO led the digital transformation of your company? A reflection of IT related challenges during the pandemic. *International Journal of Information Management*, *55*, 102166. doi:10.1016/j.ijinfomgt.2020.102166 PMID:32836631

Parguel, B., Benoît-Moreau, F., & Larceneux, F. (2011). How sustainability ratings might deter 'greenwashing': A closer look at ethical corporate communication. *Journal of Business Ethics*, *102*(1), 15–28. doi:10.100710551-011-0901-2

Park, C., & Lee, T. M. (2009). Information direction, website reputation and eWOM effect: A moderating role of product type. *Journal of Business Research*, *62*(1), 61–67. doi:10.1016/j.jbusres.2007.11.017

Parker, S. C., Gamble, E. N., Moroz, P. W., & Branzei, O. (2019). The impact of B lab certification on firm growth. *Academy of Management Discoveries*, *5*(1), 57–77. doi:10.5465/amd.2017.0068

Pathak, S., & Muralidharan, E. (2016). Informal institutions and their comparative influences on social and commercial entrepreneurship: The role of in-group collectivism and interpersonal trust. *Journal of Small Business Management*, *54*(S1), 168–188. doi:10.1111/jsbm.12289

Patten, D. M. (1992). Intra-industry environmental disclosures in response to the Alaskan oil spill: A note on legitimacy theory. *Accounting, Organizations and Society*, *17*(5), 471–475.

Patten, D. M. (2008). Does the market value corporate philanthropy? Evidence from the response to the 2004 tsunami relief effort. *Journal of Business Ethics*, *81*(3), 599–607. doi:10.100710551-007-9534-x

Pearson, C. M., & Clair, J. A. (1998). Reframing crisis management. *Academy of Management Review*, *23*(1), 59–76. doi:10.5465/amr.1998.192960

Pedersen, J. S., & Rendtorff, J. D. (2004). Value-based Management in Local Public Organizations: A Danish Experience. *Cross Cultural Management*, *11*(2).

Peloza, J., & Shang, J. (2011). How can corporate social responsibility activities create value for stakeholders? A systematic review. *Journal of the Academy of Marketing Science*, *39*(1), 117–135. doi:10.100711747-010-0213-6

Penrose, E. T. (1959). *The Theory of the Growth of the Firm*. John Wiley.

Peredo, A. M., & McLean, M. (2006). Social entrepreneurship: A critical review of the concept. *Journal of World Business*, *41*(1), 56–65. doi:10.1016/j.jwb.2005.10.007

Pérez, A. (2011). *A study of corporate social responsibility image: Its formation process and its integration in banking service users behavior* [Thesis]. University of Cantabria, Santander, Spain.

Pérez, A., López, C., & García de los Salmones, M. M. (2020). Do all CSR news affect market value equally? *Social Responsibility Journal*, *16*(8), 1107–1123. doi:10.1108/SRJ-03-2019-0116

Perrini, F., Costanzo, L. A., & Karatas-Ozkan, M. (2020). Measuring impact and creating change: a comparison of the main methods for social enterprises. *Corporate Governance: The International Journal of Business in Society.*

Perrini, F., Russo, A., & Tencati, A. (2007). CSR Strategies of SMEs and Large Firms. Evidence from Italy. *Journal of Business Ethics*, *74*(3), 285–300. doi:10.100710551-006-9235-x

Petersen, K., Feldt, R., Mujtaba, S., & Mattsson, M. (2008). Systematic mapping studies in software engineering. In *12th International Conference on Evaluation and Assessment in Software Engineering (EASE) 12* (pp. 1-10). Academic Press.

Peugeot S. A. (2019). *Corporate Social Responsibility Report*. Author.

Pfeffer, J. (2010). Building sustainable organizations: The human factor. *The Academy of Management Perspectives*, *24*, 34–45.

Phillips, R. A., & Freeman, R. E. (2010). *Stakeholders*. Edward Elgar Publishing. doi:10.4337/9781785362316

Pistoni, A., Songini, L., & Bavagnoli, F. (2018). Integrated reporting quality: An empirical analysis. *Corporate Social Responsibility and Environmental Management*, *25*(4), 489–507. doi:10.1002/csr.1474

Pizzi, S. (2018). The Relationship between Non-financial Reporting, Environmental Strategies and Financial Performance. Empirical Evidence from Milano Stock Exchange. *Administrative Sciences*, *8*(4), 76–84. doi:10.3390/admsci8040076

Poponi, S., Colantoni, A., Cividino, S. R. S., & Mosconi, E. M. (2019). The Stakeholders' perspective within the B corp certification for a circular approach. *Sustainability (Switzerland)*, *11*(6), 1584. Advance online publication. doi:10.3390u11061584

Porter, M. E., & Kramer, M. R. (2003) The competitive advantage of corporate philanthropy. Reprinted In Harvard business review on corporate social responsibility. Harvard Business School Press.

Porter, M. E., & Kramer, M. R. (2006, Dec.). Strategy and Society: The Link Between Competitive Advantage and Corporate Social Responsibility. Harvard Business Review.

Porter, M. E. (1980). *Competitive strategy*. Free Press.

Porter, M. E. (1987). From competitive advantage to corporate strategy. *Harvard Business Review*, *65*(3), 43–59. PMID:17183795

Porter, M. E. (2008). The five competitive forces that shape strategy. *Harvard Business Review*, *86*(1), 79–93. PMID:18271320

Porter, M. E., & Kramer, M. R. (2006). Strategy and society: The link between competitive Advantage and corporate social responsibility. *Harvard Business Review*, *84*(12), 78–92. PMID:17183795

Porter, M. E., & Kramer, M. R. (2006). The link between competitive advantage and corporate social responsibility. *Harvard Business Review*, *84*(12), 78–92. doi:10.1108d.2007.05623ead.006 PMID:17183795

Porter, M. E., & Kramer, M. R. (2011). Creating shared value. *Harvard Business Review*, *89*(1-2).

Porter, M. E., & Kramer, M. R. (2011). *Creating Shared Value*. Harvard Business Review.

Porter, M. E., & Kramer, M. R. (2011). Creating shared value. How to reinvent Capitalism – And unleash a wave of innovation and growth. *Harvard Business Review*, *89*(1), 62–77.

Portney, K. E. (2013). Local Sustainability Policies and Programs As Economic Development: Is the New Economic Development Sustainable Development? Cityscape: A Journal of Policy Development and Research, 15.

Potts, J., Lynch, M., Wilkings, A., Huppé, G. A., Cunningham, M., & Voora, V. A. (2014). *The state of sustainability initiatives review 2014: Standards and the green economy*. International Institute for Sustainable Development.

Powell, C. (2003). The Delphi technique: Myths and realities. Journal of Advanced Nursing, 41(4), 376–382. doi:10.1046/j.1365-2648.2003.02537.x

Procter, L., Angus, D. J., Blaszczynski, A., & Gainsbury, S. M. (2019). Understanding use of consumer protection tools among Internet gambling customers: Utility of the Theory of Planned Behavior and Theory of Reasoned Action. *Addictive Behaviors*, *99*, 106050. doi:10.1016/j.addbeh.2019.106050 PMID:31522130

Prosser, A. M., Judge, M., Bolderdijk, J. W., Blackwood, L., & Kurz, T. (2020). 'Distancers' and 'non-distancers'? The potential social psychological impact of moralizing COVID-19 mitigating practices on sustained behaviour change. *British Journal of Social Psychology*, *59*(3), 653–662. doi:10.1111/bjso.12399 PMID:32584437

Purvis, B., Mao, Y., & Robinson, D. (2019). Three pillars of sustainability: In search of conceptual origins. *Sustainability Science*, *14*, 681–695.

Purwanto, A., Fahlevi, M., Zuniawan, A., Kusuma, R. P., Supriatna, H., & Maryani, E. (2020). The Covid-19 pandemic impact on industries performance: An explorative study of Indonesian companies. *Journal of Critical Review*, *7*, 1965–1972.

Putnam, H. (2002). *The Collapse of the Fact/Value Dichotomy and Other Essays*. Harvard University Press.

PVH. (2020). *2019 CR Report*. Retrieved from https://www.pvh.com/-/media/Files/pvh/responsibility/PVH-CR-Report-2019.pdf

PVH. (2021a). *Brands*. Retrieved from https://www.pvh.com/brands

PVH. (2021b). *Responsibility*. Retrieved from https://www.pvh.com/responsibility

PwC. (2015). Make it your business: Engaging with the Sustainable Development Goals [Report]. PriceWaterhouseCoopers.

PwC. (2017). *SDG reporting challenge 2017. Exploring business communication on the global goals* [Report]. https://www.pwc.com/gx/en/sustainability/SDG/pwc-sdg-reporting-chal-lenge-2017-final.pdf

PWC. (2018). *SDG Reporting Challenge 2017 - Exploring business communication on the global goals*. PWC.

PwC. (2020). *Retos del emprendimiento social en España y su contribución para el cumplimiento de los ODS* [Report]. https://www.pwc.es/es/publicaciones/tercer-sector/informe-emprendimiento-social-pwc-y-ashoka.pdf

Qiu, S. C., Jiang, J., Liu, X., Chen, M. H., & Yuan, X. (2021). Can corporate social responsibility protect firm value during the COVID-19 pandemic? *International Journal of Hospitality Management*, *93*, 102759. doi:10.1016/j.ijhm.2020.102759

Quinn, R. E., & Rohrbaugh, J. (1981). A Competing Values Approach to Organizational Effectiveness. *Public Productivity Review*, *5*(2), 122–140. doi:10.2307/3380029

Rahim, R. A., Sulaiman, Z., Chin, T. A., Baharun, R., & Muharam, F. M. (2016). Measuring electronic word of mouth review adoption on green purchase intention using source credibility theory. *Advanced Science Letters*, *22*(12), 4283–4287. doi:10.1166/asl.2016.8129

Rahul De, N. P., & Pal, A. (n.d.). Impact of Digital Surge during Covid-19 Pandemic: A Viewpoint on Research and Practice. *International Journal of Information Management*.

Rai, S. S., Rai, S., & Singh, N. K. (2021). Organizational resilience and social-economic sustainability: COVID-19 perspective. *Environment, Development and Sustainability*, 1–18. PMID:33519297

Raman, S. R. (2006). Corporate social reporting in India – A view from the top. *Global Business Review*, *7*(2), 313–324.

Ramirez, O., Carrasco, J.M., González, R., & Fanjul, G. (2020). Resumen de ODS3+ del concepto a la implementación de la "Salud en todas las políticas" en España. *Revista Diecisite: Investigación interdisciplinar para los Objetivos del Desarrollo Sostenible,* (3), 25-42. doi:10.36852/2695-4427_2020_03.02

Ramos, A. R., & Ruiz, J. (2008). Base intelectual de la investigación en creación de empresas: Un estudio biométrico. *Revista Europea de Dirección y Economía de la Empresa*, *17*(1), 13–38.

Randle, M., Kemperman, A., & Dolnicar, S. (2019). Making cause-related corporate social responsibility (CSR)count in holiday accommodation choice. *Tourism Management*, *75*, 66–77. doi:10.1016/j.tourman.2019.05.002

Raucci, D., & Tarquinio, L. (2020). Sustainability Performance Indicators and Non-Financial Information Reporting. Evidence from the Italian Case. *Administrative Sciences*, *10*(1), 13–29. doi:10.3390/admsci10010013

Raulet, G. (2011). Legitimacy and Globalization. *Philosophy and Social Criticism*, *37*(3), 313–323.

Rawhouser, H., Cummings, M., & Newbert, S. L. (2019). Social impact measurement: Current approaches and future directions for social entrepreneurship research. *Entrepreneurship Theory and Practice*, *43*(1), 82–115. doi:10.1177/1042258717727718

Razali, F., Daud, D., Weng-Wai, C., & Jiram, W. R. A. (2020). Waste separation at source behaviour among Malaysian households: The Theory of Planned Behaviour with moral norm. *Journal of Cleaner Production*, *271*, 122025. doi:10.1016/j.jclepro.2020.122025

Reimers, F. M., & Schleicher, A. (2020). *A framework to guide an education response to the COVID-19 Pandemic of 2020*. OECD.

Reimer, T., & Benkenstein, M. (2018). Not just for the recommender: How eWOM incentives influence the recommendation audience. *Journal of Business Research*, *86*, 11–21. doi:10.1016/j.jbusres.2018.01.041

Rendtorff, J. D. (2011a). Institutionalization of corporate ethics and social responsibility programs in firms. I K. Buhmann, L. Roseberry, & M. Morsing (eds.), Corporate social and human rights responsibilities: global, legal and management perspectives (pp. 244-266). London: Palgrave Macmillan.

Rendtorff, J. D. (2011b). Business Ethics, Strategy and Organizational Integrity: The Importance of Integrity as a Basic Principle of Business Ethics That Contributes to Better Economic Performance. I C. Wankel, & A. Stachowicz-Stanusch (eds.), Handbook of Research on Teaching Ethics in Business and Management Education (pp. 274-288).

Rendtorff, J. D. (2013a). Basic concepts of philosophy of management and corporations. I C. Luetge (ed.), Handbook of the philosophical foundations of business ethics (pp. 1361-1386). Dordrecht, Heidelberg, New York, London: Springer Science+Business Media.

Rendtorff, J. D. (2013b). Philosophical theories of management and corporations. I C. Luetge (ed.), Handbook of the philosophical foundations of business ethics (pp. 1409-1432). Dordrecht, Heidelberg, New York, London: Springer Science+Business Media.

Rendtorff, J. D. (2013c). Recent debates in philosophy of management. I C. Luetge (ed.), Handbook of the philosophical foundations of business ethics (pp. 1433-1457). Dordrecht, Heidelberg, New York, London: Springer Science+Business Media.

Rendtorff, J. D. (2013d). The history of the philosophy of management and corporations. I C. Luetge (ed.), Handbook of the philosophical foundations of business ethics (pp. 1387-1408). Dordrecht, Heidelberg, New York, London: Springer Science+Business Media.

Rendtorff, J. D. (2020). The Concept of Business Legitimacy: Learnings from Suchman. Integrating Sociological, Ethical and Critical Perspectives. In Handbook of Business Legitimacy. Springer Nature Switzerland AG.

Rendtorff, J. D. (2002). Basic ethical principles in European bioethics and biolaw: Autonomy, dignity, integrity and vulnerability. towards a foundation of bioethics and biolaw. *Medicine, Health Care, and Philosophy*, *5*(3), 235–244. doi:10.1023/A:1021132602330 PMID:12517031

Rendtorff, J. D. (2009). Basic ethical principles applied to service industries. *Service Industries Journal*, *29*(1), 9–19. doi:10.1080/02642060802116404

Rendtorff, J. D. (2010). *Power and Principle in the Market Place: On Ethics and Economics*. Ashgate.

Rendtorff, J. D. (2017). *Cosmopolitan Business Ethics: Towards a Global Ethos of Management*. Challenges to Theory and Practice Series. Routledge. Finance, Governance and Sustainability. doi:10.4324/9781315574400

Rendtorff, J. D. (2019a). *Philosophy of Management and Sustainability: Rethinking Business Ethics and Social Responsibility in Sustainable Development*. Emerald Group Publishing.

Rendtorff, J. D. (2019b). Sustainable development goals and progressive business models for economic transformation. *Local Economy*, *34*(6), 510–524.

Renouard, C., & Ezvan, C. (2018). Corporate social responsibility towards human development: A capabilities framework. *Business Ethics (Oxford, England)*, *27*(2), 144–155. doi:10.1111/beer.12181

Retolaza, J. L., Ruiz, M., & San-Jose, L. (2009). CSR in business start-ups: An application method for stakeholder engagement. *Corporate Social Responsibility and Environmental Management*, *16*(6), 324–336. doi:10.1002/csr.191

Rey-Martí, A., Ribeiro-Soriano, D., & Palacios-Marqués, D. (2016). A bibliometric analysis of social entrepreneurship. *Journal of Business Research*, *69*(5), 1651–1655. doi:10.1016/j.jbusres.2015.10.033

Rezaee, Z., & Tuo, L. (2017). Voluntary disclosure of non-financial information and its association with sustainability performance. *Advances in Accounting*, *39*, 47–59. doi:10.1016/j.adiac.2017.08.001

Ribeiro-Soriano, D. (2017). Small business and entrepreneurship: Their role in economic and social development. *Entrepreneurship and Regional Development*, *29*(1-2), 1–3. doi:10.1080/08985626.2016.1255438

Richemont. (2021a). Retrieved from https://www.richemont.com/en/home/

Richemont. (2021b). *Sustainability. Our approach*. Retrieved from https://www.richemont.com/en/home/sustainability/our-approach/

Richemont. (2021c). *Sustainability Report 2020*. Retrieved from https://www.richemont.com/media/4ksenvnu/sustainability_report_2020.pdf

Richter, U. H., & Dow, K. E. (2017). Stakeholder theory: A deliberative perspective. *Business Ethics (Oxford, England)*, *26*(4), 428–442. doi:10.1111/beer.12164

Ricoeur, P. (1990). *Soi-même comme un Autre*. Le Seuil.

Rivero-Jiménez, B. R., Conde-Caballero, D., & Mariano-Juárez, L. (2020). Educación para la salud y alimentación en personas mayores. Tradición, cultura y autoridad en Las Hurdes (Extremadura-España). *Educación (Lima)*, (3), 18–25.

Rivis, A., Sheeran, P., & Armitage, C. J. (2009). Expanding the Affective and Normative Components of the Theory of Planned Behavior: A Meta-Analysis of Anticipated Affect and Moral Norms. *Journal of Applied Social Psychology*, *39*(12), 2985–3019. doi:10.1111/j.1559-1816.2009.00558.x

Roberts, D., & Woods, C. (2005). Changing the world on a shoestring: The concept of social entrepreneurship. *University of Auckland Business Review*, *7*(1), 45–51.

Robinson, H. S., Anumba, C. J., Carrillo, P. M., & Al-Ghassani, A. M. (2016). STEPS: A knowledge management maturity roadmap for corporate sustainability. *Business Process Management Journal*, *12*(6), 793–808. doi:10.1108/14637150610710936

Romi, A., Cook, K. A., & Dixon-Fowler, H. R. (2018). The influence of social responsibility on employee productivity and sales growth: Evidence from certified B corps. *Sustainability Accounting. Management and Policy Journal*, *9*(4), 392–421. doi:10.1108/SAMPJ-12-2016-0097

Rothenhoefer, L. M. (2019). The impact of CSR on corporate reputation perceptions of the public—A configurational multi-time, multi-source perspective, Business Ethics. *European Review (Chichester, England)*, *28*(2), 141–155. doi:10.1111/beer.12207

Rousseau, D. M. (2012). Organizational Behavior's Contributions to Evidence-Based Management. In The Oxford Handbook of Evidence-Based Management. doi:10.1093/oxfordhb/9780199763986.013.0004

Ruiz-Azarola, A., & Perestelo-Pérez, L. (2012). Participación ciudadana en salud: Formación y toma de decisiones compartida. Informe SESPAS 2012. *Gaceta Sanitaria*, *26*, 158–161. doi:10.1016/j.gaceta.2011.10.005 PMID:22265652

Rupp, D. E., & Mallory, D. B. (2015). Corporate social responsibility: Psychological, person-centric, and progressing. *Annual Review of Organizational Psychology and Organizational Behavior*, *2*(1), 211–236. doi:10.1146/annurev-orgpsych-032414-111505

Russo, A., & Perrini, F. (2009). Investigating Stakeholder Theory and Social Capital: CSR in Large Firms and SMEs. *Journal of Business Ethics*, *91*(2), 207–221. doi:10.100710551-009-0079-z

Russo, A., & Tencati, A. (2008). Formal vs. Informal CSR Strategies: Evidence from Italian Micro, Small, Medium-sized, and Large Firms. *Journal of Business Ethics*, *85*(S2), 339–353. doi:10.100710551-008-9736-x

Rutter, D. R., & Bunce, D. J. (1989). The theory of reasoned action of Fishbein and Ajzen: A test of Towriss's amended procedure for measuring beliefs. *British Journal of Social Psychology*, *28*(1), 39–46. doi:10.1111/j.2044-8309.1989.tb00844.x

Rynes, S. L., & Bartunek, J. M. (2017). Evidence-Based Management: Foundations, Development, Controversies and Future. *Annual Review of Organizational Psychology and Organizational Behavior*, *4*(1), 235–261. doi:10.1146/annurev-orgpsych-032516-113306

Sachs, J. D., Schmidt-Traub, G., Kroll, C., Lafortune, G., & Fuller, G. (2018). *SDG Index and Dashboards Report 2018*. New Tork: Bertelsmann Stiftung and Sustainable Development Solutions Network (SDSN).

Sachs, J. D. (2012). From millennium development goals to sustainable development goals. *Lancet*, *379*(9832), 2206–2211. doi:10.1016/S0140-6736(12)60685-0 PMID:22682467

Sachs, J., Schmidt-Traub, G., Kroll, C., Lafortune, G., Fuller, G., & Woelm, F. (2020). *The Sustainable Development Goals and COVID-19. Sustainable development report 2020* [Report]. Cambridge University Press.

Saizarbitoria Iñaki, H., Arana Landín, G., & Casadesús Fa, M. (2006). A Delphi study on motivation for ISO 9000 and EFQM. *International Journal of Quality & Reliability Management*, *23*(7), 807–827. doi:10.1108/02656710610679824

Salazar, V. A., & Katigbak, J. J. P. (2016). Financing the Sustainable Development Goals through private sector partnership. *CIRSS Commentaries*, *3*(10), 1–2.

Salvioni, D. M., Franzoni, S., & Cassano, R. (2017). Sustainability in the Higher Education System: An Opportunity to Improve Quality and Image. *Sustainability*, *9*(6), 914. https://doi.org/10.3390/su9060914

Salzmann, O., Ionescu-Somers, A., & Steger, U. (2005). The business case for corporate sustainability: Literature review and research options. *European Management Journal*, *23*(1), 27–36. doi:10.1016/j.emj.2004.12.007

Samper, L. F., & Quiñones-Ruiz, X. F. (2017). Towards a balanced sustainability vision for the coffee industry. *Resources*, *6*(2), 17.

Samson, A. (2010). Product Usage and Firm-Generated Word of Mouth: Some Results from FMCG Product Trials. *International Journal of Market Research*, *52*(4), 459–482. doi:10.2501/S1470785309201405

Sánchez, L., & Blanco, B. (2014). Three decades of continuous improvement. *Total Quality Management & Business Excellence*, *25*(9-10), 986–1001. doi:10.1080/14783363.2013.856547

Sánchez-Medina, A., Benítez-del-Rosario, J. M., & Blázquez-Santana, F. (2017). Anomia and Displacement of Responsibility as Determinants of Tourist Company Managers' Non-Involvement in Alleviating Poverty. *Sustainability*, *9*(5), 802. https://doi.org/10.3390/su9050802

Sanchez-Ruiz, L., Blanco, B., & Diaz, E. (2019). Difficulty in implementing continuous improvement – Rasch measurement analysis. *Business Process Management Journal*, *25*(6), 1228–1250. doi:10.1108/BPMJ-05-2017-0125

Sánchez-Ruiz, L., Blanco, B., & Gómez-López, R. (2019). Continuous improvement enablers: Defining a new construct. *Journal of Industrial Engineering and Management JIEM*, *12*(1), 51. doi:10.3926/jiem.2743

Sanchez-Ruiz, L., Gomez-Lopez, R., & Blanco, B. (2020). Barriers to effectively implementing continuous improvement in Spanish firms. *Total Quality Management & Business Excellence*, *31*(13–14), 1409–1426. doi:10.1080/14783363.2019.1699783

Santos, F. (2012). A positive theory of social entrepreneurship. *Journal of Business Ethics*, *111*(3), 335–351. doi:10.100710551-012-1413-4

Sanyang, S. E., & Huang, W. C. (2009). Entrepreneurship and economic development: The EMPRETEC showcase. *The International Entrepreneurship and Management Journal*, *6*(3), 317–329. doi:10.100711365-008-0106-z

Sanz-Tolosana, E. (2018). Crisis, austeridad y áreas rurales: Estudio cualitativo de las percepciones sobre los impactos en el sistema sanitario y la salud en Navarra, España. *Saúde e Sociedade*, *27*(3), 898–908. doi:10.15900104-12902018170745

Sassmannshausen, S. P., & Volkmann, C. (2018). The scientometrics of social entrepreneurship and its establishment as an academic field. *Journal of Small Business Management*, *56*(2), 251–273. doi:10.1111/jsbm.12254

Saxton, G. D., Ren, C., & Guo, C. (2020). Responding to Diffused Stakeholders on Social Media: Connective Power and Firm Reactions to CSR-Related Twitter Messages. *Journal of Business Ethics*, •••, 1–24.

Schaltegger, S., & Burritt, R. (2018). Business cases and corporate engagement with sustainability: Differentiating ethical motivations. *Journal of Business Ethics*, *147*(2), 241–259. doi:10.100710551-015-2938-0

Schaltegger, S., Ludeke-Freund, F., & Hansen, E. G. (2012). Business cases for sustainability: The role of business model innovation for corporate sustainability. *International Journal of Innovation and Sustainable Development*, *6*(2), 95–119. doi:10.1504/IJISD.2012.046944

Schein, E. (1993). *Organizational culture and leadership*. Prentice Hall.

Schein, E. H. (2017). *Organizational Culture and Leadership* (5th ed.). Jon Wiley & Sons Inc.

Scherer, Palazzo, & Seidl. (2013). Managing Legitimacy in Complex and Heterogeneous Environments: Sustainable Development in a Globalized World. *Journal of Management Studies*, *50*(2), 259-284.

Scherer, A. G., & Palazzo, G. (2007). „Toward a Political Conception of Corporate Responsibility: Business and Society seen from a Habermasian Perspective. *Academy of Management Review*, *32*(4), 1096–1120. doi:10.5465/amr.2007.26585837

Scherer, A. G., & Palazzo, G. (2011). The new political role of business in a globalized world: A review of a new perspective on CSR and its implications for the firm, governance, and democracy. *Journal of Management Studies*, *48*(4), 899–931. doi:10.1111/j.1467-6486.2010.00950.x

Scheyvens, R., Banks, G., & Hughes, E. (2016). The private sector and the SDGs: The need to move beyond 'business as usual'. *Sustainable Development*, *24*(6), 371–382. doi:10.1002d.1623

Scheyvens, R., Banks, G., & Hughes, E. (2016). The Private Sector and the SDGs: The Need to Move Beyond 'Business as Usual'. *Sustainable Development*, *24*, 371–382.

Schmeltz, L. (2012). Consumer-oriented CSR communication: Focusing on ability or morality? *Corporate Communications*, *17*(1), 29–49. doi:10.1108/13563281211196344

Schmeltz, L. (2017). Getting CSR communication fit: A study of strategically fitting cause, consumers and company in corporate CSR communication. *Public Relations Inquiry*, *6*(1), 47–72. doi:10.1177/2046147X16666731

Schmelzer, P. (2013). *Value relevance of corporate social responsibility reports* [Master's Thesis]. Erasmus Universiteit Rotterdam.

Schönherr, N., Findler, F., & Martinuzzi, A. (2017). Exploring the interface of CSR and the Sustainable Development Goals. *Transnational Corporations*, *24*(3), 33–47. doi:10.18356/cfb5b8b6-en

Schrettle, S., Hinz, A., Scherrer-Rathje, M., & Friedli, T. (2014). Turning sustainability into action: Explaining firms' sustainability efforts and their impact on firm performance. *International Journal of Production Economics*, *147*, 73–84. doi:10.1016/j.ijpe.2013.02.030

Schroeder, P., Anggraeni, K., & Weber, U. (2018). The Relevance of Circular Economy Practices to the Sustainable Development Goals. *Journal of Industrial Ecology*, *23*(1), 77–95. doi:10.1111/jiec.12732

Schumpeter, J. A. (1934). *The theory of economic development: An inquiry into profits, capital, credit, interest, and the business cycle*. Transaction Publishers.

Schwartz, S. H. (1968). Awareness of Consequences and the Influence of Moral Norms on Interpersonal Behavior. *Sociometry*, *31*(4), 355. doi:10.2307/2786399

SDGs for better fashion. (n.d.). *United Nations*. Available at: https://sustainabledevelopment.un.org/partnership/?p=28041

Sedláček, P., & Sterk, V. (2017). The Growth Potential of Startups over the Business Cycle. *The American Economic Review*, *107*(10), 3182–3210. doi:10.1257/aer.20141280

Seele, P., & Lock, I. (2015). Instrumental and/or deliberative? A typology of CSR communication tools. *Journal of Business Ethics*, *131*(2), 401–414.

Seelos, C., & Mair, J. (2005). Social entrepreneurship: Creating new business models to serve the poor. *Business Horizons*, *48*(3), 241–246. doi:10.1016/j.bushor.2004.11.006

Self-Management Resource Center. (n.d.). https://www.selfmanagementresource.com/

Sen, A. (1987). *On Ethics and Economics.* Blackwell Publishers.

Sengupta, S., & Sahay, A. (2017). Social entrepreneurship research in Asia-Pacific: Perspectives and opportunities. *Social Enterprise Journal*, *13*(1), 17–37. doi:10.1108/SEJ-11-2016-0050

Sengupta, S., Sahay, A., & Croce, F. (2018). Conceptualizing social entrepreneurship in the context of emerging economies: An integrative review of past research from BRIICS. *The International Entrepreneurship and Management Journal*, *14*(5), 771–803. doi:10.100711365-017-0483-2

Sen, S., & Lerman, D. (2007). Why are you telling me this? An examination into negative consumer reviews on the web. *Journal of Interactive Marketing*, *21*(4), 76–94. doi:10.1002/dir.20090

Septiari, E. D. (2018). The Effect of eWOM as Mediation of Website Quality and Trust. *KINERJA Journal of Business and Economics, 22*(2), 142–155. Retrieved from https://ojs.uajy.ac.id/index.php/kinerja/article/view/1810

Serafeim, G. (2020). Public Sentiment and the Price of Corporate Sustainability. *Financial Analysts Journal*, *76*(2), 26–46.

SERES. (2018). SERES, valor social 2018. V Informe del impacto social de las empresas [Report]. SERES.

Shamsrizi, M., Pakura, A., Wiechers, J., Pakura, S., & Dauster, D. V. (2021). Digital Entrepreneurship for the "Decade of Action". In M. Soltanifar, M. Hughes, & L. Göcke (Eds.), *Digital Entrepreneurship. Future of Business and Finance* (pp. 303–327). Springer. doi:10.1007/978-3-030-53914-6_15

Sharma, R. W., & Srivastava, D. (2017). Measuring Customer Response to Word-of-mouth Messages on Social Media: Development of a Multi-item Scale. *Journal of Creative Communications*, *12*(3), 185–204. doi:10.1177/0973258617722004

Sheppard, B. H., Hartwick, J., & Warshaw, P. R. (1988). The Theory of Reasoned Action: A Meta-Analysis of Past Research with Recommendations for Modifications and Future Research. *The Journal of Consumer Research*, *15*(3), 325. doi:10.1086/209170

Shevlin, T. (1996). The value-relevance of nonfinancial information: A discussion. *Journal of Accounting and Economics*, *22*(1/3), 31–42. doi:10.1016/S0165-4101(96)00441-7

Shim, J., Moon, J., Song, M., & Lee, W. S. (2021). Antecedents of Purchase Intention at Starbucks in the Context of Covid-19 Pandemic. *Sustainability*, *13*(4), 1758.

Short, J. C., Moss, T. W., & Lumpkin, G. T. (2009). Research in social entrepreneurship: Past contributions and future opportunities. *Strategic Entrepreneurship Journal*, *3*(2), 161–194. doi:10.1002ej.69

Shulla, K., Voigt, B. F., Cibian, S., Scandone, G., Martinez, E., Nelkovski, F., & Salehi, P. (2021). Effects of COVID-19 on the sustainable development goals (SDGs). *Discover Sustainability*, *2*(1), 1–19. doi:10.100743621-021-00026-x

Sia, S. K., & Jose, A. (2019). Attitude and subjective norm as personal moral obligation mediated predictors of intention to build eco-friendly house. *Management of Environmental Quality*, *30*(4), 678–694. doi:10.1108/MEQ-02-2019-0038

Sierra-García, L., García-Benau, M. A., & Bollas-Araya, H. M. (2018). Empirical analysis of non-financial reporting by Spanish companies. *Administrative Sciences*, *8*(3), 29. doi:10.3390/admsci8030029

Si, H., Shi, J., Tang, D., Wu, G., & Lan, J. (2020). Understanding intention and behavior toward sustainable usage of bike sharing by extending the theory of planned behavior. *Resources, Conservation and Recycling*, *152*, 104513. doi:10.1016/j.resconrec.2019.104513

Silva, A. C. (2015). Social entrepreneurship and corporate social responsibility: Differences and points in common. *Journal of Business & Economic Policy*, *2*(2), 85–93.

Simnett, R., Vanstraelen, A., & Chua, W. F. (2009). Assurance on sustainability reports: An international comparison. *The Accounting Review*, *84*(3), 937–967. doi:10.2308/accr.2009.84.3.937

Simpson, A. V. (2010). Analysts' use of non-financial information disclosures. *Contemporary Accounting Research*, *27*(1), 249–288. doi:10.1111/j.1911-3846.2010.01008.x

Sipior, J. C. (2020). Considerations for Development and Use of AI in Response to COVID-19. *International Journal of Information Management*, *55*, 102170. doi:10.1016/j.ijinfomgt.2020.102170 PMID:32836632

Skala, A. (2019). The Startup as a Result of Innovative Entrepreneurship. In A. Skala (Ed.), *Digital Startups in Transition Economies* (pp. 1–40). Palgrave Pivot. doi:10.1007/978-3-030-01500-8_1

Smith, T. (2000). *Viable Values. A Study of Life as the Root and Reward of Vitality*. Rowman & Littlefield Publishers.

Snider, J., Hill, R., & Martin, D. (2003). Corporate Social Responsibility in the 21st century: A view from the world's most successful firms. *Journal of Business Ethics*, *48*(2), 175–187. doi:10.1023/B:BUSI.0000004606.29523.db

Sobradillo, P., Pozo, F., & Álvar, A. (2011). Medicina P4: El futuro a la vuelta de la esquina. *Archivos de Bronconeumologia*, *47*(1), 35–40. doi:10.1016/j.arbres.2010.09.009 PMID:21190770

Social Enterprise UK. (2015). *Think global trade social* [Report]. https://www.britishcouncil.org/sites/default/files/seuk_british_council_think_global_report.pdf

Sohn, D. (2014). Coping with information in social media: The effects of network structure and knowledge on perception of information value. *Computers in Human Behavior*, *32*, 145–151. doi:10.1016/j.chb.2013.12.006

Solomon, R. C., & Flores, F. (2001). *Building Trust in Business, Politics and Life*. Oxford University Press.

Soon, J., Davies, W., Chadd, S., & Baines, R. (2012). A Delphi-based approach to developing and validating a farm food safety risk assessment tool by experts. *Expert Systems*. https://www.sciencedirect.com/science/article/pii/S0957417412002175

Spekman, R. E., & Dotson, E. (2009). *Using Social Media in the B2B Context*. Academic Press.

Srivastava, D., & Sharma, R. W. (2017). Developing a Model for Studying the Antecedents and Effects of Word of Mouth (WoM) and e-WoM Marketing Based on Literature Review. *Jindal Journal of Business Research*, *6*(1), 25–43. doi:10.1177/2278682117700307

Staats, H. (2004). Proenvironmental attitudes and behavioral change. In C. D. Spielberger (Ed.), Encyclopedia of Applied Psychology (vol. 3). Elsevier.

Stankevičienė, J., & Čepulytė, J. (2014). Sustainable value creation: Coherence of corporate social responsibility and performance of socially responsible investment funds. *Economic Research-Ekonomska Istraživanja*, *27*(1), 882–898. doi:10.1080/1331677X.2014.976058

Starbucks Social Impact Report. (2019). Accessed at: https://www.starbucks.com/responsibility/global-report

Starbucks Stories and News. (2020). *C.A.F.E. Practices: Starbucks Approach to Ethically Sourcing Coffee*. Accessed at: https://stories.starbucks.com/press/2020/cafe-practices-starbucks-approach-to-ethically-sourcing-coffee/

Starbucks Stories. (2021). Accessed at: https://stories.starbucks.com/press/2021/starbucks-commitment-to-environmental-social-and-governance-disclosures/

Starik, M., & Kanashiro, P. (2013). Toward a Theory of Sustainability Management: Uncovering and Integrating the Nearly Obvious. *Organization & Environment*, *26*(1), 7–30. doi:10.1177/1086026612474958

Statista Outlook. (2021). *Coffee Worldwide*. Accessed at: https://www.statista.com/outlook/30010000/100/coffee/worldwide

Statista. (2021). *Market Share of Selected Leading Coffee Chains in the United States as of October 2019, by number of outlets*. Accessed at: https://www.statista.com/statistics/250166/market-share-of-major-us-coffee-shops/

Stephan, U., Uhlaner, L. M., & Stride, C. (2015). Institutions and social entrepreneurship: The role of institutional voids, institutional support, and institutional configurations. *Journal of International Business Studies*, *46*(3), 308–331. doi:10.1057/jibs.2014.38

Stockdill, R. (2020). *Lululemon: The great survivor of Covid-19*. Retrieved from https://insideretail.asia/2020/06/14/lululemon-the-great-survivor-of-covid-19/

Stockholm Resilience Centre. (2016, June 14). *How food connects all the SDGs*. https://www.stockholmresilience.org/research/research-news/2016-06-14-how-food-connects-all-the-sdgs.html

Stubbs, W. (2017). Characterising B Corps as a sustainable business model: An exploratory study of B Corps in Australia. *Journal of Cleaner Production*, *144*, 299–312. doi:10.1016/j.jclepro.2016.12.093

Stubbs, W. (2017b). Sustainable Entrepreneurship and B Corps. *Business Strategy and the Environment*, *26*(3), 331–344. doi:10.1002/bse.1920

Subaru Corporation. (2020). *Corporate Social Responsibility Report*. Author.

Suchman, M. C. (1995). Managing legitimacy: Strategic and institutional approaches. *Academy of Management Review*, *20*(3), 571–610.

Suchman, M. C. (1995). Managing Legitimacy: Strategic and Institutional Approaches. *Academy of Management Review*, *20*(3), 571–610. doi:10.5465/amr.1995.9508080331

Sun, H., Li, S., Ho, K., Gertsen, F., Hansen, P., & Frick, J. (1992). The trajectory of implementing ISO 9000 standards versus total quality management in Western Europe. *International Journal of Quality & Reliability Management*, *21*(2), 131–153. doi:10.1108/02656710410516952

Sun, Y., Gonzalez-Jimenez, H., & Wang, S. (2020). Examining the relationships between e-WOM, consumer ethnocentrism and brand equity. *Journal of Business Research*. Advance online publication. doi:10.1016/j.jbusres.2019.09.040

Suzuki Corporation. (2019). *Corporate Social Responsibility and Environmental Report*. Author.

Swatch Group. (2020). *2020 CR Report*. Retrieved from https://www.swatchgroup.com/en/services/archive/2020/half-year-report-2020

Swatch Group. (2021a). *Brands & Companies*. Retrieved from https://www.swatchgroup.com/en/brands-companies

Swatch Group. (2021b). *Sustainability report & social policy*. Retrieved from https://www.swatchgroup.com/en/brands-companies

Szabo, D. G., & Sorensen, K. E. (2015). New EU Directive on the Disclosure of Non-Financial Information (CSR). *European Company and Financial Law Review*, *12*(3), 307–340. doi:10.1515/ecfr-2015-0307

Szabo, D. G., & Sorensen, K. E. (2017). Non-financial reporting, CSR frameworks and groups of undertakings: Application and consequences. *Journal of Corporate Law Studies*, *17*(1), 137–165. doi:10.1080/14735970.2016.1254449

Szabo, D. G., & Sorensen, K. E. (2018). Pursuing CSR Policy in Corporate Groups: Insights in the Operation of Groups from Consolidated Non-Financial Reporting. *European Company Law*, *15*(2), 51–60.

Tabares, S. (2021). Do hybrid organizations contribute to Sustainable Development Goals? Evidence from B Corps in Colombia. *Journal of Cleaner Production*, *280*, 124615. doi:10.1016/j.jclepro.2020.124615

Taheri, B., Gannon, M. J., Cordina, R., & Lochrie, S. (2018). Measuring host sincerity: Scale development and validation. *International Journal of Contemporary Hospitality Management*, *30*(8), 2752–2772. doi:10.1108/IJCHM-08-2017-0535

Taleb, N. N. (2007). *The Black Swan*. The Random House Publishing Group.

Tan, B. C., & Yeap, P. F. (2012). What drives green restaurant patronage intention? *International Journal of Business and Management*, *7*(2), 215.

Tarquinio, L., & Posadas, S. C. (2020). Exploring the term "non-financial information": An academics' view. *Meditari Accountancy Research*, *28*(5), 727–749. doi:10.1108/MEDAR-11-2019-0602

TaskinsoyJ. (2020). A move towards a cashless society accelerates with the novel coronavirus induced global lockdown. Available at SSRN 3747750.

Tata Motors. (2020). *Annual Corporate Social Responsibility Report*. Author.

Taufique, K. M. R., & Vaithianathan, S. (2018). A fresh look at understanding Green consumer behavior among young urban Indian consumers through the lens of Theory of Planned Behavior. *Journal of Cleaner Production*, *183*, 46–55. doi:10.1016/j.jclepro.2018.02.097

Teasdale, S. (2010). Can social enterprise address disadvantage? Evidence from an inner city community. *Nonprofit and Public Sector Marketing*, *22*(2), 89–107. doi:10.1080/10495141003601278

Teece, D. J. (2007). Explicating dynamic capabilities: The nature and microfoundations of (sustainable) enterprise performance. *Strategic Management Journal*, *28*(13), 1319–1350. doi:10.1002mj.640

Teece, D. J., Pisano, G., & Shuen, A. (1997). Dynamic capabilities and strategic management. *Strategic Management Journal*, *18*(7), 509–533. doi:10.1002/(SICI)1097-0266(199708)18:7<509::AID-SMJ882>3.0.CO;2-Z

Teece, D., & Leih, S. (2016). Uncertainty, innovation, and dynamic capabilities: An introduction. *California Management Review*, *58*(4), 5–12. doi:10.1525/cmr.2016.58.4.5

Teece, D., Peteraf, M., & Leih, S. (2016). Dynamic capabilities and organizational agility: Risk, uncertainty, and strategy in the innovation economy. *California Management Review*, *58*(4), 13–35. doi:10.1525/cmr.2016.58.4.13

Terjesen, S., Lepoutre, J., Justo, R., & Bosma, N. (2012). *2009 Report on Social Entrepreneurship*. Academic Press.

Terziev, V., & Arabska, E. (2017). Social entrepreneurship, social values and social impact. *International Journal of Research in Management, Economics and Commerce*, *7*(4), 41–46. doi:10.2139srn.3142936

The European Commission. (2011, October 25). *Corporate Social Responsibility: a new definition, a new agenda for action.* Retrieved April 2, 2021, from MEMO/11/730 website: https://ec.europa.eu/commission/presscorner/detail/en/MEMO_11_730

The Fashion Pact. (2020). *First steps to transform our industry*. Retrieved from https://cutt.ly/ybbvtee

Themudo, N. S. (2009). Gender and the nonprofit sector. *Nonprofit and Voluntary Sector Quarterly*, *38*(4), 663–683. doi:10.1177/0899764009333957

Thogersen, J., & Olander, F. (2006). The Dynamic Interaction of Personal Norms and Environment-Friendly Buying Behavior: A Panel Study1. *Journal of Applied Social Psychology*, *36*(7), 1758–1780. doi:10.1111/j.0021-9029.2006.00080.x

Thomas, S. (2018). Peace of mind: The quintessential luxury. Journal of Design. *Business & Society*, *4*(2), 151–169.

Thompson, J. L. (2002). The world of the social entrepreneur. *International Journal of Public Sector Management*, *15*(5), 412–431. doi:10.1108/09513550210435746

Thurik, R., & Wennekers, S. (2004). Entrepreneurship, small business and economic growth. *Journal of Small Business and Enterprise Development*, *11*(1), 140–149. doi:10.1108/14626000410519173

Thyssen, O. (2009). *Business Ethics and Organizational Values - A Systems Theoretical Analysis*. Palgrave-MacMillan.

Tian, Q., & Robertson, J. L. (2019). How and When Does Perceived CSR Affect Employees' Engagement in Voluntary Pro-environmental Behavior? *Journal of Business Ethics*, *155*(2), 399–412. doi:10.100710551-017-3497-3

Tien, D. H., Amaya Rivas, A. A., & Liao, Y. K. (2019). Examining the influence of customer-to-customer electronic word-of-mouth on purchase intention in social networking sites. *Asia Pacific Management Review*, *24*(3), 238–249. doi:10.1016/j.apmrv.2018.06.003

Todeschini, B. V., Cortimiglia, M. N., Callegaro-de-Menezes, D., & Ghezzi, A. (2017). Innovative and sustainable business models in the fashion industry: Entrepreneurial drivers, opportunities, and challenges. *Business Horizons*, *60*(6), 759–770. doi:10.1016/j.bushor.2017.07.003

Tongco, M. D. C. (2007). Purposive sampling as a tool for informant selection. *Ethnobotany Research and Applications*, *5*, 147–158. doi:10.17348/era.5.0.147-158

Torres-García, M., & Santana-Hernández, H. (2017). La Educación para la Salud en la formación de maestros desde el Espacio Europeo de Educación Superior. *Revista Complutense de Educación*, *28*(4), 1083–1011. doi:10.5209/RCED.51536

Toyota Motor Corporation. (2020). *Environment Reporter*. Author.

Truffer, B., & Coenen, L. (2012). Environmental innovation and sustainability transitions in regional studies. *Regional Studies*, *46*(1), 1–21. doi:10.1080/00343404.2012.646164

Trusov, M., Bucklin, R. E., & Pauwels, K. (2009). Effects of Word-of-Mouth versus Traditional Marketing: Findings from an Internet Social Networking Site. *Journal of Marketing*, *73*(5), 90–102. doi:10.1509/jmkg.73.5.90

Turker, D. (2008). How Corporate Social Responsibility Influences Organizational Commitment. *Journal of Business Ethics*, *89*(2), 189–204. doi:10.100710551-008-9993-8

Tuškej, U., & Podnar, K. (2018). Consumers' identification with corporate brands: Brand prestige, anthropomorphism and engagement in social media. *Journal of Product and Brand Management*, *27*(1), 3–17. doi:10.1108/JPBM-05-2016-1199

Ulrich, P. (2008). *Integrative Economic Ethics. Foundations of a Civilized Market Economy*. Cambridge University Press. doi:10.1017/CBO9780511488658

UN. (2021). *UN Secretary-General's annual report on SDG progress*. Accessed at: https://sdg.iisd.org/news/secretary-generals-sdg-progress-report-recaps-pandemic-impacts-on-17-global-goals/

UNESCO. (2020). https://en.unesco.org/covid19/educationresponse

United Nations (UN). (2020). *The 17 Goals*. https://sdgs.un.org/goals

United Nations General Assembly. (1987). *Report of the world commission on environment and development: Our common future*. Oslo, Norway: United Nations General Assembly, Development and International Co-operation.

United Nations. (2000). *United Nations Millennium Declaration. New York* (A/RES/55/2). https://documents-dds-ny.un.org/doc/UNDOC/GEN/N00/559/54/PDF/N0055954.pdf?OpenElement

United Nations. (2015). *Transforming our world. The Agenda 2030 for sustainable development*. Available at: https://sdgs.un.org/sites/default/files/publications/21252030%20Agenda%20for%20Sustainable%20Development%20web.pdf

United Nations. (2015). Transforming our world: The 2030 agenda for sustainable development [Report]. Author.

United Nations. (2015). *Transforming our world: the 2030 Agenda for Sustainable Development*. Author.

United Nations. (2015). *Transforming our world: the 2030 Agenda for Sustainable Development*. United Nations, A/RES/70/1, Agenda items 15 and 116, 1–35. https://sustainabledevelopment.un.org/post2015/transformingourworld

United Nations. (2020). *Global indicator framework for the Sustainable Development Goals and targets of the 2030 Agenda for Sustainable Development*. 51st session of the United Nations Statistical Commission.

United Nations. (2021). *Transforming our world: The 2030 Agenda for Sustainable Development*. Sustainable Development Knowledge Platform. https://sustainabledevelopment.un.org/post2015/transformingourworld

United Nations. (2021). *United Nations*. https://www.un.org/en/

Universidad de los Pacientes. (n.d.). *Universidad de los Pacientes*. https://www.universidadpacientes.org/

Urionabarrenetxea, K. M. (2011). La educación en bioética, camino para la profesionalidad. *Revista de Calidad Asistencial*, *26*(1), 62–66. doi:10.1016/j.cali.2010.11.007 PMID:21256065

Vadakkepatt, G. G., Winterich, K. P., Mittal, V., Zinn, W., Beitelspacher, L., Aloysius, J., ... Reilman, J. (2020). Sustainable Retailing. *Journal of Retailing*.

Vaidya, H., & Chatterji, T. (2020). SDG 11 Sustainable Cities and Communities. In I. Franco, T. Chatterji, E. Derbyshire, & J. Tracey (Eds), Actioning the Global Goals for Local Impact. Science for Sustainable Societies (pp. 73–185). Springer. doi:10.1007/978-981-32-9927-6_12

Valls-Martínez, M. C., & Abad-Segura, E. (2018, December). Satisfacción del paciente en el Sistema Nacional de Salud español. *Anales del Sistema Sanitario de Navarra*, *41*(3), 309–320. doi:10.23938/ASSN.0315 PMID:30277227

Van Der Linden, B., & Freeman, R. E. (2017). Profit and Other Values: Thick Evaluation in Decision Making. *Business Ethics Quarterly*, *27*(3), 353–379. doi:10.1017/beq.2017.1

van Doorn, J., Lemon, K. N., Mittal, V., Nass, S., Pick, D., Pirner, P., & Verhoef, P. C. (2010). Customer Engagement Behavior: Theoretical Foundations and Research Directions. *Journal of Service Research*, *13*(3), 253–266. doi:10.1177/1094670510375599

Van Hille, I., De Bakker, F. G. A., Ferguson, J. E., & Groenewegen, P. (2020). Cross-Sector Partnerships for Sustainability: How Mission-Driven Conveners Drive Change in National Coffee Platforms. *Sustainability*, *12*(7), 2846. doi:10.3390u12072846

van Marrewijk, M. (2003). Concepts and Definitions of CSR and Corporate Sustainability: Between Agency and Communion. *Journal of Business Ethics*, *44*(2), 95–105. doi:10.1023/A:1023331212247 van Mossel, A., van Rijnsoever, F. J., & Hekkert, M. P. (2018). Navigators through the storm: A review of organization theories and the behavior of incumbent firms during transitions. *Environmental Innovation and Societal Transitions*, *26*, 44–63. doi:10.1016/j.eist.2017.07.001

van Ryzin, G. G., Grossman, S., DiPadova-Stocks, L., & Bergrud, E. (2009). Portrait of the social entrepreneur: Statistical evidence from a US panel. *Voluntas*, *20*(2), 129–140. doi:10.100711266-009-9081-4

van Zanten, J. A., & van Tulder, R. (2018). Multinational enterprises and the Sustainable Development Goals: An institutional approach to corporate engagement. *Journal of International Business Policy*, *1*(3-4), 208–233. doi:10.105742214-018-0008-x

Vázquez-Carrasco, R., & López-Pérez, M. E. (2013). Small and medium-sized enterprises and Corporate Social Responsibility: A systematic review of the literature. *Quality & Quantity*, *47*(6), 3205–3218. doi:10.100711135-012-9713-4

Vega, G., & Kidwell, R. E. (2007). Toward a typology of new venture creators: Similarities and contrasts between business and social entrepreneurs. *New England Journal of Entrepreneurship*, *10*(2), 15–28. doi:10.1108/NEJE-10-02-2007-B002

Vegro, C. L. R., & de Almeida, L. F. (2020). Global coffee market: Socio-economic and cultural dynamics. In *Coffee Consumption and Industry Strategies in Brazil* (pp. 3–19). Woodhead Publishing.

Ventura, R., & Martínez-Martínez, S. L. (2020). *Global Entrepreneurship Monitor. Informe GEM Málaga 2019/20.* UMA Editorial.

Venturelli, A., Caputo, F., Leopizzi, R., & Pizzi, S. (2019). The state of art of corporate social disclosure before the introduction of non-financial reporting directive: A cross country analysis. *Social Responsibility Journal*, *15*(4), 409–423. doi:10.1108/SRJ-12-2017-0275

Verma, V. K., Chandra, B., & Kumar, S. (2019). Values and ascribed responsibility to predict consumers' attitude and concern towards green hotel visit intention. *Journal of Business Research*, *96*, 206–216. doi:10.1016/j.jbusres.2018.11.021

Vermeulen, W. J. V., & Witjes, S. (2016). On addressing the dual and embedded nature of business and the route towards corporate sustainability. *Journal of Cleaner Production*, *112*, 2822–2832. doi:10.1016/j.jclepro.2015.09.132

Vernuccio, M. (2014). Communicating Corporate Brands Through Social Media: An Exploratory Study. *International Journal of Business Communication*, *51*(3), 211–233. doi:10.1177/2329488414525400

Verstraeten, J. (2000). *Business Ethics. Broadening the perspective*. Peters.

Vial, G. (2019). Understanding digital transformation: A review and a research agenda. *The Journal of Strategic Information Systems*, *28*(2), 118–144. doi:10.1016/j.jsis.2019.01.003

Villagra, N., López, B., & Monfort, A. (2015). The management of intangibles and corporate branding: Has anything changed in the relationship between business and society? *Revista Latina de Comunicación Social*, (70), 793. doi:10.4185/RLCS-2015-1072en

Villela, M., Bulgacov, S., & Morgan, G. (2019). B Corp Certification and Its Impact on Organizations Over Time. *Journal of Business Ethics*. Advance online publication. doi:10.100710551-019-04372-9

Vitolla, F., Raimo, N., & Rubino, M. (2020). Board characteristics and integrated reporting quality: An agency theory perspective. *Corporate Social Responsibility and Environmental Management*, *27*(2), 1152–1163. doi:10.1002/csr.1879

Vivek, S. D., Beatty, S. E., & Morgan, R. M. (2012). Customer engagement: Exploring customer relationships beyond purchase. *Journal of Marketing Theory and Practice*, *20*(2), 122–146. doi:10.2753/MTP1069-6679200201

Volkswagen A. G. (2019). *Sustainability Report*. Author.

Vuorio, A. (2017). Young adults and sustainable enterpreneurship: The role of culture and demographic factors. *Journal of International Business and Entrepreneurship Development, 10*(3), 209–230. doi:10.1504/JIBED.2017.085499

Waddock, S. A., & Graves, S. B. (1997). The corporate social performance-financial performance link. *Strategic Management Journal, 18*(4), 303–319. doi:10.1002/(SICI)1097-0266(199704)18:4<303::AID-SMJ869>3.0.CO;2-G

Waddock, S., & McIntosh, M. (2011). Business unusual: Corporate responsibility in a 2.0 World. *Business and Society Review, 116*(3), 303–330. doi:10.1111/j.1467-8594.2011.00387.x

Wade, M., & Hulland, J. (2004). The resource-based view and information systems research: Review, extension, and suggestions for future research. *Management Information Systems Quarterly, 28*(1), 107–142. doi:10.2307/25148626

Wayne, N., & MacDonald, C. (2004). Getting to the bottom of the triple bottom line! *Business Ethics Quarterly, 14*(2), 243–262. doi:10.5840/beq200414211

Weber, M. (1904-1905). *Die Protestantische Ethik und der Geist des Kapitalismus*. Academic Press.

Weber, M. (1978). *Economy and society. An outline of interpretative sociology*. University of California Press.

WEF. (2021). *The Global Risks Report*. Accessed at: http://www3.weforum.org/docs/WEF_The_Global_Risks_Report_2021.pdf

Weise, K., & Conger, K. (2020). Gaps in Amazon's response as virus spreads to more than 50 warehouses. *The New York Times*.

Wernerfelt, B. (1984). A resource-based view of the firm. *Strategic Management Journal, 5*(2), 171–180. doi:10.1002mj.4250050207

Whelan, T., & Fink, C. (2016). The comprehensive business case for sustainability. *Harvard Business Review, 21*, 2012.

Whitehouse, L. (2006). Corporate social responsibility: Views from the frontline. *Journal of Business Ethics, 63*(3), 279–296. doi:10.100710551-005-3243-0

Whitmarsh, L. (2009). Behavioural responses to climate change: Asymmetry of intentions and impacts. *Journal of Environmental Psychology, 29*(1), 13–23. doi:10.1016/j.jenvp.2008.05.003

Wieland, J. (2020). *Relational Economics. A Political Economy. In Relational Economics and Organization Governance*. Springer. doi:10.1007/978-3-030-45112-7

Williams, A., Philipp, F., Kennedy, S., & Whiteman, G. (2017). Systems Thinking: A Review of Sustainability Management Research. *Journal of Cleaner Production, 148*, 866–881. doi:10.1016/j.jclepro.2017.02.002

Williams, A., Whiteman, G., & Parker, J. N. (2019). Backstage Interorganizational Collaboration: Corporate Endorsement of the Sustainable Development Goals. *Academy of Management Discoveries, 5*(4), 367–395. doi:10.5465/amd.2018.0154

Winby, S., & Worley, C. G. (2014). Management processes for agility, speed, and innovation. *Organizational Dynamics, 43*(3), 225–234. doi:10.1016/j.orgdyn.2014.08.009

Winkler, A.-L. P., Brown, J. A., & Finegold, D. L. (2019). Employees as Conduits for Effective Stakeholder Engagement: An Example from B Corporations. *Journal of Business Ethics, 160*(4), 913–936. doi:10.100710551-018-3924-0

Winter, S. G. (2003). Understanding dynamic capabilities. *Strategic Management Journal, 24*(10), 991–995. doi:10.1002mj.318

Wirtz, J., & Chew, P. (2002). The effects of incentives, deal proneness, satisfaction and tie strength on word-of-mouth behaviour. *International Journal of Service Industry Management, 13*(2), 141–162. doi:10.1108/09564230210425340

Woeld Health Organization. (2015). *Garantizar una vida sana y promover el bienestar para todos en todas las edades.* https://www.who.int/es/news/item/25-09-2015-ensure-healthy-lives-and-promote-well-being-for-all-at-all-ages

Wolor, C., Solikah, S., Fidhyallah, N. F., & Lestari, D. P. (2020). Effectiveness of E-Training, Leadership, and Work Life Balance on Employee Performance during COVID-19. *The Journal of Asian Finance, Economics, and Business*, *7*(10), 443–450. doi:10.13106/jafeb.2020.vol7.no10.443

Wong, E., Leung, R., & Law, R. (2015). How Effective Are Asian Hotels in Communicating CSR Efforts Through the Property Websites? The Case of Hong Kong. In Information and Communication Technologies in Tourism 2015 (pp. 651–663). Springer International Publishing. doi:10.1007/978-3-319-14343-9_47

Woodside, A. G., & Fine, M. B. (2019). Sustainable fashion themes in luxury brand storytelling: The sustainability fashion research grid. *Journal of Global Fashion Marketing*, *10*(2), 111–128. doi:10.1080/20932685.2019.1573699

World Commission on Environment and Development (WCED). (1987). *Our common future.* Oxford university Press.

World Commission on Environment and Development (WCED). (1987). *Our Common Future.* Oxford University.

World Commission on Environment and Development. (1987). *Brundtland' Report: Our Common Future.* https://sustainabledevelopment.un.org

World Health Organization. (2020). *WHO Director-General's opening remarks at the media briefing on COVID-19.* https://www.who.int/director-general/speeches/detail/who-director-general-s-opening-remarks-at-the-media-briefing-on-covid-19---11-march-2020

Worley, C. G., & Jules, C. (2020). COVID-19's uncomfortable revelations about agile and sustainable organizations in a VUCA world. *The Journal of Applied Behavioral Science*, *56*(3), 279–283. doi:10.1177/0021886320936263

Wright, C., & Nyberg, D. (2017). An inconvenient truth: How organizations translate climate change into business as usual. *Academy of Management Journal*, *60*(5), 1633–1661. doi:10.5465/amj.2015.0718

Wry, T., & York, J. G. (2017). An identity-based approach to social enterprise. *Academy of Management Review*, *42*(3), 407–416. doi:10.5465/amr.2013.0506

Wu, D. (2020). Empirical study of knowledge withholding in cyberspace: Integrating protection motivation theory and theory of reasoned behavior. *Computers in Human Behavior*, *105*, 106229. doi:10.1016/j.chb.2019.106229

Wuepper, D., Clemm, A., & Wree, P. (2019). The preference for sustainable coffee and a new approach for dealing with hypothetical bias. *Journal of Economic Behavior & Organization*, *158*, 475–486.

Wulandari, V., Hertati, L., Antasari, R., & Nazarudin, N. (2021). The Influence of the Covid-19 Crisis Transformative Leadership Style on Job Satisfaction Implications on Company Performance. *Ilomata International Journal of Tax and Accounting*, *2*(1), 17–36. doi:10.52728/ijtc.v2i1.185

Wu, S., & Chen, J. (2011). Comparison between manufacturing companies that are ISO certified and those that are not certified using performance measurement model. *Total Quality Management & Business Excellence*, *22*(8), 869–890. doi:10.1080/14783363.2011.593860

Wu, Y., Zhang, K., & Xie, J. (2020). Bad greenwashing, good greenwashing: Corporate Social Responsibility and information transparency. *Management Science*, *66*(7), 3095–3112. doi:10.1287/mnsc.2019.3340

Wymer, S., & Regan, E. (2005). Factors Influencing e-commerce Adoption and Use by Small and Medium Businesses. *Electronic Markets*, *15*(4), 438–453. doi:10.1080/10196780500303151

Xiao, M., Cooke, F. L., Xu, J., & Bian, H. (2020). To what extent is corporate social responsibility part of human resource management in the Chinese context? A review of literature and future research directions. *Human Resource Management Review*, *30*(4), 100726. doi:10.1016/j.hrmr.2019.100726

Yadav, R., & Pathak, G. S. (2016). Young consumers' intention towards buying green products in a developing nation: Extending the theory of planned behavior. *Journal of Cleaner Production*, *135*, 732–739. doi:10.1016/j.jclepro.2016.06.120

Yan, R.-N., Ogle, J. P., & Hyllegard, K. H. (2010). *The impact of message appeal and message source on Gen Y consumers' attitudes and purchase intentions toward American Apparel*. doi:10.1080/13527260902863221

Yan, M. (2019). Corporate Social Responsibility versus shareholder value maximization: Through the lens of hard and soft law. *Northwestern Journal of International Law & Business*, *40*(1), 47–85.

Yeasmin, S., Banik, R., Hossain, S., Hossain, M. N., Mahumud, R., Salma, N., & Hossain, M. M. (2020). Impact of COVID-19 pandemic on the mental health of children in Bangladesh: A cross-sectional study. *Children and Youth Services Review*, *117*, 105277. doi:10.1016/j.childyouth.2020.105277 PMID:32834275

Yoo, D., & Lee, J. (2018). The effects of Corporate Social Responsibility (CSR) fit and CSR consistency on company evaluation: The role of CSR support. *Sustainability*, *10*(2956), 1–16. doi:10.3390u10082956

Yusuf, A. S., Che Hussin, A. R., & Busalim, A. H. (2018). Influence of e-WOM engagement on consumer purchase intention in social commerce. *Journal of Services Marketing*, *32*(4), 493–504. doi:10.1108/JSM-01-2017-0031

Zadek, S. (2002). Mapping Instruments for Corporate Social Responsibility. Directorate General for Employment and Social Affairs. European Commission.

Zahra, S. A., Gedajlovic, E., Neubaum, D. O., & Shulman, J. M. (2009). A typology of social entrepreneurs: Motives, search processes and ethical challenges. *Journal of Business Venturing*, *24*(5), 519–532. doi:10.1016/j.jbusvent.2008.04.007

Zahra, S. A., Rawhouser, H. N., Bhawe, N., Neubaum, D. O., & Hayton, J. C. (2008). Globalization of social entrepreneurship opportunities. *Strategic Entrepreneurship Journal*, *2*(2), 117–131. doi:10.1002ej.43

Zairi, M., & Sinclair, D. (1995). Business process re-engineering and process management. *Management Decision*. https://www.emerald.com/insight/content/doi/10.1108/00251749510085021/full/html

Zhang Stephen, X., Yifei, W., Andreas, R., & Feng, W. (2020). *Unprecedented disruption of lives and work: Health, distress and life satisfaction of working adults in China one month into the COVID-19 outbreak*. https://www. ncbi. nlm. nih. gov/pmc/articles/PMC7146665/pdf/main. pdf

Zhao, C., Zhang, M., & Wang, W. (2019). Exploring the influence of severe haze pollution on residents' intention to purchase energy-saving appliances. *Journal of Cleaner Production*, *212*, 1536–1543. doi:10.1016/j.jclepro.2018.12.134

Zhou, J., Zhang, B., Tan, R., Tseng, M.-L., & Zhang, Y. (2020). Exploring the Systematic Attributes Influencing Gerontechnology Adoption for Elderly Users Using a Meta-Analysis. *Sustainability*, *12*(7), 2864. doi:10.3390u12072864

Zyglidopoulos, S. C. (2003). The issue life-cycle: Implications for reputation for social performance and organizational legitimacy. *Corporate Reputation Review*, *6*(1), 70–81. doi:10.1057/palgrave.crr.1540191

About the Contributors

Andrea Pérez is Bachelor in Business Administration (2006) and she received her PhD from the University of Cantabria (2011). She also has a Master Degree in Sustainability and Corporate Social Responsibility (2013). She is currently Associate Professor at the University of Cantabria (Spain) and she is specialized in strategic marketing, distribution and commercial communication teaching. Her research interests include corporate social responsibility, corporate communications, consumer behaviour and entrepreneurship. She has published papers in international renowned journals such as the International Journal of Hospitality Management, Corporate Social Responsibility and Environmental Management, Psychology and Marketing, European Journal of Marketing or the Journal of Business Ethics, among others. She is author of numerous books and book chapters in CSR and marketing. She has made teaching and research stays at several universities and international centers, such as the Center for Business Ethics (Bentley University, United States), the Center for Business, Organizations and Society (University of Bath, United Kingdom) and the University of Macau (China).

* * *

Mansour Naser Alraja received the PhD degree in management information systems (2010). He is currently an associate professor of management information systems (MIS) with the Department of MIS, College of Commerce and Business Administration, Dhofar University, Oman. His research interests include information technology adoption, data analytics, information security, e-commerce, and the IoT. Alraja published many papers in many reputable journals that are indexed in Web of Science and have good impact factor. He has also served as a reviewer for many well-reputed conferences, including AOM, AIB, and IEEE conferences, as well as acting as a reviewer for several reputable journals such the journal of Information Technology and People (IT&P), journal of Small Business & Entrepreneurship, IEEE Access, and Sage open. Alraja is College's Chief Accreditation Officer for AACSB. Moreover, since 2018, he has been appointed as the Chair for the Department of MIS. Alraja was a principle investigator for many funded projects. Currently, he is leading and mentoring two funded research project.

Narin Bekki graduated from the Department of International Relations and European Union and International Trade and Finance (double major degree) of Izmir University of Economics in 2011. She has a M.Sc. on European Politics and Policies at the KU Leuven, Belgium. She then obtained her Ph.D. on Business Administration at Yasar University in 2019. She worked as a cultural affairs coordinator at Municipality of Bornava (Izmir) between 2013-2016 and an assistant expert at Aegean Exporters Association' (Izmir) between 2016-2017. She now works as a Sustainability Affairs Manager at the Beksan Nail & Wire Co. Her research interests are sustainability, sustainable supply chain management, and buyer-supplier relationships.

Gönenç Dalgıç Turhan, a business professional on sales and marketing, graduated from the Department of International Relations of Izmir Dokuz Eylül University in 2001. She worked for ten years in pension and life insurance sector at managerial positions. She has M.A. degree in Management and Organization from Dokuz Eylül University in 2006 and obtained her Ph.D. on Business Administration at Yasar University in 2017. She conducted a study as a Visiting Researcher at Hohenheim University, Institute of Marketing and Management, Department of Business StartUps and Entrepreneurship between 2013-2014 and worked from 2015- 2017 as a part-time lecturer at Yasar University. She has been working at Karyatech Electrical Equipments Industry and Trade Inc. Co. as Import Manager since 2016. Her research interests are corporate sustainability, entrepreneurship, innovation and international business.

Gulen Desteli is a global marketing and commercial activation leader who has deep corporate experience in healthcare, FMCG, telecommunications and software industries across global markets. In addition, she continues her PhD studies in Business in Yasar University. She is a recognized thought leader in value-based pricing and NPI activation who has participated to many international speaking engagements related to pricing strategy and digital transformation. She has a B.A. degree in Economics from Bogazici University and an MBA from University of Virginia, Darden Graduate School of Business.

Elsa Diez-Busto is a PhD student. Her research interests focus on B Corp companies, Social Entrepreneurship, Sustainable Development, Teaching Innovation, and Continuous Improvement. Despite her short career, she is the co-author of four scientific articles, two of which have been published in prestigious journals (JCR). She has participated in numerous scientific congresses. Additionally, she is a researcher at the Yunus Cantabria Center (Yunus Social Business Center) and the Global Entrepreneurship Monitor Cantabria.

M. Banu Durukan received her bachelor's degree from Dokuz Eylul University (1993) in Turkey, her MBA from Graduate School of Management, Boston University (1995) in the U.S. and her doctorate degree from Dokuz Eylul University (1997). She is currently teaching and carrying out her research activities at Dokuz Eylul University Faculty of Business as well as University of Ljubljana, School of Economics and Business where she has been a guest professor between 2008 and 2010. Her research interest includes corporate finance, behavioral finance, corporate governance and capital structure. She has published books, book chapters and articles in national and international journals. She has also taken many administrative roles including University International Relations Coordinator, Director of Graduate School of Social Sciences, associate dean responsible from Erasmus at its initiation in Turkey. She is currently the Associate Dean of Faculty of Business and head of the Business Department.

Amr ElAlfy's background is in Corporate Social Responsibility (CSR) with an emphasis on using Big Data and Artificial Intelligence to optimize impact measurement and corporate reporting. Dr. ElAlfy spent more than eight years in business development in multinational conglomerates, namely Nestlé and 3M, where he led the marketing and CSR functions for the Middle East and Africa Region. He has applied his expertise in research, program management, CSR, impact measurement and capacity development. Dr. ElAlfy is also a co-founder and the managing director of Synergy Sustainability and Development Group.

Ana Fernández-Laviada is Associate Professor. Bachelor of Business Administration and Management (1996), Bachelor of Economics (1998) and Doctor of the University of Cantabria (2003). Accounting Expert Accredited by the CGE-ICJCE. President of Observatory of Entrepreneurship in Spain (GEM Spanish Network) since 2013 and Director of the Global Entrepreneurship Monitor (GEM) in Cantabria since 2008. Director of the Yunus Social Business Centre (YSBC) in Cantabria since 2019. Associate Editor of the Spanish Accounting Review (SAR-RC). More than 50 papers published on indexed journals as Academia Revista Latinoamericana de Administración, Entrepreneurship Research Journal, Investigaciones Regionales, Journal of Financial Regulation and Compliance, Journal of Risk Research, Managerial Auditing Journal, Revista Española de Financiación y Contabilidad, Revista Europea de Dirección y Economía de la Empresa, Journal of Social Entreprenuership, Spanish Accounting Review, Universia Business Review, Sustainability, Voluntas, among others, books and several contributions to national and international conferences. Research interest: social and educational entrepreneurship, teaching innovation in accounting and auditing and internal and financial auditing, among others.

Dolores Gallardo Vazquez is a lecturer and researcher in the Department of Financial Economy and Accounting at the Faculty of Economics Sciences and Business Administration at the University of Extremadura. She is an Economist specialized in Financial Accounting, Intellectual Capital and Corporate Social Responsibility, Expert in Implementation of International Accounting Standards, MSc in Training as University Teaching in the European Higher Education, MSc in Management of Higher Education Institutions; Fellowship at Cranfield University based on a competitive aid from Spanish Government. She has managed the Orientation and Teacher Training Service at the University for four years. Now, she is managing the University Social Responsibility Office. Her research interests range across several key areas within Intellectual Capital, Corporate Social Responsibility, Corporate Volunteering, University Social Responsibility, Social Entrepreneurship and Social Innovation. She has published in various peer reviewed journals, books, international conferences proceedings and monographs. She has also held lectureships at a wide variety of academic institutions.

Ana Isabel Gil-Lacruz is an empirical health economist at Zaragoza University (Spain). Gil-Lacruz has been recently working in the projects "Cross-National Patterns and Predictors of Life-Cycle Smoking Behavior", (sponsored by the National Institute of Health of the United States) and "Risky sexual behaviours and alcohol consumption" (sponsored by the Spanish Association of Health Economics). These research has resulted in published papers on the journals: Empirical Economics, The European Journal of Health Economics, Social Indicators Research, among others.

Marta Gil-Lacruz is a Doctor of psychology and sociology. Her thesis "The Health System and the Community" won the Zaragoza University Extraordinary Social Sciences Doctorate Award for the academic year 2002-2003. She is currently Tenured Professor of Social Psychology. Her many publications include Health and Sources of Social Support (The Centre for Sociological Research, 2000), A Didactic Guide to Social Psychology (Promolibro, 2004), Social Psychology, a Commitment Applied to Health (University Press, 2007) and numerous articles and collaborations in projects relative to theoretical aspects applied to the social psychology of health, lifestyles, and social determinants.

Mohamed Hamdoun is an assistant professor in the College of Commerce and Business Administration at Dhofar University in Oman. In addition, he is a member of the research unit "ISEFE" at University Tunis El Manar in Tunisia. He holds university habilitation from the University of Tunis (2019) and a doctorate in management sciences from the University of Manouba (2012). He received the thesis prize «Excellence» of the University of Manouba. He is member of the university research committee and chair of the college research committee. Mohamed Hamdoun's research interests focus on environmental management, corporate social responsibility, ecological preferences of consumers and global value chains. His articles have been published in leading academic journals.

Belen Lopez is Director of Corporate Social Responsibility at ESIC, PhD in Communication and she is an associate researcher at ESIC. She combines management and research on CSR as a senior lecturer since 2004. Member of the Academy of International Business (AIB) and Academy of Management (AoM) since 2010. She has participated in international conferences and published her work in international academic journals. She is a researcher at the Complutense Group for Brand Management and Integrated Communication. And she also has been an Associate Researcher at the University of Bristol and Associate Professor at Shanghai International Studies University, China.

Carlos López-Gutiérrez is an Associate Professor, teaching international finance, derivatives and financial markets, and financial management. His main research lines are corporate finance, banking and sustainable finance (Social entrepreneurship, CSR and microfinance). He has published more than forty articles in prestigious journals and books/book chapters in first-level editorials. He is referee of many prestigious international journals and has participated in national and international conferences, obtaining on four occasions prizes to the papers presented. He has supervised two doctoral theses and more than forty graduate and master projects. He has participated in numerous national and international research projects. He has held research stays at the London School of Economics and Political Science and at the London Business School. He is member of the Banking and Corporate Finance research group, the Global Entrepreneurship Monitor (GEM-Cantabria) and the Yunus Centre Cantabria.

Shafat Maqbool is research associate at Cluster University, Srinagar. He has done PhD from Aligarh Muslim University. His research oscillates between corporate strategy to Entrepreneurship. His micro focus is on corporate social responsibility, entrepreneurship, intellectual capital, and conflict economy.

Sofía Louise Martínez-Martínez is an Entrepreneurship and Innovation researcher at the Chair of Sustainable Entrepreneurship of the University of Málaga. Member of the GEM (Global Entrepreneurship Monitor) researching group of Spain and currently PhD student in Business and Economics. Double university degree in Business Management and Law. Master in Applied Sociology focused on research methods and techniques in Social Science. She has experience in developing different activities to foster the University-Business collaboration (e.g., Explorer International Entrepreneurship program, University-Business Ecosystem Forum). She develops research in the fields of Entrepreneurial University, entrepreneurial competences, academic spinoffs, innovation, sustainable development, social capital, and entrepreneurial culture.

Javier Montoya del Corte is Associate Professor of Accounting and Finance. Specialized teaching areas: accounting, auditing and internal control. Main research interests: auditing, SMEs and active teaching-learning methodologies. Extraordinary Award of Doctorate in Social and Legal Sciences (2011), Award of the Social Council for the best Dissertation in this area (2008) and Enrique Fuentes Quintana Award of the Savings Banks Foundation (2009). More than fifty papers published in indexed scientific, academic and professional journals from different countries: Argentina, Australia, Chile, Colombia, Spain, United States, Netherlands, Mexico, Panama, Poland and Venezuela. Research and teaching stays: University College Dublin (Ireland), Monterrey Institute of Technology and Higher Education (Mexico), La Salle University (Mexico) and University of Panama (Panama).

Nicholas Palaschuk is a Senior Doctoral Researcher at the University of Waterloo in the School of Environment, Enterprise and Development. With extensive experience in corporate sustainability, change management, and leadership development, his research investigates the cultural and behavioral drivers of purpose-led business transformations. Nicholas currently serves as a Doctoral Fellow with the Canadian Health and Fitness Institute and Ambassador to the North American EcoInnovation Network. His current research works collaboratively with Canadian organizations to develop, deploy, and evaluate culture change initiatives and leadership development and learning strategies.

Estefanía Palazuelos is Associate Professor teaching in the areas of accounting and auditing. Her research interests focus on auditing, SMEs' financing and active teaching-learning methodologies. She has participated in numerous scientific congresses and has participated in the elaboration of several handbooks/books in the field of accounting and auditing. She has held a national research stay at University of Cádiz (Spain), and two more abroad, at London School of Economics (UK) and at Cranfield University (UK), two of the most influential social sciences faculties worldwide.

Clara Plata Ríos is a PhD in Physics from the University of Granada, since 2010 she has been working on project management at the Vice-Rectorate for Social Innovation and Entrepreneurship of the University of Malaga, having worked on topics such as Smart Campus, Innovation, Entrepreneurship and Circular Economy. Currently she combines this work with the development of Circular Economy projects and research activities as Operations and Technology Manager in the company IPStar SEMiLLA, linked to the European Space Agency. She currently researches about Circular Economy and Industrial Symbiosis, including strategies, technologies, and new circular business models.

Celia Rangel has combined her academic career with professional experience. She has brand & communication experience in leadership roles within corporate entities, as well as in leading branding and communications agencies managing luxury brands. Research interests are advertising, communication, strategy, brands, and luxury. Her last book chapter is "Managing the Intangibles of Luxury Brands."

Jacob Dahl Rendtorff, PhD and Dr. Scient. Adm. is professor of philosophy of management at the Department of Business and Social Sciences, Roskilde University, Denmark. Rendtorff's research has a broad perspective on organization theory, management, responsibility, ethics and legitimacy of business firms and corporations, corporate social responsibility, business ethics, sustainability, bioethics and biolaw, human rights, political theory and philosophy of law. Rendtorff is educated in philosophy and political sciences in Copenhagen, Paris and Berlin, and he has been visiting professor in many universities (Utrecht, Rome, Freiburg, Boston, Stanford, Santa Clara, Louvain, Shanghai, Besancon, Paris, and Tubingen). Rendtorff has written and edited on issues of existentialism and hermeneutics, French philosophy, ethics, bioethics, business ethics and philosophy of management as well as philosophy of law. Rendtorff's recent publications are Handbook of Business Legitimacy, Springer 2020, Philosophy of Management and Sustainability, Emerald 2019, Cosmopolitan Business Ethics. Towards a Global Ethos of Management, Routledge 2017 and Stakeholder Theory a Model for Strategic Management, Springer 2016. Rendtorff is a member of the steering committee of the European Business Ethics Network (EBEN) and of the Steering Committee of FISP (International Federation of Philosophical Societies). Rendtorff is editor of the Springer Series Ethical Economy, associate editor of Social Responsibility Journal (Emerald) and European editor of Journal of Business Ethics Education. Presently, Rendtorff' s main research interests are philosophy of management, stakeholder theory, sustainability, CSR, and cosmopolitan business ethics.

Paula San-Martín is an Assistant Professor teaching in the area of accounting. Accredited as Associate Professor by the National Agency for Quality Assessment and Accreditation (ANECA). Her research interests focus on entrepreneurship education, non-financial information and active teaching-learning methodologies. She has participated in numerous scientific congresses and is technical director of the Global Entrepreneurship Monitor (GEM) in Cantabria since 2014. She has held two international research stays at EmLyon Business School (Lyon, France).

Juan de la Cruz Sánchez Domínguez is a PhD student enrolled in the PhD Program in Economics and Business of the University of Extremadura, Spain. He has a MSc of Research in Economics, Management and International Trade. His main research interests are Corporate Social Responsibility, entrepreneurship, the Sustainable Development Goals and circular economy, and how these topics are connected with each other. He speaks fluent English and Portuguese, and has basic knowledge of French and German.

Lidia Sánchez-Ruiz is Associate Professor, Business and Management Department, University of Cantabria (Spain). She is also a member in the Research Group of Health Economics and Health Service Management. She holds a PhD in Business and Management. She has been a visiting fellow at different universities along her career: University of La Laguna (Spain); Polytechnic University of Catalonia (Spain); Cardiff University (Wales); University of Algarve (Portugal); ISM University of Management and Economics (Lithuania); University of Katowice (Poland) and Technical University of Sofia (Bulgaria). Her main lines of research are focused on the operations management field, specifically on process management and continuous improvement (lean management, lean healthcare). Additionally, she is an expert on Rasch Measurement Theory and its application on different fields related with management and healthcare topics.

Mª Isabel Saz-Gil is a Lecturer at Business University of Zaragoza (Spain). Isabel Saz-Gil is member of The Third Sector's Social and Economic Studies Group, which take part and collaborate with different research networks. This research has resulted in published papers on the journals: Hacienda Pública Española, Ciriec-España: Revista de Economía Pública, Social y Cooperativa, Voluntas: International Journal of Voluntary and Nonprofit Organizations, among others.

Semen Son-Turan, throughout her 20+ years long professional career, Dr. Son-Turan has held various positions from intern, analyst, internal auditor, investment advisor, general coordinator to general manager, at companies such as Chase Manhattan Bank, Toronto-Dominion Bank, Ashmore Asset Management, Is Asset Management, Rehau, and Ford Otosan. Subsequently, Dr. Son-Turan founded her own company providing management consulting services to agribusinesses and small to medium-sized family firms. Her academic career, starting with her employment as Teaching Assistant at Penn State University's Business School in 1998 followed by an appointment as Lecturer in Accounting at the same institution, evolved in parallel to her professional career. Dr. Son-Turan has been teaching business, finance, and accounting courses in Turkish, English, and German at US, European and Turkish academic institutions as well as corporations for 23 years. At the beginning of 2014, she became a full-time faculty member at the Department of Business Administration at MEF University in Istanbul, where she is still employed as Associate Professor of Finance and Head of Vocational School. Dr. Son-Turan holds the Capital Market Activities Advanced Level License, a BA in Political Science and International Relations from Bogazici University (1998), an MBA from Penn State University (2000) where she also completed all requirements of the MS in Accounting program (2001), and a Ph.D. in Finance from Yasar University (2014). Her academic research interests include sustainable finance, higher education finance, behavioral finance, and capital markets, and financial innovation. She has published in reputed international journals and books.

Rafael Ventura Fernández is vice-president for Innovation and Entrepreneurship at the University of Málaga and Associate Professor in Business Administration. Ventura has been visiting research fellow at the Technical University of Delft (Netherlands) and the University of Stockholm (Sweden). He has received PhD Prize and Spin Off Award in the University of Málaga. His research interests are in the areas of entrepreneurship, innovation in business models, social responsibility, economy of culture and new organizational forms derived from the information technology and communication.

Jeffrey Wilson works at the interface of economic, sustainability and wellbeing research and policy. In addition to his position at SEED, he is an Affiliate with the Canadian Index of Wellbeing, member of the Waterloo Institute for Sustainable Energy, and member of the Interdisciplinary Center on Climate Change. Dr. Wilson has an established publication record with 24 peer reviewed journal articles, and six book chapters. His work is well cited, with over 900 citations as measured by google scholar. One of his articles received the Graedel Prize for best paper in the Journal of Industrial Ecology. His research has been recognized internationally. For example, in 2019, he was invited as an expert to the InterAction Council meetings in Colombia advising former heads of state. He was also an international research fellow with Shanghai Jiao Tong University (SJTU) Low Carbon College. Dr. Wilson enjoys teaching, leading classes in environment and business, corporate social responsibility, sustainability economics, and economic development theory. As an academic, Jeff takes pride in staying abreast of leading edge thinking on sustainability innovation and the green economy. Prior to joining the University of Waterloo, Dr. Wilson was a consultant specializing in sustainability measurement and strategy.

Index

www.ingramcontent.com/pod-product-compliance
Lightning Source LLC
LaVergne TN
LVHW062134300926
849161LV00010B/2526